tershire College (Worcester), Deansway, Worces

Legal Systems & Skills

Dedications

Scott Slorach:

For Becky.

Judith Embley:

To my husband, Greg, and my son, Oliver, with thanks for their help and invaluable insights into today's legal profession, as well as my daughter, Charlotte, and son, Edward, for all their support.

Peter Goodchild:

To my beautiful and long-suffering family, and in memory of my beloved Dad.

Catherine Shephard:

For Jack, who loves books and happily was content to share me with this one for a while.

Legal Systems & Skills

Scott Slorach

Judith Embley

Peter Goodchild

Catherine Shephard

OXFORD

UNIVERSITY PRESS

OXFORD
UNIVERSITY PRESS

Great Clarendon Street, Oxford, OX2 6DP,
United Kingdom

Oxford University Press is a department of the University of Oxford.
It furthers the University's objective of excellence in research, scholarship,
and education by publishing worldwide. Oxford is a registered trade mark of
Oxford University Press in the UK and in certain other countries

© Oxford University Press 2013

The moral rights of the authors have been asserted

Impression: 2

Public sector information reproduced under Open Government Licence v1.0
(http://www.nationalarchives.gov.uk/doc/open-government-licence/open-government-licence.htm)

Crown Copyright material reproduced with the permission of the
Controller, HMSO (under the terms of the Click Use licence)

British Library Cataloguing in Publication Data

Data available

ISBN 978-0-19-967619-4

Printed in Great Britain by

Ashford Colour Press Ltd, Gosport, Hampshire

Contents in brief

Contents in full

PART III **Professional development and commercial awareness**

About the authors

Professor Scott Slorach is Vice President (Education) at the University of Law, and a Visiting Professor at Strathclyde University. He has been involved in the design and delivery of legal education programmes for over twenty years, at undergraduate, postgraduate, vocational, and professional levels. A qualified solicitor with City experience, he was author of *Corporate Finance, Mergers and Acquisitions* (Oxford: OUP, 2005) and is currently co-author of *Business Law* (Oxford: OUP, 2012).

Judith Embley is an Associate Professor at the University of Law. She read History at Bristol University, then attended the University of Law and qualified as a solicitor in 1980, practising in a Lincoln's Inn firm. After a career break to bring up her three children, she began teaching law in 1999 as a Visiting Lecturer at Bellerby's College and then Anglia Ruskin University in Cambridge. She joined the Univerisity of Law in 2001, where she has taught Contract, Commercial, and Business Financial Law. She is now a course designer and is joint author of *Commercial Law and Practice*, one of the University of Law's Legal Practice Guides.

Peter Goodchild is an Associate Professor at the University of Law. He read Politics, Philosophy, and Economics at St Anne's College, Oxford, then attended the College of Law and qualified as a solicitor in 1997 in commercial practice. He joined the Univeristy of Law in 2000, where he has taught the English Legal System, Contract, Tort, Commercial, and Business Structures Law. In addition to over ten years of teaching experience, he has designed programmes on legal systems, legal skills, commercial law, intellectual property, and employability, and is a co-author of texts on the English legal system.

Catherine Shephard is a Senior Lecturer and Subject Leader of Corporate Practice at Manchester Metropolitan University. She read law at Cambridge, practised as a solicitor in corporate finance, and has ten years' experience of designing and delivering a wide range of skills, law, and practice management programmes to students at the University of Law, Manchester Metropolitan University, and to solicitors in practice. Catherine has a Postgraduate Certificate in Learning and Teaching in Higher Education with distinction, was the author of *Public Companies and Equity Finance* (London: College of Law Publishing, 2005), and is on the expert database at BBC North.

Preface

At the time of writing this textbook, both the UK and US legal education systems are the subject of scrutiny and discussion. In a lecture entitled 'Reforming Legal Education' (The Lord Upjohn Lecture, *Association of Law Teachers*, November 2012), Lord Neuberger suggested the future direction:

> It seems to me that both university and non-university legal education should develop what may be characterised as professional skills to a fuller degree than currently.

Academics, educationalists, and practitioners are debating what students and lawyers should learn during the academic, vocational, and professional stages of their education. This debate is taking place within a wider discussion on the theme of employability, and the generic skills expected of all graduates.

Lord Neuberger's suggestion was that, by developing further a 'practical skills curriculum' to complement the academic core of a degree, these skills could then be set at a higher level and honed during the vocational stage of education, potentially better preparing trainees to enter training contracts or pupillage.

The authors of this book endorse Lord Neuberger's statement. There are skills, and core areas of knowledge and understanding, the development of which during legal education enhances both that education process itself and the subsequent employability of graduates. This book developed from a review at the University of Law of the essential knowledge and skills required by, and of universal application to, law students to underpin their studies. The knowledge and skills fell within three key areas: legal systems, legal skills (including professional skills), and commercial awareness. We concluded that each of these areas is, almost without fail, relevant to the core activity of legal problem solving. That is, students—and indeed practitioners—must: understand the legal system within which the law has developed; exercise appropriate legal skills; and understand the effect of the law on individuals and businesses. The latter involves a redefinition of commercial awareness for legal studies: understanding individuals and businesses; their motivations and finances; and why and when they may have recourse to the law.

In light of this review, we wanted to write a textbook that would take a distinct approach to introducing students to the study and practice of law by:

1. drawing together material on legal systems and skills to provide a single introductory resource to underpin legal studies; and (crucially)

2. supporting the development of practical professional skills and knowledge that both enhance students' understanding of the application of the law and provide a foundation for further training and graduate employability, the latter in the widest sense of the expression.

Central to our approach is the firm belief that students should be introduced to the issues encountered and the skills required in legal practice from an early stage. This enables students to develop a more grounded and holistic understanding of the law, and helps them to prepare themselves for further training and legal practice. Moreover, we believe that this practical emphasis will, most importantly, help students to engage better with, and thus benefit more from, their legal studies.

Professor J. Scott Slorach
February 2013

How to use this book ...

Legal Systems & Skills is enriched with a range of carefully designed learning features to support development of the essential knowledge and skills you need to underpin your legal studies:

... to focus your learning

 Learning objectives

After studying this chapter you should be able to:
- Explain the concept of Parliamentary sovereignty.
- Identify different types of legislation.
- Describe in outline the process by which a statute is created.
- Recognise key issues of statutory interpretation.
- Discuss basic concepts relating to EU and European Convention on Rights (ECHR) legislation.

Learning objectives

A bulleted outline of the main concepts and ideas signposts what you can expect to learn from each chapter.

Introduction

The primary function of a court is to administer the law. Any law-m in Chapters 2 and 4) is important, but secondary. Real people ne resolved.

There are around 650 different courts at various levels in Engla numerous tribunals and other quasi-judicial bodies. To understand law and to give context to the law they create, it is vital to unders court system.

Chapter introduction

A concise outline of the chapter contents enables you to plan your learning session.

 Summary

- Firms expect their lawyers to be commercially aware. An important p awareness is understanding that a law firm is a business, with all the c faced by every other business. You need to understand how a firm ma its clients, the competition which it faces, and the environment in whi

- Like every business, law firms provide a product—legal services—for t must tailor their services to their customer base. Commercial awaren those clients, why they instruct a particular firm, and their expectatio

Summary of key points

The central points and concepts covered in each chapter are distilled into summaries, providing a useful point for you to reinforce your understanding.

... to become confident with new concepts

 Essential explanation
Appeal

An important aspect of the Rule of Law is recognition that even courts can ma an avenue to correct miscarriages of justice where, for instance, the judge or the law, or gave the wrong sentence or remedy. Because adjudicating on legal preserve of the court system, this must comprise access to a different court.

When litigants disagree with a decision of a court, they may try to appeal t have the resources and a strong enough argument.

This litigant is called the 'appellant' (whether he was claimant, prosecution

Essential explanation boxes

Quickly understand unfamiliar terminology and concepts with these useful jargon-busting explanation boxes, which can be found throughout the book.

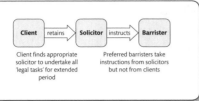

Client finds appropriate solicitor to undertake all 'legal tasks' for extended period

Preferred barristers take instructions from solicitors but not from clients

Diagrams and tables

Numerous diagrams and flowcharts are used to provide a visual representation of concepts and processes.

... to contextualize your understanding

Example 3

Facts

Jack filled his car with £60 worth of petrol from the petrol station at his local su
days later, ten minutes into a journey to the airport 100 miles from his house, Ja
power. He was forced to turn the car around and go home, his car misfiring all t
returned home, he was too late to make alternative plans to travel to the airpor
to Dublin where he had planned to spend the weekend visiting friends.
  The next day, Jack managed to drive very slowly to the nearest repair garage.
several vehicles that day with a similar problems, and there was speculation tha
wrong with the supermarket's petrol. Later that day, the garage called with a qu

Example boxes

Throughout the book, examples walk you through the key elements and applications of a concept or process.

In Part II, detailed step-by-step examples demonstrate approaches to legal skills which you can use in your studies and subsequent employment.

Case study 1

On 22 April 2010, one of BP's deep-water oil rigs in the Gulf of Mexico, the Dee
after an explosion. Eleven people died in the blast. The pipe which connected t
became disconnected and began leaking oil, and the wellhead itself was leaking
reattach the pipe and stop the leak failed and 60,000 barrels of oil per day were
It was the US's largest ever oil spill, threatening wildlife along the coast, and brir
tourist industries to a halt. President Obama suspended deep-water drilling in t
six months. BP has incurred clean-up and other costs amounting to nearly $40
immense reputational damage as a result.[1]
  What issues arise here?

Case study boxes

All chapters contain legal and real-life illustrative case studies to contextualize your understanding.

In Part III, 2 detailed case studies of the BP Deepwater Horizon disaster and the London Olympic Stadium highlight the importance of commercial awareness, with linked questions that challenge you to reflect on your current understanding.

... to think critically about law

Essential debate

UK governments have often pushed for extensions to the 14-day period for
From 2006–11, detention without charge could be extended to 28 days. The
Blair, had originally pushed to extend this to 90 days. The case for such exter
assertions that criminal investigations are sometimes complex and, especiall
terrorists, sensitive evidence can be difficult to obtain.
  By contrast, human rights groups such as Liberty and Amnesty maintain th
for complex charges relating to terrorist activities. What are your views on th

Essential debate boxes

Quickly grasp the essential debates you need to know about legal systems with these concise boxes and start to develop your own critical thinking.

? Thought-provoking questions

1. Are legal services just like any other service?
2. Should legal services be regulated just like any other service?
3. Should all defendants, no matter how odious, have legal representa
4. Is it only a matter of time before solicitors and barristers disappear?
5. Should the solicitors' and barristers' professions merge?

Thought-provoking questions

Challenge your thinking about legal systems and skills with these thought-provoking questions, great for exam and interview preparation. Guideline responses from the authors are available on the online resource centre.

Further reading

Keith Walmsley, *Butterworths Company Law Handbook* (London: Lexis
26th edn, 2012)
—this includes a collection of the main statutes, statutory instruments, an
are relevant to corporate lawyers.
Supreme Court website: http://www.supremecourt.gov.uk/decided-c
—for transcripts of Supreme Court judgments since August 2009.
British and Irish Legal Information Institute (BAILII) website: http://ww
—a good source for case transcripts (see 7.5.1).
Cardiff Index to Legal Abbreviations: http://www.legalabbrevs.cardif

Further reading

Extend your knowledge with this annotated further
reading section.

... to apply your knowledge and skills

AGREEMENT

You should define
terms which you
intend to use fre-
quently in the con-
tract. Then make sure
you refer consistently
to these terms in the
body of the contract.
Definitions should be
in alphabetical order.

Dated: [   ]
Parties: (1)
         (2)

THIS AGREEMENT is made the day of BETWEEN

(1) [Name] of [Address] (the '[defined term]'); and
(2) [Name] of [Address] (the '[defined term]').

IT IS AGREED as follows:

Annotated documents and templates

Familiarize yourself with the format of important
legal documents with these annotated resources and
document templates in Part II, great for use in study
and preparing for subsequent employment.

What the professionals say

You soon realise that everything you write is either on the clock, against the clock
combined with the need to ensure everything you write is effective in the eyes of
withstand being crawled over with a fine tooth comb if it is ever scrutinised in co
for Legal Writing skills that you didn't expect you would ever have.

Stedman Harmon, 2012-13 Trainee, DLA Piper

'What the professionals say' boxes

Enhance your employability by following the advice of
top legal services professionals, as found throughout
Part II.

 Practice tip

Trainees sit with different departments during their training contract of two y
with one department is referred to as a 'seat', and when a trainee moves to a
this is called a 'seat move'. The majority of firms offer trainees four seats each
some firms offer more seats over the two-year period. Arranging seat moves
as several trainees may indicate an interest in the same seat, and not all will o
It is important to give your best performance in all seats, even if you are not s
that department. Do not forget that the partner in your current department
with the partner in the department you want to go to next, and a positive or

Practice tip boxes

Relevant aspects of the realities of legal practice are
introduced in Part II, to provide context for your skills
development.

 Sample interview questions

1. What do you think are the main challenges/opportunities facing the legal
2. What do you know about alternative business structures?
3. Do you think that the franchising of law firms helps to provide better servi
4. Should all referral fees be banned by the government?
5. What do you think about the recent reforms of legal aid?
6. What do you think about the effects of the Legal Aid, Sentencing and Punishm

Sample interview questions

Could you answer these sample commercial awareness
interview questions? Identify areas of your commercial
awareness that you need to focus on with these
challenging questions in Part III.

How to use the Online Resource Centre

Make the most of this package by accessing your FREE online supplementary learning materials at:

www.oxfordtextbooks.co.uk/orc/slorach/

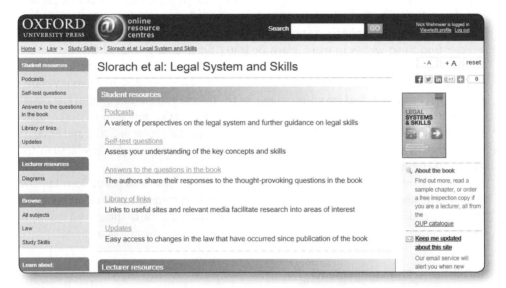

Student Resources

Free and open-access material available:

- **Podcasts** provide a variety of perspectives on the legal system and further guidance on legal skills
- **Self-test questions** arranged per chapter assess your understanding of the key concepts and skills.
- The authors share their **responses to the thought-provoking questions** in the book
- **A library of links** to useful sites and relevant media facilitate research into areas of interest
- **Regular legal updates** provide easy access to changes in the law that have occurred since publication of the book.

Lecturer Resources

Free for all registered adopters of the textbook:

- All of the diagrams in the textbook are available to download electronically and can be used in lectures to aid student understanding.

Acknowledgements

The authors would like to thank all those who took time to provide reviews and feedback on the book's development: this was both valued and greatly appreciated. We would also like to thank Eleanor Chatburn and Helen Swann of OUP for their guidance and assistance.

Judith Embley wishes to thank colleagues at the University of Law at Bloomsbury, particularly Jacqui Kempton, Susan Sang, Stuart Roberts, Judith Pothecary, Louise Mawer, and Jane Vandervlies, for their helpful suggestions and invaluable support.

Peter Goodchild wishes to thank Hugh Boileau (Parliamentary Counsel Office) and Leo Hodes (Treasury Solicitor's Department) for their contributions in relation to the drafting of legislation and the interplay between the government departments and parliamentary draftsmen; Judith Pothecary (the University of Law) for her patience and advice on the finer points of constitutional law; Ben Wilson (UK Supreme Court, Head of Communications) for his assistance in sourcing statistics in relation to the workload of the UK Supreme Court; and Amanda Powell (the University of Law) as a vital source of information on the English legal system and aspects of litigation procedure.

Catherine Shephard is grateful to Natasha Choolun, Dan Hill, Mark Keith, Tom Laidlaw, Wendy Laws, and Corryn Walker for, variously, their advice regarding advocacy, mooting, the law of tort, and legal research. Thanks also to everyone named in the chapters who took time out of their busy schedules to listen to me and provide such illuminating quotations.

Publisher acknowledgements

Crown copyright material is reproduced under Class Licence Number C2006010631 with the permission of POSI and the Queen's Printer for Scotland.

The publishers would be pleased to make suitable arrangements to clear permission for material reproduced in this book with any copyright holders whom it has not been possible to contact.

Part I

Legal Systems

It is important that law students develop an holistic and contemporary understanding of the purpose and practical application of the law. This goes beyond a basic knowledge of the English legal system.

This section therefore considers the rationale for law from social and moral perspectives, and reflects on further jurisprudential perspectives. It then focuses on the development of legal systems, illustrated with practical examples from a range of jurisdictions, and compares common law and civil law systems. Within the context of the English legal system, there is coverage of the courts, and the civil and criminal justice systems. The various sources of law are explained, with specific coverage of case law and the doctrine of precedent, and statutes.

Throughout this section, there is a theme of contemporary application: the current function of legal systems and their effect on individuals, businesses, and commerce. This leads to consideration of why and when legal services are required; the range of ways in which these are provided and by whom; the regulation and ethics of legal services provision; and the changing nature of the legal services market.

Introduction to law

 Learning objectives

After studying this chapter you should be able to:

- Explain the importance of law as a concept.
- Develop an awareness that law can (and should) be studied in its wider context.
- Relate law to its underpinnings in ethics.
- Explain in outline selected aspects of philosophies of law, known as jurisprudence.
- Discuss the importance of legitimacy in law, and in particular the idea of sovereignty.
- Understand the theoretical and practical importance of the rule of law.
- Describe the central principles relating to the doctrine of Separation of Powers, and understand its importance in maintaining the rule of law.

Introduction

In this chapter we consider law as a concept and law in its wider context.

The concept of law, in its simplest sense, is straightforward.

 Essential explanation

Law

What is law?

The Shorter Oxford English Dictionary defines 'law' in 17 different ways, but the first definition is most relevant here.

> The body of rules, whether formally enacted or customary, which a particular state or community recognizes as governing the actions of its subjects or members and which it may enforce by imposing penalties.[1]

The significant words are 'rules' and 'state': the rules by which a state operates.

Chapters 1 to 6 on Legal Systems are about the law, and how it works. Specific legal rules will be referred to by way of illustration and example. In Chapter 1 we consider law as a concept and in its context. We examine key legal concepts such as law and morality, jurisprudence, the legitimacy of laws, the Rule of Law, and the Separation of Powers, looking at these in both theory and practice.

[1] *The Shorter Oxford English Dictionary* (Oxford: OUP, 6th edn, 2007).

Chapter 2 examines how these concepts are manifested in England & Wales. Chapter 3 outlines the court system, and the general principles of its operation. Chapters 4 and 5 consider the two main types of law in England & Wales, statutes and case law, respectively.

To give access to legal rights, we need people who can help citizens use the law. This is where lawyers come in. In Chapter 6 we look at the development of the legal profession and whether, in the light of recent reforms, it provides efficient access to law.

1.1 Law in context

Law is important.

This may seem obvious, but it is easy to lose sight of how significant law is in a modern society. As law students or lawyers become absorbed in their work, they will understandably focus on the particular area they are involved in. They may reflect less on the importance of the law as a whole—practically and culturally. This context is important. In this section we look at how law relates to all citizens and how it relates to other academic subjects.

1.1.1 Law and the citizen

Evidence of the importance of law is all around us. Imagine your typical day, and think about how it involves the law. What follows is a day in the life of an imaginary citizen somewhere in England. Note the variety of laws involved in guaranteeing that our lives run smoothly. Note also the variety of institutions involved in implementing and adjudicating on the rules, including the different political entities involved:

- You wake up in the morning. Your phone alarm works. If it is faulty then this is a breach of your contract with whoever sold the phone to you, under a term of the contract implied by a statute. A statute is a law passed by Parliament.

- You go to the bathroom and take a shower. The water is uncontaminated and drinkable partly because it is regulated by UK and European legislation. If the company that provides the water breaches this legislation then the government will take action via the Department for Environment, Food and Rural Affairs, and its agency Ofwat. The company is a large Public Limited Company which is subject to extensive statutory rules and law developed by courts to protect the public if they invest in it.

- You live in a house or flat. The right to use it is governed by many different legal rules, either in statutes, or case law, or both.

- Then you go down some stairs. If built in recent decades, the stairs and in fact all of the dimensions and infrastructure of the building will have been subject to building regulations passed under the authority of Parliament.

- To make your morning coffee, you switch on a kettle that must be sold in conformity with EU regulations. The coffee beans may be imported from Brazil, under a series of contracts, governed by English and international commercial law. You add some milk—Parliament has passed legislation to ensure that all food and drink is safe. Kellogg's Cornflakes are subject to similar regulation. No other manufacturers of cereals can call their product 'Kellogg's' because of the Kellogg's trade mark, under UK and EU legislation (and related case law). You can be relatively confident that the food matches the labelling on the packet because of legislation.

- You take a quick look at the news, streamed onto your tablet computer. Statutes passed by Parliament regulate the broadcasts, along with further case law and non-binding codes of practice involved in the regulation of media. Without the WiFi connection supplied by your phone provider, this would not work. There is a contract, subject to significant regulation, plus a body of legislation regulating telecoms providers and internet service providers. This regulation exists to protect you from wrongs like overcharging, poor service, wrongful use of your data (e.g. via cookies), and so on.

- As you go outside, you lock the door and leave with the expectation that your property and goods will remain secure. You hope not to be burgled while you are out. This would constitute a crime. There are statutory penalties for people who steal from other people. These statutes are interpreted by case law.

- You get to the station and wait for your train. It is delayed. Half an hour later, there is still no train. On the platform your fellow travellers are impatient. This is likely to be a breach of contract by the rail operator and will normally trigger its compensation scheme, required by the Office of Rail Regulation under statute. There is also a large amount of UK and EU legislation relating to public transport, cars, trains, streets, etc.

- While you are waiting, you send a message to a friend on Facebook and read a Tweet with a photo of you from last night's party. Surely there are rules to protect your privacy? But then again, there must be rules to protect freedom of expression. There are both, and the Human Rights Act is at the centre of them. Thankfully no one has tweeted anything derogatory about you, but if they did, the law of defamation might provide you with help.

Your day is not even two hours old, and hundreds of laws of various types from several institutions and different eras have been relevant. The law, then, includes an astonishingly wide spectrum of rules and institutions. Human activity is enormously creative but without formal regulation is open to open-ended abuse. We need law.

Imagine a society without law. There would be no binding rules to live by. Only vague social values, religion, and family would provide any guidance on acceptable behaviour in society. The state would not be able to organise itself. Much of what we take for granted—government, taxes, utilities, infrastructure, medicine, welfare—would never have been developed. At 1.2 we consider the critical but also sometimes troubled relationship between law, social values, and morality. At 1.4 we see that the concept of the Rule of Law is critical to maintaining the rules by which society lives.

The example above illustrates the variety of issues that arise in the law. The word 'law' describes a huge and diverse body of rules and skills, involving many different people. It describes both the substance of rules, but also the procedures by which people access and use it. We have seen that it can be local, national, or international law. It can regulate the affairs of anyone from individuals to large companies. When it is applied by courts the people concerned can be subject to many types of sanction, from prison to orders that they compensate someone they have wronged. Rulings by courts can be challenged, but as we will find out in Chapter 3, few of them are. Some areas of law constantly change, and yet some remain largely the same as they were centuries ago.

There are some fundamental aspects of the question 'what is law' that all lawyers need to consider.

1.1.2 **Law and its boundaries**

It is often counterproductive to view law in isolation. Of course, if you are in the thick of focused academic study, or advising a client on a subtle aspect of (say) patent law, you may need to immerse yourself in the subject matter to some extent. But to understand law as a discipline, we must consider it in context, as part of a suite of subjects that work together and impact on each other. This contextual approach is sometimes referred to as the 'empirical' study of law.

Figure 1.1 shows law at the centre of a range of subjects. This is not to say that law is the most important of these areas, but that, as lawyers, we must have our main focus on law (for an historian, history would be at the centre of a similar range of disciplines, and so on). Law must be seen in context, and this means that when we start to study it, we should dispense with boundaries.

Law regulates people and institutions in a society and develops to reflect a combination of needs and influences. In Chapter 2 we consider its development against the background of society and history in England & Wales. There is an interplay between society's values and the law, along with ethics and religion. We examine this in 1.2. All statutes are enacted by Parliament, and Parliament is the product of politics. So much of the law you will encounter is the product of the political process. There is an example of this in Chapter 6 on the regulation of the legal profession.

Politics, philosophy, and law have always been natural bedfellows in the sense that political dogma is often implemented through law. Moreover, a lawyer should have an understanding, in theoretical terms, of how and why law works as it does—and political philosophy plays no small part in this. The study of this is called jurisprudence, and is addressed in 1.3.

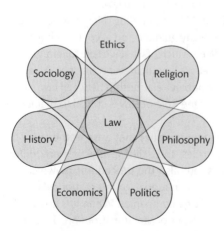

Figure 1.1 Law at the centre of an interconnected range of academic disciplines

1.2 Law, morality, and society

We saw in the Introduction that law is a system of rules by which a state operates. We have also seen that it overlaps with other disciplines. It must provide some kind of guidance about behaviour, a benchmark against which people are judged. This standard must reflect the views of the majority of the population to ensure it can be enforced. As a result, the law incorporates moral issues and also social values (which may be distinct from ethical principles).

This necessity may be illustrated by examples from history. Some laws which would have been acceptable in a different era would now be unpalatable. Until 1831 it was a capital offence to steal a sheep.[2] Over a thousand people were hanged between 1825 and 1831 for this offence. By contrast, today it would be unusual even to go to prison for theft of a sheep.

An illuminating example is the law relating to sexual offences. Homosexual behaviour was a criminal offence in England & Wales until 1967.[3] Oscar Wilde was famously sentenced to two years' hard labour for gross indecency, partly because of his own testimony that, '"The love that dare not speak its name" in this century is such a great affection of an elder for a younger man ... such as you find in the sonnets of Michelangelo and Shakespeare.'[4] The age of consent for homosexuals was only brought into line with heterosexuals in 2003.[5]

To address the interplay between law, morality, and society, we must first clarify what is meant by 'morality'.

1.2.1 What is morality?

Whole books have been written on this complex subject, however, a basic understanding will suffice to allow us to address its interplay with law. Two vital terms here are ethics and metaethics. Philosophers often refer to ethics as being the study of morality. Metaethics looks at the *nature* of morality.

 Essential debate

There are two general views on how ethics works:

- Objectivism: objectivists believe that it is possible for there to be one absolute set of moral values, although precisely what this set of values is, is clearly extremely controversial.

- Relativism: relativists argue that morals are the function of human thought and are therefore the reflection of the beliefs of people themselves, either as a society, or individually. This means that morality can change over time (e.g. the example of homosexuality referred to above) and can vary between societies, or even people. Some relativists claim that social values and morality are intertwined.

---

[2] An Act to render the Laws more effective for the preventing the stealing and destroying of Sheep 1741.
[3] Criminal Law Amendment Act 1885, Sexual Offences Act 1967.
[4] *R v Wilde* (1895) unreported.   [5] Sexual Offences Act 2003.

1.2.2 **Examples and analysis**

Introduction: legal, moral, and social duties

We have seen that there are two (much generalised) views of morality. So a moral duty is a duty owed by people to each other as a function of whatever moral or ethical system is being used; by contrast, a legal duty is a duty created by law, rather than by any system of moral values. Different again is a social duty, which is a more informal category of duties that help society work on a day-to-day basis. These are not necessarily backed up by legal sanction, and are not seen as 'moral' duties.

Example 1

Here are two contemporary examples of the uneasy relationship between legal, social, and moral values:

- Are large multinational companies morally wrong to operate offshore to avoid UK tax? In 2012 the Public Accounts Committee of Parliament criticised companies like Starbucks, Amazon, and Google for moving UK profits offshore. But their acts are lawful because they are within the rules set out by the Inland Revenue and UK statutes such as the Corporation Tax Act 2010. Is paying your plumber in cash to get a discount morally wrong? It might be argued that depriving the state of much-needed funds is wrong. Socially, the practice of tax avoidance is far more ambiguous—avoidance by the plumber and the corporation are very different situations.

- What about same-sex marriage? While civil partnerships between gay couples are legal in the UK,[6] marriage is not. In 11 countries, same-sex marriage is legal, and all political parties in the UK are committed to introducing it soon. But the Church in the UK, as well as other religious bodies, is opposed on moral grounds, as is the Campaign For Marriage. Social values, moral values, and legal reality in this area are currently in a state of flux.

Figure 1.2 shows an overlap between legal, moral, and social duties. They overlap but are not the same. It is arguable that the greater the overlap between these categories of duty, the easier it is to enforce them all, because they are more comprehensively justifiable.

Let's draw out some themes and examples.

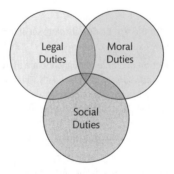

Figure 1.2 Overlap between legal, moral, and social duties

---

[6] Civil Partnership Act 2004.

Legal vs moral

Not all moral duties are legally enforceable. Adultery is not illegal in the UK (although it is against the law in some other countries, e.g. Pakistan and Saudi Arabia), but many people would contend that under most (if not all) circumstances, it is immoral.

Exclusively moral duties may not be given legal protection either because some moral rules are difficult to police, or because for whatever reason such behaviour is seen as beyond the sphere of state intervention. When a legal duty diverges too much from morality it runs the risk of becoming unenforceable without resorting to heavy-handed or violent enforcement. Statistics bear out the relationship between speeding and an increase in the risk of serious injury.[7] In 2010 in the UK, 49% of motorists exceeded 70mph in free-flowing motorway traffic.[8] All of these motorists were committing a criminal offence. Do they feel morally responsible when they do so?

This brings us to the first case study:

Case study 1

The Enabling Act and the Nuremberg Laws

Hitler became German Chancellor in January 1933. In February the German *Reichstag* (Parliament) building burned down and civil liberties were suspended. The Nazis used the state of panic as a pretext to force the passing of the Enabling Act, which allowed the Cabinet (mainly composed of Nazis) to enact legislation without reference to the *Reichstag*. The *Reichstag* became a cipher for propaganda, especially after the banning of all political parties bar the Nazi party in July that year. Between 1933 and 1945 the *Reichstag* passed only four laws, all other regulation being by decree.

Within four months of Hitler coming to power, the first laws curtailing the rights of Jewish citizens were enacted. By 1935, the political climate in Germany had been transformed by Hitler's rule.

In September 1935, the 'Nuremberg Laws' were enacted by the *Reichstag*, comprising The Law for the Protection of German Blood and German Honour, which prohibited marriages and intercourse between Jews and Germans, and The Reich Citizenship Law, which declared those of Aryan blood to be citizens and those not of Aryan blood to be merely subjects.

The Nazis had so engineered the social prejudices of a significant proportion of the German population in the 1930s that it was possible to bring in laws that were clearly amoral. There were two factors which enabled this: first, the severe penalties for those seen to flout or evade the Nuremberg Laws, and, second, the distortion of social attitudes.

Legal vs social

A government will not be able to enforce a law which is too divergent from social attitudes. The importance of social norms is often downplayed, but it is society that collectively determines good and bad behaviour.

---

[7] Department for Transport, *Relationship between Speed and Risk of Fatal Injury: Pedestrians and Car Occupants* (16 September 2010).

[8] Department for Transport, *Free Flow Vehicle Speeds in Great Britain* (June 2011).

In early societies it was natural for legal rules to reflect social values. In India, Hindus adhered to values epitomised in *Manu Smriti (Laws of Manu)*, poems of the 1st century BC, about social obligations (set out by caste or class) and the consequences of their breach. There was no differentiation between 'legal' and 'social'.

In a modern society, for laws to match social values so precisely would be problematic. If you steal something, you would expect to be punished under the criminal law. However, you would be surprised to be arrested for pushing in front of someone in a supermarket queue. It is probably a social wrong creating great annoyance. It may or may not be a moral wrong; but it is unlikely to be a legal wrong.

The illustration of the Nuremberg Laws shows how important it is for legal rules to shadow social attitudes. Hitler had to 'prepare the ground' for his anti-Semitic legislation. Legal rules must therefore attract some legitimacy from the degree to which they reflect important social values.

Moral vs social

One would hope that the social values of all societies reflect morality. To a relativist, morality will always (logically) coincide with such values.

Social values include, but are much more extensive than, mere etiquette. Etiquette would, however, seem to occupy a lower domain than morality. Take this extract from a Victorian magazine:

> Again I must conduct you back to the dining-room. Observe how highly-bred people eat asparagus. They feel with the knife where the soft part ends, and dividing the stems, they eat with the fork. It is a disgusting spectacle to see people draw out a mangled end from their mouths reduced to a ragged fringe.[9]

But social values are more important than passing the salt to the left at supper. They are at the root of major issues affecting a society, such as whether immigration is a good thing, and what a welfare state should provide. Most moral philosophers draw a distinction between morality and social values. It is possible for social values to be amoral. Anyone who believes that right and wrong exist at least to some extent separately from society would agree with this. This chapter contains many possible examples.

Referring back to Oscar Wilde, although homosexuality has become part of the mainstream in many modern moral cultures, Wilde also referred to a practice which is still unacceptable according to the values of most societies in the 21st century. It was common in ancient Greece for adult men to engage in sexual relations with pubescent or adolescent boys (see e.g. Phaedrus by Plato). Were the ancient Greeks amoral as a society?

Those who believe in an objective morality would point out that in some societies, morals and social values diverge, and where this happens, there is an opening for the law to follow malign social pressures.

Hitler's Germany again provides a chilling example. A British writer living in Germany (Christopher Isherwood) witnessed the arrest of a Jew in a Berlin cafe where German citizens turned away. Of course, it is likely that many of the citizens were not unwilling to act; merely that they were unable to act, for fear of reprisals.

---

[9] 'On Dinner', *Girl's Own Paper*, 1880.

Conclusion: reconciling legal, moral, and social duties

An ideal society would be one where law reflected social customs, and these in turn were morally justifiable. But because people are different this is virtually impossible. Whether we regard morality as objective or relative, people have different views on right and wrong, so it is difficult to see how this utopian vision would ever work. Because of cultural, technological, and industrial progress, society develops and with it opinions on morality.

However, governments and legislators do often try to translate their own ethical preferences, and society's developing customs, into law. The next section is about the degree to which real legal rules have reflected this.

1.2.3 Law and morality in practice

Ethical underpinnings of law

Ethical systems divide into three broad categories:

- virtue theories (e.g. Aristotle in his Nicomachean Ethics), which focus on developing good traits of character;
- duty theories (e.g. Locke, Kant), which seek to set out fundamental obligations (or rights); and
- consequentialist theories (e.g. Mill, Bentham), which evaluate the consequences of our actions.

All of these theories have been manifested to a greater or lesser extent in political and legal reality.

Virtue theories

Virtue theories focus on developing good traits of character.

Aristotle viewed personal virtue and happiness as being mutually reinforcing. He and like-minded philosophers believed that the ideal political unit for reflecting and fostering these virtues was the city state. The aim of Aristotle's ideal city state was the 'good life', rather than making money or conquests. Modern societies do not reflect this view of morality (although there are city states today, such as Singapore, Vatican City, Monaco, and San Marino, these are some way from the ancient cities Aristotle had in mind).

While not the subject of 'hard law' (i.e. enforceable by courts), it is common for politicians to espouse nebulous concepts of social responsibility, and the value of volunteering to help others individually and in society generally (a contemporary example is David Cameron's 'Big Society' concept). Hobbes was far more pessimistic about human nature. He saw that individuals were fundamentally self-seeking. He saw morality as an artificial framework constructed by society for everyone's mutual advancement. In his 'social contract', deviation from social norms was discouraged by punishment.

Duty and consequentialist theories do, however, find manifestation in modern legal systems.

Duty theories

Duty theories seek to set out fundamental obligations, and their flip-side, 'rights'.

Legal theorists from the Roman era onwards have referred to the importance of 'Natural Law', a set of duties whose validity does not depend on human concepts like sovereignty (see 1.4.3).

This contrasts with 'Positive Law', being the 'real' law of the land. St Augustine stated: 'An unjust law is not a law'.[10] Thomas Aquinas (in the 13th to 14th centuries) argued that there was no duty at all to obey a law contravening Natural Law. Over time such concepts were refined: Hobbes and Locke (in the 17th century) developed concepts of Natural Rights alongside duties under Natural Law.

Sir Edmund Coke, a lawyer, judge, and legal theorist in the 16th to 17th centuries, explicitly linked Natural Law and legal theory:

> this law of nature is part of the laws of England ... the law of nature was before any judicial or municipal law in the world ... the law of nature is immutable, and cannot be changed.[11]

Only sometimes are judges free to align Positive Law and Natural Law. Two common law (i.e. case law—see Chapter 5) examples follow:

- A recurring theme in ethics has been the 'Golden Rule' that we should do to others what we would want them to do to us. This traces its lineage back to Ancient Babylon, via Egypt, Greece, China, and Rome. In the Parable of the Good Samaritan, Jesus said, 'You shall love ... your neighbour as yourself'.[12]

    This is often expressed as 'Love Thy Neighbour'. In Chapters 2 and 5 we shall consider one of the most important cases in English law, *Donoghue v Stevenson*,[13] in which Lord Atkin expressly refers to this rule and places it in legal language to formulate the Neighbour Principle that underpins the modern law of negligence. It is not common for the law so clearly to reflect morality.

- Judges and lawyers in common law jurisdictions such as England, the US, and Australia (see Chapter 5) often refer to something called 'natural justice'. This is an attempt to reflect basic tenets of morality in the law and its execution. In England, natural justice is epitomised by the rule against bias, and the right to a fair hearing; in the US, by the principle of Due Process.

Most legal systems incorporate either a written constitution or a statement of rights, or both. All (or most) actors within these systems are bound by such duties and rights. Here are some examples:

- The European Convention on Human Rights 1950 as incorporated into UK law by the Human Rights Act 1998, and EU law by the Treaty of Lisbon 2007.

- The United States Constitution 1789 as amended, in particular, by the (so-called) Bill of Rights 1791, setting out fundamental rights and obligations among other provisions.

- The French Constitution (in its various forms) has always included the Declaration of the Rights of Man and the Citizen of 1789.

Such documents explicitly reflect 'duty'-based morality. The lineage of the US Constitution is clearly traceable to Hobbes, Locke, and Baron de Montesquieu (see 1.6.1). Arguably they also epitomise 'Rule Utilitarianism'.

---

[10] St Augustine, *On Free Choice of the Will*, 1.5.33 (387–395 AD) (Indianapolis: Hackett Publishing Co., 1993).
[11] *Calvin's Case* (1608) 7 Co Rep 1a, 77 ER 377.   [12] Luke 10:25–29.
[13] *Donoghue v Stevenson* [1932] AC 562.

Consequentialist, or utilitarian law?

Consequentialist theories (including Utilitarian theories) evaluate the consequences of our actions.

Jeremy Bentham's 'felicific calculus'[14] (or 'utilitarian calculus') is perhaps the most notable of these theories. He, John Stuart Mill, and their successors maintained that the moral worth of an action could be determined by a calculation of the total goodness of its consequences.

Many modern statutes are detailed in focus and contain provisions which contribute to what the government of the day sees as the greater good. These can be explained in utilitarian terms, and many ambiguities in them will be addressed on a case-by-case basis by courts in a narrow literal analysis (see 4.4.4, statutory interpretation). This is often justified using a utilitarian evaluation (or calculus)—essentially 'a means to an end'.

Conclusion

Modern law, especially in England & Wales, can derive its justification from several different moral antecedents.

Figure 1.3 summarises the degree to which these moral systems have been reflected in the laws of a generalised modern state. Some laws lie outside the moral sphere; others are justified by duties, or by utilitarian calculation, or both. Very few are classically virtue-based.

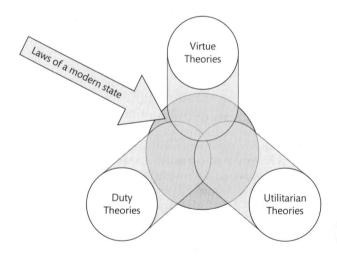

Figure 1.3 Moral ancestry of the modern state

1.2.4 **Can all law be morally justified?**

Murder and rape are universally condemned, but what about more controversial areas? For instance, euthanasia and abortion. These two cases, about the beginning and end of human life respectively, demonstrate how emotive the moral/legal nexus can be.

---

[14] Set out in *An Introduction to the Principles of Morals and Legislation* (London: 1789), ch. 4.

Abortion

In the US, one of the defining political issues for several decades, upon which any politician must have a view, is abortion. The issue is far more politicised in the US than in the UK. The 1973 US Supreme Court case *Roe* v *Wade*[15] is arguably one of the three most significant cases in that court over the last century. In it, a liberal court stated that the right to privacy derived from the US Constitution extended to a woman's decision to have an abortion, but was qualified by the state's interests in protecting the health of the mother and the life of the foetus as it matured.

To be taken seriously, American politicians must have an opinion on this—they must be either 'pro-life' or 'pro-choice'. It is the barometer by which the political make-up of the Supreme Court is tested, and its initial 7 to 2 majority ruling in 1973 has been subject to fluctuation in later cases reconsidering the issue. These fluctuations have, by-and-large, reflected public opinion, as measured in polls.[16]

So in the US the law, as enunciated by the Supreme Court, tends to reflect social values. This is even more the case in state (as opposed to federal) courts, where the population is often more homogenous than in the US as a whole.

Euthanasia/'mercy killing'

It is currently against the law in the UK to help someone to commit suicide, which suggests that society places a supreme moral value on the preservation of life. Maybe you believe this is wrong and that it should be left to individuals to decide whether or not they wish to live.

Case study 2
Diane Pretty

Diane Pretty suffered from motor neurone disease, an illness making it impossible for her to move or communicate easily. Despite having full mental capacity, she required round-the-clock care. She wanted her husband to be able to help her die, as she was unable to take her own life. On her website, she said, 'I want to have a quick death without suffering, at home surrounded by my family so that I can say good-bye to them'. Under s. 2(1) of the Suicide Act 1961, this would make her husband guilty of assisted suicide.

The House of Lords refused to order the Director of Public Prosecutions to undertake not to prosecute under the Act.[17] They reasoned that the Right to Life under the Human Rights Act 1998 did not include the right to choose to live, and that therefore it was not discriminatory (under the Human Rights Act) to prevent assisted suicide of the incapacitated by loved ones. To allow this would open the door to doctors being pressurised to accelerate the demise of elderly or infirm patients by unscrupulous relatives. In parallel litigation, the European Court of Human Rights refused to declare that the actions of the UK government violated the European Convention on Human Rights.[18]

---

[15] *Roe* v *Wade*, 410 US 113 (1973).

[16] Harris Interactive, 'Support for Roe v. Wade Increases Significantly, Reaches Highest Level in Nine Years' (9 November 2007).

[17] *R (Pretty)* v *DPP and Secretary of State for the Home Department* [2001] UKHL 61.

[18] *Pretty* v *UK*, App. no. 2346/02 (2002) 35 EHRR 1.

As suggested in 'Conclusion: reconciling legal, moral, and social duties' at 1.2.2, an ideal society would be one where individual morality and social values coincided and were reinforced by legal duties in all cases. The two examples here have shown that this is unlikely ever to be possible. Section 1.2 has shown that morality is very difficult to pin down. We have seen that people have a wide variety of values on many issues. As a result it is inconceivable that any system of law in a modern context could also perfectly reflect morality and social values.

1.3 Jurisprudence

1.3.1 Justifying jurisprudence

'Laws are like sausages. It's better not to see how they are made', Otto von Bismarck (the First Chancellor of Germany) is reputed to have said in 1849. To any lawyer, the opposite must be true. We need to know exactly how and why law is made, to make sense of it.

 Essential explanation

Jurisprudence

Jurisprudence constitutes the formal study of themes of law, including the nature of law as a concept. This may seem very academic, but hundreds of books have been written on the subject. It is important to any lawyer, academic or vocational, because it shows how and why law is created as it is. It places law in its historical, political, social, and philosophical context. The discussion in which we engaged in 1.2, on law, society, and morality, was a jurisprudential one.

The term 'jurisprudence' is occasionally used in another sense, meaning the body of law created by a court or judge, for example the jurisprudence of the European Court of Justice or of Lord Bingham. In this section we are using the term in the wider sense, namely the nature of law as a concept.

In 1.4 we consider the Rule of Law, a very important concept within jurisprudence. Lord Bingham (a former Master of the Rolls, Lord Chief Justice, and Senior Law Lord) made it very clear why it is important for practising lawyers to understand key legal theories like the Rule of Law: 'we are not, as we are sometimes seen, mere custodians of a body of arid prescriptive rules but are, with others, the guardians of an all but sacred flame which animates and enlightens the society in which we live'.[19] Jurisprudence allows lawyers to reflect on why the law is so important in the real world.

1.3.2 An overview of jurisprudence

There are many ways to characterise jurisprudence. Focusing on the main philosophies in roughly chronological order, there have been the following approaches to legal theory:

- Natural Law.
- Positivism.
- Realism.
- Critical Legal Studies.

[19] Lord Bingham, 'The Sixth Sir David Williams Lecture: The Rule of Law' (November 2006).

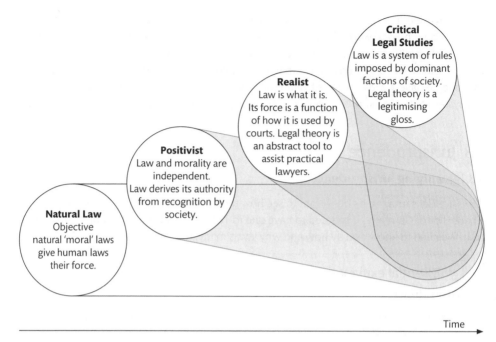

Figure 1.4 The historical development of approaches to jurisprudence

These are clearly labels, and many theories of law defy such neat categorisation. These theories draw out different aspects of the law and of legal systems. It might be said that to evaluate, for instance, Positivism against Realism or Feminist Critical Legal Studies, is like comparing the merits of lychees with the benefits of ladders. Figure 1.4 summarises this view.

We can now draw out a few general themes.

Natural Law

We saw in 1.2 that there is a complex relationship between law and morality. Early theorists like Aristotle and Aquinas thought that law derived its authority from having moral underpin-nings. This is the Natural Law model of jurisprudence.

Natural Law remains a significant element of judicial reasoning, for instance in human rights law. Modern contemporary theorists like Dworkin still promote principles of Natural Law, and argue that contemporary views of legal authority cannot be complete without acknowledging the importance of moral force.

Islamic Law can be related to this model. *Fiqh* constitutes much of the practical legal principles of Islamic jurists, but it is based on *Sharia* (taken from the Qu'ran), expressed to be the moral principles underlying *fiqh*.

Legal positivism

By the 19th century, another school of thought was developing. Positivists believed that the search for a relationship between law and morality was of secondary importance, and that more significant was an understanding of how law obtained its authority in society.

Initially, philosophers like Bentham and Mill (drawing from Hobbes) saw the threat of sanctions as the incentive for people to do what was good for them. More recently, writers like Hart and Kelsen have seen law as deriving authority as a system of rules. These rules draw legitimacy from fundamental laws accepted as basic to a society. The discussion at 1.4 uses this reasoning. Natural Law—giving law moral underpinnings—and Legal Positivism—giving law authority because it is a set of rules recognised by society—are generally seen to be difficult to reconcile.

Legal realism

Realists emerged in the 20th century. They felt that all this theorising was rather missing the point. The celebrated American judge Oliver Wendell-Holmes said: 'The life of the law has not been logic, it has been experience.'[20] The law is what it is, and is determined by factors as prosaic as who represented the parties, who was on the bench, and, most importantly, the facts of the cases being heard or appealed. Llewellyn (a famous realist), stated: 'The real rules ... are on the level of *isness* and not *oughtness* ...'[21] (italics added).

Critical legal studies

The Critical Legal Studies movement evolved during the 1970s, and is difficult to define, partly because there are many strands to it, and partly because it is still evolving. One of the themes is a recognition that 'all law is politics', in other words it is difficult or impossible to disentangle political motivations from legislative and judicial acts. A second theme is an agenda of removing external bias from the creation and administration of law.

By the mid-20th century, politically active philosophies such as feminism and communism took centre stage, and provided critiques on legal rules as inherited from the *ancien regime*. To feminists, law was created in patriarchal societies and reflected this; to Marxists, law has been one of the tools of the bourgeoisie, and the nobility before them, in reinforcing economic relationships favourable to them, and detrimental to the proletariat. In your study of contract law, for instance, you will find that many early cases were decided in favour of the employer and not the employee. Marxists would find such outcomes more than coincidental. Indeed the fact that domestic and European employment law was significantly reformed in the second half of the 20th century, reflecting the political mood of the time (discussed in more detail at 2.4.3 and 6.4) would serve to confirm that at least some 'law is politics'. This more socially responsible legal environment can be identified not just in employment law, but elsewhere, for instance in consumer law.

Summary

A simplified summary of the development of jurisprudence would be as follows: over time analysis of the law has moved from placing law within its moral context, to an acknowledgement that law is one of many social constructs, and need not necessarily be elevated to such an ethical level. Many of the features of each movement have been adopted by successive scholars over time, so that many theorists now use a variety of analytical tools taken from a

---

[20] Oliver Wendell-Holmes, *The Common Law* (Boston: Little, Brown & Co., 1881), p. 461.
[21] Karl N. Llewellyn, *Jurisprudence: Realism in Theory and Practice* (University of Chicago Press, 1962).

jurisprudential toolbox. This is reflected in disciplines such as statutory interpretation, which we examine in Chapter 3.

1.4 How legitimate is law?

1.4.1 Importance of the question

We have seen that law has some moral underpinnings, but that law and morality do not always coincide. So why are laws obeyed? This is a key jurisprudential question. Is it just that, as Hobbes said, if we didn't obey the law, we would be punished? Is it laziness, a lack of imagination, or an inherent respect for order?

A more common contemporary view is that, irrespective of the morality of a given rule of law, we need to respect the *legitimacy* of the law. Senior lawyers earning over £1 million per annum may well not agree that they should pay high levels of tax on most of their income, but they will usually respect their legal obligation to do so.

In the following example, we shall trace the *legitimacy* of this tax rule.

Example 2

Legitimacy of legal rules

Assume it is 2014. Frank Mackworth, chairman of Valuebank plc, has failed to pay his £1 million-plus tax bill, on the ground that he morally objects to the imposition of the additional rate of tax at 45% on all income above £150,000.

- The First-Tier Tax Tribunal, on appeal from Her Majesty's Revenue & Customs (HMRC), has imposed a penalty on Frank.

- The Tribunal derives its authority to impose penalties from the Tribunals, Courts and Enforcement Act 2007.

- Under the authority of the Taxes Management Act 1970, s. 59B(3), Frank is liable to a penalty for not paying his income tax to HMRC by the due date.

- Income tax is charged under the Income Tax Acts, which include the key statute, the Income and Corporation Taxes Act 1988, and the Income Tax Act 2007 as amended by the Finance Acts 2009 and 2011.

- These are all statutes passed by Parliament, comprising the House of Commons, the House of Lords, and the Monarch.

- The Enrolled Act Rule states that no court can challenge the validity of an Act.

- Parliament is given sovereignty (see 1.4.3) by the Bill of Rights 1688, enacted by the revolutionary Convention Parliament.

Because the Glorious Revolution of 1688 replaced the sovereignty of the Monarch alone, it is the Bill of Rights that gives all subsequent statutes their legitimacy.

There are two themes here: one is that we can (in theory) trace the legitimacy of all law in a jurisdiction back to one fundamental legal rule. We explore this at 1.4.2. The other is that, usually as a result of that rule, an actor (or combination of actors) in a political system is given something called 'sovereignty', which entitles them to make law unconstrained by other actors. We first (at 1.4.2) examine the idea that there might be a fundamental legal rule, and then (at 1.4.3) the importance of sovereignty.

1.4.2 **One solution: the *gründnorm***

The importance of the *gründnorm*

Legal theorists sometimes give a name to a law which provides legitimacy to subsequent laws: the term '*gründnorm*'.

 Essential explanation

The *gründnorm*

'Gründnorm', coined by Kelsen,[22] means 'basic rule'.

The idea is that all law in any jurisdiction can be characterised as 'norms'—in English this means 'rules'. Each can be quite specific, for example the application of case law to a specific narrow circumstance. Each norm derives its legitimacy from a wider and more basic principle until one can legitimise no further. This rule is called the *gründnorm*.

In any jurisdiction where there is a rule of law (see 1.5) there will be a *gründnorm*. In the US, the *gründnorm* is the US Constitution, which gives each actor in the legal and political system its authority, and defines basic principles.

The example of Nazi Germany illustrates this well. The Rule of Law was increasingly a sham in the Third Reich but Hitler paid lip-service to the legitimacy of his regime. You will remember from Case study 1 that it was the Reichstag that in 1933 passed the Enabling Act, devolving its powers to the Cabinet. The Act was renewed in 1937 and 1941, giving a theoretical legitimacy to his regime. The Enabling Act was passed by the Reichstag under the constitution of the Weimar Republic that preceded Nazi rule. The Weimar Constitution of 1919 ended a year of constitutional uncertainty after the demise of the German Empire. It is arguable, therefore, that the *gründnorm* in Nazi Germany was this document.

The *gründnorm* will usually change if there is a revolution, and a different regime is recognised. This occurs when society begins to acquiesce to the new legal and political order.

This process is illustrated in Figure 1.5. Time is important in this analysis, as we must look back in time to find the rules (or 'norms') that legitimise any given legal rule. So, starting from the most recent legal rules on the right of Figure 1.5, we can trace their legitimacy back, until we arrive at the *gründnorm*. In the case of the Frank Mackworth example, the intricacies of tax legislation and case law occupy the area on the right of Figure 1.5. They are dependent on earlier norms for their legitimacy.

As we saw in the example, the *gründnorm* from which many legal rules in the current UK political settlement derive their legitimacy is the Bill of Rights 1688.[23] This created parliamentary sovereignty (sovereignty is defined at 1.4.3 and parliamentary sovereignty is explored at 4.1.1). All previous norms (laws) are no longer considered automatically legitimate. The slate is wiped clean at that point.

[22] Hans Kelsen, *The Pure Theory of Law* (1943).   [23] Actually enacted in 1689.

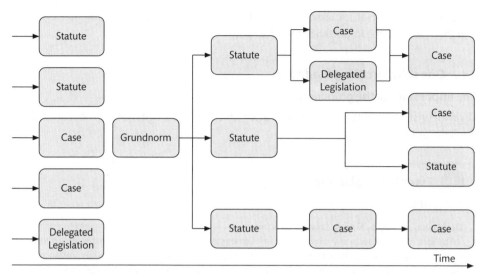

Figure 1.5 Role of the *gründnorm* in justifying subsequent law

The *gründnorm* in practice

The UK (for simplicity we will restrict our discussion here to England) is a special case. While England's political settlement was the Glorious Revolution, so that the Bill of Rights 1688 is the *gründnorm*, there is a significant amount of prior law that also has legitimacy.

This is either because the *gründnorm* as a concept does not suit a country that has developed organically like post-1066 England; or it is because the concept of the *gründnorm* is flawed because it attempts to impose an intellectual framework on an enormous variety of realities.

 Essential debate

Is the concept of the *gründnorm* flawed?

Kelsen posited the theory that in any jurisdiction the law could be traced back to one fundamental rule or norm, called the *gründnorm*. Does this work?

Should we regard the idea of the *gründnorm* as a one-size-fits-all concept that provides a useful analytical tool, or as an interesting but flawed attempt to provide logical structure to complex and possibly arbitrary historical and legal developments?

One conclusion is this:

Provided the *gründnorm* permits it, courts are free to adopt previous laws, but only under the authority of the *gründnorm*, and their legitimacy now flows from that *gründnorm*, and not any previous one. This has occurred in the UK where some very old cases and statutes remain good law. So the relationship between *gründnorm* and dependant law is not necessarily one that flows with time.

So, for instance, parts of Magna Carta 1215[24] (e.g. s. 1, confirming the liberty of freemen in England) are still recognised as good law, but only because post-1688 cases have done so. In your study of contract law, you will encounter a case from 1602, *Pinnel's Case*,[25] which is central to the study of the doctrine of consideration.

Many of the US states enacted 'reception statutes' under the Declaration of Independence (and then the US Constitution) which formally incorporated relevant prior English case law. Hong Kong retained English case law in the same way when it reverted to China in 1997. This formal adoption of aspects of previous law is more common than the unusual piecemeal approach taken in the UK.

Another conclusion is that a country can have more than one *gründnorm*, depending on the area of law concerned. In the UK we have adopted EU law. The European Communities Act 1972 incorporated it into UK law, and in such matters, it is the Treaty on the Foundation of the EU (originally the Treaty of Rome 1957) that is the *gründnorm*. It is possibly by similar reasoning that Magna Carta still has legitimacy.

1.4.3 The importance of sovereignty

Sovereignty is a very complex concept and the subject of much debate among constitutional and legal scholars. Its importance is that law made by a sovereign actor in a state has legitimacy.

 Essential explanation

Sovereignty

A notoriously difficult concept to pin down. Here we use it in the following sense: sovereignty (sometimes called 'supremacy') is the characteristic of an actor in a state who can impose its will on all the other actors without constraint.

   Although a sovereign power can devolve authority to make rules, that power is always given with the authority of the Sovereign.

Positivists like Hobbes believed that the idea of laws that were legitimate by virtue of nature was misguided. They believed it to be more important to recognise that the law was given legitimacy because the law was the law prevailing in that jurisdiction at that time. In Hobbes' state of nature, each person has complete freedom to do what they want—so everyone is sovereign. In such a situation, it would be impossible to resolve disputes—there would be anarchy. We consider this further in the context of the Rule of Law at 1.5. Hobbes (in his *Leviathan*[26]) and others reasoned that at some point in the distant past, individuals gave up their sovereignty for a degree of protection and support from the state and its machinery. This was called the 'social contract'.

Many legal and political theorists say that the necessary consequence of sovereignty is that a sovereign body cannot bind its future self irrevocably. This is because to do so would undermine its own later freedom to do what it wants.

[24] Originally issued in 1215, but the version now in force is Magna Carta 1297.
[25] *Pinnel's Case* (1602) 5 Co Rep 117.
[26] Thomas Hobbes, *Leviathan* (1651).

In the UK, sovereignty is said to be vested in 'The Queen in Parliament', namely the Queen, the House of Lords, and the House of Commons. This is called 'parliamentary sovereignty' or 'parliamentary supremacy' (see 4.1.1). Some theorists refer to *'de facto* sovereignty', as distinct from *'de jure* sovereignty'. *De jure* sovereignty resides in the body that has formal authority to make laws; *de facto* sovereignty resides in those people who *actually* make the decisions. In the UK *de facto* sovereignty normally resides in the Cabinet—when the government has a working majority.

Historically, sovereignty vested in monarchs; prior to the English Interregnum (in 1649-60, when there was no monarch) it was generally accepted that by 'divine right' God had vested His authority in the King or Queen, so the monarch had sole sovereignty. The monarch in the UK is still referred to as the 'Sovereign', though in practical terms the monarch is no longer sovereign because he or she cannot make law independently of other actors in the system.

Any powers exercised by local authorities in the UK do not give them legal sovereignty. This is because they are granted (or devolved) by Parliament. The UK is said to be 'unitary' in this respect.

In contrast, the US and Germany are examples of countries where sovereignty is shared federally, that is to say it is shared between federal (national) institutions and those of the 50 states/16 *länder*. The US Constitution (Tenth Amendment) states that any powers not expressly conferred on the federal government are reserved for the states. So some powers are reserved for the states and some are ceded to federal institutions. This has a profound impact on the consciousness of citizens in that their political loyalty is in many circumstances to their state more than to their nation. It also affects the degree of acceptance they may or may not have for decisions made (and politicians) at a federal level.

Sovereignty is often shared between different institutions within a state. Sometimes it is difficult to pin down exactly where sovereignty lies. For instance, in the US, there is a true Separation of Powers, with different powers vested (by the Constitution) in the three branches of the federal government (executive (President), legislature (Congress), and judiciary (Supreme Court)). Indeed it is arguable that in the US, it is the citizens, through the Constitution, who are sovereign. In theory, the people created and can amend the Constitution and it is the people who can amend it. Famously, the US Constitution opens with the words, 'We, the People ...'.

1.5 **The Rule of Law**

'The Law is King', wrote Thomas Paine.[27] He meant that in a free country the law itself must be sovereign, and not any one individual or body. Nobody is 'above the law'.

To many lawyers, one of the vital ingredients of civilised society is something called the 'Rule of Law'. To an academic lawyer the idea of the Rule of Law is notoriously difficult to pin down. To the politician, it is an easy rhetorical shortcut to the moral high ground. Dwight D. Eisenhower, President of the US 1953-61 (and famous World War II general) opined: 'The clearest way to show what the rule of law means to us in everyday life is to recall what has

---

[27] Thomas Paine, *Common Sense* (1776) (London: Everyman's Library, 1994), p. 279.

happened when there is no rule of law.'[28] Eisenhower was referring to the terror of the 'knock on the door in the middle of the night' in Nazi Germany, and warning about what he saw as the future in Communist states. These were states where the regimes aimed to exert total power, without reference to the niceties of legality. At the other extreme are states or ghettoes within states where there is no law at all, and people revert to what Hobbes would call a 'brutish' state of nature.[29]

1.5.1 Defining the Rule of Law

The Rule of Law is therefore a concept used to describe a group of characteristics necessary for a functioning and civilised state. Lord Bingham was noted for his advocacy of human rights and the Rule of Law. Among the many proponents he was one of the most influential. In his seminal lecture on 'The Rule of Law',[30] he identified eight 'sub-rules':

1. The law must be accessible, intelligible, clear, and predictable.
2. Questions of legal right and liability should ordinarily be resolved by application of the law and not the exercise of discretion.
3. The laws of the land should apply equally to all, save to the extent that objective differences justify differentiation.
4. The law must afford adequate protection of human rights.
5. Means must be provided for resolving, without excessive cost or delay, civil disputes which the parties cannot resolve themselves.
6. Ministers and public officers must exercise the powers conferred on them reasonably, in good faith, for the purpose for which the powers were conferred and without exceeding the limits of such powers.
7. The adjudicative procedures provided by the state should be fair.
8. The state must comply with its obligations in international law.

A more concise definition was given by theorist John Finnis, who said the Rule of Law is 'the name commonly given to the state of affairs in which a legal system is legally in good shape ...'.[31]

Referring back to Eisenhower's statement, there are various factors which prejudice the Rule of Law:

- arbitrariness;
- lack of protection for some or all citizens;
- lack of an independent judiciary; and
- legitimacy replaced by coercion.

---

[28] Dwight D. Eisenhower, Speech, Law Day, 5 May 1958 .
[29] Thomas Hobbes, *Leviathan* (1651), chs. XIII–XIV.
[30] Lord Bingham, 'The Sixth Sir David Williams Lecture: The Rule of Law' (November 2006).
[31] John Finnis, *Natural Law and Natural Rights* (Oxford: OUP, 2nd edn, 2011), p. 270.

1.5.2 **Absence of the Rule of Law**

Imagine a state with no laws at all. Sovereignty would vest in the individual. Freedom would be complete. Hobbes painted a dire picture in his seminal work, *Leviathan*, a key source for all modern political and legal theorists.

> In [the state of nature] ... where every man is enemy to every man; ... men live without other security, than what their own strength, and their own invention shall furnish them with all. In such condition, there is no place for Industry; because the fruit thereof is uncertain; and consequently no culture of the earth; no navigation, nor use of the commodities that may be imported by sea; no commodious building; no instruments of moving, and removing such things as require much force; no knowledge of the face of the Earth; no account of time; no arts; no letters; no society; and which is worst of all, continual fear, and danger of violent death. And the life of man, solitary, poor, nasty, brutish, and short ...[32]

The state would not be a 'state' in the conventional sense. The weak would be at the mercy of the strong, and everyone would fight to assert themselves over all but their immediate family. Hobbes wrote that we had to give up much of our personal sovereignty in return for the state guaranteeing us a structured society. This was his 'Social Contract'. Figure 1.6 shows how the Rule of Law occupies a middle ground between anarchy and totalitarianism (i.e. where the state seeks to exert total control over its subjects); and how the individual gives up some personal sovereignty in exchange for a system of laws.

The following passage is taken from *Dangerous Society (Detroit's Inner City Gangs)*,[33] by Carl Taylor:

> In the Third City, you have citizens, noncitizens—people who participate in an underground economy, but not in mainstream civic life—and anticitizens—people who defy authority and accept criminal activity as normative.
>
> There's a strong identity of 'us' against 'them'—the white power structure and the black bourgeoisie.
>
> The Third City is held together by common values often at loggerheads with mainstream ones.
>
> The thug is perceived as the underdog. I was taught to walk away from a fight. In the Third City, parents are likely to tell kids to never back down—even to carry a gun. Their biggest resentment is hypocrisy. When major systems fail it only affirms the feeling that everything is rigged to favour whites and the rich.

This is a modern day version of anarchy. In theory, Detroit is governed, maintained, and policed by the Detroit City Council at local level, the state of Michigan at state level, and the US government at a federal level. In practice, the apparatus of state has disintegrated in some parts of Detroit and the Rule of Law has disappeared from areas of the city, as graphically portrayed in the film *Eight Mile*, starring Eminem.

In the wider world today, there are some states that are said to have 'failed', in that many of the indicators of the Rule of Law are absent. A failed state index is generated

---

[32] Thomas Hobbes, *Leviathan* (1651), ch. 13, para. 9.

[33] Carl S. Taylor, *Dangerous Society (Detroit's Inner City Gangs)* (Michigan State University Press, 1990).

annually[34] by analysing social, economic, and political components, many of which overlap with factors of the Rule of Law (e.g. adherence to human rights, and the security apparatus being above the law). In 2012, the three most failed states were listed as Somalia, the Democratic Republic of Congo, and Sudan.

There have been societies where the Rule of Law was shunned or had not yet developed. Evidence suggests that Iron Age societies were organised around survival and, where necessary, cooperation and barter. After the disintegration of the Tsarist regime in 1918, the Ukraine was proclaimed (by Nestor Makhno) as an anarchist community on similar principles. The instruments of state control and the Rule of Law were eschewed. The experiment was extinguished by Lenin's communists after four years.

At the other extreme are totalitarian systems (such as Lenin's) where state control aims to be absolute. Many would say that the Rule of Law is suffocated under these regimes. However, some theorists like Raz[35] argue that, on the contrary, the Rule of Law in these states is strong. Raz refers to the 'sharp knife' of the Rule of Law, in that it can be used for both good and bad ends.

In Figure 1.6, at the totalitarian end of the spectrum, there is no freedom, where all sovereignty is vested in an individual: an autocracy (one person has ultimate power) is one type of totalitarian approach.

Case study 3

President Niyazov of Turkmenistan

After the dissolution of the Soviet Union in 1990, Suparumat Niyazov became President of Turkmenistan. He attempted to fill the legal and cultural vacuum left by communism with a quasi-dictatorial rule combined with a cult of personality. His regime was noted not only for these features but also for its idiosyncrasy. Among his many decrees, Niyazov:

- banned the use of sound recordings at cultural events on the ground that they stifled creativity;
- forbade opera, ballet, and the circus on account of their being 'decidedly unturkmen-like';
- excluded dogs from the capital because of the smell;
- ordered the building of a 'palace of ice', so that those living in the desert country could learn to skate;
- ordered that men should no longer wear beards or long hair;
- prohibited television personalities from wearing make-up because he believed Turkmen women were already beautiful enough;
- outlawed gold teeth to encourage dental health; and
- renamed months and days of the week after notable Turkmens, including himself.

One of the characteristics of the Rule of Law is that laws must not be arbitrary. Citizens must be able to anticipate the nature of the obligations they have to the state. The situation in Case study 3 is an illustration of the exercise of arbitrary power. There are many examples from history where such exercise of power has been used to more malign ends.

---

[34] Fund for Peace, *Failed States Index*, http://www.fundforpeace.org.

[35] Joseph Raz, 'The Rule of Law and its virtue' in *The Authority of Law* (Oxford: OUP, 2nd edn, 2009), pp. 210–32.

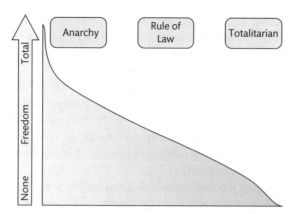

Figure 1.6 Relationship between personal freedom and types of state

If we generalise different systems into a spectrum from total control, through various types of democracy, to anarchy, we can broadly conclude that the Rule of Law probably typifies any system where laws are created and administered in a democratic and fair context. This is a generalisation as it is culturally slightly blinkered to equate democracy with the Rule of Law; many cultures do exhibit many of the characteristics outlined by Lord Bingham, but are not necessarily democracies.

1.5.3 The nature of the Rule of Law

While the Rule of Law is absolutely central to the self-image of a modern state, Lord Bingham has warned of the dangers of the concept becoming so misappropriated and watered-down that it becomes 'the jurisprudential equivalent of motherhood and apple pie'.[36]

Here we need to refer back to the discussion of jurisprudence at 1.3. You may recall that Natural Lawyers (see 1.2.3) regard law as deriving its underpinnings from moral arguments. They would say that the Rule of Law must depend for its legitimacy on minimum standards of morality and predictability. Many of Lord Bingham's 'sub-rules' would seem to reflect this.

But positivists would claim that a clear and consistent body of rules does not necessarily need to be moral, or conform to certain social or political ideals. This is Joseph Raz's 'sharp knife' argument again. They would say that the main virtue of the Rule of Law is to allow subjects (not necessarily called 'citizens') to plan their lives. The philosopher and economist Freidrich von Hayek most clearly summarised this position:

> Stripped of all technicalities this means that government in all its actions is bound by rules fixed and announced beforehand—rules which make it possible to foresee with fair certainty how the authority will use its coercive powers in given circumstances, and to plan one's individual affairs on the basis of this knowledge.[37]

---

[36] Lord Bingham, 'The Sixth Sir David Williams Lecture: The Rule of Law' (November 2006), p. 4.
[37] Freidrich Hayek, *The Road to Serfdom* (1944), p. 72.

In the light of this, the positivist view would mean that it does not really matter how fair a system of law is, merely that it exists and conforms to its own clear rules. Thus, all systems but anarchic systems or arbitrary tyranny would conform to the Rule of Law.

1.5.4 **The Rule of Law in practice**

'Window dressing'?

For the purposes of this book, we will adopt the more ambitious ideal of the Rule of Law, as set out by Lord Bingham at 1.5.1. Lord Bingham's concern that the term is used as 'window dressing' remains valid. The Rule of Law might be termed an aspiration, rather than a reality.

Governments do openly aspire to follow the Rule of Law. Leaders as polarised as US President Barack Obama and Robert Mugabe, President of Zimbabwe, seek to adopt the legitimacy of the term 'the Rule of Law', but these states can fall short because aspects of the Rule of Law (as defined by academics) are not adhered to, for instance because laws are applied arbitrarily or because human rights are disproportionately compromised. In the debates over whether the invasion of Iraq in 2003 was legal, the then British Prime Minister Tony Blair expended a great deal of effort to show that, in his view, the invasion was legally justified.

By contrast, governments sometimes adopt a more pragmatic attitude to observing the doctrine. When Anthony Eden (British Prime Minister 1955-7) ordered the invasion of Suez in Egypt, he stated: 'We should not allow ourselves to become involved in legal quibbles ...'.[38]

One legal scholar analysed the US in 2008, stating, 'the Rule of Law has yet to be reinstated in the US battle on terror. The problem started when the Bush administration rejected the Geneva conventions which are intended to apply to every armed conflict in the World.'[39]

Cultural considerations

The Rule of Law may seem like a basic constituent requirement of a state, but it is arguable that it is (like democracy, which so frequently accompanies it) a construct of Western academics. This links with sociology because different cultures have different approaches to rights and obligations—even on the need for laws.

Here is one example. Contract law is an absolutely central element of law in Western countries and in many others. But it is not an entirely familiar idiom in parts of the world where barter and bribery have historically been more commonplace forms of business. In the Middle East, Africa, and the Far East it was long acknowledged that reciprocal gift-giving and trade were perfectly acceptable bedfellows.[40] The idea that a bribe is culpable was alien in some cultures. Squeamishness about gifts and incentives is sometimes seen as a view held only in certain Western democracies.

---

[38] *Armed Intervention in the 1956 Suez Crisis: The Legal Advice tendered to the British Government* quoted by Geoffrey Marston, (1988) 37 ICLQ 773, 777, taken from Lord Bingham, 'The Sixth Sir David Williams Lecture: The Rule of Law' (November 2006).

[39] Barbara Olshansky, The Center for Constitutional Rights.

[40] For more on this issue, see e.g. M. Mauss, *The Gift. The Form and Reason for Exchange in Archaic Societies* (1954) (New York: WW Norton, 1990).

For instance, some societies have been more recently tribal. Many tribes existed on a smaller scale to Western societies and so did not need the machinery of state that has typified the latter in the last few centuries. This is closer to the Hobbesian state of Nature (see 1.5) where administrative creations such as legally binding obligations are unfamiliar. To individuals in such societies, replacing long-established customs with laws might seem unnecessary and inappropriate. Many studies have focused on Africa as an example, where the number of tribes (over 3,000 according to one study[41]), languages, or ethnic groups, far exceeds the number of countries (55). Even the idea of a country or state was (it is argued) superimposed on these societies by European empires. All the apparatus that comes with a state (including legal systems) could be said to be unsuitable.

An analogy might be drawn with the idea of cultural imperialism. This is a term used by sociologists, among others, to characterise the spread of (usually) Western culture into other civilisations. This extends to the adoption of the English language, and the incorporation of Western popular culture, be it sporting, musical, or cinematic. This has accelerated with the stimulus of information technology. Whether the Rule of Law is an aspect of 'cultural imperialism' is a matter of opinion.

The alternative view is that, as the world shrinks and becomes interconnected, so it is more important to have common ground in doing business and politics; hence essential legal concepts such as legally enforceable contracts and internationally comprehensible law have to be projected on to local cultures.

Compliance with the Rule of Law today

Studies have been made of the degree to which modern states comply with the Rule of Law. An organisation called the World Justice Project has attempted to rank notable states by conformity with indicators of the Rule of Law, which by and large mirror those of Lord Bingham above.

While the Rule of Law World Report breaks down the indicators into factors, some general observations are sufficient to provide us with evidence of the Rule of Law in practice:

- Even the top-ranked nations (Sweden, Norway, New Zealand) fell some way short of the ideal, with around 20% shortfall overall using the factors in the report.
- There is a strong correlation between prosperity and the indicators, but not a necessary one. One view is that the Rule of Law is a luxury afforded to states who can afford it. Alternatively, it could be said that the Western democracies with higher scores have a culturally different attitude to the role of the law and the status of the citizen.

The most common limitations on the Rule of Law (even in otherwise high-scoring nations) were the prevalence of police discrimination, and the difficulty (owing to expense) of accessing civil justice.

- China scored highly in criminal justice and security, but low in fundamental rights and judicial independence. Interestingly it scored very highly on open government.
- Corruption and high crime rates were rife in South America and the Caribbean, as well as lack of government accountability.
- Middle East and North African countries scored highly in lack of crime but poorly on government accountability.

[41] The Joshua Project, http://www.joshuaproject.net/.

1.6 The Separation of Powers

1.6.1 **Separation of Powers in theory**

Many of the indicators or sub-rules (to use Lord Bingham's language) of the Rule of Law can be safeguarded to some extent by a simple constitutional device, the Separation of Powers, by which a division of powers within a state will prevent accumulation of too much power in the hands of one body or person. It is necessary to give a brief account of this doctrine, although a fuller discussion is properly the preserve of public law.

 Essential explanation

The Separation of Powers

The Separation of Powers doctrine was first advocated by the Ancient Greeks, but was given its modern expression by Baron de Montesquieu in the 18th century. He believed that a division of the roles of the state between three branches would provide a safeguard to the tyranny of one of them, most especially the executive branch.

   Under the doctrine, each 'branch' of government has a different role to play in the idealised constitution. In its purest form, there should be no overlap between the branches, either in function or personnel. If overlap occurred, then power would concentrate and open the door to arbitrary or oppressive government.

   Normally powers are divided between three functions of state (as in Figure 1.7):

- the legislature makes law;
- the executive (the government) implements law; and
- the judiciary resolves disputes relating to the law, between the state and its citizens.

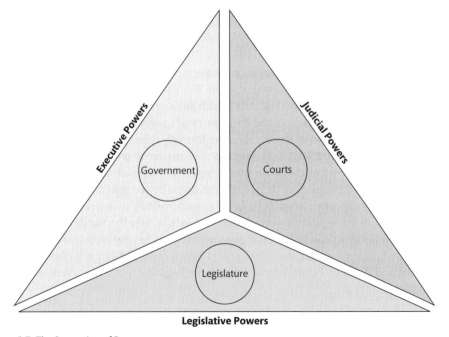

Figure 1.7 The Separation of Powers

1.6.2 Separation of Powers in practice

In the UK at national level, the executive is Her Majesty's Government, the legislature is Parliament, and the courts constitute the judiciary. Although the normal model has three branches, there are variations around the world: China, for instance, has five branches.

In several of the case studies, this ideal has broken down. President Niyazov of Turkmenistan reinforced the Soviet concentration of power in the hands of the President, notionally the executive. There was no legislature, and the judiciary was staffed by political appointees.

In Nazi Germany, the position was summarised in this extract from the Nuremberg War Trials:

> Independence of the judiciary was destroyed. Judges were removed from the bench for political and 'racial' reasons. Periodic 'letters' were sent by the Ministry of Justice to all Reich judges and public prosecutors, instructing them as to the results they must accomplish. Both the bench and bar were continually spied upon by the Gestapo and SD [intelligence agency], and were directed to keep disposition of their cases politically acceptable. Judges, prosecutors and, in many cases, defense counsel were reduced in effect to an administrative arm of the Nazi Party.[42]

The doctrine also states that the branches cannot operate in isolation and that there should be a system of 'checks and balances' so that each branch can keep the others in check and maintain a balance of power. So, for instance, in England & Wales, the doctrine of judicial review allows courts to ensure that public bodies (formally within the 'executive' branch) act within the powers they have been granted and do not exceed or abuse those powers. In England & Wales judicial review does not extend to questioning the merits of the decisions of the state (unlike in the US, for instance) but merely that the decisions are made in the right way.

The US Constitution was conceived deliberately to reflect Montesquieu's doctrine, and the success of the Constitution in this respect is the source of sustained debate among political and legal theorists. The repeated 'budget impasses' where a President from one party refuses to sign into law the budget drawn up by a Congress with majorities of the other party, are evidence of these checks and balances at work. Periodic rebalancing occurs if one branch sustains political primacy for too long, usually with the Supreme Court (the judiciary's highest court) moderating the behaviour of the President or of Congress.

In the UK, the Separation of Powers is not so formally reflected as in the US, though the Constitutional Reform Act 2005 tidied up many of the loose ends (e.g. the anomaly that the Lord Chancellor was at the same time a senior member of all three branches). The Queen remains at the head of all three branches but is by convention unable to exert any real power in any capacity. Because the UK is a parliamentary democracy, ministers in the government sit in the legislature—unlike in the US where only the Vice-President has any role to play in Congress—and hence the government straddles the executive and legislative branches. In Chapter 5 we see that some courts have a quasi-legislative (as well as judicial) role in England & Wales. Figure 1.8 summarises the Separation of Powers within the UK at national level.

---

[42] *United States v Altstotter*, Nuremerg Military Tribunals case no. 3 pg 7 indictment count 1 (1947).

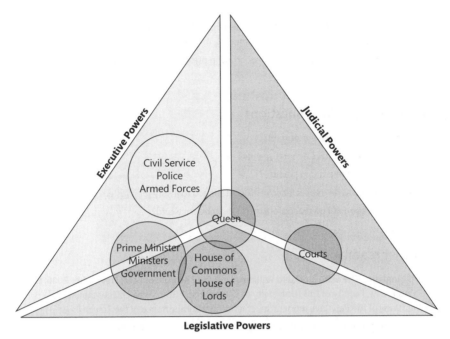

Figure 1.8 The Separation of Powers in the UK

It is quite clear that 'successful' states depend on the embodiment of various characteristics of the Rule of Law, importantly including a separation of powers. Without clearly delineated and balanced participants, it is unfortunately human nature that power will be abused. 'Power tends to corrupt, and absolute power corrupts absolutely.'[43]

➕ Summary

- Law is a system of rules by which a state operates.
- Law touches on every aspect of our day-to-day lives.
- Law cannot be viewed in isolation from other related areas.
- Morality is difficult to define and analyse, but this is a worthwhile exercise as it helps us understand the relationship between law and ethics. This relationship should be viewed in the context of social values.
- Jurisprudence is the study of key concepts in law, and has developed over time.
- One important issue in legal theory is the legitimacy of law, and a common means of providing legitimacy is to find an acceptable *gründnorm* (or basic rule).
- Sovereignty is important in a legal system—it describes which actor in that system has power over other participants.

[43] John Dalberg-Acton, Letter to Bishop Mandell Creighton (5 April 1887).

- Another important legal concept is the Rule of Law, by which we can analyse certain characteristics of a healthy state. If the Rule of Law disappears, the individual will usually suffer.
- The Separation of Powers is a central doctrine in preserving the Rule of Law, and with it the rights of citizens.

Thought-provoking questions

1. Why do you think law is important?
2. Should law-makers have a moral agenda?
3. Is jurisprudence relevant in practice?
4. Is the Rule of Law an intellectual construct, designed to justify the Western democratic state?
5. Is the Separation of Powers appropriate in the modern world?

Further reading

Lord Bingham, 'The Sixth Sir David Williams Lecture: The Rule of Law', November 2006, Centre for Public Law, Faculty of Law, University of Cambridge, http://www.cpl.law.cam.ac.uk/
—this is one of the definitive modern statements on the importance of the Rule of Law.

John Finnis, *Natural Law and Natural Rights* (Oxford; OUP, 2nd edn, 2011)
—includes authoritative discussions on the Rule of Law.

Thomas Hobbes, *Leviathan* (1651) (Oxford: OUP, 2008)
—a text demonstrating early concepts of the social contract.

Hans Kelsen, *The Pure Theory of Law* (1943) (The Lawbook Exchange Ltd, 2009)
—one of the important texts incorporating the idea of the **gründnorm**.

Joseph Raz, 'The Rule of Law and its virtue' in *The Authority of Law: Essays on Law and Morality* (Oxford: OUP, 2nd edn, 2009), pp. 210–32
—where it is argued that the Rule of Law can be taken to undesirable extremes.

For the authors' reflections on the thought-provoking questions, additional self-test questions, podcasts offering a variety of perspectives on legal systems and skills, and a library of links to useful websites, visit the free Online Resource Centre at **http://www.oxfordtextbooks.co.uk/orc/slorach/.**

2

Sources of law in England & Wales

 Learning objectives

After studying this chapter you should, in relation to England & Wales:

● Be aware of the key jurisdictions that are relevant to a lawyer.

● Be familiar with sources of law.

● Be aware of fundamental distinctions between types of law.

● Be able to use essential terms in use by lawyers.

● Demonstrate a basic understanding of the development of case law and statutes.

Introduction

In Chapter 1 we looked at general theories of law, and placed the law in its political, cultural, and historical context. In this chapter we look at how this is manifested in England & Wales.

The first thing that might surprise you is the term, 'England & Wales'. This is not a function of any bias among lawyers in relation to Scotland or Northern Ireland, merely that their legal systems are largely different from those of England & Wales.

This chapter, then, is about the basic language of law in the jurisdiction of England & Wales. ('Jurisdiction' is defined at 2.1.) An understanding of the essential terms introduced in this chapter is essential for any lawyer.

Lawyers need to know *where* they are practising. Section 2.1 concerns the fundamental issue of which law a lawyer in England & Wales will be working with. Section 2.2 deals with the issue of where that law comes from: you are unlikely to be surprised that there is no single source of law in England & Wales, and that it is a fascinating hybrid of different types of law, not all of which are wholly compatible with the others. Section 2.3 establishes and clarifies key terms you will come across every day.

Finally, once we have identified these basic concepts, we review the development of the two fundamental sources of law in England & Wales—statutes and case law. This groundwork is essential before we explore in more detail the court system, statutes, and case law, in Chapters 3, 4, and 5 respectively.

2.1 What is the 'legal system'?

2.1.1 What is a 'legal system'?

A lawyer's ability to practise is limited by matters of 'jurisdiction'.

 Essential explanations

Jurisdiction

'Jurisdiction' is a term you will come across often.

It is most commonly used to refer to a political entity where a particular law has application. This could be the EU, the UK, Greater London, the London Borough of Camden, or even a local parish. This is context in which this book will use the term.

You may also occasionally read that an entity does not have 'jurisdiction' over a particular issue. What this means is that it does not have the power to make law or settle disputes on that area of human endeavour. So, for instance, a particular court may not have jurisdiction to decide on certain issues of immigration.

Legal system

In many ways, a 'legal system' is synonymous with a 'jurisdiction'. The idea of a jurisdiction is essentially political. A political scientist would call the actors in the political system the 'polity'.

The legal system describes the body of institutions that make, execute, and resolve disputes on the law of a jurisdiction, together with the law dealt with, taken as a whole. You may encounter the term 'legal system' in a narrower sense, meaning the courts of a jurisdiction.

As you can see, the boundaries between the legal and the political frames of reference are very blurred. We saw at 1.1.2 that this is by no means an inappropriate analysis.

These key concepts are not merely academic. They have practical significance to lawyers in many situations. For instance, in a modern contract two important common clauses are about 'jurisdiction' (where litigation happens if there is a dispute in relation to the contract) and 'choice of law' (which country's law applies to that dispute).

2.1.2 Legal systems in Britain

The legal system in the 'British Isles' (this very loose term is used deliberately) is idiosyncratic and complex. There are overlapping jurisdictions for different types of law. What is peculiar is the variety of combinations of states and nations which have, to varying degrees, been associated with, or unified with, England. As a result, there is a multiplicity of different forums. This is very much an accident of history.

This is not unusual; for instance many nations like Germany or the US have several layers of law. But the legal systems in the 'British Isles' do have a quirkiness that bemuses even some practising lawyers.

Another eccentricity is the continuous, evolutionary, and extended development of the political system. Each change has left a legacy in the legal system. Figure 2.1 summarises the key distinctions.

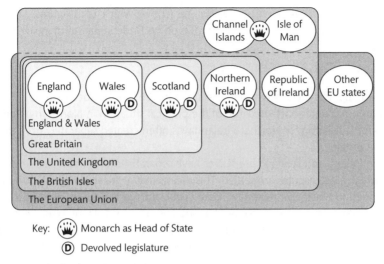

Key: Monarch as Head of State

D   Devolved legislature

Figure 2.1 Jurisdictions within the British Isles

We start by looking at all the British Isles, and gradually narrow the focus. At 2.2.3 we broaden the focus again, to place these jurisdictions in the EU context.

'The British Isles'

The British Isles is a geographical, rather than legal or political, term. It is made up of two sovereign states: the Republic of Ireland and the United Kingdom. The Monarch (currently Queen Elizabeth II) (symbolised by a crown in Figure 2.1) is Head of State in all of these Islands, except the Republic of Ireland. The Republic gained independence in 1922, ending a state of affairs that had existed from 1801, when the formerly separate kingdoms of Great Britain and Ireland were united.

The Republic of Ireland (also known as Eire in the Irish language) is therefore entirely separate from the rest of the UK in political and legal terms, although both Ireland and the UK are members of the EU. The summary diagram at 2.12 places some of these changes in historical context.

Guernsey, Jersey, and the Isle of Man are Crown Dependencies, and are independent of the UK, having their own governments, legislatures, and court systems. They are usually represented internationally by the UK. None is a member of the EU, though some trading aspects of the EU do apply to these islands.[1] Often the UK Parliament is asked to extend the jurisdiction of statutes to these dependencies, but it has no formal sovereignty there.

The United Kingdom

The United Kingdom (formally, 'The United Kingdom of Great Britain and Northern Ireland') is the state in which 'British' people live and which acts on the international stage. The default position for any legislation produced by Parliament is that its jurisdiction is the whole of the UK. It includes the countries of England, Northern Ireland, Scotland, and Wales. Northern Ireland,

---

[1] Treaty on the Functioning of the European Union, Art. 355(5)(c).

Scotland, and Wales all have devolved legislatures (shown with a 'D' in Figure 2.1) which have varying degrees of competence or jurisdiction (i.e. power) independently of the UK Parliament.

Great Britain

Great Britain does not include Northern Ireland. 'Great Britain' is not a commonly used term (except in international sport). Because of the political situation in Northern Ireland during 'the Troubles', legislation for Northern Ireland was often created separately from that applying to Great Britain.

Northern Ireland and Scotland are said to have separate 'legal systems', in the sense of the forum in which legal disputes are settled. This means that a citizen living in Northern Ireland would be tried in Northern Ireland or make civil claims in the courts of Northern Ireland. Likewise a citizen living in Scotland would be tried or make civil claims in the Scottish courts. Although the Northern Irish system resembles that of England & Wales, and is common law in nature (see 2.3.2 for more on the contrast between common law and civil law), the Scottish system does not mirror that of England & Wales. The court system is particular to Scotland, and the law itself is an amalgam of civil, common, and customary law, with certain academic publications having almost the force of law.

England & Wales

This leaves England & Wales—the 'English legal system'. References to 'English' normally imply 'Welsh' too in this context. Wales was annexed to England in 1282. The law English lawyers use is that of England & Wales, and is administered by the English courts. The main focus of this book is the law applicable in the English legal system, although viewed in a wider context.

Summary

The map in Figure 2.2 offers what is perhaps a more familiar summary. Table 2.1 provides a key to the map as well as drawing out important features of each jurisdiction highlighted.

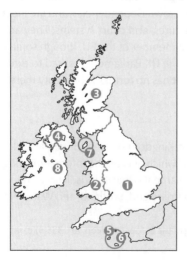

Figure 2.2 Legal map of the British Isles

Table 2.1 Key to Figure 2.2: Legal and political systems within the British Isles

	Entity	Legal system	Political system
1.	England	England & Wales	Part of the UK and the EU
2.	Wales	England & Wales	Part of the UK and the EU; devolved legislature
3.	Scotland	Scottish	Part of the UK and the EU; devolved legislature
4.	Northern Ireland	Northern Irish	Part of the UK and the EU; devolved legislature
5.	Bailiwick of Guernsey	Guernsey, Privy Council is final court of appeal	Crown dependency. Adopts some UK legislation. Has dependent territories of its own—Alderney and Sark; not part of the EU.
6.	Bailiwick of Jersey	Jersey, Privy Council is final court of appeal	Crown dependency. Adopts some UK legislation; not part of the EU.
7.	Isle of Man	Isle of Man, Privy Council is final court of appeal	Crown dependency. Adopts some UK legislation; not part of the EU.
8.	Republic of Ireland	Irish	Republic of Ireland, part of the EU.

2.2 Sources of law in England & Wales

English legal tradition places a lot of emphasis on the 'sources' of law. It is important to find which institution 'made' or 'recognised' a legal rule, and to identify exactly when it was made, so that you can decide which rule takes precedence.

In England & Wales, by an accident of history, the legal system has a varied combination of sources. This is not unique. Most countries possess a blend of legal cultures. As an example, in Norway civil law has been superimposed on common law and customary law.

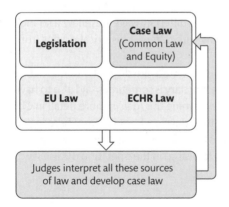

Figure 2.3 Sources of law in England & Wales

Figure 2.3 summarises the current situation: there are four main sources of law in England & Wales—statutes, case law, EU law, and ECHR law. This was not always so. For a long time, the two principal institutions which were said to 'make' law in the English legal system were Parliament and the courts, although (as we saw in 1.4.3) Parliament was ultimately sovereign. In 2.2.4 we briefly explore the separate status of international law.

2.2.1 **Statutes**

Parliament consists of the House of Commons, the House of Lords, and the Queen, although the monarch's role is largely ceremonial. The government usually has a majority in the House of Commons, and is responsible for introducing most of the laws made by Parliament, called 'Acts of Parliament', 'statutes', or 'legislation'. Legislation can be divided into primary legislation made by Parliament, and secondary (and tertiary) legislation made with the authority of Parliament, but not by it. It is discussed in detail in Chapter 4.

2.2.2 **EU law and ECHR law**

In the modern English legal system, both Parliament and the courts also need to take into account EU law, incorporated into UK law by the European Communities Act 1972, and the European Convention on Human Rights (ECHR) (via the Human Rights Act 1998). It is vital to understand that EU law and ECHR law are entirely separate from each other. Both of these changes are illustrated in their historical context in the summary diagram at 2.12.

Both areas of law are having a profound and increasing effect on the English legal system. We look in detail at the status and impact of EU Law at 4.5 and the Human Rights Act at 4.6. Law emanating from the European Court of Human Rights is technically a type of international law—we look at its status at 2.2.4. Although both areas of law govern relations between states, both also create rights enforceable by individuals.

2.2.3 **Case law**

The courts consist of independent, non-elected, judges. By contrast, in some jurisdictions, judges have a more political focus, the epitome being in the US, where they are commonly appointed by politicians.

Senior judges create case law by reaching decisions on the cases before them. This is sometimes referred to as the 'common law' to distinguish it from legislation; at 2.4.1 we see that the term 'common law' can be used in different ways. Case law also includes equity, which is a largely separate body of case law with different historical origins from common law. We explore this in more detail at 5.2.

We saw at 1.6 that the functions of the state are divided into distinct roles: the legislature, the executive, and the judiciary. The judiciary is sometimes said also to have a quasi-legislative role when it produces case law. We examine this idea in more detail in Chapter 5.

Judges have a law-making role: they develop law in areas where legislation is sparse (e.g. the law of negligence), and, if necessary, fill the gaps in legislation. Figure 2.3 summarises the sources of law in England & Wales, focusing on the operation of case law.

2.2.4 **International law**

International law is not part of the law of England & Wales but clearly has significance. It is a type of law binding between states. It generally concerns only relations between states rather than their citizens, though there are some notable hybrids. In 3.5.3 and 3.5.4 we examine two international tribunals—the European Court of Human Rights and the International Criminal

Court. The United Nations Charter is also an example of international law to which the UK is signatory. The reason international law is not part of national legal systems is that it requires the consent of participating nations for it to be enforceable. State sovereignty prevails. You might be interested to note that space law is a category of international law, purporting to govern the rights and obligations of Earth's states in space.[2]

2.3 Classification of law in England & Wales

Lawyers have gradually classified the law into a number of broad areas. Every lawyer needs to be aware of some key terminology. As always in England & Wales, use of some terms is not always clear-cut, in particular in relation to the terms 'common law' and 'civil law'. This section draws out some of these important, but sometimes overlapping, concepts.

2.3.1 Public law and private law

One classification of the law is into public law and private law.

 Essential explanations

Public law

Duties owed to or by the state are matters of public law. Public law is often said to include not only things like administrative law, constitutional law, and human rights, but also criminal law.

Private law

Duties owed to or by individuals (including corporate individuals like companies) are generally matters of private law. Private law includes (among other things) tort, contract, land, and equity. Company law is mainly private because it concerns relations between private people (a company is a legal person, as opposed to a natural person) rather than the state.

Figure 2.4 offers a simple summary of this categorisation of law in England and Wales.

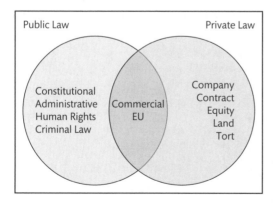

Figure 2.4 Categorisation of law in England & Wales: public and private

---

[2] E.g. the 1967 Treaty on Principles Governing the Activities of States in the Exploration and Use of Outer Space, including the Moon and Other Celestial Bodies.

The division between public and private law is not always clear-cut; for example, EU law is a hybrid, as it covers relations between individuals, relations between states, and relations between individuals and the state.

2.3.2 Common law

Common law can be contrasted with three other concepts: civil law, equity, and statute law. Figure 2.5 summarises the position.

At 2.4 we look at the development of the English legal system from largely local customs, into law 'common' to the country ('common law'). The development of this type of law may be contrasted in three different ways. At this stage, we need only introduce these key themes; they are developed in later chapters.

Common law vs civil law

This is a significant contrast which is explored in more detail at 4.4 (in the area of case law) and 5.1 (with reference to legislation). At this stage we introduce the basic attributes of common law and civil law jurisdictions.

There are some other typical distinctions between the two types of system. The vast major-ity (but not all) of the legal systems in the world fall into one of these categories, as illustrated in Figure 2.6. We explore this further at 5.1.

In this book we generally use the terms 'common law' and 'civil law' to describe the nature of a legal system, although there are other ways of using both expressions, if the context re-quires. We will make it clear if we are using the terms in a different sense (for instance in this section). At 2.3.3 we look at the different functions of the term 'civil law'. Lawyers need to be careful to make clear in which context they are referring to such terms.

Common law vs equity

Equity also contrasts with common law. It developed in the 14th century to mitigate the worst problems with the common law. Until the mid-19th century it comprised an entirely separate system of law to the common law. While this is no longer the case, there remain two distinct

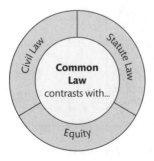

Figure 2.5 Common law and its contrasts

Essential explanations

'Common law' jurisdiction

A common law jurisdiction (e.g. England & Wales, the US, Australia, and others in the same tradition) has a system of binding judicial precedent which generates a body of case law. In short, principles of law stated in some courts will bind many later judges.

These jurisdictions tend to use legislation that grows organically to meet demands and deal with problems as they arise. This means that in a given area there may be many relevant statutes.

'Civil law' jurisdiction

Unlike common law jurisdictions, civil law (sometimes called, 'civilian') jurisdictions, including, for example, France and Germany, tend not to have binding case law. They do, of course, have litigation, but cases do not coalesce into a self-standing system of legal principles.

Instead civil law systems usually adopt one or more comprehensive 'codes' which attempt to define all the rules in a given area. This model, including much of the content of early civil codes, was derived from Roman law, which originated in Ancient Rome.

Civil law jurisdictions also normally use constitutional legislation stating overriding aims and principles by which all subsequent behaviour (including legislation) is to be measured. There is an increasing tendency in common law states (even the UK) for law in some areas to be codified into statutes more resembling civilian codes. We examine this aspect of the civil law/common law contrast at 4.4.3.

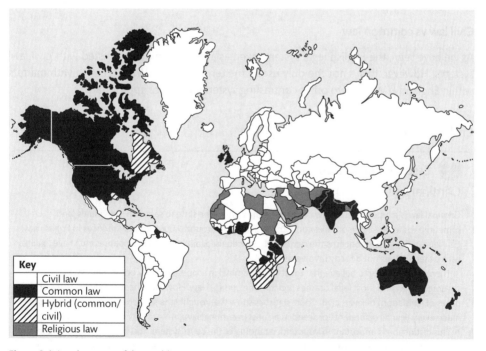

Key

	Civil law
	Common law
/////	Hybrid (common/civil)
	Religious law

Figure 2.6 Legal systems of the world

bodies of case law—common law and equity—the latter being considerably more flexible than the former. We explore this in more detail at 2.4.

Common law vs statute law

Case law as a whole (comprising both common law and equity) can be contrasted with statute law, which we look at in detail in Chapter 4.

2.3.3 Civil law

Civil law can itself be contrasted in three ways. These are summarised in Figure 2.7.

Figure 2.7 Civil law and its contrasts

Civil law vs common law

As we have seen, the English legal system taken as a whole can be contrasted with 'civil law' systems. However, this is not the only use of the term 'civil law'. When dealing with matters within England & Wales, two other contrasting systems are more appropriate.

Civil law vs criminal law

 Essential explanations

Criminal law

Criminal law is a type of public law concerning the right of the state to sanction individuals (and sometimes other legal persons like companies). There are around 9,000 criminal offences in English law. Civil law (in this sense) concerns the rights that individuals (again including companies etc.) have against each other—it does not directly involve the state.

There is a tendency to believe that most law is criminal in scope, probably because most media coverage of law and most legal dramas concern the criminal law. However, the majority (in terms of pages of legislation) of law is civil. Court statistics show that roughly the same number of civil claims is made every year as defendants proceeded against in criminal law.

This distinction is important in your understanding of the court system. You may encounter the terms 'civil jurisdiction' and 'criminal jurisdiction'. This refers to the (mainly) separate courts that administer justice in each area. We look at this in more detail in Chapter 3.

The same set of facts can create liabilities in both areas of law, as illustrated in Example 1.

Example 1

If Ben has stolen a car, and sold it to John, the state (represented by the Crown Prosecution Service—CPS) can prosecute Ben in criminal law under the Theft Act 1968.[3] Then, usually after the prosecution has run its course, John can make a civil claim against Ben in contract, under the Sale of Goods Act 1979,[4] because Ben did not have a right to sell the car.

Table 2.2 sets out some important differences between criminal law and civil law.

Table 2.2 Key contrasts between criminal and civil law in England & Wales

	Criminal	Civil
Nature of proceedings	A criminal case is called a prosecution.	A civil case is called an action or claim.
Who will initiate proceedings?	A prosecution will normally be started by the state in the form of the police arresting and charging someone. The victim of a crime does not normally commence proceedings. The prosecution will be continued or discontinued by the CPS (lawyers who are civil servants independent of the police).	Proceedings are commenced by the victim—the person who has suffered damage. Disputes can also involve wills or family matters.
The parties	The CPS is called the 'prosecution'; the accused is called the 'defendant'. See 3.1.1 for an explanation of these terms.	The person who makes the claim is referred to as the 'claimant' (prior to 1998, the 'plaintiff'), and the person against whom the claim is made is called the 'defendant'. See 3.1.1 for an explanation of these terms.
Standard of proof	Beyond all reasonable doubt: the prosecution will do this by providing evidence of each of the necessary elements of the offence.	On the balance of probabilities.
Onus (or burden) of proof	CPS/prosecution.	Claimant.
Objective of proceedings	Punishment (and sometimes rehabilitation).	The claimant will normally seek compensation for the losses suffered (though in intentional torts e.g. deceit and defamation, damages may be punitive).
Defendant will be ...	Guilty: defendant will be convicted. Not guilty: defendant will be acquitted.	Liable. Not liable: case will be dismissed.
Possible outcome	A defendant who is found guilty will be sentenced to e.g. imprisonment, a fine, or a community sentence (e.g. a community penalty order).	A remedy (e.g. damages) will be given to the claimant.

[3] Theft Act 1968, s. 1(1).   [4] Sale of Goods Act 1979, s. 12.

Civil law vs ecclesiastical and military law

Ecclesiastical and military law are both specialised areas of law concerning discrete areas of activity. Both areas have their own forums for litigation, with their own procedures. In this context, any law not within the relevant specialist area of law is called 'civil law'.

The legal implications of actions by members of a body such as the clergy or soldiers can be the subject both of litigation in the specialist courts (e.g. courts Christian and courts martial), and if necessary the 'civil' courts, which are those courts that have jurisdiction over citizens generally.

Ecclesiastical courts derive their authority directly from the Crown, as the monarch is the Supreme Governor of the Church of England, and courts martial derive theirs from the Armed Forces Act 2006.[5]

2.4 Development of the English legal system

2.4.1 Why study the history of the English legal system?

In Chapter 1 we looked at the concept of the *gründnorm*. The origins and the legitimacy of a body of law are significant. In addition, in Chapter 1 we saw that the law does not operate in isolation, and is one of a suite of disciplines.

History and politics weigh heavily as they impact directly on how the law develops. Throughout this section you may wish to keep track of this interaction using the timeline in Figure 2.12. In this section we look at the development of the two 'traditional' sources of law in England & Wales—case law and statutes.

2.4.2 Case law

All 'common law' (as distinguished from 'civil law') states can trace their legal systems back to the pre-Victorian English legal system—most were at one time colonies of Great Britain. In Chapter 5 we see that a disproportionately high number of G20 states are 'common law'. In the US, for instance, however strongly the founding fathers of the US desired independence, they felt that the legal system of England was suitable at both state and federal level. Figure 2.8 shows states formerly associated with the British Empire, which may be compared to the common law states illustrated in Figure 2.6.

The equivalent for civil law systems is Roman law (see 'Common law vs civil law' at 2.3.2), still a staple of many university courses as it is the direct ancestor of civil law codes today. It is important to note that many English legal principles (in particular those in equity) also borrow from Roman law. The standardisation of rules within the EU also owes much to the ideas of codification within Roman law.

You may wish to refer to Figure 2.12 as you read on to help keep each feature in context.

Development of the common law

William the Conqueror invaded England from Normandy in 1066. He realised that it would be easier to control the country if he also controlled the legal system. He imposed his authority

---

[5] Armed Forces Act 2006, s. 50.

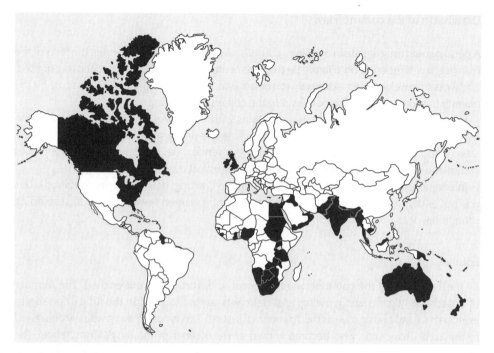

Figure 2.8 States formerly in the British Empire

by travelling around the country accompanied by his court, listening to and then ruling upon his subjects' grievances. The King would literally sit on a bench to hear these cases, which is why the most important court became known as the Court of King's Bench. This name is still used today, although it is currently called the Queen's Bench.

Later monarchs were less conscientious and this role was gradually delegated to Justices, who held 'Assizes' (sittings) of the royal courts. There was no unified or national set of laws. Local customs were applied. The local sheriff and later justices of the peace would deal with less serious offences. The King's courts gradually achieved ascendancy over local courts as the preferred forum for resolving disputes, when litigants (the parties) had a choice.

The system was formalised under Henry II (1154–89). Henry divided the country into 'circuits' or areas for the judges to visit on a regular basis. Judges as a group began to adopt the best of the local customs, and eventually a 'common' law emerged. If you turn to the timeline in Figure 2.12, you can see this interaction between Norman high politics and the need for legal uniformity.

This system of circuit judges from the King's Bench and the Assizes was not abolished until 1971, and a version of this system still exists in the US. The Rule of Law was so well entrenched by Henry's reign that, when he was accused of ordering the death of his Archbishop of Canterbury, Thomas Becket, the King accepted the punishment of a public whipping.

Respect for the Rule of Law required some consistency, and the 'common law' gradually coalesced into a body of binding case law. This doctrine of *stare decisis*, which means 'standing by previous decisions', still exists.

Drawbacks of the common law

A person could only litigate in the King's courts if a 'writ' was available, covering the facts of the case (e.g. a writ for entry onto land). By the 13th century, the number of writs became limited. The writs themselves were extremely formulaic and inflexible, and the slightest error by the plaintiff (now the 'claimant') would lead to the collapse of the case.

For example, there were particular problems with mortgages: in common law, once the loan repayment date had passed the land became the property of the lender and the borrower had no title to the land. It was common for lenders deliberately to make themselves unavailable on the date for payment, so the borrower lost the land.

In addition, only one remedy was available for civil wrong: damages (compensation). This was not always appropriate, for instance if the plaintiff wanted the defendant to stop doing something, or to perform his obligations.

Equity

By the 14th century the common law had become distorted and entrenched. The number of dissatisfied litigants was growing, and claimants started to petition the King in person to exercise his royal prerogative as the 'fountain of justice'. This function was gradually delegated to the Lord Chancellor, who became known as the 'Keeper of the King's Conscience'. The Court of Chancery evolved and the Chancellor began issuing decrees in his own name by 1474, separately from the King and the common law courts.

The Chancellor (as the Court of Chancery) developed the law of equity (see Figure 2.12). No writ was necessary and cases were determined purely on grounds of fairness. Remedies were not limited to damages, and procedure was simple—litigants made their claim to the Chancellor.

To take the example of the trust, in common law no writ was available in respect of a trust, a vital concept in law today. But equity recognised trusts very early in its development, during the Crusades (1095–1291). Nobles would leave the country for years at a time to fight holy wars in the Middle East. Often, landowners would transfer their property to a trusted friend, on the understanding it would be used for the crusader's family if he did not return. The legal interest in the land vested in the 'friend'. This is known as 'legal title', and was enforceable at common law. The family did not have legal title, and therefore had no rights at common law.

Until equity developed, crusaders' families were frequently left homeless. Equity imposed a 'trust' where the friend held the land as trustee for the benefit of the crusader and his family

Essential explanation

A trust

A trust arises when one person (the 'trustee') is obliged to hold property on behalf of another person (the 'beneficiary') so that the benefit of the property is ultimately given to the beneficiary.

A trust allows the separation of administration and enjoyment of property. The trustee has management and control of the property subject to the trust (the 'trust property'), but the beneficiary is the 'real' owner in the sense that he will eventually enjoy the benefit of the property.

as beneficiaries. They had 'equitable title'. The friend was obliged to transfer legal title to the crusader or his family on request.

The trust is still a significant element of most common law legal systems. It is used by individuals in tax planning, the shared ownership of property, or in making provision for dependants. It is also important in matters of corporate or public interest, such as pension funds and charities.

Paradoxically, one criticism of equity was that it was simply too erratic:

> Equity is a roguish thing: for law we have a measure, know what to trust to; equity is according to the conscience of him that is Chancellor, and as that is larger or narrower, so is equity. 'Tis all one as if they should make the standard for the measure we call a foot, a Chancellor's foot; what an uncertain measure would this be? One Chancellor has a long foot, another a short foot, a third an indifferent foot: 'tis the same thing in a Chancellor's conscience.[6]

Take a look at Figure 2.9. In the top box you will see that principles of equity gradually emerged and equity became a separate branch of the law with its own rules and procedure, rather than simply being the application of natural justice to a case.

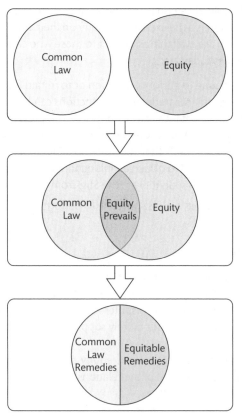

Figure 2.9 Development of the relationship between common law and equity: initially separate legal systems (top box) overlap causing conflict (middle box). The lower box illustrates the unified legal system created by the Judicature Acts.

---

[6] John Selden, *Table Talk* (1689) (London: JR Smith, 1856).

Equitable maxims

You will read about equitable 'maxims'. These were developed by the Court of Chancery and remain relevant when using equity today. There are at least 20, but important ones include:

- Equity looks on that as done which ought to be done: this means that equity will observe the parties' intention instead of rigid procedure. This means that it is more flexible and litigation less formulaic.
- He who comes to equity must come with clean hands: an equitable remedy is not available to a claimant who is not acting in good faith.
- Delay defeats equity: a claimant cannot wait too long before making a claim as this may prejudice the other party. This is frequently a problem for litigants who seek injunctions to stop others from doing something.
- Equity will not suffer a wrong to be without a remedy.

Equitable remedies

Equitable remedies developed because receiving damages in common law was not always adequate. These remedies still have a vital role in English law. They remain discretionary: the court has discretion as to whether litigants deserve the exercise of equity on their behalf. This contrasts with common law remedies, which are available as of right to those who can prove their case. Two significant equitable remedies today are:

- An injunction: here the court orders someone to perform an action or to refrain from an action, for example to stop using the claimant's trade mark. Injunctions can be issued in a matter of hours if they are equitable. For instance, if a celebrity seeks to prevent a newspaper from publishing a defamatory story, or if someone wants to prevent the publication of confidential information about them, they may seek an injunction to prevent publication. The BBC, for instance, failed to obtain an injunction preventing publication of Ben Collins' memoirs revealing his identity as 'The Stig' from *Top Gear*.[7]
- A decree of specific performance: here the court orders someone to perform their obligations under a contract or trust.

Discord between common law and equity

You will often read that 'Equity follows the law'. Today this means that the common law position is normally considered before any equitable rules. Originally this meant that it supplemented the common law, often as an alternative forum for settling disputes. Conflicts arose between it and the common law. By the 16th century, equity did not merely supplement the common law, but directly challenged it.

In 1615, James I personally decided that in cases of conflict, equity should prevail over common law.[8] You can see this stage in the development of the relationship illustrated in the middle box in Figure 2.9.

[7] 'Top Gear court case: The Stig revealed as racing driver Ben Collins', *The Telegraph*, 1 September 2010.
[8] *Earl of Oxford's Case* (1615) 21 ER 485, 1 Rep Ch 1.

This resolution lost much of its value as equity itself hardened into a system of law with rules which sometimes became as inflexible as those of the common law. Both jurisdictions needed reform by the 19th century. There were too many courts with overlapping jurisdictions and it was expensive and slow to obtain justice.

Amalgamation of courts of common law and equity

The courts of common law and equity were merged by the Supreme Court of Judicature Acts of 1873 and 1875. Both systems of law remained but these were administered by all courts when it was necessary to discuss equity. Some significant effects were:

- Civil courts can now grant both common law and equitable remedies in the same action, which you can see in the lower box in Figure 2.9. For example, an injunction to stop unlawful behaviour can be ordered, in addition to damages for losses accrued to date. In a classic Lord Denning case,[9] it was found that the repeated hitting of 'sixes' out of a cricket ground into neighbours' gardens constituted a private nuisance. The court was happy to award damages for losses, but (and this romanticism was a theme of Denning's judgments) used its discretion not to award an injunction to stop the cricket. Rights in common law and in equity are recognised by the same courts, for example an equitable right of way over land held at common law by someone else, or an equitable interest in shares held at common law by another.
- Equity sometimes provides defences to common law claims. In contract law, for instance, you will read about a defence to a common law debt claim, called promissory estoppel. It was developed almost singlehandedly by Lord Denning, to prevent creditors going back on promises to ease repayments by debtors.

Equity may have developed in England & Wales, but it was inherited by most of the common law jurisdictions, and in many, most notably the US, it continues to play an important role in the courts.

 Essential debate

In India, equity was a key element of the law until independence from Great Britain in 1947. In 1963, the Indian Parliament abolished and replaced most equitable rights and remedies with statutory rights.[10]

  Is there an argument for replacing the idiosyncratic principles of equity in England & Wales with a statement of rights and remedies in a statute? Would this be more open and authoritative? What drawbacks would there be?

2.4.3 Statutes

In England & Wales, there are records of the formal enactment of statutes from the accession of William the Conqueror in 1066, and written evidence of laws purporting to be statutes going back to Anglo-Saxon times (around 600). The *legislation.gov.uk* website reveals a trickle

---

[9] *Miller v Jackson* [1977] QB 966.   [10] Specific Relief Act 1963.

of statutes in force starting in 1262, and increasing significantly in volume after the 'Glorious Revolution' in 1688. If you look at the timeline in Figure 2.12, you can appreciate the historical context to this development. But this is only part of the story. Incredibly, the early statutes listed on that website are still in force. As the role of the state has increased, so statutes have replaced the common law as the primary source of law in England & Wales.

Until the 15th century, however, a 'statute' was merely a law passed with Royal authority. Try to look at old statutes today, and you may find the variety surprising and content often unfamiliar.

In the 15th century, the consent of the House of Commons became necessary when a statute was passed, a process formalised by the Tudors in the 16th century.[11] The 17th century saw a struggle for supremacy between the Monarchy and Parliament, resolved initially by the *Case of Proclamations*[12] in which it was declared that 'The King has no prerogative but that which the law of the land allows him', and eventually confirmed by the 'Glorious Revolution' of 1688 (see Figure 2.12). This was a key moment in English law, as it confirmed (via the Bill of Rights 1688) parliamentary sovereignty.

As the country expanded, so the territorial extent of statutes also grew. Social and industrial development (particularly associated with the industrial revolution of the 18th and 19th centuries) required a significant expansion in regulation. Bigger cities and more dangerous workplaces combined with an antiquated electoral system to create pressure for social and political reform. Look again at Figure 2.12; the Reform Acts of 1832, 1867, and 1884 were reactions to the clamour for greater representation of the growing middle and working classes. The same pressures, along with rapidly evolving attitudes within the House of Commons, led to early workplace safety legislation.

The 20th century saw further significant changes in society and politics. Up to 900,000 servicemen perished and a further 1,700,000 were wounded in the World War I (1914-18) (see Figure 2.12). Resentment grew against the ruling elites around Europe that were seemingly out of touch and unwilling to countenance wholesale changes to the structure and politics of their countries. Revolutions occurred around mainland Europe as a reaction to these related factors. Without recognition for the sacrifices of ordinary people, there would almost certainly have been revolution in the UK. Parliament passed unprecedentedly interventionist housing, health, and welfare legislation, including the establishment of a state pension. Many women got the vote in 1918.[13]

In the 19th and 20th centuries, Parliament, and hence also statutes, reflected the democratisation of society. World War II (1939-45) witnessed another terrible death toll (around 400,000 UK military deaths) and an enormous growth of the state to drive forward war production and the control of infrastructure. In 1945, a Labour government was elected on a platform of extensive state intervention, including the establishment of the National Health Service, and the extension of welfare 'from the cradle to the grave'. Wide-ranging legislation was necessary in the short term[14] but also thereafter, and it continues to this day.

[11] T. F. T. Plucknett, *Concise History of the Common Law* (London: Butterworth, 5th edn, 1956), p. 322.

[12] *Case of Proclamations* (1611) 12 Co Rep 74.   [13] Representation of the People Act 1918.

[14] E.g. Family Allowances Act 1945, National Insurance Act 1946, National Insurance (Industrial Injuries) Act 1946, National Health Service Act 1946, Town and Country Planning Act 1947, National Assistance Act 1948, Children Act 1948, Housing Act 1949.

Eventually even primary legislation could not keep up with the demand for regulation, and secondary legislation (i.e. not passed directly by Parliament) such as statutory instruments (see 4.2.2) grew in importance.

Some rather sensationalist headlines have bemoaned a jump in regulatory legislation in recent years, allegedly burdening businesses with red tape; others lament the torrent of criminal legislation overwhelming the justice system with new offences.[15] Lord Phillips of Sudbury has said, 'We legislate more than any other major democratic country. I'm talking 200-300 per cent more. And you don't need to be a soothsayer to see that the downstream consequences of all that law-making are parlous—more bureaucratisation, centralisation, more demoralisation.'[16]

Rather surprisingly, the number of statutes has decreased consistently since the 1960s, although there has been a significant increase in the amount of statutory instruments. Figure 2.10 shows how the volume of legislation has increased since the early 20th century.[17]

Although the number of statutes has actually declined, the complexity and comprehensiveness of Acts has increased—look at the number of pages of legislation per year (an average for each decade is set out in the graph). Until the 1950s, the pages of legislation emanating from Parliament numbered in the low hundreds; since the 1950s there has been a steady (and seemingly inexorable) rise to the 2000s level of roughly 3,000 each year.

The Companies Act 2006 is an illuminating example. It was passed to bring together the content of several preceding statutes and to give statutory footing to common law and equitable principles. It also amended the law in some areas. It runs to 1,300 sections, divided

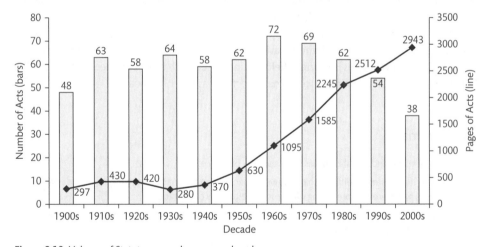

Figure 2.10 Volume of Statutes, annual mean per decade

[15] See 'Lord Judge tells Jack Straw: the UK has too many crime laws', *The Telegraph*, 15 July 2009.

[16] Lord Phillips of Sudbury, quoted in *The Times*, 31 May 2012.

[17] Statistics derived from (for 1950-2007) Richard Crackness, *Acts & Statutory Instruments: Volume of UK legislation 1950-2007* (House of Commons Library, 2008); (for pre-1950 Acts) *Chronological Table of Statutes* (TSO, 2010); (for pre-1950 statutory instruments) *Halsbury's Statutory Instrument Citator 2012* (N.B. numbers estimated according to statutes cited); for average number of pages per piece of legislation prior to 1950, figures derived from Crackness. Mean figures for statutory instruments 1900s and 1910s, figures extrapolated from mean for 1920s.

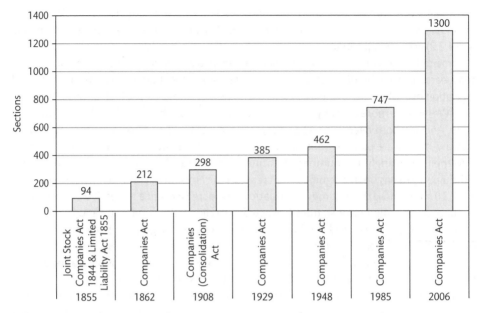

Figure 2.11 Size of the Companies Acts

into 47 parts. It also includes 16 schedules. The Act totals 571 pages. This is before we consider the 32 statutory instruments relating to its implementation, passed by mid-2012.

A study[18] examined the length of companies legislation since 1844, providing an excellent illustration of the increased volume of law passed by Parliament. Figure 2.11 shows that the volume of legislation in this important field has increased each time it has been legislated. The Companies Act 2006 contains twice as many sections as the 1985 Act.

Summary

- Law in England & Wales comes from a variety of sources.
- The 'legal system' is difficult to pin down, depending on the context. In reality there are several legal systems each comprising different combinations of countries.
- Lawyers and legal academics categorise the English legal system in various ways. Each brings out important elements and concepts relating to its operation.
- To understand how and why case law operates as it does, we need to look at its historical development.
- To understand the importance of statutes, again, we need to look at their historical development.Figure 2.12 summarises the interaction between important events in the political and legal history of England and related jurisdictions. You may wish to use it as a reference source throughout the legal systems chapters.

[18] John Armour, 'Codification and UK Company Law', in Association du Bicentenaire du Code de Commerce (ed.), *Bicentenaire du Code de Commerce 1807–2007: les Actes des Colloques* (Paris: Dalloz, 2008), pp. 287–310.

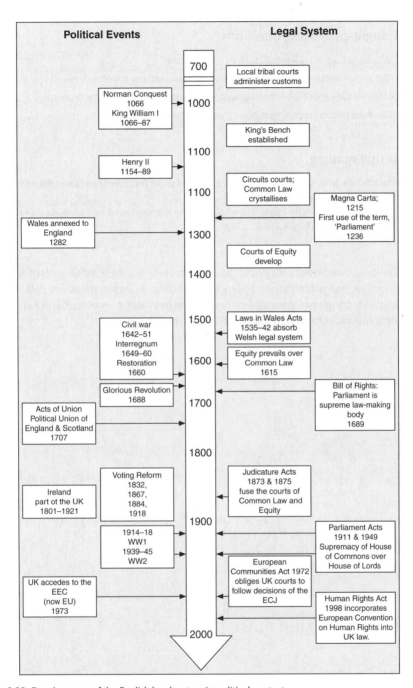

Figure 2.12 Development of the English legal system in political context

Thought-provoking questions

1. Why is the English legal system such an 'unusual case'?
2. Can we understand the English legal system properly without knowing its history?
3. Is there an argument for dispensing with 'equity' altogether? Is it an anachronism?
4. Can there be too much legislation on the statute books?

 ## Further reading

**Robert Pearce, John Stevens, and Warren Barr, *The Law of Trusts and Equitable Obligations*
(Oxford: OUP, 5th edn, 2010)**
—one of the leading modern texts on the law of equity, it addresses key questions on the role of equity
in the modern English legal system.

 *For the authors' reflections on the thought-provoking questions, additional self-test
questions, podcasts offering a variety of perspectives on legal systems and skills,
and a library of links to useful websites, visit the free* Online Resource Centre *at*
http://www.oxfordtextbooks.co.uk/orc/slorach/.

3 The court system of England & Wales

Learning objectives

After studying this chapter you should be able to:

- Discuss key themes in the English court system.
- Be familiar with the structure of the court system in sufficient depth to understand the background to case law.
- Understand in outline the criminal and civil court systems, including trial courts and appeals courts.
- Develop an awareness of other courts and tribunals important to the law of England & Wales.

Introduction

The primary function of a court is to administer the law. Any law-making role (as discussed in Chapters 2 and 4) is important, but secondary. Real people need to have real disputes resolved.

There are around 650 different courts at various levels in England and Wales, as well as numerous tribunals and other quasi-judicial bodies. To understand how they administer the law and to give context to the law they create, it is vital to understand the structure of the court system.

Good litigation lawyers will be able to navigate their way through labyrinthine rules of legal proceedings. At this stage in your studies you may not yet have knowledge of these intricacies. However, in this context it is the bigger picture of the system, rather than specific rules, that matters. Considering the wider picture provides a firm and workable foundation for the study of the law. To assist in providing this picture, occasionally some generalisations have been made in this chapter, so be aware that some themes covered may involve greater complexity, and may also be, over time, the subject of variation.

First, this chapter examines important themes and concepts that are essential for understanding the structure and mechanics of the English courts. We then look at criminal and civil courts in detail. The chapter ends with an examination of courts and other forums that have significance in the English legal system but which are not part of the court system in England & Wales. You can refer to the Appendix for a summary of the courts discussed with key facts.

3.1 Key themes

The starting point in a study of the English court system is to grasp some key elements:

- civil vs criminal litigation;
- trial vs appellate courts (including a distinction between facts and law); and
- superior vs inferior courts.

 Essential explanation

Parties to the case, and the case name

The most important people in any given case are the parties, called the 'litigants'. While lawyers will consider legal principles deriving from a case, it is the parties who are directly affected by the decision.

In 2.3 we saw that in the civil jurisdiction, the parties are called the 'claimant' and the 'respondent', but in criminal trials, the equivalents are the 'prosecution' (usually the Crown, represented by the Crown Prosecution Service), and the 'defendant'.

The case name will usually derive from the parties, so:

- A civil case is named after the parties concerned, for example *Donoghue* v *Stevenson*.[1] Sometimes more than one party is claiming or defending the claim. Here, the full case name will have the names of all the parties on each side, often abbreviated to 'and others'. Another example of a civil case name is *Re Vandervell (No. 2)*.[2] This type of case is about ('re') something, such as a trust settlement, a will, or a patent application. Sometimes only one party is involved, such as in a procedural application to court.

- A criminal case name will normally take the form *R* v *Smith*.[3] 'R' is the Crown, and Morgan Smith was the defendant. Some older criminal cases will use the name of the prosecuting police officer, such as *Fisher* v *Bell*.[4]

- In public law, a judicial review of the actions of a state body[5] will also mirror the parties' names. In Chapter 4[6] we briefly examine an example in connection with the Hunting Act, *R (Countryside Alliance and others)* v *Attorney General and another*,[7] meaning the Crown, on behalf of the Countryside Alliance (and others), against the Attorney General.

3.1.1 Civil vs criminal litigation

In England & Wales (with some exceptions) criminal trials (and appeals) are usually conducted in different courts from those in which civil proceedings occur. The two types of law are dealt with by court systems which, for the most part, operate independently from each other. These

---

[1] *Donoghue (or M'Alister)* v *Stevenson* [1932] AC 562, which is discussed in depth in Chapter 5 on case law and in Chapter 7 on reading and understanding law.

[2] *Re Vandervell (No. 2)* [1974] Ch 269.

[3] *R* v *Smith (Morgan)* [2001] 1 AC 146, discussed in Chapter 5 on legislation.

[4] *Fisher* v *Bell* [1961] 1QB 394.   [5] Examined briefly at 1.6.2.   [6] At 4.4.4.

[7] *R (Countryside Alliance and others)* v *Attorney General and another, R (Derwin and others)* v *Same* [2007] UKHL 52.

courts have different expertise and, because of the fundamental importance of protecting individual liberty in criminal trials, different procedures. In addition the civil system includes largely self-contained courts specialising in family and administrative law; these are areas of law which you will come to later in your studies.

In Chapter 2 we explored basic differences between criminal and civil law. The principal objectives of the criminal courts are to decide guilt or innocence according to the criminal law, and then to sanction the wrong-doer. In contrast, the principal objectives of the civil courts are to decide disputes between members of society, or between the state and individuals, and to grant an appropriate remedy (usually compensation) to the victim.

The same event, such as a road accident, may lead to proceedings both in the criminal courts (e.g. to punish the careless motorist) and in the civil courts (to compensate the injured pedestrian). Normally the civil case will wait until the criminal proceedings are concluded.

Although it is a helpful introductory generalisation that there are two largely distinct streams of court (civil and criminal), some courts do in fact have both criminal and civil jurisdictions. In fact, only the Crown Court (exclusively criminal) and county courts (exclusively civil) conform entirely to this generalisation; other courts, like the Court of Appeal, do consider both types of proceeding, but often with separate procedures and administration.

3.1.2 Trial courts vs appellate courts

The importance of appeals

Another distinction is between a trial (or 'first instance') court, and an appeal (or 'appellate') court.

Essential explanation

Appeal

An important aspect of the Rule of Law is recognition that even courts can make errors. There must be an avenue to correct miscarriages of justice where, for instance, the judge or magistrates misapplied the law, or gave the wrong sentence or remedy. Because adjudicating on legal issues is generally the preserve of the court system, this must comprise access to a different court.

When litigants disagree with a decision of a court, they may try to appeal to a higher court, if they have the resources and a strong enough argument.

This litigant is called the 'appellant' (whether he was claimant, prosecution, or defendant in the case), and the party seeking to prevent the success of the appeal is called the 'respondent'.

Trial courts are contrasted with courts of 'appeal', of which *the* Court of Appeal is only one. In most legal systems there are trial courts, then one or two levels of appeal court (e.g. the Court of Appeal of England & Wales), and finally a supreme court (of which the UK Supreme Court, examined later, is an example). Figure 3.1 summarises this generalised appeals system. There are a number of different procedures to follow depending on the court involved.

Figure 3.1 Generic appeals system

Normally a trial court will apply law to the facts, deciding mainly on issues of fact or evidence, whereas an appeal court will normally consider appeals from one or other party, to decide whether to reverse the decision of the lower court by interpreting the law differently.

Under most circumstances, litigants will need permission (sometimes called 'leave') to appeal. Normally they will seek leave from the court which handed down the initial decision, and if this is refused, they may instead, under certain conditions, seek leave from the potential appeal court. Frivolous appeals need to be discouraged as they would be expensive and would clog up the court system—for example some appellants may be unwilling to accept the law as it stands, even in cases where the law is well established.

Courts of first instance are where all trials and cases start, and most (around 99.5%) stop. Her Majesty's Courts and Tribunals Service[8] statistics state that the total number of first instance proceedings commenced (most of which will settle or not be tried in full) is annually around 3.4 million, evenly split between criminal and civil proceedings. The total number of appeals, in any of the courts of appeal, is normally around 20,000 (around 0.5%). This statistic can be viewed in two ways. One might be that 99.5% of proceedings reach a satisfactory conclusion at first instance. A contrasting view would be that for most litigants it is prohibitively expensive to seek justice beyond the initial trial stage.

Note that the law reports—officially reported case law, comprising the bulk of case law studied by lawyers, judges, academics, and students—comprise but a tiny proportion of the overall number of court cases. Only a minority, including appeals, are reported.

Fact vs law

The distinction between facts and law is very important in the English legal system. To distinguish between questions of fact and questions of law we will use the case of *Donoghue* v *Stevenson*.[9] This may be the most famous case in the law of England and Wales. Paradoxically, it is a case that originated in Scotland. In Chapter 5 we examine the case in the context of case law.

---

[8] *Judicial and Court Statistics 2011* (Ministry of Justice, 2012). Note that in this chapter the authors have used rounded figures; for precise figures, see the Ministry of Justice website.

[9] *Donoghue (or M'Alister)* v *Stevenson* [1932] AC 562 (HL).

Case study 1

Donoghue v *Stevenson*

In August 1928, Mrs May Donoghue joined a friend for a drink in the Wellmeadow Café in Wellmeadow Place, Paisley, Glasgow.

The friend bought the drinks. The owner poured some ginger beer from an opaque bottle into Mrs Donoghue's glass (which may or may not have had some ice cream floating in it). She took some swigs and then poured the rest of the contents into her glass. To her horror the remains of a decomposing snail presented themselves to her. Mrs Donoghue later complained of stomach pains and shock, both a result of gastroenteritis.

On appeal, the House of Lords found that the manufacturer would owe a Duty of Care (that is, a duty not to carelessly cause harm) to the consumer. The case was later settled.

Further detail in relation to the case itself can be found at 7.5.3, which analyses extracts from the case report.

Questions of fact can be settled without considering the law. These questions can be resolved by looking at the evidence; in other words, issues such as 'was it ginger beer on its own or was it an "ice cream float"?', (a question that remains unresolved) and, 'did Mrs Donoghue suffer any loss of earnings as a result of the gastroenteritis?' These questions are almost exclusively the preserve of courts of first instance.

Unlike questions of fact, questions of law can be answered without reference to the evidence of a particular case, for instance, 'does a manufacturer owe a duty of care to consumers not to cause them unintended physical damage?' Indeed this was an important question of law dealt with in the *Donoghue* case.

When considering appeals, the facts of a case are generally settled in the first instance court. This means that it is very rare that a lawyer would call any witnesses before an appeal court. The higher courts normally accept the facts as found by the first instance court and then focus on issues of law. It is very difficult to show that a trial judge misunderstood or misused the facts presented to the court. It is easier to suggest that the judge misinterpreted the law. However, there may be situations where facts are disputed, so, occasionally, some appeal courts also have jurisdiction to reconsider disputed issues of fact.

Mixed questions of fact and law are the province of first instance courts, for instance, 'did Stevenson cause Mrs Donoghue actionable harm?' This question was never actually answered by a court. While the House of Lords did decide on the question of law, as discussed earlier, this was a preliminary point. The trial, in the Scottish trial court, to determine whether Mr Stevenson had actually caused Mrs Donoghue actionable harm, settled, partly because Mr Stevenson died before the trial commenced. Whole websites are devoted to the niceties of the case.[10]

3.1.3 **Superior court vs inferior court**

Superior courts have unlimited jurisdiction—they can try cases from any part of the country and for claims of any value. Generally, they try the most important and difficult cases. They are: the Supreme Court, the Court of Appeal, the High Court, and the Crown Court. The 'Senior

[10] E.g. http://www.thepaisleysnail.com.

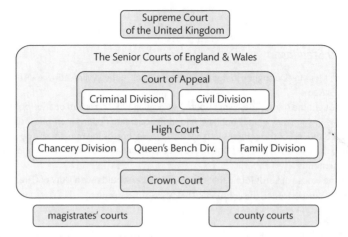

Figure 3.2 The courts of England & Wales

Courts' of England & Wales comprise the superior courts, not including the Supreme Court—the latter having UK-wide jurisdiction in most matters. Before 2005, different terminology was used—a researcher on this issue therefore needs to take care when reading materials from before that date.

All other courts, called inferior (or subordinate) courts, have limited geographical and financial jurisdiction, and deal with less important cases. But inferior courts are important as they try the vast majority of cases. These courts are the magistrates' and county courts.

3.2 Introduction to the courts of England & Wales

3.2.1 The courts

Now that we have the basic concepts, we can develop them. Figure 3.2 sets out the main courts in England & Wales.

Use Figure 3.2 to get a sense of the hierarchy of the courts, and their different names. Courts of High Court level and above are considered 'courts of record', which means that law reporters generally report some of the cases from these courts.

The modern court structure was created by the Supreme Court of Judicature Acts 1873 and 1875 (already encountered under 'Amalgamation of courts of common law and equity' at 2.4.2). Prior to that, there were separate court systems of equity and common law, which made litigation artificially complex and difficult to access. Key themes in the development of common law and equity were examined at 2.4.2.

Her Majesty's Courts and Tribunals Service, an agency of the Ministry of Justice, is responsible for the operation of the courts. The Ministry of Justice was formerly known as the Department for Constitutional Affairs and, before that, the Lord Chancellor's Department. The Lord Chancellor (at the time of writing, Chris Grayling) is responsible for this department. Detailed information on the court system, including statistics, can be found on the Ministry of Justice's website.[11]

---

[11] http://www.justice.gov.uk/.

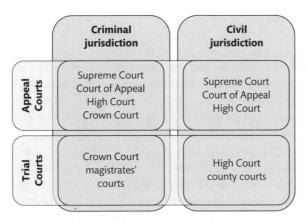

Figure 3.3 Thematic categorisation of courts in England & Wales

3.2.2 **Jurisdiction and appeals**

We can use two of the distinctions set out at 3.1 to create a simplified categorisation of the legal system: see Figure 3.3.

As a general rule, it is the superior courts such as the High Court, the Court of Appeal, and the Supreme Court which are the appellate courts. Two courts have a dual role of being both a trial and an appellate court—the High Court and the Crown Court. The Crown Court hears retrials and some appeals from the magistrates' courts; the High Court hears appeals on points of law from the magistrates' courts and, more commonly, appeals from the county courts. Often appellate courts have more than one judge, and first instance courts usually have a sole judge. Magistrates' courts usually use a bench of three lay magistrates.

It is possible (though rare, because complex cases are normally tried first in the High Court) for a civil case to begin in the county court at first instance and to conclude in the Supreme Court on appeal.

In the detailed description of the court system that follows, reference will be made to the Appendix, which comprises a summary of each of the key courts. The facts are for illustration and background only.

We now look separately at the criminal and civil jurisdictions.

3.3 **The criminal courts of England & Wales**

3.3.1 **Criminal courts of first instance**

The criminal courts of first instance are the magistrates' courts (245 courts) and the Crown Court (one court, with 76 centres). Many offences, for example ignoring red traffic lights on a bicycle,[12] possession of cannabis,[13] etc., are often dealt with by the use of on-the-spot fines and cautions, issued by police, and bypassing the court system altogether.

---

[12] Road Traffic Act 1988, s. 361.

[13] Possession of a Class B drug under the Misuse of Drugs Act 1971, s. 5(1), is subject to a warning or an on-the-spot fine of £80.

The magistrates' courts

The magistrates' courts deal with 97% of all criminal prosecutions each year. Offences dealt with by magistrates are less serious and more common than those dealt with by the Crown Court. That said, magistrates deal with only twice as many *full* trials as the Crown Court. This is because many trials in magistrates' courts fail to reach a full trial, either because the defendant pleads guilty (so-called 'cracked' trials) and goes straight to sentencing, or because the trial collapses, for example through lack of evidence.

A panel of three magistrates adjudicates on both matters of fact and law. Most magistrates are 'lay people' who are not qualified lawyers. Although they are given training, lay magistrates are advised on the law by a legally qualified clerk. There are some professional magistrates, district judges, who deal with some more complex cases tried in magistrates' courts. In order to convict a defendant, the magistrates must be satisfied that the prosecution has proved beyond all reasonable doubt that the defendant committed the offence.

The Crown Court

The 76 Crown Court centres in England and Wales normally try just under 100,000 cases each year. Around 70% of defendants who appear in the Crown Court plead guilty. The Old Bailey is a Crown Court situated in London (formally, the Central Criminal Court), albeit one that often deals with high-profile crimes.

In the Crown Court a judge presides over proceedings, but innocence or guilt (on the facts of the case) is normally decided upon by a jury of 12 citizens chosen at random. The judge directs the jury on the law, but the jury are at liberty to make their own minds up on the verdict. Although the jury must normally reach a unanimous verdict, a majority verdict with one or two dissenters is permitted, if it is taking too long for the jury to reach a unanimous verdict.[14]

The pre-trial stage

While detailed criminal procedure is beyond the scope of this book, it is worth understanding how a criminal case comes to trial.

If the police have reason to believe a criminal offence has been committed, they will arrest the suspect and investigate by questioning them and any witnesses, and by obtaining evidence. There are other agencies with similar powers in specific areas (e.g. Her Majesty's Revenue & Customs, the Health and Safety Executive, or the trading standards departments of local authorities).

The Crown Prosecution Service (CPS), headed by the Director of Public Prosecutions (DPP), is responsible for prosecuting suspects. While the CPS is separate from the police, the two agencies work closely together. The CPS is comprised of around 9,000 employees, a third of whom are lawyers.[15] Solicitors from the CPS are responsible for collating the evidence on which they seek to rely as prosecutors. It is usually the CPS (rather than the police) which will

---

[14] Juries Act 1974, s. 17.   [15] For information about the CPS, see http://www.cps.gov.uk.

issue a charge if it decides there is enough evidence to ensure a realistic prospect of conviction, and that issuing proceedings is in the public interest.

The controversy over how long a suspect can be held in custody without a charge being issued relates to this stage of proceedings. The current maximum period is three days for most suspects, and 14 days for terrorist offences.

 Essential debate

UK governments have often pushed for extensions to the 14-day period for detention without charge. From 2006–11, detention without charge could be extended to 28 days. The then Prime Minister, Tony Blair, had originally pushed to extend this to 90 days. The case for such extensions has been backed by assertions that criminal investigations are sometimes complex and, especially in relation to suspected terrorists, sensitive evidence can be difficult to obtain.

By contrast, human rights groups such as Liberty and Amnesty maintain that 14 days is too long, even for complex charges relating to terrorist activities. What are your views on this?

Once the decision to charge has been taken, the charge will be read out and handed to a defendant in person by the police. Alternatively, if the defendant has not been held in custody, a summons will be sent to the defendant through the post—this method is normally used for driving offences. The defendant will then make her first appearance before the magistrates' court. The magistrates will ask the defendant to confirm her name and ask the prosecution to confirm the offence with which the defendant is charged. What happens next will depend on the classification of offence with which the defendant is charged.

Mode of trial

The key factor determining the forum of the trial is the severity of the offence. Criminal offences are categorised as:

1. Summary only offences, including driving without insurance and common assault. These are minor offences and must be dealt with in the magistrates' court.

2. Indictable only offences, such as murder and robbery. These are serious offences and can be tried only in the Crown Court, because only the Crown Court has the power to sentence defendants accordingly.

3. Either way offences, including theft and fraud. These are offences which are capable of being more or less serious depending upon the facts of the case. These can be dealt with in either a magistrates' court or the Crown Court. Theft[16] is the classic either way offence. A shopper snatching a magazine from a shop is committing a theft, as is a company's director using millions from his company's accounts for his own purposes. The former would likely be tried in a magistrates' court, and the latter in the Crown Court.

The process for determining the trial court is summarised in Figure 3.4.

[16] Theft Act 1968, s. 1(1).

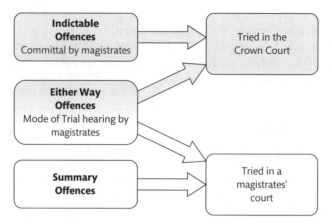

Figure 3.4 Criminal mode of trial

For either way offences, there will be a mode of trial hearing in a magistrates' court, in which the magistrates will decide whether to retain jurisdiction or to commit the trial to the Crown Court. The magistrates base their decision on various guidelines, but most importantly whether the offence, if proved, is likely to lead to a sentence within their sentencing powers (up to six months' custodial sentence). While the magistrates decide on the venue for full trial, the defendant can overrule this decision if the magistrates wish to retain jurisdiction but the defendant elects a Crown Court trial. The defendant cannot elect to stay in the magistrates' court if the magistrates themselves decide the case to be suitable only for the Crown Court.

There is a perception among defendants that the jury in a Crown Court is more likely to acquit than the (allegedly) case-hardened magistrates. This is despite the risk of a harsher sentence if found guilty. Looking at CPS statistics it is true that, of cases where the defendant has pleaded 'not guilty,' a slightly higher proportion is acquitted in a Crown Court than by magistrates. However, this may be due to factors other than the identity of the decision-maker;[17] for instance, those who are truly innocent may be more determined to take their case to the higher court than others.

The importance of the jury

Jury trial is based on the premise that everyone should have the right to be tried by their peers, rather than a judge who (the theory goes) may have a bias towards the establishment.

The jury system has been a valued aspect of the English legal system since the 12th century, and was an important part of Magna Carta in 1215. An alternative to juries was 'Trial by Ordeal'. For instance the defendant would be thrown into the water (often attached to millstones) and if she was guilty, she would sink. If God saw fit to spare the defendant, she was innocent. The law of England and the laws of physics worked together to produce 'justice'. The jury system became subject to abuse as monarchs reasserted their power. Juries were

---

[17] The *CPS Annual Report and Resource Accounts 2010–11* shows that roughly 50% of not guilty pleas in the Crown Court end in acquittal, compared with roughly 40% in the magistrates' courts.

often composed of placemen or were threatened into agreeing the desired result. Only the advent of the English Civil War (1642–51) saw juries restored to their former status.

In a criminal case, the jury merely state that the accused is either guilty or not guilty, and give no reasons. The decision cannot be disputed, as the jury deliberate in secret, and is arrived at on the basis the jury choose, according to the evidence and their conscience. The judge then decides on the appropriate sentence.

The jury trial is a comparative rarity. Only 2–3% of all criminal cases reach the Crown Court. Of these, less than a third are jury trials, as there are many pleas of guilty without a full trial taking place.

The expense and administrative difficulty of jury trials is significant. The continued use of juries is the subject of detailed, and often passionate, debate. There is extensive literature on the issue.[18] The many perceived problems include:

- in controversial trials (e.g. involving charges of rape) there is a perception that it is difficult for jurors to retain their objectivity;
- some research[19] shows that juries at certain Crown Court centres (e.g. Snaresbrook) have very low conviction rates, suggesting that at least some juries act contrary to objective standards of justice;
- juries may find factual and legal complexity challenging;
- there is a risk of 'jury-tampering'—a practice whereby the independence of jurors is compromised by threats or bribes; and
- a jury sit in secret, so their deliberations are not transparent.

Most commentators consider that the drawbacks of trial by jury are outweighed by the benefits. These include:

- the right of citizens to be tried by their 'peers', namely people like them, with similar values;
- the perception that, even after having been directed by the judge as to the law, juries decide on the basis of 'natural justice';
- the ability of a jury to decide according to perceived common sense, but contrary to unhelpful precedent;
- the ability of the jury to focus on character and facts, and not legal niceties; and
- 800 years of largely successful history.

Because of the potential for problems with the use of juries, in 2003 the law was changed to allow a Crown Court trial by a judge without a jury in cases where there was likelihood of 'jury tampering', but with safeguards for defendants.[20] The first non-jury criminal trial in the Crown Court commenced in January 2010,[21] after three previous jury trials collapsed (relating to a

[18] E.g. Cheryl Thomas, *Are Juries Fair?* (Ministry of Justice, February 2010).
[19] Cheryl Thomas, *Are Juries Fair?* (Ministry of Justice, February 2010).
[20] Criminal Justice Act 2003, Part 7.
[21] *R v Peter Blake, John Twomey, Glenn Cameron and Barry Hibberd*. Trial for armed robbery and firearms offences, Central Criminal Court sitting at Royal Courts of Justice, London before Treacy J sitting without a jury, January–March 2010 (unreported at Crown Court, but reported on appeal as *R v Twomey* [2011] EWCA Crim 8).

£1.75 million robbery from a warehouse at Heathrow). Non-jury Crown Court trials are rare— the detailed level of guidance issued by the CPS[22] illuminates the contentious and legally delicate nature of the procedure.

Trial by jury is a sensitive issue, and the recent changes have been controversial. The policy director of Liberty, Isabella Sankey, has said:

> The right to jury trial isn't just a hallowed principle but a practice that ensures that one class of people don't sit in judgement over another and the public have confidence in an open and representative justice system. What signal do we send to witnesses if the police can't even protect juries?[23]

3.3.2 **Criminal appeal courts**

Criminal appeals—introduction

If a defendant in a criminal case is convicted she may appeal against conviction. Alternatively, she can accept her conviction but appeal against the sentence if she feels it is unduly harsh. The prosecution may also appeal against the length of the sentence if they feel it is unduly lenient, but may not appeal against an acquittal. The CPS can appeal against decisions of higher courts that favour the defendant. Much depends on where the case was tried—in a magistrates' court or in the Crown Court. Permission (or 'leave') is not always required for a criminal appeal; by contrast, appeals in civil law cases usually require leave.

Appeals from magistrates' courts

Figure 3.5 shows the basics of the appeal procedure in relation to summary offences or either way offences tried in a magistrates' court. An explanation of key concepts follows the diagram.

A retrial in a Crown Court (normally around 14,000 annually) is much more common than an appeal to the High Court (around 100 annually). The distinction is that in the former there is essentially a retrial of the case, including fresh consideration of factual evidence. In the latter, the Divisional Court of the High Court (Queen's Bench Division) hears an appeal on the ground that the magistrates were wrong in law. This is called an 'appeal by way of case stated', referring to the magistrates, who must state their case. 'Divisional Court' refers to the High Court in its appellate (multi-judge) incarnation. The system is skewed in favour of the defendant, as the CPS can only appeal via the High Court.

Any further appeals in relation to summary offences are rare. Appeals from the High Court (Queen's Bench Division) Divisional Court would be to the Supreme Court, and the appellant must be granted 'leave' to appeal. Often there are no such appeals in a given year.

Details of the High Court and the Supreme Court are set out in the Appendix. The Supreme Court took over the functions of the Appellate Committee of the House of Lords in 2009. You will encounter many cases from the House of Lords—they have the same status and authority as equivalents appealed in the UK Supreme Court.

---

[22] http://www.cps.gov.uk/legal/l_to_o/non_jury_trials/index.html.

[23] Interviewed in 'First trial without jury approved', *BBC News*, 18 June 2009, http://news.bbc.co.uk/1/hi/uk/8106590.stm.

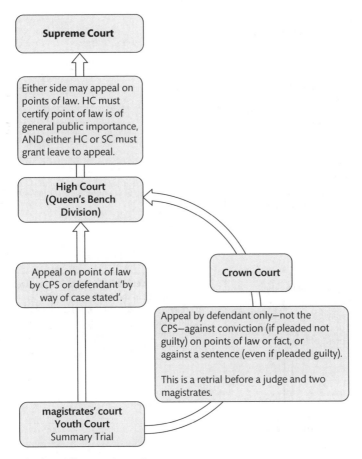

Figure 3.5 Appeals after trial in a magistrates' court

Appeals from the Crown Court

Figure 3.6 shows the basics of the appeals procedure in relation to indictable offences or either way offences tried in the Crown Court. An explanation of key concepts follows the diagram.

If a defendant has been tried in the Crown Court, he may appeal to the Court of Appeal, if he has obtained permission. An appeal may be on a point of law or fact, against conviction or against the sentence imposed. There are normally around 1,500 appeals against conviction and 5,500 against sentence annually. While the Court of Appeal refuses to accept most applications for leave to appeal, a slim majority of defendants' appeals are successful.

Thereafter, either side may seek leave to appeal to the Supreme Court. There are normally only around five such appeals each year from the Court of Appeal (Criminal Division).

Criminal appeals—summary

Depending on which court was the trial court, the route of appeal follows one of two main routes. The criminal appeal routes are summarised in Figure 3.7.

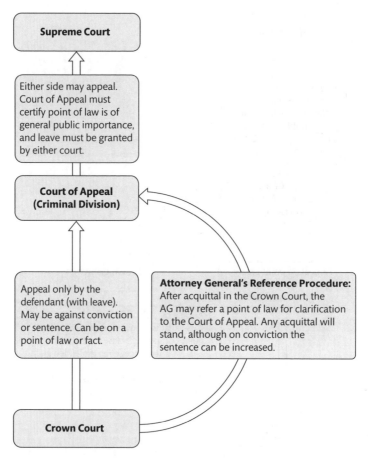

Figure 3.6 Appeals after trial in the Crown Court

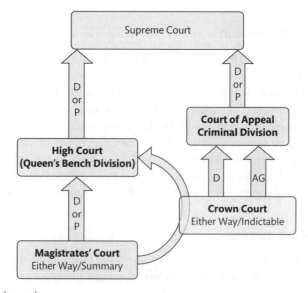

Figure 3.7 Criminal appeals—summary

3.4 **The civil courts of England & Wales**

In Chapter 1 we saw that access to civil justice is a key indicator of the health of the Rule of Law in a country, and that the US in particular lags behind many other jurisdictions because of the expense of civil litigation.

The UK has a less pronounced, but still sizeable, deficit in access to civil justice. The main factors are the cost of civil litigation (e.g. pursuing a debt) along with the complexity, length, and stress of the process. In 1996, to remedy these problems, Lord Woolf's report *Access to Justice* triggered substantial reforms, via the Civil Procedure Rules[24] and the Access to Justice Act 1999. Central to these reforms is the 'overriding objective',[25] which emphasises putting the parties on an equal footing, saving expense, dealing with cases proportionately and expeditiously, and allocating court resources efficiently. More recently, a report by Sir Rupert Jackson has made further recommendations intended to promote access to justice at proportionate cost, the bulk of which came into effect in April 2013.[26]

In this section we examine the courts in which civil claims are made.

3.4.1 **An outline of civil litigation**

The civil courts of first instance are the 165 county courts and the High Court, which is based in the Royal Courts of Justice in London but has 137 district registries around the country. Proceedings are commenced by a claim form, issued by the relevant court and served by the claimant on the defendant. If the defendant wishes to contest the claim, she must file a defence at the court and serve it on the claimant. The Woolf reforms attempted to incentivise parties to settle early, or to use Alternative Dispute Resolution (ADR) (see 3.7), to reduce the cost of civil claims and the burden on the court system. Since the reform, the number of proceedings has indeed declined.

If the case does come to trial, it will be before a judge, sitting alone. At the trial, the judge will listen to the evidence from both parties and to any legal arguments. He will then apply the law to the facts to decide whether or not the claimant has proved its claim on the balance of probabilities. The judge will award judgment (note the spelling of 'judgment' in this context) to either party, and the defendant will be found to be either liable or not. 'Guilty' is an unsuitable term in civil proceedings.

In a debt claim, the agreed sum is the main remedy, and in most other actions damages is the most common remedy. You may recall (from Chapter 2) that equitable remedies, such as injunctions, are often appropriate. The court decides who pays the legal costs of the matter. The losing party will usually be ordered to pay the winner's legal costs. Under the small claims procedure (see 'Choice of forum—civil claims', below), the loser will only pay court fees, and both parties will normally bear their own costs. While costs are dealt with at the end of the trial, they loom over the proceedings from the start. The fear of paying substantial amounts in costs (not to forget protracted argument and worry) is a major factor in cases being settled or not even being commenced.

---

[24] Civil Procedure Rules 1998 (SI 1998/3132), under the Civil Procedure Act 1997.
[25] Civil Procedure Rules 1998, r. 1.1.
[26] Sir Rupert Jackson, *Review of Civil Litigation Costs: Final Report* (TSO, 2010).

Here we describe each court, before examining the basis upon which the case is allocated to one of them.

The county courts

County courts were introduced in 1846 so that claims could be heard more quickly and cheaply without using the Queen's Bench (forerunner of the High Court). They deal with the bulk of civil actions—in most years, over 1.5 million claims are issued, around 97% of civil claims.

Most county court claims take between six and 12 months from the issue of proceedings to a decision. The cost and expense of this still drawn-out process may help explain why the vast majority (around 90%) settle before the decision is made.

Because county courts are where most civil matters are resolved, it is helpful to have some perspective on what these courts actually deal with. Table 3.1 sets out the proportion of claims in the county courts in 2011:[27]

Table 3.1 Proportion of claims in the county courts, by type: 2011

Type of claim	Proportion of claims in county courts
Debt action	69%
Repossession	14%
Personal injury	13%
Insolvency petition	4%

The High Court

Only complex or higher-value cases are considered in the High Court. Although we have already encountered the High Court in its appellate jurisdiction, its main workload is as a court of first instance. The court is split according to the type of cases considered:

- The Queen's Bench Division: this considers claims in contract and tort, and also incorporates various specialised courts, for example the Commercial Court and the Technology and Construction Court.
- The Family Division: this considers family claims including divorce, adoption, and wardship.
- The Chancery Division: this deals with wills and probate, trusts, land and mortgage actions, company law, intellectual property, and bankruptcy. It derives its competence from the old courts of Chancery, the courts of Equity prior to the Judicature Acts. It also incorporates specialised courts, including the Court of Protection (persons under disability), the Patents Court, and the Companies Court.

Each year, around 16,000 claims are issued in the Queen's Bench Division of the High Court, and 36,000 in the Chancery Division. Only a small percentage of those reach a full trial.

[27] *Judicial and Court Statistics 2011* (Ministry of Justice, 2012).

Choice of forum—civil claims

Where claimants (termed 'plaintiffs' until 1999) should issue their claim is mainly a matter of value, but also complexity. The Civil Procedure Rules make it clear that proceedings may not be started in the High Court unless the value of the claim is more than £25,000. Around 90% of civil claims settle before a trial formally starts.

The Woolf reforms introduced a track system, designed to make the formality and rigour of proceedings proportionate to the nature and size of the claim. A county court will normally allocate a claim of up to £5,000 to the small claims track. Typically, these claims concern consumer disputes and the court does not expect parties to be legally represented. Claims exceeding £5,000 and up to £25,000 are usually allocated to the fast track. While parties will usually have legal representation on this track, the court will tightly control costs, as well as the type and amount of evidence each party can rely on. In particular, the expectation is that a single joint expert should be used by the parties where expert evidence is necessary, and the trial must be conducted within one day (effectively five hours). Claims exceeding £25,000 are usually allocated to the multi-track.

As a claim cannot be started in the High Court unless it exceeds £25,000, all claims in that court are dealt with on the multi-track. The position is set out in Figure 3.8.

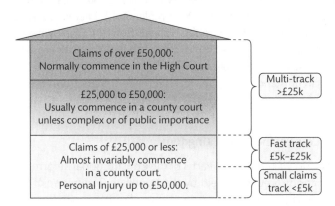

Figure 3.8 Courts of first instance—civil courts

3.4.2 **Civil appeals**

Civil appeals—introduction

The civil appeals system was rationalised in 2000 as a result of the Woolf report.[28] Any detailed analysis of the rules and time limits associated with appeals is beyond the scope of this book. However, as a general principle, it is harder to obtain leave to appeal in civil (as distinct from criminal) litigation because liberty is not at stake. Leave will only be given either if the court considers that the appeal has a real prospect of success or if there is some other compelling reason why the appeal should be heard. This also prevents the system being clogged by implausible appeals.

[28] Lord Woolf, *Access to Justice* (HMSO, 1996).

The High Court

We have already looked at the High Court's role as a court of first instance. It is also an appeal court, in which the majority of appeals from the county court will be heard. Very occasionally, appeals from a county court will be heard in a county court, and, also very rarely, they may be heard in the Court of Appeal, bypassing the High Court.

An avenue through which the inferior courts can be supervised is the Administrative Court, part of the High Court Queen's Bench Division. Its main role is to supervise public bodies—including courts—by means of judicial review. This is not an appeals procedure. This is a key concept of public law. There are around 13,000 such cases received annually, many relating to asylum and immigration decisions.

Appeals from the High Court will almost always be to the Court of Appeal (Civil Division), but very occasionally will be direct to the Supreme Court under the 'leapfrog' procedure. Some appeals will be made within the High Court. As you have probably realised, there are many variations on the general themes discussed in this chapter.

The Court of Appeal (Civil Division)

The Court of Appeal (Civil Division) deals with 1,000–1,500 cases annually. Established by the Supreme Court of Judicature Act 1873, it replaced 12 different courts of appeal. It is exclusively an appeal court. It also considers appeals from the Employment Appeals Tribunal, which itself hears appeals from the Employment Tribunal (tribunals are discussed at 3.6.1).

County court cases are very rarely appealed beyond the High Court to the Court of Appeal. In exceptional circumstances an appeal can be made straight from the county court to the Court of Appeal.

The Supreme Court of the United Kingdom

The Supreme Court was created by Part 3 of the Constitutional Reform Act 2005, assuming the judicial functions previously held by the Appellate Committee of the House of Lords in October 2009. The change was made to formalise the Separation of Powers between the House of Lords in its legislative capacity and the Appellate Committee of the House of Lords. In reality, Lords who were not legally qualified ceased to take part in judicial matters in 1876.[29] Law Lords, by convention, did not vote at all, and did not speak on controversial matters, though this rule was not well-defined. The Constitutional Reform Act also gave the Supreme Court a separate building and administration commensurate with its status.

Very few cases go on to the Supreme Court, which is the ultimate court of appeal in the whole of the UK for civil matters and for criminal matters outside Scotland. It only deals with cases of real public importance—in 2011, 56 civil appeals from the Court of Appeal were heard.[30]

[29] Appellate Jurisdiction Act 1876.

[30] Figure derived from *Judicial and Court Statistics 2011* (Ministry of Justice, 2012), with thanks to Ben Wilson, Head of Communications, UKSC.

The Supreme Court can hear appeals direct from the High Court under the 'leapfrog' procedure. This procedure is reserved for matters certified by the Supreme Court to be of general public importance—the type of issue which would ultimately be appealed from the Court of Appeal in any event. There are normally a few of these direct appeals from the High Court each year.

Civil appeals—summary

We have seen that the civil appeals system can operate at up to four levels. Figure 3.9 summarises the system. Remember that the majority of appeals conform to the 'ladder' of courts, and that appeals bypassing courts and appeals within single courts are rare.

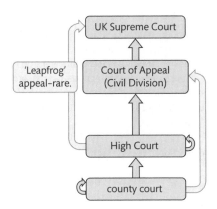

Figure 3.9 Civil appeals—summary

3.5 Other important courts

The UK has many international commitments of different types. Some give supranational courts a degree of jurisdiction within the UK (and therefore England & Wales).

3.5.1 The European Court of Justice

Based in Luxembourg, the Court of Justice of the European Union (often referred to as the European Court of Justice or simply the ECJ) has jurisdiction to make rulings interpreting law emanating from EU institutions. Usually these rulings are then applied by our national courts. The ECJ has a very limited power to deal with actions brought by individuals. Chapter 5 discusses how decisions of the ECJ have force of law in the UK. The relevant procedure is not strictly an appeal, but instead is called a 'reference' procedure.

The ECJ's role under the Treaty on the Functioning of the EU (TFEU—see 4.5) is 'to ensure that in the interpretation and application of the Treaties the law is observed'. The EU has competence in the UK in relation to the single market (e.g. trade and competition) and some social policy. Article 267 TFEU states that the ECJ has jurisdiction to give rulings on interpretation of the TFEU and the acts of EU institutions (i.e. including EU legislation—see Chapter 4).

English courts can make an 'Article 267 reference' to the ECJ on matters of EU law. There is no restriction on the level of court that can do this. There is a significant amount of important jurisprudence resulting from Court of Appeal and House of Lords/Supreme Court references. At the same time, magistrates' courts have jurisdiction in Sunday trading cases, and have made related Article 267 references to the ECJ.[31] The English court will formulate a question of law to be resolved by the ECJ (either the CJEU or the General Court—a 'lower court' set up to deal with the high caseload of the ECJ). The ECJ will then give judgment, and send an answer back to the relevant English court. The English court will then give a judgment. Case study 2 gives a famous example of the Article 267 reference at work.

Case study 2

Mrs Murphy vs Sky

In 2006, a pub landlady in Portsmouth was convicted under criminal provisions of the Copyright, Designs and Patents Act 1988 for breach of copyright in using a Greek satellite channel to broadcast Premier League matches. Use of the Greek decoder was significantly cheaper than signing up to Sky's package. The landlady appealed to the High Court on the ground that the Act was discriminatory because it restricted the free movement of cross border services.[32]

The High Court sought a preliminary reference under Article 267 TFEU on matters of EU competition and intellectual property law set out in the TFEU[33] and various EU Directives.[34]

The ECJ decided[35] that the relevant provision of the Copyright, Designs and Patents Act 1988 was unenforceable. The High Court then quashed her conviction.[36]

3.5.2 The European Court of Human Rights

Based in Strasbourg, the European Court of Human Rights is set up under an international treaty: the European Convention on Human Rights (ECHR). These rights can be enforced in our national courts (under the Human Rights Act 1998—see 4.6).

The Convention gives a citizen of a signatory state the right to apply to the European Court of Human Rights for an order for compensation on the grounds that there has been a breach by the state of the Convention, either directly (e.g. by the actions of the police), or indirectly (e.g. because the approach of the courts has constituted a lack of access to a fair trial under Article 6). However, this procedure is both expensive and lengthy, the latter due to the need first to exhaust domestic avenues of justice, and the logjam of cases before the European Court of Human Rights.

The UK government normally shows great attention to detail in observing judgments of the European Court of Human Rights. It is important to realise that the enforceability of the court's judgments is very much a matter of national governments opting in. This is because decisions

---

[31] E.g. Case C-145/88 *Torfaen Borough Council* [1989] ECR 3851.

[32] *Murphy v Media Protection Services* [2007] EWHC 3091 and [2008] EWHC 1666 (Admin).

[33] E.g. Art. 101 TFEU.   [34] E.g. Conditional Access Directive 98/84/EC.

[35] Joined Cases C-403/08 and C-429/08.

[36] *Murphy v Media Protection Services Ltd* [2012] EWHC 466 (Admin)

are binding on states only as a matter of international law (see 2.2.4) under Article 1 ECHR and are not directly binding in domestic law. For instance, the UK government observed the initial judgment of the European Court of Human Rights[37] (under Article 6—right to a fair trial) that the government could not deport the controversial and radical Islamic cleric Abu Qatada to Jordan without specific guarantees from that country that evidence obtained through torture would not be used against him in trial. By contrast, the Italian government ignored similar rulings four times between 2005 and 2012.[38]

However, the UK government has refused to legislate to change the law, in defiance of a ruling from Strasbourg[39] that, by removing the right to vote from prisoners, the UK government was in breach of Protocol 1, Article 3 ECHR (right to regular, free and fair elections). So, unlike the ECJ, the European Court of Human Rights has no direct (enforceable) jurisdiction within the UK.

3.5.3 The International Criminal Court

Based in The Hague, Netherlands, the ICC has jurisdiction under the Rome Statute of the International Criminal Court (2002)[40] to prosecute individuals for genocide, crimes against humanity, and war crimes. Muammar Gadaffi's son, Saif al-Gadaffi, is among its more notable defendants. Like the European Court of Human Rights, its jurisdiction is subject to ratification by member states, and their cooperation. Important non-ratifiers include the US and Russia. The ICC has not yet exercised its authority within the UK, but in theory has the right to do so.

3.5.4 The Judicial Committee of the Privy Council

This court, which has largely overlapping membership with the UK Supreme Court, hears appeals from 23 Commonwealth countries and four independent republics. The decisions of the Privy Council are not binding on English courts. Nor does the Privy Council have any appellate capacity within the English legal system (except in very rare and particular circumstances, e.g. ecclesiastical courts).

Although not binding, Privy Council decisions are highly persuasive in English case law (see Chapter 5), because of the seniority of the Judicial Committee's personnel. The court disposes of between 30 and 50 appeals each year. Civil matters recently considered have included a challenge on environmental grounds to the construction of a dam in Belize and an appeal from New Zealand on the extent to which the law of defamation applies to Members of Parliament. Criminal appeals, mainly from Trinidad and Tobago, have related to the mandatory death penalty. Its role is likely to decline in future as more Commonwealth countries (e.g. Belize, New Zealand) establish their own final courts of appeal.

---

[37] *Othman (Abu Qatada) v UK* App. no. 8139/09 (2012) 55 EHRR 1.

[38] Alexander Horne and Melanie Gower, *Statistics: Deportation of Individuals who may face Torture* (House of Commons Library, 14 February 2012).

[39] *Hirst v UK (No. 2)* App. no. 74025/01 (2005) 42 EHRR 41.

[40] Rome Statute of the International Criminal Court Rome, 17 July 1998, United Nations Treaty Collection. Entry into force, 1 July 2002, in accordance with Art. 126.

3.6 Other judicial forums in England & Wales

3.6.1 Tribunals

While not strictly courts, tribunals have a quasi-judicial role, largely mirroring the lower courts in the court system in specific fields.

Tribunals are established by statute to deal with certain types of claim only; members of tribunals (unlike judges in courts) have specific relevant expertise. They range in jurisdiction from individuals challenging their benefit entitlement in the Health, Education and Social Care Chamber, to multinational corporations arguing over sizeable tax liabilities in the Tax Chamber. They are generally less formal than courts. Bringing claims in tribunals is often cheaper and faster than in the court system. These characteristics are aimed to promote justice.

In 2007, most tribunals were organised into a unified structure,[41] in a move towards accessibility and transparency of access to justice (at 1.5.1 we saw that such characteristics are important to the Rule of Law). First Tier tribunals are equivalent to trial courts (such as county courts) and appeals on questions of law are heard by Upper Tier tribunals. Figure 3.10 draws parallels between the court system and the tribunals system, and gives examples of tribunals at each level.

Although formally outside the First Tier system, employment tribunals are perhaps the best known tribunal at this level. They hear complaints from employees and former employees who believe that they have been unfairly or wrongfully dismissed, or have been subject to discrimination. Appeals are to the Employment Appeals Tribunal.

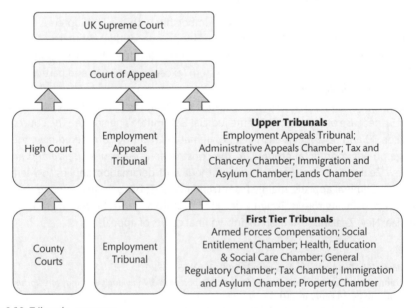

Figure 3.10 Tribunals—summary

[41] Tribunals, Courts and Enforcement Act 2007.

Further appeals beyond the tribunal system are to the Court of Appeal. Another way of challenging tribunal decisions is by the judicial review procedure, on the ground that the tribunal's decision-making was in some way flawed. As we saw at 3.4.2, judicial review is not a type of appeal.

3.6.2 Statutory inquiries

Statutory inquiries (not to be confused with judicial inquiries) are established by statute to examine common specific situations where courts may not necessarily have the expertise or appropriate procedures. An example of an inquiry is when the Charity Commission investigates misconduct in the management of a charity. Planning inquiries[42] are a common means of hearing appeals from interested parties in relation to decisions allowing or disallowing the development of land.

3.6.3 Judicial inquiries

Judicial inquiries are established on an *ad hoc* basis to deal with specific issues of public interest, and are often run like court cases, frequently by senior members of the judiciary. However, they do not necessarily reach a 'decision' in the judicial sense—instead they investigate facts and reach conclusions. Many are established by Parliament with wide-ranging powers to call and question witnesses. The Bloody Sunday Inquiry was authorised in 1998 and reported in 2010.[43] This inquiry involved an international panel of judges chaired by Lord Saville, a Law Lord and Supreme Court Justice.

Others are launched by the government, for example, the Chilcott Inquiry (which began in 2009 but has yet, as of January 2013, to report), established to examine how and why the UK's involvement in Iraq started, and what lessons can be learned. In 2012 the Leveson Inquiry reported on the role of the press and police in phone-hacking.[44]

3.7 Alternatives to litigation

This chapter started with the statement that the primary function of a court is to administer the law. Courts (including tribunals) do not, however, have a monopoly on settling legal disputes.

Example 1

Imagine that you are in a dispute over a business contract. You receive a letter from a court together with a document entitled 'particulars of claim' setting out your alleged breach and what is claimed. This formal document sets out the claimant's case, and refers to you as the 'defendant'. There is a list of damage, and then of monetary losses, and a claim for damages. You can see months of expense and stress, and conflict with a once-valuable client. If you lose, you may have to pay all the other side's costs and court fees. The other side is probably mindful of the same issues.

---

[42] Under the Town and Country Planning Act 1990, and related secondary legislation.

[43] The Rt Hon. Lord Saville of Newdigate, The Hon. Mr William L. Hoyt, The Hon. Mr John L. Toohey, *Report of the Bloody Sunday Inquiry* (15 June 2010).

[44] The Rt Hon. Lord Justice Leveson, *An Inquiry into the Culture, Practices and Ethics of the Press* (HMSO, November 2012).

Example 1 illustrates why it is often said that litigation should be used as a last resort. This was an explicit consideration in Lord Woolf's report[45] (see 3.4). Important alternatives to formal litigation include ADR, mediation, arbitration, access to ombudsmen, and negotiation. They are not, however, alternatives to using the law. The rights and obligations created by the law continue to provide the basis of parties' assertions when using these procedures and are observed by the practitioners involved in facilitating them. Indeed, the use of these avenues reinforces respect for the law and the Rule of Law, by making access to the law more feasible to private and commercial parties.

3.7.1 Alternative Dispute Resolution

In its widest sense, ADR is a term used to describe any dispute resolution outside the courts, so it is often said to include arbitration, mediation, and similar schemes. ADR is often used in a narrower sense to describe a procedure where the parties agree that an independent third party should help them reach a solution. It is normally confidential. The decision of the third party is not legally enforceable (with the exception of arbitration, see 3.7.2).

Mediation is a type of ADR often used in matrimonial and commercial matters. Because the independent third party is unable to bind the parties, the proceedings are intended to be less confrontational than litigation or arbitration.

3.7.2 Arbitration

Many business contracts contain a clause whereby the parties agree to refer their disputes to a named arbitrator. An arbitrator is an independent third party who considers the parties' arguments and reaches a binding decision on the dispute. The parties can agree to go to arbitration when a dispute arises even without an arbitration clause in their contract. Arbitration proceedings are governed by the Arbitration Act 1996. Crucially, and in contrast to other forms of ADR, the decision of the arbitrator is binding and legally enforceable.

Arbitration is often cheaper and less formal than litigation. Parties have some scope to determine the format of proceedings, with the result that they may be less confrontational. Proceedings may also be private if the parties wish. The arbitrator does not (and cannot) award all the remedies available to a court, but the parties and the arbitrator can formulate more practical solutions, such as agreeing to amend a contract.

Sharia law (see 'Natural law' at 1.3.2) is used in some Muslim communities in the UK. In general this does not constitute an attempt to impose an alternative legal system; instead, in certain areas like divorce, civil (not criminal) disputes within the Muslim community can be settled under the Arbitration Act by the Muslim Arbitration Tribunal, a network of Sharia courts. This means that the rulings of these courts can be enforced by English courts, provided they do not conflict with English law. Other religions have similar practices, such as the Beth Din, which are courts in the Jewish community also operating under the Arbitration Act.

---

[45] Lord Woolf, *Access to Justice* (HMSO, 1996).

3.7.3 **Ombudsmen**

Ombudsmen are usually established by statute[46] and given delegated authority to investigate and settle minor complaints. Examples include the Financial Ombudsman Service, and the Property Ombudsman, which provide consumers and businesses with independent advice and investigation relating to disputes with service providers in various sectors.

The template for ombudsmen in the UK was the Parliamentary Ombudsman (officially the Parliamentary and Health Service Ombudsman). The Parliamentary Ombudsman is responsible for considering complaints about poor administration by government departments, made by members of the public via their MPs. Parties are normally free to litigate if they disagree with decisions by ombudsmen.

3.7.4 **Negotiation**

It is always open to the parties to dispense with third parties altogether, and negotiate a settlement of their disputes. This is, in reality, the most frequent means of dispute resolution without recourse to litigation. As with all forms of ADR, the balance of legal rights and obligations between the parties will exert a strong influence on the ultimate outcome.

 Summary

- Trials take place in different courts depending on the type of law and the degree of harm.
- The appeals systems differ for criminal law and civil law. Within each type of law there are variations depending on the trial court.
- Other bodies also assume judicial or quasi-judicial roles.

 Thought-provoking questions

1. How long should detention without charge be permitted to last?
2. Should trial by jury be required for all Crown Court cases?
3. Was it necessary to replace the Appellate Committee of the House of Lords with the UK Supreme Court?
4. Should religious 'courts' be permitted as a form of arbitration? Do they undermine the importance of the English court system?
5. Is the Privy Council an anachronism?

 Further reading

Lord Woolf, *Access to Justice* (HMSO, 1996)
—this report highlighted the contemporary barriers to access to justice in England & Wales and triggered the opening-up of litigation procedure.

---

[46] The Financial Ombudsman Service was established by the Financial Services and Markets Act 2000 and the Consumer Credit Act 2006; the Property Ombudsman was approved under the Estate Agents and Redress Act 2007.

Cheryl Thomas, *Are Juries Fair?* (Ministry of Justice, February 2010)
—a very modern take on the old question. This debate extends to the more fundamental question of whether it is desirable to abolish trial by jury.

Judicial and Court Statistics 2011 (Ministry of Justice, 2012)
—this puts together useful information relating to the court system in England & Wales, and, in the online version, contains tables of source statistics.

The Right Honourable Lord Justice Leveson, *An Inquiry into the Culture, Practices and Ethics of the Press* (HMSO, November 2012)
—an illuminating example of a report from a judicial inquiry.

Refer to the Appendix for a useful collection of key facts about all the courts discussed in this chapter.

For the authors' reflections on the thought-provoking questions, additional self-test questions, podcasts offering a variety of perspectives on legal systems and skills, and a library of links to useful websites, visit the free Online Resource Centre *at* **http://www.oxfordtextbooks.co.uk/orc/slorach/.**

4   Legislation

 Learning objectives

After studying this chapter you should be able to:

- Explain the concept of Parliamentary sovereignty.
- Identify different types of legislation.
- Describe in outline the process by which a statute is created.
- Recognise key issues of statutory interpretation.
- Discuss basic concepts relating to EU and European Convention on Human Rights (ECHR) legislation.

Introduction

The most important source of English law is now legislation. Unlike case law, which only applies to England & Wales, and in the absence of specific provisions to the contrary, statutes apply to England, Wales, Scotland, and Northern Ireland.

 Essential explanation

'Legislation' is often used as a synonym for 'statute'. However, strictly speaking, a statute is an Act of Parliament, whereas 'legislation' is a generic term that includes other types of legislation such as secondary legislation (see 4.2.2) and EU legislation.

In this section we use the terms 'Act' and 'statute' interchangeably—this reflects normal practice.

Statute is the primary source of law in England & Wales. This is a key consequence of the doctrine of parliamentary sovereignty, also known as parliamentary supremacy, which gives Parliament an unfettered power to legislate. Therefore, even though the English legal system is a common law jurisdiction, no court may overrule any statute. Unlike in some other jurisdictions, a court can do no more than interpret statutes. We examine this in more detail in at 4.1.

There have been statutes in one form or another ever since there were governments. Before statutes came customary law (remnants of which survive in some jurisdictions—especially Scandinavian—today). All modern states have statutes made by law-making bodies. In contrast with (for instance) case law, a statute has the advantage of being a definitive statement of law, passed with the authority of whatever institution has sovereignty.

This chapter addresses the key issue of parliamentary sovereignty, before looking at the rise of the statute as a source of law in the UK. It then categorises statutes and examines the importance of the various types of legislation. We then look at how courts and lawyers interpret statutes before moving on to consider the impact of two of the most fundamental changes in our legal history: the incorporation into our law of EU law and the European Convention on Human Rights (ECHR).

4.1 Parliamentary sovereignty

We examined the concept of sovereignty at 1.4.3. In the UK, Parliament is sovereign. The noted constitutional theorist, Professor A. V. Dicey, said:

> The Principle of Parliamentary Sovereignty means neither more nor less than this: namely, that Parliament ... has, under the English constitution the right to make or unmake any law whatever; and further that no person or body is recognised by the law ... as having the right to override or set aside the legislation of Parliament.[1]

Parliament is therefore the supreme law-making body in the UK.

Even though England & Wales remains a common law jurisdiction, with a sizeable body of judge-made law, Parliament is at liberty to reverse the common law, and no court can challenge the validity of an Act of Parliament. Courts often shy away from making law in areas deemed too sensitive; they defer to the democratic legitimacy of Parliament. In the Diane Pretty case on assisted dying (discussed at 1.2.4), Lord Steyn stated: 'In our Parliamentary democracy ... such a fundamental change cannot be brought about by judicial creativity.'[2]

The 'Enrolled Act' Rule confirms that courts cannot question the validity of an Act, or disregard it,[3] on any grounds. For instance, the Hunting Act 2004 was challenged on the basis that it had not been passed by the House of Lords. The House of Lords (in their judicial capacity; the forerunner to the Supreme Court) unanimously stated that, because the Act had received Royal Assent (see 4.3.1), its validity could not be challenged in court.[4]

4.1.1 Challenges to parliamentary sovereignty

It has been said that parliamentary sovereignty has been eroded over the last century or so, and that, while Parliament is said to be the 'supreme' law-making body in the UK, it is no longer entirely sovereign. In three areas in particular Parliament has ceded sovereignty, but in each of these there are arguments that formal sovereignty has remained with Parliament.

Devolution

The Scotland Act 1998, the Government of Wales Act 1998, and the Northern Ireland Act 1998, established the Scottish Parliament, the Welsh Assembly, and the Northern Ireland Assembly, respectively. These statutes devolved certain powers to those institutions.

---

[1] A. V. Dicey, *An Introduction to the Study of the Law of the Constitution* (1885), p. 36.

[2] *R (Pretty) v Director of Public Prosecutions, Secretary of State for the Home Department intervening* [2001] UKHL 61, at [55].

[3] *Edinburgh & Dalkeith Railway Co. v Wauchope* (1842) 8 C & F 710; *Pickin v British Railways Board* [1975] AC 765.   [4] *R (Jackson) v Attorney General* [2005] UKHL 56.

The legislation produced by those institutions and executed by the executive of each country, is limited in its extent by the Westminster Parliament, and, strictly speaking, the Westminster Parliament may repeal or amend the relevant statutes (and has in the past suspended the Northern Ireland Assembly), although it would be politically difficult to do so.

International treaties

Under the Royal Prerogative (detailed examination of which is beyond the scope of this book) the UK government has signed many international treaties, and therefore adheres to many different bodies of international law (e.g. the ECHR 1950, the Berne Copyright Convention 1887). While the government exercises these powers, Parliament can take them away, because it is sovereign. Parliament long had the power to ratify treaties, and this was recently codified in the Constitutional Reform and Governance Act 2010. If an international treaty purports to affect citizens within the UK itself, Parliament must legislate to give this legal force. For instance, the UK was a founder signatory to the ECHR, but it only became directly enforceable within the UK after the Human Rights Act 1998 (HRA). Ungoed-Thomas J said in the *Cheney v Conn* case, 'international law is part of the law of the land, but it yields to statute'.[5]

The European Union

Possibly most controversially, the European Communities Act 1972 incorporated into UK law the Treaty on the Functioning of the European Union (then the Treaty of Rome). The UK became a member of the European Union (then the EEC—see 4.5 in relation to EU terminology). In the *Factortame*[6] case, the House of Lords (after consulting the European Court of Justice (ECJ)) confirmed that, in any area of EU competence, EU law would take precedence over conflicting UK legislation. Again, however, it is clear that Parliament could (in theory) legislate to pull out of the EU, just as it sanctioned the entry into the EU in 1972. This would, of course, be politically contentious, and economically hazardous.

4.2 Types of legislation

We saw in 2.4.3 that the state has grown considerably in the last two centuries. This has required a prodigious amount of statutory implementation, with the consequence that the body of legislation has grown enormously. Although it is the job of Members of Parliament to legislate, there is a limit to how much work they can do. They certainly cannot debate and consider all of the thousands of pages of legislation necessary to provide the framework for regulation of the UK, extending to welfare, tax, health, education, etc. Parliament cannot legislate for every aspect of our lives in intricate detail, nor would anyone want it to.

It is a fact that government in the UK is big. But central and local government require more than even the yearly 3,000 pages of statutes to guide them. This means that it is

---

[5] *Cheney v Conn (Inspector of Taxes); Cheney v Inland Revenue Commissioners* [1968] 1 All ER 779.
[6] *R v Secretary of State for Transport, ex parte Factortame (No. 2)* [1991] AC 603.

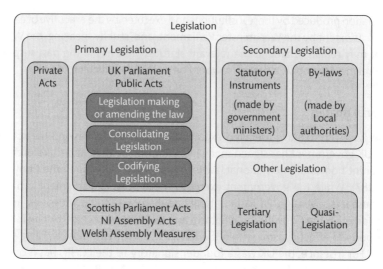

Figure 4.1 Types of legislation in the UK

impracticable for all legislation required at all levels of government to be in the form of statutes. There are therefore several types of domestic legislation in the UK. Figure 4.1 summarises the main types of legislation in the UK; you may wish to refer to it as you read about each type of legislation.

4.2.1 Primary legislation

Public and private Acts

Acts are known as primary legislation to distinguish them from secondary legislation, also known as delegated legislation. Before it is enacted, a statute is called a 'Bill', rather than an 'Act'. Public Bills are introduced to Parliament by Members of Parliament (usually government ministers) and concern matters affecting the public as a whole, whereas private Bills are submitted to Parliament by a person or body who needs parliamentary authority to get something done.

A well-known public statute is the Sale of Goods Act 1979, which applies to all of us virtually every day. All public statutes proceed through Parliament as Bills, either government Bills, introduced by a minister as part of the government's legislative programme, or private members' Bills, which are non-government sponsored Bills introduced by backbench MPs.

Private members' Bills are public Bills, but they are not introduced on behalf of the government, and so do not benefit from the weight of any government majority. The Hunting Act 2004 illustrates the distinction neatly. It eventually passed as a government Bill, but was preceded by at least six private members' Bills on the same subject, unsuccessfully introduced in Parliament since 1949.

Private Bills are quite distinct from private members' Bills. Private Bills (including a category called local Bills) affect particular persons or a particular locality, such as a Bill to build a new section of railway line or a reservoir. They were more prolific in the 19th and early 20th centuries before statutory instruments became the preferred method of legislative micro-management. A memorable example was an Act of 1727,[7] giving George Handel (the composer) citizenship of Great Britain. Outdated as they may seem, private Bills have performed an important role as society has developed:

> Every citizen of this country, whenever he mounts an omnibus or tram or gets into a railway train, whenever he turns on a water tap ... ignites a gas burner ... whenever he walks in a well-paved and lighted street, saunters on an esplanade, or listens to a band playing in a municipal bandstand ... is profiting from the results of private Bill legislation.[8]

While this role has diminished, many major infrastructure projects still require (and benefit from) Parliamentary authority as private Bills. For instance, the London Local Authorities and Transport for London Act 2008 concerned parking penalties and rail penalty charges in Greater London.

UK and devolved legislation

It is a presumption that all primary legislation will apply throughout England, Wales, Scotland, and Northern Ireland unless the statute specifically states that it does not apply in any of these jurisdictions. (A presumption in law is a rule that is presumed to apply in certain situations. Presumptions are often rebuttable. A presumption is rebuttable when the legal rule concerned can be disapplied if there is enough evidence to the contrary.)

Since the devolution statutes were passed (the Scotland Act 1998, the Government of Wales Act 1998, and the Northern Ireland Act 1998), each of the devolved legislatures has had the power to pass primary legislation in its jurisdiction, in a limited number of areas of competence (including health, education, the Scottish legal system, and transport, but notably not raising taxes).

Categories of public Act

Most legislation makes or changes law. The Hunting Act 2004 is an example of a statute creating new law. It created the offence of hunting wild mammals with dogs, where no such law existed beforehand. The Welfare Reform Act 2012 is an example of amending legislation. It purported to simplify the welfare benefits system and improve work incentives. You will encounter some statutes which attempt to do neither; instead they are 'tidying-up' exercises.

Consolidating Acts

Consolidation occurs where one statute re-enacts law which was previously contained in several different statutes. There is a presumption that consolidation does not materially change earlier legislation (the presumption is rebuttable by an express statement in the Act or by the promoter of the Act).

This is sometimes of great importance. The last Labour government embarked on a project to rewrite tax law, the aim of which was stated to be 'to rewrite the UK's primary direct tax

---

[7] Act of naturalisation of George Frideric Händel and others 1727.

[8] O. Cyprian Williams, *The Historical Development of Private Bill Procedure and Standing Orders in the House of Commons* (HMSO, 1948), p. 1.

legislation to make it clearer and easier to use, without changing the law'.[9] In 2010, it proudly announced that the project was complete, with ten statutes having been enacted since 2001. The law was changed only to a limited extent by these statutes.

Codifying Acts

Codification occurs where all the law on a topic, which may previously have been covered by common law, custom, and even statute(s), is brought together in one new statute. The codifying statute may, if necessary, change the pre-existing law (e.g. the Theft Act 1968).

The law relating to the sale of goods is an illuminating example. The law originated in medieval mercantile custom, which eventually crystallised into case law. The law was then codified by the Sale of Goods Act 1893. Over the course of nearly a century, this Act was the subject of a number of statutory amendments, which changed and repealed parts of it. These were then consolidated into the Sale of Goods Act 1979. The 1979 Act, amongst other things, makes a seller of goods liable to the buyer if the goods supplied are not of satisfactory quality. However, that Act has since been the subject of further amendment, notably by the Sale and Supply of Goods Act 1994.

4.2.2 Secondary legislation

 Essential explanation

Secondary legislation

Also called 'delegated' or 'subordinate' legislation.

Any law not made directly by Parliament or a devolved legislature is called secondary legislation. It is typically made with the authority of Parliament by local authorities, the Crown (i.e. the government), or ministers.

The authority to make secondary legislation is usually contained in a 'parent' Act, which creates the framework of the law, but then delegates the power to add the detailed provisions to others.

Statutory instruments

As mentioned earlier, it would be impractical for Parliament to be expected to consider and debate every detail of each Act. To overcome this, ministers and their departments are given authority to make regulations and orders (i.e. statutory instruments) in areas for which they are specifically responsible. For example, in 2012, the Chancellor of the Exchequer exercised his authority under the European Communities Act 1972 to extend sanctions against Iran.[10]

Parliament has always had this power, but it is now used to such an extent that the amount of secondary legislation far exceeds Acts of Parliament. In the early decades of

---

[9] http://www.hmrc.gov.uk/rewrite/.

[10] Iran (European Union Financial Sanctions) (Amendment) Regulations 2012 (SI 2012/190).

the 20th century around 1,200 statutory instruments were made each year; by the middle of that century, the number was around 2,100, and by the beginning of the 21st century, around 3,000 each year, that is around 90 times more statutory instruments than statutes (totalling a yearly average of around 10,000 pages). Thus the balance has shifted from statutes to statutory instruments over time. According to http://www.legislation.gov.uk, in 2012, 3,328 UK statutory instruments (or SIs) were made compared with the passing of just 23 Acts of Parliament. Why is this?

As the state has expanded, the need for extremely technical secondary legislation has increased. Statutory instruments enable Parliament to call upon technical expertise to assist in drafting regulations such as those relating to health and safety or road traffic matters. Delegation can be extremely useful in dealing quickly with emergencies, such as the outbreak of foot-and-mouth disease in 2000.

It might seem that statutory instruments run contrary to the spirit of parliamentary sovereignty, except in so far as they are created under the authority of Parliament. But all statutory instruments are subject to the approval of Parliament and to judicial review, under which courts can strike down a statutory instrument if it is outside the scope of the parent statute.

The move toward delegating legislative functions has culminated in secondary legislation occasionally being made without specific parliamentary delegation. Since 1994, ministers have had limited powers to legislate without specific prior parliamentary authority. Most controversially the Legislation and Regulatory Reform Act 2006 extended these powers significantly, so that a minister can make a regulatory reform order changing existing primary or secondary legislation if reform is needed, or to implement recommendations by the Law Commissions. Although there are limitations on this power (e.g. it cannot be used to amend the taxation regime, and must be used proportionately), it can extend even to creating new minor criminal offences.

 Essential debate

Legislation and Regulatory Reform Act 2006

Look at Case study 1 at 1.2.2 on the Enabling Act 1933, under which the *Reichstag* in Germany delegated its authority to Hitler's cabinet. Then read s. 1 of the Legislation and Regulatory Reform Act 2006, in addition to the contents page.

During the debates leading to the Act, David Howarth MP called the Bill the 'Abolition of Parliament Bill'. The main criticism of the Act is that it is anti-democratic in that it undermines parliamentary power. Former parliamentary draftsman Daniel Greenberg wrote, 'if an anti-democratic and dictatorial regime were to acquire significant political power in the United Kingdom, it would be able to bypass Parliament and legislate in an extreme and controlling way on a troublingly wide range of subjects, all through reliance on powers that have been duly granted by Parliament, with very little controversy'.[11]

The very existence of these powers, it is alleged, is a problem. The contents page reveals that the powers are currently heavily circumscribed. Even acknowledging that they are used responsibly in the current political climate, if a less well-meaning government were ever to take power, critics argue that they might be able to take advantage of the Act to force undesirable policies into law without Parliamentary scrutiny.

Do you think the Act—like the Enabling Act—is an unjustified erosion of democracy?

---

[11] Daniel Greenberg, *Laying Down the Law* (London: Sweet & Maxwell, 2011), pp. 214–15.

By-laws

Sometimes spelled 'bye-laws', these are made under the authority of parliamentary statute. They are usually made by local authorities to deal with issues within their own area. For example, public bathing is regulated by local councils under the authority of s. 231 of the Public Health Act 1936. In 2010 Greater Manchester City Council controversially considered a by-law increasing the price of alcohol in local shops. Occasionally other bodies make by-laws, such as public transport operators, utilities, or the National Trust.[12] For instance, queuing (among many other activities) on the London Underground is regulated by by-law.[13]

By-laws cannot take effect until they are confirmed by the appropriate minister. As government control of local matters has increased, so the need for by-laws has reduced.

4.2.3 **Other legislation**

Primary and secondary legislation are both created with some degree of legislative scrutiny. Government is so complex that some rules need to be made by government departments without any formal Parliamentary examination. This is sometimes categorised as tertiary legislation. For instance many tax forms have the force of law but, although they are made with parliamentary *authority* they have not necessarily had any *scrutiny* by the legislature. Important examples include:

- codes of practice made by the Home Secretary under s. 66 of the Police and Criminal Evidence Act 1984, which regulates police procedure, and
- rules and guidance of the Financial Conduct Authority (FCA), the body created by the Financial Services Act 2012 to supervise all firms to ensure that business across financial services and markets is conducted in a way that advances the interests of all users and participants. The Financial Services and Markets Act 2000, as amended by the Financial Services Act 2012, delegates powers and functions to the FCA. Rules made by the FCA are therefore delegated legislation.

Yet another, even less formal, category of rules exists. Quasi-legislation (sometimes called 'soft law') is a category of rules passed with the authority of Parliament, but in the form of guidance, for example some codes of practice. It often has force of law. If you have read the Highway Code, then you have already encountered 'quasi-legislation'.

4.3 **The creation and enforcement of statutes**

A statute becomes law when it receives Royal Assent. The Bill becomes an Act. The Act is then brought into force, often at a later date, and is enforced by the executive. This is often the end of an arduous process. The legislature (Parliament) creates statutes, but it is the executive (the government) that enforces them.

---

[12] Under the National Trust Acts 1907, 1919, 1937, 1939, 1953, and 1971.

[13] The Transport for London Railway Byelaws were made under para. 26 of Sch. 11 to the Greater London Authority Act 1999, confirmed by authority of the Secretary of State for Transport on 6 September 2011.

4.3.1 **The creation of statutes**

Parliament consists of the Queen, the House of Commons, which is democratically elected, and the House of Lords, which is not. The UK is a constitutional monarchy, which means that, although it has the machinery of a democratic state, the monarch still has a formal role as Head of State—this is why Bills are signed into law by (or on behalf of) the Monarch.

   Both Houses are involved in the process of creating statutes. An Act will begin its life as a document known as a Bill. Only when it has passed through all the stages set out below will it eventually become an Act of Parliament. There are three clear phases in the creation of a statute: the pre-parliamentary stage; the debates in Parliament; and finally its enactment and commencement. You may wish to refer to Figure 4.2 as you digest the description that follows.

Before Parliament

Before a Bill starts its progress through Parliament, there is usually an extensive gestation period.

   Governments are formed after general elections. Historically these have occurred every four or five years unless an emergency election is needed (e.g. there were two elections in 1974 because the first failed to yield a decisive result). As a result of the passing of the Fixed Term Parliaments Act 2011 general elections will normally be held every five years. The political parties campaign using a platform of policies contained in a manifesto. The manifesto is key

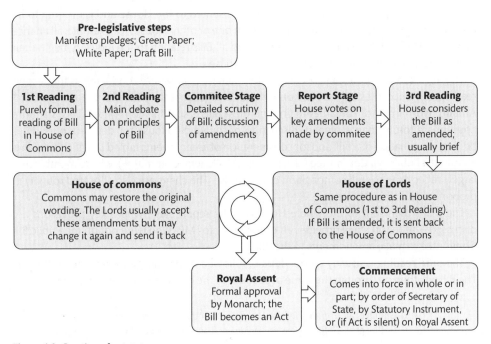

Figure 4.2 Creation of a statute

to democratic legitimacy. Regardless of whether voters actually read the manifesto or summaries of it in the media, it is important that a government is elected with a mandate to do certain things by introducing appropriate legislation into Parliament. Politically sensitive Bills are often trailed as manifesto pledges.

A government green paper is a consultation document. It will address an issue with a view to possible reform, inviting responses from interested parties to the relevant government department. A white paper will then follow. More authoritative, and less open to discussion, it will set out future government policy. The publication of a draft Bill forms an interim stage, allowing examination and consultation on the detail of the Bill before it is formally debated in Parliament. Not all Bills are subject to all (or sometimes any) of these stages. The draft Bill will form the underpinnings of a Bill to be put before Parliament.

Debates and readings within Parliament

A Bill must normally pass through all the stages set out here in both houses, before receiving Royal Assent.

There are some constitutional limits (set out in the Parliament Acts 1911 and 1949) on the House of Lords' ability to delay or prevent passage of Bills that have been passed in the House of Commons, especially in the case of 'money Bills' (e.g. the Finance Acts that contain budget provisions), and Bills that start life as manifesto pledges. Have a look at the Hunting Act 2004. If you read the enacting formula (the words beginning 'Be it enacted ...' at the start of the Act) you will see that the Act did not receive the approval of the House of Lords, but became law anyway because it was a Labour manifesto pledge, albeit a very controversial one.

The first reading is purely formal. The Bill is presented to the House and is ordered to be printed. Different types of Bills begin their lives in one or other House. For example, all finance Bills must first be debated in the Commons, and all Bills relating to the judiciary begin their lives in the Lords. Other Bills can start in either House.

The most controversial stage, where the key plenary debates are conducted, is the second reading, but it occupies only around one-fifth of the Parliamentary time for the average Bill.[14] Around two-thirds[15] of Parliament's time on most Bills is spent in committee. This is a more appropriate forum than a plenary discussion of the whole House for detailed, often line-by-line, examination of a Bill, and for consideration of amendments tabled by MPs. Each Bill is allocated a Public Bill Committee (also known as a General Committee), whose membership largely reflects the overall composition of the House. The chairs are also allocated roughly in proportion to political balance.

The Bill is then sent to the whole House for the report stage where key provisions are discussed. The report stage provides an opportunity for MPs who were not on the Public Bill Committee to make amendments to the Bill.

The third reading is usually a brief debate, followed by (usually) a single vote on the Bill. The Bill will then go through the same procedure in the other House. This 'ping pong' stage,

---

[14] J. A. G. Griffith et al., *Griffith & Ryle on Parliament* (London: Sweet & Maxwell, 2003), p. 17.
[15] J. A. G. Griffith et al., *Griffith & Ryle on Parliament* (London: Sweet & Maxwell, 2003), p. 17.

when the two Houses try to resolve their disagreements, is frequently the stage at which Bills are amended most substantially. If the two Houses cannot reach agreement, there is deadlock. This is when the House of Commons (subject to procedural limitations) can use the Parliament Acts to force a Bill through to Royal Assent without the approval of the House of Lords.

Royal Assent and commencement

All legislation requires Royal Assent to become law. In theory the sovereign has power to refuse Royal Assent, but this has not been done since 1707, and would be unimaginable in today's world. It should be noted, however, that ex-prime ministers have revealed that Queen Elizabeth II has offered advice to them, especially on Commonwealth matters.

A statute may be 'on the books' and 'law' in the formal sense, long before it comes into force. Legislation requires complex implementation, so this is often fleshed out by the use of statutory instruments. Sections of statutes are brought into force in phases, by statutory instrument or directly by the appropriate Secretary of State. The most extreme example is the Easter Act 1928, which was an Act to regulate the date in the UK of Easter Day. The Act, though it received Royal Assent over eight decades ago, has not yet been brought into force.

Debate is essential to democracy; the word 'Parliament' itself comes from the Norman French meaning 'talking shop'. Controversial Bills can therefore take a considerable amount of time to become Acts. For example, it took five years and 700 hours of parliamentary time before the Hunting Act 2004 received Royal Assent.

Rules of parliamentary procedure dictate that most legislation takes less than a year from first reading to Royal Assent. Parliament can, however, respond quickly to crisis. In the recent banking crisis, the Banking (Special Provisions) Act 2008, giving the government power to nationalise banks (in particular, Northern Rock), made the journey through Parliament in a day. One of the most infamous statutes is the Dangerous Dogs Act 1991, which took only two months from first reading to commencement, including all three readings in the Commons in one day's sitting. This Bill was generated after a very brief period of drafting against a background of tabloid fury at maulings of children by certain breeds of dogs. These breeds are now effectively banned or severely restricted. There has been a swathe of criticism in relation to this Act. Critics cite this 'knee-jerk' legislation as being overly restrictive, as a result of insufficient debate within Parliament.

4.3.2 The implementation of statutes

By the time a statute is in force, the means to implement the statute should be in place. This is the role of the executive, namely the government. The executive is split into government departments, 24 of which have an appointed government minister, and all of which are run by civil servants. Most of these departments delegate enforcement to various agencies. For a criminal statute this often means the police, with the Crown Prosecution Service (CPS) providing lawyers to act for the Crown. Her Majesty's Courts and Tribunals Service is an agency of the Ministry of Justice. In the civil context, 'enforcement' is often simply a matter of individuals using the rights created within a statute, such as a consumer returning a broken alarm clock to the shop. In legal terms the consumer is claiming against the retailer for breach of the term implied into a contract by s. 14(2) of the Sale of Goods Act 1979 that the goods will be of satisfactory quality.

Certain executive powers are devolved by Parliament (mainly under the Local Government Act 1972) to various levels of local government:

- devolved Administrations (in Scotland, Wales, or Northern Ireland);
- county, then district, then parish councils; and
- unitary authorities.

Local government (especially in England & Wales) is very complex in structure with many regional variations. All of these local authorities have some sort of election, and many have a split between legislature and executive.

4.4 Statutory interpretation

Statutes set out laws which regulate a population. People live complex lives, constantly creating new legal issues which require laws to be interpreted and applied. Over time, judges and lawyers have developed a set of rules by which statutes can be interpreted to apply to millions of individuals living real lives in a constantly changing country.

This section starts by focusing on the nature of the problem of statutory interpretation. Next, we look at the tools available to the lawyer in resolving ambiguities. We then use a case study to apply some of those rules, before drawing some conclusions on statutory interpretation in general.

4.4.1 The problem

Statutes are required to give legal effect to what often starts as loose political rhetoric. Politicians create policy. Government lawyers (in the Government Legal Service) then advise the politicians on how to give policies legal effect, and instruct parliamentary draftsmen. These draftsmen give concrete statutory shape to government policy. The draftsmen and the lawyers have to turn the results of debate and compromise into unambiguous, consistent, and adaptable form. The detailed wording of the statute is critical—this is what the courts will pore over in difficult cases. The slightest drafting error can have great ramifications, and statutes regularly need to be applied in a world beyond the imagination of the most far-thinking of draftsmen. Sometimes legislation is deliberately drafted loosely, in an attempt to avoid confrontation, but this may lead to ambiguity.

Although Parliament is the source of the statutes, the courts play a vital role. When the courts apply the statutes, they will have to ascertain the intention of Parliament. This can be extremely difficult. There are a number of actors in the process that might be able to personify Parliament's intention:

- The minister: the passing of a Bill involves the minister who initiates the new law. But that person's intention may have changed or the wording may have been changed by the amendments introduced so that the Bill, as finally enacted, is very different from the one originally submitted to Parliament.

- The lawyers in the Government Legal Service who advise the minister on the legal implementation of their policies: they are the interface between the politicians and the draftsmen. They also directly draft some legislation, most commonly statutory instruments.

- The draftsman: the draftsmen are the people who write the words of the statute at every stage from Bill to Act. If anyone knows what the words mean, surely they do. But they are not part of the decision-making process and, in theory, just translate the intent of others into print.

- The legislators: MPs debate the Bill in the House of Commons, and some of the MPs will discuss the Bill in detail in committees. Their deliberations reveal why the Bill is changed before it becomes law. But their deliberations are politically motivated, and perhaps are not appropriate as a source of assistance in statutory interpretation.

So the intention of Parliament emerges as an artificial and elusive concept which can pose all sorts of problems. Even straightforward phrases can have more than one meaning. Take this example from s. 1(1) of the Street Offences Act 1959:

> It shall be an offence for a common prostitute to loiter or solicit in a street or public place for the purpose of prostitution.

In *Smith v Hughes*[16] the defendant was inside her home, tapping on the window, to attract the attention of potential clients. Did the prostitute need to be in the street, or did the soliciting need to be there? The High Court (Queen's Bench Division) decided that only the soliciting had to be in the street and that therefore the defendant was guilty under the Act. They decided this to reflect the reason behind the passing of the statute. We look at this technique under 'The mischief rule' at 4.4.3.

4.4.2 Drafting legislation in the UK

Statutory interpretation is especially important in the UK because Parliament was created in a common law (as opposed to civil law) tradition. We examined the interaction of statute law and case law in Chapter 2.

In most civil law jurisdictions, legislators aim for statutes to be comprehensive and continuously updated legal codes. These combine very general core principles with often exhaustive codification of detailed rules. There are many variations on this picture, but possibly the most extreme is in France, where all national level law is contained within forty-plus codes in specific areas (e.g. a criminal code), each amended frequently. The basic version runs to over 3,000 pages. It has existed in some form since the *Code Napoleon*

---

[16] *Smith v Hughes* [1960] 2 All ER 859.

in 1804. Statutes in these jurisdictions attempt to specify all matters that may be litigated, including procedure and remedy (or punishment). English lawyers find this rationale difficult to visualise:

> In a judicial utopia, every statute ... would be expressed with such clarity and would cover every contingency so effectively that interpretation would be straightforward and the only task of the courts would be to apply their terms. Utopia has not yet arrived ... and judges facing the interpretation of ambiguous or obscure provisions must use the well-worn tools of statutory construction to arrive at a result.[17]

In common law jurisdictions, the body of legislation (like case law) tends to grow organically. There is rarely an attempt in English law to create a comprehensive 'code' in any area, and there are no overriding written constitutional principles. It is rare for a statute to attempt to provide an answer for every situation in which a statute may be relevant. The common law frequently fills the gaps left (intentionally or not) by the legislators. Consequently, legislators can legislate in the knowledge that they can leave some issues (in many areas of law) to the courts to resolve.

Four examples draw out key ramifications of this 'common law' style of drafting:

Example 1
Reasonableness and exemption clauses—letting the courts fill in the gaps

A typical example is the concept of 'reasonableness' which is central to the Unfair Contract Terms Act 1977 (UCTA). Under this Act, certain attempts to exclude liability in contract and tort are enforceable only if they are 'reasonable'.

While there is some guidance in the statute as to what constitutes a 'reasonable' exclusion of liability, subsequent case law has fleshed out the concept considerably, including the seminal case of *Smith* v *Bush*,[18] consideration of which is usually essential in any discussion of UCTA reasonableness.

Example 2
Companies Act 2006—reliance on an established body of case law

Even the Companies Act 2006, which was drafted to be comprehensive and to codify the law (in the civil as distinct from common law tradition), leaves key concepts open to judicial interpretation, by explicitly relying upon accepted case law. The key area of directors' duties epitomises this approach. See, for example, s. 178:

Civil consequences of breach of general duties
(1) The consequences of breach ... are the same as would apply if the corresponding common law rule or equitable principle applied.
(2) The duties in these sections ... are, accordingly, enforceable in the same way as any other fiduciary duty owed to a company by its directors.

---

[17] Lord Carswell in *Smith* v *Smith* [2006] UKHL 35, at [79].
[18] *Smith* v *Bush (Eric S) (A firm); Harris* v *Wyre Forest District Council* [1990] 1 AC 831.

Example 3

Hunting Act 2004—letting courts deal with controversial issues?

This statute consumed a significant amount of Parliamentary time. It would seem important, in legislation regulating the hunting of foxes, to define the word 'hunt'. The draftsmen deliberately avoided providing a definition, perhaps conscious of the ability of courts to fine-tune the law to suit complex situations.

It has been suggested that the draftsmen were striving to give effect to a key election pledge without making the legislation so draconian that it would be unenforceable. According to a leading text,[19] an early private member's Bill on the subject demonstrated the problems associated with attempts to draft too specifically. Had that Bill become law, courts would have been invited to determine the intention, not of the huntsmen, but of the dogs.

Example 4

Copyright, Designs and Patents Act 1988—an example of 'future-proof' drafting?

Partly because UK statutes are not all-encompassing codes, their wording becomes strained when society and technology develop. The Copyright, Designs and Patents Act 1988 was drafted at a time when widespread use of computers was in its infancy, and digital file sharing (and so-called 'format-shifting') was science fiction for most people. The statute (with some modification) is still the primary source of law in the area, thanks to some flexible drafting and imaginative judges in key cases.

For instance, s. 16 of the Act states that the owner of copyright in a 'work' (e.g. a book, a photograph, or a painting) has the exclusive right to copy the work or any substantial part of it. In 1988, whether 'a substantial part' could be construed to include the overall structure of a computer program (its 'architecture') was still a question that could not be accurately legislated for. But the words 'substantial part' have since been found to include a program's architecture.[20]

However, even so, there are still limitations, and increasing demands for amendment of this particular statute only serve to show how difficult is the balancing act for draftsmen.[21]

So a UK statute attempts to provide general rules but also seeks precision when necessary. Taxation statutes tend to leave little to the discretion of courts, whereas others (like the Hunting Act, above) may adopt a looser style. A parliamentary draftsman seeks to create rules that are 'justiciable', that is to say that the courts can apply to everyday situations.

The result of this is that, as drafted, statutes may often contain ambiguities. What are the techniques used for resolving these ambiguities?

4.4.3 **Rules of interpretation**

Just as a mechanic might have boxes containing tools with which to fix cars, so a lawyer (and, in particular, a judge) has a mental box of tools with which to interpret statutes. These are

---

[19] Daniel Greenberg (ed.), *Craies on Legislation* (London: Sweet & Maxwell, 9th edn, 2008), p. 359.

[20] E.g. *Cantor Fitzgerald v Tradition (UK)* [2000] RPC 95.

[21] See Ian Hargreaves, *Digital Opportunity: A Review of Intellectual Property and Growth* (May 2011), http://www.ipo.gov.uk/ipreview-finalreport.pdf.

called rules of interpretation, although they are not 'rules' in the strictest sense of the word. They are very much tools of the trade from which lawyers can choose, if there is an ambiguity, to help interpret the provision concerned. They are free, within reason, to choose the means they believe most appropriate for the task.

 Essential explanation

Key rules of statutory interpretation

- Rules of construction: what meaning to give words, and why,
- Rules of language: how to read specific words in context, especially when used in lists.
- Presumptions: at 4.2.1 under 'UK and devolved legislation' presumptions were defined as rules that are presumed to apply in certain situations. Statutory presumptions are rebuttable, but they can be used to settle finely balanced arguments about meaning.
- Statutory aids: sources of guidance on the meaning of words in a statute both inside and outside the statute itself.

There is no particular order of priority, though each type of rule has a different role to play, and the rules of construction usually drive the judge's reasoning.

Lawyers rarely refer to the various rules of interpretation by name. The list of techniques here, however, is given to allow you to familiarise yourself with the tools at a lawyer's disposal. Continuing the analogy, a mechanic rarely sets out all of his tools while working on a car, but he does need to know instinctively which sort of tool will suit a given job.

Rules of construction

For this section we use the Hunting Act 2004 as an example. The primary offence created by this statute is as defined in s. 1:

> A person commits an offence if he hunts a wild mammal with a dog, unless his hunting is exempt.

Imagine that you have been charged with this offence by the CPS after riding a horse in the countryside with a pack of terriers. You were carrying a gun to shoot any foxes that might be pursued by the hounds. Your lawyer would challenge the CPS to explain why it had construed the statute so that 'hunts' included your activities. The CPS lawyer would justify its interpretation by using a rule of construction.

The literal rule

The court will always look first at the literal rule, applying the language of a statute using the ordinary and natural meaning of the words. A dictionary often helps with this.

Here, a terrier is a dog, and you were riding with hunting dogs and a gun. *The Oxford English Dictionary* defines 'hunt' to include, 'pursue (wild animals or game ...) for sport or food; ... use (horse or hounds) for hunting'. You were hunting.

The golden rule

Sometimes, as we saw in relation to *Smith* v *Hughes*[22] at 4.4.1, the literal rule may give rise to an ambiguity. The golden rule is designed to mitigate some of the problems which can arise with the literal rule. So, if the literal rule leads to manifest absurdity or an offensive result, the court will depart from the literal meaning—but only if there is any ambiguity. A lawyer may also argue that the golden rule can be used even if the literal interpretation is clear, but this 'wider' approach is not universally accepted.

Here, your defence lawyer might argue that the literal interpretation argued by the CPS is manifestly absurd. Its argument was that because you had a pack of dogs and a horse, you were clearly hunting; but this could mean that any person walking a dog, while on horseback (possibly irrespective of the presence of a gun) could potentially be caught by the Act. Horse-riding is, after all, a sport, as included in the dictionary definition of 'hunting'. As this is absurd, this interpretation should not be used and therefore you should not be guilty.

The mischief rule

The mischief rule strives to allow interpretation of a statute in line with the intent of Parliament. The court tries to ascertain why the legislation was introduced with this wording. It asks itself, 'what was the mischief which Parliament was trying to address?' and then seeks to resolve any ambiguity in the wording to reflect the legislative intention. One of the ways it can do this is by looking at *Hansard*, the official record of proceedings in Parliament.

In 4.4.1, we examined the problems of trying to divine the intention of Parliament. *Hansard* may help. So your lawyer might argue (using a *Hansard* report) that Alun Michael, then a minister at the Department for Environment, Food and Rural Affairs, had maintained during debates in the Hunting Bill Committee on 4 February 2003 that:

> The intentions or actions of the hunter determine what is going on. Hunting has an ordinary meaning: 'to hunt' is the intention to pursue a wild mammal. Without that intent, a person is not hunting and is not covered by the offence.

However the circumstances in which *Hansard* can be used in court are limited: see *Pepper* v *Hart* under 'Extrinsic aids', below.

The purposive approach

The purposive approach involves the court interpreting legislation bearing in mind its purpose. It often yields similar results to the mischief rule but by a different means. Judges look at the reasons why the statute was passed and its purpose, even if it means distorting the ordinary meaning of the words. This approach has been influenced by our membership of the EU as it is widely used in European law, which is drafted with the expectation that judges will consider the policy behind the words. However, the principle is not confined to EU law and UK judges frequently adopt a purposive approach when considering all types of statute.

In relation to EU law: under s. 2(4) of the European Communities Act 1972, the court must adopt a purposive approach in construing EU-related legislation, and in particular UK provisions implementing EU law. This is the same approach as is taken in civil law jurisdictions.

---

[22] *Smith* v *Hughes* [1960] 2 All ER 859.

EU legislation is drafted in a very different way from English statutes. It follows the civil law tradition—although it is exhaustive, there is an emphasis in key parts of EU legislation on a high degree of generalisation. For instance, an EU Directive often starts with a summary of the policy behind the legislation, including its aims. This means that a purposive approach is vital when interpreting legislation, so that questions of wider economic or social aims are often considered by the courts, including in the UK.

Case study 1

Litster v Forth Dry Dock and Engineering Co. Ltd[23]

A statutory instrument[24] had implemented the EU Employee Rights on Transfer of Business Directive.[25] It provided that a transferee (the new owner of a business) should not terminate the contract of any person employed 'immediately before the transfer'.

In this case, dockworkers were dismissed one hour before a business was transferred to a new owner. The employees claimed they were unfairly dismissed.

The House of Lords (now the Supreme Court) read into the provision the additional words 'or would have been so employed if he had not been unfairly dismissed before the transfer'. This was necessary to achieve the purpose of the EU Directive, which was to protect the employees on the transfer of a business.

In relation to the Human Rights Act: the purposive approach is also used in relation to human rights law. The HRA incorporated into UK law most of the rights set out in the ECHR. Under s. 3 of the Act, legislation must be read, so far as it is possible to do so, in a way compatible with the rights enshrined in the Convention.

In our 'hunting' example, your lawyer might argue that the Hunting Act 2004 as a whole is incompatible with citizens' rights (e.g. the right to privacy,[26] and to freedom of assembly[27]) under the Act. This was argued—albeit unsuccessfully—in the *Countryside Alliance*[28] case that tested the enforceability of the Act in the House of Lords.

Analysis: because very broad principles are set out in these areas of law, courts can interpret legislation in line with these principles. This is sometimes called a 'teleological' approach. As a consequence UK courts have to adopt an explicitly aims-based or policy-driven approach to EU-derived legislation, and also where the ECHR is involved. This approach is incrementally superseding the 'mischief' approach traditionally used by English courts in interpreting legislation. Although the purposive approach is strongly reminiscent of the mischief rule, there are differences:

- When using 'traditional' principles of statutory interpretation, courts are unable to change (or 'do violence to', as judges often say) the wording of the legislation. Parliament,

---

[23] *Litster v Forth Dry Dock and Engineering Co. Ltd* [1989] 1 All ER 1134.

[24] Transfer of Undertakings (Protection of Employment) Regulations 1981 (SI 1981/1794), reg. 5.

[25] Employee Rights on Transfer of Business Directive 77/187.

[26] Art. 8 ECHR.   [27] Art. 11 ECHR.

[28] *R (Countryside Alliance and others) v Attorney General and another, R (Derwin and others) v Attorney General and another* [2007] UKHL 52.

remember, is sovereign. With the purposive approach, even where there is no ambiguity in the wording for the courts to play with, courts may do some violence to the statutory provision, by adding or substituting words, as they bring it into line with the perceived aims of the legislation.

- The two rules also operate differently: the purposive approach looks forwards (or even upwards) at the aims of the original legislation. By contrast, the mischief approach looks backwards to the root of the problem before the relevant statute was passed.

Rules of language

Rules of language are technical tools to help you use the language in a statute to resolve any ambiguity. You will often use them in the context of lists. We examine four of the key rules of language, by translating them, discussing them, applying each of them to a sample statute, and then looking at an example of their application from case law. The rules have Latin names, but the techniques are quite straightforward and in practice you rarely need to use the Latin expressions.

To illustrate these rules we use the Dangerous Wild Animals Act 1976 (DWAA).

Case study 2
Dangerous Wild Animals Act 1976[29]

This statute was enacted to regulate the import and keeping of exotic pets. The aim was to reduce the risk of injury to the public and maltreatment of the animals concerned. The regime requires anyone who wishes to keep such an animal to obtain a licence from the local authority.

Section 1(1) states, 'no person shall keep any dangerous wild animal except under the authority of a licence granted in accordance with the provisions of this Act by a local authority'. The animals concerned are listed in a schedule to the DWAA.

Imagine you have a spider in your possession, very similar to the notorious Black Widow spider. It is however of a different genus and unlike any other spider. Like the Black Widow, it can kill or paralyse with its bite. Section 1 creates the obligation to keep a licence if a person keeps a dangerous wild animal. What is such an animal? Do you need a licence? We look below at how each of the chosen rules of language applies to the DWAA and could assist in interpreting the statute, and answering these questions.

Expressio unius est exclusio alterius

Translation: to say one thing is to exclude the others.

Explanation: sometimes a court will decide that a list is clearly intended only to include all the relevant items, and so if something (e.g. a mouse in a list of mammals) is not specifically listed, then it must be excluded. This is a very literal and often common-sense approach, and could certainly be used in tandem with the literal rule.

Application to DWAA: most statutes have an interpretation section, usually towards the end of the statute. Longer legislation may have a series of sections, forming a distinct part

[29] Text available at http://www.legislation.gov.uk.

of the statute. These sections contain definitions of important terms in the relevant statute. Part II of this book gives more detail on techniques of reading statutes.

Section 7(4) states that '"dangerous wild animal" means any animal of a kind for the time being specified in the first column of the Schedule to this Act'. This incorporates the schedule into the Act. Schedules are frequently used to contain lengthy detail that might undermine the clarity of the main (or operative) parts of the Act.

Go to the end of the schedule and you will find a list of spiders which require a licence. At the end of the list is 'Theridiidae of the species of the genus Latrodectus', explained in the second column as, 'The black widow spider (otherwise known as redback spider) and its close relatives'. The list, therefore, does not expressly include your spider. Indeed, the Secretary of State has not seen fit to amend the list in the schedule under powers conferred by the statute. Are you therefore entitled to keep this spider outside the protective regime of the DWAA? Using the *expressio* rule, yes. It is not on the list, so you do not need a licence.

Example from case law: in *R v Secretary of State for the Home Department, ex p Crew*,[30] *expressio* was used to exclude the father of an illegitimate child from rights under immigration law, because the definitions section mentioned the mother alone. (The law has since changed.)

Noscitur a sociis

Translation: known by the company it keeps.

Explanation: the meaning can be taken from the surrounding words and context; this could extend as far as all relevant parts of the statute. It is usually used to interpret words in an *exhaustive* list (i.e. where there is a list of specific things to which that provision of the statute applies, with no general words to allow the inclusion of unforeseen alternatives). This is often used in conjunction with the mischief rule, because the context of the statute is important. The rule is often used in opposition to an *expressio* argument.

Application to DWAA: you would be ill-advised not to apply for a licence for keeping your spider. The argument used by the local council (and then the CPS) would be that, while not expressly mentioned in the Act, the spider should be taken to be a 'close relative of' the Black Widow. It would therefore be a dangerous wild animal because all the other spiders listed, indeed the scorpions too, are potentially very harmful. The CPS might also use the mischief rule to help reinforce this argument, namely that regulating animals like yours was exactly what this statute was designed for.

Example from case law—*Pengelly v Bell Punch Co. Ltd*:[31] the Factories Act 1961 required that all 'floors, steps, stairs, passageways and gangways' had to be kept free from obstruction. The court had to decide whether a floor used for storage came under the provisions of the Act. It held that as all the other words were used to indicate passage, a floor used exclusively for storage did not fall within the Act. This was a negative use of the rule; but note how the rule goes further than *expressio*, because it examines the context of the words to help interpretation.

---

[30] *R v Secretary of State for the Home Department, ex parte Crew* [1982] Imm AR 94.
[31] *Pengelly v Bell Punch Co. Ltd* [1964] 1 WLR 1055.

Eiusdem generis

Translation: of the same type.

Explanation: this rule is used where general words need interpretation. This is usually the case with *non-exhaustive* lists, where the list allows for as yet unforeseen possibilities, often using general words. (Compare this with *noscitur a sociis*, above, which is useful when dealing with *exhaustive* lists.) If a general word follows two or more specific words, that general word will only apply to items of the same type as the specific words. There is a considerable overlap in application between *eiusdem* and *noscitur*.

Application to DWAA: the 'cat' section of the schedule is more appropriate as an example here, because it contains general words that may need interpretation. A client has acquired a Bengal cat, a hybrid breed of cat, formed by the cross of a domestic feline and an Asian leopard cat. It is not a pure domestic cat, though many are kept as pets. Do they need a licence? Looking at the schedule the relevant provision states that a keeper needs a licence for '*Felidae*, except the species *Felis catus*': that is, all cats except domestic cats.

The explanation clarifies this as: 'The bobcat, caracal, cheetah, jaguar, lion, lynx, ocelot, puma, serval, tiger and all other cats (the domestic cat is excepted)'. So we need to look at the rest of the provision. 'All other cats' seems quite unequivocal—it includes the Bengal cat. The client might argue that the list of cats is a list of potentially dangerous cats not commonly kept in the home. This list reflects the mischief the Act was designed to address. The general words, 'all other cats', require interpretation. Does this include domestic/wild hybrids? These general words need to be construed *eiusdem generis*. The list of cats includes dangerous wild undomesticated cats. 'All other cats' (you might argue) means 'all other wild undomesticated cats', and therefore not your Bengal cat. Bengal cats are not dangerous wild cats like the others.

You may wish at this stage to look at how the statute has been updated. The Dangerous Wild Animals Act 1976 (Modification) (No. 2) Order 2007[32] was enacted to deal with this exact problem, and the exception has been explicitly expanded to include so-called hybrid cats.

Example from case law—*Wood* v *Commissioner of Police of the Metropolis*:[33] the Vagrancy Act 1824 was enacted to deal with a sudden influx of ne'er-do-wells, including soldiers discharged from the Napoleonic Wars and refugees fleeing hostile absent landlords in Scotland and Ireland. Section 4 of the Act defined offensive weapons as 'any gun, pistol, hanger, cutlass, bludgeon or other offensive weapons'. Mr Wood was charged with an offence under this Act after using a piece of broken glass, which had fallen out of his front door, as a weapon. It was held that the words 'other offensive weapons' were to be construed as being confined to articles made or adapted for use for causing injury to the person. The glass was no such article, so it was not *eiusdem generis* with the specific items caught by the statute and therefore no offence was committed by the defendant.

In pari materia

Translation: upon the same matter or subject.

Explanation: the meaning of an ambiguity in a statute can be determined in light of other statutes on the same subject matter, provided the ambiguous statute concerned does not expressly mention another statute. This promotes consistency and transparency of law.

---

[32] SI 2007/2465.   [33] *Wood* v *Commissioner of Police of the Metropolis* [1986] 1 WLR 796.

Application to DWAA: s. 5 of the Act exempts certain keepers from the requirement to license, mainly because they are subject to alternative regimes. The section states:

The provisions of this Act shall not apply to any dangerous wild animal kept in:

(1) a zoological garden;

(2) a circus;

(3) premises licensed as a pet shop under the Pet Animals Act 1951;

(4) a place registered pursuant to the Cruelty to Animals Act 1876 for the purpose of per-forming experiments.

The rule of language does *not* apply to s. 5(3) and (4) because these refer explicitly to other statutes. But s. 5(1) does not refer to another statute. The proprietors of a zoo could however (in the event of doubt) point to the Zoo Licensing Act 1981. Section 1(2) of this Act defines the term 'zoo' (the definition is quite lengthy and does not need to be repeated here). If they are within this definition, then they are likely to be within the definition of a 'zoological garden' for the DWAA.

Example from case law—*R (ZA (Nigeria)) v Secretary of State for the Home Department, R (SM (Congo)) v Secretary of State for the Home Department*:[34] a claimant's asylum claim under a statute[35] was denied on the basis that previous asylum claims under earlier secondary legislation[36] had also been denied.

Rules of language—conclusion

It is worth remembering that these rules often reiterate common sense, and sometimes it is better to ignore their Latin labels. They are not 'rules' in the normal sense of the word in that there is no obligation to use them. It may be better to think of them, along with principles of construction—with which they overlap—as a set of techniques and tools that you can use in any combination to support interpretation of statutes. You should also remember that these rules apply to most legal documents, from a residents' association constitution, through con-tracts, to Acts of Parliament. Therefore, it is also important to bear in mind how these rules could affect the potential interpretation of a legal document when you are drafting.

Aids to interpretation

These are resources inside and outside statutes which can help the courts in interpreting meaning. The courts can in theory use anything to ascertain the intention of Parliament, although they place greater reliance on some sources than others.

Intrinsic aids

Anything in the same Act is 'intrinsic', therefore the first port of call is always the relevant statutory provision. Definitions will usually be at the start of the relevant part of the Act, or

---

[34] *R (ZA (Nigeria)) v Secretary of State for the Home Department, R (SM (Congo)) v Secretary of State for the Home Department* [2010] EWCA Civ 926.

[35] Borders, Citizenship and Immigration Act 2009, s. 53.

[36] *Statement of Changes in Immigration Rules* (1994) (HC 395), r. 353 (as inserted by *Statement of Changes in Immigration Rules* (2004) (HC 1112)).

towards the end in an interpretation section. Chapter 7 contains a detailed explanation of the structure of a typical Act.

Other parts of the Act are helpful but not binding in the same way, so, for instance, headings and marginal notes or the Long Title—if the Act has one—may help determine its meaning. While the Long Title is formally part of the Act, it cannot be used to displace the text of provisions themselves in the statute. The Short Title, and any headings used in the Act are not considered operative parts of the statute but are helpful for reference. Chapter 7 examines the Long and Short Titles in more detail.

Extrinsic aids

Courts can look beyond the statute using an almost limitless array of extrinsic aids. In particular:

- The Interpretation Acts: these supply general assumptions for interpreting statutes, for example that the masculine includes the feminine in the absence of a contrary express statement in a specific Act.

- Dictionaries: a lawyer or court might use a dictionary to provide a meaning of a word.

- Explanatory notes: these are guidance on the majority of statutes passed since 1999 prepared by the Government Legal Service to make the Act accessible to non-lawyers.

- Other statutes: the use of other statutes can change depending on the circumstances, indeed sometimes depending on the point the advocate is trying to argue. Often a statute will expressly refer to definitions in previous statutes, but sometimes this helpful approach may not be taken. Courts may be obliged to interpret a statute in line with an earlier one if instructed expressly by the statute, or if a court considers the Acts to constitute a 'package' of measures.[37] Alternatively courts may be compelled not to follow the earlier legislation, again either expressly within the later statute, or where each statute clearly needs different application. For instance, different statutes define 'groups' of companies in different ways. Alternatively it may be a matter of discretion, and left for lawyers to argue.

- *Hansard*: as seen above, this is a record of the proceedings of Parliament, and helps to determine the intention of law-makers. It is particularly helpful when applying the mischief rule. In *Pepper v Hart*[38] the House of Lords set out some rules relating to the use of *Hansard*—it may only be used in relation to speeches by the relevant minister or promoter of a Bill, and even then only when the statute itself is ambiguous.

- Academic know-how: a court may refer to articles or books written on controversial areas of law by legal academics.

- Previous cases: under the doctrine of precedent one court is bound to follow the reasoning of some previous courts on a particular statute, and may be persuaded by the reasoning of others (see Chapter 5).

The list of extrinsic aids is endless, and the lawyer's skill is to give due weight to any resources used or encountered.

---

[37] E.g. the concept of 'honest practices in industrial or commercial matters' is used as part of a defence to infringement of the Olympic Association right in the Olympic Symbol etc. (Protection) Act 1995. It is clear from case law that courts should follow jurisprudence developed in relation to the same phrase as used in the Trade Marks Act 1994.

[38] *Pepper v Hart* [1993] AC 593.

Presumptions

At 4.2.1 we saw that a presumption is a rule that is presumed to apply in certain situations. Presumptions are often rebuttable. A presumption is rebuttable when the legal rule concerned can be disapplied if there is enough evidence to the contrary. A statutory presumption is one about the intention of Parliament. Presumptions help clear up ambiguities in relation to common or fundamental issues. All these presumptions (there are many more than the most important ones listed below) are rebuttable if the Act under consideration has express statements to the contrary. Indeed there are some statutes with retrospective effect.

Certain presumptions in relation to statutes are important to the mechanics of England's legal system:

- There is a presumption against statutes altering the common law. The theory is that these two sources of law—statute and case law—should sit comfortably alongside one another. This is sometimes difficult when statute is superimposed upon existing areas of law.

- It is presumed that no statute applies retrospectively, otherwise something which was lawful when you did it might be rendered unlawful after the event. This presumption is rebutted very rarely, especially in criminal or tax matters. Occasionally, legislation is specifically stated to have retrospective effect, such as the War Crimes Act 1991, which allows the prosecution of those suspected of committing acts of atrocity during World War II.

- In criminal statutes it is presumed that any ambiguity be construed in favour of defendants as it is their liberty which is at stake—this is of course rebuttable in the face of conflicting arguments. It is also presumed that commission of an offence requires a 'guilty mind' (intent) unless it is stated that no intent to commit the crime is needed on the part of the defendant.

- There is a presumption against ousting the jurisdiction of the courts.

You should always keep the major presumptions in the back of your mind when considering ambiguities in statutes.

4.4.4 Statutory interpretation—conclusion

Issues of interpretation are sometimes quite difficult. Mr Justice Donaldson said: 'The duty of the courts is to ascertain and give effect to the will of Parliament as expressed in its enactments ... the interpretation of statutes is a craft as much as a science.'[39] As we have seen, the intention of Parliament is a critical concept; over time techniques for interpreting this intention have evolved.

A lawyer has many different tools to call on when interpreting a statute.

Case study

There have been few ambiguities in statutes more controversial than that in s. 3 of the Homicide Act 1957, now repealed because the deliberate ambiguities in its wording created so many problems. After the extract from the statute we summarise two cases which tested it (literally) to destruction.

---

[39] *Corocraft Ltd v Pan American Airways Inc.* [1969] 1 QB 616, at 638.

Case study 3
Homicide Act 1957, s. 3 (now repealed)

The Homicide Act put on a statutory footing various defences to a charge of murder.

Where on a charge of murder there is evidence on which the jury can find that the person charged was provoked (whether by things done or by things said or by both together) to lose his self-control, the question whether the provocation was enough to make a reasonable man do as he did shall be left to be determined by the jury; and in determining that question the jury shall take into account everything both done and said according to the effect which, in their opinion, it would have on a reasonable man.

Scenario 1: *R v Smith (Morgan)*[40]

The defendant killed his friend, by stabbing him several times with a carving knife, after spending the evening 'in drinking and recrimination'. He claimed he had been provoked into doing so as a consequence of a number of grievances, the latest being his belief that the victim had stolen his carpentry tools. The defendant suffered from a depressive mental condition which had the effect of reducing his self-control below that of an ordinary person. He pleaded provocation as a defence to the charge of murder.

Scenario 2: *Attorney General for Jersey v Holley*[41]

The defendant killed his girlfriend with an axe, after spending the afternoon 'drinking heavily and arguing'. They were both alcoholics. She told him she had just had sex with another man. He picked up the axe, intending to leave the flat and chop wood. When the deceased said, 'You haven't got the guts', he struck her with the axe seven or eight times. He pleaded provocation.

In both cases the stakes were very high. The reason it was so important to the defendant to succeed in establishing provocation was because the murder charge would then be reduced to one of manslaughter. Whereas murder attracts a mandatory life sentence, the sentence for manslaughter is discretionary. These two cases produced very different results because of the way the courts approached the ambiguity in the section.

The first step is to identify the ambiguity. What is the ambiguity in s. 3 of the Homicide Act 1957? The main uncertainty which required interpretation was the term 'reasonable man'. In assessing the reasonable man can we take into account any medical conditions or personality traits?

 Essential explanation

The 'reasonable man'

You will encounter the so-called reasonable man frequently in legal discourse, particularly in the contexts of criminal, contract, and tort law. The normal use of the term is as a means of measuring a person by purely objective, dispassionate, and neutral standards.

This objective standard is to be contrasted with a subjective standard. The latter is a standard matched to the characteristics of the person being discussed.

In the case study, if we are able to adapt the reasonable man to reflect the characteristics of someone with a depressive mental condition with reduced levels of self-control (as in

---

[40] *R v Smith (Morgan)* [2001] 1 AC 146.   [41] *Attorney General for Jersey v Holley* [2005] UKPC 23.

R v *Smith (Morgan)*[42]), then the defendant in that case would be more likely to reach that standard, and be able to use the defence of provocation under the Homicide Act. He would be found guilty only of manslaughter. In *Holley*,[43] if we are able to adapt the reasonable man to reflect the characteristics of someone suffering from alcoholism (in the sense of the recognised medical affliction), then (again) Holley would be found not guilty of murder, and guilty only of manslaughter.

In these circumstances we need to use principles of statutory interpretation. In Table 4.1 are just a few of the rules that we might use (some of which were used by the Lords of Appeal in the cases).

Both the case decisions surprised academics and lawyers, albeit for different reasons.

In *R* v *Smith (Morgan)*,[44] the House of Lords confirmed the Court of Appeal's decision that Smith was not guilty on the ground that juries could take into account any circumstances which they regarded as relevant, including any personal characteristic of the defendant which made him particularly susceptible to losing his self-control.

In *Attorney General for Jersey* v *Holley*[45] the Privy Council decided that juries could not take account of the personal characteristics of defendants when deciding the issue of provocation. The standard was an objective one (would the *reasonable* man have lost control in these circumstances), not whether this defendant had.

The first decision was surprising because it seemed to make a mockery of the objective test. The second was surprising because, despite being more justifiable, it ran counter to the doctrine of precedent (see 5.2). The literal rule had effectively won the day; Lord Nicholls in *Holley*, impliedly restated its importance:

> Their Lordships consider there is one compelling, overriding reason why this [*Smith*] view cannot be regarded as an accurate statement of English law. It is this. The law of homicide is a highly sensitive and highly controversial area of criminal law. In 1957, Parliament altered the common law relating to provocation and declared what the law on this subject should henceforth be. In these circumstances, it is not open to judges now to change ('develop') the common law and thereby depart from the law as declared by Parliament.[46]

He went on to state there should be a uniform, objective standard of behaviour which everyone is expected to meet. If there are mental health reasons as to why a person cannot meet this standard, he would have to use the alternative defence of diminished responsibility. This ambiguity created so many problems that eventually Parliament legislated to change the defences to murder, and abolish the defence of provocation.[47]

A possible approach to statutory interpretation

We can see from Case study 3 that the tools at the disposal of a lawyer when considering statutory ambiguity are varied and flexible. Aside from starting with a literal interpretation it is vital to remember that there is no particular order of priority, and that you can use these

---

[42] *R* v *Smith (Morgan)* [2001] 1 AC 146.   [43] *Attorney General for Jersey* v *Holley* [2005] UKPC 23.
[44] *R* v *Smith (Morgan)* [2001] 1 AC 146.   [45] *Attorney General for Jersey* v *Holley* [2005] UKPC 23.
[46] *Attorney General for Jersey* v *Holley* [2005] UKPC 23, at [22] (Lord Nicholls).
[47] Coroners and Justice Act 2009, ss. 54–5.

Table 4.1 Use of statutory interpretation: Homicide Act 1957, s. 3

Rule	Type of rule	Favours murder or manslaughter?	Reasoning
Literal	Construction	Murder	Defendants with such medical conditions are not acting as reasonable persons if they kill people. The reasonable man does not suffer from depression, nor is he an alcoholic
Golden	Construction	Either	It is arguably absurd that provocation is limited only to such provocation as would provoke mentally 'normal' people.
			Equally, it might be absurd to say that provocation can be adapted to suit the person provoked. There is a contradiction in terms—schizophrenics do not come within the usual definition of a 'reasonable man'.
			Taken too far, the concept could become meaningless. It would lead to absurd questions such as: would the reasonable 50-year-old overweight schizophrenic who had suffered abuse as a child have lost control when taunted about his inadequacies? A jury would find this a very difficult question to answer.
Mischief/ Purposive	Construction	Neutral	The purpose of the legislation was to mitigate the harshness of the death penalty for murder in certain circumstances. The section recognises the fact that everyone has a breaking point if they are provoked far enough.
			However, perhaps this exception was not designed to help people who have mental impairments—see argument for 'noscitur' below.
Noscitur a sociis	Language	Murder	In view of the wider context—including the presence of other exceptions (like diminished responsibility)—this exception was not designed to deal with defendants with mental impairments.
Interpretation Act 1978	Extrinsic aid	Neutral	Section 6 states that (in all legislation) unless expressly stipulated otherwise, the masculine includes the feminine. The 'reasonable man' thus becomes the 'reasonable person'.
Presumption against deprivation of liberty	Presumption	Manslaughter	In the event of an ambiguity, it must be presumed that Parliament did not intend to deprive defendants of liberty (in this case by increasing the sentence).

rules whenever you feel they will benefit your legal argument relating to a statute. There are no absolute rules.

Having said that, while getting used to using techniques of interpretation you might wish to adopt the following approach:

1. Start with a literal interpretation of the provision.

2. Use an alternative rule of construction either:

   - if the literal rule produces unsatisfactory results, or,

   - in relation to EU or ECHR law, when a purposive approach is required.

3. Support your interpretation. Tools for this include:

   - rules of language (in particular for lists), and

   - aids to statutory interpretation.

4. If the statute is still ambiguous, use presumptions.

4.5 **EU law**

The jurisdiction and institutions of the EU are entirely separate from those of the ECHR (although the EU is a signatory to the ECHR).

The UK became a member of the European Economic Community (EEC) on 1 January 1973 (having signed the Treaty of Rome 1957 in the previous year). As the UK is a member of the EU it follows that EU law applies throughout the UK. The EEC (as it was then) was created in 1957 to promote trade within the European common market (then constituting six member states) by seeking to create a level playing field for commercial activity in Europe. The EU's role is now significantly greater, incorporating a wide range of economic matters (notably monetary union), justice, education, health, and foreign relations. As of February 2013 it has 27 member states, with Croatia expected to join in July.

International law is not regarded as part of our legal system (see 2.2.4), so it was necessary to enact the European Communities Act 1972. As a result of this Act, EU legislation can be incorporated into our law without Parliament having to legislate on each separate occasion. The UK system in this context is known as a 'dualist' system because EU law is not automatically binding; it needs to be incorporated into domestic legislation by Parliament, via the European Communities Act. So (in theory) Parliament could pass legislation to abolish the European Communities Act, and with it the incorporation of EU law into UK law. In contrast, some other jurisdictions (e.g. France) are 'monist' in that, on ratification of the EU Treaty (then the EEC Treaty) by the French government, (French) domestic legislation was not needed for EU law to become part of domestic law.

Some of our national law (e.g. land law) is not affected by membership of the EU, but certain highly significant areas are, for example, commercial and consumer law, employment law, the environment, and freedom of movement. Between 1957 and 2009, the EU had created 666,879 pages of legislation[48] which, laid end-to-end, would equate to 120 miles of legislation, enough to stretch from London to Birmingham.

---

[48] Source: http://www.openeurope.org.uk/.

Essential explanation

EU terminology

There are several terms that are, or have historically been used to, describe fundamental features of what is now the EU and its law.

- The EEC, or European Economic Community, created by the Treaty of Rome 1957.
- The EC, or European Community, created under the Maastricht Treaty 1992.
- The EU, or European Union, also established under the Maastricht Treaty 1992.

There have been key differences in the jurisdiction of each body.

Under the Maastricht Treaty in 1992, the EC replaced the EEC, and also the EU was created. The EU at this stage comprised three 'pillars'—the EC, which had a legal system; the Common Foreign and Security Policy; and Police and Judicial Cooperation in Criminal Matters. The EU did not itself have a legal system, so the law within the EU was called 'EC law'.

The Lisbon Treaty, signed in 2007, and which came into force on 1 December 2009, unified the three 'pillars' of the EU into one legal entity. At this stage 'EC law' became 'EU law'. The Lisbon Treaty had many effects; importantly in this context, the Treaty of Rome was at the same time retrospectively renamed the Treaty on the Functioning of the European Union (TFEU).

In this section we look first at the institutions (4.5.1), then at the legislation they produce (4.5.2). The effect of that legislation (4.5.3) is then examined before looking at how this impacts on each type of legislation (4.5.4).

4.5.1 **EU institutions**

The institutions identified

To understand how EU law is made, it is important to have an understanding of the EU institutions. These descriptions should be read in conjunction with Figure 4.3, which places them in a traditional framework of Separation of Powers:

- The Council of Ministers (formally, the Council of the European Union) consists of a government representative from each member state. It has a legislative role—the 'co-decision' procedure (formally, the 'ordinary legislative procedure')—in tandem with the Parliament, and it approves the EU budget. It also has an executive role, being the main decision-making body of the EU, most significantly for economic policy.

- The European Commission develops and implements policy. It consists of independent Commissioners appointed by national governments, but who must work independently of national loyalties, and who make proposals for legislation and oversee implementation of legislation.

- The Parliament has a limited legislative role including the ability to veto some types of legislation. This is called the 'co-decision' procedure (with the Council of Ministers). With the Council of Ministers, it approves the EU budget. It also has oversight over the Commission. It is made up of elected members.

- The Court of Justice of the European Union, the senior court of which is the ECJ, consisting of judges nominated by each of the Member States. Its role is to ensure that EU law is observed

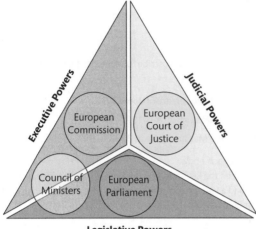

Legislative Powers

Figure 4.3 Separation of Powers within the EU

throughout the Community. It has the power to judicially review the actions of the other institutions. Be careful not to confuse the ECJ with the European Court of Human Rights.

● The European Council, not to be confused with the Council of the European Union, is a label given to the heads of government (or heads of state) of the member states, meeting on an *ad hoc* basis (around six times each year). Their role is to give overall impetus to the EU.[49]

The institutions compared

In this context, we need only look at what legislation emanates from which EU institutions. However, this is also an appropriate point at which to compare their key features (summarised in Table 4.2). We look in detail at the different types of legislation at 4.5.2. Figure 4.4 summarises the legislative process within the institutions of the EU.

4.5.2 **EU legislation identified**

EU legislation can be split into primary and secondary legislation.

The primary legislation comprises the founding treaties, such as the Treaty on the Functioning of the European Union (TFEU), the Treaty on European Union (often known as the Maastricht Treaty), and the Lisbon Treaty. These treaties are agreed by member states in various ways. Although formally signed by heads of state or prime ministers, they are normally subject to ratification by national legislation, or referendums, both of which have historically been fraught processes (the European Constitution failed in 2005 as a result of two adverse national referendums). The European Communities Act 1972 approved the UK's accession to the EEC. Primary legislation is binding on member states and EU institutions, and it cannot be challenged in national courts or the ECJ.

The secondary legislation which emanates from the institutions described above takes the form of regulations, directives, and decisions. For a complete picture we can also include

[49] Art. 15 TFEU.

Table 4.2 Summary of EU institutions

Institution	Composition	Overall role	Legislative role	Legislation produced/ decisions taken
European Commission	One Commissioner per member state,[50] each with a portfolio approved by Council of Ministers and Parliament.	One of two executive branches: implements and enforces policy.	Makes formal proposals for legislation; drafts the EU budget.	Decisions (in competition law). Recommendations and opinions. Regulations are sometimes passed by the Commission alone.
Council of Ministers (Council of the EU)	One member per member state, normally votes by qualified majority voting.	One of two executive branches for some issues, e.g. foreign policy. Coordinates economic policies of member states.	Can request Commission to propose legislation. Co-decision procedure with Parliament.[51] Approves the EU budget.	Regulations and directives. Some decisions. Recommendations and opinions.
European Council	Heads of government.	Gives overall impetus to the EU.[52]	None.	None.
European Parliament	754 MEPs directly elected in proportion to member states' population.	Supervises Commission and legislates.	Can request Commission to propose legislation. Co-decision procedure with Council in many areas of competence. Approves Commission's draft budget.	Regulations and directives.
European Court of Justice	One judge per member state in both the General Court and ECJ.	Preliminary rulings:[53] references from national courts on EU matters. Judicial review of validity of the acts of other EU institutions.[54] Actions against member states by the Commission[55] or other member states.[56]	Rules on EU law.	Rulings.

[50] Art. 245 TFEU.   [51] Art. 294 TFEU.   [52] Art. 15 TFEU.   [53] Art. 267 TFEU.
[54] Art. 263 TFEU.   [55] Art. 258 TFEU.   [56] Art. 259 TFEU.

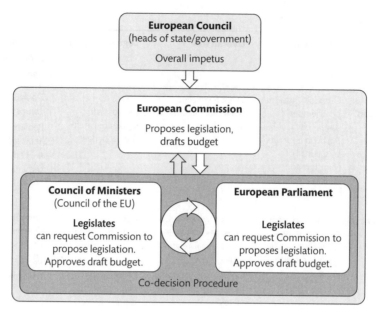

Figure 4.4 Creation of EU legislation

non-binding recommendations and opinions emanating from the Commission and Council, particularly in competition law. Despite being non-binding, these are classified as legislation. Lawyers will usually use the TFEU in combination with secondary legislation. They will also often refer to ECJ rulings in the same area.

Figure 4.5 summarises the main types of EU legislation, including how they are created and their legal effect.

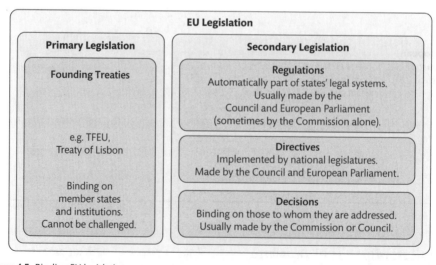

Figure 4.5 Binding EU legislation

4.5.3 **The effect of EU legislation**

The enforceability of EU legislation is complex, because of the variety of legislation emanating from the EU. It is crucial to understand some key terminology, even for a basic understanding of the functioning of EU law in the UK. The terms below describe various characteristics of EU legislation; they are not necessarily mutually exclusive.

Direct effect

Directly effective legislation gives rise to rights and obligations which individuals may enforce in their national courts. There are two categories of directly effective legislation:

- Vertical direct effect: this describes a situation where EU legislation allows an individual (i.e. a legal person including companies etc.) to make a claim in a national court against the state (or its 'emanations', i.e. public bodies).
- Horizontal direct effect: this allows individuals to make claims against each other in EU law.

There are strict criteria to determine whether a piece of EU legislation has direct effect, set out in the *Van Gend en Loos*[57] case. These are beyond the scope of this book.

Direct applicability

Some directly effective legislation is also said to be directly applicable. This means that the legislation becomes part of the national legal system without the need for further implementation by national legislatures (e.g. Parliament). If EU legislation requires implementation (e.g. by an implementing statute) then it is not directly applicable to EU citizens. If you think this is complex, you are not alone. The ECJ commonly uses the terms 'direct effect' and 'direct applicability' interchangeably.

Indirect effect

Under Art. 4(3) TFEU, member states must take all appropriate measures to ensure the fulfilment of their EU obligations. This requirement falls on all member state authorities including, importantly, courts. This means that courts must interpret national law in line with the relevant EU legislation.

Any EU legislation which requires national implementation will need to be legislated by the national legislature. If an individual believes the legislature has failed to legislate correctly (e.g. by giving them insufficient rights, or by failing to legislate at all within the EU time limits) then that individual can ask the national court to interpret domestic legislation in line with the relevant EU legislation. This is called 'indirect effect'. The extent of this principle is still unclear.

---

[57] *Van Gend en Loos v Nederlandse Administratie der Belastingen* [1963] ECR 1.

4.5.4 **EU legislation in detail**

Let us now look at each type of EU legislation in the light of how it affects a UK individual (both natural and legal, i.e. companies etc.). For each type of legislation we describe it, look briefly at how that type of legislation becomes part of UK law, give a fictional illustration, and then an historical example. We use the fictional illustration to provide a direct comparison between the effects of the legislation in the same factual context.

Treaty articles

- Treaties are the EU's primary legislation, and are often (but not always) framed in very general, teleological (aims-based) terms.
- Articles of the TFEU form part of the legal systems of all member states. They are directly applicable. They may also be directly effective, which means an individual can rely upon rights granted by treaty articles and enforce them, if necessary, in the national courts.
- A fictional example might be the EU adopting a treaty article stating, 'Anyone working within the EU must wear clothing appropriate to their employment, because it ensures workers around the EU are equally protected.'
- For example, Art. 157 TFEU states: 'Each Member State shall ensure that the principle of equal pay for male and female workers for equal work or work of equal value is applied.' In *Defrenne* v *SABENA*,[58] SABENA paid its female flight attendants less than comparable male flight attendants. Ms Defrenne was able to use Art. 119 (now 157) TFEU to claim equal pay from her employer.

Regulations

- Regulations are detailed secondary legislation made under the co-decision procedure by the Council and Parliament, or by the Commission alone. At the time of writing, there were 9,159 regulations in force.
- Once a regulation has been passed, it automatically becomes part of the legal systems of all member states. It is directly applicable. Like treaty articles, regulations may also be directly effective.
- A fictional example might be a regulation directly requiring anyone working on a building site to wear appropriate protective clothing, including a hard hat and footwear with protective toecaps.
- One example of an important regulation is Commission Regulation (EC) No. 2790/1999, which deals with competition law. It permits a supplier to appoint distributors and to accept restrictions on their activities, despite the fact that restricting market behaviour is potentially anti-competitive and in breach of the TFEU. Like many regulations it is very complex and requires advanced understanding, not only of EU law but also economics.

[58] Case 43/75 *Defrenne* v *SABENA (No. 2)* [1976] ECR 455.

Directives

- Directives are detailed secondary legislation that the EU believes is best left to Member States to implement because of the wide variety of national characteristics. They are made by the Council and Parliament under the co-decision procedure. At the time of writing, there were 1,931 directives in force.

  They are binding as to the result to be achieved on each Member State but leave implementation (e.g. how it is to be administered and the range of remedies available) to the national legislature. The UK will usually (but not always) implement a directive into national law by passing secondary legislation containing the provisions specified in the directive. Because they give individuals rights and obligations, directives have direct effect. However, if a member state does not implement a directive, or implements it incorrectly, it may then have indirect effect, and an individual can rely on it in the national courts, but only against the state or a state body.

- A fictional directive might require member states to legislate in line with EU policy on building site protective clothing, including their requirements in relation to hard hats and protective toe caps.

- You will encounter statutes like the Consumer Protection Act 1987 and the Trade Marks Act 1994 where national implementation has been via primary legislation. Occasionally, citizens of member states are sceptical about regulation coming from the supra-national EU. If implementation of EU law is via the national legislature, the legislation concerned may have greater 'legitimacy' in the eyes of a sometimes sceptical public. This process has inherent drawbacks—both these statutes have been the subject of debate in the courts in relation to whether the implementing legislation truly reflected the parent directive.[59]

Decisions

- Decisions are made either by the Commission or the Council (sometimes by co-decision procedure with the Parliament). They are secondary legislation, binding on those to whom they are addressed—specified member states or individuals. They are very common in competition law. They are very focused in their ambit. At the time of writing, a total of 15,823 decisions had been made by the Commission or Council over the lifetime of the EU.

- EU decisions are directly effective and directly applicable.

- A fictional example of a decision might be the EU telling the UK, or even a building contractor in the UK, what their policy on hard hats should be.

- In 2007, attention in the UK focused on a series of Commission decisions relating to the export of British beef during the foot-and-mouth crisis.[60] Another famous example is

---

[59] Council Directive 85/374/EEC of 25 July 1985 on the approximation of the laws, regulations and administrative provisions of the Member States concerning liability for defective products; Council Directive 89/104/EEC of 21 December 1988 to approximate the laws of the Member States relating to trade marks.

[60] E.g. Commission Decision 2007/663/EC of 12 October 2007 amending Decision 2007/554/EC concerning certain protection measures against foot-and-mouth disease in the United Kingdom (notified under document number C(2007) 4660).

Table 4.3 Summary of EU legislation

Type of legislation	Directly applicable?	Directly effective?	Capable of indirect effect?	Institution
	Automatically part of legal system	Gives enforceable rights to individuals	Reinterpretation of domestic legislation by national courts	
Treaty article	Yes	Sometimes	N/A	N/A
Regulation	Yes	Often	N/A	Commission, or Council and Parliament
Directive	No	Yes	Yes	Council and Parliament
Decision	Yes	Specific addressees only	No	Commission or Council (sometimes with Parliament)

the EU Commission decision under the TFEU[61] that Microsoft had abused its dominant economic position by preventing interoperability elements of its Windows bundle with rivals' products. The Commission ordered Microsoft to disclose relevant information to competitors, and levied a fine of €497,196,304.

Summary of EU legislation

Key aspects of EU legislation are summarised in Table 4.3.

4.5.5 Interpreting EU law

Because the original EU (then EEC) member states all had civil law systems (see 2.3.2 and 5.1 on civil vs common law), EU law was based on civil law traditions. The ECJ therefore uses an inquisitorial, rather than adversarial, system. This means that the court is aiming for the truth, as well as a winner, and the court will be more active in respect of evidence and witnesses. There are no minority judgments or dissents—for more details of the ECJ see 3.5.1.

The ultimate source of law in a civil system is a Code—in the EU this is the EU Treaty (TFEU). This sets out the principles on which the rest of the law is based. The ECJ then interprets the law by applying those principles in the circumstances of each particular case.

The ECJ would (like an English court) normally start with a literal approach (see 4.4.3), but it may (even if there is no ambiguity) depart from this with a purposive approach. In the SABENA case mentioned at 4.5.4 a literal interpretation would only have protected the air

---

[61] Commission Decision 2007/53/EC of 24 May 2004 relating to a proceeding pursuant to Art. 82 of the EC Treaty and Art. 54 of the EEA Agreement against Microsoft Corporation (Case COMP/C-3/37.792 – Microsoft) (notified under document number C(2004) 900).

hostess had she been a state employee. The ECJ purposively interpreted the article to include private employers as being subject to the obligation.

The ECJ does not adopt a strict system of precedent, but, rather like the UK Supreme Court, it will try to follow a principle of consistency. All EU national courts are bound by the rulings of the ECJ.

4.5.6 EU law and UK law—revisiting Parliamentary supremacy

Sections 2(1) and 3 of the European Communities Act 1972 oblige all UK courts to give effect to any EU law which is directly effective and to follow decisions of the ECJ. UK courts are required to apply directly effective EU law in preference to domestic law and to interpret all domestic law to comply with EU law, as far as possible. While the TFEU does not state that EU law is supreme over national law, the ECJ has developed key principles that have entrenched this supremacy. It is increasingly recognised in the English legal system that EU law has supremacy over Parliament and is therefore a limitation on Parliamentary sovereignty.

An example of the way in which the UK courts now acknowledge the supremacy of EU law can be seen in Case study 4.

Case study 4
R v Secretary of State for Transport, ex parte Factortame (No. 2)[62]

Some Spanish fishermen set up a UK company to operate trawlers with the intention of exploiting the UK fishing quota in the North Sea. The Merchant Shipping Act 1988 was enacted to prevent this practice. The Spanish fishermen who found themselves excluded by this rule argued that the Act was contrary to the TFEU.

The ECJ agreed that the Merchant Shipping Act was indeed contrary to the TFEU. This case was significant because the ECJ stated that national courts were to ignore any national law which ran contrary to directly effective EU law. The House of Lords was given no choice by the ECJ but to ignore the relevant provision of the UK statute, and grant the injunction.

This was clearly a watershed decision, but it is worth noting that the House of Lords (and now the UK Supreme Court) has not yet declared UK statutes void in whole or part, as happens under the doctrine of judicial review in the US.

As we saw in 4.1.1, it can be argued that Parliament remains sovereign in that it has the power to abolish the European Communities Act 1972 and with it EU law supremacy. This is only an option for 'dualist' systems like the UK, where, international and/or EU law is not automatically part of domestic law. By contrast, in 'monist' systems, such as the Netherlands, all international law is given constitutional supremacy. Abolition of the European Communities Act 1972 and withdrawal from the EU would, however, be politically exceedingly controversial, so we can conclude that in areas of EU competence, EU law is in practice supreme.

---

[62] *R v Secretary of State for Transport, ex parte Factortame (No. 2)* [1991] 1 AC 603.

4.6 **The Human Rights Act 1998**

The HRA was passed to give UK citizens protection of certain rights in the UK courts. It was a key pledge in the manifesto of the Labour Party before its landslide victory in 1997. The white paper that preceded this Act contained a foreword by the then Prime Minister, Tony Blair, which shows how important the Act was to the government:

> The Bill marks a major step forward in the achievement of our programme of reform. It will give people in the United Kingdom opportunities to enforce their rights under the European Convention in British courts rather than having to incur the cost and delay of taking a case to the European Human Rights Commission and Court in Strasbourg. It will enhance the awareness of human rights in our society. And it stands alongside our decision to put the promotion of human rights at the forefront of our foreign policy.[63]

The issue of human rights is contentious in British politics. Prime Minister David Cameron said in 2011 (a day after widespread riots had caused extensive damage):

> But what is alien to our tradition—and now exerting such a corrosive influence on behaviour and morality, is the twisting and misrepresenting of human rights in a way that has undermined personal responsibility. The interpretation of human rights legislation has exerted a chilling effect on public sector organisations, leading them to act in ways that fly in the face of common sense, offend our sense of right and wrong, and undermine responsibility. We're working to develop a way through the morass by looking at creating our own British Bill of Rights.[64]

Statutory interpretation had hit the headlines. David Cameron was referring to certain defensive administrative practices that may have developed such as, for instance, police needing to keep one eye on duties under the HRA towards suspects and witnesses, or (the example David Cameron used in the interview concerned) a prison van being driven nearly 100 miles to transport a prisoner 200 yards when the prisoner was willing to walk.

The HRA is unique in its pervasive effect on the operation of the English legal system, and sits alongside the European Communities Act 1972 as one of the most important statutes of recent times. This book does not look in detail at the substance of human rights law, but instead gives an outline of its effect on the English legal system.

4.6.1 **Before the Human Rights Act**

Prior to the coming into force of the HRA, the UK was a (founder) member of the Council of Europe, meaning that it was a signatory to the ECHR, adopted in 1950. The Convention was a response to the atrocities of World War II and Nazi Germany, and also intended as a barrier against the totalitarian practices of the Soviet bloc. The aim was to prevent large-scale violations of human rights.

The rights specifically defined in the Convention include the rights to life, freedom from torture or inhumane or degrading treatment or punishment, and the right to a fair trial by an

---

[63] *Rights Brought Home: the Human Rights Bill* (HMSO, 1997, Cm. 3782).
[64] David Cameron, speech, 15 August 2011.

impartial tribunal. Schedule 1 to the HRA lists the 'Convention Rights'. The Convention gives a citizen of a signatory state the right to apply to the European Court of Human Rights for an order for compensation on the ground that there has been a breach by the state of the Convention, either directly (e.g. by the actions of the police) or indirectly (e.g. because the approach of courts has constituted a lack of access to a fair trial under Art. 6). However, this procedure is expensive, and lengthy, because of the need to exhaust domestic avenues of justice, and because of the logjam of cases before the European Court of Human Rights. It is said to take five years to get a case to the court, and cost on average £30,000.[65]

The HRA was passed to give citizens remedies for breach of their human rights without having to go to the European Court of Human Rights. The key mechanisms are:

- making it unlawful for a public body to act incompatibly with the Convention rights;
- ensuring courts take into account European Court of Human Rights jurisprudence in their decision making; and
- ensuring courts interpret legislation compatibly with the Convention.

4.6.2 The rights protected

The protection of key rights and freedoms is an important attribute of the Rule of Law (see 1.5). The rights are classified in three ways:

- Absolute rights: these do not allow for any exception at all. For instance, it is always a breach of the Convention for a signatory state to use torture against its citizens (Art. 3).
- Limited rights: these can be suspended in times of war or emergency, for example the right to a fair trial (Art. 6).
- Qualified rights: these require a balance between the rights of individuals and (if the state is involved) the needs of the state. So, for instance, while a newspaper may claim that revealing private information about a celebrity is an important aspect of freedom of expression (Art. 10), the individual concerned would counter that it is an infringement of her right to privacy (Art. 8). Many of the sensationalist headlines of newspapers tend to ignore that many rights within the Convention (and HRA) are subject to the principle of 'proportionality'. This means that the impact of the HRA must not be out of proportion to the importance of the allegedly infringing action by the state.

Some of the key rights are listed in Table 4.4.

4.6.3 Using the Human Rights Act

The HRA gives additional rights to UK citizens using two mechanisms: vertical and horizontal effect. It also affects statutory interpretation and the operation of case law. In this section we look at how individuals can use the HRA; an understanding of this will help in many different areas of law.

---

[65] *Rights Brought Home: the Human Rights Bill* (HMSO, 1997, Cm. 3782), para. 1.14.

Table 4.4 The Convention rights

Absolute rights	Qualified or limited rights
Art. 2: Right to life	Art. 5: Right to liberty and security
Art. 3: Prohibition of torture	Art. 6: Right to a fair trial
Art. 4: Prohibition of slavery	Art. 8: Right to respect for private and family life
Art. 7: No punishment without law	Art. 9: Right to freedom of thought, conscience and religion
	Art. 10: Right to freedom of expression
	Art. 11: Right to freedom of assembly and association
	Art. 12: Right to marry
	Art. 1 of the 1st Protocol: Right to protection of property
	Art. 2 of the 2nd Protocol: Right to education
	Art. 3 of the 2nd Protocol: Right to free and fair elections

Vertical effect

A rule of law with 'vertical' effect can be used by a person against the state (we have already seen this in the context of EU law at 4.5.3). Section 6 of the HRA states that it is unlawful for a public authority (e.g. the police) to act in a way that is incompatible with Convention rights unless it is left with no choice to do so by statute. In public law there has long been a doctrine called 'judicial review'. This is a mechanism which enables the courts to ensure that the government and other public bodies exercise the powers which they have been granted in the proper way and so do not breach the rule of law. The HRA has given a significant impetus to the doctrine of judicial review.

Horizontal effect

This is perhaps the most radical effect of the Act in terms of its effect on the English legal system. As we have seen in the context of EU law (4.5.3) any rule of law that has 'horizontal' effect can be used by one person against another. This means that in some contexts a person can say that another private person or organisation has infringed his rights. There is no express statement to this effect in the HRA. The process is indirect.

It has already been said that s. 6 of the HRA requires public authorities to act compatibly with Convention rights. This, crucially, includes the courts. Baroness Hale has said: 'The 1998 Act does not create any new cause of action between private persons. But if there is a relevant cause of action applicable, the court as a public authority must act compatibly with both parties' Convention rights.'[66] So the Convention right needs to 'piggyback' on another claim.

On 30 March 2008, the *News of the World* published an article, the 'sting' of which was that Max Mosley (former President of the Federation Internationale de l'Automobile and leading contemporary Formula 1 figure) had employed five prostitutes to act out allegedly pseudo-Nazi prison camp sex scenes. He successfully sued the paper.[67] The claim was made under what Mr Justice Eady called an 'old fashioned breach of confidence'. 'Breach of confidence' is

[66] *Campbell* v *Mirror Group Newspapers* [2004] UKHL 22, at [132].
[67] *Mosley* v *News Group Newspapers Ltd* [2008] EWHC 1777 (QB).

a tort. However, Mr Justice Eady used Art. 6 of the Convention (Respect for private life) to help him come to the conclusion that the tort had been breached. Prior to the HRA, this avenue would not have been available to him. Some commentators felt that (despite Mr Justice Eady's protestations to the contrary) this let a new tort of privacy in through the back door.

This mechanism has been used in many other important areas of law, including defamation and negligence.

4.6.4 The impact of the Human Rights Act on statutes

The purposive approach under s. 3

We saw in 4.5.4 that the European Communities Act 1972 requires UK courts to give effect to any EU law which is binding. Likewise, s. 3 of the HRA provides that 'so far as it is possible to do so, primary and secondary legislation must be read and given effect in a way which is compatible with the Convention rights'. If a court cannot achieve this, it may make a declaration of incompatibility in respect of the relevant piece of legislation.

Section 3 of the HRA implies that a purposive approach must be adopted by courts in relation to the Convention rights (as listed in Table 4.4). This purposive approach was alien to English courts, except in the context of EU law. Lady Justice Arden has said that courts have been 'feeling their way towards a set of rules and canons of construction that will apply where section 3(1) is in point'.[68] The application is less strict than for EU law and the words 'so far as it is possible to do so' in s. 3 of the HRA clearly envisage that some statutes are beyond compliance with Convention rights and cannot be adapted.

An example of the application of the purposive approach in this context is seen in *R (Sim) v Parole Board*[69] in which s. 44A of the Criminal Justice Act 1991 (no longer in force) was considered in the light of the obligation under s. 3 of the HRA. The Criminal Justice Act set out circumstances in which a prisoner might be brought back into custody after having been released on parole. It required that further release was required when 'it is no longer necessary for the protection of the public'. The court needed to determine the construction of the word 'necessary'. This was done flexibly to allow release of the prisoner, giving effect to Art. 5(4) of the Convention (Right to liberty–continued detention).

Because of s. 3 of the HRA and the court's obligations as a public authority under s. 5, the doctrine of precedent under which case law develops has also been modified–see 5.2.1 for more on this effect of the HRA.

Procedural requirements of the Human Rights Act

Section 4 of the HRA gives judges at the level of the High Court and above the power to make a declaration of incompatibility, if it is found that an Act of Parliament cannot be used consistently with the relevant Convention rights. This has occurred roughly four times a year since the passing of the HRA.[70]

---

[68] 'The Interpretation of UK Domestic Legislation in the Light of European Convention on Human Rights Jurisprudence' (2004) Stat LR 165, at 179.

[69] *R (Sim) v Parole Board* [2003] EWHC 152 (Admin).

[70] Houses of Parliament Joint Committee on Human Rights, *Sixteenth Report* (HL86/HC111, 2007), part 4.

To guard against this possibility, s. 19 of the HRA requires the minister who introduces the draft legislation into Parliament to state whether or not the Bill is compliant with the Act. This mechanism, called a 'statement of compatibility', can stimulate early debate on human rights issues inherent in proposed legislation. Ministers almost always state legislation to be HRA-compatible, even if the compatibility is subject to some debate. For instance, much of the anti-terrorism legislation passed since 2001 is arguably very restrictive of human rights, especially with regard to privacy and detention. But ministers have often stated such legislation to be HRA-compatible. This requirement can be suspended under the Convention in the context of an emergency.

Under s. 10 of the HRA, if a court makes a declaration of incompatibility with Convention rights in relation to a statute, the government can (under parliamentary scrutiny) enact statutory instruments (called 'remedial orders') to amend primary legislation in order to remove any incompatibility. Between 2000 and 2007, only 24 declarations of incompatibility were made by courts.[71] The Joint Committee on Human Rights is a select committee comprised of members of both Houses of Parliament with a remit to consider human rights issues in the UK. It scrutinises government Bills for human rights implications, and also examines government remedial orders.

Summary of effect of the Human Rights Act on statutes and interpretation

The HRA therefore contains many procedural protections of the Convention rights, which impact on elements of parliamentary sovereignty and the doctrine of precedent. These are summarised in Figure 4.6.

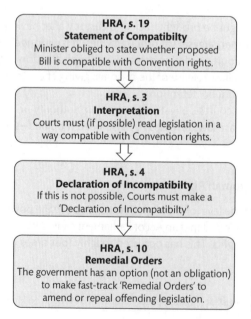

Figure 4.6 HRA process in relation to statutes

---

[71] Houses of Parliament Joint Committee on Human Rights, *Sixteenth Report* (HL86/HC111, 2007).

 **Summary**

- Statutes are the primary source of law in the UK.
- Legislation is passed by or with the authority of Parliament.
- Parliament is said to be 'sovereign', meaning that it is the supreme law-making body, and that no other institution can unmake laws passed by it.
- Parliamentary sovereignty has been subject to challenges, especially in the context of law derived from the EU and the ECHR.
- Statutes can be ambiguous, and lawyers have developed techniques of interpretation to help resolve these ambiguities.
- EU law can be broken down into several different types, and the impact of this legislation varies.
- The HRA has had profound implications for parliamentary sovereignty and the interpretation of statutes.

 Thought-provoking questions

1. Does the Regulatory Reform Act have a place in a democracy like the UK?
2. Is Parliament still sovereign?
3. Are human rights adequately protected by the mechanisms of the HRA?

Further reading

A. V. Dicey, *An Introduction to the Study of the Law of the Constitution* (1885)
—this contains the definitive statement of parliamentary sovereignty by one of the earliest modern constitutional theorists.

Daniel Greenberg, *Laying Down the Law* (London: Sweet & Maxwell, 2011)
—an accessible account by a legislative draftsman of the realities of drafting legislation in the UK.

Daniel Greenberg (ed.), *Craies on Legislation* (London: Sweet & Maxwell, 9th edn, 2008)
—a detailed guide to the interpretation of statutes.

Houses of Parliament Joint Committee on Human Rights, *Sixteenth Report,* HL86/HC111, 2007
—analyses the constitutional, legislative, and judicial impact of the HRA in the first decade since its coming into force.

Michael Zander, *The Law Making Process* (Cambridge: CUP, 6th edn, 2004)
—the definitive critical analysis of the law-making process.

 For the authors' reflections on the thought-provoking questions, additional self-test questions, podcasts offering a variety of perspectives on legal systems and skills, and a library of links to useful websites, visit the free Online Resource Centre at **http://www.oxfordtextbooks.co.uk/orc/slorach/.**

5 Case law

 Learning objectives

After reading this chapter you should be able to:

- Describe the distinction between common law and civil law jurisdictions.
- Explain in outline the operation of the doctrine of precedent.
- Use basic terminology relating to the case law of England & Wales.
- Develop an opinion on whether judges should make law.

Introduction

'Someone must be trusted. Let it be the judges.'[1] Most commentators agree that judges make law. And yet, every four or five years, in the UK, we elect a House of Commons to lead the law-making process. Indeed, roughly two-thirds of countries today are democracies[2]—so why should judges make law?

In this chapter we look more closely at the distinction between common law and civil law jurisdictions. We examine the operation of the doctrine of precedent. Finally, we address the arguments for and against the development of judge-made law.

5.1 Common law contrasted with civil law

To most people, a court is where issues of law are tried by judges. But in many countries, courts and judges have an additional role. Courts, especially appeal courts, are also called upon to make law, either where statutes leave room for interpretation, or where there is no statutory coverage.

At 2.3.2 we saw that a common law jurisdiction is a legal system where case law (as well as other forms of law, like statute law) has a significant role. It is normally contrasted with a 'civil law' jurisdiction, with some clear differences to be drawn between the two types of system. These are set out in Table 5.1.

Although it is common to refer to a common/civil law dichotomy, in reality there is a spectrum of jurisdictions.

England & Wales is probably the jurisdiction with the most extreme common law attributes. In some areas of law, such as negligence or the formation of contracts, there is almost total reliance on binding judge-made law, with little or no impact from statutes or

---

[1] Lord Denning, *What Next in the Law* (Oxford: OUP, 1982), p. 330.
[2] World Forum on Democracy, 25–7 June 2000, Warsaw.

Table 5.1 Contrasting features of common and civil law systems

	Common law	Civil law
Legal rules	Significant role for binding of case law.	No formal role for case law.
Constitutional rules	Have little or no impact on interpretation of statutes.	Comprehensive codes help with interpretation of statutes.
Development	Body of case law built up over time, often from English jurisprudence.	Derived from Roman *Corpus Juris Civilus* and reinterpretations.
Conduct of litigation	Largely 'adversarial', with judge as arbiter.	Largely 'inquisitorial', with judge questioning either side, examining the evidence.

codes. Why? One reason may be, as we saw in Chapter 2, that it is so old. The development of the English legal system largely pre-dated the rediscovery of Roman law in Continental Europe.

By contrast, France has an almost entirely codified system. Its code is derived from the *Code Napoleon* (and prior to that the Roman *Corpus Juris Civilis*), created by Napoleon Bonaparte in 1804, and still used in updated form today. To reinforce this, the French *Cour de Cassation*, their supreme court, is not permitted to give decisions supported by written judgments referring to the facts of a case, so there is little scope for the formation of a body of binding or persuasive case law in that jurisdiction.

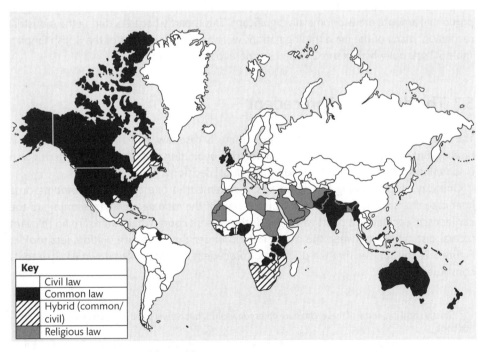

Key

	Civil law
	Common law
	Hybrid (common/ civil)
	Religious law

Figure 5.1 Legal systems around the world

Table 5.2 States, categorised by type of legal system, in order of GDP (G20 states are named)

Common law systems	Civil law systems	Hybrid/other
Around 40 states, including:	Around 150 states, including:	Around 20 states, including:
US (excl. Louisiana—civil), UK (excl. Scotland—hybrid), Canada (excl. Quebec—hybrid), India, Australia.	China, Japan, Germany, France, South Korea, Brazil, Italy, Russia, Mexico, South Korea, Turkey, Indonesia, Argentina.	Saudi Arabia (Islamic), South Africa (hybrid).

In between these two extremes, the US, and most of the states comprising it,[3] inherited a heavy reliance on common law and equity. Indeed the states' constitutions expressly refer to pre-Independence jurisprudence[4] as surviving. The US has a common law system but with a codified Constitution (of 1789), which incorporates the Bill of Rights (of 1791). The Constitution forms a codified cornerstone on which much US jurisprudence is built. This gives a 'civilian' flavour even to binding US case law.

Another hybrid is the jurisprudence of the European Court of Justice (ECJ), the decisions of which are binding on the courts of member states (almost all of which are 'civil law' jurisdictions), in order to bring consistency to the implementation of EU law.

There are other types of legal systems. Some are mainly reliant on Islamic law. Others, for example the Kyrgyzstan system, place emphasis on customary law. Some of the remaining communist states employ socialist law.

Look at Figure 5.1 to get a sense of the balance between these predominant systems. While the predominant type of system is civil, if we look at *which* systems are common law, a disproportionate amount are economically significant. This is partly because, during the industrial revolution, many of the main trading nations were at some stage part of the British Empire. Table 5.2 sets out which of the G20 states adhere to each system.

5.2 The doctrine of precedent

The doctrine of precedent exists wherever there is case law, whether or not that law is binding. But in England & Wales there is a doctrine of binding precedent, or *stare decisis*, as it is sometimes called—literally, 'to stand by [previous] decisions'.

One way of formulating it is as follows: a statement in one case will be binding on a later case if it is a statement of law, which is part of the *ratio decidendi* (reasoning) of the earlier case, decided in a court which binds the present court, where there are no relevant factual distinctions between the cases. To help understand this formulation, let's look at Figure 5.2. You can see that the doctrine of precedent can be broken down easily into its constituent parts.

---

[3] Strictly speaking, some of these states are commonwealths, but we will use the generic term, 'states', in this book.

[4] In the context of this chapter, the term 'jurisprudence' will be used to describe a body of case law, rather than the study of legal theory.

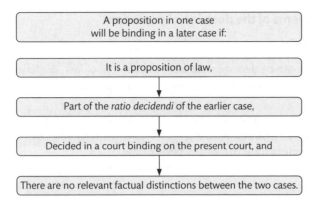

```
┌─────────────────────────────────────────────┐
│          A proposition in one case          │
│          will be binding in a later case if: │
└─────────────────────────────────────────────┘

┌─────────────────────────────────────────────┐
│          It is a proposition of law,        │
└─────────────────────────────────────────────┘
                      ↓
┌─────────────────────────────────────────────┐
│    Part of the ratio decidendi of the earlier case, │
└─────────────────────────────────────────────┘
                      ↓
┌─────────────────────────────────────────────┐
│   Decided in a court binding on the present court, and │
└─────────────────────────────────────────────┘
                      ↓
┌─────────────────────────────────────────────┐
│ There are no relevant factual distinctions between the two cases. │
└─────────────────────────────────────────────┘
```

Figure 5.2 The doctrine of precedent

This chapter now examines each aspect of the doctrine in turn. We first look at each aspect of the doctrine before drawing out some important themes.

To help us with this, we use the case study introduced in Chapter 3, *Donoghue* v *Stevenson*.[5] Here are the key case facts again:

Case study 1

Donoghue v Stevenson

In August 1928, Mrs May Donoghue joined a friend for a drink in the Wellmeadow Café in Wellmeadow Place, Paisley, Glasgow.

The friend bought the drinks. The owner poured some ginger beer from an opaque bottle into Mrs Donoghue's glass (which may or may not have had some ice cream floating in it). She took some swigs and then poured the rest of the contents into her glass. To her horror the remains of a decomposing snail presented themselves to her. Mrs Donoghue later complained of stomach pains and shock, both a result of gastroenteritis.

On appeal, the House of Lords found that the manufacturer would owe a duty of care (that is, a duty not to carelessly cause harm) to the consumer. The case was later settled.

There is also an annotated extract from this case at 7.5.2, should you wish to look in more detail at the legal themes referred to here.

Why should this quaint-sounding case be so important in English law, and indeed in many jurisdictions? It is because the case addressed the fundamental question, 'Who is my neighbour?'

We are using *Donoghue* here as an example to aid the study of the doctrine of precedent; you will cover the law of negligence itself in detail in your study of tort law. The case was never decided on the facts—it was settled after the House of Lords decided on the preliminary issue of whether a duty of care was owed.

[5] *Donoghue (or M'Alister) v Stevenson* [1932] AC 562.

5.2.1 **Basic elements of the doctrine of precedent**

A statement of law ...

A statement of law can be distinguished from a statement of fact. We have already seen that the difference between questions of fact and law is a key concept in the study and operation of legal systems.

Fact: from the information we have in the Scottish Law Reports, we know that Mrs Donoghue contracted gastroenteritis after drinking contaminated ginger beer. This is a statement of fact and cannot form part of any body of law.

Law: from the *Donoghue* case it is possible to derive many statements of law, for instance:

1. You must not injure your neighbour.
2. 'You must take reasonable care to avoid acts or omissions which you can reasonably foresee would be likely to injure your neighbour', as stated by Lord Atkin in his speech.[6]
3. A duty of care does arise when the person or property of one person is in such proximity to another that, if due care is not taken, she might suffer physical and consequential damage.[7]
4. '... a manufacturer of products, which he sells in such a form as to show that he intends them to reach the ultimate consumer in the form in which they left him with no reasonable possibility of intermediate examination, and with the knowledge that the absence of reasonable care in the preparation or putting up of the products will result in an injury to the consumer's life or property, owes a duty to the consumer to take that reasonable care ...'[8]
5. A manufacturer of ginger beer must take care to prevent molluscs from entering and contaminating its products, thus causing gastroenteritis in anyone resident in Glasgow.
6. A duty of care should not extend to everyone injured by a defect in a product, irrespective of proximity. It would be difficult for trade to be carried on.

All of these are statements of law. Only some of them are of importance. In fact, *Donoghue* is unusual in that there are so many statements of law that are of general importance. You may note that only (2) and (4) are quotations (from Lord Atkin's leading speech).

When you study tort law, you will find that statements (2), (3), and (4) are vital to an understanding of the modern law of negligence.

... part of the *ratio decidendi* ...

Ratio decidendi, usually abbreviated as *ratio*, means 'the reason for the decision'. The *ratio* is the most important statement of law in the case. Every statement in the case which is not part of the *ratio* is called *obiter dictum*, which means 'said in passing'.

Look at Figure 5.3. The decision in a case is guilty/not guilty in criminal proceedings, or liable/not liable in a civil case. This is the outcome of the case, and is what the litigants and

---

[6] *Donoghue (or M'Alister) v Stevenson* [1932] AC 562, at 580.

[7] This statement of law is adapted from a quote made in Lord Atkin's speech, from *obiter* comments in an earlier Court of Appeal case, *Heaven v Pender* (1883) 11 QBD 503.

[8] *Donoghue (or M'Alister) v Stevenson* [1932] AC 562, at 599.

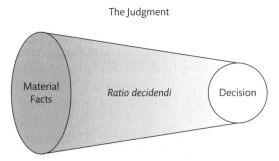

The Judgment

Material Facts — *Ratio decidendi* — Decision

Figure 5.3 *Ratio*: the reasoning necessary to get from the material facts to the decision

their lawyers want to know. In a civil law system, as contrasted with common law, it is common for the decision to be the only information reported, with no reasoning. However, observing lawyers want to know the reasoning or *ratio*. This is the 'law' in 'case law'. This reasoning derives from the court's application of the law to the material facts.

A case may have more than one *ratio*, either because the law is complex and requires lengthy reasoning, or because the *ratio* is disputed, or because different judges reached their decisions in different ways. We explore these issues at 5.2.2.

Statements (2), (3), and (4) in *Donoghue* have all been accepted as *ratios* (or *rationes*) arising from the case. Statement (6) summarises part of Lord Atkin's reasoning, but is only a statement made *obiter*.[9] Note that the *ratio* does not need to be a quotation from a judgment. The *ratio* is the underlying principle of law. This helps give the concept its flexibility.

... decided in a court binding on the present court ...

Most legal systems divide their courts into three types (see 3.1.2). Trial courts deal with all litigation and most of it stops there. Issues of law can then go to appeal. Most legal systems have one level of appeals court, although in England & Wales we have both the High Court in its appellate capacity and the Court of Appeal. Finally there is a final court of appeal, often called a supreme court. Until 2009 in the UK this was the House of Lords; it is now the Supreme Court of the UK.

In general:

- All courts are bound by superior courts (i.e. courts above them in the court hierarchy)— vertical *stare decisis*. The reason for this is to ensure consistency and reinforce the case law-making primacy of the supreme courts.
- Some courts are usually bound by previous decisions of their own court (or their predecessors)—horizontal *stare decisis*. The reason for this is to reinforce consistency in their jurisprudence unless absolutely necessary for reasons of justice.
- Courts are never bound by courts of a lower level.

A generic representation of common law *stare decisis* (i.e. not specific to England & Wales) is set out in Figure 5.4.

[9] *Donoghue (or M'Alister) v Stevenson* [1932] AC 562, at 576.

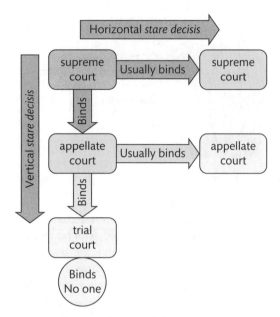

Figure 5.4 Generic representation of common law *stare decisis*

In England and Wales this situation is manifested as follows (see also Figure 5.5):

Vertical stare decisis

All courts are bound by higher courts. So the law made by the House of Lords in *Donoghue* would bind any High Court or Court of Appeal judge considering questions relating to product liability in negligence.

Only appellate courts are called 'courts of record', which means courts where the case is reported in a recognised series of law reports (see 7.5.1). Some decisions of lower courts are however reported in newspapers or on legal databases like Lawtel. Partly as a consequence of this, only statements from appellate courts have binding effect.

The jurisprudence of the ECJ is binding (in all 27 member states) on matters of EU law, even though it is a court founded on civil law principles under EU law.

There is in theory one limitation on vertical *stare decisis*. Under s. 6 of the Human Rights Act 1998 it is unlawful for any public authority (including courts) to act inconsistently with the Convention rights (see 4.6.3). This means that a court has a strong (though not binding) obligation to ignore precedent case law which is incompatible with Convention rights, even if it would otherwise be bound. There have not yet been any reported cases where this has occurred. It has, so far, been possible to interpret binding case law compatibly with Convention rights.

Horizontal stare decisis

In the past the House of Lords bound itself. While this led to consistency, it also caused its jurisprudence to become embedded and inflexible. So since 1966 the House of Lords (now the Supreme Court) has been able to depart from its own earlier decisions. It does so rarely, in what is estimated to be only around 25 times since 1966.[10]

---

[10] A figure of 20 occasions is quoted for 1966–2005 in Jacqueline Martin, *The English Legal System* (London: Hodder Arnold, 4th edn, 2005), p. 25.

For reasons of consistency the Court of Appeal also tends to follow its own earlier decisions, although the Criminal Division is more liable to change its approach, because the liberty of individuals is at stake. There are exceptions[11] which are applied infrequently. The same approach applies to the High Court—remember that only its appellate decisions have binding authority.

Other courts

It should not be thought that other courts' decisions are irrelevant. Statements of law in other courts, either lower in the hierarchy, or in other jurisdictions, are persuasive. A persuasive authority is not binding but may be used in reasoning.

Case law of the Privy Council is only persuasive authority unless it expressly states otherwise. Also persuasive is the reasoning of the European Court of Human Rights (under s. 2 of the Human Rights Act 1998). However, it would be a brave court to decide contrary to the jurisprudence of either court where English law was similar to the law applied in the earlier authority. Another example of a persuasive authority is the Old Bailey. It is nominally a Crown Court, yet some of its decisions involve consideration of important issues of law, and have been variously reported.

Decisions of foreign courts are frequently important. The laws of tort and contract in the US and England & Wales have developed in parallel, and authority from one jurisdiction is frequently highly persuasive in the other. *Shuey* v *US*[12] is a US Supreme Court case which is important in English contract law. Much of the reasoning in *Donoghue* v *Stevenson* is derived from a New York state Supreme Court case.[13] *Donoghue* is itself highly persuasive authority in the US.

Figure 5.5 sets out the full hierarchy of courts in England and Wales. Note that the court hierarchy echoes the appeals system discussed at 3.1.2, but describes a separate mechanism.

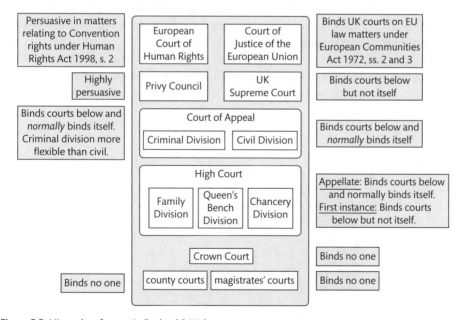

Figure 5.5 Hierarchy of courts in England & Wales

---

[11] Set out in *Young* v *Bristol Aeroplane Co. Ltd* [1944] KB 718.   [12] *Shuey* v *US* 92 US 73 (1875).

[13] *MacPherson* v *Buick Motor Co.*, 217 NY 382, 111 NE 1050 (1916) (New York Court of Appeals, equivalent to the Court of Appeal in England & Wales).

... where there are no relevant factual distinctions between the cases ...

We have already learned that if the earlier case was decided in a higher court, its *ratio* is binding on lower courts. However, you will recall that the *ratio* is the application of the law to the material facts; it is the later court which determines both what is the *ratio* of the earlier case and the material facts of both cases.

If a court considers a case before it to be different in some material way from the precedent cited, either on the facts or the law, that earlier case need not be followed. The new case will then be said to be 'distinguished' from the earlier case and, as a consequence, the court can decide not to apply the prior *ratio*. Indeed, where the court is anxious not to be bound by a particular precedent, some distinctions are drawn which are very fine.

Therefore, the more a case is distinguished, or confined to its facts, the narrower its *ratio* is likely to be. We explore this technique next.

5.2.2 **Key themes in the doctrine of precedent**

Alternative *ratios*

As we saw at 5.2.1 there may be many possible *ratios*. Some are unworkably narrow and others are impossibly wide. The importance of this is that the *ratio* will be used by lawyers in later cases to promote their arguments about the impact of the earlier authority.

It is the number of facts considered to be material which will make the *ratio* either narrower or wider. These are the concepts of narrow and wide *ratio*. The more general the statement of facts, the greater the number of subsequent cases which will be 'caught' by the principle. You can see from Figure 5.6 that this effect makes the *ratio* 'wider'. The formulation of the judgment will be an important factor. It would be unlikely in many cases that the narrowest and widest statements would actually be considered to be *ratios*.

An advocate seeking to employ too wide a *ratio to* bring his argument within the ambit of a previous line of authority will find his arguments are likely to be too spurious to have any impact. Likewise using too narrow a *ratio* in order to distinguish authority will be unlikely to succeed.

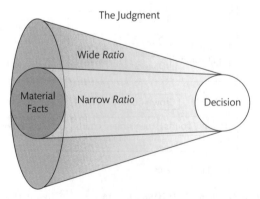

Figure 5.6 Wide and narrow *ratio*: the more general the facts considered relevant, the 'wider' the *ratio*

The example of *Donoghue* brings this out well:

1. You must not injure your neighbour.

    This would be an unmanageably wide *ratio*, and would apply to any two people when any harm occurs. Any advocate seeking to use this would be going beyond the realm of law into statements hitherto the province only of morality. If this were accepted as *ratio*, floodgates would be wide open to indeterminate litigation.

2. 'You must take reasonable care to avoid acts or omissions which you can reasonably foresee would be likely to injure your neighbour', as stated by Lord Atkin in his speech.

    This statement of law seems quite wide: the material facts are that there are two parties, who are legally proximate, with damage causing foreseeable harm. This is however the accepted statement of the neighbour principle in *Donoghue*, and is called the 'wide rule', the wide *ratio* of the case. It has since been refined slightly by case law, and in particular the crucial *Caparo*[14] case.

3. A duty of care does arise when the person or property of one person is in such proximity to another that, if due care is not taken, she might suffer physical and consequential damage.

    Here, the material facts are that there are two parties with no contract and some injury with consequential economic losses. This statement of law is important in defining the limits of the neighbour principle as Atkin saw it. Importantly, negligence could only cover physical damage, and its consequences. Purely 'economic' damage, not arising from physical damage, was properly the province of contract law and not negligence. Such a *ratio* would now be considered too restrictive, based on too narrow an interpretation of *Donoghue's* material facts.

4. '... a manufacturer of products, which he sells in such a form as to show that he intends them to reach the ultimate consumer in the form in which they left him with no reasonable possibility of intermediate examination, and with the knowledge that the absence of reasonable care in the preparation or putting up of the products will result in an injury to the consumer's life or property, owes a duty to the consumer to take that reasonable care ...'

    Here, the material facts narrow again—a manufacturer has caused a foreseeable consumer physical injury or property damage and consequential harm. This statement of law is the accepted 'narrow rule' from *Donoghue* and this *ratio* has generally recognised importance in the area of product liability law. No lawyer would attempt to distinguish this rule.

5. A manufacturer of ginger beer must take care to prevent molluscs from entering and contaminating its products, thus causing gastroenteritis in anyone resident in Glasgow.

    Here, the material facts are that there was a manufacturer of ginger beer, a snail, a stomach-related illness, and the events occurred in Glasgow. A statement of law derived from this would be far too narrow to form the basis of useable precedent. No lawyer would attempt to confine the impact of *Donoghue* to its facts in this way.

In conclusion, using the example of *Donoghue*, we can see that one person's reading of the judgments in a case may yield a subtly different *ratio* from another's, although the statements (2) and (4) set out above have become accepted in respect of the case. This can be quite

[14] *Caparo Industries plc v Dickman* [1990] 2 AC 605.

liberating for the lawyer or legal scholar seeking to use a precedent case in argument. It is critical at an early stage of your study to realise that to some extent *ratio* is, like beauty, in the eye of the beholder.

Finding a *ratio*

When we look for a *ratio*, we are trying to distil the legal reasoning in the case which is essential for the decision. Sometimes, it is straightforward to determine the *ratio* of a case. One can ask a rhetorical question, 'What's the key legal question being asked?' The answer to that legal question will be the *ratio*.

For instance, if we refer back to Case study 3 in Chapter 4, summarised below, the question is: 'In judging the actions of a reasonable man for the purposes of provocation under s. 3 of the Homicide Act 1957, can we take a subjective view, reflecting relevant characteristics of the defendant?' The answer was 'yes', and then became 'no', before legislation put a stop to the debate. The legal principles derived from these answers were the *ratios* of the cases in which they were considered.

Case study 2

Homicide Act 1957, s. 3 (now repealed)—summary

The Homicide Act put on a statutory footing various defences to a charge of murder.

> Where on a charge of murder there is evidence on which the jury can find that the person charged was provoked (whether by things done or by things said or by both together) to lose his self-control, the question whether the provocation was enough to make a reasonable man do as he did shall be left to be determined by the jury; and in determining that question the jury shall take into account everything both done and said according to the effect which, in their opinion, it would have on a reasonable man.

But often it is not quite so hard and fast. *Ratios* are sometimes difficult to find. There are four main difficulties:

- The first problem is that often judgments are lengthy and judges say many things. So the *ratio* may be buried amongst a mass of other statements, and is not often highlighted or labelled in any way.

- Second, and at the other extreme, occasionally judges take care to highlight the key parts of their reasoning. Even this raises issues. If a judge purports to state the law in any definitive way, this should sometimes be viewed with caution, as the judge concerned may have a policy agenda. They may be going beyond the reasoning necessary to reach a decision. One possible example—depending on your interpretation of the case—is the principle of law claimed to be decisive by Glidewell LJ in the *Williams* v *Roffey*[15] case in contract law. Not all judgments are definitive like Lord Atkin's in *Donoghue*.

- A third issue is that judges frequently have more than one reason for their decision: it can often be hard to determine which their main line of argument is.

---

[15] *Williams* v *Roffey Bros. & Nicholls (Contractors) Ltd* [1991] 1 QB 1.

- Finally, there may also be more than one judge, not necessarily giving the same reasons. Where multiple judge courts are concerned, one needs to distinguish between the reasoning of the individual judge and the *ratio* of the court as a whole. Each judge must have a reason for her decision, but it does not follow that there is any single reason for the decision of the court as a whole, since each of the judges may give different reasons which may be inconsistent. In one infamous contract law case,[16] of the five judges in the House of Lords, one dissented from the final judgment (which was therefore a majority decision of 4:1) and no more than two of the other judges delivered similar *ratios* on any point. In other words, the court as a whole produced no discernible *ratio*. The case has since been written off as inconclusive.

Obiter dicta and dissent

We have already seen that if reasoning is part of the majority reasoning but is not necessary for the decision of the court as a whole, then this is not *ratio* but *obiter* instead. *Obiter* is, like decisions of foreign courts, persuasive in value. There is no magic formula for the strength of persuasive authority. You simply give the persuasive authority the weight it deserves.

For instance, there is an *obiter* discussion in the *High Trees* case;[17] without any prior knowledge of the judge involved, one might give the authority little value. The reasoning constitutes the musings of a second-year High Court judge at first instance, railing against unhelpful unanimous House of Lords authority. This has since formed the basis of the equitable doctrine of 'promissory estoppel' (which is a defence to a contract debt claim), which survives today. The judge later became Lord Denning, whose jurisprudence in private law is given great weight; the doctrine of promissory estoppel has been approved by the Court of Appeal on numerous occasions (sometimes, admittedly, by Denning himself).

Judges in multi-judge courts, who do not agree with the decision, give a dissenting opinion. In *Donoghue* v *Stevenson*,[18] of the five Lords of Appeal, two disagreed with the majority decision. Some of these dissents carry persuasive weight in later cases. They may be approved or referred to when the law subsequently develops. For example, Lord Denning dissented from decisions early in the development of the law of negligence (relating to purely economic damage) after *Donoghue*. His dissents gave impetus to later developments in the law in this area. In *Donoghue*, the reasoning in Lord Buckmaster's dissent (he was the senior Law Lord at the time) helps lawyers analyse the background to Lord Atkin's leading judgment (see 7.5.3 for more on how to use dissenting judgments).

Figure 5.7 illustrates the status of *obiter* and dissent. Neither is part of the *ratio* of a case, although dissenting reasoning does stem from the material facts and leads to an alternative decision.

You may well have realised that what one lawyer states to be *ratio*, to another is *obiter*, and non-binding. Lawyers are free to make any sensible interpretation. Eventually, a later court will decide which one is correct.

[16] *Esso Petroleum Co. Ltd v Commissioners of Customs and Excise* [1976] 1 WLR 1.
[17] *Central London Property Trust Ltd v High Trees House Ltd* [1947] KB 130.
[18] *Donoghue (or M'Alister) v Stevenson* [1932] AC 562.

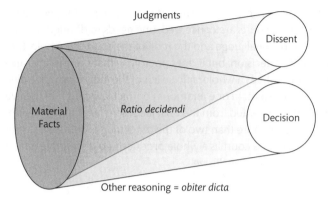

Figure 5.7 *Ratio, obiter,* and dissent

Evolving *ratios*

Zhou Enlai, the first Premier of the People's Republic of China, was once asked to assess the impact of the French Revolution, nearly 200 years previously. He replied, 'It's too soon to say' (this story is sometimes said to be apocryphal).

Likewise, the *ratio* often crystallises with time and perspective. A case may be analysed by academics and lawyers, and considered in later cases. Eventually, like a picture coming into focus, the reasoning of a case becomes refined and clear.

Figure 5.8 illustrates this. In your study of tort law you will see that the law of negligence has evolved in this way in several areas. One example was the area of product liability

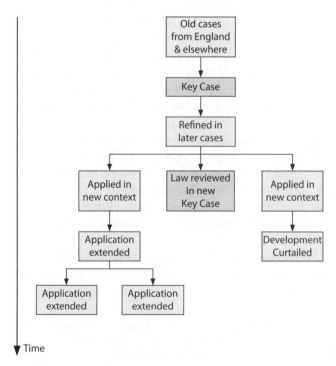

Figure 5.8 Evolution of *ratio*–generic diagram

developing from the *Donoghue* case study. The so-called 'narrow rule' (described at 5.3.2) has been applied and refined in many different contexts—including cars, lifts, and even irritant chemicals in undergarments. Another, closely related, example is where courts have refined principles relating to economic losses when they result from statements rather than from physical damage. The case law in this area has witnessed many twists and turns.

5.2.3 Terminology of the doctrine of precedent

When reading about how courts deal with precedent, it is important to understand the terminology used. The explanations given below can be read in conjunction with Figure 5.9.

Distinguishing, applying, or following

A lower court must normally **apply** or **follow** an earlier ruling of a higher court. The only way to disagree is to **distinguish** that ruling.

For example, a litigant could find himself in court, faced with unhelpful precedent. We have seen that a statement in one case will bind a court in a later case unless there are relevant distinctions between the two cases. Therefore, the litigant could argue that the facts of the case at hand are materially different to those from the problematic precedent, and consequently that the court is not bound to follow the earlier precedent. That is, the litigant would be asking the court to distinguish the earlier ruling from the instant case.

Overruling, disapproving, and approving

A higher court can **approve** the decision of a lower court or it may **disapprove** or **overrule** it, if it disagrees.

The latter occurs when a principle laid down by a lower court is declared incorrect and not followed by a higher court in a different later case. The higher court will set a new 'correct' precedent.

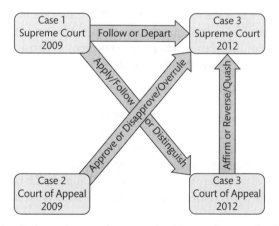

Figure 5.9 Precedent terminology: what can a later court do with an earlier precedent?

Departing or following

A court can follow or depart from an earlier case.

The Supreme Court normally **follows** its own earlier decisions (and those of the House of Lords) but it can **depart** from them if it wishes to change its approach to the law in a particular area. This is what the Court did when departing from the *Smith* decision in *Holley*, which we looked at in Case study 3 in Chapter 4.

Reversing, quashing, or affirming

If a case is appealed from a lower court to a higher court, then the higher court can **confirm**, or **affirm**, the decision of the lower court, if the appeal is dismissed. However, if the appeal is allowed, the decision of the lower court will be **reversed**, and if it is a criminal case, the sentence may be **quashed**.

Reversing therefore occurs where the decision of a court in the same case is altered by a higher court on appeal. It is thus different in nature from the other terms considered, because it does not relate to the doctrine of precedent. For example, the Court of Appeal may come to a different conclusion from the High Court on a point of law; in this situation, it will reverse the decision made by the High Court.

5.3 Judges as legislators

England & Wales is a common law jurisdiction. This means that there is a significant role for case law. If judges make law, does this mean they are legislators? This section discusses this controversial issue.

5.3.1 Do judges legislate?

Yes, judges do legislate

At the most basic level, judges clearly make law. According to the American legal theorist John Chipman Gray, 'in truth all law is judge-made law ... the courts put life into the dead words of the statute'.[19] So even first instance judges such as district judges or magistrates make law.

The main debate is not about law-making in this literal sense. The main academic discussion in this area concerns whether judges make law in the sense of legal principles that can be used in the future by other lawyers and courts.

It is clear that certain areas of law, such as formation of contracts, negligence, and equity, are largely judge-made, with little statutory intervention. It is also clear that other areas are mainly created by statute, such as tax law and health and safety legislation. There are other areas where the two types of law-making sit alongside each other, such as land law, where a large body of case law sits alongside and around certain key statutes like the Law of Property Act 1925. In such areas case law predating statutes still applies, if it has not been expressly replaced by the statute, and is sometimes expressly referred to in the statute.

---

[19] John Chipman Gray, *The Nature and Sources of the Law* (1909), pp. 119–20.

An example is the codification of directors' common law and equitable duties to a company in the Companies Act 2006.[20] Section 170(4), for instance, states that: 'The general duties shall be interpreted and applied in the same way as common law rules or equitable principles, and regard shall be had to the corresponding common law rules and equitable principles in interpreting and applying the general duties.'

An alternative situation is where judges make law to 'fill the gaps' in statutes, especially by interpreting them (see 4.4 for a full discussion of statutory interpretation). This is sometimes called 'interstitial' law-making.

In other countries, judges' law-making takes on a different character entirely. Perhaps the most extreme example is in the US, where the Supreme Court can declare Acts of Congress unconstitutional.[21] It has done so over 160 times since the early 19th century.[22] Partly this is a function of the fact that the US has a written Constitution, and that the Supreme Court quickly assumed a role as its guardian. This role is common to many US state Supreme Courts, and courts around the world. This process is more common in civil law jurisdictions, where a court is frequently given power to protect the code or constitution, although this court is usually a separate constitutional court, such as the *Bundesverfassungsgericht* in Germany or the *Conseil Constitutionnel* in France.

In England & Wales, the UK Supreme Court does not have power to overrule any legislation. It does, however, have the ability to make a declaration of incompatibility under s. 3 of the Human Rights Act 1998, although this has no formal effect on the legislation concerned. The House of Lords/Supreme Court has on occasion ignored UK statutes that are ruled by the ECJ as incompatible with EU law, as we saw at 4.1.1 in the *Factortame*[23] case.

No, judges do not legislate

An alternative analysis of English judicial law-making is the now largely defunct 'declaratory theory', in which it is maintained that judges merely *declare* the law as it subsists at the time of the events in question. This is reminiscent of the civil law approach where judges decide on the facts of a case. But this is clearly not the case in England & Wales. Lord Reid, a famous House of Lords judge, once said, 'We do not believe in fairy tales any more, so we must accept the fact that for better or worse judges do make law.'[24]

Judges do legislate, but they are not legislators

It is, however, arguable that the extent of judicial law-making in many common law countries is overstated, and that in civil law countries it is understated.

Many commentators view judicial law-making as increasingly 'interstitial', that is to say filling in the gaps left by or between statutes. The most common view is that because statutes are made by legislators in Parliament they are the primary source of law. Statutes necessarily leave room for interpretation; they cannot, and indeed should not normally, seek to provide

---

[20] Companies Act 2006, ss. 170–81. [21] *Marbury* v *Madison*, 5 US (1 Cranch) 137 (1803).

[22] US Government Printing Office Database, 2002.

[23] *Secretary of State for Transport, ex parte Factortame (No. 2)* [1991] AC 603.

[24] Lord Reid, 'The Judge as Lawmaker' (1972) 12 *Journal of the Society of Public Teachers of Law* 22.

for each and every scenario explicitly. Look again at Figure 2.3 summarising how judges make law in England & Wales.

You may recall, for instance (as in Case study 3 in Chapter 4), that the defence of provocation was replaced by the defence of 'loss of self control' after the confusion of *Smith* and *Holley*. Section 54 of the Coroners and Justice Act 2009 still requires that, for the defence to be available, 'a person of D's sex and age, with a normal degree of tolerance and self-restraint and in the circumstances of D, might have reacted in the same or in a similar way to D'. Against this background, it is quite clear that the legislators saw the courts as qualified to fill in the gaps in relation to concepts like 'normal'. The techniques of statutory interpretation examined in Chapter 4 were developed by judges and are a pivotal part of law-making in England & Wales.

What about civil law jurisdictions? The term 'civil law' is a broad term for many varied legal systems. The key distinction we are examining here is the nature and impact of judicial law-making.

While in general there is no doctrine of *binding* precedent in civil law jurisdictions, there is a doctrine of *non-binding* precedent, often called the doctrine of judicial consistency. It would be seen as erratic if a court changed its approach to a legal question too much. Without this dependability it would be more difficult for people to rely on the decisions of courts.

An extreme example is the French *Cour de Cassation* (their supreme court), which adopts an approach of 'imperial brevity', ruling only on narrow legal questions, an approach which constrains its ability to set useable precedent. Most other French courts give decisions without revealing their reasoning—this means that a body of case law based on judicial reasoning cannot emerge at all. By contrast, the jurisprudence of the ECJ is frequently lengthy and comprehensive. It is rare for the ECJ to amend or overrule its earlier reasoning. Further, the jurisprudence of the ECJ is binding on national courts.

It is therefore evident that judges do have some sort of law-making function in the UK and in other parts of the world, including most 'civil law' systems. Is this a desirable outcome?

5.3.2 Should judges legislate?

There are several criticisms of judicial legislating, or 'activism' as it is sometimes known. These are that:

- legislating is the job of legislatures such as Parliament, and no branch of state should have more than one function;
- courts are somehow 'undemocratic', and should not be legislating;
- judges are 'out of touch', or worse still, make arbitrary or immoral decisions; and
- judge-made law is inflexible and prone to paralysis.

Let's take these criticisms in turn. In each we set out a challenge to the legitimacy of judges' law-making role. This will be followed by an answer to that challenge:

That judicial law-making offends the principle of Separation of Powers

In Chapter 1 we saw that many constitutional theorists regard the doctrine of Separation of Powers as the cornerstone of a modern state. Let's examine the courts' role in a little more detail.

In a 'pure' theory of Separation of Powers, the role of the courts would be limited entirely to resolving legal disputes. Taking this to extremes, the role of an appeals court would simply be to rule on ambiguities in the law on a case by case basis. There would be no point in reporting judgments because they would have no future value. This hypothetical situation was set out in Figure 1.7.

In a common law system like England & Wales, the role of the courts is more ambiguous. When the courts of a common law jurisdiction hear appeals, the reasoning leading to their decisions becomes binding precedent. Not only are they acting in their judicial capacity, they are arguably also adopting a legislative role. This situation was summarised in Figure 1.8. To the casual observer, this would seem to be an encroachment by the courts on a role properly the province of Parliament.

The answer to this challenge is that the Separation of Powers is a theoretical concept and that no legal and political system can hope to reflect it fully. The US Constitution was drafted explicitly to reflect Montesquieu's doctrine of the Separation of Powers, but even this incorporates 'checks and balances'. This means that each branch has a limited role outside its core powers, to prevent too much power accumulating in one 'branch' of the system.

Further, modern courts are arguably aware of the limitations of their role, and bear in mind some of the criticisms levelled at their law-making role. At 1.2.4 we looked at the case of Diane Pretty, and saw that the House of Lords refused to order the Director of Public Prosecutions not to prosecute under s. 2(1) of the Suicide Act 1961. Lord Hope, in his judgment, said, 'In the present uncertain climate of public opinion, where there is no consensus in favour of assisted suicide and there are powerful religious and ethical arguments to the contrary, any change in the law which would make assisted suicide generally acceptable is best seen as a matter for Parliament.'[25]

There are also rare examples where courts have gone too far in their law-making function, and it is clear that Parliament does legislate to limit this. A line of tort cases concluded[26] with liability being imposed on employers for compensating workers for certain diseases where it was impossible to determine when the disease was caused, and therefore by whom. This was unfair on employers as it was impossible to determine whether they were at fault. The Compensation Act 2006[27] put an end to the courts' law-making in this area. At 4.4.4, we saw another instance when Parliament stepped in to prevent further judicial confusion on the issue of provocation as a defence to murder.

That judicial law-making is undemocratic

In the UK General Election of 2010, roughly 30 million people voted for 650 Members of Parliament to represent them in the House of Commons. In India (the world's largest democracy), roughly 426 million voted in their 2009 General Election. Whatever objections one might have to the electoral systems adopted by modern democracies, there is no disputing that the laws passed by legislatures in such nations are, to a significant extent, legitimate.

By contrast, in England & Wales, there are 159 judges serving in appellate courts, comprising 108 High Court Judges, 39 Lords Justice of Appeal, and 11 Supreme Court Justices.[28] They are

---

[25] *R (Pretty) v DPP and Secretary of State for the Home Department* [2001] UKHL 61, at [96].
[26] *Barker v Corus UK Ltd* [2006] UKHL 20.   [27] Compensation Act 2006, s. 3.
[28] Figures correct as February 2013.

appointed by the Judicial Appointments Commission, comprised of 15 members. They are drawn from a very narrow background—only 4% of judges are non-white, and only a fifth of judges in England & Wales, and only one of the 13 current Supreme Court Justices, is female.[29] It is true to say that the selection of the judiciary is undemocratic, and that judges do not have a popular mandate.

In answer to this assertion, it is worth asking whether judges *should* have a mandate. Certainly in their judicial capacity, it is strongly arguable that this is not a relevant consideration. Mere arbiters of legal liability should not need to be elected. The problem is, the more that we conclude that judges make law, the more it is arguable that they should be accountable to the people who are subject to those laws, namely elected. Much of the discussion reduces to an evaluation of the nature of the judges' law-making (see 5.3.1).

Another counterargument is that the comparison with legislatures is not as unflattering as it might at first seem. There are many arguments about how truly democratic legislatures are around the world. While it is not the aim of this chapter to discuss the merits of democratic institutions, we can at least acknowledge that Parliament in the UK, the European Parliament, and the US Congress are frequently cited as suffering from a 'democratic deficit'.[30] The latter in particular is said to be stymied by 'pork barrel politics'. This happens when the interests of powerful pressure groups or voters in marginal districts dictate the positions of some key congressmen during consideration of legislation in committee. In return, pet projects are given funding out of proportion to their public value.

That judicial law-making is out of touch, arbitrary, and immoral

Jeremy Bentham, a philosopher mentioned in Chapter 1, was an ardent critic of judicial law-making, about which he wrote sarcastically:

> But King, Lords and Commons are a dull and slow set determining nothing about facts till after they been poring over as well as prying into facts. How more easily are these things managed by a learned Judge! When at any time *he thinks it worthwhile* to make a law it need cost him but a word nor is it necessary even to that word to contain *thought* or any such heavy matter at the bottom of it.[31]

The implication was that judges can make law, if they wish, arbitrarily or by whim.

One of the most infamous examples of judicial activism in the face of the opposition of a legislature is the *Dred Scott* case in the pre-civil war US.[32] The Missouri Compromise, an Act of the US Congress, had partitioned the states of the US into states where slavery was, and states where it was not, permitted. Dred Scott (a slave) had lived in so-called 'free' states for some time and sued for his freedom, when it was denied to him. The US Supreme Court, in *obiter*, stated that the Missouri Compromise was unconstitutional, much of the impetus coming

---

[29] *2012 Judicial Diversity Statistics*, taken as at 1 April 2012, http://www.judiciary.gov.uk.

[30] See e.g. Patrick Wintour, 'European Parliament should be abolished, says Jack Straw', *The Guardian*, 21 February 2012, quoting a poll by the Institute for Public Policy Research, and *Report of the Independent Commission on the Voting System (the Jenkins Commission)* (HMSO 1998, Cm. 4090).

[31] Jeremy Bentham, *The Elements of the Art of Packing as Applied to Special Juries ...* (E. Wilson, 1821), p. 157 (emphasis added).

[32] *Dred Scott* v *Sandford*, 60 US 393 (1857).

from the activist Supreme Court Chief Justice, Roger Taney. This is seen as one of the most politically motivated, immoral, and controversial decisions in US legal history.[33]

In England, Lord Denning, a popular champion of private rights, had a notorious reputation in the area of public law. In his 1982 book, *What Next in the Law*, he seemed to suggest that immigrants were unsuitable to serve on juries because they had different moral standards to a native Englishman.

An answer to this challenge also comes from the US. In Chapter 1 we saw that the US Constitution is the archetype of constitutions drafted to preserve the Separation of Powers. Much of its content was based upon reasoning by the 'Founding Fathers' in the Federalist Papers. Alexander Hamilton insisted:

> the independence of the judges may be an essential safeguard against the effects of occasional ill humors in the society.[34]

So the 'arbitrary' argument can be turned on its head. Indeed, Hamilton went on to say:

> To avoid an arbitrary discretion in the courts, it is indispensable that they should be bound down by strict rules and precedents, which serve to define and point out their duty in every particular case that comes before them; and it will readily be conceived from the variety of controversies which grow out of the folly and wickedness of mankind, that the records of those precedents must unavoidably swell to a very considerable bulk, and must demand long and laborious study to acquire a competent knowledge of them. Hence it is, that there can be but few men in the society who will have sufficient skill in the laws to qualify them for the stations of judges.[35]

So the very weight of precedent lends gravitas to the case law it generates.

That judicial law-making is inflexible

If we accept that significant swathes of law are still judge-made, then we meet a problem. Common law systems adhere to a binding doctrine of precedent (see 5.2). Because of this, it is not open to courts to develop law if they are faced with awkward precedents.

It is very unusual in England & Wales for a case to be stated as the definitive statement of the law in a given area. One rare example was a case[36] which sought to state comprehensively the law on 'undue influence' in contract law. This relates to how mortgages could be set aside, on the ground that a person had unduly influenced their spouse into guaranteeing their debts.

In general, case law in a given area needs to be refined as issues are litigated. Only rarely will these issues be appealed to courts that have the power to depart from earlier decisions, and even then only the part of the decision which is directly relevant to the material facts will be accepted as *ratio* and therefore binding law. Figure 5.10 summarises the process.

---

[33] Paul Finkelman, 'Scott v. Sandford: The Court's Most Dreadful Case and How it Changed History' (2007) 82 *Chicago-Kent Law Review* 3.

[34] Alexander Hamilton, *The Federalist Papers No. 78* (1788).

[35] Alexander Hamilton, *The Federalist Papers No. 78* (1788).

[36] *Royal Bank of Scotland plc v Etridge (No. 2)* [2001] UKHL 44.

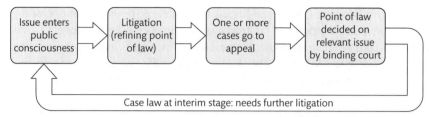

Figure 5.10 The process by which case law develops to reflect changes in society

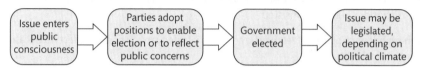

Figure 5.11 The process by which legislation develops to reflect changes in society.

Equity provides a little more flexibility, for example with the creation by Lord Denning of the doctrine of promissory estoppel, in the face of countervailing House of Lords authority. However it is often argued that case law all too often moves too slowly to meet the needs of an evolving society.

By contrast, it is theoretically easy for a new statute to be passed if there is enough pressure. Figure 5.11 illustrates how public mores and morality are sometimes reflected in legislation. Given enough impetus, a government can implement important manifesto planks or pressing social needs. A good example is the swift implementation in 1945–7 of the comprehensive welfare state (requiring several significant Acts of Parliament). Public pressure led to the passing of the Dangerous Dogs Act 1991, which made it illegal to own certain breeds of dog; however that piece of legislation is often cited as an example of a rushed and botched law.[37]

So is judicial law-making inflexible? In practice, many proposed statutes are victims of lack of parliamentary time, insufficient political will, or decaying mandate. A commonly cited example is the further reform of the House of Lords, which has been part of the manifestoes of all three major UK parties, but is as yet still unlegislated, despite taking up much parliamentary time.

The interstitial nature of case law allows principles to be refined in situations too narrow to be legislated, in either primary or secondary legislation. Also, case law allows legislation to be applied in circumstances beyond the contemplation of legislators, such as applying rules of contract, or in creating duties in tort in a new world of instantaneous and detailed communication.

Bearing in mind the justification for the role of interstitial judicial law-making, any democratic deficit might be argued to be an irrelevance in the modern political world.

That judicial law-making is unclear or uncertain

At 5.2.1 we looked at the challenges of finding a *ratio*. Judgments in case law are infamous for using too many words to get to a decision, and for being difficult to interpret. In addition,

---

[37] See, e.g. 'The Lords is the more democratic house', *Daily Telegraph*, 13 April 2004; Ian Hollingshead, 'Whatever happened to dangerous dogs?', *The Guardian*, 5 November 2005.

it is sometimes difficult to reconcile two cases in the same area. This leads to uncertainty. In contract law, some of the rules relating to 'consideration', or the price paid for the other party's promise, are difficult to reconcile.

It is straightforward to counter this argument. The flip-side of the inflexibility encountered above is certainty: it is no coincidence that much of contract law in the Anglo-Saxon world is based on clear legal principles, creating the backdrop for making bargains with predictable consequences. Benjamin Cardozo, the esteemed US Supreme Court justice, declared:

> The judge ... is not to innovate at pleasure. He is not a knight-errant roaming at will in pursuit of his own ideal of beauty or of goodness. He is to draw his inspiration from consecrated principles. He is not to yield to spasmodic sentiment, to vague and unregu-lated benevolence. He is to exercise a discretion informed by tradition, methodized by analogy, disciplined by system, and subordinated to the primordial necessity of order in the social life.[38]

Clear law means that contracting parties can bargain with confidence. Commercial contracts are often given jurisdiction in England & Wales, or New York or Delaware, as the law of con-tract in these forums is so robust.

In defamation and privacy law, newspapers can publish with a degree of certainty about the boundaries of what is legally acceptable, though it is instructive that the goalposts have moved with the more 'civil law', codified approach of the Human Rights Act 1998, and the certainty provided by the common law has been somewhat vitiated.

5.3.3 Judges as legislators: conclusions

Because England & Wales is a common law jurisdiction, case law has a significant role to play. While judges make law in most (but not all) jurisdictions, their role in England & Wales is comparatively substantial. Many criticisms have been levelled at the practice of judges con-tributing to the body of law to which all citizens are subject.

Lord Reid, a notable Law Lord, once wrote:

> There was a time when it was thought almost indecent to suggest that judges make law—they only declare it. Those with a taste for fairy tales seem to have thought that in some Aladdin's cave there is hidden the Common Law in all its splendour and that on a judge's appointment there descends on him knowledge of the magic words Open Sesame. Bad decisions are given when the judge muddles the password and the wrong door opens. But we do not believe in fairy tales any more.[39]

But most of those criticisms can be countered or at least put into perspective. The reality is that the courts have a limited but important role to play in the law-making system in England & Wales, and that it would be very difficult to remove this role without undermining the whole apparatus.

---

[38] Benjamin Cardozo, *The Nature of the Judicial Process* (1921).
[39] Lord Reid, 'The Judge as Lawmaker' (1972) 12 *Journal of the Society of Public Teachers of Law* 22.

Summary

- Judges and courts are given different roles in different countries; the degree to which they are given power to make, as opposed to only adjudicating on, law is a controversial issue.
- Case law operates via a doctrine of (usually) binding precedent. A statement of law from one case will bind lower courts provided there are no relevant factual distinctions between the cases.
- Skilled lawyers can feel liberated to use case law in many ways to argue points for their clients.
- It is possible to argue that the existence of binding case law offends the principle of Separation of Powers, but history shows us that case law has many benefits and can be flexible if times change.

 Thought-provoking questions

1. Should judges be restricted to the role of adjudication between litigants?
2. Should law be generated by cases, or just by Parliament?
3. Lord Denning famously thought that the Court of Appeal should be free to depart from unhelpful House of Lords (now Supreme Court) precedent (see *Broome* v *Cassell*[40]). Would you agree?

 Further reading

Lord Denning, *What Next in the Law* (Oxford: OUP, 1982)
—this is widely regarded as one of the definitive statements of Lord Denning's jurisprudence, including, controversially, on the rights of immigrants. At the time, Lord Denning saw the book's publication as a rallying cry for change.

Alexander Hamilton, *The Federalist Papers No. 78* (1788)
—Hamilton, as one of the 'founding fathers' of the US Constitution, used this paper to explain why he felt that judges should have some law-making powers in a democracy.

 For the authors' reflections on the thought-provoking questions, additional self-test questions, podcasts offering a variety of perspectives on legal systems and skills, and a library of links to useful websites, visit the free Online Resource Centre at **http://www.oxfordtextbooks.co.uk/orc/slorach/.**

---

[40] *Broome* v *Cassell* [1971] 2 QB 354.

Legal services

 Learning objectives

After reading this chapter you should be able to:

- Explain the importance of a strong legal profession.
- Understand the central role played by ethics in a lawyer's work.
- Describe the basic structure of the legal profession in England & Wales.
- Gain an awareness of the legal profession in its wider context.
- Discuss how the increased importance of market forces has been reflected in the legal profession.

Introduction

We have looked at the law as a concept (Chapter 1), how it is created (Chapter 2), and where it is litigated (Chapter 3). We have seen that a key factor in entrenching the Rule of Law was the ability of the individual to access justice effectively. But this entire framework lacks impact without an accessible and strong legal profession.

In this chapter we focus on the legal profession in the UK, where major regulatory changes have been made to the provision of legal services. In the changing context in which lawyers operate, we look at why it remains important to have a robust legal profession with strong values.

This chapter is designed to complement Chapter 15. While this chapter looks at the importance of legal services, and their evolution, Chapter 15 focuses on law firms as businesses and the commercial challenges they face as a result of the changing economic and regulatory environment.

6.1 Lawyers as professionals

Service industries generate 76% of the UK's Gross Domestic Product (GDP).[1] Lawyers make a major contribution to this—in 2009, the legal services market had a turnover of £24.7 billion.[2] However, while lawyers are one of the UK's service industries, they are also members of a profession. First we examine the idea of a profession, before focusing on lawyers as professionals.

---

[1] Office of National Statistics, *Economic Review, October 2011* (1 November 2011).

[2] Office of National Statistics, *ONS Statistical Bulletin: Quarterly National Accounts, 4th Quarter* (30 March 2010).

6.1.1 **What is a professional?**

 Essential explanation

A **professional** is someone who works in a profession. The Royal Commission on Legal Services 1979 defined a 'profession' as an occupation that:

- requires central organisation;
- is self-regulated;
- has required minimum standards of training;
- places significant importance on duty to the client; and
- involves the giving of specialist advice.

Other 'professions' include accountants, architects, dentists, doctors, engineers, pharmacists, and teachers. The list is open-ended, but these are good examples.

Lawyers are legal professionals. In the recent past there have been many initiatives aimed at removing lawyers' monopolies in areas such as domestic conveyancing and will drafting. Despite the erosion of lawyers' monopolies (see 6.4.3), lawyers remain professionals.

6.1.2 **What is a legal professional?**

In the widest sense, this includes:

- judges at all levels (although magistrates are said to be 'laypeople', so not practising lawyers);
- solicitors and barristers, who are qualified lawyers entitled to practise law by offering their advice professionally;
- paralegals, trainee solicitors, and pupil barristers, none of whom have yet qualified to offer their services; and
- academic lawyers, who write about or teach the law.

Traditionally, the legal profession in England & Wales has been made up predominantly of solicitors and barristers, both of whom exhibit the traits of a profession. They are centrally organised and regulated—solicitors by the Solicitors Regulation Authority (SRA), and barristers by the Bar Standards Board (BSB). Each body places substantial emphasis on high standards of training and qualification, and on professional ethics (which we examine at 6.3.4). Both carry out statutorily defined[3] areas of work such as litigation and representing clients in court.

Other legal services providers, such as legal executives, patent attorneys, and trade mark attorneys, are also regulated by their own regulatory bodies. However, this chapter focuses on the two main branches of the profession.

Over time, changes have impacted upon the work of both professions, such as solicitors getting rights of audience in superior courts (see Chapter 3 in relation to the court system),

---

[3] Legal Services Act 2007, s. 12.

and the opening up of traditional solicitors' monopolies (such as domestic conveyancing and the drafting of wills) to non-lawyers. Arguably the biggest change has occurred recently, as a result of the Legal Services Act 2007. We examine these changes at 6.4.

Although it is perhaps artificial to create an exhaustive list of legal services, a lawyer will provide some or all of the following legal services. The first group lists legal services which are 'reserved activities'. These must be undertaken by a qualified lawyer under the Legal Services Act:[4]

- advocacy in court;
- administration of oaths;
- the conduct of litigation;
- handling probate matters;
- notarial activities; and
- reserved instrument activities.

The second group contains examples of legal services which are not reserved activities. Historically, they were almost always provided by qualified lawyers; however, this monopoly is being eroded. Areas of practice that are not reserved include non-contentious (i.e. not involving litigation or advocacy) aspects of, among other areas:

- commercial law, including international trade (including contract drafting, competition law, and marketing agreements);
- corporate finance (including banking, debt finance and capital markets);
- corporate regulatory compliance (including company procedure, directors' duties, shareholders' rights, and mergers and acquisitions);
- domestic conveyancing;
- employment law (including workplace safety, redundancy, unfair and wrongful dismissal, and discrimination);
- environmental and planning law;
- family law (including non-contentious aspects of divorce, abuse, rights of children);
- financial services law (although advising on specific financial products is itself regulated);
- housing law (including eviction, housing benefit, and private and public sector lettings);
- immigration law (including asylum and deportation);
- insurance law (including claims handling, reinsurance, the Lloyd's market);
- media and intellectual property law (including licensing and media finance);
- professional negligence;
- tax compliance by individuals and businesses; and
- the legal aspects of new media and the internet.

[4] Legal Services Act 2007, s. 12.

As you can see, legal practice involves a vast range of disciplines. Yet beyond this, some lawyers' work is non-legal, for example advising on the merits of transactions, acting as 'wise counsel' to clients, etc. In addition, many non-lawyers, such as licensed conveyancers, accountants, Citizens Advice Bureaux, Legal Advice Centres, etc., provide legal services, including some of the 'legal' services identified above.

At 6.4 we look at the continuing changes to the regulation and character of the legal profession and its work: the nature of lawyers' work, the structure of the profession, and those permitted to undertake work formerly the sole preserve of solicitors and barristers, are all changing.

6.2 The importance of legal services

We have already noted the importance of access to justice. 'Justice' should be seen in the widest sense: not only enforcing rights but also establishing rights, obligations, and relationships within the legal framework adopted by society.

Because they concern people's rights, obligations, and freedoms, the legal services that assist individuals' access to justice are qualitatively different from other services. Over the years, a mystique has built up around them—in popular culture the law provides powerful drama derived from its traditions and significance; countless novels and films feature lawyers as role models, heroes, or villains.

The legal profession has also developed a mixed reputation outside legal circles: it can be expensive to use the law, and lawyers' fees are an obvious (if often unjustified) target. The press are quick to make generalisations on the rare occasions that lawyers are found to be guilty of breaches of ethics. Also, what for some may epitomise the gravitas of a profession, may appear to others (rightly or wrongly) arcane or insular: the complexity of the law, professional traditions, even the architecture of the Inns of Court.

However, the fact remains that a healthy legal profession providing accessible legal services is vital to the Rule of Law and to the wider economy. This is what we shall explore in this section.

6.2.1 Lawyers and the Rule of Law

In Chapter 1 we saw that a key factor in entrenching the Rule of Law was the ability of the individual (including legal persons like companies) to access justice effectively. Lord Bingham's definition included: 'Means must be provided for resolving, without excessive cost or delay, civil disputes which the parties cannot resolve themselves.' In a study undertaken by the World Justice Project, the UK ranked 11th in access to civil justice, with a 72% score using their methodology,[5] Norway ranked 1st with 82%, and the US ranked 22nd with 65%. For criminal justice the UK ranked 11th with 75%, Finland 1st with 87%, and the US 26th with 65%.

Recent history has shown that the winds of change that have blown through the wider economy, in the shape of market forces, have also impacted on the legal profession. While this has created significant challenges, it must also be hoped that, in opening up the profession,

---

[5] World Justice Project, *Rule of Law Index 2012–2013*, http://worldjusticeproject.org.

it will allow non-lawyers to understand a little more the importance of lawyers. A healthy legal profession is very important in the functioning of a modern state.

We saw in Chapter 1 that anarchy is undesirable for anyone who wants a stable framework within which to live their lives. Societies need rules. The daily actions and rights of individuals and businesses are governed and regulated by the law. It follows that anyone acting within a society needs to know what those rules are. In a mature society, legal rules are necessarily detailed and very carefully formulated; we have seen in Chapter 2 that the law is extensive, varied, and frequently complex. Laws are often difficult to find and interpret.

Consider, by analogy, the rules of a sport. Football has something called 'the Laws of the Game'. There are 17 rules, and most football players know most of these rules. However, the detail of the rules is set out in a book occupying 50 pages. Not many footballers would profess to an intimate understanding of everything written in that book. In a modern society, 'the rules of the game' are not 50 pages long. A visit to a law library will reveal how long are 'the rules of the game' in England & Wales. Whole walls are filled with so-called black letter law, namely simply the statutes, statutory instruments, and law reports, as well as commentary on those sources. (In Chapter 8 we discuss the role of paper legal resources in a digital world.)

The stakes are higher in law than in football. In civil law, there could be billions at stake. For most people, if they are presented with a claim for £1,000, this is a major issue. A convicted criminal might be sentenced to decades of incarceration. In international law, people's lives, and the fate of whole countries is in the balance.

Some areas of law are familiar to most people and do not require legal advice. For instance, most people know that if they drive at over 70mph on a UK motorway, they are committing an offence. But in many other areas, people require expert help. The lawyer is this expert.

Example
Why people need lawyers

Imagine you are a newspaper editor. You have found out that a prominent MP, Norbert Samm, is making money from operating a pensions scam via a company. You think it is important that you expose this potentially illegal conduct by a public servant. You also need to sell newspapers, and the headline, 'MP Samm's Pension Scam' would certainly increase the paper's circulation.

Which areas of law might be relevant? How much time would it take to research them? Could you understand all the nuances while doing your normal day's work? What if you get something wrong?

We can see from this relatively simple example that some legal rules need a professional to find, interpret, and enforce them.

Thus lawyers are important because they assist in maintaining the stable framework and Rule of Law by providing individuals and businesses with access to justice. The lawyer will know where to take the argument, to which court or tribunal. She will be able to tell the client whether it is worth spending any money to argue his case, or whether instead it is a lost cause.

At a more pragmatic level, lawyers can provide a valuable expert service by interpreting and applying the law to assist individuals and businesses in maintaining rights, complying with regulation, creating legal relationships, and protecting property, etc. A lawyer will know where to look to find the relevant rules (or 'law'); the lawyer will know which issues are open to interpretation, and what the best arguments are for the client.

6.2.2 **Lawyers and the economy**

Kenneth Clarke, who, among many other positions, has held the office of Secretary of State for Justice, stated in 2011: 'The UK may no longer be able to boast it is the workshop of the world, but the UK can be a lawyer to the world.'[6]

Legal services contribute significantly to the UK economy, generating £24.7 billion[7] (or 1.8% of the UK's GDP[8]) in 2011. The profits of the 100 largest law firms together amount to around £4 billion. Around £2 billion is spent on legal aid by the government each year, and a similar figure is generated through the export of legal services. Law firms therefore make a significant contribution to the country's economy.

6.3 **The legal profession in England & Wales**

6.3.1 **History and structure**

The legal profession has changed beyond recognition since the Victorian era. Charles Dickens wrote in *Bleak House*: 'Mr. Vholes's chambers are on so small a scale that one clerk can open the door without getting off his stool, while the other who elbows him at the same desk has equal facilities for poking the fire'. He wrote of an office, 'blending with the smell of must and dust, the fretting of parchment forms and skins in greasy drawers'.[9] Modern multinational law firms are a world away from this cramped, stuffy picture of a bygone age. They operate from elegant space-age glass towers, and their websites proclaim worldwide practices offering one-stop legal services for huge corporate and banking clients.

England & Wales is one of only three jurisdictions that have a divided legal profession. Solicitors have traditionally constituted only one branch of the legal profession; barristers (collectively, 'the Bar') form the other. This is a historic division in the profession, and has been likened to the division between general practitioners and specialist doctors in medicine. This analogy is increasingly inaccurate as more solicitors specialise in a particular field of law or take up rights of audience in courts.

The two branches of the profession are organised separately. The General Council of the Bar—the Bar Council—is the governing body for the Bar, and barristers are regulated by the BSB. The Law Society represents the interests of solicitors, and the SRA regulates their conduct. Both barristers and solicitors have detailed Codes of Conduct (see 6.3.4). For all branches of the legal profession (including legal executives, patent and trade mark attorneys, etc.) the regulatory bodies are overseen by the Legal Services Board under the Legal Services Act 2007.[10]

6.3.2 **Barristers**

The circuit courts historically travelled around the country to dispense justice (see 'The development of the common law' at 2.4.2), accompanied by a retinue of lawyers, to act for those

---

[6] Kenneth Clarke MP, speech at CityUK Future Litigation event, 14 September 2011.

[7] Office of National Statistics.

[8] 'Profits of UK law firms increase despite global fee income slowdown', *TheCityUK*, 10 February 2011.

[9] Charles Dickens, *Bleak House* (1852–3) (Wordsworth Editions Ltd, 1993), p. 626.

[10] Legal Services Act 2007, s. 2 and Sch. 1.

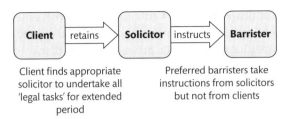

Figure 6.1 Roles of solicitors and barristers

who needed representation. These lawyers evolved into barristers, and were generally drawn from the same class and background as judges. Most judges were drawn from their ranks.

Traditionally, the Bar was viewed as the senior branch of the profession, both for its historic roots and because almost all the senior judges were appointed from barristers. 'The Bar', incidentally, is derived from a physical bar that separated the public (including solicitors) from those in the 'well' of the court—that is, the barristers and judges.

The Bar is comparatively small—there are nearly 10,000 practising barristers, with the majority based in London, compared with over 127,000[11] practising solicitors. Barristers operate as consultants, offering specialised services as advocates in court and giving opinions and advice on specific areas of law. Clients do not normally go directly to barristers (although this situation is changing—see 6.4.4); rather it is the solicitor who instructs 'counsel', as lawyers usually call barristers (see Figure 6.1).

Until 1990, only barristers were entitled to appear in the superior courts (the High Court, the Court of Appeal, and the Supreme Court) and, for most purposes, the Crown Courts. Now, rights of audience—as the right to appear in court as an advocate is known—depend instead only on ability and qualification as an advocate.

Unlike solicitors, barristers are not permitted to enter into a professional partnership with other barristers. Instead, they are members of Chambers, a form of association which is less formal than a partnership and which provides, among other things, for the sharing of office expenses and other resources with fellow barristers. Practising barristers have to be members of one of the four Inns of Court: Lincoln's Inn, the Inner Temple, the Middle Temple, and Gray's Inn.[12] Each Inn's main function is to maintain a collegiate framework for the Bar, and foster legal education and standards of professional conduct. In order to qualify, a barrister has to be 'called to the Bar' by one of the Inns.

6.3.3 Solicitors

Originally, solicitors were court officers (called 'attorneys'), who helped their clients bring their case before the local courts. Their representative role was normally confined to local courts. It was useful for litigants to engage a solicitor to find the appropriate barrister. Over the centuries this crystallised into the rule that an attorney did not have rights of audience before a court, while a barrister did. In London, lawyers performing a mainly clerical role 'solicited'

---

[11] SRA Statistics, October 2012.

[12] Formally, the Honourable Society of Lincoln's Inn, the Honourable Society of the Inner Temple, the Honourable Society of the Middle Temple, and the Honourable Society of Gray's Inn.

actions in the Court of Chancery. In 1831 solicitors and attorneys merged and received a Royal Charter. The Law Society (which represents solicitors) was created in 1845.

Historically, there was a formal distinction between the roles of solicitors and barristers, the solicitors' role being to advise the client and to instruct a barrister, if advocacy was necessary on behalf of the client (as in Figure 6.1). In addition, the work of most solicitors was more general than that of many barristers. This is still the most common situation—a solicitor is the first point of contact for most individuals or organisations seeking legal advice. Solicitors may have to deal with a wide variety of problems; however, they do increasingly specialise in particular areas of legal work, and the formal distinction between the roles of solicitors and barristers is not as clear cut as it used to be (see 6.4.4).

Unlike barristers, solicitors are entitled to practise in partnership with other solicitors. Most of them do this, although sole practitioners still make up almost half of the total number of firms.

The structure and size of the solicitors' profession in England & Wales can be seen from the following statistics, released by the Law Society.[13] Of around 169,000 qualified solicitors,[14] approximately 127,000 have practising certificates (around 42,000 solicitors do not practise). There are just over 10,000 law firms. Every year roughly 5,000 people begin training contracts and 8,500 new solicitors qualify.

Chapter 15 examines the range of firms in which solicitors work. Not only is the solicitors' profession distributed among many different types of firm, it is also changing rapidly in composition. An increasing proportion of lawyers do not work for a firm, but directly 'in house', for example exclusively for a large company or for the government, as an employee of that entity. The number of solicitors employed outside private practice has increased by 10% in the decade 2000–10.

In the period 2000–11, the number of women practising as solicitors went up by nearly 80% (although their average age is much lower than their male counterparts, suggesting that the profession may not yet uniformly accommodate women seeking to balance the pressures of a career in practice with the demands of family life.)

Figure 6.2 shows the proportion of solicitors in 2011 in each of these important groups. It also shows the proportion from 2000, to illustrate how quickly the profession is changing its composition. At 6.4.4 we examine the considerable structural changes also occurring in the delivery of legal services.

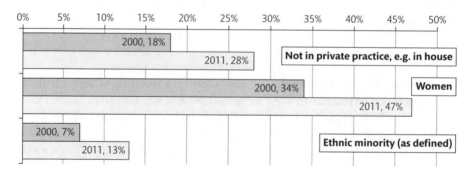

Figure 6.2 The changing social composition of the solicitors' profession

[13] Law Society, *Annual Statistical Report 2011*.   [14] SRA Statistics, October 2012.

6.3.4 **The importance of ethics**

At 1.2 we touched on the important but occasionally uneasy relationship between law and morality. The ethics of any profession are of vital importance. But because of the sensitive relationship between law and morality, when considering legal services, ethics assume an even more acute role. Lawyers are intimately involved with some of the most important decisions people make in their lives and they have to confront many interesting ethical challenges. Almost all activities carried out by lawyers have ethical implications. The legal profession is special not merely because (like other professions) it demands probity from its members, but also because its work is *about* probity. So, just as doctors adhere to ethical codes (e.g. the 'four principles', and the Hippocratic Oath, to practise honestly and ethically), lawyers also have comprehensive rules about ethical behaviour.

There is plenty of cynicism about lawyers, especially in the tabloid press, but the vast majority do adhere to the very high ethical standards which the profession sets itself. A lawyer's probity and competence will have a critical impact on a client, for example:

- Will the client succeed in business deals?
- Will the client be able to have contact with his children?
- Can the client avoid going to prison?
- Will the client receive compensation for her injuries?

The lawyer is often in a position of great power: entrusted with enormous sums of money and with confidential information about the most important and delicate aspects of people's lives. This brings great responsibility.

The practising lawyer owes ethical obligations not only to the client, but also to the court, and to other lawyers. Because lawyers are among the custodians of the Rule of Law, they also owe less formal ethical obligations to the world at large. Lawyers earn their living by acting for clients. Ethical issues can arise over whether you as a lawyer are willing or able to act for a specific client. Paedophiles, rapists, fraudsters, traffickers, terrorists, torturers, and murderers all look for lawyers to represent them.

 Essential debate

Would you act?

Imagine you are a solicitor specialising in criminal law. A potential client comes to see you, in your capacity as an advocate. He asks you to appear for him in court. He has been charged with rape. He says that the woman consented. You instinctively don't believe him.

Would you represent him, notwithstanding your suspicions, or would you refuse to act?

As a result of the critical nature of ethics in a lawyer's role, the lawyer must abide by an extensive rule book—the SRA Handbook runs to 650 pages, and the BSB Code of Conduct is 207 pages long. These provide for disciplinary action to be taken against any member of the profession who does not comply.

Lawyers in both professions generally take complaints and ethics very seriously, but if clients are unhappy with their lawyer they will normally complain first to the firm or barrister concerned. In the event that this does not produce the required result, or is inappropriate, the client can then contact the Legal Ombudsman who will consider the complaint. If the lawyer or firm is in breach of professional rules, the case is then referred to the SRA or BSB as appropriate.

This introduction to the legal profession does not require a full discussion of these rules, but a list of the key responsibilities provides a flavour of the ethically intensive nature of legal practice:

- a duty to act in the client's best interests (even if the effect is to reduce your own fees, because it is not in the client's interests to proceed);
- a duty to keep a client's affairs confidential (think of the sensitivity of the personal, commercial, or financial information lawyers will keep in relation to their clients); and
- a duty not to deceive the court or the other side (e.g. if your client tells you half way through a trial that he is guilty after all).

These duties often clash with each other, and lawyers need a strong grasp of the detail and spirit of the rules by which they operate.

6.4 The changing face of the legal profession within society

The size and organisation of the solicitors' profession has changed out of all recognition in recent decades, and probably not even Charles Dickens could have imagined the changes which have produced the typical law firm (if there is one) of the 21st century. Why?

Law does not exist in a bubble. Radical changes affecting lawyers and the legal system today are a reflection of wider changes in society and politics. While it is not the role of this book to explore theories of social and political evolution, we will explore very general themes in the progression of politics and society, and at each stage examine how these changes have affected the development of the legal profession. We also highlight reforms in the legal system where they illuminate changes within the profession. You may find it helpful to refer to Figure 6.3 as an overview while reading this section.

6.4.1 Early development

Society

Western societies developed over time into highly organised but often very stratified and partitioned states. England & Wales, for instance, was organised from before the Norman conquest (1066) on decentralised, 'feudal' lines, where national institutions were of limited importance and function. Power and bureaucracy became centralised over many centuries. By the Elizabethan era (1558–1603), the state began to assume a slightly more influential role, and legislation such as the Poor Laws evidenced an admission that the state did have a narrow role to play in subjects' lives.

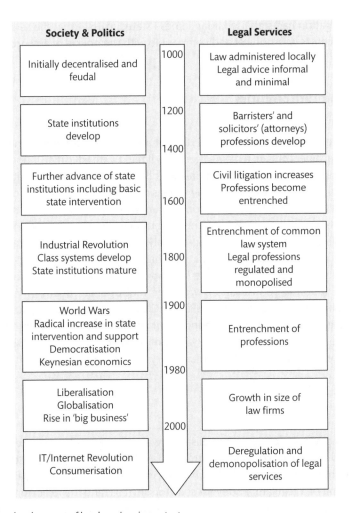

Figure 6.3 The development of legal services in context

Legal services

While the litigation of criminal matters had long been established (at least at a local level), civil litigation (particularly in London) began to boom in the 16th century, and the court system matured into the prototype of the system we have today (see Chapter 2). Between 1500 and 1600 the central civil courts (in those days called the Court of Common Pleas and the King's Bench) saw a sixfold increase in litigation.[15] At roughly the same time the solicitors' profession crystallised out of the abundance of court clerical workers.

By the death of Elizabeth I in 1603, the machinery of law was becoming institution-alised, and the two professions entrenched. Despite the political upheavals of the 17th century (with civil war, the Commonwealth, and then the 'Glorious Revolution'), the court

---

[15] C. W. Brooks, *Pettifoggers and Vipers of the Commonwealth: The 'Lower Branch' of the Legal Profession in Early Modern England* (Cambridge: CUP, 1986), p. 360.

system and litigation had stabilised. King James I stated in 1614 that the settlement of disputes outside courts was 'not just and compatible with the policie of any orderly or stayed government'.[16]

6.4.2 **18th and 19th centuries**

Society

The industrial revolution of the 18th and 19th centuries created clear and often inflexible class systems. The machinery of state remained generally limited, with education, poor relief, etc. provided on a piecemeal basis by local communities. Political systems and state institutions became more organised to reflect their sporadically increasing roles, for example in providing prisons, customs, minimal levels of relief for the poor, and rudimentary industrial safety regulation.

Early institutions (like local government, government departments, courts, and professional bodies) were slowly put on a progressively more formal footing. Gradually central taxation replaced more local finance that had harked back to feudal times. For instance, the Home Office was created in 1782; the Metropolitan Police service was formed in 1829; and the first London-wide institutions were the Metropolitan Board of Works in 1855, and the London County Council in 1889. The Civil Service was largely ad hoc until the 1854 *Northcote-Trevelyan Report* pronounced it inadequate for the efficient functioning of a modern state. It is estimated that there were only 8,000 civil servants in 1832, and 14,000 in 1898.[17] Only incrementally did the machinery of the state resemble what we take for granted today.

Legal services

In the law this gradual process of formalisation was reflected by the requirement for legal practitioners to be subject to regulated admission, in the Attorneys and Solicitors Act 1728. A solicitors' monopoly was established in conveyancing in 1804.[18] This formalisation continued with the creation of a regulatory body for solicitors in 1831, and the Judicature Acts 1873–5, which reorganised and consolidated the court system (see 'Amalgamation of courts of common law and equity' at 2.4.2).

6.4.3 **1900 to 1979**

Society

The 20th century saw state intervention in society increasing, mainly as a result of the two World Wars. Populations required welfare and health. The civil service numbered only around 50,000 in 1910, rising to 221,000 at the end of World War I in 1918,[19] over a million during

---

[16] King James I Royal Proclamation, 4 February 1614, as quoted in J. F. Larkin and P. L. Hughes (eds.), *Stuart Royal Proclamations* (Oxford: Clarendon Press, 1973).

[17] Source: Imperial Calendars, interpreted by Oliver Morley in 'Did we Rule the Empire with 4000 Civil Servants?', National Archives blog, 1 August 2012, http://blog.nationalarchives.gov.uk.

[18] Stamp Act 1804.

[19] *Mandate and Departmental Returns*, Civil Service Statistics, http://www.civilservice.gov.uk/about/facts/statistics.

World War II, and a post-war peak of 733,800 in 1977.[20] Ruling classes became aware of the moral and political need to support and involve the middle and working classes. Institutions which had developed in the previous century became entrenched and grew to reflect larger populations and bigger, more active states.

The field of economics became ever more important in society and politics. Many economists felt that, while the private sector was very effective at generating wealth, some of the decisions made by the sector as a whole created inefficiencies at a national level. The most famous of these economists was John Maynard Keynes (see also 14.2.2). By the 1950s largely Keynesian theories of economics became the default in most Western economies. Political theorists write about a 'Post-War Consensus'. In Continental Europe this entailed most states adhering to a social democratic model which, in the context of the UK, according to Dennis Kavanagh,[21] was epitomised by five 'planks':

- a commitment to full employment;
- promotion and consultation of trade unions by government;
- a mixed economy, with a significant role for state ownership of utilities and central planning (including restrictive state controls within the financial sector);
- a strong and comprehensive welfare state including a 'cradle to the grave' National Health Service; and
- a belief that government had a role in ensuring social equality.

As a consequence political systems in many countries 'froze' into a left/right division,[22] but based on these social democratic principles. In the UK, both Labour and the Conservatives agreed on these tenets, particularly when faced with the realities of operating the levers of power.

While most of Europe reaped the rewards of post-war reconstruction, the UK was hobbled by industrial unrest and economic decline. By the mid-1970s, it was possible to argue that the country was 'ungovernable'. The February 1974 General Election epitomised the breakdown, as the Prime Minister, Edward Heath, asked 'Who governs Britain?' (after that election, it was not him). There was a sense that Britain and its institutions had become so complacent, its institutions so ossified, that it could not function effectively, either politically or economically. The 'Winter of Discontent' of 1978–9 was the culmination of this process, as the country was crippled by a series of strikes. Something had to change. At 6.4.4 we describe what happened.

Legal services

This entrenchment was echoed by the monopolies within the law. Only solicitors and barristers could practise law. Only barristers had rights of audience in the courts. Under the

---

[20] Rodney Lowe, *The Official History of the British Civil Service: Reforming the Civil Service, Volume I: The Fulton Years, 1966-81* (Government Official History Series, Routledge, 2011).

[21] Dennis Kavanagh, *Thatcherism and British Politics: The End of Consensus?* (Oxford: OUP, 1987).

[22] As expressed in Seymour Martin Lipset and Stein Rokkan (eds.), *Party Systems and Voter Alignments* (New York Free Press, 1967).

Solicitors Act 1974[23] unqualified persons were prohibited from acting as solicitors, commencing litigation, or preparing documents relating to probate (handling the administration of a person's estate after their death). These monopolies were significant and long-standing, and were justified by the need to prevent fraud and maintain high standards of service and probity. Barristers' rights of audience in superior courts (now 'senior courts'—see 3.1.3) had been entrenched since the Bar emerged in the 12th century.

In this period, a client would use a very rigid mechanism to obtain legal advice. If a client already had a reliable solicitor, he would normally continue to employ that solicitor. If not, then he would research an appropriate solicitor, either by word of mouth, or by using published directories. Advertising was not permitted for the provision of legal services. The client would retain that solicitor, who would then, if necessary, instruct a barrister (usually a preferred counsel, with an established relationship with the solicitor's firm) for any expert advice or representation in a higher court. This traditional position is summarised in Figure 6.1.

A possible additional reason for this conservatism is the legal system itself. We have seen that the English legal system is a common law system, and that one criticism of it is that there is an inherent inertia which operates as a drag on the development of legal principles. The legal profession since the 19th century has arguably reflected this. The argument goes that lawyers, schooled in entrenched case law, become naturally conservative and resistant to change. These lawyers rose up the career ladder to manage their firms, with the effect that managers in the profession were arguably focused on maintaining the status quo, rather than embracing any changes developing within society and the wider economy.

Other professions also became entrenched by monopolistic or anti-competitive regulation. Accountants, engineers, and architects were prime examples. In 2001, the Office of Fair Trading (OFT) investigated the regulation and deregulation of professions in the UK and around the world. It highlighted certain restrictions which were characteristic of the traditional regulation of professions:

- entry restrictions (i.e. the requirement for professionals to have undergone a formal professional training course like the Legal Practice Course or the Bar Professional Training Course);
- price regulation;
- the prohibition of certain business structures (e.g. not allowing limited liability for professions);
- prohibition of joint practices combining more than one profession (e.g. lawyers and accountants); and
- restrictions on advertising, placing emphasis on word of mouth recommendation.[24]

The OFT's survey concluded that in most professions, many of these restrictions were generally negative in their effect on quality of service. Since that report, things have moved on.

---

[23] Solicitors Act 1974, s. 21.

[24] Office of Fair Trading, *Competition in Professions—A Report by the Director General of Fair Trading* (March 2001, OFT328).

6.4.4 **The changing world**

Society

Here, we focus on two (linked) themes: the growth in very large companies, and the loosening up of key features of the Post-War Consensus mentioned at 6.4.3.

Very large companies became ever more important to Western economies. Many developments came together to encourage this expansion:

- globalisation of markets as transport and information improved;
- liberalisation of stock markets allowing a surge in demand for publicly tradable shares, and the rise in investment opportunities (e.g. taking over rivals);
- increased relevance of economies of scale in relation to infrastructure (e.g. information technology, buildings, and plant), and employment;
- greater ability of larger companies to meet regulatory requirements;
- the need to meet manufacturing challenges from the Far East (most particularly, in the 1980s and 1990s, Japan);
- expansion of companies' portfolios horizontally (i.e. by taking over or merging with rivals) and vertically (i.e. by expansion into new fields); and
- lowering of taxes (particularly in the US) to encourage the growth of businesses and investment.

Chapter 14 discusses the economics behind these market changes in more detail.

The UK was the first major Western economy to embrace an alternative to social democracy, most emphatically during the administrations of Prime Minister Margaret Thatcher in the period 1979–90. Whether 'Thatcherism' was, from the start, a conscious or planned programme of national transformation, is the subject of whole books. Suffice it to say that a decisive victory for the Thatcher government, in the 1987 General Election, served as proof that a significant number of voters had accepted that state intervention, union involvement, and other aspects of the Post-War Consensus were over.

They were replaced by 'free market' or 'laissez faire' principles (see 14.2.5). Free market theorists (such as Milton Friedman and Freidrich Hayek[25]) believed that a market would find its own equilibrium, most typically through the mechanisms of supply and demand rather than national planning. One means by which services can be provided efficiently (according to free market theories) is by removing barriers to entry into markets. Increased competition forces existing suppliers to reduce prices and/or improve quality. The counter-argument is that the free market forces most actors to prioritise short-term gains over longer-term investment and quality.

Taking Kavanagh's five planks in turn, we can examine the breaking down of the Post-War Consensus:

- A commitment to full employment: this was abandoned as impracticable in the mid-1970s.
- Promotion and consultation of trade unions by government: trade unions were excluded from decision-making, and their activities progressively regulated, in the early years of

---

[25] Particularly in Friedrich Hayek, *The Road to Serfdom* (London: Routledge, 1944).

the Thatcher administrations (1979–90)—the angry, and often violent, miners' strike of 1984–5 being the key showdown in this battle.

- A mixed economy, with a significant role for state ownership of utilities and central planning: the balance between state and private ownership of utilities was significantly tilted in favour of 'private' by the progressive privatisation of utilities in the 1980s, opening these utilities up to market investment and market pressures.

- A strong and comprehensive welfare state including a 'cradle to the grave' National Health Service: this has remained largely intact, although the NHS has gradually been permitted to subcontract aspects of its service to private companies.

- A belief that government has a role in ensuring social equality: this has been gradually replaced by a commitment instead to creating the environment for equality of opportunity.

The theme, then, is the opening up—or liberalisation—of the economy to the involvement of private institutions and the removal of institutional and economic restrictions on participation. Successive governments sought to reduce inefficiencies based on procedure and regulation, and to modernise the machinery of state, with an emphasis on transparency where possible. Roles hitherto the preserve of the state were contracted out to private service providers, such as service industries providing the government with IT, etc. As of 1999, the civil service had shrunk to 460,000.[26] Over 2 million houses owned by local authorities were sold off to their tenants between 1980 and 1995 under 'Right to Buy' schemes (Housing Act 1980), again reflecting a wish to reduce the role of public ownership and emphasise the economic incentives of private ownership. In the UK there is an unusually high level of home ownership (although many homes are in fact mortgaged to financial institutions).

The information and communications technology revolution has had a major impact on both businesses and consumers over the past 20 years. The growth of internet-based commerce is pervading all parts of the economy. Information is readily available to consumers and businesses at all levels, and decision-making is thus more informed. In many areas this has led to increased competition and greater consumer choice.

We can see the results of these changes today, with highly active financial markets, an often wide-ranging array of choices for basic services and utilities, and a consumer-led market economy. Market transparency and information transparency have become increasingly important to allow businesses and consumers to make informed choices. In turn, those more traditional professions that advise businesses and consumers have had to respond and adapt their services.

Legal services

Any changes to the profession must be seen not only in the wider context of society, but also in the context of the law as a whole. This liberalisation process has been mirrored by parallel changes in both the efficiency of the legal system and the provision of legal services; changes

---

[26] *Civil Service Statistics 1999*, http://webarchive.nationalarchives.gov.uk.

which overlap and cross-fertilise. The courts of England & Wales and their procedure have been radically overhauled. A summary of these changes is as follows:

- The Civil Procedure Rules 1998 (the Woolf Reforms) revolutionised the way civil claims were pursued in courts. Reflecting attempts to reduce red tape in society as a whole, their express aims included speeding up pre-trial procedure and reducing the cost of litigation.

- The Constitutional Reform Act 2005 removed archaic overlaps between the judiciary, the legislature, and the executive (see Chapters 1 and 5), and created the Supreme Court of the UK. Its procedures are more open than those of its predecessor, the Appellate Committee of the House of Lords.

- A Ministry of Justice was created, removing responsibility for the judiciary from the Lord Chancellor's Department.

- Her Majesty's Courts and Tribunals Service brought together the administration of all courts and most tribunals under one umbrella.

So the legal *system* is more open and clearly defined than before. But what have these wider changes meant for the legal *profession*?

There have been two key changes in delivery of the law and legal services, roughly in parallel with the changes in society and politics described at 6.4.4.

First, large law firms have mushroomed in size since the 1980s. The advantages of scale in exploiting IT, training, marketing, and premises have largely mirrored those available to large companies in mainstream industries. As clients grew, so did the need for large (often international) law firms that could cope with the demands of huge multinational clients, for example in the growth area of corporate finance. Mergers among law firms are very common, often for similar reasons as in the mainstream economy, such as diversification or the strengthening of market share. In 1986, the Law Society allowed its members to advertise directly to the public, following the more market-driven pressures of the economy as a whole. The largest law firms in the UK employ thousands of lawyers, with even more support staff. These trends continue and developments in IT and marketing are adopted by smaller firms as they also grow.

Second, the trend to liberalisation has been echoed in the legal profession. The Courts and Legal Services Act 1990, the Access to Justice Act 1999, and the Legal Services Act 2007 have changed the landscape of legal services (see Table 6.1). Indeed it is arguable that they created a concept of 'providers of legal services', built around the existing core legal profession. To give a flavour of the context of these statutes, the Courts and Legal Services Act 1990 has a stated objective:[27]

> The general objective ... is the development of legal services in England and Wales (and in particular the development of advocacy, litigation, conveyancing and probate services) by making provision for new or better ways of providing such services and a wider choice of persons providing them, while maintaining the proper and efficient administration of justice.

---

[27] Courts and Legal Services Act 1990, s. 17.

Table 6.1 Summary of reforms to legal services

Solicitors Act 1974	Puts existing solicitors' monopolies on a formal footing.
Administration of Justice Act 1985[28]	Breaks solicitors' monopoly in conveyancing.
1986	Law Society permits solicitors to advertise their services to the general public.
Courts and Legal Services Act 1990	Rationalises civil courts. Allows solicitors higher rights of audience.
Access to Justice Act 1999	Increases flexibility on funding access to law. Allows other professions the right to litigate.
2004	Bar Council permits barristers to accept direct instructions from the public (rather than via a solicitor) ('public access').
Legal Services Act 2007	Redefines professional bodies approved to authorise several aspects of key legal work (e.g. trade mark and patent attorneys, licensed conveyancers, legal executives, law costs draftsmen). Allows alternative business structures (ABS) for lawyers, i.e. beyond partnerships, including multi-disciplinary practices where lawyers and non-lawyers (e.g. accountants) are in partnership.

Remember that this statute was not drafted in isolation. Milton Friedman (the intellectual figurehead of free market capitalism) stated:

> So that the record of history is absolutely crystal clear, that there is no alternative way so far discovered of improving the lot of the ordinary people that can hold a candle to the productive activities that are unleashed by the free-enterprise system.[29]

Table 6.1 summarises the key relevant statutes in this transformation, and these trends are drawn out by Figure 6.4.

All of these regulatory changes have the aim of liberalising the provision of legal services and making access to justice more transparent. The most far reaching is the Legal Services Act 2007, which implemented elements of the Clementi Report of 2004.[30] The Act has stated objectives, which are worth repeating:

(a) protecting and promoting the public interest;

(b) supporting the constitutional principle of the rule of law;

(c) improving access to justice;

(d) protecting and promoting the interests of consumers;

(e) promoting competition in the provision of services ...;

(f) encouraging an independent, strong, diverse and effective legal profession;

(g) increasing public understanding of the citizen's legal rights and duties;

(h) promoting and maintaining adherence to the professional principles.

[28] Administration of Justice Act 1985, Pt II.   [29] Milton Friedman, interview, 1979.

[30] Sir David Clementi, *Review of the Regulatory Framework for Legal Services in England and Wales—Final Report* (TSO, 2004).

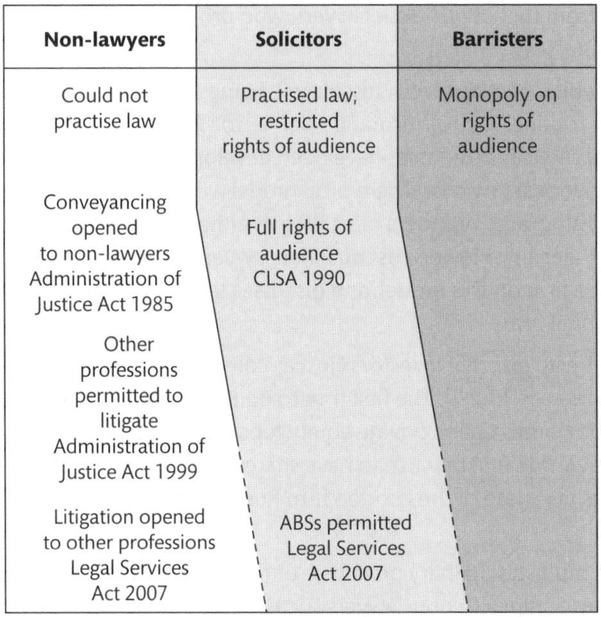

Non-lawyers	Solicitors	Barristers
Could not practise law	Practised law; restricted rights of audience	Monopoly on rights of audience
Conveyancing opened to non-lawyers Administration of Justice Act 1985	Full rights of audience CLSA 1990	
Other professions permitted to litigate Administration of Justice Act 1999		
Litigation opened to other professions Legal Services Act 2007	ABSs permitted Legal Services Act 2007	

Figure 6.4 Development of the new legal regulatory framework—summary

All of these objectives echo key themes in this chapter.

The Act put regulation of all branches of the profession on a more consistent footing, promoting openness to client complaints, among many other benefits. For solicitors, though, the other significant change was permitting new ways of organising their businesses. This reflects the drive, in a market-led world, for businesses, including legal businesses, to appeal to consumers, and to offer them a comprehensible choice. Any business, legal or not, must respond to such pressures. This freeing up of regulation has led to the provision of legal services being marketed in more varied and entrepreneurial ways:

First, ABSs were permitted, allowing non-lawyers to manage or own law firms. By November 2012, only 40 ABS authorisations had occurred,[31] although it is clear more will follow. Examples of ABSs include:

- 'Tesco law'. The best publicised outcome of these changes has been the concept of so-called 'Tesco law', the provision of legal services to the public by organisations that have traditionally provided non-legal services. The Co-op, for instance, historically provided retail services then, like a number of retailers, it expanded into banking and financial services. It now offers legal services to its customers. One of its core businesses, funeral services, has a natural fit with certain legal services, including advice on probate law, which deals with a person's assets on death. The offer to consumers is a combination of a trusted brand and value for money. Note that this mode of delivering legal services is

---

[31] SRA Register of Licensed Bodies (ABS), http://www.sra.org.uk/absregister.

very different from that of in-house lawyers, who provide legal advice exclusively *within* non-legal businesses.

- 'Factory law' (which overlaps with 'Tesco law'). Some areas of legal work can be comparatively routine, such as insurance claims, road traffic accident claims, and debt recovery. Legal services businesses have been developed to manage high volumes of these types of work at low cost. The typical model will have low numbers of qualified lawyers supervising large numbers of paralegals either in the UK or, increasingly, outsourced paralegals or lower-cost qualified lawyers based overseas. 15.1.9 examines 'Lawyers2You', a firm on this model, and discusses the threat which businesses like this pose to traditional firms.

- Law firms can invite external investors (just as companies can issue shares to people who are not directors—see 13.2.7). The first firm to do this was Knights, which has secured investment from James Caan's private equity fund. The Australian firm Slater & Gordon, which was the world's first practice to have shares listed on a stock exchange, is entering the fray with its purchase of the London firm Russell Jones and Walker for £53.8 million in April 2012.

- The advent of 'multi-disciplinary practices', or MDPs, an ABS in which lawyers can practise in partnership with non-lawyers such as accountants, with obvious economies of scale and efficiencies of service, especially for corporate clients.

Other reforms under the Legal Services Act 2007 have reinforced the liberalisation of legal services:

- The inception of legal disciplinary practices (LDPs) in which different types of lawyers, such as solicitors, barristers, and foreign lawyers, can enter into partnership. By October 2012, 484 LDPs had been registered with the SRA.

- The marketing of groups of local solicitors as networks, such as QualitySolicitors[32]— visit their website and you will be met with testimonials from customers (rather than clients) about the quality of service provided. Administrative intermediaries match the lawyer to the client. This is a very different business model from the traditional high-street law firm.

- The opening up of some reserved legal activities (see 6.1.2) to defined groups beyond solicitors and barristers, such as registered foreign and European lawyers, notaries, legal executives, licensed conveyancers, patent agents, trade mark agents, and law costs draftsmen.

- The marketing of barristers on a direct access basis, again through intermediaries. Stobart Barristers,[33] for instance, run by the Stobart Group (of transport fame) offers the public direct access to appropriate counsel.

A key word here is 'marketing'—the legal sector increasingly resembles other service industries, for example the financial services sector. For more on the impact of advertising and marketing on lawyers, see 15.1.4.

---

[32] http://www.qualitysolicitors.com.   [33] http://www.stobartbarristers.co.uk.

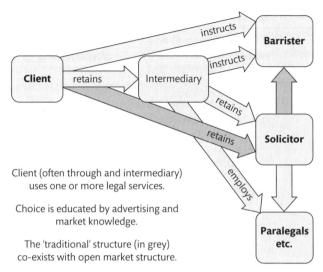

Figure 6.5 The developing legal market

So, does this mean 'The End of Lawyers?', a concept being discussed actively by academics?[34] Most probably not. It can be analysed, again, against the wider backdrop. Privatisation of utilities has not dispensed with the need for gas, electricity, water, or trains; they are merely provided in a different and, some would say, more efficient way. Equally, legal services have been liberalised. They are provided, still mainly by lawyers, in a different, and evolving, way. In Chapter 15 we discuss the challenges these changes are likely to present to lawyers of the future.

There is still a role for law firms in the traditional image (from high-street to City firms), especially in more complex contentious and commercial areas where the advice of an experienced and expert lawyer is essential; but increasingly they need to market and structure themselves imaginatively in response to the freeing up of the market. It is quite clear that law firms must adapt quickly or face an uncertain future.

Figure 6.5 is a simplified representation of the new open market structure for the provision of legal services. Take time to contrast it with Figure 6.2, the traditional model.

6.4.5 Arguments

Over the last few decades, governments and regulators have performed a difficult balancing act between freeing up lawyers to market efficiencies, and maintaining standards through tight regulation of lawyers' business practices.

There are arguments for, and against, the liberalisation of legal services. The balance of these arguments is clearly shifting as society becomes less entrenched in its structure. These arguments are summarised in Table 6.2.

[34] E.g. Richard Susskind, *The End of Lawyers?* (Oxford: OUP, 2008).

Table 6.2 Arguments for and against the liberalisation of legal services

	In favour of the traditional model	In favour of deregulated provision of legal services
Probity	Lawyers should feel able to be selective about the work that they do, and in decisions relating to ethics, their only concern should be integrity; profit should not be a factor. Multi-disciplinary practices in particular risk exposure to conflicts of interest.	Regulation will be more in line with other industries. A Legal Ombudsman takes initial legal complaints handling away from the professions, promoting probity in a more open way. A properly regulated service will prevent a drop in ethical standards.
Quality of service	Market pressures may force lawyers and their firms to 'cut corners' in the search for short term profit.	Specialised knowledge is often joined with a high degree of exclusivity, jargon, and impenetrability.
Cradle to grave service/one stop shop	A highly defined marketplace allowed people to know where to look for advice. Solicitors were the people you went to for legal advice: that was all they did.	ABSs allow law firms to employ non-lawyers, and non-law firms to employ lawyers, e.g. accountants and solicitors working together, or lawyers providing services to the public, working for banks in the high street (like the Co-op). Another alternative is solicitors and barristers working together in partnership. These structures prevent duplication of costs. The ideal is a 'one stop shop' for legal and related services.
Consumer focus	The established model of the law firm, though it has its problems, is very good at providing a tailored or personal service, with emphasis on strong bonds between solicitor and client, e.g. in the high street.	The express objectives of the Legal Services Act 2007 (s. 1) included improving access to justice and protecting and promoting the interests of consumers. The market will of necessity promote transparency and value for money.
Independence	An independent legal profession promotes democracy and liberty, by giving lawyers, and hence the law, special status.	There is no reason why liberties should be endangered by (for instance) changing business structures.

 ## Summary

- A legal system cannot be analysed in isolation from history or society, and neither can lawyers.
- Lawyers, whatever their formal role or job description, are vitally important to the maintenance of the Rule of Law. A legal profession must (in theory) provide access to high-quality legal advice when it is needed.
- The legal profession has largely developed as a reflection of wider trends in society and politics. Figure 6.3 summarises this process.

- Recent reforms have sought to improve market efficiency in the provision of legal services, also in the name of quality.
- At this point, these changes have yet to permeate the profession fully. Only time will tell whether the new freedoms are compatible with the integrity which is so important to the Rule of Law.

 ## Thought-provoking questions

1. Are legal services just like any other service?
2. Should legal services be regulated just like any other service?
3. Should all defendants, no matter how odious, have legal representation?
4. Is it only a matter of time before solicitors and barristers disappear?
5. Should the solicitors' and barristers' professions merge?

 ## Further reading

Office of Fair Trading, *Competition in Professions—A Report by the Director General of Fair Trading* (March 2001, OFT328)
—a report by a government department which symbolised a perceived need to identify restrictions within professions (including the legal profession) that prevented, restricted, or distorted competition to the detriment of consumers.

Sir David Clementi, *Review of the Regulatory Framework for Legal Services in England and Wales—Final Report*, (TSO, 2004)
—commissioned by the Department for Constitutional Affairs in 2003, the Clementi report triggered the Legal Services Act 2007. It contains discussion about the possible extent of legal services reform.

Richard Susskind, *The End of Lawyers?* (Oxford: OUP, 2008)
—this attention-grabbing question crystallises a series of issues identified by the author, which together present the challenges for the legal profession in the current environment. Susskind argues that the concept of 'legal work' is changing quickly, and that lawyers need to adapt equally fast.

World Justice Project, http://www.worldjusticeproject.org
—an organisation set up in 2006 by the American Bar Association to promote the Rule of Law, and to draw attention to examples of states exhibiting the presence or absence of these characteristics. In the context of this chapter there is extensive discussion and analysis of access to lawyers and justice.

 For the authors' reflections on the thought-provoking questions, additional self-test questions, podcasts offering a variety of perspectives on legal systems and skills, and a library of links to useful websites, visit the free Online Resource Centre *at* **http://www.oxfordtextbooks.co.uk/orc/slorach/.**

Part II

Legal Skills

The legal skills which law students are required to develop and demonstrate on undergraduate programmes are fundamental to the continued development of professional legal skills. It is therefore imperative both to develop these skills and to build foundations for the future in a structured manner.

This section is therefore designed to assist students to develop their own strategies to research, read, and understand law more effectively; to analyse and apply the law to solve legal problems; and to communicate legal concepts and solutions in writing and orally. It does so by demonstrating step by step approaches that students can employ both immediately, in their undergraduate studies, and also beyond, as professionals. The section also includes a number of demonstrations of how core legal skills are later employed in professional practice, to provide a wider understanding of the competencies required.

In accordance with accepted educational theory and practice, this part of the book seeks to engage students with its subject by showing them not only 'what' is good practice but also providing guidance on 'how' to develop good practice.

7

Reading and understanding law

 Learning objectives

After studying this chapter you should be able to:

- Appreciate that your approach to reading law will differ from your approach to reading in general.
- Develop your own practical strategies to help you to read law more effectively.
- Follow guidance to read and understand a statute, statutory instrument, and a case effectively.

Introduction

It used to be a rite of passage for a law student to walk into a law library for the first time and be overawed by the sheer volume of law and commentary on that law, all in books, some ancient, all beautifully bound and displayed, volume by volume, shelf by shelf. Now that these sources of law are available electronically, and physical law libraries are shrinking, this is an experience modern law students might miss. So before we begin, it is useful to reflect on the simple fact that there really is a huge amount of law. Chapters 2 to 3 examine the sources of this law in some detail.

After a moment's reflection, it is perhaps important also to consider that you will not be expected to read or understand all of this law at any stage in your legal career. This can often come as a surprise and slight disappointment to a non-lawyer, who might ask you a question about a speeding fine, divorce, and a company director's duties all in the same breath, and look puzzled when you cannot answer all three questions immediately without looking anything up. A lawyer knows that law is diverse, and it is also changing constantly. For that reason, it is usual for a lawyer to specialise, either in one particular area of law, or several related areas of law. It would be unusual, for example, for the same lawyer to be advising on a catastrophic injury claim one day and a stock market flotation the next. However, it is in fact at the beginning of your career, as a student (and later if you decide to go into the legal services industry, as a trainee), when you will be exposed to the most diversity in terms of the areas of law you will be expected to read and understand. You need, therefore, to hone your skills of reading and understanding law at an early stage in your legal career. If you decide to pursue a training contract these skills will become time critical (because, as Chapter 15 explains, you will charge clients based on the time you spend on their work).

Let's now consider how you can make the process of reading law as efficient and enjoyable as possible. We will then examine how we can make sure you understand what you have read, because, as you will read in Chapter 9, when you practise law it is not enough to be able to say what the law is. You must *understand* it so that you can *apply* it in order to solve a client's legal problem.

Of course, once you have mastered the art of reading and understanding sources of law, you will have developed your skills of analysis, synthesis, and summarising to a point where you will notice that your reading and understanding of other everyday reading material, be it newspapers, history books, or political manifestos, seems considerably easier. Conversely, you will find that you can adopt an approach to your everyday reading material in a way which will assist your reading and understanding of law. This is a skill for life.

7.1 Practicalities of reading

Lawyers spend quite a lot of time reading. Whether you are reading a statute, statutory instrument, case, commentary, or anything else, it is fair to say that legal text can be quite dense and reading it can be relatively heavy going. In light of this, it is helpful to consider what practical steps you can take to make this process as effective as possible.

Increasingly, lawyers are accessing electronic sources of law, because they have advantages in terms of being updated on a timely basis, and they are portable on a laptop, tablet, or smartphone. You should consider whether you have any particular issues with reading on a screen. Adjusting the brightness of the screen, the font size, and colour can help you to focus more clearly on your reading. Accessibility Options (on a PC) and Universal Access (on a Mac) can also help address any specific needs you may have in this regard.

If you are using paper sources of law or decide to print your online sources in order to read them more comfortably, then there are also steps you can take to help with your reading. If the source is photocopied, make sure you adjust the contrast settings so that the print is clear. It is not uncommon for people to find that reading copious amounts of black text on a stark white background can be difficult. In this case you may find that printing onto coloured paper, or simply putting a sheet of coloured perspex over the white page, can help to stop the text jumping around. However, sometimes all that is needed is a break, and so in that regard you should make sure you set aside enough time to read. Of course, time is money in a law firm, so you also need to be able to navigate sources of law effectively, and understand which parts, if any, you can skim read or not read at all, and which you must read in detail.

Make sure you are free from distractions when you are reading. You will not read effectively if you are checking your email or your text messages every five minutes. If possible, move to a quiet place where you will not be distracted.

 Practice tip

Do not assume that in practice your desk will be a quiet place. Law firms are busy places and lawyers are often discussing the law, either face to face with their colleagues or over the telephone with others. Increasingly lawyers share offices or even work in open plan offices with lots of other lawyers in the same room. Most law firms however, and particularly those which have chosen to have an **open plan** office layout, will provide work spaces which are suitable for and can be used for quiet work, e.g. the library or a room referred to as a **breakout room** or **space**.

7.2 Sources of law

Your strategy for reading law effectively will depend on the nature of what you are reading. Chapters 4 and 5 explained that there are two primary sources of law in England and Wales, namely legislation (statutes and statutory instruments) and case law, and that there are numerous secondary sources of law which comment on these primary sources. We will now take each source in turn and consider how it is likely to be set out, and the best approach to reading and understanding the law it contains.

7.3 Statutes

Chapter 4 considers the nature of a statute in some detail. Broadly, you will remember that Parliament produces statutes and that statutes set out our rights, or alternatively impose obligations on us (and often set out the sanctions we will face if we fail to comply) in some detail.

7.3.1 Structure of a statute

Helpfully, most statutes are set out in a similar way, so once you are familiar with this structure you should be able to navigate around any statute, regardless of the subject matter.

Let us consider the layout of a statute called the Unfair Contract Terms Act 1977. It is set out in Figure 7.1 below, together with guidance as to what is being referred to. When you have read Figure 7.1 you should continue reading at 7.3.2 below.

7.3.2 How to read and understand a statute

Wherever you are currently in your legal career, if you are reading this book then undoubtedly you will consider that you have mastered the art of reading. However, you are about to learn that your approach to reading law will differ quite significantly to the approach you have will have adopted in your reading to date. It is a common error for junior lawyers to attempt to read a statute like a book. The temptation to turn to the first page and start reading is great. Although technically this may work with some statutes, usually it is not the most effective approach. When you consider that, for example, the Companies Act 2006 comprises over 1,000 sections, in some cases it is just is not a workable option at all. Instead, you should aim to read the *relevant* parts of the statute. The skill is to determine which parts of the statute are relevant to your needs.

You have just learned how most statutes are structured. This knowledge will help you to navigate around a statute effectively, to find the law which is relevant to your needs at any particular time. The following approach will help you to read any statute effectively.

Read as part of a wider research strategy

You should not expect to obtain an holistic understanding of the statute simply by reading it. Your reading is likely to form part of a wider research strategy to ensure you have a sound understanding of the relevant law, and this is explored in Chapter 8.

Figure 7.1 Once you have finished reading Figure 7.1 continue your reading at 7.3.2 above.

Unfair Contract Terms Act

1977[1]

1977 CHAPTER 50[2]

An Act to impose further limits on the extent to which under the law of England and Wales and Northern Ireland civil liability for breach of contract, of for negligence or other breach of duty, can be avoided by means of contract terms and otherwise, and under the law of Scotland civil liability can be avoided by means of contract terms.[3]

[26th October 1977][4]

Annotations:

Commencement Information

I1   Act not in force at Royal Assent; Act wholly in force at 1.2.1978 see s. 31(1)[5]

Table of Contents[6]

PART I [7]

AMENDMENT OF LAW FOR ENGLAND AND WALES AND NORTHERN IRELAND

Introductory[8]

PART II

AMENDMENT OF LAW FOR SCOTLAND

1 Short Title

This is the short title of the statute and its year of publication, the 'Unfair Contract Terms Act 1977'. It is the normal way to describe a statute, but it is common for lawyers to refer to the most regularly used statutes using an abbreviation. For example, the Unfair Contract Terms Act is often referred to as the 'UCTA' (pronounced 'uc-ta') and sometimes the year is also referred to, e.g. 'UCTA77'. The Sale of Goods Act 1979 is often referred to as the 'SoGA' (pronounced to rhyme with yoga) or 'SoGA79'. You will learn from experience which statutes tend to be referred to by abbreviated names.

2 Citation

This is the official citation for the statute. Each statute passed in any one year is given its own number, known as the chapter number. The UCTA is the 50th Act of 1977. The citation 1977 Chapter 50 refers to this statute alone. In the official citation, 'chapter' is often abbreviated to 'c'.

3 Long Title

The long title gives some indication of the statute's general purpose. Here the long title is the wording, 'An Act to impose ... can be avoided by means of contract terms' and it indicates that the purpose of the UCTA is to impose further limits on the extent to which liability for breach can be avoided, and gives some indication of how the statute differs in scope between the different jurisdictions within the UK.

4 Royal Assent

This is the date when the statute received Royal Assent. A statute will take effect on the date that it receives the Royal Assent unless the statute says otherwise (which the UCTA and many other relatively recent statutes do).

5 Commencement

There is usually a commencement section near to the end or beginning of the statute. If the statute does not take effect on the date that it receives Royal Assent, then, like the UCTA, it may take effect on a fixed date stated in the Act. Here you can see that s. 31(1) provides that the UCTA will come into force just over three months following its Royal Assent, namely on 1 February 1978. (Note that the year in the short title is the year the statute received Royal Assent, not the year it came into force.) Alternatively, a statute can grant power to a government minister to decide when it should become law. In this case the minister would bring the statute (or part of it) into effect by issuing a commencement order, which is a form of delegated legislation. If it is intended that the statute should apply to anything that pre-exists the statute itself, then the statute must specifically provide for this. This reflects the principle that a statute does not take effect retrospectively.

6 Table of Contents

The table of contents provides a useful summary of what you will find in the statute.

7 Parts

You can see that the statute is subdivided into different parts, and that each part has a heading which indicates what that part deals with. Here, the parts are divided according to which jurisdiction within the UK the provisions apply to.

8 Headings

Within each part, there are headings which group together certain sections of the statute. For example, ss. 5–7 all deal with liability arising from the sale or supply of goods, so they are grouped together under an appropriate heading. Sections 2–4 deal with other types of liability and so are grouped together under another heading, and so on. The headings are part of the statute.

9 Sections

Within each part, and grouped together under appropriate headings, are the sections of the statute. Each section contains a different rule of law and is given a number and a useful heading to let you know what it is about. When you refer to a rule of law contained in a statute, you should identify where it can be found. It is usual to abbreviate 'section' to 's.' so that s. 1 refers to section 1. If you are referring to more than one section, it is usual to refer to 'ss.', e.g. 'see ss. 5–7 of the UCTA'. You will see when we consider the body of the statute that the sections are subdivided into:

- subsections, e.g. s. 1(2)
- paragraphs, e.g. s. 1(1)(a)
- subparagraphs, e.g. s. 3(2)(b)(i) (however the table of contents does not drill down into this detail).

10 Definitions

The definitions (sometimes referred to as **interpretation** or **explanatory provisions**) provide an explanation of the meaning of certain words to which the statute refers. The meaning will not necessarily be the meaning that a non-lawyer would understand to be the meaning of a word (and indeed you should assume that a definition in a statute applies only to that statute unless it states otherwise). It is very important to find and read any definitions in order to understand the legislation.

PART III

PROVISIONS APPLYING TO WHOLE OF UNITED KINGDOM

Miscellaneous

SCHEDULES[11]

PART I[12]

AMENDMENT OF LAW FOR ENGLAND AND WALES AND NORTHERN IRELAND

Annotations:

Modifications etc. (not altering text)

C1   Pt. I applied (3.1.1995): by 1973 c. 13, **s. 11A** (as inserted (3.1.1995) by 1994 c. 35, ss. 7, 8(2)(3), **Sch. 2 para. 4(6)**); by 1979 c. 54, **s. 61(5A)** (as inserted (3.1.1995) by 1994 c. 35, ss. 7, 8(2)(3), **Sch. 2 para. 5(9)(c)**); by 1982 c. 29, **s. 18(3)** (as inserted (3.1.1995) by 1994 c. 35, ss. 7, 8(2)(3), **Sch. 2 para. 6(10)**)

Introductory[13]

1   **Scope of Part I**[14]

(1) For the purposes of this Part of this Act, "negligence" means the breach—

(a) of any obligation, arising from the express or implied terms of a contract, to take reasonable care or exercise reasonable skill in the performance of the contract;

(b) of any common law duty to take reasonable care or exercise reasonable skill (but not any stricter duty);

(c) of the common duty of care imposed by the [M1] Occupiers' Liability Act 1957 or the [M2] Occupiers' Liability Act (Northern Ireland) 1957.

(2) This Part of this Act is subject to Part 111; and in relation to contracts, the operation of sections 2 to 4 and 7 is subject to the exceptions made by Schedule 1.

(3) In the case of both contract and tort, sections 2 to 7 apply (except where the contrary is stated in section 6(4)) only to business liability, that is liability for breach of obligations or duties arising—

(a) from things done or to be done by a person in the course of a business (whether his own business or another's); or

(b) from the occupation of premises used for business purposes of the occupier; and references to liability are to be read accordingly [**F1** but liability of an occupier of premises for breach of an obligation or duty towards a person obtaining access to the premises for recreational or educational purposes, being liability for loss or damage suffered by reason of the dangerous state of the premises, is not a business liability of the occupier unless granting that person such access for the purposes concerned falls within the business purposes of the occupier].

(4) In relation to any breach of duty or obligation, it is immaterial for any purpose of this Part of this Act whether the breach was inadvertent or intentional, or whether liability for it arises directly or vicariously.

Annotations:

Amendments (Textual)

F1   Words added by Occupiers' Liability Act 1984 (c. 3, SIF 122:2), **s. 2** (E.W.) and by the **Occupiers' Liability (Northern Ireland) Order 1987 S.I. 1987/1280 (N.I.15), art 4**

Marginal Citations[15]

M1   1957 c. 31

M2   1957 c. 25 (N.I.)

Avoidance of liability for negligence, breach of contract, etc

2   Negligence liability.

(1) A person cannot by reference to any contract term or to a notice given to persons generally or to particular persons exclude or restrict his liability for death or personal injury resulting from negligence.

(continued . . .)

11 Schedules

Some statutes have schedules to them. This can be for several reasons, but it is often to separate reference or administrative material from the detail in the body of the statute. For example, a schedule can contain specific detail relating to provisions in the main body of the statute, it can expand or define phrases in the statute, or it can contain detailed amendments of any earlier legislation. Typically the final schedule will set out which earlier statutes it repeals. In the UCTA, Schedules 1 and 2 provide detail, Schedule 3 sets out which earlier statutes it amends, and Schedule 4 sets out the earlier statutes it repeals. Schedule can be abbreviated to 'Sched.' or 'Sch.' and the terminology is to refer to a schedule 'to' (not 'of') the statute. The schedule itself may be divided into paragraphs, which can be abbreviated to 'para.' and the correct terminology is a paragraph 'of' a schedule.

12 Parts

See n. 7 above.

13 Headings

See n. 8 above.

14 Sections

See n. 9 above.

15 Marginal Citations or Notes

There may be short marginal citations or notes by each section explaining its contents. Unlike headings, the marginal notes are not part of the statute. Here, for example, the marginal citations provide the citations for other statutes referred to in s. 1(1)(c) of the UCTA.

(2) In the case of other loss or damage, a person cannot so exclude or restrict his liability for negligence except in so far as the term or notice satisfies the requirement of reasonableness.

(3) Where a contract term or notice purports to exclude or restrict liability for negligence a person's agreement to or awareness of it is not of itself to be taken as indicating his voluntary acceptance of any risk.

Annotations:

Modifications etc. (not altering text)

C2   S. 2(2) excluded (11.11.1999, but subject to s. 10(3) of the amending Act, does not apply in relation to a contract referred to in s. 10(2)) by 1999 c. 31, **ss. 7(2)**, 10(2)(3)

3   Liability arising in contract.

(1) This section applies as between contracting parties where one of them deals as consumer or on the other's written standard terms of business.

(2) As against that party, the other cannot by reference to any contract term—

(a) when himself in breach of contract, exclude or restrict any liability of his in respect of the breach; or

(b) claim to be entitled—

(i) to render a contractual performance substantially different from that which was reasonably expected of him, or

(ii) in respect of the whole or any part of his contractual obligation, to render no performance at all,

except in so far as (in any of the cases mentioned above in this subsection) the contract term satisfies the requirement of reasonableness.

Annotations:

Modifications etc. (not altering text)

C3   S. 3(2)(b) extended (1.11.1998 and 1.7.1999 in relation to certain contracts and 7.8.2002 insofar as not then in force) by 1998 c. 20, s. 14(2) (with s. 12); S.I. 1998/2479, arts. 2,3; S.I. 1999/1816, art. 3(1); S.I. 2002/1673, **art. 2**

4   Unreasonable indemnity clauses.

(1) A person dealing as consumer cannot by reference to any contract term be made to indemnify another person (whether a party to the contract or not) in respect of liability that may be incurred by the other for negligence or breach of contract, except in so far as the contract term satisfies the requirement of reasonableness.

(2) This section applies whether the liability in question—

(a) is directly that of the person to be indemnified or is incurred by him vicariously;

(b) is to the person dealing as consumer or to someone else.

Liability arising from sale or supply of goods

5   "Guarantee" of consumer goods.

[omitted for the purposes of this book]

6   Sale and hire purchase.

(1) Liability for breach of the obligations arising from—

(a) [F2 section 12 of the Sale of Goods Act 1979] (seller's implied undertakings as to title, etc.);

(b) section 8 of the M3 Supply of Goods (Implied Terms) Act 1973 (the corresponding thing in relation to hire-purchase),

cannot be excluded or restricted by reference to any contract term.

(2) As against a person dealing as consumer, liability for breach of the obligations arising from—

    (a) [**F3** section 13, 14, or 15 of the 1979 Act] (sellers's implied undertakings as to conformity of goods with description or sample, or as to their quality or fitness for a particular purpose);

    (b) section 9, 10 or 11 of the 1973 Act (the corresponding things in relation to hire-purchase), cannot be excluded or restricted by reference to any contract term.

(3) As against a person dealing otherwise than as consumer, the liability specified in subsection (2) above can be excluded or restricted by reference to a contract term, but only in so far as the term satisfies the requirement of reasonableness.

(4) The liabilities referred to in this section are not only the business liabilities defined by section 1(3), but include those arising under any contract of sale of goods or hire- purchase agreement.

Annotations:

Amendments (Textual)

F2   Words substituted by Sale of Goods Act 1979 (c. 54, SIF 109:1), ss. 62, 63, **Sch. 2 para. 19**(*a*)

F3   Words substituted by Sale of Goods Act 1979 (c. 54, SIF 109:1), ss. 62, 63, **Sch. 2 para. 19**(*b*)

Marginal Citations

M3   1973 c. 13.

7   Miscellaneous contracts under which goods pass.

[omitted for the purposes of this book]

Other provisions about contracts

[omitted for the purposes of this book]

Explanatory provisions[16]

11   The "reasonableness" test.[17]

(1) In relation to a contract term, the requirement of reasonableness for the purposes of this Part of this Act, section 3 of the **M6** Misrepresentation Act 1967 and section 3 of the **M7** Misrepresentation Act (Northern Ireland) 1967 is that the term shall have been a fair and reasonable one to be included having regard to the circumstances which were, or ought reasonably to have been, known to or in the contemplation of the parties when the contract was made.

(2) In determining for the purposes of section 6 or 7 above whether a contract term satisfies the requirement of reasonableness, regard shall be had in particular to the matters specified in Schedule 2 to this Act; but this subsection does not prevent the court or arbitrator from holding, in accordance with any rule of law, that a term which purports to exclude or restrict any relevant liability is not a term of the contract.

(3) In relation to a notice (not being a notice having contractual effect), the requirement of reasonableness under this Act is that it should be fair and reasonable to allow reliance on it, having regard to all the circumstances obtaining when the liability arose or (but for the notice) would have arisen.

(continued . . .)

---

16 Explanatory provisions

See n. 10 above.

17 This section sets out the reasonable test referred to in several sections of the UCTA. Section 11(2) makes clear that you also need to refer to Sch. 2 in relation to ss. 6 and 7.

(4) Where by reference to a contract term or notice a person seeks to restrict liability to a specified sum of money, and the question arises (under this or any other Act) whether the term or notice satisfies the requirement of reasonableness, regard shall be had in particular (but without prejudice to subsection (2) above in the case of contract terms) to—

    (a) the resources which he could expect to be available to him for the purpose of meeting the liability should it arise; and

    (b) how far it was open to him to cover himself by insurance.

(5) It is for those claiming that a contract term or notice satisfies the requirement of reasonableness to show that it does.

Annotations:

Marginal Citations

M6	1967 c. 7
M7	1967 c. 14(N.I.)

12 "Dealing as a consumer".

(1) A party to a contract "deals as consumer" in relation to another party if—

    (a) he neither makes the contract in the course of a business nor holds himself out as doing so; and

    (b) the other party does make the contract in the course of a business; and

    (c) in the case of a contract governed by the law of sale of goods or hire-purchase, or by section 7 of this Act, the goods passing under or in pursuance of the contract are of a type ordinarily supplied for private use or consumption.

[**F7** (1A) But if the first party mentioned in subsection (1) is an individual paragraph (c) of that subsection must be ignored.]

[**F8** (2) But the buyer is not in any circumstances to be regarded as dealing as consumer—

    (a) if he is an individual and the goods are second hand goods sold at public auction at which individuals have the opportunity of attending the sale in person;

    (b) if he is not an individual and the goods are sold by auction or by competitive tender.]

(3) Subject to this, it is for those claiming that a party does not deal as consumer to show that he does not.

Annotations:

Amendments (Textual)

F7	S. 12(1A) inserted (31.3.2003) by The Sale and Supply of Goods to Consumers Regulations 2002 (S.I. 2002/3045), reg. **14(2)**
F8	S. 12(2) substituted (31.3.2003) by The Sale and Supply of Goods to Consumers Regulations 2002 (S.I. 2002/3045), reg. **14(3)**

13 Varieties of exemption clause.

(1) To the extent that this Part of this Act prevents the exclusion or restriction of any liability it also prevents—

    (a) making the liability or its enforcement subject to restrictive or onerous conditions;

    (b) excluding or restricting any right or remedy in respect of the liability, or subjecting a person to any prejudice in consequence of his pursuing any such right or remedy;

    (c) excluding or restricting rules of evidence or procedure; and (to that extent) sections 2 and 5 to 7 also prevent excluding or restricting liability by reference to terms and notices which exclude or restrict the relevant obligation or duty.

(2) But an agreement in writing to submit present or future differences to arbitration is not to be treated under this Part of this Act as excluding or restricting any liability.

14   **Interpretation of Part I.**[18]

In this Part of this Act—

"business" includes a profession and the activities of any government department or local or public authority;

"goods" has the same meaning as in [[F9]the Sale of Goods Act 1979];

"hire-purchase agreement" has the same meaning as in the [M8] Consumer Credit Act 1974;

"negligence" has the meaning given by section 1(1);

"notice" includes an announcement, whether or not in writing, and any other communication or pretended communication; and

"personal injury" includes any disease and any impairment of physical or mental condition.

Annotations:

....

Amendments (Textual)

F9   Words substituted by Sale of Goods Act 1979 (c. 54, SIF 109:1), ss. 62, 63, **Sch. 2 para. 20**

Marginal Citations

M8   1974 c. 39

PART II

[omitted for the purposes of this book]

PART III

[omitted for the purposes of this book]

PROVISIONS APPLYING TO WHOLE OF UNITED KINGDOM

Miscellaneous

[omitted for the purposes of this book]

General

31   **Commencement; amendments; repeals.**[19]

(1) This Act comes into force on 1st February 1978.

(2) Nothing in this Act applies to contracts made before the date on which it comes into force; but subject to this, it applies to liability for any loss or damage which is suffered on or after that date.

[X2](3) The enactments specified in Schedule 3 to this Act are amended as there shown.

(4) The enactments specified in Schedule 4 to this Act are repealed to the extent specified in column 3 of that Schedule.

(continued . . .)

18 Interpretation
See n. 10.

19 This section reiterates the commencement information provided at the beginning of the statute.

Annotations:

Editorial Information

X2   The text of s. 31(3)(4) is in the form in which it was originally enacted: it was not reproduced in Statutes in Force and does not reflect any amendments or repeals which may have been made prior to 1.2.1991.

32   Citation and extent.[20]
(1) This Act may be cited as the Unfair Contract Terms Act 1977.
(2) Part I of this Act extends to England and Wales and to Northern Ireland; but it does not extend to Scotland.
(3) Part II of this Act extends to Scotland only.
(4) This Part of this Act extends to the whole of the United Kingdom.

SCHEDULES[21]

SCHEDULE 1   Section 1(2).

SCOPE OF SECTIONS 2 TO 4 AND 7

1   Sections 2 to 4 of this Act do not extend to—
(a) any contract of insurance (including a contract to pay an annuity on human life);
(b) any contract so far as it relates to the creation or transfer of an interest in land, or to the termination of such an interest, whether by extinction, merger, surrender, forfeiture or otherwise;
(c) any contract so far as it relates to the creation or transfer of a right or interest in any patent, trade mark, copyright [**F28**or design right], registered design, technical or commercial information or other intellectual property, or relates to the termination of any such right or interest;
(d) any contract so far as it relates—
  (i) to the formation or dissolution of a company (which means any body corporate or unincorporated association and includes a partnership), or
  (ii) to its constitution or the rights or obligations of its corporators or members;
(e) any contract so far as it relates to the creation or transfer of securities or of any right or interest in securities.

Annotations:

Amendments (Textual)

F28   Words inserted by Copyright, Designs and Patents Act 1988 (c. 48, SIF 67A), s. 303(1), **Sch. 7 para. 24**

Modifications etc. (not altering text)

C7   Sch. 1 para. 1(c) extended by Patents, Designs and Marks Act 1986 (c. 39, SIF 67A), ss. 2(3), 4(7), **Sch. para. 1(2)(f)**
C8   Sch. 1 para. 1(c) extended by S.I. 1987/1497, reg. 9(2), **sch. 2**Sch. 1 para. 1(c) amended (31.10.1994) by 1994 c. 26, s. 106(1), **Sch. 4 para. 1(1)(2)**; S.I. 1994/2550, **art.2**
2   Section 2(1) extends to—
(a) any contract of marine salvage or towage;
(b) any charterparty of a ship or hovercraft; and
(c) any contract for the carriage of goods by ship or hovercraft; but subject to this sections 2 to 4 and 7 do not extend to any such contract except in favour of a person dealing as consumer.

3   Where goods are carried by ship or hovercraft in pursuance of a contract which either—
     (a) specifies that as the means of carriage over part of the journey to be covered, or
     (b) makes no provision as to the means of carriage and does not exclude that means, then
         sections 2(2), 3 and 4 do not, except in favour of a person dealing as consumer, extend to the
         contract as it operates for and in relation to the carriage of the goods by that means.
4   Section 2(1) and (2) do not extend to a contract of employment, except in favour of the
     employee.
5   Section 2(1) does not affect the validity of any discharge and indemnity given by a person, on
     or in connection with an award to him of compensation for pneumoconiosis attributable to
     employment in the coal industry, in respect of any further claim arising from his contracting that
     disease.

SCHEDULE 2   Sections 11(2) and 24(2).

"Guidelines" for Application of Reasonableness Test

The matters to which regard is to be had in particular for the purposes of sections 6(3), 7(3) and (4),
20 and 21 are any of the following which appear to be relevant—
     (a) the strength of the bargaining positions of the parties relative to each other, taking into
         account (among other things) alternative means by which the customer's requirements could
         have been met;
     (b) whether the customer received an inducement to agree to the term, or in accepting it had
         an opportunity of entering into a similar contract with other persons, but without having a
         similar term;
     (c) whether the customer knew or ought reasonably to have known of the existence and the
         extent of the term (having regard, among other things, to any custom of the trade and any
         previous course of dealing between the parties);
     (d) where the term excludes or restricts any relevant liability if some condition was not complied
         with, whether it was reasonable at the time of the contract to expect that compliance with that
         condition would be practicable;
     (e) whether the goods were manufactured, processed or adapted to the special order of the
         customer.

X3 SCHEDULE 3   Section 31(3).

Amendments of Enactments

Annotations:
....

Editorial Information
X3   The text of Sch. 3 is in the form in which it was originally enacted: it was not reproduced in Statutes
      in Force and does not reflect any amendments or repeals which may have been made prior to
      1.2.1991.

(continued . . .)

20 Citation

This section reiterates the short title
provided at the beginning of the
statute.

21 Schedules

See n. 11 above.

Annotations:

Amendments (Textual)

F29   Entries repealed by Sale of goods Act 1979 (c. 54, SIF 109:1), s. 62, Sch. 3

Annotations:

Amendments (Textual)

F29   Entries repealed by Sale of goods Act 1979 (c. 54, SIF 109:1), s. 62, Sch. 3

In the [M11] Supply of Goods (Implied Terms) Act 1973 as originally enacted and as substituted by the [M12] Consumer Credit Act 1974)—

(a) in section 14(1) for the words from "conditional sale" to the end substitute " a conditional sale agreement where the buyer deals as a consumer within Part I of the Unfair Contract Terms Act 1977.
. . . . [F30] ".

(b) in section 15(1), in the definition of " business", for "local authority or statutory undertaker" substitute " or local or public authority ".

Annotations:

Amendments (Textual)

F30   Words repealed by Statute Law (Repeals) Act 1981 (c. 19), **Sch. Pt. XII**

Marginal Citations

M11   1973 c. 13
M12   1974 c. 39

Annotations:

Amendments (Textual)

F30   Words repealed by Statute Law (Repeals) Act 1981 (c. 19), **Sch. Pt. XII**

Marginal Citations

M11   1973 c. 13
M12   1974 c. 39

[X4] SCHEDULE 4   Section 31(4).

REPEALS

Annotations:

Editorial Information

X4   The text of Sch. 4 is in the form in which it was originally enacted: it was not reproduced in Statutes in Force and does not reflect any amendments or repeals which may have been made prior to 1.2.1991.

Chapter	Short title	Extent of repeal
56&57 Vict. c. 71.	Sale of Goods Act 1893.	In section 55, subsections (3) to (11). Section 55A. Section 61(6). In section 62(1) the definition of "contract for the international sale of goods".
1962 c. 46.	Transport Act 1962.	Section 43(7).
1967 c. 45	Uniform Laws on International Sales Act 1967.	In section 1(4), the words "55 and 55A".
1972 c. 33.	Carriage by Railway Act 1972.	In section 1(1), the words from "contract for the international sale of goods" onwards.
1973 c. 13.	Supply of Goods (Implied Terms) Act 1973.	Section 5(1). Section 6. In section 7(1), the words from "contract for the international sale of goods" onwards. In section 12, subsections (2) to (9). Section 13. In section 15(1), the definition of "consumer sale".

The repeals in sections 12 and 15 of the Supply of Goods (Implied Terms) Act 1973 shall have effect in relation to those sections as originally enacted and as substituted by the [M13] Consumer Credit Act 1974.

Annotations:

Marginal Citations

M13   1974 c. 39

Annotations:

Marginal Citations

M13   1974 c. 39

> **Changes to legislation:**
> There are currently no known outstanding effects for the Unfair Contract Terms Act 1977.

If you turn to Figure 8.1, which summarises the strategy in a flowchart, you will note that 'analysing the primary source', such as a statute, is just one aspect of finding all relevant law. In particular, where available you should first have read a secondary source, such as a textbook or *Halsbury's Laws*, which describes the key aspects of the law enshrined in the statute.

Read the long title of the Act as a guide to its general purpose

For example, if you have found a term in an employment contract which appears to be unfair, and you have chosen to read the UCTA because it sounds like it might be relevant, the long title will explain that the unfair terms it is seeking to address are certain terms which avoid liability. If the reason your term appears unfair is because it obliges your client to work for 18 hours a day without a break, then reading the long title will have helped you to identify at the earliest opportunity that the UCTA is unlikely to help you.

Check whether the statute is in force, in part or as a whole

A statute may not yet have come into force, or it may even have been repealed. Bear in mind that some sources give the text of statutes as originally passed by Parliament, while others give the text as amended by later provisions and statute, and some offer both, so you should check that you are reading the version you wish to read.

Identify the sections you may need

You should begin by analysing the table of contents. The headings and titles of each section in particular will help you to find what is most likely to be relevant. While a statute itself does not include an index, typically a publisher will publish a text which includes the most common statutes in a subject area, and it will include a helpful consolidated index for those statutes. For example, corporate lawyers will usually have a copy of *Butterworths Company Law Handbook* which includes an indexed collection of the main statutes, statutory instruments, and European material that are relevant to corporate lawyers. Similarly, if you can access a statute using an online database, you will be able to search the statute on screen to find a specific word.

Skim read the sections that you have identified as possibly relevant, to check whether they do appear to be relevant.

Locate the definition or interpretation sections

Again, the table of contents may help here, but some definitions are hidden within sections and this may not be evident from the title of any section. There is no general rule as to where you will find the definitions section (sometimes called the interpretation section), although often you will find it in one or more of the following places:

- near the beginning of the statute;
- near the end of the statute;
- within the section where the term(s) feature;
- near the end of the part of the statute where the term(s) feature.

In the UCTA the definitions for Part I are in s. 14 (at the end of Part I) and there are also separate explanatory provisions is ss. 11–13. The definitions for Part II are in s. 25 (at the end of Part II). There are also some definitions within the section where the terms feature (e.g. s. 12 sets out the meaning of 'dealing as a consumer' which features in s. 6(2) and (3)). Note that the meaning of a word in a statute will not necessarily be the meaning that a non-lawyer would understand to be the meaning of that word. Nor can you assume that the definition of a word in one statute will be the same as the definition of the same word in another statute. It is very important to find and read any definitions in order to understand the legislation.

Carefully read the relevant parts of the statute

Once you have used this approach to identity the relevant sections, you should now re-read the sections slowly and with care, having attended to the practicalities of reading referred to at 7.1. The general rule is that a statute means precisely what it says, so each word of the statute is important. You must focus and pay attention to what you are reading. The following guidance will help you.

Rights, obligations, and prohibitions

It is vital to identify when a statute is granting a right; that is, saying someone can do something. The statute might use words such as 'can' or 'may' to do this. Be alert too for any wording that restricts the right in any way. The statute might use words such as 'only in so far as', 'subject to', or 'provided that' to do this. For example, s. 6(3) of the UCTA grants a limited right ('can ... but only in so far as ... satisfies the requirement of reasonableness') for a contract term to exclude liability for breach of various obligations ('the liability specified in subsection 2') when the term is in a contract with someone who is 'dealing otherwise than as consumer'.

Conversely, you must also be able to identify when a statute is imposing a positive obligation; that is, saying someone must do something. The statute might use words such as 'must', 'shall', or 'will' to do this. Again, the statute might limit the scope of the obligation, or render it subject to the court's discretion. For example, s. 11(2) of the UCTA states that, when considering whether a contract term satisfies the requirement of reasonableness under s. 6 of the UCTA, there is an obligation on the court ('regard shall be had') to consider 'the matters specified in Schedule 2'. However the statute makes clear that this obligation would not prevent a court or arbitrator 'in accordance with any rule of law' from striking out a term even if it appears to be reasonable in light of Sch. 2.

Finally, look out for wording which imposes a negative obligation, or prohibition, that is, saying someone must not do something. The statute might use words such as 'cannot', 'must not', 'shall not', or 'will not' to do this. For example, s. 6(2) of the UCTA prohibits a term of a contract from excluding liability for breach of the obligations referred to in that section when the term is in a contract with someone who is 'dealing as consumer'.

Cross-references

It is common for a section of a statute not to 'stand alone' but instead to require reference to another section of or schedule to that statute, or even to another statute entirely. This adds to the complexity of your reading, as you need to read the section in conjunction with something else. We have already seen examples of this, such as that the reference in s. 6(3) to the requirement of reasonableness needs to be read in light of s. 11 which sets out the 'reasonableness' test, which in turn must be read in light of Sch. 2, which sets out the guidelines for the application of the test. While s. 11(2) clearly signposts back to s. 6 and forward to Sch. 2, in fact s. 6 is silent even as to the existence of s. 11 and Sch. 2.

A further example is the reference to 'that party' in s. 3(2). This can only be explained by looking at the previous subsection. Reading s. 3(1) it becomes clear that the reference to 'that party' in s. 3(2) is a reference to a party to a contract who either deals 'as consumer' or alternatively in accordance with the other party's 'standard terms of business'.

Another example is the cross-references in s. 6(2) to various obligations arising under a different act entirely to the UCTA, namely the Sale of Goods Act 1925 (the 'SOGA').

You can see why some students actually never get round to reading the sections, having given up trying to navigate their way to an answer. Chapter 8 explains how reading secondary sources of law, such as textbooks and *Halsbury's Laws*, before you read the statute itself, can really assist your reading and understanding of a particular statute, the jargon it contains, and how best to navigate around it.

Section structure

The sections of a statute are often drafted as subsections of a central 'stem', and the subsections may end with 'and', 'or', or nothing at all. It is important to understand this structure in order to understand fully the meaning of the section. To take s. 3 as an example, you can see that the central stem in s. 3(2) is 'As against that party, the other cannot by reference to any contract term' and this stem then needs to be read in front of two subsections, (a) and (b). The word 'or' at the end of s. 3(2)(a) clearly shows that there are two things that the 'other party' cannot do, one set out in (a) and one set out in (b). These are in the alternative; that is the 'other party' will be in breach if she does (a) or (b), not just if she does (a) and (b). You will then note that there is an exception at the end of s. 3(b), 'except in so far as (in any of the cases mentioned above in this subsection) the contract term satisfies the requirement of reasonableness'. When reading this exception, you need to be clear that it applies just to s. 3(2)(b) and definitely not to s. 3(2)(a). How can you ascertain this? The exception wording alludes to this by referring to 'in any of the cases mentioned above in *this subsection*'. However, even if it did not say so, you can tell by the alignment of the exception. Can you see that the word 'except' is aligned under 'claim'? Contrast that with s. 6(1). There the final part of the section, 'cannot be excluded or restricted by reference to any contract term', is aligned under the stem 'Liability for breach of the obligations arising from', indicating that those words must be read onto the stem, not just a subsection.

'Reading in' the facts

Clearly a statute uses generic wording and will not refer to the facts of the legal issue you are facing. It is for you to 'read in' to the statute the facts of your legal issue, in order to understand better the statute you are reading.

For example, if Jane buys a box of chocolates from Retailer Ltd as a consumer, you might therefore read s. 3(2) as 'As against Jane, Retailer Ltd cannot by reference to any contract term ... (a) when Retailer Ltd are in breach of contract, exclude ..., or (b) (i) claim to be entitled to render a contractual performance substantially different from that which was reasonably expected of Retailer Ltd', and so on.

Case law

Chapter 4 details how to interpret a statute and how case law can affect this interpretation. For example, it may be that case law has interpreted and refined the guidelines which are set out in Sch. 2 to the UCTA regarding the application of the reasonableness test . This may not be obvious from the statute itself; it may not be annotated anywhere on the page. This is why it is not enough simply to read the statute in isolation, but instead as part of a wider legal research strategy, and this is explored further in Chapter 8.

Updating information

You may have noticed that the statute contains square brackets or other punctuation or text formatting that you were not expecting to see. This is likely to relate to the updating of the statute, and is code to tell you whether something is in force, pending, or has become obsolete. Chapter 8 provides further guidance on this.

7.4 Statutory instruments

Chapter 4 considers the nature of a statutory instrument in some detail. As a reminder, statutory instruments are secondary legislation made under powers delegated by Parliament, usually to government ministers. There are various reasons for their use. Statutes can progress more quickly through Parliament if some of the detail is left to be set out in a statutory instrument at a later date. Sometimes statutory instruments are needed to bring statutes up to date with modern life (e.g. to include reference to civil partners alongside existing references to spouses and other family members).

7.4.1 Structure of a statutory instrument

Helpfully, as with a statute, most statutory instruments are set out in a similar way. Figure 7.2 sets out the Sale and Supply of Goods to Consumers Regulations 2002, a statutory instrument referred to in s. 12 of the UCTA. The statutory instrument is annotated with some explanations about its structure, to help you to follow the basic structure of any other statutory instrument. You should read Figure 7.2 before returning to read 7.4.2 below.

7.4.2 How to read and understand a statutory instrument

Generally, you should read a statutory instrument in the same way as a statute. However, there are some minor differences in the approach you should adopt. As Chapter 4 explains, a statutory instrument is secondary legislation, made under powers conferred by an Act of Parliament (often referred to as the **parent statute** or the **primary legislation**). You should expect to see references in the statutory instrument to the parent statute and sometimes to other relevant statutory instruments, some of which may have been made under the same parent statute. To understand the statutory instrument fully, you must understand the context in which it was made. This means that you must be prepared to refer back to the parent statute and across to any other relevant statutory instruments and any case law which relate to it.

2002 No. 3045[1]

CONSUMER PROTECTION[2]

The Sale and Supply of Goods to Consumers Regulations 2002[3]

Made - - - -	*10th December 2002*
Laid before Parliament	*11th December 2002*
Coming into force - -	*31st March 2003*[4]

THE SALE AND SUPPLY OF GOODS TO CONSUMERS REGULATIONS 2002

Table of Contents[5]

1.   Title, commencement and extent
2.   Interpretation[6]

Amendments to the Sale of Goods Act 1979[7]

3.   Additional implied terms in consumer cases
4.   Amendments to rules on passing of risk and acceptance of goods in consumer cases
5.   Buyer's additional remedies in consumer cases
6.   Other amendments to the 1979 Act

Amendments to the Supply of Goods and Services Act 1982

7.   Additional implied terms in cases where goods are transferred to consumers—England, Wales and Northern Ireland
8.   Additional implied terms in cases where goods are transferred to consumers—Scotland
9.   Transferee's additional remedies in consumer cases
10.   Additional implied terms where goods are hired to consumers—England, Wales and Northern Ireland
11.   Additional implied terms where goods are hired to consumers—Scotland
12.   Other Amendments to 1982 Act

Amendments to the Supply of Goods (Implied Terms) Act 1973

13.   Additional implied terms in consumer cases
14.   Amendments to the Unfair Contract Terms Act 1977
15.   Consumer guarantees Signature Explanatory Note

The Secretary of State[8] Figure 7.2, being a Minister designated(**1**) for the purposes of section 2(2) of the European Communities Act 1972(**2**)[9] in relation to measures relating to consumer protection, in exercise of the powers conferred on her by that subsection, makes the following Regulations:

Title, commencement and extent

1.–   (1) These Regulations may be cited as the Sale and Supply of Goods to Consumers Regulations 2002 and shall come into force on 31st March 2003.
      (2) These Regulations extend to Northern Ireland.

Interpretation[10]

2.   In these Regulations—
      "consumer" means any natural person who, in the contracts covered by these Regulations, is acting for purposes which are outside his trade, business or profession;

      "consumer guarantee" means any undertaking to a consumer by a person acting in the course of his business, given without extra charge, to reimburse the price paid or to replace, repair or handle consumer goods in any way if they do not meet the specifications set out in the guarantee statement or in the relevant advertising;

"court" in relation to England and Wales and Northern Ireland means a county court or the High Court, and in relation to Scotland, the sheriff or the Court of Session;

"enforcement authority" means the Director General of Fair Trading, every local weights and measures authority in Great Britain and the Department of Enterprise, Trade and Investment for Northern Ireland;

"goods" has the same meaning as in section 61 of the Sale of Goods Act 1979(**3**); "guarantor" means a person who offers a consumer guarantee to a consumer; and "supply" includes supply by way of sale, lease, hire or hire-purchase.

(1)   S.I.1993/2661.
(2)   1972 c. 68.
(3)   1979 c. 54.

AMENDMENTS TO THE SALE OF GOODS ACT 1979

[omitted for the purposes of this book]

AMENDMENTS TO THE UNFAIR CONTRACT TERMS ACT 1977[11]

14.–   (1) The Unfair Contract Terms Act 1977(**7**) is amended as follows.
(2) In section 12, after subsection (1) there is inserted the following subsection–
   "(1A) But if the first party mentioned in subsection (1) is an individual paragraph (c) of that subsection must be ignored.".
(3) For subsection (2) of section 12 there is substituted the following subsection–
   "(2) But the buyer is not in any circumstances to be regarded as dealing as consumer–
      (a) if he is an individual and the goods are second hand goods sold at public auction at which individuals have the opportunity of attending the sale in person;
      (b) if he is not an individual and the goods are sold by auction or by competitive tender.".

(continued . . .)

1 Citation

The year and serial number of the statutory instrument. SI 2002 No. 3045 means that this was the 3,045th statutory instrument of 2002, and this is the definitive way to identify it. The serial numbering reverts to '1' at the start of each calendar year.

2 Subject matter

This SI is about consumer protection.

3 Title

The Sale and Supply of Goods to Consumers Regulations 2002.

4 Date

The SI was made on 10 December 2002. It was laid before Parliament the next day. As the SI was not intended to come into force until some months later, it clearly states the commencement date of 31 March 2003 here and also in s. 1. Note that the year in the title is the year the SI was made, not the year it came into force.

5 Table of Contents

The table of contents provides a useful summary of what you will find in the statutory instrument (SI) and can help you to navigate around the SI.

6 Interpretation

As with a statute, the Interpretation section provides an explanation of the meaning of certain words (sometimes referred to as Definitions) which the statute refers to. The meaning will not necessarily be the meaning that a non-lawyer would understand to be the meaning of a word (and indeed you should assume that a definition in a SI applies only to that SI unless it states otherwise). It is very important to find and read any definitions in order to understand the legislation.

7 Structure

The body of a SI is divided. The names of these divisions depend on the form of the title. If (as here) it is entitled 'Regulations', the divisions are also known as regulations. If it is an 'Order', the divisions are known as articles. If it is entitled 'Rules', the divisions are also known as rules. A subdivision of a regulation, article, or rule is always referred to as a paragraph.

8 Minister

The minister who signed the SI (in this case the Secretary of State). You will find the name of the minister at the end of the SI. Here it was Melanie Johnson.

9 Authority

The authority under which the statutory instrument is made, which in this case is the European Communities Act 1972.

10 Interpretation

See n. 6 above.

11 See n. 7 above

(4) In section 25—
    (a) in subsection (1), the definition of "consumer contract"—
        (i) after the word "means" there is inserted "subject to subsections (1A) and (1B) below";
        (ii) the words "(not being a contract of sale by auction or competitive tender)" are repealed.
    (b) after subsection (1) there is inserted—
      "(1A) Where the consumer is an individual, paragraph (b) in the definition of "consumer contract" in subsection (1) must be disregarded.
      (1B) The expression of "consumer contract" does not include a contract in which—
        (a) the buyer is an individual and the goods are second hand goods sold by public auction at which individuals have the opportunity of attending in person; or
        (b) the buyer is not an individual and the goods are sold by auction or competitive tender.".

Consumer guarantees

15.– (1) Where goods are sold or otherwise supplied to a consumer which are offered with a consumer guarantee, the consumer guarantee takes effect at the time the goods are delivered as a contractual obligation owed by the guarantor under the conditions set out in the guarantee statement and the associated advertising.

(2) The guarantor shall ensure that the guarantee sets out in plain intelligible language the contents of the guarantee and the essential particulars necessary for making claims under the guarantee, notably the duration and territorial scope of the guarantee as well as the name and address of the guarantor.

(3) On request by the consumer to a person to whom paragraph (4) applies, the guarantee shall within a reasonable time be made available in writing or in another durable medium available and accessible to him.

(4) This paragraph applies to the guarantor and any other person who offers to consumers the goods which are the subject of the guarantee for sale or supply.

(5) Where consumer goods are offered with a consumer guarantee, and where those goods are offered within the territory of the United Kingdom, then the guarantor shall ensure that the consumer guarantee is written in English.

(6) If the guarantor fails to comply with the provisions of paragraphs (2) or (5) above, or a person to whom paragraph (4) applies fails to comply with paragraph (3) then the enforcement authority may apply for an injunction or (in Scotland) an order of specific implement against that person requiring him to comply.

(7) The court on application under this Regulation may grant an injunction or (in Scotland) an order of specific implement on such terms as it thinks fit.

10th December 2002

Melanie Johnson[12]

Parliamentary Under-
Secretary of State for
Competition, Consumers and
Markets, Department of
Trade and Industry

EXPLANATORY NOTE[13]

(This note is not part of the Regulations)

These Regulations implement Directive 1999/44/EC of the European Parliament and of the Council of 25th May 1999 on certain aspects of the sale of consumer goods and associated guarantees, referred to below as "the Directive" (OJ No. L 171, 7.7.99, p. 12).

The Regulations make amendments to existing legislation on the sale and supply of goods and unfair terms in order to provide additional remedies to consumers in certain circumstances. The Regulations also contain provisions on the legal status of guarantees offered to consumers and place obligations on guarantors in relation to such guarantees.

Regulation 3 makes amendments to section 14 of the Sale of Goods Act 1979 ("the 1979 Act") in order to give effect to the provisions of Article 2 of the Directive which relate to the seller's liability for public statements made by the seller, the producer or his representative.

Regulation 4 makes amendments to the rules in the 1979 Act governing passing of risk and acceptance of goods in consumer cases.

Regulation 5 introduces a new Part 5A into the 1979 Act in order to give effect to the new rights for consumers set out in Article 3 of the Directive. Where goods fail to conform to the contract of sale at the time of delivery, then under Part 5A the buyer firstly has the right to require the seller to repair or replace the goods within a reasonable time and without causing significant inconvenience to the buyer. If repair or replacement is impossible or disproportionate, or if the seller fails to repair or replace the goods within a reasonable time and without significant inconvenience to the buyer, then the buyer may require the seller to reduce the purchase price of the goods by an appropriate amount, or rescind the contract.

Regulations 7 and 8 make amendments to the Supply of Goods and Services Act 1982 ("the 1982 Act") for England and Wales and Scotland respectively in order to give effect to the provisions of Article 2 of the Directive which relate to the transferor's liability for public statements made by the transferor, the producer or his representative.

Regulation 9 introduces a new Part 1B into the 1982 Act in order to give effect to the new rights for consumers set out in Article 3 of the Directive. Where goods fail to conform to the contract of sale at the time of delivery, then under Part 1B the transferee firstly has the right to require the transferor to repair or replace the goods within a reasonable time and without causing significant inconvenience to the transferee. If repair or replacement is impossible or disproportionate, or if the transferor fails to repair or replace the goods within a reasonable time and without significant inconvenience to the transferee, then the transferee may require the transferor to reduce the purchase price of the goods by an appropriate amount, or rescind the contract.

Regulation 10 makes amendments to the 1982 Act in relation to the hire of goods by consumers in England and Wales which shadow the changes made to the 1979 Act by Regulation 3.

Regulation 11 makes amendments to the 1982 Act in relation to the hire of goods by consumers in Scotland which shadows the changes made to the 1979 Act by Regulation 3.

Regulation 13 makes amendments to the Supply of Goods (Implied Terms) Act 1973 in relation to the hire-purchase of goods by consumers which shadow the changes made to the 1979 Act by Regulation 3.

Regulation 14 makes amendments to the Unfair Contract Terms Act 1977. The definition of "Dealing as consumer" is modified in that the condition in section 12(1)(c) does not apply where the consumer is an individual. Changes are also made to section 12(2) concerning sales at auction.

Regulation 15 provides that where goods are sold or otherwise supplied to a consumer which are offered with a consumer guarantee, the consumer guarantee takes effect as a contractual obligation. The Regulation sets out the requirements for the form and content of consumer guarantees and gives powers to enforcement authorities to apply for an injunction or (in Scotland) an interdict against the guarantor or offeror in the event of non-compliance.

A transposition note setting out how the main elements of the Directive are transposed into law and a regulatory impact assessment have been placed in the libraries of both Houses of Parliament. Copies are also available from the Consumer and Competition Policy Directorate, Department of Trade and Industry, 1 Victoria Street, London SW1H 0ET.

12 Minister

This is the name of the minister who signed the SI and who is referred to, but not by name, at the beginning of the SI.

13 Explanatory Note

As stated in this explanatory note, it does not form part of the SI. As here, it may summarise the purpose of the SI, whether it amends or revokes any previous legislation, or note the implementation of EU legislation.

Figure 7.2 Once you have finished reading Figure 7.2 continue your reading at 7.4.2 above.

7.5 **Case law**

As Chapter 5 explains, case law is a primary source of English law. That chapter also explains the doctrine of precedent (concerning when courts are bound to follow previous decisions) and various other information you need to be aware of if you are to read and understand case law effectively. This chapter considers the practice of reporting a case, the structure of a case report, and how to read and understand that case report effectively.

7.5.1 **Reporting cases**

Where cases are reported

Cases are published in various places. Higher courts will keep a record of the cases they hear, which are often referred to as **transcripts**. The internet is a good source of transcripts. For example, the Supreme Court publishes its judgments on its website and the British and Irish Legal Information Institute (BAILII) publishes judgments from a variety of courts in the UK (details of both websites are set out in the 'Further reading' section of this chapter). Electronic subscription databases such as Lawtel and Lexis®Library also publish transcripts of judgments.

Commercial publishers will choose to report some judgments which they consider to be of particular interest, perhaps because they changed the law or applied it differently. These cases are likely to be ones heard in the higher courts and typically it is these reported cases which you will be reading as a student or junior lawyer. A publisher will help you to read and understand a case by providing useful navigation tools and summaries such as a head-note. You will find these law reports in a variety of places. Three general series report the most significant cases across all areas of the law: the Law Reports (divided into Appeal Cases, Chancery, Family and King's/Queen's Bench), the Weekly Law Reports, and the All England Law Reports. There are also specialist reports (e.g. the Road Traffic Reports and the Family Law Reports), reports in weekly practitioners' journals (such as *New Law Journal* and the *Solicitors' Journal*), and reports in newspapers including *The Times*.

Case citation

You can find cases by using the case citation. This is a list of abbreviations which are used in citations to refer to the most well known series of law reports. You can look up other abbreviations in the Cardiff Index to Legal Abbreviations, further details of which are set out in the 'Further reading' section at the end of this chapter.

AC	Appeal Cases (Law Reports)
All ER / AER	All England Law Reports
CL	Current Law
CLJ	Cambridge Law Journal
CLY	Current Law Year Book
CMLR	Common Market Law Reports
Ch	Chancery (Law Reports)
Cr App R	Criminal Appeal Reports
Crim LR	Criminal Law Review

ECR	European Court Reports
ER	English Reports
FLR	Family Law Reports
Fam	Family Division (Law Reports)
ICR	Industrial Cases Reports
IRLR	Industrial Relations Law Reports
KB	King's Bench (Law Reports)
LJR	Law Journal Reports
LQR	Law Quarterly Review
LR	Law Reports
LS Gaz	Law Society's Gazette
LT	Law Times
LTJ	Law Times Journal
Lloyd's Rep	Lloyd's List Reports (1951 onwards)
MLR	Modern Law Review
New LJ / NLJ	New Law Journal
P	Probate, Divorce & Admiralty (Law Reports)
QB	Queen's Bench (Law Reports)
RTR	Road Traffic Reports
SJ	Solicitors' Journal
WLR	Weekly Law Reports

An example and explanation of a case citation is provided in the extract from the *Donoghue* v *Stevenson* case set out in Figure 7.3.

A new system of neutral citation of judgments was introduced in 2001. The court gives a neutral citation to every judgment, and numbers every paragraph of the judgment. This citation should then feature in every subsequent publication of that judgment, whether online or in hard copy, and paragraphs of the judgment can be referred to by number.

The neutral citation takes the form:

[year in square brackets]	Abbreviation of the name of the court	Serial number (which reverts to 1 each calendar year)

Examples of abbreviations of the name of the courts are:

UKSC	Supreme Court
EWCA Civ	Court of Appeal (Civil Division)
EWCA Crim	Court of Appeal (Criminal Division)
EWHC Admin	High Court (Administrative Division)

Example 1

Smith v *Jones* [2012] EWCA Crim 3 at [49]

This is a reference to paragraph 49 in the judgment of *Smith* v *Jones*, which was the third judgment of the year 2012 in the Court of Appeal (Criminal Division).

[1932] A.C. 562[1]

[HOUSE OF LORDS.][2]
M'ALISTER (OR DONOGHUE) (PAUPER) ... APPELLANT
AND
STEVENSON ... RESPONDENT[3]

1932 May 26.[4]

Lord Buckmaster, Lord Atkin, Lord Tomlin, Lord Thankerton, and Lord Macmillan.[5]

Negligence - Liability of Manufacturer to ultimate Consumer - Article of Food - Defect likely to cause Injury to Health.[6]

By Scots and English law alike the manufacturer of an article of food, medicine or the like, sold by him to a distributor in circumstances which prevent the distributor or the ultimate purchaser or consumer from discovering by inspection any defect, is under a legal duty to the ultimate purchaser or consumer to take reasonable care that the article is free from defect likely to cause injury to health:-[7]

So held, by Lord Atkin, Lord Thankerton and Lord Macmillan; Lord Buckmaster and Lord Tomlin dissenting.[8]

George v. Skivington (1869) L. R. 5 Ex. 1 approved.

Dicta of Brett M.R. in Heaven v. Pender (1883) 11 Q. B. D. 503, 509-11 considered.

Mullen v. Barr & Co., Ld., and M'Gowan v. Barr & Co., Ld., 1929 S. C. 461 overruled.[9]

APPEAL against an interlocutor of the Second Division of the Court of Session in Scotland recalling an interlocutor of the Lord Ordinary (Lord Moncrieff).

By an action brought in the Court of Session the appellant, who was a shop assistant, sought to recover damages from the respondent, who was a manufacturer of aerated waters, for injuries she suffered as a result of consuming part of the contents of a bottle of ginger-beer which had been manufactured by the respondent, and which contained the decomposed remains of a snail. The appellant by her conde-scendence averred that the bottle of ginger-beer was purchased for the appellant by a friend in a café at Paisley, which was occupied by one Minchella; that the bottle was made of dark opaque glass and that the appellant had no reason to suspect that it contained anything but pure ginger-beer; that the said Minchella poured some of the ginger-beer out into a tumbler, and that the appellant drank some of the contents of the tumbler; that her friend was then proceeding to pour the remainder of the contents of the bottle into the tumbler when a snail, which was in a state of decomposition, floated out of the bottle; that as a result of the nauseating sight of the snail in such circumstances, and in consequence of the impuri-ties in the ginger-beer which she had already consumed, the appellant suffered from shock and severe gastro-enteritis. The appellant further averred that the ginger-beer was manufactured by the respondent to be sold as a drink to the public (including the appellant); that it was bottled by the respondent and labelled by him with a label bearing his name; and that the bottles were thereafter sealed with a metal cap by the respondent. She further averred that it was the duty of the respondent to provide a system of working his business which would not allow snails to get into his ginger-beer bottles, and that it was also his duty to provide an efficient system of inspection of the bottles before the ginger-beer was filled into them, and that he had failed in both these duties and had so caused the accident.

The respondent objected that these averments were irrelevant and insufficient to support the conclu-sions of the summons.

The Lord Ordinary held that the averments disclosed a good cause of action and allowed a proof.

1 Case citation

This tells you that the report of the case of *Donoghue* v *Stevenson* starts at page 562 of the Appeal Cases series of the Law Reports for 1932.

Each series of law reports has its own abbreviation. A list of the most common abbreviations is set out in this chapter.

Note that in this citation the year is in square brackets. This is code to show that the year is essential information for finding this case, because volumes of the Law Reports are consecutively numbered within each year. In some citations the year is in round brackets, which is code to show that the information about the year is superfluous as the other information in the citation will allow you to find the case.

This case was reported before the neutral citation system was implemented.

2 Court

It is important to understand which court heard the case, in this instance the House of Lords, because of the doctrine of precedent explained in Chapter 5. A House of Lords decision is really significant, a Court of Appeal decision still important, but less so, and so on.

3 Case name

This is a civil matter, so you should pronounce the case name as 'Donoghue and (not 'v' 'vs' or 'against') Stevenson'. This is an appeal case, so Donoghue, who is bringing the appeal, is referred to as the appellant, and Stevenson, who won in the last hearing, is called the respondent. As Chapter 3 explains, the first time a civil case is heard the person bringing the claim is referred to as the claimant (formerly the plaintiff) and the person against whom the claim is brought is referred to as the defendant.

Criminal cases are set out as 'R v [Name of person being prosecuted]'. You pronounce these case names as 'The Crown against [Name]'. Until 1985, in the magistrates' court, the name of the senior police officer was used instead of 'R'. The person bringing the criminal claim is called the prosecution and the person defending the claim is called the defendant.

4 Dates

Here the date indicates that the judges heard the case and gave judgment on it on the same day, 26 May 1932. If, after the hearing, the judges left to consider the issues and present a full written judgment at a later date (referred to as deferring judgment), then this date would also be stated here.

Note that the date of the report can be different from the date of the decision (it might not even be the same year as the decision).

5 Judges

These are the names of the five House of Lords judges who considered this case. This is useful information as the seniority or reputation of judges can affect how a decision is regarded. The judges deliver their judgments in order of seniority so you can tell that Buckmaster was the most senior Law Lord (although, as discussed at summary of the judgments below, he was in dissent).

6 Subject matter

The editor of the report will choose some words to put here (in italics) as a guide to the subject matter of the case.

7 Headnote

The editor of the report will prepare a summary of the facts of the case and put it here as a headnote. The headnote should summarise the case accurately and if you read this in conjunction with a secondary source of law (e.g. a textbook or *Halsbury's Laws*) it will be extremely helpful in allowing you to ascertain the key points of the case. During legal research (see Chapter 8) the headnote can also help you to consider whether you have found a case which is relevant to the issue you are researching. So there is no doubt that the headnote is useful. You will soon hear, however, if you have not already, the mantra that you really should not read the headnote as an alternative to reading the case itself (which is of course precisely what law students with long reading lists are tempted to do). The reason for this is that the headnote will state what the reporter considers is the

decisive legal principle in the case, but a later case may take a different view or place a different emphasis on the case. The headnote is not authoritative, it is only a summary, and cannot capture the detail of the legal arguments that you will need to understand and apply as a lawyer. A good strategy is to use the headnote and secondary sources to shortlist relevant cases in order of priority, but then make sure you proceed to read those relevant cases (following the guidance set out below). It is interesting, for example, that the headnote of *Donoghue* v *Stevenson* does not really do anything to highlight that the case had the potential to be seen as groundbreaking. You would really have to have read a secondary source of law to ascertain this before proceeding to read the case itself.

8 Summary of the judgments

This says that Lords Atkin, Thankerton, and Macmillan agreed with each other and their judgment prevailed. Lord Buckmaster (the most senior judge) and Lord Tomlin agreed with each other but not with the other judges, so their judgments are referred to as dissenting. It is important to read and understand not only the prevailing judgments, but also the dissenting ones. You can tell that this case was controversial, as the judges only reached a 3:2 majority decision.

9 Relationship with existing case law

The headnote will often indicate what the effect of the decision of this case is on existing case law. We can see here that *Donoghue* v *Stevenson* approved one case, considered one case, and overruled another. Other terms which could be used to describe the effect of a case on existing case law are explained at 5.2.4.

Approved: the House of Lords is stating that this case was correctly decided.

Considered: the House of Lords simply discussed this case.

Overruled: The House of Lords overturned this decision of another court in a different case.

The Second Division by a majority (the Lord Justice-Clerk, Lord Ormidale, and Lord Anderson; Lord Hunter dissenting) recalled the interlocutor of the Lord Ordinary and dismissed the action.[10]

1931. Dec. 10, 11. George Morton K.C. (with him W. R. Milligan) (both of the Scottish Bar) for the appellant. The facts averred by the appellant in her condescendence disclose a relevant cause of action ... [omitted for the purposes of this book]

W. G. Normand, Solicitor-General for Scotland (with him J. L. Clyde (of the Scottish Bar) and T. Elder Jones (of the English Bar)) for the respondent. In an ordinary case such as this the manufacturer owes no duty to the consumer apart from contract ... [omitted for the purposes of this book]

George Morton K.C. replied.[11]

The House took time for consideration.
1932. May 26.
LORD BUCKMASTER (read by LORD TOMLIN).
LORD ATKIN.
LORD TOMLIN.
LORD THANKERTON.
LORD MACMILLAN.[12]

[The full text of each judgment is made available for you on this book's Online Resource Centre or you could choose to look up the case yourself on sites such as BAILII. You are recommended to read this text in conjunction with the guidance below. Chapter 5 considers the judgments and the ratio of the case in some detail and 7.5.3 summarises the key points.]

> *Interlocutor of the Second Division of the Court of Session in Scotland reversed and interlocutor of the Lord Ordinary restored. Cause remitted back to the Court of Session in Scotland to do therein as shall be just and consistent with this judgment. The respondent to pay to the appellant the costs of the action in the Inner House and also the costs incurred by her in respect of the appeal to this House, such last mentioned costs to be taxed in the manner usual when the appellant sues in forma pauperis.*
>
> *Lords' Journals, May 26, 1932.[13]*

Agents for the appellant: Horner & Horner, for W. G. Leechman & Co., Glasgow and Edinburgh.

Agents for the respondent: Lawrence Jones & Co., for Niven, Macniven & Co., Glasgow, and Macpherson & Mackay, W.S., Edinburgh.[14]

10 Details of the Appeal

This provides some background information about the case. It often also includes a short summary of the facts, as here (where the facts are particularly intriguing). It ends with a summary of all the courts that have previously considered this case. It is important to understand this. The first time this case was heard, the Lord Ordinary (the first instance judge for this case in Scotland) found for Donoghue, who had drunk the ginger beer. Stevenson, the manufacturer of the ginger beer, then appealed against this decision to the Second Division, and won. This case is an appeal by Donoghue against the decision of the Second Division. (Do not worry if the court names appear unfamiliar; remember this case was heard in Scotland.)

11 Counsel's submissions

Here are the names of the barristers (also referred to as counsel) who represented each party. Senior barristers are called QCs (Queen's Counsel) when the monarch is female and KCs (King's Counsel) when the monarch is male. At the time of this case George V was King.

As a solicitor it can be useful to know which barristers appeared in a particular case, as you might wish to instruct them in future. However clearly this is no help when the case was decided in 1932.

There is a summary of the legal arguments each barrister put to the court, together with the names of previous cases that they asked the court to consider. (These summaries are omitted in this extract.)

12 Judgment

The judgment is the most important part of any case. (Note that 'judgment' is the correct spelling to use in a legal context, not 'judgement'.)

Judges are each entitled to deliver their own judgment, however here Lord Tomlin reads Lord Buckmaster's judgment. The senior judge usually gives the first judgment, or decides who should. The judges following may give a brief concurring judgment (which can be 'I agree', or a full judgment of their own) and will either support the decision of the other judges, or dissent.

The decision of each judge is key and will be summarised towards the end of their judgment.

Of course before you read these judgments you already know that two of the judges dissent, from the summary of the judgments provided earlier in the report.

_____

13 Decision
The overall decision of the court is stated here. You need to make sure you understand what this is, as it can be less than clear in appeal cases. Here, Donoghue's appeal is being

allowed. The original judgment of the Lord Ordinary (referred to above), finding, in favour of Donoghue, that Stevenson owed Donoghue a duty of care, is restored. The appeal decision of the Second Division, finding in favour of Stevenson, is reversed.

_____

14 Solicitors
The names of the solicitors who represented each party are set out here.

Figure 7.3

7.5.2 **Structure of a case**

As with a statute and a statutory instrument, the layout of a case follows a particular convention. Again, this means that the more familiar you are with this layout, the easier it will be for you to navigate, read, and understand the case effectively. The case of _Donoghue_ v _Stevenson_ is set out in Figure 7.3 below, together with guidance as to how the case is set out. You may recognise this case; it is 'the one about the snail and the ginger beer' and is one of the most famous cases in British legal history. The case concerns the law of tort, and in particular the law of negligence. It is introduced and analysed in Chapters 3 and 5.

7.5.3 **How to read and understand case law**

Chapter 5 gives guidance on how to find the _ratio_ of a case and how to identify what is _obiter dicta_, and considers this specifically in the context of _Donoghue_ v _Stevenson_. This chapter focuses on the practical skill of how to approach your reading of a case.

Read as part of a wider research strategy

As with a statute, you should not expect to obtain a holistic understanding of a case simply by reading the case. Again you can refer to Figure 8.1, which makes clear that 'analysing the primary source' such as a case is just one aspect of finding all relevant law. In particular, where available you should first have read a secondary source, such as a textbook or _Halsbury's Laws_, which describes the key aspects of the case.

Preparing to read the judgments

The key to reading and understanding the judgments effectively is to prepare for your reading of those judgments. You should not read the judgments, wondering, as you do when you read a novel, what the ending will be. Instead, you should have 'done your homework' first, and use the information set out before and after the judgments before you become embroiled in the detail of the case.

The _Donoghue_ v _Stevenson_ example above shows where you can find this information. To recap, the headnote provides a significant amount of important basic information about the case. You should read this first and digest that information. You should also read the important information that, as the example highlights, you can find at the end of the case, particularly the overall decision of the court. This means that, when you begin reading the judgments, which can be heavy work, you are reading from an informed position. You will already know, for example, before you start reading any judgment, the basic facts of the case, the area of law it concerns, what the decision of the case is, which judges agreed with the decision, and which judges dissented from it. You should also have worked out whether it is a decision at first instance, or on appeal. You need to know who the parties are, and have worked out which party actually won the case. In an appeal case this can take a little concentration, as the report might simply say 'appeal dismissed' or 'appeal granted'. When you know what the ending is, and what the starting point is, it is so much easier to concentrate on reading through the judgments and searching for the *ratio* of the case.

How to focus your reading of case law

You need to use your analytical skills when you read a case. The following list of questions should help you to capture the essential facts in context. Answers are provided in relation to the *Donoghue* v *Stevenson* case as an example of how asking yourself these questions can help you to identify the key points in your reading. You will be able to answer some of the questions from the information set out before and after the judgments, but you will not be able to answer all of the questions comprehensively until you have read the judgments too. Referring to these questions before, during, and after your reading can help you to remain focused and analytical and avoid drifting into reading them as a narrative story.

To what area of law does this case relate?
The law of tort.

What principles of law are considered?
The law of negligence and in particular the duty of care.

What level of court did this case reach?
The House of Lords.

What are the relevant facts of the case?
You may remember that the facts were summarised for you at 3.1.2 as follows:
   In August 1928, Mrs May Donoghue joined a friend for a drink in the Wellmeadow Café in Wellmeadow Place, Paisley, Glasgow.
   The friend bought the drinks. The owner poured some ginger beer from an opaque bottle into Mrs Donoghue's glass (which may or may not have had some ice cream floating in it). She took some swigs and then poured the rest of the contents into her glass. To her horror the remains of a decomposing snail presented themselves to her. Mrs Donoghue later complained of stomach pains and shock, both a result of gastroenteritis.
   On appeal, the House of Lords found that the manufacturer would owe a duty of care (that is, a duty not to cause harm carelessly) to the consumer. The courts were considering the issue of whether a duty of care was owed as a preliminary point of law which needed to be established. The case was never tried on its facts as it later settled out of court, so the court did not, for example, ever even consider the issue of whether it was actually the snail which caused Donoghue's gastroenteritis.

Note that sometimes you will not need to refer to the actual facts of a case; all that you will need will be the principle established in the case. However, sometimes it can be very helpful to know the facts to compare or contrast with the facts of a problem you are considering. Chapter 9 explores this further in giving guidance on how to answer problem questions.

Why is this case important?

It forms the basis of the law on the duty of care between a manufacturer and a consumer. Before this case, the law of negligence had evolved piecemeal to impose liability in the absence of a contract, but there had been no attempt to state generally when a duty of care would arise. Instead it had been examined and extended on a case-by-case basis and largely confined to situations where there was a pre-existing relationship between the parties. This case was notable because it established that a duty of care could arise between two parties in the absence of a pre-existing relationship, in any situation where two very general criteria were satisfied (namely that the parties are legally 'proximate' and the damage is 'reasonably foreseeable'). Most think that the wide and general nature of this decision reflects that the majority of the judges were attempting to encourage a more general approach to establishing a duty of care than had gone before.

What decisions did the Court reach?

That the manufacturer, Stevenson, owed a duty of care to Donoghue as the consumer and end user of his products.

Who gave the lead judgment?

Lord Atkin. Note that this is sometimes not immediately obvious. For example, Lord Atkin's judgment is not the first judgment set out in the case. You should look for the judgment with which the majority of other judges agree (or 'concur'). Sometimes the other judges simply say 'I agree' or 'I concur' with the judge giving the leading judgment, but sometimes, as in this case, they will set out their judgments in more detail. In *Donoghue* v *Stevenson* it was with Lord Atkin's judgment that the majority of the other judges, that is Lord Thankerton and Lord Macmillan, agreed.

What was the ratio decidendi *of the case, that is, the reason for the decision?*

Again, you may recall that this was discussed in some detail at 5.2.2. It is not always clear what the *ratio decidendi* of a case is, and you should use the Chapter 5 guidance to help you. However, in *Donoghue* v *Stevenson* the *ratio decidendi* is very clear, because Lord Atkin made it so. He said (at 580, emphasis added):

> You must take reasonable care to avoid acts or omissions which you can *reasonably foresee* would be likely to injure your neighbour. Who, then, in law is my neighbour? The answer seems to be—persons who are so closely and directly affected by my act that I ought reasonably to have them in contemplation as being so affected when I am directing my mind to the acts or omissions which are called in question.

Most think Lord Atkin was seeking to establish a more general approach to a duty of care, which was consistent with the case-by-case approach adopted previously, but which in future might make it easier to anticipate when a duty might be found. He also said (at 599):

> A manufacturer of products, which he sells in such a form as to show that he intends them to reach the ultimate consumer in the form in which they left him with no reasonable possibility

of intermediate examination, and with the knowledge that the absence of reasonable care in the preparation or the putting up of the products will result in an injury to the consumer's life or property, owes a duty to the consumer to take that reasonable care.

Both of these quotations are accepted as *ratios* arising from the case (the second being narrower than the first). However, as explained at 5.2.2, a *ratio* does not have to be quoted from a judgment. A further *ratio* arising out of *Donoghue* v *Stevenson* which is not directly quoted from Lord Atkin's judgment, but which might be implied from his definition of 'who is my neighbour', is that a duty of care arises when the person or property of one person is in such *proximity* to another that, if due care is not taken, she might suffer physical and consequential damage.

Were there any other notable majority judgments?

As stated above, Lord Thankerton and Lord Macmillan did not simply state 'I concur'. When Lord Macmillan states (at 619) 'the categories of negligence are never closed', this can be interpreted to support the view that the majority of judges were seeking to use this case to establish a more general approach to duty of care.

Were there any notable dissenting judgments?

Yes, two of the five law lords dissented, which is significant dissent. In fact, the first judgment you read is Lord Buckmaster's dissenting judgment (because he is the most senior law lord amongst the judges). His judgment comes first (read by Lord Tomlin who also dissented). However, you should have been aware before you started reading, from the information provided before the judgments, that his judgment was dissenting. It is easy to see how you would not have a hope of understanding what happened in this case if you had not prepared properly for reading the judgments and had given up after reading the most senior law lord's (Buckmaster's) judgment. Unlike Lord Atkin, Lord Buckmaster was very dismissive of Donoghue's case and cautioned against extending the reach of a duty of care.

How old is this case?

The parties made their submissions in 1931 and judgment was passed in 1932.

Why is this case relevant today?

This case is still relevant to the law of negligence and is the basis of the law on duty of care between a manufacturer and a consumer. Although the 'wide *ratio*' has been refined by *Caparo Industries plc* v *Dickman* (see 5.2.3), the case has not been overruled and, due to the doctrine of precedent, the law in *Donoghue* v *Stevenson* would bind any High Court or Court of Appeal judge considering questions relating to product liability in negligence.

How to capture, assimilate, and synthesise what you have read

You need to develop a good technique to capture what you have read and understood in a way that will help you assimilate the information logically, put it into context and, crucially for a student, help you to revise effectively. Your answers to the questions set out above will focus your reading and ensure you extract essential information from a case. However, you then need to place what you have read into the wider context and assimilate it with other relevant law in the same area. You can use a spreadsheet very effectively to do this.

Let's consider how you might create a spreadsheet which collates the cases you have read and makes sense of them. We will take as an example the area of contract law, but of course this technique can apply equally well to any other area of law. You could create a separate sheet for each topic of contract law you cover, and label the tabs of the sheets with those topics, such as agreement and intention, consideration and agency, damages, remedies, frustration, pre-contractual terms, duress and undue influence. Within each sheet, you could summarise the key findings from your reading of each case you have read on that topic. How much information to capture is up to you, but for most cases the basics would be name, date, facts, and key findings. For key cases you may wish to include the other information covered by the questions set out above. One of the distinct advantages of using a spreadsheet to record this information is that you can then easily re-order and collate the cases logically under headings. Consider, for example, the sheet on exemption clauses. Most cases in this area are on incorporation, construction, or reasonableness of the clause. Some cases cover third party liability. You could use these as headings, and order the cases beneath those headings. Creating the spreadsheet in itself will therefore help you to identify the relevant legal issues in relation to each topic (e.g. exemption clauses) within an area of law (e.g. contract). It also means that if you subsequently read another case on that issue, you can slot it in at the correct point with ease, e.g. under the reasonableness heading, which of course you cannot do with handwritten notes. You can also easily annotate and amend your work throughout the course as your understanding increases and clarifies. Working with the spreadsheet in this way will familiarise you with the relevant material and make your revision easier.

The example at Table 7.1 is a sample from a basic exemption clause spreadsheet that a student might create on contract law. It covers just the name and key principle learned from the student's reading of the case. The student can develop this using the guidance above, and could also abbreviate words to make it more concise.

Being able to distil complex reading into a summary of key facts is a skill which will benefit from practice, so the sooner you start a working spreadsheet, the earlier you can start to hone this particular skill. Of course, you can practise this skill in other ways too. Even trying to summarise the newspaper article you read over breakfast, and identifying its key message, will help you on your way to an effective method of reading and understanding law.

7.6 European Union law

Chapter 4 provides an analysis of EU law and how it affects law in the UK. You will have realised that you need to be able to find, read, and understand EU legislation and cases.

7.6.1 European Union legislation

As Chapter 4 explains, the primary legislation of the European Union (comprising the founding Treaties that established the European Communities, along with later amending treaties) is very much a framework. It is the secondary legislation which contains the detail. The authoritative text of both primary and secondary legislation appears in the Official Journal of the European Communities (OJ) L-series (for 'legislation').

Table 7.1 A spreadsheet aiming to capture, assimilate, and synthesise reading about exemption clauses in contract law

Incorporation	
Chapelton v Barry	Clause must be in document of contractual nature (deckchair ticket is not)
L'Estrange v Graucob	If clause signed, even if not read, is incorporated...
Curtis v Chemical Cleaning	...provided no misrepresentation
Parker v SE Railway	If clause unsigned, 'reasonable notice' test—by time contract signed
Olley v Marlborough	Exemption clause in hotel bedroom—too late (in absence of regular course of dealings)
Thornton v Shoe Lane	The more onerous the clause, the more needs to be done to bring to notice (here, excluded liability for personal injury)
Interphoto v Stiletto	Applying above. Very high penalty for later return of photos
Hollier v Rambler	Car serviced 3/4 times in 5 yrs is not 'continuous course of dealings'
Kendall v Lillico	Risk of incorporation if seen clause before

Construction	
Houghton v Trafalgar	Ambiguity construed against person who suggested the wording ('contra proferentum')
Stewart Gill v Horatio Myer	Won't blue pencil within one term; immaterial if some parts of clause might have been reasonable in isolation So draft discrete clauses eg <u>Watford</u> (and more liberal approach taken there)
Thomas Witter v TBP	Excluding misrepresentation would mean fraudulent misrepresentation also excluded, so unreasonable. Cf (contrast) <u>Phillips Products v Hyland, Skipskredittforeningen</u>
Phillips Products v Hyland	Excluded liability for negligence, which would include death and personal injury. But case turned on other loss.
Skipskredittforeningen	Court should not focus too much on fact clause would fail by reference to unlikely situations

Reasonableness	
Watford Electronics v Sanderson	Court reluctant to find unreasonableness when bargaining power equal eg Business 2 Business Saw price cap term as distinct from other unreasonable term, so would 'blue pencil' one term.
Smith v Bush	Negligence other than death/personal injury. House buyer brought negligence claim against building society's surveyor. Had signed disclaimer. Guidelines: ● bargaining power? ● reasonably practicable to obtain from alternative source? ● how difficult was task? ● practical consequences?

Third party liability	
Adler v Dickson	Cannot rely on contract if not party to it. Exception in Contract (Rights of Third Parties) Act 1999

The most common types of secondary legislation you are likely to have to read are:

- Regulations (directly applicable in Member States): these are cited by running number then year, so that 1/99 is the first Regulation of 1999.
- Directives (require Member States to pass implementing legislation within a certain timeframe): these are cited by year then running number, so that 99/1 is the first Directive of 1999.

You can find EU legislation on the Europa website and the EUR-Lex website (see the 'Further reading' section at the end of this chapter) as well as the commercial databases such as Lawtel, Lexis®Library, and Westlaw UK.

7.6.2 **Reporting of European Union case law**

The European Court Reports contain the authoritative reports of EU judgments. In the UK the monthly Common Market Law Reports also publish some decisions of the European Court of Justice and some decisions before courts of other Member States that have a bearing on EU law. There is also a European Cases series of the All England Law Reports.

Cases before courts in the EU can proceed differently from cases in courts in the UK, and this in turn affects the reporting of case law. For example, judgments are preceded by an 'opinion' of the Advocate General which, although not binding, is usually followed. Applications to the court that concern the same area of law may be joined together. This means that the names of parties can be very long, and so lawyers often abbreviate the case name when referring to those cases. Law reports, however, may use the full name rather than the abbreviated name by which the case has come to be known.

Citations also differ. Cases have a case number, comprising a running serial number followed by the year of application or reference to the Court. A full citation comprises:

Case number	Parties	Citation of the authoritative report in the European Court Reports

> ### Example 2
> Case C-295/95 *Farrell* v *Long* [1997] ECR I-1683
>
> Since 1989, when the Court of First Instance was created, cases are prefixed by 'C-' (Court of Justice, or 'Cour' in French) or 'T-' (Court of First Instance, or 'Tribunal' in French).

 Summary

- Reading law requires a structured approach.
- The primary sources of law are a statute, a statutory instrument, and a case.
- There are practical steps you can take to enhance your reading skills.
- Do not read a statute from beginning to end, but navigate the statute to find the relevant law.
- Before you read judgments in a case, make sure you have a good understanding of the basic facts.

Thought-provoking questions

1. What was your experience of reading (online) the judgments in the *Donoghue* v *Stevenson* case? If you lost focus, consider why you did and what you might be able to do differently next time to read them more effectively.

2. How would you describe what (i) a statute and (ii) a case look like in terms of structure and layout?

3. Can you summarise the guidance in this chapter into three tips you would give to someone about to read (i) a statute and (ii) a case for the first time?

What the professionals say

No-one finds reading a case for the first time an easy task. The key is to approach your reading in an analytical way, looking beyond the particular facts of the case and identifying the principles of law that are being discussed. Visiting court to see how practising lawyers deploy their research and apply legal principle to argue their client's case can really help you to understand what you are aiming to achieve from your reading. Putting these observed skills into practice during a moot will help you further in identifying the principle rather than unnecessary detail. Then read, read and read some more. It will get easier. The hard work put in at this stage will equip you with a range of analytical skills which will prove invaluable wherever your career may take you.

Katherine Pierpoint, Criminal Barrister, Lincoln House Chambers, Manchester

 Further reading

Keith Walmsley, *Butterworths Company Law Handbook* (London: LexisNexis Butterworths, 26th edn, 2012)
—this includes a collection of the main statutes, statutory instruments, and European material which are relevant to corporate lawyers.
Supreme Court website: http://www.supremecourt.gov.uk/decided-cases
—for transcripts of Supreme Court judgments since August 2009.
British and Irish Legal Information Institute (BAILII) website: http://www.bailii.org
—a good source for case transcripts (see 7.5.1).
Cardiff Index to Legal Abbreviations: http://www.legalabbrevs.cardiff.ac.uk
—an online index of the abbreviations used in citations to refer to law reports (see 7.5.1).
Europa website: http://europa.eu/eu-law/index_en.htm
—general information on EU law (see 7.6.2)
EUR-Lex website: http://eur-lex.europa.eu/en/index.htm
—a good source of European legislation (see 7.6.2).

 For the authors' reflections on the thought-provoking questions, additional self-test questions, podcasts offering a variety of perspectives on legal systems and skills, and a library of links to useful websites, visit the free Online Resource Centre *at* **http://www.oxfordtextbooks.co.uk/orc/slorach/.**

8

Legal research

◎ Learning objectives

After studying this chapter you should be able to:

- Explain the purposes of legal research.
- Describe the types of material to be located to fulfil particular research objectives.
- Explain the main features of primary and secondary sources of law.
- Devise appropriate strategies for carrying out research.
- Apply appropriate techniques to ensure that materials are in force, up to date, and relevant to issues in hand.
- Record and report effectively on the process and results of your legal research.

Introduction

All lawyers need good legal research skills. As we shall see in subsequent chapters, legal research is an intrinsic requirement for law students in being able to write high quality essays and answer problem questions. For lawyers in practice, the skill is a fundamental requirement in being able to advise clients and solve their problems. In both cases, the skill is much more than simply 'finding the law'. There will be frequent occasions when you need information *about* the law or *related to* the law, as well the law itself. In addition, as we shall see when we address problem solving (see Chapter 9) and legal essays (see Chapter 11), considering the purpose of any question, problem, or skill is a major factor in ensuring a high level of performance in the subsequent task or application of the skill.

Therefore this chapter first explores the purposes of legal research: why might you be carrying it out and, more importantly, what are the results you require from it? With these in mind, we then discuss approaches and strategies you can apply to carry out legal research and develop your skills. While we consider various reference sources, we do not intend to provide a comprehensive, exhaustive list of legal and other sources. There are various and numerous sources of law (see Chapter 2). As a law student, your faculty and library and information personnel will provide you with comprehensive guidance on the specific content and 'physical location' (much of course will be located in electronic databases) of these sources of law, and how to access them. Our guidance on legal research is therefore aimed at strategic skills development: how best to plan and carry out legal research in a structured and efficient way, to achieve the results you need.

8.1 The purpose of legal research

The purpose of your legal research will determine your research strategy: the sources you first consult, why, and what you will do with your findings. The other factor involved is your level of knowledge: how well do you know the law in an area and the specific sources of that law? When these factors are combined, you will see that different people carry out differing levels of research to find differing types of material: as we said above, legal research goes beyond simply finding the law.

8.1.1 Research: what materials are required?

The simplest way to illustrate this is to consider some examples, all of which require some research into s. 4 of the Public Order Act 1986. This section deals with the offence of causing fear or provocation of violence.

Examples

A. As part of a criminal law module, a student reading list includes: 'Section 4 Public Order Act 1986'.

B. An essay title: 'There is an overlap between the types of conduct required for offences under section 91 Criminal Justice Act 1967, and sections 4, 4A and 5 Public Order Act 1986. Discuss.'

C. An undergraduate problem question: 'Adrian is working as a steward at a football match. At the end of the match, Colin, a supporter of the losing side, ran down the steps of the stand towards Adrian. The latter thought that Colin was going to attempt to run on to the pitch. When Adrian stood his ground, to prevent Colin from getting to the pitch, Colin screamed abuse at Adrian, including the words: "if you don't get out of my way right now, I'll make you ... I'm going to take your head off ...".'

D. A practising criminal lawyer has a client who has been charged under s. 4 of the Public Order Act 1986. The lawyer believes that she may be able to argue that her client did not commit this offence by reason of having committed a lesser offence.

Let's examine each of these examples, considering the purpose of the legal research and the research tasks that would be undertaken as a consequence.

Example A

Here, the student has been given the name of a statute, together with a section number. (Similarly, reading lists will provide the names of cases to be read.) The research task would simply involve locating that section. Most likely, the student will either print out or copy the section, or make a note of its provisions. The intended result—without further instruction on any application of that law—is simply that the student should *know the law* created by that section.

Example B

Here, as in Example A, the student is given a specific direction to statutory material, so the first research task is to locate the material. Again, the student will print, copy, or make notes of the relevant provisions. However, the intended result is not simply to know the law. The purpose of a legal essay is also that a student should be able not only to state *what* the law is, but also show a wider understanding of the purpose and effect of the law, and be able to apply specific intellectual skills (see 11.1.2). One of these, as in this case, is the ability to discuss the law. A general requirement is to demonstrate critical thinking, which involves being able to show that you understand, have considered, and have a view on the discussions and arguments which have surrounded the development, interpretation, and application of the law.

So, Example B not only requires the student to research:

(a) *what* is the law; but also

(b) *how* that law has developed, and been interpreted and applied (thus, *commentary* on the law), focusing on the areas of overlap mentioned in the question; and

(c) *what* have been the views of academics and other experts on all of the latter (*opinion* on the law).

Only once the student has researched (b) and (c) will he be able to apply critical thinking skills. The student might also wish, to develop and demonstrate a broader understanding, to research (d): material *relating to* the law. In this case, finding out the number of convictions for each of the offences created under each of the sections could provide interesting supporting material. Note that in the example given, the student has been given explicit directions as to what is the specific applicable law. The question could have been posed without specific reference to the sections, perhaps referring more broadly to 'public order offences'. In this case, the student would first have had to locate the specific law, before moving on to the other types of research.

Example C

This differs from Example B in that the student is not given any explicit directions on the law. In many cases, the student would know that the problem involved a public order offence, perhaps because it was set at the time of teaching on public order offences or, if part of an assessment on criminal law, through having revised the subject. If so, the student would have at least an area of law within which he might narrow down his search to the offence in question. If not, then we have an example where the student may neither have knowledge of the applicable law nor the sources of that law. That being the case, the student will have to carry out initial fact and problem analysis (see 9.2), and apply a series of search terms (see 8.3.1) to identify the broad area of law—public order offences—within which to research. Then, within that area, the student will have to research further to identify the specific sources of the law that cover the offence in question.

In the same way as in Example B, the student will certainly have to research both *what* the law is and some *commentary*. The latter will provide material on *how* the law has been applied: application of the law is one of the major steps in legal problem solving (see 'Application' at 9.1.3). If there are differing views as to how the law should or might be applied, this will be found in *opinion* pieces. Depending on the particular issues posed by the problem, there might be cause to consider additional material about the law, but this would be less prevalent.

Example D

Here, the practitioner knows the offence and particular section under which the client has been charged. She also appears to know a lesser offence that she believes she can argue was the *actual* offence committed, and we can expect that she would be capable of finding the relevant statute and section. In these circumstances, depending on experience, some practitioners might know the precise wording of each statute, *and* which words are most important in defining and establishing the offence, *and* how these important words have been interpreted in previous cases. However, even experienced practitioners will often take a prudent approach and carry out either or both of: a check of the precise wording of each section (hence the law); and reference to some form of *commentary*—most likely a practitioner text—on how the wording is usually applied.

8.1.2 **Types of materials—summary**

If we summarise the various types of legal research which were applied in the above examples, we can see that, depending on the purpose and person involved, research may be carried out to locate materials which provide:

- the relevant law;
- commentary on the law;
- opinion on the law; and
- 'non-legal' material relating to the law.

The important point in terms of developing your skills is that you should consider, for any task, the required result and therefore what types of materials you should seek. This is a major part of developing a research strategy, which we consider in 8.2 and 8.3, together with which are the best sources for locating each of the types of materials summarised above, and some techniques for effective and efficient research.

The flowchart at Figure 8.1 summarises the essential steps for conducting effective and efficient legal research. Chapter 9 builds further on this to create a comprehensive problem-solving flowchart (see Figure 9.1).

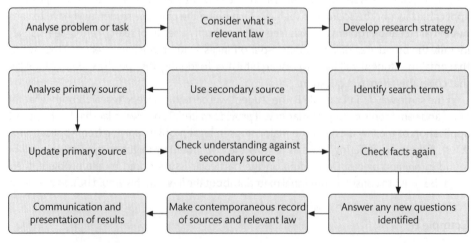

Figure 8.1 Legal research flowchart

8.2 Strategy: planning your research

8.2.1 First steps

From 8.1, you can see that legal research is not just 'finding the law' and that the latter is not the first stage of legal research. If you embark prematurely on finding the law, as many students do, there will be a fair chance that you will not have a clear idea of what you are looking for. You then risk wasting time in taking notes, and printing and reading law which is wholly irrelevant to your research task. Once you have taken this route, it can be quite difficult to go back and start again. So, however tempting it may be, delay your search for the relevant law until you have:

- analysed your task and any related facts;
- clearly identified the legal issues it raises (which, as we have seen, might require some initial research);
- considered what types of materials (including the relevant law) you need to locate as part of your research; and
- thought about a strategy which will be both efficient and effective in locating the specific materials which will best suit your requirements.

As part of an efficient research strategy, you should consider which search terms (see 8.3.1) are most likely to help you locate relevant law most quickly. The above is all essential ground-work for effective legal research.

8.2.2 What is the relevant law?

At 8.2.1 we have used the expression 'relevant law'. This would appear to be rather obvious: you should locate the law relevant to your task, whether it be reading, problem-solving, es-say-writing, or advising. However, frequently students struggle to understand the meaning of relevant law, particularly when researching case law. When looking for relevant case law, you are looking first and foremost for cases which feature the same *legal principles* which you think are *relevant* to your task. Many students will search only for cases with the same, or strik-ingly similar, facts as the problem they have been asked to research. Although any such cases are likely to be relevant and helpful, in practice you are unlikely always to find a case which is factually similar to the legal problem you are researching.

To illustrate what we mean about featuring the same legal principles, we shall look at the case of *Donoghue* v *Stevenson*, set out in Chapter 7. The facts in that case are both memor-able and specific, featuring decomposing snails and ginger beer. To the author's knowledge, there have been no reported cases with the same facts. The case however established a principle that a manufacturer owes a duty of care to the consumer and end user of its prod-ucts. It is therefore a relevant case to consider in relation to any problem where a consumer wants to sue a manufacturer, regardless of the type of goods manufactured. However, the legal principles established in *Donoghue* on owing and measuring a duty of care are not limited to manufacturing situations and product liability: these principles have been applied in cases where the facts concern, for example, personal injury or occupiers' liability. The principles in *Donoghue* v *Stevenson* may be *relevant law* to consider when dealing with a range of matters in tort.

Having considered what is relevant law, we will now develop a research strategy to help you to find it efficiently. First, we shall consider secondary and primary sources, before looking at some particular search techniques.

8.2.3 **Starting with secondary sources**

Overviews

A good strategy in legal research is to use what is referred to as a **funnel approach**. This involves casting a wide net to begin with by first reading an overview of the area law in question. This is invariably valuable even if you have been directed to a specific case or statute, as in examples A and B (see 8.1.1).

You will usually be able to find an overview of a common legal issue in an undergraduate textbook. However, if you feel you need an alternative, or if the legal issue you need to research is more specialised, then consider *Halsbury's Laws* (see inset box below), which has commentary on a wide range of legal issues.

Whether you start with a textbook, *Halsbury's Laws*, or another commentary, these are all known as 'secondary sources' of law because they are not the original source of the law (that will be legislation or a case), but instead they discuss or comment on it. This is useful in two ways. First, the secondary source should identify the primary source(s) of the relevant law. Second, the secondary source should help to give you an initial understanding of the primary source and hence its relevance to your particular task. Depending on the type of secondary source, it may provide valuable material of some or all of the types summarised in 8.1.2.

Halsbury's Laws

This is a really useful secondary source, and is available as a paper resource or electronically using Lexis®Library.

Paper resource

You should search against the broad legal context in the Index to find the volume, edition, and paragraph number. When you read the paragraph, it will provide a commentary on the law, and there are likely to be lots of footnotes. It is essential to read these footnotes, as you will often find the detail about the primary sources of law there. You then need to consult the *Cumulative Supplement* to check if there has been any change to the law since the volume you have read was published. The *Cumulative Supplement* cross-refers to the volume you have just read. It will note any changes that have been made to any paragraphs of that volume. If there have been no changes, there will be no listing in the *Cumulative Supplement*, so do not worry if there is no update for the paragraph you have read. Finally, you should check the *Noter Up*, again by volume then paragraph, for any changes to the law since the *Cumulative Supplement* was published.

Electronic resource

You can access *Halsbury's Laws* through Lexis®Library. The UPDATE paragraph towards the bottom of the page is the electronic equivalent of both the *Cumulative Supplement* and the *Noter Up*.

In addition to an undergraduate academic textbook or *Halsbury's Laws*, which can provide a good starting point when researching a particular area of law, you should also consider, particularly in the context of the type of material you are seeking (see 8.1.2), the following secondary sources.

Encyclopaedias

You should consider consulting this type of secondary source for detailed explanation of and commentary on the law. *Halsbury's Laws* is in the form of an encyclopaedia. It differs from most other legal encyclopaedias in the comprehensive nature of its contents: commentary on the law of England & Wales. Other encyclopaedias tend to focus on a single area of law: for example EU law, competition law, or employment law. Although a secondary source, some may also include relevant primary legal materials. Given their depth, they are often compiled and kept up to date by a team of authors and editors, which may include both academics and practitioners, thus providing a rounded and detailed explanation of the law in an area.

Journals

Legal journals are a valuable source of opinion on the law (see 8.1.2). As such, they are an excellent resource when carrying out research for a legal essay or longer piece of writing, such as coursework. They are published by academic institutions and commercial publishers on a periodic basis. Many are also available in electronic form. They may be general in nature, such as the *Law Quarterly Review*, or more specialised, such as the *Journal of International Banking Law & Regulation*. Depending on its target readership, a journal may adopt an academic or more practical approach to the law. To that extent, journals may also provide a source of commentary on the law. The *Legal Journals Index* is the main resource which you can use to locate UK published legal journal articles.

Practitioner texts

These texts provide guidance, explanation, and commentary on how the law in a particular area is applied in practice. Commonly used by practitioners (as the description suggests), they can also be a very useful resource when dealing with problem-solving questions. Practitioner texts may vary in depth and complexity: some may resemble encyclopaedias, while others may be in a handbook in format. Depending on the subject matter in question, practitioner texts may also include guidance on legal procedures, such as court actions and company administration matters.

Websites

These can provide materials of all the types summarised at 8.1.2. For example, the progress of new UK legislation can be tracked on http://www.legislation.gov.uk, which also provides access to vast tracts of UK legislation, some of it dating back to 1267. Many other government websites give you access to the law, commentary and guidance on the law, and 'non-legal' materials relating to the law. Examples include http://www.hmrc.gov.uk on all aspects of revenue law, http://www.companieshouse.gov.uk on company formation and administration, and https://www.gov.uk/government/organisations/department-for-business-innovation-skills, which provides a wide range of guidance on business law and employment. The Crown Prosecution Service website, at http://www.cps.gov.uk, provides a range of legal resources, including guidance on the application of a number of criminal statutes. You can also find data and statistics on prosecutions on this website, an example of non-legal materials which you might use in an essay. Again, government websites are a good source of these materials.

Outside the government websites, there are a host of other sources of legal and non-legal material, including websites and blogs hosted by law firms, practitioner groups, and interest or campaigning groups. For an example of a practitioner website, see the Society of Trust and Estate Practitioners site at http://www.step.org, which, amongst its publication resources, has a series of leaflets explaining wills and trusts matters to the public. For examples of interest or campaigning groups, search for the websites of Liberty, the Consumer Action Group, and Amnesty International.

A final note on websites: while they can be a rich source of material, it is generally neither good practice nor efficient to rely on general internet search engines for legal research. You should have a rationale—being clear as to what particular type of material you are searching for—before searching. You should also consider the reliability of any website: is it a trustworthy, up-to-date reference source that you would be happy to cite in your work? Government websites and those belonging to major and well-respected organisations are likely to be more reliable.

8.2.4 **Primary sources**

As explained in Chapter 2, the original source of law will be legislation and/or case law. These are referred to as 'primary sources' of law. Reading a secondary source first will help you to identify and understand the primary source. However, if you are to develop both your general skills as a lawyer and your specific research skills, you should not rely solely on secondary sources. To be a good lawyer you must develop the confidence and the skills to read and interpret the primary source of law.

You will find *legislation* in a variety of books and databases including *Halsbury's Statutes*, *UK Parliament Acts*, Westlaw UK, and Lexis®Library. *Case law* is found by undertaking a case search, using resources such as *Current Law Case Citator*, Westlaw UK, and Lexis®Library. Guidance on finding current legislation and case law is set out at 8.3.3.

To a new user, these sources can feel impenetrable. Wording may appear complex, definitions from one section of a statute have to be 'read in' to other sections, and there is no denying that many pieces of legislation are long. Attempting to read a statute or even a part of a statute in its entirety will be difficult. However, if you use the guidance in Chapter 7 on how to read and understand law, you will be able to read the law more effectively and the process should be significantly easier. As with any skill, the more you practise reading primary sources, the easier you will find it.

8.3 **Research techniques**

Having considered the materials you need to locate, and why, and planned where you are going to find those materials within secondary and primary sources, we now turn to research techniques which you can employ.

8.3.1 **Identifying search terms**

Whether you are using paper or electronic versions of sources, you need to consider which search terms will best assist you to locate your material. Search terms should be key words relevant to the issues of law you are seeking to research. The wording of a question or facts of a problem will help you to identify some of these key words. You should then use these key words to search in an index (for paper resources) or in a database search engine (for electronic resources) using the techniques explored below to narrow your results.

Example 1

Consider a problem where you were advising on the rights of someone who had bought a domestic washing machine. The door seal of the appliance was faulty, which led to the buyer's kitchen being flooded. As a result, the buyer had to replace two adjoining kitchen units, the bases of which had become saturated with the water from the washing machine. The appliance had been sold on the basis of a standard form contract which included a term which purported to exclude any liability for damage other than to the appliance itself.

In these facts, examples of search terms which may be suitable are:

- Sale
- Goods
- Faulty
- Liability
- Exclusion
- Remedies

You may be able to think of others. Be prepared to try variations of your original search terms if they prove fruitless. For example, if 'faulty' does not return any helpful material, try 'poor quality', 'defective', 'unsatisfactory quality', and so on.

8.3.2 Techniques for using electronic resources

The following techniques will improve the effectiveness of your search of electronic resources, and help you to reduce your results to a manageable number.

Truncation

Typing 'excluding' into a search engine will only find examples of that particular word. It will not look for 'exclude' or 'exclusion'. A search with a truncated word is better because it will extend your search to find all permutations of that word. So, if a leading case on excluding liability did not include the word 'excluding', but referred throughout to 'exclusion', using phrases such as exclusion of liability, exclusion clauses and so on, a search using the term 'excluding' would not find this case. It is useful therefore to truncate the word. The technique will vary from database to database; however, a common way is to type 'exclu*', or 'exclu!'. The following further examples demonstrate how truncating search terms can keep open your search options:

- Pollution (Pollut*—finds pollute, pollutes, pollution, polluting, and pollutants)
- Penalties (Penalt*—finds penalty and penalties)
- Taxation (Tax*—finds tax, taxes, taxation)
- Infestation (Infest*—finds infest, infests, infestation)
- Injury (Injur*—finds injury, injuries)

Wild card characters

Wild card characters work within a word just as truncation works at the end of a word. For example, 'm*n' would search for both 'men' and 'man'.

Connectors

The words 'and', 'or', and 'not' are such common words that they are not useful as search terms. Electronic databases recognise this, and generally will not use them as search terms but will instead take them to be commands as follows:

- Joining two search terms with:
  - 'and' will retrieve results only where both words appear;
  - 'or' will produce results where either of the search terms appear.
- Using 'not' will exclude results in which the search term appears.

Phrase searching

If you consider that a source will use words in a phrase, such as 'sale of goods' or 'exclusion clause', then you should search for that phrase. The most common technique is to put the phrase in quotation marks, so, for example, you would search for 'exclusion clause' rather than search for 'exclusion' and 'clause'. Using this guidance, we might refine our search terms as follows:

- 'Sale of Goods' and Fault*
- Limit* and liability
- Exclu* and liability
- Exclusion clause
- Remed* and 'sale of goods'

8.3.3 Ensuring primary sources are up to date

The fact that the law continues to change and evolve makes legal research particularly challenging. Unfortunately, it can be relatively easy to find law which is out of date. The challenge is to find out whether it has changed and, if so, how. Set out below is guidance as to how to check that the law you find is current and in force.

Legislation

Potential problem 1: is it in force?

Chapter 7 shows where you can find the commencement date of legislation, and explains that this may be after the date in the short title of the legislation, which refers to the date of Royal Assent (see 7.3.1). When you are researching legislation, it is therefore vital to check whether the version you refer to has actually come into force yet.

Consider the following example, an extract from the Treasure Act 1996. Section 8(3) of this statute sets out the penalty which can be imposed on someone who finds treasure (as defined elsewhere in this statute) but fails to comply with the obligation to notify the coroner (as set out earlier in s. 8(1)).

Example 2

8. Duty of finder to notify coroner

(3) Any person who fails to comply with subsection (1) is guilty of an offence and liable on summary conviction to—

(a) imprisonment for a term not exceeding *three months* [51 weeks]

Sub-s (3): in para (a) words 'three months' in italics repealed and subsequent words in square brackets substituted by the Criminal Justice Act 2003, s280(2), (3), Sch26, para 48.

Date in force: to be appointed: see the Criminal Justice Act 2003, s336(3).

This statute contains public sector information licensed under the Open Government Licence v1.0.

The question is: what is the maximum term of imprisonment under the statute? The answer to this depends on whether s. 336(3) of the Criminal Justice Act 2003 is in force. Given that the commencement date of a statute can be after the date it is made and laid before Parliament, it is perfectly possible that a statute with the year 2003 in the title, or part of that statute, is not yet in force. The words 'to be appointed' indicate that s. 336 was not in force at the time this version of s. 8 was printed; however, it could have been printed some time ago. You would need to use your legal research skills to check the position using an electronic database or paper resource. If s. 336(3) is in force, it will have repealed the words 'three months' and imposed the new maximum sentence of 51 weeks. If s. 336(3) is not yet in force, the maximum sentence remains at three months.

Potential problem 2: has it been amended or repealed?

Statutes are amended over time, or even repealed altogether. Again, you need to check before relying on the source.

Locating current legislation using paper resources

Halsbury's Statutes and *Halsbury's Statutory Instruments* are paper resources you can use to find legislation. The steps to follow are:

1. Look up the legislation in the index. This will give you the volume and page you need.

2. When you find the legislation in the volume, check the commencement date (see 7.3.1) not only for the legislation as a whole, but also for the particular sections you are reading. You cannot assume every part of the legislation is in force.

3. Next, consult the *Cumulative Supplement* to check whether there have been any changes since the volume you have just read was published. The *Cumulative Supplement* is an annual volume that updates all the main volumes up to the end of the previous calendar year.

4. Then, check the *Noter Up* for changes made since the date of publication of the *Cumulative Supplement*. The *Noter Up* is issued monthly and updates the *Cumulative Supplement*.

In both the *Cumulative Supplement* and the *Noter Up* you will search against the name of the Act then against the section you are using. If the section is not referred to, you can assume that the legislation in the volume is up to date.

Locating current legislation using electronic databases

The most common general electronic databases are Lexis®Library and Westlaw UK. Both databases employ techniques to highlight updating issues, but the techniques they use are different.

At the time of writing, Lexis®Library uses text formatting such as square brackets, italics, underline, and ellipsis to identify issues such as prospective repeals, repeals, prospective insertions, and insertions. An explanatory document is maintained on their website to 'translate' the text formatting you will see. Lexis®Library also features useful click-through buttons on the face of the legislation. 'Stop press' will identify the latest news about legislation, 'Date in force' will make absolutely clear, not surprisingly, whether the legislation is in force, and 'Related cases/commentary' will make it easy for you to find related law and descriptions of the law you have found.

At the time of writing, Westlaw UK uses status icons to indicate whether the law is in force, whether amendments are pending or prospective, or whether the provision has been superseded or repealed. These icons are explained in a document maintained on their website. Westlaw also uses click-through buttons such as 'Version in Force', 'Legislation Analysis', and 'Annotations', the titles of which are self-explanatory.

Case law

Potential problem: has the case been reversed or overruled?

Chapter 5 explains that cases can be reversed by a higher court on appeal or overruled by a higher court in a subsequent case (see 5.2.3). The potential problem is that you may therefore, in the course of your research, find a judgment that is no longer current law. The guidance below will ensure that you use only current case law.

Locating current case law using paper resources

Current Law Case Citator provides information on all English cases which have been judicially considered since 1947. It is set out as an alphabetical index of cases in volumes according to the period indicated on the spine. For each case, there will be provided details of when and where it was reported, together with any articles or journals in which the case was commented upon. There will also be a reference to a digest of the case in the *Current Law Yearbook*. The *Citator* will also indicate whether the case has been applied, considered, distinguished, or overruled, and, if so, in which case or cases. A reference to the location of these cases in the relevant *Current Law Yearbook* will also be provided. When considering more recent cases, the *Current Law Monthly Digest* provides similar information.

Locating current case law using electronic databases

Lexis®Library has a CaseSearch function, and at the time of writing uses status icons (rather than the text formatting it uses for legislation) to indicate whether a decision has been reversed, disapproved, overruled, had doubt cast on it, received positive treatment, and whether or not it has been considered.

Westlaw has a Case Analysis function which uses a different set of status symbols, to indicate how a case has been treated and its currency.

Both databases maintain explanatory lists of their respective status symbols. (Note also when searching for cases there is an option to search by relevance, which is not the default option but which can be very useful when you do not know the name of the case you are looking for.)

8.3.4 **Checking your understanding of primary sources**

A good way to check your understanding of a primary source is to check your interpretation of the law against the commentary in a secondary source *after* you have analysed the primary source. As this is a verification stage, it may be helpful to use an alternative secondary source (e.g. an encyclopaedia or practitioner text—see 8.2.3) rather the original one (e.g. an academic text or *Halsbury's Laws*) you may have used at the outset. This verification process will also help to consolidate your understanding of the relevant area of law.

8.3.5 **Continue to check facts**

If you are dealing with problem questions or advising, you should continue to check the facts as you carry out your research. This is for two reasons:

1. It is easy to forget about an important fact when you have been researching another issue for a while. It is a surprisingly common error in legal research to overlook a important fact. In Example 1 about the washing machine, for instance, it would be possible to become consumed by the purported limitation on liability and to forget to consider the central issue of the defective product. A mind map, setting out the main facts and issues (see 9.2.3), can help to avoid this problem.

2. Sometimes you will not have realised the importance of a fact until you have read the law. For example, if you discover that a penalty applies only to someone who is over 18, you may need to go back to the facts if, at the time you originally considered them, you had not realised that age would be a relevant factor.

8.3.6 **Answer any new questions raised by your research**

Often the answers you find to one question will raise further questions of their own. You must approach the answers you find with a questioning mind, and leave no relevant question unanswered. By way of example, let's return to the Treasure Act 1996.

Example 3
Treasure Act 1996, s. 8(3)

Any person who fails to comply with subsection (1) is guilty of an offence and liable on summary conviction to—

(a) imprisonment for a term not exceeding *three months* [51 weeks];

(b) a fine of an amount not exceeding level 5 on the standard scale; or

(c) both.

If you have found that there has been an offence under s. 8(1), it is essential that you undertake further research to find the 'standard scale', and find out what 'level 5' means, so you can state exactly the maximum fine that can be imposed. If you do not do this, then you will not be providing full information, whether to a reader, examiner, or client.

8.4 Recording and presenting your research

We considered at 8.1 the purposes of legal research and the type of tasks that will require you to employ research skills. Where those tasks are part of your undergraduate studies, the results of your research will usually be translated and incorporated into either a piece of written work, or a presentation or other contribution in a class. An exception to this would be, for example, a legal skills module including stand-alone research skills tasks, where you might be required to produce a form of research report (see 8.4.2). Chapters 9 to 11 provide detailed guidance on legal writing (on both problem questions and essays) and oral communications. One point to remember in relation to all these formats is that part of the skill of presenting the findings of legal research is being selective. That is, you should only present material that is relevant to the task you were set, using language appropriate to your audience. As to the former, there is always a risk that you become too close to your research or feel that you have to present every last detail you found, no matter how irrelevant it is to the issues in hand. You should always think about the outcomes of legal research in terms of quality rather than quantity.

The quality of your output will be determined by both how you record your research as you carry it out, and how you present the final version of your findings, whatever the required format. Given the guidance in Chapters 9 to 11 on other formats, this section provides further guidance in the context of producing a research report for a client in practice. However, do note the commonality of skills required as between practice and, in particular, dealing with problem-solving questions on an undergraduate programme. In addition, during your studies, the recording techniques set out in 8.4.1 should be adopted when you are required to cite sources.

8.4.1 Contemporaneous record

You should make a contemporaneous record of your research, to help you create the final report of your research when you have finished. A contemporaneous record involves noting what you do and when you do it, as you do it. As it is for your own reference, you may wish simply to annotate a written or diagrammatic record of the facts, or you may wish to produce a separate written record. However you make your contemporaneous record, it should include what you have found at each stage plus:

- the date your research was carried out (this is particularly important when working with online sources, where content can change daily);
- the titles of the sources consulted;
- search terms used during searches;
- page references or website addresses for important pieces of information;
- dates of publication (including the date of the latest release for a looseleaf source);
- any dates to which the law as stated is claimed to be up to date by the publisher;
- how you made sure the law you found was up to date.

The reasons for the additional details are to allow you to (a) easily locate the material again should you wish to check a point or an additional question arises from later research; (b) correctly cite sources should your final piece of work based on the research require this; and (c) remind yourself to take steps to ensure that your primary sources are up to date (see 8.3.3).

8.4.2 Producing a research report

Once you have completed your research, you need to present your findings in a way which the recipient of your findings will find helpful. In undergraduate skills modules, you might be asked to produce a formal written report of your research. In legal practice, you might be asked to produce a formal report or, less formally, summarise your research to your supervisor by email. You might even be asked to produce the first draft of a letter of advice or legal opinion, based on your research.

Your contemporaneous record will help you to compile a research report, albeit the latter will look very different to the former. It is important that you do not include anything in this report which you do not fully understand, as it is common, particularly in practice, for the recipient of your report to ask you to explain it, or part of it, verbally.

Purpose

A research report is normally only required for internal purposes. Once reviewed by a supervising lawyer, it will usually then be used as the basis for written or oral advice, or some other action. Your research report should therefore fulfil two purposes. It should:

- Highlight and summarise the main issues and your key findings. The person you have undertaken research for is likely to be busy. A wordy, lengthy research report with the answers buried within it may demand time to digest that the recipient simply cannot spare (or justify from a fees perspective).
- Provide enough detail so that the reader could replicate your research if necessary, and check that your conclusions are properly supported. A report that is too brief will leave the recipient with no way of verifying its accuracy.

One common format is to begin the report with a conclusion that summarises the main issues and your key findings, followed by the detail of the research supporting that conclusion. This may seem counter-intuitive, but it has the advantage for recipients that they will know immediately what the result of your research is, before moving on to the more detailed rationale. (In practice, you might even summarise the conclusion in a covering email or memorandum as well as in the report itself.) The following section provides an example of a research report format that adopts this approach.

Research report format

In practice, some law firms often have their own preferred format which they will recommend you use. Equally, a tutor may recommend a particular approach to recording and reporting research. What is produced below demonstrates common elements of a research report in a format that would create a useful report for a recipient. It also illustrates various elements commonly required in practice, such as client details.

In practice, each client and each matter for that client will be given a reference, which might be numerical or some letters derived from the client's name, or a combination of those. It is helpful to include these references here (e.g., Client: CHL, Matter: 1234-5678) so it is clear where to file your report and to ensure that any time spent on this report, for example reading it, can be recorded against the correct file.

[CLIENT]
[MATTER]
[FILE REFERENCE]
DATE [OF REPORT]

CLIENT'S OBJECTIVES

Your list of the client's known objectives.

LEGAL ISSUES

Your own summary of the legal issues that you cover in your report. You may have been given these issues to research or you may have had to deduce them yourself by analysing the facts and the legal problems arising out of them (see 9.2.2 for a practice-based example of this).

CONCLUSION

Here you provide 'the answer' to the problem. This requires application of the research law to the facts and identification of the options for the client (see 9.3.1 and 9.3.2 for a practice-based example of this). You should aim to provide an unequivocal conclusion about how the law affects this particular client. It takes confidence to do this. Do not 'hedge your bets' or be inconsistent. Students often use language such as 'it seems that it might' or 'probably'. If this is to express a *genuine* doubt that exists, having applied the law to the facts correctly, then fine. However do not use this language simply because you are not confident that your answer is correct. Make sure you use the facts properly here. Do not say 'If X is Y' if the facts are clear that X is Y; say 'As X is Y' instead.

Your conclusion as to the effect of the law must be both clear and complete. It should be clear enough so that your supervisor could cut and paste it, for example into an email to the client. You should not include explanatory detail, such as citing your authority, here. Supporting detail is very important, but you will put it in the report section below. It should be complete, such that you neither leave anything unanswered, nor make a point that raises further questions that you do not address.

It may seem strange to provide your answer first, without explanation, but it is for the reader's benefit. The report is not intended to be a contemporaneous or chronological note of your research. You should have completed your research before you begin to write your report. If you think of any worked example you may have seen, you will appreciate that it is easier to follow reasoning when you already know the answer. A busy supervising lawyer will also find it helpful to have the answer summarised at the beginning of your report for ease of reference.

ADVICE

Your report must form the basis for advising a client, so it should set out your overall advice here, including any practical advice. This is where you need to evaluate the options (see 9.3.3) and provide advice on which might be the most appropriate (see 9.3.4). The difference between conclusion and advice is explored in section 9.3; however, to give an example, you might conclude that the client has a legal right to sue, but advise not to sue because, for example, it would be too expensive, or it is better to preserve a working relationship with the other party.

For more simple research tasks, one report will suffice. For more complex tasks, raising several issues, it may be helpful to prepare a single summary of issues and conclusions, with a separate supporting research report for each issue. Each of the latter would then require report two further headings, 'Issue' and 'Conclusion', which you would cross-refer to the summary document.

SUPPORTING RESEARCH REPORT

HOW THE LAW APPLIES TO THE FACTS OF THE PROBLEM

This is where you explain how you reached the 'answer' set out in your conclusion. This is the main part of your report, and you will detail how the law applies to the facts of the legal issue. You should follow the guidance in Chapter 9 as to how to apply the law to the facts effectively, and the guidance in Chapter 11 as to how to write clearly and concisely. Your explanation should be easy to read and it should refer expressly to the facts of the question.

You must identify the primary source(s) of law here. It is good practice to include details of the relevant ratio of a case and/or the text of the relevant parts of the legislative provision. Do not simply copy out chunks of legislation or judgment though: cite only that which is relevant. It can occasionally be helpful to attach extracts of the primary source, but again only attach relevant extracts. In general, however, be cautious about attaching extracts. Many practitioners, with some displeasure, recount tales of junior lawyers having been asked to undertake research and presenting their supervisor with a sheaf of photocopied extracts from primary and secondary sources. Legal research is not limited to finding material: it is about identifying relevant material for the purpose of a specific task. If you have been asked to produce a report, it will be expected that the latter will be the result not only of research but also analysis and application of the law.

As stated above, your report is not meant to be a chronological guide to how you conducted your research. You will have used the 'funnel approach' (see 8.2.3) when conducting your research, starting with a secondary source then progressing to the primary source. However your report should take the opposite approach and detail the primary sources first, as they represent the main source of law. It is possible that the source of your answer is case law only, or legislation only, or it may be both.

METHODOLOGY

This part of your report should provide enough detail about how you conducted your research and found the relevant law, so that your supervisor or tutor could easily replicate your research in your absence. If the source is a book, give the volume and page or paragraph number. When using computer-based sources you should give a brief description of how to find the material again quickly. For example, include the search terms you used (if the search produces quick results), or the path or URL that your supervisor can use to browse straight to the relevant material.

However, note the words 'enough detail' in the first line of the paragraph above. You do not need to detail every step you actually took while conducting your research, providing a blow by blow account of 'what I did at my desk and in the library yesterday afternoon'. While you may not have taken the most direct route to the answer, you should only detail here the most direct route which you are now aware of, in hindsight. This is not 'cheating' or seeking credit for something you did not do, it is simply reflecting the practical reality that whilst you may have taken an indirect route to the answer, the recipient of your report should not have to. The reader should be able to follow this part of your report and directly find the relevant material that you found.

(continued . . .)

It can be useful to reassure your supervisor by stating that you have checked that secondary sources are consistent with your conclusion, and identify those sources. However, if you started your research by using a very basic source such as a legal dictionary, and this adds nothing now that you have progressed on to more reliable legal sources, then there is no merit in including a reference to this source. In other words, recognise that there may be some sources which helped you make a start, but would not now help your supervisor because they add nothing to your report. You should not, for example, be mentioning particular internet search engines anywhere in this report.

UPDATING

You need to show that you have checked that your research is up to date. You will need to explain how you made sure that you have used current, in force, law and valid cases (see 8.3.3). Give the date to which the research is up to date (which may be the date of your report).

References to the Cumulative Supplement and Noter Up will help you to show that you have ensured paper versions of Halsbury's (Laws, Statutes or Statutory Instruments) are up to date. You should mention you have checked these even if all they showed was that the law you found had not been amended.

As electronic databases are kept up to date by the suppliers and usually updated daily, they tend not to provide the specific date on which they were last updated. If you have used an electronic database, then explain which site or source you used and the steps you took to make sure that there are no further relevant points of law. Refer to the symbols and text formatting of electronic databases to evidence that you have checked the law is up to date. You should also detail here whether any changes to the law are imminent.

If your research has led you to legislation then you must check that the legislation has come into force and give the date of commencement (again, see 8.3.3).

TIME TAKEN

In practice this would be required to be recorded to assist time management and be used in calculating the overall cost of the matter for the client. (See Chapter 13 for more detail on the costs of legal services.) You should always state the actual time taken.

Summary

- Legal research is seldom conducted in isolation. It is usually undertaken as part of a particular task, such as solving a legal problem.

- You should consider the purpose of the research *and* task to assist you to identify the types of material you need to locate.

- Before starting your research, take a strategic approach, and plan which secondary and primary sources are most likely to provide the material you need.

- Use appropriate techniques to ensure that the law you refer to is in force, up to date, and relevant to the issues in hand.

- Keep a contemporaneous record of your research as you progress.

- Consider the recipient of your research, and use appropriate written and oral communication skills to provide them with your conclusions and advice.

What the professionals say

The benefit of practising and developing your legal research skills while at university and on the LPC should not be underestimated.

Students often concentrate so much on obtaining good grades that they forget how important other skills are. As a trainee you will complete a large amount of research and your ability to do so in a timely and cost effective manner will be valued as much as the actual results.

At my interview, my firm were impressed that I had a strong working knowledge of online resources such as Lexis Nexis Butterworths and this knowledge has served me well throughout my training contract. It is a great way of standing out in your department either by producing high quality research notes or by being the 'go to' person when someone in your team has a question about how to complete their research task.

Louise Verrinder, 2011–13 trainee, CMS Cameron McKenna

Don't underestimate just how many research tasks you will be given in practice. Law firms pay anything up to tens of thousands of pounds a month for their legal research searches and resources. Your employer will want to know that you can find the relevant law as efficiently as possible and they need to have confidence that what you find is current and that you have not missed anything. They will judge you on that. If you can show that you can use resources well then you will become the 'go to' person for research and will be given the best work to do. My advice would be to appreciate the freedom you have as a student, from the pressure of time recording and having to justify search costs and your salary. Now is the time to practise these skills, to make mistakes and to learn from them. Apply for certification using online schemes such as those provided by Westlaw UK and LexisNexis Butterworths. Good legal research skills will make you more employable and help you to stand out from the crowd.

Corryn Walker, Law Librarian, Manchester Metropolitan University, and former Librarian at Freshfields LLP and the Inner Temple

Thought-provoking questions

1. When analysing a legal problem, how would you describe the distinction between the client's objectives and the legal issues?

2. What are the benefits of starting (rather than ending) a report with your conclusion and advice?

3. What criteria would you apply to decide whether a case you have found is relevant to your legal problem?

Further reading

Christina L. Kunz et al., *The Process of Legal Research: Authorities and Opinions* **(Aspen Publishers, 7th edn, 2008; new edn due 2013)**
—this US text relates legal research to client problems, and provides a number of alternative models and frameworks for research.

Mike McConville and Wing Hong Chui, *Research Methods for Law* **(Edinburgh University Press, 2007)**
—this text analyses a range of research methods (legalistic, empirical, comparative, and theoretical) which can be employed by undergraduate and postgraduate students when carrying out legal research projects.

For the authors' reflections on the thought-provoking questions, additional self-test questions, podcasts offering a variety of perspectives on legal systems and skills, and a library of links to useful websites, visit the free Online Resource Centre at **http://www.oxfordtextbooks.co.uk/orc/slorach/.**

9 Problem solving

 Learning objectives

After studying this chapter you should be able to, in relation to legal problems:

- Analyse the facts.
- Identify the legal and practical issues arising.
- Identify law relevant to solving the problem.
- Apply the law to the facts.
- Advise on the issues raised.
- Develop and apply processes for problem solving.
- Understand the personal, commercial, and financial issues that arise in practice.

Introduction

A good lawyer is a problem solver; someone who not only knows and understands what the law states, but can also apply that law to specific situations, and advise clearly on the potential outcomes and possible solutions.

As a lawyer, you will first encounter problem solving in your legal studies, most likely in the form of 'problem questions', which are common to most assessments. This chapter therefore considers a simple but effective problem-solving model, endorsed by many lecturers, which you can apply to problem questions. As you progress your studies, you will be presented with more complex legal problems. We therefore consider how to develop your skills and the initial model to deal with these.

A number of legal education programmes employ 'problem-based learning'. This is a particular learning methodology based around problems, usually presented in a less defined manner than traditional questions and often requiring additional analysis of the facts and problem presented, and identification of further facts required to solve the problem. Similar skills are a major part of problem solving in practice: where the ultimate goal is to find a solution to a client's problem. The background to these problems is often complex, requiring the lawyer to collate and analyse a great deal of factual information before dealing with the law and its application. This chapter therefore also discusses the skills of problem and fact analysis, and of advising clients.

Problem solving in its widest sense incorporates a range of skills considered elsewhere in this book. In Chapter 8 we discussed the skills of legal research and a range of sources of law and commentary. You will use these skills and draw upon these sources repeatedly when problem solving. Chapter 7 explained how to read the law you find in the most effective way. Whether as part of your studies or in practice, you will have to present your analyses of and solutions to problems in both oral and written form, using many of the communication skills covered in Chapters 10 and 11.

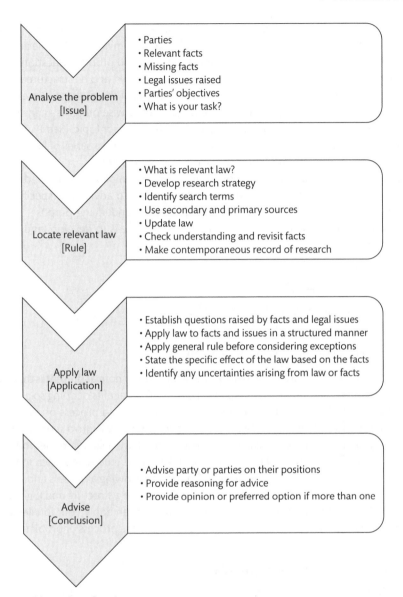

Figure 9.1 Problem solving flowchart

So, you will require a range of these skills to solve legal problems. The flowchart at Figure 9.1 incorporates the elements of the legal research flowchart (see Figure 8.1) to demonstrate a comprehensive problem-solving approach.

9.1 Dealing with problem-solving questions

9.1.1 The purpose of problem-solving questions

Problem-solving questions and essays share some common purposes. Both require you to demonstrate your understanding of a particular area of law. They also have an aim of developing (and assessing) your ability to reach reasoned conclusions, backed by evidence. Some of the intellectual skills you will need to apply may be similar, for example analysis and evaluation. Your presentation of your responses to essays and problem questions, whether oral or written, should demonstrate good communication skills, and be structured and clear.

The main difference in purpose derives from the format of the question. An essay either presents a proposition to be discussed or evaluated, or otherwise presents an instruction or question to be dealt with in the context of a particular law, case, or topic. (See 11.1 for further discussion of legal essays.) A problem question is usually based on a series of facts describing particular events, and, in the vast majority of cases, asks you to 'advise'.

The facts and events can often, on first reading, appear complex and involved. They may well involve more than one party, and you could be asked to advise one specific party or more. Whatever the scenario you are presented with, the underlying purpose, and hence your approach and output should be the same. The purpose is to develop (and ultimately assess) your ability to:

- analyse facts;
- identify the legal issue(s) they raise;
- identify and explain the law relevant to the issue(s);
- apply that law; and
- advise accordingly as directed by the question.

We look at these steps in more detail below. The main point to note at present is that answering a problem question requires you to follow *a process*. The benefits of doing so are twofold. First, however complex the facts with which you are presented, a process provides a structured approach for you to deal with them, breaking down your task into a series of individual steps. Once you understand what each step involves, you have a standard method to apply in solving any problem presented to you. Second, taking a structured approach to problem-solving provides the structure for your answer. That is, by following a process and setting out the results of your thinking at each stage, your answer will have a structure and logic to it. This will help to demonstrate how you understand the law and can apply your intellectual skills to problems. Our next step, therefore, is to consider further the process of problem solving.

9.1.2 A simple problem-solving model

A simple model which you can apply to solve legal problem questions is IRAC (see Figure 9.1): issue; rule; application; conclusion. This follows the process described above:

- Issue—analyse the facts to identify the legal issue(s) raised.
- Rule—identify and explain the law relevant to the issues.
- Application—apply that law.
- Conclusion—advise accordingly as directed by the question.

9.1.3 Applying the model

To demonstrate the application of the IRAC model, we shall look at a very simple problem. The answer provided has also been simplified for the purpose of the demonstration, to allow you to see more easily the process to follow when addressing problem questions. Following the example, we shall look in more detail at each stage of the process, which will show you how the actual answer would be expanded.

Example 1

Facts: Nina was driving through Kettering town centre behind a contractor's pick-up truck. She could see that the tailgate of this vehicle had been left down. As the truck rounded a bend, a large container of paint slid along the bed of the truck, before falling out. The container hit the road directly in front of Nina's car, and burst open. The front of Nina's car, a silver 2011 Mercedes A Class, was sprayed with paint. In addition, the container also hit and then cracked the front bumper of her car. The estimated cost of replacing the bumper, and cleaning, then respraying, the affected areas of her car is £1,800.
  Advise Nina.

Applying the IRAC model:

Issue: Analysing the facts, they can be summarised as follows. Nina's car has been damaged by paint and a container which fell from a vehicle whose tailgate had been left down. The estimated cost of repairing the damage is £1,800. The issue is whether Nina has a legal claim against the contractor, the owner of the vehicle from which the container fell.

Rule: The relevant area of law to consider is that of tort and, specifically, negligence. The general principles of the law of negligence were established in the leading case of *Donoghue v Stevenson* (1932) and have been developed through a number of subsequent cases. The main elements of law to consider are: duty of care; standard of care; breach of duty; and damages. The applicable principles are:

(a) for a claim of negligence, it is necessary first to establish that a duty of care exists;

(b) then to consider what standard of care is required;

(c) and then assess whether that standard was observed or the duty was breached.

If the duty was breached, the question of damages arises, where the applicable principles are that:

(a) actual damage must occur;

(b) the damage must be caused by the breach of duty of care; and

(c) any damages must be reasonably foreseeable as resulting from the breach.

The general purpose of damages in tort is to put injured parties back into the position they were in before the relevant event occurred.

Application: Applying the law to the facts means that we have to establish the following:

(a) Did the contractor owe Nina a duty of care?

(b) If so, what standard of care was owed by the contractor to Nina?

(c) Did the contractor fail to meet the required standard?

(d) Did actual damage occur?

(e) Was the damage caused as a result of contractor's breach of duty?

(f) Was the damage a reasonably foreseeable result of the contractor's breach of duty?

(g) What amount of damages would be required to put Nina back into the position before her car was damaged by the container and paint?

Conclusion: Assuming that each of questions (a)–(f) was answered in the affirmative, you would conclude that Nina would have a claim in negligence against the contractor, under which she would look to claim damages. The amount of those damages would be based on the answer to (g).

It is valuable to reflect on the example to see the benefits you gain by applying this model or process in dealing with the problem:

- It gives you a logical order for working: only once you identify the issue can you consider the relevant law, and only once you have the relevant law can you apply it to the facts, and only once you have done that can you conclude with appropriate advice.

- This logic extends into the narrative of your answer: each subsequent section and point is the one that the reader would want to come next, so it gives you the required clarity and structure.

- In terms of structure, as a piece of legal writing or communication, it also provides you with the required elements of: an introduction (setting out the issue(s) in hand); a body (the law and its application); and a conclusion.

- Perhaps best of all, if you use the model as the basis of planning the answer to your problem question, it makes the overall task much easier.

On this last point, look back at the answer given in the example. By applying the IRAC model, you have produced have a structured plan or 'skeleton' for your answer. You will also have a fairly good idea of what your final advice will be. All that you now need to do is expand the various areas through a combination of: explanation; citing authorities; answering the questions you have posed; and tailoring your advice based on the facts. The following, again based on the IRAC model, provides further guidance on both how to complete your answer and the individual elements of the model.

Issue

In the example the facts (assisted by the question) were such that it was easy to identify what was the issue. You may be presented with problems which are based on more complex facts and which raise more than one issue. During your legal studies, this should not raise too many difficulties, as you will usually be set problems based on the current areas of law being studied. Therefore, you will already know the type of issues that are presented by that area. By the time you are assessed, you will have both a broad knowledge of these issues and a developed instinct for the type of facts and scenarios that give rise to them: you will know facts that present a negligence issue when you see them.

Your main task is to isolate the relevant facts and each issue they present, and summarise these. The approach in the example is a good one to adopt: summarising the facts which give rise to the issue; then summarising the issue itself, with reference to the facts. As to the former, this involved analysing which facts are relevant, and including only those *which give rise to the issue* in the summary. In our example, the issue arose because of damage to a car resulting from a container falling from an open truck. The make of Nina's car and the specific detail of the repairs (which might be relevant as to the amount of damages) are irrelevant as far as the issue itself is concerned. Note that, when summarising issues, it is good practice to identify the parties involved in respect of each issue. This helps to avoid any confusion as you continue to work on the problem and is also a fundamental element of case analysis (see 10.4.2).

Rule

As with the issue, the subject areas you are studying, and your developing instinct as a lawyer will provide you with a good indication of both the general (in our example, tort) and specific (negligence) area of law. Clearly indicate these in your answer. You will need to apply legal research skills (see Chapter 8) to identify the specific law—in the sense of legal rules—relevant to the issues identified. In our example, the 'rules' derive from case law. They could equally be the subject of statute or other regulations (see Example 2). As you carry out your research, you should not only summarise the relevant law but also note its source. That will allow you, when stating a rule in your answer, to support it with relevant authority, for instance the case that established it or a statutory reference. Remember to follow any required conventions on citation.

If there are specific facts which determine *why* a particular rule is relevant, this should also be noted in your answer: it is a good means of demonstrating your understanding of the law. By both summarising and ordering the applicable law, you should make your task easier when you come to apply it. The example above illustrates the ordering of the law, in this case following the standard order of the tests or definitions that have to be met to establish negligence.

Application

Your task here is to apply the law to the particular facts and issue in hand. The approach illustrated in the example above—that of posing a series of questions—can work well when applying a series of tests or definitions to evaluate whether a claim or particular rights exist. This is effectively mirroring the process taken by a court, the role of which is to decide a case based on what it judges the effect of the law to be on the facts, evidence, and argument before it.

Do not be afraid of stating the obvious during this stage, when applying the law to the facts: if your interpretation is that, because of particular words during a phone call, X made an offer to Y for the purchase of goods at a set price, then say exactly that, and justify (i.e. explain *why*) with reference to decided cases.

You can use cases in two main ways:

- As authority for a legal principle (see 'Rule' above). Here you are unlikely to need to refer to the facts of the case.
- As a comparison with the facts of the legal problem, for example if the facts are similar to a case, or similar but with a significant difference. Here you will need to refer to the facts of the case, for instance 'case X is relevant, as it is very similar on the facts, however in that case the defendant was a business and in this case the defendant is a consumer ... therefore will the court imply the same test?'

If you think an exception applies, state the general rule first before you explore whether the exception applies. For example, if someone has posted an acceptance, you should state the general rule that acceptance must be communicated *before* you consider, for example, whether the postal rule exception applies.

It is worthwhile spending some additional time considering the application stage of the process, as it is likely to be both the largest and most important part of your answer.

In educational terms, you will be using higher-level intellectual skills. For example, we have already seen that you will be:

- synthesising facts and law;
- analysing the effect of and applying law and principles in respect of the issues in hand;
- evaluating the application of law in similar cases and critically comparing it to the current situation; and
- drawing preliminary conclusions as a result.

In summary, and more practical terms, you are 'multi-tasking'. To that end, it is important to take a measured, structured approach when applying the law. A broad discursive approach will lack structure and increase the risk of missing out important points. At the end of this section on problem-solving questions, there features a second example, with two answers to compare, and some further guidance on how best to apply the law and structure your answer (see 'Further guidance' below). There is a further demonstration of the application of law in Example 3.

Conclusion

Before finalising your conclusion, read the facts and the question again, then check that your conclusion will answer *that* question. It is not uncommon, during the application stage, to start moving off course and rephrasing the question in your head as you write your answer.

Given that most questions require you to advise, make sure that your conclusion (a) clearly advises the relevant party on her position and (b) provides, concisely, the reasoning behind the advice. So, in our example above, the first part of your conclusion could be that, based on the facts, Nina has a strong case in tort to bring an action for negligence against the contractor. This would be on the ground that the latter had breached his duty of care to her to take reasonable steps to avoid damage resulting from his trade activities.

If your analysis is that there are two possible answers (e.g. you may be unable to conclude categorically whether a general rule or the exception applies), you must consider the effects of both possibilities, before stating which option you personally are most persuaded would be the most appropriate outcome. Do not, however, do this to 'hedge your bets' in circumstances where you should, on the facts given, be able to draw a clear conclusion.

Structuring your answer

Consider how best to structure your answer. With single-issue or otherwise simple problems, following the structure of IRAC will generally be straightforward. If you identify multiple issues, you should consider whether following the RAC stages for each issue at a time would produce a clearer, more structured answer than attempting to deal with all of the law for all of the issues, then applying the law to each issue. Equally, if there are several characters or several events, you may wish to deal with each separately. In all 'multiple aspect' cases, using headings to make clear which issue, character, or event you are discussing will discourage you from mixing up different issues or revisiting an issue you have already dealt with.

Further guidance

The following example has been included as a means of providing you with further guidance on problem-solving questions and, in particular, application of the law. It also gives you an example of application of regulation as opposed to case law. The specific regulations applicable to the facts have been summarised and simplified, and are expressed as 'Rules'. You may wish, before reading the sample outline answers that show how the Rules were applied, to attempt to apply the Rules yourself. You can then compare your answer to the sample answers.

Example 2

Predator plc ('Predator') wants to buy all the shares in Target plc ('Target'). Both companies' shares are traded on the London Stock Exchange. Currently Predator does not own any shares in Target. It decides to buy the shares in Target gradually, preferably in secret, in case Target does not want to be bought by Predator. So Predator will buy Target shares on the Stock Exchange from the existing shareholders of Target.

- On 9 September Predator buys 2% of Target's shares.
- On 28 September it buys a further 0.9%.
- On 2 October it then buys another 7.1%.
- On 31 October it buys another 0.9%.

This brings Predator's total shareholding in Target to 10.9%.
Advise Predator whether it will be able to keep its share purchases secret from Target.

Using your research skills, you found the following rules which are relevant to the issue in hand:

1. *Rule 2 applies only to shares that you have bought or sold in a company which is a public company that trades on a UK stock market.*

2. *You must tell a company the percentage of shares you own if, having bought or sold shares, the percentage of shares you own either reaches or exceeds each of 3%, 4%, 5%, 6%, 7%, 8%, 9%, 10%, and each 1% threshold thereafter up to 100%.*

3. *You must comply with Rule 2 as soon as possible and in any event no later than two days after you bought or sold shares.*

4. *When you calculate percentages for Rule 2, you should round down any fractions.*

You now apply the above rules to the facts in order to advise Predator on the issue of whether it will be able to keep the share purchases secret.

Good answer

Applying the Rules to Predator's share purchases:
First, does Rule 2 apply? Yes, because:

- Predator owns shares in Target;
- Predator has bought shares in Target (on four separate occasions);
- Target is a public company ('plc' stands for public limited company) and trades its shares on the London Stock Exchange, which is a UK stock market.

(continued . . .)

Rule 2 therefore applies as a result of Rule 1 and therefore we now have to work through each of the four purchases in turn, analysing the relevant percentages at each stage, to establish if and when Predator would have to tell Target about them.

- Predator can keep secret the purchase of 9 September as it does not take Predator's shareholding to the minimum threshold of 3% referred to in Rule 2. Predator owns only 2% of Target shares.

- Predator can keep secret the purchase of a further 0.9% on 28 September. Following this purchase Predator owns only 2.9% of Target shares. This fraction will be rounded down to 2% under Rule 4, and so still does not reach the 3% threshold in Rule 2.

- Predator cannot, however, keep secret the purchase of 7.1% on 2 October. Following this purchase Target will own 10% of Target shares, and 'reaching 10%' is one of the thresholds referred to in Rule 2. Predator will have to tell Target about this purchase. Under Rule 3, Predator must tell Target as soon as possible after the purchase on 2 October. 'As soon as possible' is not defined, but it cannot be longer than two days after that day. So we can be certain that Predator would have to disclose its 10% shareholding to Target by 4 October at the latest, and by 2 October at the earliest.

- Predator would not have to tell Target when it buys a further 0.9% on 31 October, taking its shareholding to 10.9%. This is because under Rule 4 this shareholding would be rounded down to 10% and so would not take the shareholding through another 1%, which would be the triggering event for another notification under Rule 2.

Therefore, to conclude, Predator will not be able to keep all of its share purchases secret from Target, as under Rule 2 Predator must notify Target when Predator's shareholding reaches 10%. This will occur following the purchase of 7.1% on 2 October, and Predator must notify Target as soon as possible, and no later than two days after the purchase, namely 4 October. Predator does not have to notify Target of its further purchase on 31 October because the resulting shareholding does not exceed the relevant threshold for a further notification.

Note that this answer is good for the following reasons:

- It does not just cite the law. At each stage, it refers to the actual facts of the problem, for example to the percentages of shares Predator bought and to actual calendar dates and deadlines.

- As there are four purchases, it analyses each one, in chronological order. This is a good approach whenever a problem details a series of events.

- No time has been wasted in copying out the law first in its entirety, then repeating it when applied to the facts. Instead, efficiently, it refers to the law (in this case by reference to Rule numbers), and applies it to the facts, as it goes along.

- The structured, consistent application of the law to the facts means that, if there were an error at any point (there is not), causing the wrong conclusion to be drawn, then an experienced reader (a marker of an assessment or a supervising solicitor checking your work in practice) is likely to be able to identify this and possibly infer what the correct answer should have been. This means that the answer is still useful to the reader, compared to an answer comprising only conclusions with neither explanations nor references to the law.

- It uses active language, for instance it does not just say Predator needs 'to notify', or that Target needs to 'be notified'; it identifies that Predator should notify Target.

- It provides a clear, reasoned conclusion.

Compare the above with the following, less good, answer.

Less good answer

Rule 2 states that you must tell a company of the percentage of shares you own if, having bought or sold some shares, the percentage of those shares reaches, exceeds, or falls below certain thresholds, one of which is 10%. As the company now holds 10.9%, it must notify within two days.

This answer is less good in several respects:

- The majority of it is copying out the law (i.e. the Rules).

- The only fact against which the writer has applied the law is the final shareholding of 10.9%. It does not analyse each chronological event. As a result, the answer is vague as to the exact date which Predator must notify, and specifically which of the four purchases crosses the Rule 2 10% threshold and triggers notification.

- Compared to the first example, there is far less evidence of application of the law to the facts. This has resulted in an imprecise conclusion.

- It lacks detail. For example, it does not identify who must notify or be notified, or consider the actual dates of notification. Predator would need to know these practical issues.

- It does not clearly conclude, by reference to the question, that Predator cannot build its stake in secret.

For these reasons, this answer would be awarded a lower mark in an assessment compared with the example above of a good answer. In legal practice, it would amount to unhelpful, imprecise advice.

9.2 Problem and fact analysis

At 9.1, we considered how to deal with problem-solving questions, as traditionally set for students on undergraduate law programmes. The skills developed by working on these problems are transferable to legal practice: that is one of the reasons for the use of these questions. The majority of scenarios used in problem-solving questions are at least derived from actual events, if not based directly on them.

However, it is fair to say that these questions cannot replicate all of the aspects of problem-solving in practice. A client may not always provide all the facts required, and may provide many facts that are irrelevant to the matter in hand. The lawyer may identify the additional facts required early on, or might only do so after an initial analysis of the problem based on the facts in hand at that time. Even then, some initial research may be required just to identify the issues. Thus, while lawyers may employ the steps of a model such as IRAC, it can often be a less structured, more iterative process. There will also be both personal and commercial considerations and objectives of the client that have to be factored into both identifying issues and ultimately providing advice. Finally, there may also be additional parties (sometimes referred to as 'stakeholders') whose interests need to be considered, even though they may not be directly involved in the matter.

In the Introduction to this chapter, we mentioned problem-based learning, which can be designed so as to incorporate some of the additional aspects experienced in practice. For example, students may only be given minimal facts: they may not be able fully to isolate the problems and issues to be addressed without additional facts, and so they will need first to identify what those facts are. Alternatively, they may be given more facts than are needed, so that they have to analyse and evaluate which are relevant to the case in hand, In addition, more law programmes are including commercial awareness in their curriculum, some of them integrating elements of this into problem-solving questions. Therefore students have to think like practising lawyers, taking into account clients' personal and commercial considerations when advising on problems (see Chapters 13 and 16), such as the effect on ongoing relationships or the financial risks of pursuing court action as against the likelihood of success. (For a specific example on advising in practice, see 9.3).

The effect of all of the above is that it is often necessary to spend more time analysing facts and problems *before* carrying out research into the law, applying that law, and advising. This section therefore considers these wider aspects of problem and fact analysis. In addition to their application in the areas discussed above, they can enrich the skills of legal research (see Chapter 8), issue identification (see 9.1.3), and case analysis (see 10.4.2), aspects of which you may identify below. A case study, set in legal practice, followed by an analysis, has been used by way of illustration. It runs from the point of receiving initial instructions, through problem and fact analysis, to the point at which the issues and client's objectives can be summarised and the main areas of legal research identified. The guidance given includes some diagrammatic techniques which can be used to assist problem and fact analysis.

9.2.1 **Case study**

It is August. You act for Stentor Limited ('S'), a company that manufactures and sells high-quality brass hardware, including buckles and locks. A director of S, Georgia King, has asked your firm for advice. In the spring, S was approached by Britbag plc ('B'), which manufactures high-quality handbags. B was interested in buying a large consignment of buckles and locks for its new 'Catherine' handbag, ready for a high-profile advertising campaign to be launched in the autumn. To secure the order, S gave B a 10% discount off the normal list price of the buckles and locks.

S and B entered into a contract for sale of the goods on the basis of S's standard terms and conditions of sale. Clause 9 of that contract is reproduced below.

Case study 1

Extract from contract

9. LIABILITY

9.1 In the event of any defect in the Goods, the Seller shall at its option repair or replace such Goods or refund the price of such Goods. Subject to clause 9.3, the Seller shall have no further liability in respect of the Goods.

9.2 Subject to clause 9.3, the Seller shall not be liable for any claims for damages whether consequential or otherwise, howsoever caused.

9.3 Nothing in clauses 9.1 or 9.2 excludes or limits the Seller's liability for death or personal injury caused by the Seller's negligence or fraudulent misrepresentation.

S delivered the buckles and locks on 1 June and B paid for the goods on 15 June, in accordance with the terms of the contract.

The bags are not yet ready to be sold in shops, but 25 prototypes have been made up and tested by volunteers. This resulted in the buckles and locks discolouring and spoiling the handbags' appearance. Scientific testing revealed a fundamental weakness in the buckles and locks as a result of the poor quality brass used.

B has told S it no longer has faith in S and would not be interested in any replacement goods. B is insisting on returning to S the remaining unused buckles and locks and is demanding a refund from S for those. B has also made clear that it will strip out the buckles and locks it has already used in the prototype bags and wants a refund for those too. B wants S to meet the cost of buying replacement buckles and locks from other suppliers (to the extent that the refunds do not cover that cost).

Georgia has told you that S accepts that the goods are not representative of S's usual standards, although she is a little puzzled because, having read the contract, there does not seem to be anything in it about the standard the goods should meet. Nevertheless S is prepared to replace the buckles and locks 'to honour S's obligations under the contract'. However, S 'refuses to go any further than this' and does not want to give B a refund for any of the buckles and locks, or reimburse B for the cost of buying replacements from any other supplier.

Advise.

9.2.2 Analysis

Who is the client?

While it may often appear obvious, it is important, at the start of any analysis leading to advice, to be sure who you are advising. When companies are involved, there can be potential for confusion, as the company and each of its directors are separate persons in law. Although Georgia King is asking your firm for advice, she is asking on behalf of the company of which she is a director. It is this company, S, which is the client.

Fact analysis

The next stage is to analyse the information received so far from your client and, based on what you currently understand the main issues to be, isolate, summarise, and order the *relevant* facts. This will, in turn, make it easier to focus on what are the legal issues, without being distracted by irrelevant material. So, in this case, the relevant facts are:

- S has sold brass buckles and locks to B at a 10% discount.
- B has used these items on 25 prototype bags and they have discoloured.
- B commissioned testing of the bags: this showed that the discoloration was due to the poor quality brass used in S's product.
- B wants to:
  - **reject** the unused buckles and locks;
  - **claim a refund** for all the buckles and locks, used and unused; and
  - **be reimbursed** for the cost of buying replacement buckles and locks, to the extent that the cost of replacement is more than the refunds it receives from S.

- B does not want any replacement goods from S.
- S accepts liability for any faulty goods, but is willing only to provide replacements.
- Clause 9 of the contract between S and B appears to limit S's liability by giving S the choice of whether to offer a repair, replacement, or refund, and providing expressly that S is not liable for damages.
- S has informed us that it understands that the contract is silent on the standard the bags and locks should have met.

Compare the note above with the initial information set out at 9.2.1, in terms of clarity and order.

Recording and representing the relevant facts

An initial analysis of the relevant facts is set out above. The act of summarising and recording these is a valuable process in embedding these facts in your mind. Some lawyers find a visual approach valuable, either as an alternative or in addition to words.

 Practice tip

In practice, lawyers often distil legal arrangements and transactions into diagrammatic form, to aid understanding of the facts and also to make it easier to explain the problem to other people who may need to understand it.

Diagrams

Diagrams can be very useful for setting out transactions and contractual relationships. They are also frequently used to set out corporate structures, showing, for example, a groups of companies and their interrelationships. Figure 9.2 provides a simple representation of the legal transaction in the case study.

Mind maps

A **mind map** or **spider diagram** is also a useful visual way to both record facts and set out potential issues. It can be useful in the legal research process: by setting out potential issues and questions, you are providing a focus for your research. Also, if you find law relevant to several areas of the mind map, it can help you to identify that this law is likely to be important. There are several ways of preparing a mind map. Figure 9.3 builds on the transaction diagram above to show more of the facts and issues.

Figure 9.2 Diagram showing the transaction between S and B

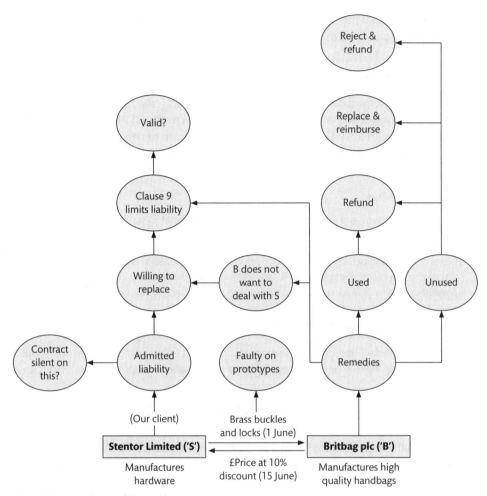

Figure 9.3 A mind map of the problem

You will use the facts you identify at this stage as a basis to start your legal research. However, as mentioned above, you will need to be open to the fact that you may need to come back to this stage in the near future, based on the results of your research and any additional facts you elicit.

Additional facts or questions

Our fact analysis summarised the relevant facts based on the information we have received to date. That process, together with an initial analysis of the issues, may make you realise that you need additional facts or want to ask further questions. The latter can relate to legal or commercial matters. In this case, for example:

- Can you have a copy of the signed contract between S and B?
- Even if there is nothing in the contract about the required standard of the goods, was anything said in this respect before the contract was signed?

- Is S willing to jeopardise the prospect of a good working relationship with B in the future in pursuing a solution to this problem?

Additional stakeholders

As S is a company, it must consider the interests of its owners (called **shareholders**), its employees, and also anyone to whom it owes money (called **creditors**). This is because, if S has to give any remedy to B, S will be worse off than it is now from a financial perspective. However, it may be able to preserve its business reputation, which can bring long-term benefits.

The client's objective

From all of the above, you should now be able to distil what is your client's situation and objective. For example:

> S has accepted liability for the substandard goods and is prepared to provide a remedy in the form of giving replacement goods to B. However, its objective is that it does not want to give B the remedies that B is seeking, namely rejection, refund, and reimbursement.

The legal issues for research

The process of the fact analysis and setting out the client's situation and objective should, together, raise the legal issues you now have to investigate through research. In this case these include:

- What is the basis of S's liability for providing faulty goods to B if the contract itself is silent on this issue?
- Is clause 9 effective in limiting S's liability to providing replacement goods to B?
- Is B entitled to seek the remedies it is seeking from S (rejection, refund, and reimbursement)?

Conclusion

The above case study is an illustration of the benefits, both in practice and in dealing with complex problem questions and scenarios, of investing time early on in analysing facts and the issues they raise. Your return on this investment is the focus that it will give your legal research, application of the law to these facts, and advice.

9.3 Advising in practice: presenting options

At 9.2, we began to explore some of the practicalities faced by lawyers when problem solving in practice such as: clients providing insufficient or too much information, taking account of clients' personal and commercial objectives, and considering other stakeholders' interests. In the concluding section to this chapter it is appropriate to consider in more detail the conclusion of problem solving in practice: advice to the client. We saw at 9.1 that when working on undergraduate problem-solving questions your aim is to come to a reasoned conclusion on, say, a situation, or rights, or claims. In practice, having concluded as to the effect of the law, it is the responsibility of the lawyer to provide advice to the client. The lawyer must take into account the client's objectives, and his personal or business situation and interests. In very many situations, there may be options, such as asserting legal rights, negotiation, or even walking away from the situation. The lawyer should present the client not only with the options but the advantages and disadvantages of each, and what might be most appropriate given the client's objectives. Whilst ultimately it is up to the client to decide which option to pursue, it is the lawyer's role to ensure that the decision is an informed choice.

To demonstrate this, we shall use a worked example based on a problem scenario. As you will see, we are no longer limited to considering the effect of a single area of law: elements of tort, contract, and commercial law would be considered. The scenario will be developed from the point at which you have completed your legal research and are about to apply the law. The relevant law has been provided in the form of rules, to simplify the example, and no supporting cases have been cited. This allows you to focus on the application of the law, its effect, the options available to the client, and the advantages and disadvantages of those options.

Example 3

Facts

Jack filled his car with £60 worth of petrol from the petrol station at his local supermarket. However, two days later, ten minutes into a journey to the airport 100 miles from his house, Jack's car seemed to lose power. He was forced to turn the car around and go home, his car misfiring all the way. By the time Jack returned home, he was too late to make alternative plans to travel to the airport and he missed his flight to Dublin where he had planned to spend the weekend visiting friends.

The next day, Jack managed to drive very slowly to the nearest repair garage. They said they had seen several vehicles that day with a similar problems, and there was speculation that there was something wrong with the supermarket's petrol. Later that day, the garage called with a quote for repairing the car of £700.

The garage said that Jack had made the problem worse by driving his car after the power had failed, and they were also having to work 'round the clock' to meet demand, as many cars had been affected locally. Jack was shocked at the amount of the quote but, as he uses his car as a taxi three days a week, he paid the garage the sum, and the next day collected his repaired car. The garage said Jack's car had received the last part they had in stock, and it was going to take them two weeks to take delivery of replacement parts for their other customers whose cars had suffered a similar fate.

Jack has since seen various reports on the television speculating that petrol from one particular terminal had become contaminated and that this petrol had been supplied to several supermarket petrol stations. The contaminated petrol is thought to be causing cars to break down. This has prompted Jack to seek advice from you as to whether he can 'seek compensation' for the £700 he has paid the garage, and 'whether there is anything else he can claim for'. Advise Jack.

Law

Using your research strategy, you found the following rules in contract, commercial and tort law:

1. *If a seller sells goods in the course of a business, a term will be implied into the contract that the goods are of satisfactory quality and are fit for purpose.*

(continued . . .)

2. *It is no defence to a seller who is in breach of Rule 1 that the breach was not the seller's fault.*

3. *A buyer who wants to sue a seller for damages for breach of contract must prove that he has suffered loss or damage as a result of the breach of contract.*

4. *The object of damages for breach of contract is to put the buyer into the position he would have been in if the contract had been properly performed.*

5. *The buyer will not be able to recover damages for any loss which is too remote a consequence of the breach of contract.*

6. *Even if the seller is in breach of contract, the buyer must do what is reasonable to minimise his own loss.*

7. *A buyer can only recover damages for breach of contract from another party to the contract.*

8. *A buyer can recover damages in tort from anyone who owes him a duty of care.*

9. *The object of damages in tort is to put the buyer into the position he would have been in if the tort had never happened.*

9.3.1 **Application**

Set out below is the application of the above rules to the facts.

There is a contract here between the seller of the petrol (the supermarket, 'S') and the buyer of the petrol, Jack. As S is selling in the course of its business, there is an implied term in that contract that the petrol is of satisfactory quality and is fit for purpose (Rule 1). If the television reports are correct, and the petrol S has sold to Jack has caused his car to break down, then there has been a breach by S of this implied term as the petrol is not of satisfactory quality and is not fit for its purpose. Jack will have a cause of action against S for breach of contract. S will not be able to use the defence that the petrol was contaminated at the terminal before it reached S, and not through any fault by S (Rule 2).

Jack will be able to use this cause of action to recover loss or damage resulting from the breach, that is, the sale of contaminated petrol which caused Jack's car to break down (Rule 3). We can advise Jack that he does have the right to damages. He can seek these from S, the other party to the contract (Rule 7). The measure of damages is to put Jack into a position as if the contract had been properly performed, that is to say had the petrol been of satisfactory quality and fit for its purpose (Rule 4).

In advising Jack what he can claim for, we need to consider the two limiting factors of remoteness and mitigation. The effect of Rule 5 is that Jack cannot seek to recover any loss which is too remote. The effect of Rule 6 is that Jack cannot seek to recover any loss which reasonably he could have avoided incurring. Taking each of Jack's losses in turn:

- The £60 Jack paid for petrol which made his car break down is a loss directly related to the breach and so Jack should be able to recover this amount from S.

- If the television reports are correct, and the contaminated petrol caused Jack's car to break down, this is also a loss flowing directly from the breach, and Jack should be able to recover the amount required to repair his car. However, it is likely that S will resist paying Jack the full £700. S should argue that it would have been reasonable to expect

Jack to have obtained at least one other quote to check that the figure of £700 was reasonable. Jack may be able to counter this argument by finding out the average repair cost for other cars which suffered similar damage, and he can also point out that garages were busy meeting increased demands on their time as a result of the extent of the contamination (as evidenced by the fact that the garage he used ran out of spare parts). S should also want to analyse the extent of the work done by the garage. It will probably find out that Jack made the problem worse by driving the car after the damage was apparent, rather than calling breakdown services, and may resist compensating Jack for this element of the repair.

- Jack will also be able to claim damages for any other loss directly flowing from the breach, so we should ask him what other expenses he has incurred due to the breakdown. From the facts provided, we know that Jack has missed his flight. We need to advise him that while he could seek to claim this loss from S, S is likely to be advised to resist this, on the basis that it is too remote and does not flow directly from the breach. We also know that Jack is a taxi driver. On the facts it does not appear that Jack missed any work due to the breach. However if he did, again, S is likely to be advised to argue that any loss relating to this is too remote. Unless S and Jack can come to some agreement on these matters, they would have to ask a court to decide.

It may be that Jack is also party to other contracts which could help him to recover his loss. A contract of insurance may give Jack the ability to recover certain costs from the other party to that contract, the insurer. A contract of warranty may give Jack the right to recover certain costs from the other party to that contract, the car manufacturer.

Under Rule 7, Jack cannot claim for contractual damages against the supplier and distributor ('D') who supplied the contaminated petrol to S, because Jack is not a party to any contract with D. However, if Jack can show that D owed him a duty of care, then Jack could seek 'compensation' from D in the law of tort (Rule 8). Jack would have to prove that by supplying contaminated petrol to S, D breached its duty of care to Jack, the ultimate consumer of that petrol. The measure of tortious damages would be to put Jack in the position that he would have been in had D not provided the contaminated petrol to S (Rule 9).

9.3.2 Identifying all the options

Having considered the potential claims identified above, and then combining them with potential practical approaches, we can identify that the following options are open to Jack:

1. Use his legal rights in contract law to sue S for damages.
2. Use his legal rights in tort law to sue D for damages.
3. Do nothing.
4. Seek to negotiate with S using the threat of pursuing his legal rights as leverage to obtain a quicker and more cost efficient settlement.
5. Seek to negotiate with D using the threat of pursuing his legal rights as leverage to obtain a quicker and more cost effective settlement.

6. Rely on any other contract Jack is party to, such as an insurance or warranty contract.

9.3.3 Evaluating the options

Having identified the options, the lawyer's role is then to inform the client of the advantages and disadvantages of each.

Table 9.1 Evaluating the options open to Jack

Option	Advantages	Disadvantages
Use Jack's legal rights in contract law to sue S for damages.	Jack will be able to seek contractual damages to achieve his aim of being 'compensated'. Jack may be able to use the small claims court which is a quicker and simpler way to pursue his claim than using other parts of the courts system. We need to research what the small claims court thresholds are.	Litigation can be a costly and time-consuming process, and, given the relatively small losses Jack may have incurred, the legal bills alone might outweigh what Jack could seek to recover. The issues of remoteness and mitigation discussed above will limit Jack's claim. Jack will have to obtain and provide comprehensive evidence to support his claim.
Use Jack's legal rights in the law of tort to sue D for damages.	Jack will be able to seek tortious damages to achieve his aim of 'compensation'. As above, Jack may be able to use the small claims court.	Jack would have to prove that D owes him a duty of care. Jack will have to obtain and provide comprehensive evidence to support his claim. As above, the costs of litigation might outweigh what Jack could seek to recover.
Do nothing.	This will not involve Jack incurring any further cost or time on this matter.	Jack will not be able to achieve his aim of recovering the losses he has incurred.
Seek to negotiate with S using the threat of pursuing his legal rights as leverage to obtain a quicker and more cost efficient settlement.	Jack may be able to achieve his aim without recourse to litigation and the related cost and time implications. S may be particularly receptive to this approach, given that it is a consumer-facing business and needs to protect its brand and reputation going forward. It would appear that this is not an isolated incident and this may help to encourage S to provide an accessible solution to all who have suffered loss due to the contaminated petrol, not just Jack.	Jack may require further advice regarding whether to accept any offer S makes. Jack will still have to obtain and provide some evidence to support his claim. S may decide not to enter into negotiations with Jack.
Seek to negotiate with D using the threat of pursuing his legal rights as leverage to obtain a quicker and more cost effective settlement.	As above, this may achieve Jack's aim without recourse to litigation.	As above, Jack may require further advice. Jack will still have to obtain and provide some evidence to support his claim. D may be less receptive than S to this approach, as it does not rely on consumers like Jack for ongoing custom. D's concern will be to establish its reputation with its own customers such as S.

Option	Advantages	Disadvantages
Rely on any contract of insurance Jack may have, to recover his loss from the insurer.	If suitable cover is in place, Jack may be able to achieve his aim of recovering his loss, even though this is not in the form of 'compensation'.	There may be an excess to pay. Making an insurance claim is likely to result in Jack having to pay more for his insurance next year, and may cause him to lose any 'no claims bonus' he has accrued. The insurance contract is likely to limit the losses for which Jack can claim. It may not cover the damage at all if it was caused by Jack putting contaminated petrol into the car and Jack did not elect to cover 'accidental damage' in a comprehensive policy. Jack will have to obtain and provide some evidence to support his claim.
Rely on any contract of warranty Jack may have with his car's manufacturer.	As above, if suitable cover is in place, Jack may be able to achieve his aim of recovering his loss, even though this is not in the form of 'compensation'. Jack may not have to show any link between the breakdown and the contaminated petrol.	As above, the warranty is likely to limit the losses for which Jack can claim, and may not cover the damage at all if it was caused by Jack putting contaminated petrol into the car.

9.3.4 Advising on the most appropriate option

It appears that Jack's objective is to recover what he can to cover the losses he has incurred as a result of buying the contaminated petrol. Before advising on the most appropriate option, we would check with Jack that we have correctly understood his aims and objectives.

We have identified several options which allow Jack to achieve his objective, which involve him seeking payment from S, D, or his insurer. Jack has used the word 'compensation' but, all things being equal, it is unlikely that Jack is concerned about the particular source of any reimbursement he can obtain. We would also check this with Jack.

Finally, we have now checked and know that, currently, the small claims court can be used for claims up to £5,000 but that, even if a claim is within this limit, a judge reserves the right to decide that the case is too complex to be heard as a small claim. The small claims court can still take several months to reach a judgment.

With the above in mind, we can begin to discuss what might be the most appropriate option.

The differentiating factors between the options we have identified appear largely to do with: (i) additional costs and (ii) further work required by Jack. Two important questions to ask Jack are:

Additional costs vs how much is Jack seeking to recover?

The issue here is balancing what might be the additional costs of taking steps to obtain compensation against the amount he might actually recover. This will involve:

- helping Jack to identify each potential loss following from the sale of contaminated petrol, so we can calculate the total loss Jack thinks he has incurred;
- advising Jack on which losses might not be recoverable (in particular managing his expectations about recovering any loss regarding his missed weekend away and any missed taxi-driving work);

- providing Jack with an estimate of the likely costs of pursuing each option and comparing and contrasting that with the likely amount he stands to recover under each option.

It may be that, as a result of this analysis, Jack decides he no longer wishes to pursue the matter.

If the loss he would be claiming for is relatively low, Jack may also decide he does not wish to affect his future insurance premiums by making a claim under his insurance contract.

However, we could advise that, for relatively little further cost, Jack could make an attempt to negotiate. With whom should he try to negotiate, S or D? Our analysis showed that, as a consumer, Jack has more negotiating power with S than with D. Unless D was a substantially safer proposition financially (unlikely, given that S is a household-name supermarket) it is probably best for Jack to start to negotiate with S. We would advise Jack to gather evidence in support of his claim, such as:

- proof of his purchase of petrol (receipt, credit card, or bank statement);
- anything the repairing garage can provide such as a petrol sample, or any parts it removed from the car;
- any other evidence of loss, such as Jack's flight ticket;
- a written record of events (which Jack should compile while they are relatively fresh in his mind).

Jack would not need to make a decision just yet about whether to pursue his claim in the courts if his negotiation attempt fails, but, if the estimated value of his claim is as low as expected, the possibility of pursuing the claim in the small claims court might offer him further bargaining power in persuading S to settle his claim.

Further work: how much time is Jack able to devote to recovering his losses?

This question may be key in helping Jack to make a final decision between (i) doing nothing and (ii) attempting to negotiate a settlement with S.

9.3.5 **Conclusion**

The example you have just seen might appear complex, particularly when considering the relative merits of options and what would be the most appropriate course of action. However, both the range of options available to clients, and the considerations which determine a course of action are comparatively generic (see 10.6.10). What is important, as with problem-solving in general, is to follow a process. By so doing, due consideration is given at each stage, and a properly informed—both by the law and practical factors—decision can be made.

 Summary

- It is the combination of a good knowledge and understanding of the law on the one hand, and sound legal skills on the other hand, which makes a lawyer.
- The legal skills which underpin problem solving are fact and problem analysis, legal research, application of the law to facts, and advising.

- Follow a structured process—such as IRAC—when applying your skills to problem solving (see Figure 9.1).
- More complex problems require higher levels of analysis at an early stage to make the later stages of problem solving more efficient and effective.
- When seeking solutions to the problems of clients, lawyers need to consider personal and business factors, and present options.

What the professionals say

As a student you will learn the law and how to apply it to a client's problem. However, practice has taught me that while legal acumen is fundamental to the delivery of quality legal advice, it must be underpinned by a true commercial awareness. A lawyer needs to understand the client's objectives and the environment in which they operate, and that the legal options available will not always produce the best commercial solution for that client. As an insolvency lawyer, I deal regularly with businesses who are in a state of crisis. In order to deliver clear pragmatic advice, it is not enough simply to know and understand the relevant law. I also need to understand the client, what they do, the market in which they operate, their objectives and the objectives of the other stakeholders such as the bank, directors and administrators. Only then can we go on to identify the very best solution to the problem they are facing.

Matthew Tomlinson, Solicitor, DLA Piper

 ## Thought-provoking questions

1. Has your understanding of what a lawyer does changed as a result of reading this chapter, and if so, how?

2. How will you improve your commercial awareness so that you can provide a client with all the options, not just those which follow the letter of the law?

3. Do you think a lawyer's fees should relate to the value of the solution provided?

 ## Further reading

Paul Brest and Linda Hamilton Kreiger, *Problem Solving, Decision Making, and Professional Judgment: A Guide for Lawyers and Policymakers* (Oxford: OUP, 2010)
—this text examines the steps involved in the process of legal problem-solving, in addition to exploring the behavioural aspects of decision-making and exercising professional judgement.

Stephen Nathanson, *What Lawyers Do—A Problem-Solving Approach to Legal Practice* (London: Sweet & Maxwell, 1997)
—this illustrates the key processes which underpin legal problem solving. It adopts the context of legal practice but is directed very much at law students, to develop their wider understanding.

 For the authors' reflections on the thought-provoking questions, additional self-test questions, podcasts offering a variety of perspectives on legal systems and skills, and a library of links to useful websites, visit the free Online Resource Centre *at* **http://www.oxfordtextbooks.co.uk/orc/slorach/.**

10 Communication

 Learning objectives

After studying this chapter you should be able to:

- Appreciate the need for good communication skills.
- Describe effective communication skills.
- Practise and develop these skills during your legal studies and in everyday life.
- Practise techniques to help you deliver effective presentations.
- Appreciate what makes a good advocate.
- Prepare effectively for a moot.
- Communicate effectively in one to one and group situations.

Introduction

This is the first of two chapters on communication skills. Chapter 11 discusses specifically communication in the form of writing and drafting. This chapter deals with other forms of communication, including verbal and non-verbal communication. Of all the skills referred to in this book, it is these with which you will be most familiar. From the moment you were born, even before you could speak, you could communicate your need to feed, sleep, or play.

As you progress through your legal studies, seek employment opportunities and then start developing your career, communication skills will be fundamental. They are the primary means by which you impart what you know and what you think. *How* you communicate not only dictates the extent to which a recipient will understand what you are attempting to communicate: it will also result in the recipient forming a view of your ability to communicate.

There are a range of situations in which you will need to employ verbal and non-verbal communication skills during your studies: contributions in tutorials and seminars; making presentations; competing in a moot; being involved in pro bono or similar initiatives; vacation placements or other work experience schemes. They will be a fundamental part of the interview process as you look to develop career opportunities. In providing professional advice and services, lawyers have to communicate with clients, other lawyers, officials of public bodies, and a range of other professionals. Their communication skills will be employed in diverse situations, such as interviews, meetings, telephone calls, negotiations, presentations, and court appearances. These skills, even advocacy, have generic qualities that are transferable. That is, they can be employed in other contexts and careers. The requirements or job specification for nearly every profession and career will stipulate 'communication skills'. This chapter is therefore designed to help you develop and strengthen your communication skills. As these skills develop during your 'work'—your studies and career—you should also notice that they develop in your non-working life too.

Reading about communication skills, in isolation from practising these skills, may, at times, appear a little basic. However, it is a fundamental communication skill to be able to communicate complex ideas in a way that is easy to understand, and there is no value in dressing them up as more complex than they actually are. Like most skills, developing your communication skills predominantly requires some preparatory thought, the application of common sense, and subsequent reflection. This chapter aims to reflect that.

It would be unrealistic to ignore the requirement of a level of self-confidence. It is often the case that, when faced with a real recipient of their communication, in a situation where there is a little pressure and where they may have to think 'on their feet', the communication skills of both students and professionals are the first things to suffer. Unfortunately this also tends to be the first thing the recipient notices and, in professional circumstances, can result in criticism. A good level of self-awareness, reflective practice, and simply recognising the importance of communication skills will help you to develop the confidence to avoid these situations. Confidence is, to a large extent, a function of familiarity: this chapter has therefore been written on the basis that the more familiar you become with the basics early on, the more confident you will become in your communication.

Finally, remember that communication is a basic human interaction, and is what allows us to develop relationships of all types. To explore and become further aware of the variety of ways that communication can take place, both verbally and non-verbally, whether intentional or not, can be a fascinating and enriching experience.

10.1 What are communication skills?

The term 'communication skills' refers to several different skills which you use together to allow you to convey effectively information, opinion, and advice, and to receive the same from others.

10.1.1 Non-verbal communication

Before you even begin to speak, you communicate through your body language. When dealing with any complex issue or difficult situation, we may be deep in thought, or nervous. This can have a major effect on our eye contact and body language. Naturally pleasant and outgoing people can look distracted, or even severe and unapproachable. Even accomplished, talented professionals can find themselves unable to look anyone in the eye or offer a firm handshake. The good news is that much of this can be overcome through awareness, preparation, practice, and experience. The first step is to be aware of what you should be aiming for.

Eye contact

Eye contact is extremely powerful. In Western cultures, avoiding eye contact can be deemed to be a sign of dishonesty, which is obviously a particularly bad message for anyone, and particularly a lawyer, to communicate. Conversely, good eye contact can be very reassuring, instil confidence, be persuasive, and also allow you to pick up on cues others are making with their eyes. Eye contact is therefore important: if you struggle with it, and many do, then it is something to work on. You can practise making good eye contact in everyday life. Experimenting with eye contact in situations where you are comfortable can help develop the skill, so that you can then deploy it when you are outside your comfort zone. A good tip is to focus just behind a person's head to begin with. This helps to practise the habit and gives the other person the impression of eye contact. When you are comfortable doing this, progress to looking at their eyes, which has the added advantage of allowing you to read the eye signals they are communicating. Do take care to avoid becoming locked into eye contact. Being able to break off eye contact, and then seamlessly re-establish it, is another skill you can practise and master.

If you have Autism or Asperger's Syndrome, you may find eye contact particularly challenging. Even if you have learned to make eye contact, it may be that you still do not pick up on any cues from other people's eye contact. In this case, simply being aware of the importance of eye contact, and the messages it conveys, can be helpful. You may, for example, feel comfortable where appropriate to explain that just because you are not making eye contact does not mean you are not listening or paying attention to what someone is saying. This in itself is demonstrating a high level of self-awareness and good communication skills.

Body language

Our bodies can betray feelings that we would prefer to keep to ourselves. To some people, this is not desperately important. If the bass player in a band comes across as surly, hyperactive, or very shy, no one will use this to judge her ability to play guitar. However, in contrast, a lawyer must project a professional persona at all times. We need to be particularly alert to, and actively manage, the messages our bodies may be sending. Folding your arms looks defensive and hostile. Any persistent habits, such as foot jiggling, pen tapping, hand waving, hair flicking, or pacing around can detract significantly from what you are saying. Poor posture, including staring at your feet, sends the message that you are not interested. Scowling suggests you are unapproachable. A nervous demeanour can communicate itself to recipients such that they become nervous on your behalf, which can, in turn, impair the communication you are trying to make.

Part of being an effective communicator is being self-aware. We all do something inadvertently, but not all of us are aware of that fact. Painful though it may be, the best way to identify this is to ask someone you trust to be brutally honest, or alternatively record and analyse yourself. This latter technique is an established form of teacher and media training. Smartphones make this process much more accessible than it used to be. Simply recording yourself talking about your favourite subject for five minutes is likely to reveal what aspects of your body language may let you down. Failing this, watching yourself in a mirror can also help.

So far we have discussed inadvertent body language, but it is also worth considering how to use body language deliberately to send messages to others. During a negotiation, for example, you may wish to convey that you are open to hearing what others have to say. A relaxed, open position, smiling and with palms open (but in a natural position) can convey this very effectively. Nodding and making eye contact can denote that you are listening to what is being said. When you want to make a point firmly, putting your palms together and pointed subtly towards the person to whom you are making that point can help display conviction.

Appearance

It is a fact of life that some people will judge you by your appearance. Compare a lawyer who arrives at a meeting driving a Porsche and wearing a bold pinstriped suit, to a lawyer who arrives driving a Fiesta and wearing polyester. Consider the interview candidate who wears scuffed shoes and has a button missing from his jacket. Have you made a judgment about them already, before they have started to speak? Without advocating that you change your personal style, it shows good self-awareness at least to consider the impression your appearance might convey to others, and whether it aligns with the image you want to convey.

Any judgment that people may make is, of course, a first impression, which may be refined or even dramatically changed by what you go on to say or do (see the film *Legally Blonde*). That said, there is the risk that others might adhere to the adage that 'first impressions never lie' and you will find yourself fighting an uphill battle to retrieve a situation. Chapter 12 gives some tips as to how to you might dress for interviews or the office for the first time if you are unsure (see 12.1.3).

10.1.2 **Verbal communication**

Verbal communication includes not just what you say, but also how you say it. As a lawyer, your legal knowledge and skills are vital to ensure that what you say is technically correct. However, communication should not only be correct, it should also be effective. A client receiving legal advice is likely to assume that every lawyer would have delivered the same advice, in terms of the law. The client is much more likely to judge the lawyer on *how* the advice was delivered, as it is this which ultimately determines the effectiveness of the communication. Let us consider some factors which can affect the effectiveness of verbal communication.

Jargon

Lawyers should avoid jargon wherever possible when communicating with non-lawyers. Most will not understand what is being talked about, and why should they? You would not appreciate a doctor telling you that you have had a vasovagal syncope when instead she could have explained simply that you had fainted and why.

Tone

The tone of verbal communication is very important. It can help you to convey a range of messages: empathy, sympathy; humour; whether something is problematic. If you are not communicating face to face, for example when using the telephone, very subtle changes in tone can be important. Does your tone indicate that you are pleasant and smiling, or that you are grumpy or bored? You may find that when you are concentrating on something you can slip into a monotone. Make sure you vary the tone of your voice to add interest. Note, that people tend to 'mirror' emotions and so if you are pleasant to them, they are more likely to be pleasant to you.

Accent

Provided that you are clear in your speech, having an accent should not pose a problem in communicating. If you do think that your accent may cause difficulties with clarity, however, then simply slowing down your speech can help. Remember that colloquialisms (or slang phrases) are not appropriate in any professional office. So, for example, while it is fine to speak clearly with a Newcastle accent, it would not be fine when speaking to a client to refer to a good outcome as 'canny' (unless of course that client was a fellow Geordie).

Mannerisms

Just as you may do things inadvertently which affect your communication, you may also say things inadvertently. Asking for feedback or listening to a recording of yourself can also be helpful in revealing these traits. Common examples are saying 'erm' frequently rather than simply pausing. You may have a word you use frequently to punctuate or to fill a gap, such as 'ok', 'yeah?', 'hmm, hmm', 'fine', 'great', or 'like'. You need to eliminate this as soon as you can, because it can be very irritating, distracting, and often quite inappropriate. It is not entirely uncommon to hear a lawyer respond to a long tale of woe, be it death or impending insolvency, with a positive-sounding 'great', to the bewilderment of the client and the embarrassment of everyone else in the room.

10.1.3 Listening skills

Everyone likes to be listened to. If you can show someone you are listening they will automatically be predisposed towards you. The term 'active listening' refers to the fact that it is not enough that you are actually listening; you must be *seen* to be listening too. Body language is clearly important here and, as mentioned above, nodding and eye contact convey that you are listening. You should also react appropriately to what is being said, for example by laughing at jokes. Generally you need to show that you are engaging with what is being said. The person who is speaking will appreciate these signs and will remember those people who helped him to feel comfortable when speaking. This is true for large groups as well as for small groups. Presenters love a nodder.

Remember also that if you are speaking, you are not listening. Do not be tempted to chat through a presentation. The presenter *will* notice. Also, take care not to interrupt someone who is speaking. This is a common error on the part of lawyers, who tend to like to be in control and, being bright individuals, often pre-empt what is about to be said. Often, they think that they have thought of a solution before they have really listened to a problem in full, then interrupt the client to present that solution. Lawyers need to be open to hearing what clients are trying to tell them (and this includes listening to their feelings as well as their words). Test your discipline not to interrupt. In a suitable situation, try to concentrate *only* on listening to someone and digesting what he is saying (rather than, say, appearing to listen whilst actually rehearsing in your head what you are going to say next). You will be surprised at the value of the further information which may be revealed to you, and the other person will feel infinitely more valued by being allowed to have his say.

10.1.4 **Confidence**

Lawyers, like all professionals, need to inspire confidence. This is easier if you are confident yourself. If you are not confident in your own abilities, you are unlikely to persuade others to have confidence in you. Confidence is not the same as arrogance or brashness, however, and the line is a fine one to draw. It can help if you can think of someone you admire who inspires confidence and use them as a role model. What is it that they do which impresses you? How do they strike the right balance between confidence and arrogance? Then consider how you might incorporate some of their talents into your own communication skills.

Experience would dictate that those people who come across as truly confident often would not consider themselves to be naturally confident. However, they are people who are aware enough to understand that, to succeed, they need to project confidence. As with most skills, the more you practise looking and sounding confident, the more adept you will be at it, until you are so good it begins to come naturally.

10.1.5 **Communications skills**

Example 1

The following example paints a scene that you can observe or listen to daily in any shop or call centre in the country, and which provides the most basic illustration that knowledge alone does not equip you to achieve your objectives. (Of course, if you have worked in retail, it is also an example of how you could use your work experience to date, however apparently mundane, to show a professional employer what you have learned from it.)

Let's imagine that you bought a T-shirt last month. Yesterday you washed it for the first time and it has shrunk. You take it back to the shop where you bought it. From your study of law, you know that you have a statutory right, under the Sale of Goods Act 1979, to return faulty goods, and that this right is separate from any store policy in relation to the return of goods.

Consider the following two scenarios:

Scenario 1

Shop assistant:	Hello, can I help you?
You:	*Folds arms* I'd like to see the manager please. I'm appalled by what's happened to this T-shirt. It's clearly not of satisfactory quality or fit for purpose. I'm studying law. I know my rights. I want to speak to someone in charge so I can get my money back. And I'm not happy that I've had to make this journey into town. *Scowls*
Shop assistant:	Do you have a receipt?
You:	*Rolls eyes, raises voice* A receipt is completely irrelevant in these circumstances. I am not using your returns policy. This is about my rights as a consumer under the Sale of Goods Act. A T-shirt at this price should not have shrunk like this.
Shop assistant:	Yes, but I need to see how much you paid for it if I'm to refund you.
You:	*Avoids eye contact* Oh, I see. Yes, here it is. *Quietly* Thanks.

(continued . . .)

Scenario 2

Shop assistant:	Hello, can I help you?
You:	*Gives eye contact, smiles* Hello. I'm sorry to bother you, but I wonder if you could help me with a problem I've had with this T-shirt I bought here. As you can see, it has shrunk.
Shop assistant:	Oh, yes. It does seem a little small! How did you wash it?
You:	*Nods, gives eye contact, still smiling* I followed the instructions on the care label to the letter, but it went in a size 12 and seems to have come out a size 2. *Smiles* The receipt is here. I bought it a month ago for £20, but obviously I only discovered the problem when I washed it for the first time, and that was yesterday.
Shop assistant:	I see. Unfortunately as you bought it a month ago I think we can only give you a replacement.
You:	*Gives eye contact, still smiling* I wonder if you might be able to check that for me? I thought that if the T-shirt is clearly faulty then under the Sale of Goods Act you could still give me my money back, regardless of the store policy. I'm sorry; it is just that I cannot really spare the time to come back in if the same thing happens again.
Shop assistant:	In the circumstances, yes we can refund you. I'm sorry you've had a problem with it.
You:	*Gives eye contact, still smiling, audible so others can hear* Thanks so much for your help. I really appreciate it. Have a good day.

Let's analyse how communication skills made a difference here. In both scenarios you achieved your aim of obtaining a refund. However, in Scenario 1 it is unlikely that either you or the shop assistant found the experience to be a positive one. Contrast that with Scenario 2. The shop assistant was helpful and received good feedback. You both achieved what you set out to achieve, remaining pleasant and cheerful. The relationship between the two of you was positive: you would be highly likely both to go back to that shop and to speak positively of the experience to others. If we translate this snapshot of daily life into a professional scenario, remember that many lawyers rely on repeat work or word of mouth to receive their next instructions. Someone with the skills shown in Scenario 2 is likely to be considerably more successful in this regard than the person in Scenario 1.

You had the same technical knowledge of the law in both scenarios. In Scenario 2 it was your communication skills, underpinned by that technical knowledge, which made the difference. At the beginning of the exchange you made clear that you intended to be pleasant. You did this through choosing your words carefully and thinking about your body language. You used humour to engage with the shop assistant. You listened to him and remained courteous throughout. You were no pushover; you did assert your knowledge to your advantage, but only as and when necessary, and without arrogance. Finally, you remembered to say thank you, and did so genuinely and with conviction.

10.2 Using communication skills

We noted in the introduction the range of those scenarios when you will use communication skills during your studies. We also considered the communication skills required in professional life and the scenarios in which they are used. The following sections of this chapter consider a number of these scenarios. Some are set in the context of your studies (e.g. mooting) and some are set in the context of professional legal practice (e.g. advocacy). However, all provide guidance on communication skills, and how you can develop and use them to good effect. The guidance is intended to help you make your first attempt in any of these situations a positive experience.

10.3 Presentations

10.3.1 Purpose

During your legal studies, you will most likely be asked to present on a legal topic. The purpose, as with essays and other written pieces of work, is for you to demonstrate your understanding of and opinions on a particular area of law. In addition, unlike written work (unless you are asked to read it out), you will be informing your peers about the law and your opinions.

There are several reasons why you might deliver a presentation in legal practice. One is to pitch for new work. In effect this presentation is to sell the firm to a client, and the stakes are high as a good presentation can secure high-value work from a reliable client over a sustained period of time. Another reason is to deliver training, either internally to trainees, your colleagues, or other departments in the firm, or externally, perhaps to clients or institutions such as a law school. In this type of presentation you need to convey your message clearly and succinctly in a way which will appeal to your audience. Finally, you may be delivering a presentation in order to recruit new trainees, in which case your presentation needs to fulfil both the selling and training criteria. It is quite common for junior lawyers to be involved in any of these types of presentation.

 Essential explanation

Larger clients put their legal work out to competitive tender, which is sometimes referred to as a **beauty parade** (because it involves law firms showing how attractive they are in order to win the competition). This involves a panel of people from each firm presenting to a panel of people from the client as to why they are the best firm for the job. This presentation is known as a **pitch**. Lawyers and members of the firm's business development team will invest a significant amount of time preparing the pitch and tailoring the selling message to the client.

Law firms visit universities to advertise their graduate vacancies, with a view to recruiting the best candidates to work for them. This is known as the **milk round**, to reflect the atypical position that the employers are delivered to the students at their universities, just like milk is delivered to people at their homes. Most firms no longer recruit directly in the milk round but instead will advertise why they are a good place to work as a lawyer and encourage students to apply using their centralised and uniform (often online) application process.

The following guidance is not particularly complicated. As noted above, often communication skills are often simply the application of common sense, together with some thinking ahead. Part of this is considering your audience: the guidance below should be adopted or adapted as appropriate depending on the size and nature of your audience, and your familiarity with them. Nothing will enhance your presentation skills more than actually presenting. The more familiar and comfortable you become with presentation skills, the more you will be able to concentrate on the subject matter of that presentation without losing your audience.

10.3.2 **Structure**

Your presentation should have a clear structure with a definite beginning, middle, and end, which makes it easy for your audience to follow. You should share this structure with your audience. This is a technique known as **signposting**. It might seem obvious to you, but your audience will appreciate it.

Beginning

Even experienced and professional presenters can feel nervous before starting. However, you need to develop a veneer of confidence as this is your chance to make a good impact. Chapter 12 discusses techniques to control nervousness (see 12.10.3), and you should experiment with these to discover what works best for you. Note, however, that a little nervousness is a good thing as it will produce adrenalin to enhance your performance.

Employ good body language from the outset, smile and make eye contact with everyone in the room if possible. Remember that people like to mirror, so you must be enthusiastic and energetic if you want your audience to react to your presentation in this way. Introduce yourself, and any other presenters, very clearly. Now is the time to check that everyone can hear you, to avoid the embarrassment of someone asking later if you can speak up, or, worse, getting to the end of your presentation only to discover that no one has heard a word you have said.

The best presentations are interactive; they engage the audience and make them active contributors rather than passive observers. Depending on the size and nature of your audience, you may wish to set the interactive tone from the outset by asking them to introduce themselves. If appropriate for the audience in question, you may wish to have name cards or badges for them; it can be very impressive if you can refer to them by name when you interact with them during your presentation.

In terms of content, here you will let the audience know what is in store. It is good practice to set out the specific aims of the presentation, namely what you hope your audience will be able to do at the end of your presentation, as a result of it. One model which can be adopted for the aims is SMART. This provides that your aims should be:

- **S**pecific: clear and unambiguous.
- **M**easureable: capable of being measured against objective criteria.
- **A**chievable: can be accomplished by your audience.
- **R**elevant: suitable for and of appeal to your audience.
- **T**ime-appropriate: achievable within the time frame of your presentation.

The learning objectives at the beginning of each chapter of this book are examples of SMART objectives. Consider how your lecturers use learning outcomes, which are aligned with what your assessments will test, to help you to prepare, consolidate, and revise your class work. You should seek to help your audience in a similar way, to help them to place your presentation in context.

Middle

This is where you will deliver the bulk of the content of your presentation. You need to use all of the communication skills discussed in this chapter to keep your audience engaged during this period. Be succinct, use humour where appropriate, continue to use effective body language, and provide examples that are tailored to and will appeal to your audience.

 Practice tip

Thinking about your audience is the key to preparing and delivering a good presentation. Throughout, their needs are paramount. A presentation should not be generic. For example, an employment lawyer should not be able to use a presentation delivered to employees, as a presentation for employers. This would indicate that it was not tailored to the needs of the audience. Employees, for example, will be interested in learning about their rights, and how to enforce them against their employer. Employers will be more interested in hearing about how they as employers should act in a way that does not infringe those rights of their employees. Both presentations will cover the same law, but the emphasis needs to be different to engage the different audiences.

Having tailored the content of your presentation to your audience, you should consider how else to appeal to it. Address your audience directly. If you are presenting to employers, say 'You, as employers, will need to bear this cost' rather than, say, 'This cost is borne by employers'. You are looking to produce 'light bulb moments'; when what you say truly resonates with your audience. Involve your audience at this stage wherever possible. Ask them questions. Ask their opinions. Give them a short time to discuss something with the person next to them. Do anything and everything to keep them engaged. Just as varying the tone of your own voice can add interest, a change of presenter can also renew your audience's enthusiasm. Think about whether there is a timely point in your presentation when a change of presenter might be well received.

Do not be afraid of reiterating your key messages. The maxim 'say what you're going to say; say it; then say it again' is a good one (see 'Performance' at 11.1.1 for its application in written communications). As a minimum you should deliver your key message three times. Signpost in the introduction what you intend to say. In the middle, say it, then, at the end, summarise what you have said.

Relax, smile, be yourself, and try to enjoy the experience.

End

This is the stage where you must draw everything together. Summarise the key points of your presentation. Remind your audience of the aims of the presentation and check whether they have achieved those aims, in an interactive way if possible. Leave the audience with a good lasting impression. Ask if they have any questions. If they do not, do not end on that note. Wrap up the presentation properly and enthusiastically, signposting clearly that it has come to an end. If appropriate, ensure everyone has your name and your contact details and make clear you are available for one to one questions afterwards. It is common for audience members to be shy about asking questions in front of others, but relish the chance to speak to you one to one.

10.3.3 **Timing**

You will usually be given a target time frame for delivery of the presentation. You must make sure that it does not run significantly under or over this time frame, so practise your presentation in advance to check the timing. You can add some flexibility to the final presentation by preparing some extra items that you can bring in, and identifying some items that you can cut out, if necessary.

10.3.4 **Visual aids**

Often you will be given the option of preparing visual aids. Visual aids have several advantages. They can:

- help to focus your audience by:
  - highlighting key points;
  - appealing to visual learners;

 Essential explanation

People learn in different ways, and these ways are referred to as **learning styles**. If you prefer to read a book rather than listen to a presentation on the same topic, like lecturers to use slides or write on a whiteboard rather than just speak, and find it helpful to distil information into a mind map or diagram, then you are likely to be what is known as a **visual learner**. If conversely you would much rather attend a lecture to listen to a speaker, or download a podcast, then you may be an **aural learner**. There are other learning styles on which further reading is suggested at the end of this chapter.

- add interest to your presentation;
  - images and catchphrases can appeal to your audience;
  - however, choose them wisely as some can detract from the professional quality of your presentation;
  - check the copyright position when using images;
- act as your prompt:
  - this allows you to dispense with any other prompt (such as a script);
  - however do not overload the slides; this should not be their primary purpose (and do not read out the slide contents verbatim—if they are visual aids, they are for the *audience* to read);
- give the audience something else to look at other than you.

Used well, slides can add significant impact to a presentation. However, you must use them with caution. Many presenters use slides poorly, and 'presentation' is frequently misinterpreted as 'slide show'. Remember to use slides to supplement what you say, not to replace it. These are the hallmarks of a *poor* presentation, and they may already be familiar to you:

- put everything you want to say on the slides;
- create lots of slides;
- fill each slide with as many words as you can;
- add some token clipart;
- choose your favourite colours, regardless of whether they are easy to read;
- fail to proof-read the slides properly;
- do not leave enough time to familiarise yourself with the projection equipment;
- progress too many slides at once and leave the audience hanging while you work out how to go back one slide;
- read out the slides, and read from the screen so that your back is facing the audience and they cannot see or hear you.

Compare the two slides at Figure 10.1. They both convey the same messages in the same basic font and colour. However, even using these basic tools, you can see that the slides look very different. The first slide is a good visual aid. It captures key points and lets the audience know what is to come. It has been proof read properly. This slide needs a good presenter to embellish these key points.

The second slide attempts to convey the entire message in full sentences. It will need to be read out because the audience towards the back of the room may not be able to read it. The rest of the audience will not be listening to the presenter while they are reading the slide. This will probably not be a problem however, because the presenter may not be audible as she will be facing the screen to read the slide. As they will be focusing all of their attention on this slide, the audience will notice the inconsistent use of full stops, the erroneous comma, and the misspelling of reliant.

Which slide do you prefer? This may depend on whether you are considering the slide from the perspective of the presenter or the audience. From the audience's perspective, the first slide is clear, readable, and prepares them to listen to the presenter. The second slide could be a good note to take away (if corrected), but the presentation is likely to add little to it.

From the presenter's perspective, the second slide does provide a safety net in terms of content. However it will actually detract from her ability to use the communication skills set out in this chapter. The first slide provides a decent prompt, but will encourage the presenter to be familiar with the content of the presentation and to employ effective communication skills to engage the audience.

The second slide is attempting to fulfil not only the role of slide, but also of script and notes. A good presenter should not rely on a script, and a slide is not the ideal way to provide notes. If you would like your audience to have a note to take away, then prepare a separate note for them. Most software packages have a function to allow you to prepare and print notes next to the slides.

Visual Aids	How to prepare an effective visual aid for your presentations

• **Not too much text**
 	
• **Not too full**
 	
• **Key points only**
 	
• **Add interest**
 	
• **Supplement presentation**
	• Try not to prepare too many slides.
	  - This will detract from your presentation
	• It is not a good idea to write in full sentences on the slide
	  - Your presentation will add the detail
	• Restrict what you say on the slide to the key points of your presentation
	  - Otherwise you might as well just mail the audience the slide set
	  - You are adding nothing to the presentation if you just turn up and read the slides
	• Try to make your slides as interesting as possible
	  - Law firms tend to have a house style layout for slides, but links to websites and video clips can add verve to your presentation.
	• Images can also help to make your presentation memorable
	  - Although query whether they might make it memorable for the wrong reasons
	• As a basic rule, imagine you could not use your slides. If you would still be able to present, then your slides are supplementing your presentation. If you would have to cancel, you are too relient on your slides and are delivering a slide show not a presentation,

Figure 10.1 Examples of good and bad slides

10.3.5 **Scripts and prompts**

If you read from a script it will severely inhibit your ability to use the communication skills discussed in this chapter, including eye contact and body language, and is bound to detract from your presentation. The audience will definitely notice this. They will not definitely notice if you omit to mention one esoteric point because you were not reading from a script. On balance, the risks of reading from a script far outweigh the risks of jettisoning a script and being prepared for a few minor omissions. Never read out a pre-prepared presentation.

The best presenters do not use separate prompts either. Instead, as discussed, they will rely on a basic prompt from the visual aids they have prepared for the benefit of the audience. If you really cannot do without a prompt, restrict yourself to bullet points on cards or to using the slide software's notes facility.

10.3.6 **Setting up the room**

The layout and set up of a room can make a difference to your presentation. You need to consider this from the audience's perspective. Set out below are a number of factors to consider. Having the right set up can be as important as preparing the presentation: however good the presentation, it can be ruined if the room and facilities do not 'work'. As a presenter, you should take responsibility both for checking in advance and at the time of the presentation that the set up meets your requirements.

Will the audience hear you?

Test the acoustics. Consider whether there is likely to be any background noise. Check if there is a microphone you can use. If the audience are struggling to hear, they will switch off. Always ask the audience at the beginning of the presentation if they can hear, and encourage them to let you know during your presentation if they can no longer hear you. Also remember to ask the audience to turn off their mobile telephones, and always remember to switch off your own.

Will the audience be able to read your slides?

We have discussed what you can do to make your slides readable. However, the layout of the room may prevent the audience from reading even the best slides. Check if there is anything impeding the audience's view, or whether people at the back are too far away, and change the layout of the room accordingly. Take hard copies of the slides with you in case you cannot overcome any problems with audience members being able to read the screen.

Will you be able to interact?

The best presenters engage with their audience. This can be difficult to do if you are far away from them, or on a stage. Do what you can with the room to make it as intimate as possible. When you have exhausted the possibilities for this, there are other steps you can take to interact. If everyone sits at the back of the room, encourage them to come to the front before you start. If you are on a platform or stage, leaving it from time to time, to walk among your audience, can be very effective. In a large room, you will need a wireless microphone and a mouse to do this most effectively, so that the audience can still hear you and you do not have to return to the stage to progress your slides.

Do the audience need anything?

In professional situations, it is usual to leave at least a pen and some paper for each member of the audience, in case they arrive unprepared for taking notes. (Most law firms have branded pens and paper for this purpose, which help with business development, as do business cards, brochures, and other publications.) You may have prepared a handout for use during the session, so it is helpful to put this out in advance too, and to leave copies on spare chairs for any latecomers. If you have prepared notes to take away, consider whether you want to give these out at the beginning or the end. The risk with the former is that the audience will read them rather than listen to your presentation.

Delivering in unfamiliar premises

If you are delivering a presentation at someone else's premises, perhaps as part of an interview process or for business development purposes, do not assume you have no control over the layout. If you can show that you are putting the needs of your audience first, then your enquiries are likely to be well received by the person who has control of the room.

Always arrive well in advance of your presentation too. You will need to factor in time for some or all of the following: taking longer to get to the venue than you thought; going to the toilet; checking your appearance; setting up (sometimes completely re-arranging) the room; dealing with any IT glitches; writing up any information on a whiteboard or flip chart; and checking you have all the equipment and materials you need.

10.3.7 **Equipment**

You may be asked what equipment you need, or told what equipment will be available. The following list of equipment is a good guide as to what you might need: most items have already been referred to above. There is certainly no magic to them; however, if your presentation relies on any of them and they are not there, it can be difficult to work around their absence. Thinking about what you need and checking in good time that it will be there reduces the risks.

- Laptop or computer;
- memory stick loaded with presentation (even if a copy is pre-loaded onto the computer, as back-up);
- projector and screen;
- cordless mouse;
- cordless microphone;
- flipchart;
- whiteboard;
- marker pens;
- pens and paper for the audience;
- handouts or other materials;
- name cards or badges.

10.3.8 **Preparation and developing your skills**

As discussed, recording yourself and critically appraising your performance is the best way to prepare for a presentation. In the absence of any recording equipment, you can always present to a mirror. Check any bad habits, such as waving your arms about or playing with your hair. Seek feedback from others too. It can be helpful to seek the opinion of a non-lawyer as well as from another lawyer.

Think about someone—a lecturer, a colleague, or someone on television who you think presents well. Watch them. What are they doing (or not doing) that makes them so good? Do not make the mistake of thinking what they are doing is spontaneous. It will not be. To be a good presenter takes rigorous practice. It is not by chance that television presenters stand in the correct place, look at the correct camera, and deliver an effortless joke which is absolutely suitable for their target audience. Talented presenters practise. Now think of someone who you consider to be a poor presenter. What are they doing (or not doing)? Why do you think they continue to do this, even as a professional? As with most performance skills, observation and reflection will show you what works and what does not, as well as a reserve of ideas about what will work best for you.

10.4 Advocacy

10.4.1 What does an advocate do?

A barrister or a solicitor can be an advocate. Broadly, an advocate is someone who appears in court to argue her client's case before a judge. As you will no doubt be aware from watching television dramas, the role of an advocate is to persuade the court to find in their client's favour. However, they must be aware at all times that although they represent the client, they do so as an officer of the court. This means that advocates cannot mislead the court to help their client (e.g. by presenting evidence which they know is untrue). They must be ethical and maintain professional standards.

 Practice tip

A reference to **court** may conjure up a specific image in your head. The layperson often thinks of a court as comprising a judge—in full wig and gown—and a jury, all sitting in a room with wooden panels. However, in practice, this is not always the case. Serious criminal offences will be tried before a judge and jury, while less serious offences and most civil cases are heard before a judge sitting alone. Court dress differs depending on the court in question, with full wigs retained mainly for ceremonial purposes. Tribunal judges and magistrates generally wear suits. Many court-rooms are now more modern in decor.

In brief, advocates will:

- present evidence to the court (witnesses can provide evidence in written form or they may attend court to give oral testimony);
- present the relevant law, as it applies to that evidence (referred to as legal submissions). This typically involves inviting the court to apply the law as it was found to be in previously decided cases where the principles are similar to the present case;
- ask the court to find in favour of their client.

10.4.2 What makes a good advocate?

The role of an advocate involves presenting the client's case to the court. The guidance in this chapter on effective communication and presentation skills is very relevant in the context of advocacy. Making good eye contact with the judge, varying the tone of your voice, and speaking clearly, succinctly, and at an appropriate volume and pace (usually the pace at which you would normally speak) are all skills required of an effective advocate.

However, we need to consider some of these skills specifically in the context of advocacy, given that there are some key differences between presenting and being an effective advocate. For example, questions during or after a presentation tend not to be adversarial. With advocacy, however, you can expect someone to be ready to dispute or call into question what you have said.

 Practice tip

Legal work can be categorised as **contentious** or **non-contentious** work. Contentious work involves the resolution of disputes, some of which may result in proceedings in court (or other dispute resolution forums), and non-contentious work does not. As you progress in your legal career, it is usual to find that you prefer one type over the other, however many lawyers do not discover this until they have progressed quite significantly through a training contract or pupillage (and some not even by then).

The practice of corporate and commercial law are examples of non-contentious legal work. Litigation (sometimes called dispute resolution) is clearly an example of contentious work. Some departments can involve both contentious and non-contentious work, such as employment law, where you may be drafting an employment contract (non-contentious) or defending a claim for unfair dismissal (contentious).

Case analysis

This is a skill vital for contentious lawyers, as it provides an analysis of the fundamental aspects of a dispute. It is vital to the preparation for any formal proceedings in a court or other forum, and hence to advocacy. It is also, in relation to your legal studies, an approach which you can apply in developing your problem-solving skills (see Chapter 9).

You need to analyse the facts of your client's case well. You will have to establish what you need to prove, and how you can prove it. This will involve using your legal reading, research, and problem-solving skills (see Chapters 7, 8, and 9) to find not only the relevant law which will help you, but also any relevant law which your opponent may seek to rely on. Thus, part of case analysis involves anticipating your opponent's arguments and planning how you would answer them in favour of your client. Detailed knowledge of any cases or regulations likely to be referred to in court is vital.

Case analysis therefore requires you to identify:

- Who is the claimant?
- Who is the defendant?
- What is the loss that has been suffered?
- What is the relevant law (e.g. contract law or the law of tort)?
- What is the relevant cause of action (e.g. if tort, is it nuisance, trespass, negligence)?
- What are the necessary elements of that law (e.g. with negligence this would include a duty of care, breach of that duty, and causation)?
- How does that law apply to the specific facts of your case?

Example 2

Let's consider an example where there has been a breach of contract and one party (the claimant) considers that it has suffered a loss of around £500,000 due to the breach. This party seeks legal advice on the matter, and its solicitor advises that it has an excellent chance of recovering this amount if they take the other party (the defendant) to court. The defendant then offers the claimant an out of court settlement of £300,000. The claimant refuses. The matter goes to court and the court awards the claimant just £100,000 in damages, and also orders the claimant to pay some court costs. The claimant then considers whether it has a case against its solicitor for damages based on negligent advice. Analysing the case:

- *The claimant* in this negligence action is the claimant in the original breach of contract action, who had suffered a contractual loss and sought advice from its solicitor on how to recover the loss.
- *The defendant* is the solicitor who advised on the claimant's chances of success in litigating the breach of contract.
- *The loss* the claimant has suffered can be estimated as the difference between the £300,000 it was offered to settle (but rejected in the belief that it would receive more by going to court) and the £100,000 (less court costs) it eventually received.
- *The relevant area of law* is the law of tort.
- *The relevant cause of action* is negligence.
- *The necessary elements of that law* are duty of care, breach of that duty, and causation.
- You would then *apply this law* to the specific facts of the question, to establish and explain whether:
  - the defendant solicitor owed the claimant a duty of care;
  - the solicitor breached this duty with the advice given to the claimant;
  - any breach of duty actually caused the claimant to suffer the loss identified above.

As the claimant's advocate your role would be to:

- present the claimant's factual evidence to the court (to satisfy the court that your client did in fact receive clear advice from the defendant to litigate against the other party to the contract); and
- present legal argument to satisfy the court that as a matter of law the claimant is entitled to a remedy in the law of tort, because:
  - the defendant owed the claimant a duty of care;
  - the defendant breached that duty of care by advising the claimant that it had excellent prospects of recovering its entire loss through litigation;
  - the advice to litigate did cause the claimant to suffer the loss identified above.

Preparation

As with a good presenter, good advocates will make the task before them look entirely spontaneous, but it will not have been. Preparation and rehearsal, so that you are familiar with all aspects of your case analysis, are essential if you are to assimilate and process information quickly in court. There will of course be occasions where an opponent raises something that takes you completely by surprise, and you will have to react spontaneously and 'think on your feet'. However, this should be the exception and not the rule.

Court-room etiquette

This is the name for the series of conventions that have developed over time regarding how advocates should present their case in court. They should not detract from your communication skills: the conventions are simply to be learned and adhered to. The most important principles are set out below.

Language

As an advocate you represent your client, but you are not the client. Your role is to submit the relevant law and evidence to the court, not to offer a personal view on the case. Take care that when you make submissions to the court you do not use language which suggests that you have adopted the client's case as your own. In particular, avoid subjective language such as 'I think', 'in my case', and 'in my opinion' and instead learn to adopt objective phrases such as 'it is submitted' and 'it is the claimant's case that'.

How to address the court

How an advocate addresses the judge will depend on the type of judge who is sitting. For example, you should address a District Judge who sits in the county court as Sir or Madam. Typically you should address a High Court or Court of Appeal judge as My Lord or Lady. The website of the Judiciary of England and Wales explains in detail how to address judges (see 'Further reading' at the end of this chapter).

Other advocates should be addressed as 'my friend' or 'my learned friend'.

Dress

Advocates should wear smart, professional attire that is navy blue or black. In criminal courts they must wear a wig and gown, but this is not the case in all courts. You would not require a wig in family court proceedings, and increasingly judges are allowing advocates to remove their wigs during civil cases (especially in the summer months).

The art of persuasion

A significant part of the role of advocates is to persuade the judge, and jury if appropriate, to decide in favour of their client. A good advocate will have the power of persuasion. This is often discussed as if it is an inherent talent. To some degree this is correct. You probably already have some idea whether you are naturally adept at persuading others to see your point of view. If so, then this is a good foundation on which to build in order to be a successful advocate. However, the power of persuasion is really a skilful combination of good communication and presentation skills together with effective case analysis, preparation, and knowledge of court-room etiquette referred to above, all of which can be practised and honed.

Although within the formal setting of a court-room, an advocate will use verbal and non-verbal skills to communicate with the judge, other advocates and, in some cases, a jury. Thus, variation of the voice, correct pace, and eye contact can all be employed. As noted above, these skills are all part of the skill of persuasion: the judge (and jury) need to be able to hear, understand and feel sufficiently confident in what is being said in order to agree with it.

As with presentations, reading out notes will neither engage nor inspire confidence, so is highly unlikely to be persuasive.

Visiting the court

The advocacy employed in most courts and other dispute resolution forums is rarely of the type often portrayed in television and film court-room dramas. To improve your understanding of the skills required of an advocate, and assist you in developing your own advocacy skills (see also 'Mooting' at 10.5), a visit to a court is highly worthwhile.

The vast majority of our courts are open to the public and you should visit at least one during your studies to enhance your understanding of how the law works in practice. Court visits offer you a valuable insight into what practising advocates do on a daily basis. You will be able to observe how lawyers use the law and apply it to the facts of the case, how a judge reaches a conclusion, and the court procedure generally.

You should take care to comply with the rules of the court that you visit. There is a link to a helpful guide to visiting court in 'Further reading' at the end of this chapter. The reception staff and court ushers will be happy to help you when you arrive at the court. You should simply explain that you are a law student and would like to observe the court proceedings.

10.5 Mooting

10.5.1 What is a moot?

A mooting competition, referred to as a moot, is a fictitious court hearing. Generations of law students have used mooting to help them develop both their knowledge of the law and their advocacy skills. It involves presenting to the court the legal arguments that relate to a particular written problem provided to you in advance. Typically, moots are presented as appeals, so you present to an appellate court. This requires you to accept the facts and issues as they are presented in the written problem and focus exclusively on presenting legal arguments (also known as **submissions**). You should aim to participate in a moot during your studies. This is another way you can demonstrate to a prospective employer that you have developed the skills referred to in this chapter. The process of mooting may also reveal to you whether you enjoy contentious work or prefer non-contentious work (see 'Practice Tip' at 10.4.2).

Example 3

Example 2 regarding the negligent solicitor could be presented as a moot problem. You would be given the facts of the problem in writing. Appeal cases are based on an error on a point of law and you would be told what the grounds for the appeal are. If you represent the claimant (now referred to as the appellant because it is bringing the appeal), you need to persuade the Court of Appeal that the judge at first instance made an error in law and should have found in favour of the appellant. If you represent the solicitor defendant (now known as the respondent because it is responding to the appeal), then you need to persuade the Court of Appeal to the contrary.

10.5.2 **How a moot is structured**

You will receive the written moot problem in advance of the moot and you will be told whether you represent the appellant or the respondent. In most national competitions there will be two grounds of appeal, so your team would comprise two people who take one ground each, thus testing team-working skills too (see 12.2). There will be moot rules which need to be carefully observed. These will include rules about how long you have to make your submissions and the maximum number of legal authorities on which you can rely.

You and your partner will then undertake case analysis and preparation, as described above in relation to advocacy. You will research the moot problem and prepare your legal submissions either to support or oppose the grounds of appeal. This will involve deciding which authorities you wish to rely on and why you say they are relevant and binding.

Some moots require you to present a written summary of your submissions (known as a **skeleton argument**) in advance of the moot. A skeleton argument is exactly what the name suggests. It is the bones of the argument and you will put the flesh on those bones through your skilful advocacy in the moot. Typically a skeleton argument will comprise one page that details your basic submissions and the cases or other authorities that you will rely on. You may be asked to take copies of those authorities to the moot for use by the judge and your opponent.

When the moot begins, the team representing the appellant will present their submissions first and answer any questions that the moot judge may have arising out of those submissions. The team representing the respondent will then make their submissions. When they have finished, the team representing the appellant will often be given a very short amount of time to reply to the submissions for the respondent. The moot judge will then give a judgment on the law and, in a competitive moot, declare the team whose submission the court found most persuasive to be the winner.

10.5.3 **Mooting skills**

The judge will be judging your mooting skills, which are very similar to those you require to be an effective advocate, as referred to at 10.4. These include your ability to:

- analyse your case well (including the grounds of appeal);
- work as a team;
- manage your time;
- present your submissions effectively;
- structure your arguments;
- think on your feet;
- use court etiquette.

Note that it does not necessarily follow that the team that succeeds in the appeal will win the moot. One team may have the law on their side, for example.

As with advocacy, case analysis is key. You should pay particular attention to this because it is an area in which students can struggle. If you can show that this is a particular area of strength for your team, you will have a distinct advantage. You can do this in the following way.

- Present authorities which are binding on the moot court.
  - For example, if you are in the Court of Appeal, a decision by the House of Lords or the Supreme Court will bind the court, but a High Court decision will not. There is further guidance about this at 5.2.1.
- Be prepared to summarise the facts of the authority.
- Be able to explain which **principle** of law the authority establishes and why you consider that the authority should be followed or distinguished.
  - Students tend to focus their legal research efforts on trying to find a case with similar **facts**, but as Chapter 8 explains, finding a case which establishes or distinguishes a similar legal **principle** is the key.
- You must read the whole authority and not just the headnote in order to build a persuasive argument.
  - This is critical.
  - The judge or your opponent may highlight passages of a judgment which are less helpful to your client, and you must be able to deal with this.

10.6 **Face-to-face communication**

Many law programmes offer opportunities to become involved in pro bono schemes or law clinics. A small but growing number offer programmes or modules which involve client-based scenarios or simulations. These programmes offer you valuable experience in developing face-to-face communication skills. These skills are the foundation of the majority of professional relationships, whether with clients or other professionals. The guidance given below is in the context of a lawyer meeting with a client for the first time. If any of your law programme activities involve you in meeting real-life clients, you will be able to employ the various techniques described. Similarly, if you undertake work experience or a placement, you will be very likely at least to see these skills in practice, if not practise some yourself. Note that much of the above can also be said in relation to the telephone communication skills discussed at 10.7.

  If you do not have any of the above opportunities during your studies, the guidance shows you how you can focus on practising skills such as listening and note-taking, so that when the time comes to meet a client for the first time, you will find the process easier. It will also develop your understanding of the communication skills which are important for developing professional relationships: this understanding and any relevant experience, in any context, is a topic frequently explored in job interviews. While the guidance below is set in the context of a first meeting between a lawyer and client, it goes without saying that the communication skills employed are applicable to face-to-face meetings in a range of other professional contexts.

10.6.1 **First meeting: introduction**

Your first meeting with any client is pivotal. If you make a good impression, this could be the basis of a long and mutually beneficial working relationship. If you make a poor impression, you are unlikely to see them again, and may have damaged your own and your employer's reputation. As you gain experience, first meetings will come naturally to you and you may vary more the particular structure or format employed. However, experience shows that as a student practising this skill, or trainee or junior lawyer trying it for the first time in practice, it can be helpful to follow a structure to ensure that you remember everything you need to do. This will free you to concentrate on listening to clients and communicating well with them. The flowchart at Figure 10.2 breaks down the meeting into manageable sections and will help you to structure your meeting logically. You can annotate it and take it into a meeting with you. The following commentary will help you to think about how you can communicate best at each stage. (Note that before qualification this skill is often referred to as 'interviewing and advising'. However this focuses exclusively on what the lawyer is doing and does not really capture the point that the client plays a pivotal role too. Few practising lawyers would refer to 'interviewing' a client, except in very specific circumstances.)

Most clients will be meeting you in the hope that you can solve a legal problem for them. The guidance set out in Chapters 8 and 9 is therefore relevant here too. Remember that Chapter 11 provides guidance about how to communicate with a client in writing. The guidance below focuses on a face-to-face first meeting with a client of a law firm, but as noted in the introduction to this paragraph, much of it transfers equally well to other professions and activities.

10.6.2 **Prepare for the meeting**

Preparation is essential for any professional meeting: any failure to understand either the objectives of meeting, the issues involved, and the subject matter in question, will become very obvious to any other party involved. As the objective of the current meeting is to advise a client with a legal problem, you should analyse what you know about the problem in advance of the meeting, identify the relevant facts, and find all relevant law (subject of course to any instructions and considerations about incurring costs).

Without suggesting that you read from a script in the interview itself—this would severely inhibit rapport between you and the client—you can and should prepare many aspects of the first client meeting in advance. Examples of questions are given below, but you can think of others which reflect your own personal style.

10.6.3 **Begin the meeting**

As with a presentation, the beginning of a meeting is crucial. The client will form an immediate impression and you want it to be a good one. You should arrive on time and be professional and confident from the outset, to reassure the client that she is in good hands and has chosen her adviser wisely. The client may also be nervous at this stage, so do what you can to put her at ease. A question about her journey to your office, or the weather, and taking

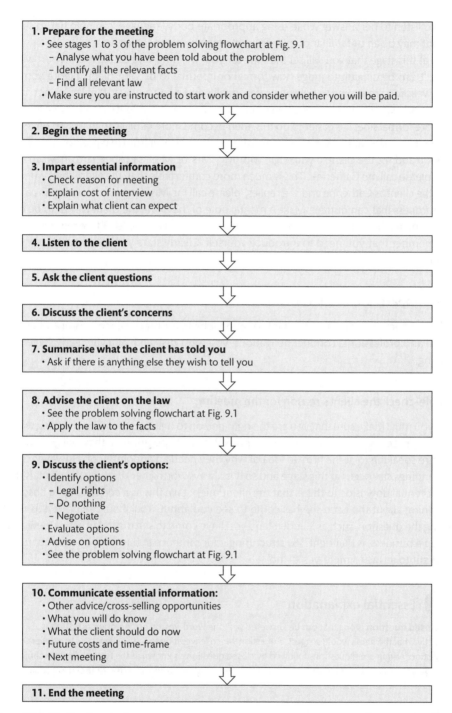

Figure 10.2 Meeting flowchart

time to listen to her answer while using appropriate body language, can help her to settle in to what may be an unfamiliar or even intimidating environment for her.

It is at this stage that you will set the tone for your meeting, and establish a rapport with the client. It can be difficult to judge how formal or informal to be with clients before you know them well. You are aiming to behave professionally, and if you are over-familiar, or not familiar enough, this will fall short of professional behaviour. As a general rule, it is good advice to start on the more formal side. It is easier to do this, then become more familiar, than to start off in a way the client considers to be over-familiar and then have to recover from that position. Apply this to how you address the client. If you begin with 'Mr', 'Mrs' or 'Miss', say, Shephard, they can always reply 'please call me Catherine'. This is much more comfortable than the alternative, where you greet the client as Catherine and she replies, 'please call me Miss Shephard', which can cause an awkwardness that can distract. Make a mental note of the name the client wishes to be called, use that name throughout the meeting, and note it on the client file for future reference.

Remember that you need to introduce yourself. Clearly state your name, and your status or role.

10.6.4 **Impart essential information**

There are a few essential pieces of information which, for practical reasons or to fulfil your ethical and professional conduct obligations, you must deal with at a very early stage of the meeting.

Double-check the client's reason for the meeting

First, you must make sure that you are the right person to help this client, by checking why she has come to see you. Usually when clients book their first appointment they will give whoever they are speaking to at the firm an idea of why they need an appointment. However, misunderstandings can occur at this stage and so it is always worth checking why the client is there. The potential downside to this is that the client might take this as a cue to tell you absolutely everything about the issue she has come to see you about. You should manage this risk by closing the question, such as 'I understand you have come to see me today with a view to setting up a business, is that right?' By structuring your sentence in this way you are encouraging the client to answer simply 'yes' or 'no'.

> **Essential explanation**
>
> A **closed question** is one that can be answered with the word 'yes' or 'no'. An **open question** is exactly what the name would suggest, a question which leaves it open to the client how to answer the question. Asking open questions followed by closed questions is known as the **funnel down** technique. Conversely asking closed questions followed by open questions is known as the **funnel up** approach.

Explain the cost of the meeting

The next information you must give to the client is about the cost of the meeting. Some firms do not charge for first meeting, in which case you can say this. However, assuming your firm is charging, then for ethical and practical reasons the client needs the opportunity to walk away at an early stage, and you also need to fulfil your obligations in this regard under the **Solicitors Code of Conduct**.

Many lawyers can feel embarrassed talking about costs at all, but particularly early on. They think it can give the (false) impression that they are only concerned about money and not about helping the client with the law. This is interesting, because client feedback often reflects the exact opposite, namely that clients think lawyers focus overly on the technicalities of the law at the expense of client service, which includes giving information about costs. Think also about whether lawyers' fears about discussing costs are actually well founded. When you go into a shop, you do not wait until you reach the checkout before you know what you have to pay. You know before you select the product from the shelf, because the seller will have clearly labelled it with its price. Similarly, when you go to the dentist, he does not say I will fill your tooth and then we can discuss what it will cost. He will tell you beforehand, so you can make an informed choice as to whether to have your tooth filled or not. So, the client will expect you to discuss what the meeting will cost, and to discuss it before the meeting is in full swing.

You should explain that you charge on a time basis. Then let the client know your hourly rate and how long you expect the meeting will last. This will allow you to provide an estimate for the cost of the meeting. You then need to ask the client if she is happy to proceed on that basis. The client is now in an informed position as to whether she wishes to pay for your advice or not, before you have given it.

 Essential explanation

The **Solicitors Regulation Authority**, which regulates the profession, publishes a **Code of Conduct** which solicitors must follow. Chapter 1 of the Code sets out obligations regarding client care. It includes obligations about fee arrangements, including discussing with clients whether the outcome will justify the expense and risks, clearly explaining your fees, warning clients about other fees for which they will be responsible, and providing this information in a clear and accessible form. Students learn about this Code during their vocational stage of training, but useful information can be found on the SRA website (see 'Further reading' at the end of this chapter).

Explain what the client can expect to happen in the meeting

Finally, remember that while you have a clear idea of what will happen in the meeting, the client may not. It can be helpful in terms of reassuring the client and building rapport just to give her a brief outline of what will (e.g. you will listen to what she has to say, ask a few questions, consider the issue and give some advice which you will follow up in writing) and will not (e.g. decide to go to court, make any final decision) happen in your meeting.

10.6.5 **Listen to the client**

You are now ready to listen to the client's issue. It is a good idea to use the funnel down technique for this (see 'Essential explanation' at 10.6.4). As discussed, lawyers have a tendency to pre-empt what a client is about to say. This is not helpful, because the lawyer must give accurate, tailored advice on the client's actual issue, rather than the issue the lawyer thinks the client has. Consider, for example, a client who mentions he has come to see you about a partnership. It is impossible to pre-empt what the client wants at this stage. He may want to set up a partnership, exit from a partnership, or even enter into a civil partnership. Remember that everyone likes to be listened to, so do not think the client will be wondering why you are not speaking. He will enjoy being given the opportunity to explain his issue fully to you.

Prepare a good open question, for example 'Now please could you tell me about the issue you have come to see me about today', to signal to the client that this is his cue to tell you everything. Use your active listening techniques, discussed earlier (see 10.1.3), to encourage the client to continue to speak. You may need to practise your 'poker face', as clients can sometimes disclose information at this stage that is unexpected, salacious, or downright alarming, but you must maintain a professional demeanour at all times.

You will want to take notes, but bear in mind that this can inhibit rapport and may also prevent you from properly digesting what the client is saying (think of taking notes in a lecture and not knowing what you have written about until you read them through after the lecture). Depending on the complexity of the information being imparted at this stage, it can be a good idea to resist taking notes at the very start. If you must take notes at this stage, try to make sure you do so in a way which avoids these problems.

Do not interrupt the client. At best, you will come across as rude; at worst you may prevent the client from telling you a pivotal fact. If, on reflection, you think that you have a tendency to interrupt, then resisting the urge to do this is something you can practise in your conversations with friends and family.

10.6.6 Ask the client questions

When the client has answered your initial open question, you will probably need to ask further questions. Following the funnel down technique, you should continue to ask open questions to begin with, and then move on to closed questions. Good open questions are:

'Could you tell me some more about ...?'
'What in particular is the problem with ...?'
'How does everyone else feel about ...?'

The reason for the funnel down approach is that it should capture more information. For example, if you ask the closed question, 'Are you worried because of X?', then a client may say yes. However, if you had asked the more open question, 'Why are you worried?', the client may answer 'X, Y, and Z'. The closed question did not reveal the existence of Y and Z, but the open question did. Y and Z might be absolutely crucial in determining the advice to give.

Also bear in mind that your client is unlikely to be the only person involved in the issue. You need to remember to ask questions about other people, who they are, whether they are in a position of strength or weakness, and how they might affect your client's position. Be inquisitive and explore all aspects of what the client has told you. You can adopt good habits now of asking questions of people rather than talking about yourself (which many lawyers are guilty of). You may be surprised by the results.

You should start to take notes at this stage if you have not already. You may think that you will remember all the information until you return to your desk, but frequently you will be diverted into something else on the way back, and by the time you do return to your desk your head will be full of other information. Chapter 11 provides some guidance as to how to take good notes (see 11.2.2). You should give some thought to how to do this in the context of a client meeting. One effective method is to divide your page into quarters. You can then use each quarter for a different purpose, for example one to record basic facts, one to record information you want to ask the client more about when the opportunity arises, one to record legal issues which occur to you that you must include in your advice, and another to record further action you or the client agree to take.

 Practice tip

If, as a trainee, you sit in to observe your supervisor's meeting, in the absence of any express instruction always assume that you should take a note of what is being said. Solicitors often expect that their trainee will take a note so they do not have to, but sometimes they are not very good at telling their trainee this in advance.

10.6.7 **Confirm the client's concerns**

When you have finished asking the client about his issue, you should have a good understanding of his concerns. However, it is an excellent idea to ask the client a direct question, such as:

'It seems to me your concern here is X. Is that true or do you also have other concerns?'
'What would be your ideal outcome here? And your worst outcome?'

Do not just rely on assumptions you have made, or consider that asking this type of question is somehow an admission that you do not know something. In fact, this type of question really shows that you are thinking from the client's perspective, and the client will appreciate it. It is also vital information for you if you are to help the client reach the best solution.

10.6.8 **Summarise what the client has told you**

You will have received a lot of information in a relatively short time. It may feel a bit laboured, but summarising to the client what he has told you in the meeting can be useful in three ways. It allows:

- you time to digest the facts of the client's issue before you advise on it;
- the client a chance to check you have understood everything correctly;
- the client to identify anything he has forgotten to tell you or which you have not remembered.

After summarising it is worth asking the client if there is anything else he would like to tell you before you start to advise him. This gives the client a final chance to disclose information to you, and recognises that the facts are crucial to identifying the correct solution for a client.

10.6.9 **Advise the client on the law**

Here you will use your legal knowledge and problem-solving skills (Chapters 8 and 9) to apply the relevant law to the facts of the client's issue (see the problem solving flowchart at

Figure 9.1). This can be complex, and it is quite appropriate to explain to the client that you are going to take a few moments to consider the issue before you advise. Students and junior lawyers often feel that this is somehow cheating or not expected, because they are under the misapprehension that advising on the law is about immediately bestowing their legal knowledge upon the client. You should have realised by now that, in fact, advising clients on the law is about applying legal knowledge to the facts of a client's problem. This requires careful analysis of the client's problem, the relevant law, and, most importantly for the client, the effect of the law on that problem. Therefore, do not worry about a short period of silence while you carry out this analysis. It may seem interminable to you, but rest assured that, having answered all of your questions, the client will be happy to have a short rest.

Once you are ready to advise, you must do so in a way which is best for the client. If you are nervous about advising, and many junior lawyers are, you must resist the temptation to speak more quickly and to avoid catching the client's eye. Instead, use your communication skills to engage the client and make sure you advise in a way that is not only accurate but is clear to the client. This means you will need to decipher any jargon and speak slowly and clearly. If you do anything else, then it does not matter how good the quality of your advice is, the client will leave unimpressed with your performance.

10.6.10 Discuss the client's options

As referred to at 9.3.2, when solving legal problems, the client's options tend to fall within the following three general categories:

1. *Use your legal rights or follow your legal obligations to the letter (litigate, end the business, get divorced, sue, make a payment).* You will need to explain clearly what these options involve. It is not enough, for example, to say, 'You could litigate'. You must be clear about the claim the client would be making, the time and costs involved, and the likelihood of success.

2. *Negotiate another option and consider bargaining power.* Again, the client will need your advice in this regard. Do not be tempted to say, 'one option is to negotiate, let me know how you get on'. You need to understand and explain what the client might be able to negotiate and analyse his bargaining power to advise on his chances of success. For example, if the client has a legal right to sue, he could use that as a bargaining chip, along the lines of 'I will agree not to sue you if you agree to do X' (e.g. pay me a sum now which is less than the amount I could sue for but enough to keep me happy). If the client has a weaker bargaining position, then again you need to advise him of this, so that he can approach negotiations in a more conciliatory manner.

3. *Do nothing.* Take care about how you present this as an option. You should mention it, but you must do so in the context that the client has come to you for help to resolve matters. Nevertheless, it may be that when the client understands the cost and time involved in resolving matters, the current situation seems more tolerable than it did previously.

Remembering these three general categories will help you to think on your feet and to formulate some options for the client to discuss during the meeting. With each category, you not only need to explain the options carefully, but you should also be clear about the advantages and disadvantages of each option (see 9.3.3). Only then can you help the client to choose the option that suits him best (see 9.3.4). The problem-solving model at Figure 9.1 will help you with this.

10.6.11 Communicate essential information at the end

Once again, you need to remember to impart some information towards the end of the meeting for both ethical and practical reasons, and to meet your professional conduct obligations.

Can your firm help with anything else?

Chapter 15 explains that a law firm is a business, and you should recognise that having a new client in front of you is a business development opportunity. This is a key chance, if appropriate, to 'cross-sell' the services of another department, or to obtain some further work from the client for your department. Use this stage of the meeting to:

- enquire whether the client has any other issue that he would like to discuss with a solicitor (e.g. if you have just advised on business acquisition, does the client need advice with more personal matters such as a will);

- discuss anything the client has raised at the meeting which you think may merit further attention from a legal perspective (e.g. if you have just advised on a business acquisition of a property rental company, you might ask if the client is interested in being introduced to your talented property law colleague).

 Practice tip

Firms are very keen to encourage **cross-selling**. This is where a solicitor in one department in the firm identifies and takes opportunities to promote to clients the work done by solicitors in other departments of the firm. Historically, partners' profit-sharing arrangements did not motivate partners to do this, as a partner in one department would see no personal benefit if a partner in another department brought in more fees. In fact, sometimes this could jeopardise a partner's position, as by promoting the success of a colleague, the partner risked looking less productive. Unbelievably, this led to situations where, for example, a large insurance company client of the property team may not have even been aware that the firm had expertise in advising on insurance law. However, cross-selling is now encouraged and often incentivised.

Let the client know what you will do now

You will always follow up the first client meeting with a letter, confirming the advice you gave in the meeting, following up anything else you promised to deliver and reminding the client of anything you need from him. Tell the client this; it will reassure and impress him. It is worth checking the client's contact details at this stage, and how he prefers to be contacted.

Let the client know what he should do now

Even though you will include this in your letter, remind the client now of anything he needs to do. If he agreed to meet someone with a view to attempting to negotiate a matter himself, make sure he is clear as to what he needs to do and when. Be clear about any deadlines in relation to anything he has agreed to do.

Discuss future costs and time frame

You need to link this back to the options you discussed earlier in the meeting. It is unlikely that the client will have selected a firm option at this stage, but if he has, you can tie your time frame and costs estimate into that. If the client has yet to choose a way forward, then go through each option and give your best estimate. If you do not have enough information to come up with a meaningful estimate at this stage, remind the client of your hourly rate and that you will keep him up to date with the costs incurred in the meantime.

Discuss your next meeting

It may be that the client has decided to do nothing further for the moment, in which case you will not need a next meeting. However, if a meeting is needed, then now is a good opportunity to be proactive and discuss when and where might be appropriate.

10.6.12 End the meeting

Just as it is important to create a good first impression, it is also important to leave the client with a good lasting impression. Bring the meeting to an end within your estimated time frame, if at all possible. If the meeting overruns, this will have costs implications. Be clear, both verbally and with your body language, that the meeting is coming to an end. Give a firm handshake, make good eye contact, and walk with your client back to reception. Part with a closing comment about how pleased you are to have met the client, and make sure he has your name and contact details by giving him your business card.

10.7 Communicating by telephone

Much of the guidance of how to communicate face to face applies equally when communicating by telephone. However, it is worth giving some consideration specifically to the skills required to develop a professional telephone manner.

10.7.1 Why telephone skills are important

Notwithstanding that text messaging and email may have overtaken telephone conversations as a way of communicating in your personal life, and the internet enables a panoply of bookings to be made that would previously have been made by telephone, telephone skills remain important in developing professional relationships and providing services. They are skills required by trainees and junior lawyers from day one. It is common for many first interviews to take place and initial instructions to be given by telephone. It is also a means by which transactions and matters are progressed, either on a one-to-one or telephone conference basis.

In light of this, take every opportunity to practise a professional telephone manner; complaints tend to remain the preserve of telephone call centres rather than being dealt with online, so next time you make a complaint, see if you can distinguish yourself by making your point clearly and firmly yet politely.

Try not to become too dependent on email. It may feel like an easy way of avoiding having to think on your feet, but the fact is that some matters are better handled by speaking to a client. Delivering an unpalatable message, such as that you are not going to meet a deadline, is the kind of matter that it is tempting to deal with by email so that you do not have to deal with the client's immediate reaction. However, it is precisely this kind of issue which is better handled by telephone. It is much easier to avoid errors in tone by telephone; emails can often be misconstrued and if the subject matter is delicate this can be exacerbated. Also, if you can call a client to deliver an unpalatable message, you will demonstrate to that client that you are an honest and confident lawyer with good communication skills, and most clients will appreciate this.

10.7.2 Begin and end a call with confidence

This sounds obvious, and again it is not complicated, but it is commonly performed quite poorly.

If you are making a call, introduce yourself properly, stating clearly and in an appropriate tone who you are, the capacity in which you are calling, and the reason for your call.

If answering a call, the common practice is to give your name along with the greeting. You will find that many firms encourage all their employees to answer with a uniform greeting, and to pick up within a certain number of rings. You may also be expected to pick up a colleague's telephone if it has been ringing without being answered.

When ending a call, make sure everyone is clear what needs to happen after the call, that everyone has the contact details they need, and that you leave a good impression.

Listen to how the professionals you encounter (on work experience, during pro bono work, and suchlike) do this, and emulate those you are impressed by.

10.7.3 Listening skills

The importance of these skills is set out at 10.1.3. On the telephone, it is more difficult to demonstrate that you are actively listening. When the other person is talking, particularly if she is providing a series of facts, the occasional 'yes', 'okay', or 'mm-hmm', provided it is not obtrusive, indicates that you are listening and taking in what is being said. The other aspect of listening skills on telephone calls is that not interrupting, and responding appropriately, become even more crucial.

10.7.4 Tone

We have already explored the effect of first impressions. On the telephone, your voice will be the thing you are judged on, so consider what impression you want to give, and make sure your tone conveys this. This is particularly important when recording your voicemail greeting. So many people sound at best flat and indifferent, and at worst cold and hostile. It may sound trite, but if you smile while you record your message, this will come through in that message.

10.7.5 Clarity

Ensure you pace your speech carefully and avoid jargon. Mobile telephones can also present problems in this regard. If the caller comes in and out of range, and you cannot hear properly, do not be embarrassed to say that you really cannot hear her. This is one instance where it is professional to interrupt.

10.7.6 Taking a telephone message

If you do pick up a telephone for colleagues, take care about what you might imply about them. Saying that they are still at lunch, or you do not know where they are, or that they have not arrived at the office yet, may be true but the caller may draw adverse inferences. It is standard practice simply to say 'I'm sorry, X is not at his desk at the moment, can I help you or would you like to leave a message?' If you take a message, make sure you take the caller's full name (ask her to spell it if necessary), the capacity in which she is calling, her contact details, the time she called, and establish what she is expecting in terms of a response and by when. If the client opts to ask you to help instead, do not be afraid to say that you do not know something but you can find out.

10.7.7 Call processing skills

How adept you are at using the features of a telephone will impact on how professional the caller perceives you to be. Dropping callers while transferring them is particularly frustrating for them. If you do not know how to operate the telephone system, ask someone to show you as soon as possible. As a minimum you should learn how to pick up a call that is not being answered, how to transfer a call, and how to join another caller into a conference call.

 Summary

- Communication skills are fundamental, both in education and employment.
- Communication skills include verbal and non-verbal communication skills, listening skills, and having confidence.
- Always consider the effect of your communication from the other person's perspective.
- You will need good communication skills when delivering presentations, as an advocate, when mooting, meeting clients and other professionals, and talking by telephone.
- First impressions and last impressions are particularly important.
- Communication skills are basic skills, but they are often forgotten in times of stress, which is often when you need them most.
- Clients may make the decision as to whether to give further instructions based upon their experience of their lawyer's communication skills.

What the professionals say

What do I value in a lawyer? As a client I expect all of our professional advisers to understand our business and to use their expertise to provide advice tailored to us and our strategic vision. I'm looking for the ability to listen, to work together to solve problems and create solutions, and to advise clearly and concisely in a way that resonates with me and on which I can act. For lawyers particularly to become 'go to' trusted advisers, they not only have to know the law, that's a given, but they also need the skills to deploy that knowledge effectively. It shouldn't be a chore to speak to a lawyer or to understand what they are advising, and if it is, clients will vote with their feet.

Chris Morris, CEO at The LateRooms Group

 ## Thought-provoking questions

1. What do you do in terms of body language that you need to pay attention to? What effect might this have on your communication skills?

2. Have you ever asserted your consumer rights? Did you achieve your aim? Having read this chapter, is there anything you would do differently next time?

3. What is your preferred learning style? What would you do in a presentation to make sure you appealed to those in the audience who have a different learning style from you?

4. Who do you admire for their communication skills? Can you articulate precisely what it is that they do that you admire? Is this transferable into what you do now, as a student, or will do later, as a professional?

 ## Further reading

P. Honey and A. Mumford, *The Manual of Learning Styles* **(Maidenhead: P. Honey, 1986)**
– a useful source of further information on learning styles (see 10.3.4).

D. Kolb, *Experiential Learning: Experience as the Source of Learning and Development* **(Englewood Cliffs, NJ: Prentice Hall, 1984)**
–a useful source of further information if you wish to explore your own preferred learning style.

Judiciary of England and Wales website: http://www.judiciary.gov.uk
–a useful resource for students who wish to learn more about court etiquette (see 10.4.2).

Solicitors Regulation Authority website: http://www.sra.org.uk/solicitors/handbook/code
–contains a wide range of material for students and trainees but if you navigate to the 'For solicitors' section you can familiarise yourself with SRA Code of Conduct (see 10.6.2).

Andrew Gillespie, *The English Legal System* **(Oxford: OUP, 4th edn, 2013) Online Resource Centre: http://www.oup.com/uk/orc/law/els/gillespie_els4e/**
–visit the Online Resource Centre and click 'Visiting Court' under 'Student Activities' for useful tips that you can use in planning your first court visit (see 10.4.2).

David Pope and Dan Hill, *Mooting and Advocacy Skills* **(London: Sweet & Maxwell, 2nd edn, 2011)**
–a helpful short mooting and advocacy guide (see 10.4 and 10.5).

 For the authors' reflections on the thought-provoking questions, additional self-test questions, podcasts offering a variety of perspectives on legal systems and skills, and a library of links to useful websites, visit the free Online Resource Centre at **http://www.oxfordtextbooks.co.uk/orc/slorach/.**

11 Writing and drafting

 Learning objectives

After studying this chapter you should be able to:

- Understand the fundamental legal writing skills required during your studies.
- Develop approaches to writing legal essays and other pieces of written work.
- Describe the characteristics of good writing.
- Improve your own writing and drafting skills.
- Describe the writing and drafting skills required by lawyers and professionals.

Introduction

You may consider that, to get to this stage in your education or career, you have mastered the skill of writing. You will doubtless have written numerous essays and reports, prepared pieces of coursework, and drafted a range of letters and emails. However, your legal studies will require you to develop your writing and drafting skills further, taking them to new levels. In the increasingly competitive market for employment, it is expected that graduates should have high levels of written communication skills. In both these areas, as we shall see, there is a vast difference between simply being able to write and being able to communicate effectively.

This chapter is designed to assist you in developing your writing and drafting skills as you develop your understanding of the law. Essays are a cornerstone of most law programmes, and so we shall consider approaches to producing good essays. They are also one of the most common means by which your legal knowledge and intellectual skills will be assessed. Your goal is to understand how best to use the medium of writing to communicate and demonstrate the quality of your knowledge and skills. As we shall see, the quality of any essay or other piece of legal writing will be diminished by failing to employ fundamental writing skills. These skills will be examined in the context of both legal studies and subsequent employment. Finally, this chapter demonstrates both the relevance and importance of writing and drafting skills in legal practice and professional life generally.

11.1 Writing legal essays

In this section, we are going to concentrate on the development of writing skills in the context of a legal essay. The approaches discussed apply equally to other types of writing you might be asked to produce, such as reports, discussion documents and pieces of coursework. Most are also applicable in the context of problem-solving questions; however, the latter have already been considered in Chapter 9.

Writing is like any other skill in terms of development: improvement requires conscious consideration of the fundamental elements of the skill. With practice, these become part of your subconscious. Professional golfers help develop their technique by spending hours on a range, repeatedly practising their swing, consciously thinking about the various elements which affect performance: stance, grip, movement, ball contact, and so on. The goal of 'subconscious competence' is described by many golfers as not really remembering any part of it when they hit a perfect shot. The point of this analogy is twofold. First, you should set yourself a similar goal of subconscious competence, of being able almost instinctively to write to a high standard. Second, to achieve this goal requires conscious thought and practice of the various elements of the skill. Set out below is a simple model to adopt, adapt, and, most of all, practise to help you produce the required result of a good quality legal essay.

11.1.1 **The 5 Ps**

You may be familiar with the expression to 'mind your Ps and Qs'. While there is debate about its origin, its meaning is generally accepted as being an instruction to think about what you say, to be careful about your language. It is also a useful way of remembering a model for approaching legal essays. Later we shall consider the importance of the 'Q'—the question—but first let us consider five 'Ps':

- Purpose
- Plan and Prepare
- Perform
- Polish

These incorporate the various elements and skills that, when applied together, will produce a good legal essay.

Purpose

We said in the introduction that essays are a cornerstone of most legal education programmes, and are a common means of assessing students' knowledge and skills. Since time immemorial, students have viewed essays as a combination of a necessary evil and a rite of passage, producing 'essay crises' as deadlines loom. However, proper consideration of the underlying purposes of a legal essay will make your subsequent tasks much simpler. There are both general and specific purposes to consider.

The general purposes of a legal essay are to enable students to develop and demonstrate, and tutors to assess (both formatively and summatively), understanding of the law, and the application of a range of intellectual skills. Examples of the latter include explanation, analysis, persuasive argument, critical evaluation, and legal reasoning. An essay also has the purpose of developing and demonstrating writing skills. There is a connection between these purposes. The better you can write, the more likely you are to demonstrate clearly your understanding of the law and the application of intellectual skills: the clearer that demonstration, the better you are likely to perform in an assessment.

Remembering these general purposes makes considering the specific purposes of an essay much easier. You can now take the question or title you have been set and ask two questions:

- What is the area of law of which I am being asked to demonstrate understanding?
- What intellectual skills am I being asked to demonstrate: what am I being asked *to do*?

(It should be taken as read that you are also being asked to demonstrate writing skills.)

While the answers to these questions may sometimes appear obvious, they provide a vital starting point for the preparation and planning of your essay. On the first question, if the answer is not explicit in the question, you should be able to work it out by reference to the subject matter of cases, statements, or propositions within the question.

Already this begins to define the boundaries of your essay. While you might occasionally make comparisons with other areas of law outside these boundaries, as a general rule you will not receive credit for any writing on extraneous topics. In terms of demonstrating understanding of an area or areas of law, think about what this actually means.

Consider this example. In the children's novel, *When Hitler Stole Pink Rabbit*, by Judith Kerr, a young boy is sent to have French lessons and is asked by his tutor to write an essay. He writes that there was a party and, at that party, 'they ate ...' and there follows a page of various nouns, copied from a dictionary. He takes the same approach in his next essay, and his tutor realises the boy's limitations. He is not demonstrating any understanding (and it is debatable whether he is even showing any real knowledge) of French.

The point is that demonstration of understanding of the law requires much more than setting out *what the law is*. The specific additional requirements will be influenced by the intellectual skills demanded by the question; however, in general, you should be prepared to demonstrate that you understand:

- What is the purpose of the law in a particular area?
- How does it operate and what is its effect?
- What are the practical implications for those affected by the law?
- How and why has the law developed in a particular way (including the leading cases)?
- What difficulties have been faced in interpreting and applying the law?

You should then identify, from the question or title of the essay, the specific intellectual skills to be demonstrated, that is, what are you being asked. A good start is to underline or highlight the key word (or words) which indicates the skill required. Common examples are:

- Explain (e.g. a term or statement, or the effect of a piece of law)
- Discuss (e.g. a statement or proposition)
- Consider (e.g. the impact or effect of a case or statute)
- Evaluate
- Compare
- Analyse

Then, consider what this word is actually asking you *to do*. Table 11.1 sets out some guidance which you may find helpful.

Table 11.1 What is the essay question asking you to do?

Explain	On the face of it, this appears straightforward and only requires you to set out an account of *what* is meant by a particular term or *what* the effect of a particular piece of law is. There is a risk in narrowly interpreting 'explain': a rather dry, factual essay may be the result, failing to meet the general requirement to demonstrate understanding. You need to think beyond dealing with *what*, and consider the *how* and *why* questions set out above, e.g. *why* did Parliament enact the statute in question, *how* has the meaning of a particular term been interpreted over time, *why* has the particular piece of law been important.
Discuss	If a tutor asked you to discuss a statement or proposition in a classroom environment, you would expect to hear different views, reasons why those views were held, arguments for and against the proposition and suchlike. The same applies to a written invitation to discuss: the difference being that you, individually, have to set out and structure the discussion. Again, a dry factual account of a topic will not work: if you proffer only one viewpoint, there is no discussion. You should indicate which viewpoint you favour, and why.
Consider (or Examine)	This is asking for your view or opinion on a particular statement, proposition, case, or piece of law. This should be supported by argument and evidence. You should also be able to demonstrate awareness of contrary views or opinions.
Evaluate (or Assess)	To evaluate a particular statement, proposition, case, or piece of law, you should examine the importance and effect of the item in question, weigh up related arguments and evidence, and come to a reasoned conclusion.
Compare (or Contrast or Distinguish)	You are being asked to identify and discuss, in relation to the subject matter, those elements which are common and those which differ. You should discuss the importance and impact of the differences.
Analyse	This indicates that you should be examining the subject matter in depth and in a very structured manner. The latter might be chronological, if you are analysing the development of law, or involve breaking down the constituent parts of a proposition. Your analysis should refer to arguments and evidence relating to the subject matter, and should result in a reasoned conclusion.

You will have noted that there are emerging common themes and features, which will apply to most or all essay types. Many of these relate back to the general purpose of demonstrating understanding. Setting out those arguments and evidence which support, and those which undermine, a proposition will demonstrate that you understand not only that differing views are held but *why* they are held. Providing the *why* also applies to the conclusions you should provide: the purpose of an essay is not only for you to demonstrate *what* you have concluded from the process of producing it but *why* you have reached that conclusion. As before, evidence should play a major part in this, and we examine below where this can come from.

Another common theme related to the purpose of an essay is the expectation that you will demonstrate 'critical' thinking. This is often made explicit in the title, for example 'Critically evaluate the statement that ...', but should be treated as implicit in every essay. To think critically about, say, a proposition, is not the same as to criticise it. Critical thinking is an approach rather than simply an action. It is about:

- taking a proposition;
- demonstrating understanding of its meaning and importance;
- considering objectively the arguments for and against the proposition;
- evaluating the supporting evidence for those arguments; and
- reaching a reasoned conclusion.

If you go back to look at the various questions that you should be able to answer to demonstrate your understanding of an area of law, you will see that all of them can play a role in demonstrating critical analysis.

We have spent some time considering both the general and specific purposes of legal essays. However, as with planning and preparation, the time invested in thinking about the purpose of an essay will pay dividends by making easier the actual task of writing it.

Planning and Preparation

We will now consider planning and preparation together. The two are closely linked and there is an iterative nature in this stage of developing your essay. That is, your plan can lead you to undertake a particular piece of preparatory work (say, reading a specific text) which might then cause you to revise elements of your plan.

Given the purposes of an essay, the end product should be a structured, reasoned piece of writing, demonstrating understanding of the law and the application of intellectual skills, and showing an ability to think critically about propositions and issues. This might be seen as labouring the points made in the previous section; however the point here is that the likelihood of producing a good essay without planning and preparation is extremely low.

The first stage of planning is to establish the purpose of the essay. Do this *before* any preparation. So, if you receive a reading list with an essay title at the top or bottom, do not give the latter a cursory glance, conclude 'it's an essay about contractual remedies', and start working through the directed reading. Thinking through the factors discussed under 'Purpose' above and forming a plan as to how you will fulfil the essay's purpose will make your preparation more focused and, again, make the eventual writing easier.

Example 1

Essay title:
   There has been a noticeable increase in delegated legislation. Discuss the proposition that the advantages of delegated legislation outweigh any disadvantages.
Purpose:
   Demonstrate understanding of delegated legislation (including rationale for increase):

- What is the purpose of delegated legislation? Sources: lecture notes; texts.
- How does delegated legislation operate and what is its effect? Sources: as above plus examples of delegated legislation to illustrate.
- How and why has the use of delegated legislation increased? Sources: lecture notes; texts; plus search for statistics to illustrate.
- What are the practical implications of this? Sources: as above plus journal articles.

Demonstrate intellectual skill of discussion:

- What are the advantages and disadvantages of delegated legislation? Sources: lecture notes; texts; journal articles; possibly cases?
- What are the arguments in support of the above, in other words why are they perceived as advantages and disadvantages? Sources: as above, primarily journal articles.
- Based on those arguments, what is my conclusion as regards the proposition and *why*?

The second stage is then to set out what material and evidence you will need to fulfil the purpose and consider likely sources of these. The following example illustrates a simple approach, whereby (a) posing a series of questions, and (b) noting likely sources, can provide a head start in planning and a focus to your preparation.

What you have now created is both a plan for your preparation and an outline structure for your essay itself. This shows the importance of thinking about the purpose of the essay: by doing so, you can create the plan without any detailed knowledge of the subject area. You can now begin your preparation, using legal research skills (see Chapter 8) to locate material within the various sources you have identified. Highlight or note the material relevant to each of the elements in your plan. As you do so, think how you might use the material, what it might illustrate, and how you can best present it within your structure. An important consideration is the relevant intellectual skill: in this case, 'discuss'. You should, as part of your preparation, collate and begin to order the material that will form the basis of the discussion. You could also summarise each of the main arguments as you find them, which will help you when you come to write up your essay.

Once you have all your material, you can refine your plan and better define, if necessary, the structure of your essay. This should include thinking about your introduction and conclusion, which we shall now consider as part of the next stage.

Performance

You now have to 'perform' the skill of writing. This really means that you have to use your writing skills to demonstrate your legal knowledge and skills within the context of the subject matter in hand. That you are expected to demonstrate good writing skills should go without saying: guidance as to what is expected is set out at 11.3. One aspect of good writing is structure, which, in this context, includes the introduction and conclusion to your essay. A couple of simple guides as to what should be the content of the introduction, body, and conclusion of an essay are:

- 'answer the question; answer the question; answer the question'; and
- say what you're going to say; say it; then say it again.

These are useful starting points, but try to be a little more creative, and certainly avoid any noticeable repetition between the text of your introduction and conclusion. Think about how you can demonstrate understanding from the start of your essay: rather than simply restating the proposition. Compare the following, where student A restates the proposition and student B shows deeper understanding, using some of the answers to the planning questions:

Example 2

- **Student A.** The fact that there has been a noticeable increase in the amount of delegated legislation means that it is important to discuss the advantages and disadvantages of this form of law.
- **Student B.** In the three years from 2010–12, there were enacted 89 UK Public General Acts. In the same period, 9,429 UK Statutory Instruments were made, an average of over 3,000 per year. In the ten years to 2012, that average was under 2,000. Both the prevalence and growth of delegated legislation raise the following important questions, which will be discussed in this work.

A similar approach should be taken in the body of your essay: you must do more than simply state the law. You have already considered what is the purpose of the essay: as you write, consider 'what is the point?' This is not a deeper philosophical version of this question but rather means asking yourself what each piece of writing is adding to your essay. This can be extended to the commonly used 'PEA' model: Point; Evidence; Analysis. That is: what point am I making; what objective evidence do I have to support it; what is my analysis of that evidence? The following example is annotated to show application of the PEA model.

Example 3

In an essay on duress (a concept in contract law) you might want to demonstrate your understanding of the latter, by showing that you know that there is a difference between someone entering into a contract under duress as compared to legitimate commercial pressure:

(P) There is a distinction between duress and legitimate commercial pressure. (E) In *Pao On v Lau Yiu Long (1979)*, Scarman LJ held that, for there to be duress, there must be the presence of some factor 'which could in law be regarded as a coercion of [his] will so as to vitiate his consent' to the contract. (A) This requirement of coercion suggests that, for duress to be found, it would not be enough that a party held a stronger bargaining position and used that commercial advantage to bring pressure on another party to enter into a contract on particular terms.

(Note that, in relation to the evidence element, a case has been cited. You must cite and reference sources of evidence. Different law schools, and even different tutors, may adopt variations in approach to citation. You should receive guidance on the preferred approach that you should follow, and so detailed citation conventions do not form part of this chapter.)

It would be highly unfeasible—and result in a rather odd essay—to have a body that comprised only repetitions of the above model. There will be a need for introductory, linking and concluding sentences for paragraphs and sections, to ensure a smooth narrative. A good narrative is easier to read and understand, and, as such, is a demonstration of good writing skills. A useful test of narrative is to check that, certainly within a paragraph or section, you could point to a clear link between a particular sentence and those that precede and follow it. See how this works in the example we looked at above, where there has been added an introductory (I) and a linking (L) sentence. (Once you have done this, if minded, you could re-read this paragraph to assess the links between sentences and hence the smoothness of narrative.)

Example 3 (continued)

(I) To understand fully the concept of duress, it is beneficial to consider it in the context of commerce. (P) There is a distinction between duress and legitimate commercial pressure. (E) In *Pao On v Lau Yiu Long (1979)*, Scarman LJ held that, for there to be duress, there must be the presence of some factor 'which could in law be regarded as a coercion of [his] will so as to vitiate his consent' to the contract. (A) This requirement of coercion suggests that, for duress to be found, it would not be enough that a party held a stronger bargaining position and used that commercial advantage to bring pressure on another party to enter into a contract on particular terms. (L) To determine whether this is the case, it is instructive to compare the facts of the following cases where duress was alleged.

- I links to P by introducing commerce, which is picked up in P by the reference to commercial pressure.
- P refers to a distinction between duress and legitimate commercial pressure, which is picked up in E by the reference to what must be present for there to be duress.
- The requirement of coercion in E is picked up in A and analysed.
- The initial conclusion reached in A is then picked up in L, which describes how that conclusion will be tested.
- You can now imagine what the first sentence of the next paragraph would be, taking a lead from L.

Your conclusion should bring together the threads of your essay in a clear, reasoned manner. There should be a link to the intellectual skill aspect of the essay's purpose. If it was a discussion essay, then conclude where you stand on the debate, and *why*. If you were asked to evaluate a proposition, then give your conclusion on the extent to which the proposition is valid or correct, and *why*. The 'and *why*' ensures that your conclusion will be reasoned.

Polish

The majority of written work now has to be submitted in word-processed form. This means that there is no excuse for not carrying out this final element of producing a good quality essay. That is, you do not physically have to write a series of drafts of your essay.

You will get the best results if you leave a period of time between completing your first draft and the 'polishing' element. Divide this final element into two stages:

- a check of content and approach; then
- a final edit.

The first stage involves checking aspects that have already been discussed. Ask yourself the following questions *and* only answer them positively if, *on a fresh reading*, you can see sufficient evidence in your essay to support that answer:

- Have I consistently demonstrated understanding of the required area of law, and *how*?
- Have I consistently demonstrated the intellectual skills required by the essay, and *how*?
- Is there an identifiable introduction, body, and conclusion?
- Does my introduction not only inform readers but also motivate them to read on, and *how*?
- Within the body of the essay, have I supported each point made with evidence (properly cited) and followed up with my analysis of that evidence (the PEA model)?
- Is my conclusion clear, reasoned, and aligned with the required intellectual skill?
- Have I consistently demonstrated the characteristics of good legal writing (see 11.3)?

Be honest in the above assessment. You can also consider swapping an essay with a colleague for the purpose of this critique (bearing in mind the issues on plagiarism set out at 11.1.2 below). (See also 11.5.3 on checking work and proof-reading.) Once you have made any resulting changes, carry out a final edit. This should deal with any outstanding legal writing points and also have the aim of ensuring that your writing is clear and concise. You may have been set a word limit or target; however, in this context, writing concisely refers to individual sentences and paragraphs. It is the skill of communicating clearly what you want to communicate, using as few words as necessary, and avoiding unnecessary verbiage (unlike this sentence, as we shall see). This skill takes time to develop but is invaluable. Consider the following versions of the sentence before last.

Example 4

A. It is the skill of communicating clearly what you want to communicate, using as few words as necessary, and avoiding unnecessary verbiage.

B. It is the skill of communicating clearly using as few words as necessary.

Within the context of the previous paragraph, version B uses nine, or 41%, fewer words to communicate the same information. It has been shown that readers' understanding of a sentence decreases as word count increases. Therefore, even if your eyes are on a word count target, do not meet that target by using longer sentences than you need or, worse still, padding out original sentences. It is a false economy as it will affect both the content and quality of your essay, and, ultimately, your mark.

11.1.2 Plagiarism and Pitfalls

Plagiarism

The sixth and seventh 'Ps' have not been included in the model above, for the simple reason that both plagiarism and pitfalls should be avoided.

 Essential explanation

Plagiarism

The Shorter Oxford English Dictionary defines plagiarism as 'the taking and using as one's own the thoughts, writings or inventions of another'. Plagiarism results more often from negligence, carelessness, or misunderstanding, than from deliberate action. You should receive, as part of your studies, clear guidance as to what will be viewed as plagiarism and the penalties that can result. Read this carefully and, if in doubt, seek clarification. The following are the most common actions that will be viewed as plagiarism:

- Using the words of others in your work as if they were your own. This will still be viewed as plagiarism even if you rephrase or paraphrase a phrase, sentence, or passage.
- Presenting the ideas of others in your work as they were your own.
- Linked to both the previous actions, failing properly to acknowledge words, ideas, and facts that you have obtained from the work of others.

Of course, a major part of your learning will result from consulting the work of others: that is how you will develop your knowledge and views on a subject. What you must do is properly acknowledge that work of others by providing full reference details of any source used. Again, your institution should provide you with guidance on its specific requirements at the start of your studies. Equally, what you should not do is to write an essay the majority of which is a compilation of fully referenced and acknowledged work and views of others. Remember the concept of 'critical thinking': you must show that you have given critical thought to the work and views of others, and present your own reasoned viewpoints on those.

Pitfalls to avoid

Taking the positive steps set out above, including a rigorous polish, should mean that you avoid most of the pitfalls. However, for the sake of completeness, here is a selection of the more popular. If you find yourself indulging in any of the following, take corrective action.

Using the title as the introduction

There is no need to repeat verbatim the title or question of the essay in your introduction. The person who set the title knows it; and, in any event, it should be at the top of your essay, before the introduction, and have been read already. Worse still is the introduction that re-phrases the title into an expanded sentence or series of sentences.

Unsubstantiated assertions

> **Example 5**
>
> 'This was a landmark case, the facts of which raised a series of interesting questions about the important issue of the measure of damages in tort, and resulted in a major change in the law.'

If you are going to use adjectives like these, then you should be able to substantiate: *why* it was a landmark case; *why* the questions were interesting; *why* the measure of damages in tort is important; and *how* the change in the law was a major one.

The 'case list'

Most legal topics will involve you in referring regularly to cases and regulations in your essays. They are primary sources and, as such, are valuable points of reference and evidential material. However, you should not refer to a specific case or statute unless it is clear from your narrative *why*. A statement of the law as decided in case A followed by 'as has subsequently been applied in case B, case C and case D' fails to do any more than give factual information. What is the significance of that subsequent application? Were the facts similar or different? Does it show that case A provided a wide or narrow definition? Merely listing lots of cases only demonstrates that you know, or have found, lots of cases on the subject: without demonstrating that you have read them, thought about them, and understand their significance, you will not be able to demonstrate the required critical thinking skills.

Lengthy quotations and regulatory extracts

This follows from the previous pitfall. As well as showing that you understand the significance of a case or regulation, you also need to pinpoint the *specific* aspect of it that makes it significant. Therefore, if a single sentence in a judgment provides a legal definition, you do not need to include the entire paragraph which contains that sentence. Similarly, if the crux of a case is the interpretation of one word in a statute, you need only include sufficient wording to place that word in context. Selectivity and conciseness are both skills to be demonstrated.

The conclusion sitting on the wall

Example 6

'Thus it can be seen that this is both an important and interesting area of law which has promoted a great deal of discussion, with some legal academics claiming that it has had a wider effect than originally intended by Parliament.'

There is a strong case for saying that the previous sentence is not even a conclusion at all: it is merely a loose combination of fact and opinion, offering neither a viewpoint nor any evidence of critical thinking.

11.2 Further developing writing skills during your studies

11.2.1 Reading

You should take advantage of every opportunity to develop your writing skills during your studies. The more legal writing you read, the more examples of good and bad writing practice you will be able to draw on and experiment with in your own written work, so read as much as possible, including other students' work. Ask your subject tutors for feedback specifically on your writing, and reflect on it to improve your written work. Find and read as many examples of legal writing as you can. In terms of essays, good journal articles will display many of the features referred to above. Law firms publish legal update bulletins which you can subscribe to using their websites. Find a subject that interests you and read the policy documents surrounding it (e.g. in 2012 the Department of Business, Innovation and Skills published a consultation document on implementing employee ownership status, and the Law Society issued its own response to this document).

11.2.2 Note-taking

You can also help develop your written skills in the context of note-taking. An important skill for all lawyers is the ability to summarise, that is to distil information down to its key points. When you take notes in a lecture or other class, you are practising this skill. There are various effective methods of taking good notes, but the first thing to consider is why you are taking notes. For example, in a lecture, are you seeking to take a note of absolutely everything the lecturer is saying, or simply the main points? Most students seek to do the former. However, in taking notes in this way, you may be missing an opportunity to digest and understand what is being said, because if you are writing, you are not actively listening (see also 10.6.5). Your decision might be informed by the other preparatory work you are set. For example, if you also have to read around the same subject, there is an argument that you should not seek to take comprehensive notes from both sources, namely the lecture and your reading. Rather you can use the lecture as an introduction to the subject, where you aim to note the main issues, understand them and put them in context. You can then use your reading to consider the detail and produce a more comprehensive note. You can then annotate this note during subsequent class work, consolidation, and revision. The key point is to analyse the purpose of your note-taking and approach it in a smart way, rather than just write down everything because that is what everyone else is doing.

Once you have decided your approach to note-taking, think about how to structure your notes. Use headings and bullet points to order your notes logically. If you are not word processing your notes, consider writing on alternate lines so that you can supplement your notes later without rendering them illegible. You do not have to write in full sentences. Consider whether you need to note down the content of any visual aids, or whether your lecturer can provide you with electronic or hard copies. Most smartphones can now take good images of visual aids, and there are apps which can convert them to pdf documents.

11.2.3 **Advising**

You will frequently encounter problem-solving questions on your law programme. In addition, many programmes now incorporate specific legal skills modules and some even include 'clinical' modules. The latter involve dealing with real life legal problems and clients. The common factor is that all of these elements require you to present advice on the law in one form or the other. In Chapter 9, there is guidance on problem-solving questions. The characteristics of good writing (see 11.3) apply equally to legal advice. In addition, you will also be able to apply many of the points of guidance on professional writing in 11.4.

11.3 **Characteristics of good writing**

Whether writing a legal essay or answering a problem question, you are expected to demonstrate good legal writing skills. In the introduction to this chapter, we also noted the expectations of employers in terms of graduates' written skills. This will be explored further at 11.4. However, legal concepts are often complex and, whether in the context of legal studies or legal practice, the best lawyers are those who can clearly and concisely communicate in writing the effect of the law in a given set of circumstances.

Before considering the fundamental characteristics of good legal writing, it should be noted that no lawyer can write well without sound legal knowledge and understanding. You should never begin writing until you understand the law and its effect. When you do start writing, you must consider each of the characteristics set out below and ensure high standards. If you do not, then, at worst, you will fail to communicate what you actually mean which can result in lost marks and, in practice, lost clients. At best, you will appear careless. Note that we have used the word 'expectation' in relation to writing skills. They are expected of you. Therefore, you will not receive great plaudits for getting them right: however, you will lose credibility if you get them wrong. While there is not necessarily a correlation between the two, a reader may well conclude that if you make errors in your writing, then your legal knowledge and advice may not be completely sound either.

Set out below are the main criteria against which a recipient of your written work is likely to judge you, together with guidance as to how you can make sure you are judged positively. Common mistakes are also discussed, on the basis that the more familiar you are with the potential errors you could make, the less likely you are to make those errors.

11.3.1 **Spelling**

Good spelling is essential. While most spelling errors will be picked up by a spell-check facility, an amount sufficient to be noticeable will not. Some words are easily confused with others which sound alike. Common examples include 'complimentary/complementary', 'there/their/they're', 'were/ we're' and 'its/it's'. So if, for example, you say 'X did not accept that there goods were faulty', the spell-check facility will not identify that 'there' should be spelled 'their'. Another common example is 'judgment/judgement'. In a legal context, the correct spelling is 'judgment', however the spell-check will not know that you are discussing the law and so will not detect this error. You will need to learn to identify these errors. If this does not come naturally to you, consider keeping your own checklist of words like this to remind you what to look out for, or invest in a book to help you such as *i before e (except after c)*, details of which are provided in the 'Further reading' section at the end of this chapter.

In addition to the standard words that can evade a spell-check, there will be legal terminology and proper nouns, such as case names. Again, there are no excuses for misspelling these.

11.3.2 **Punctuation**

You need to be familiar with how and when to use punctuation, including capital letters, full stops, exclamation marks, question marks, colons, semicolons, commas, and apostrophes. Your sentences should be properly punctuated, as punctuation can change the entire meaning of a sentence. Lynne Truss refers to some excellent examples in her book about punctuation called *Eats, Shoots and Leaves: The Zero Tolerance Approach to Punctuation* (see the 'Further reading' section at the end of this chapter). This example illustrates the point very effectively.

Example 7

How would you punctuate this sentence?
A woman without her man is nothing
You may have used some commas, to this effect:
A woman, without her man, is nothing.
However, consider the entirely different meaning if you had punctuated differently:
A woman: without her, man is nothing.

You should always pay particular attention when using an apostrophe, as this tends to be the most commonly misunderstood and misused punctuation mark. If you struggle to put apostrophes in the right place, or simply do not use them at all (which is becoming increasingly common), you must address this.

You should also make sure you use punctuation consistently. For example, you may choose whether to put a full stop after a bullet point. However, if you choose to use the full stop, make sure you do so after each bullet point.

If punctuation is something you find difficult, then Truss' book is a good place to start, as is the BBC adult literacy website. Details of both resources are set out in 'Further reading' at the end of this chapter.

11.3.3 **Grammar**

Your sentences should be grammatically correct. As with spell-check, the grammar-check of your word processing software can help but it is not infallible. You must write sentences in prose and they must contain a verb. Do not write in note form. You should not start sentences with conjunctions such as 'and' or 'but'. Make sure you do not write as you might speak, for example writing 'could of' and 'should of'. These are common errors. The correct grammar is 'could have' and 'should have'.

You should also pay attention as to how you structure your sentences. It is possible to write an active sentence, 'I opened the door', or a passive one, 'The door was opened'. In certain scenarios, using the passive can be quite helpful. Consider, for example, how the passive sentence, 'It appears that a mistake has been made', can have a conciliatory effect compared to the active 'It appears that you have made a mistake'. However, in law, as a general rule you should avoid the passive. This is because, in law, it is very important to identify where obligations and liability lie. If you fail to do so, you risk ambiguity, which can be read as not being confident about a viewpoint or piece of advice. Compare the following examples.

Example 8

Passive:	The goods were not delivered on time.
Active:	X did not deliver the goods on time.
Passive:	Liability could arise for failure to take steps to prevent accidents.
Active:	Y could be held liable for failing to take steps to prevent accidents.
Passive:	The form must be filed at Companies House within 14 days.
Active:	The company must file the form at Companies House within 14 days.

In writing generally, and in professional correspondence specifically, you should take care with reflexive pronouns, as they are increasingly misused. 'Yourself' and 'myself' are not more sophisticated versions of 'you' and 'me'. It is perfectly correct to use 'you' and 'me' in a sentence in a professional context. 'If you have any questions, please contact me' is correct. In contrast, 'If you have any questions, please contact myself' is not. 'You and Jack must attend the meeting' is correct. Again, 'Yourself and Jack must attend the meeting' is not. 'Yourself' and 'myself' have a specific grammatical use as reflexive pronouns, which means they must refer back to an earlier pronoun in the same sentence, such as 'I cut myself'. They can also be used correctly as intensive pronouns, to provide emphasis, 'You, yourself, knew this at the time'.

11.3.4 **Structure**

You do not want the recipients of your legal writing to find reading your work a difficult task. Therefore, your writing should follow a logical structure which enhances clarity. Consider how you will structure your writing before you start to write. When you are quite new to legal writing it helps to sketch out a short plan of relevant headings and content before you start.

Short sentences are both easier to write and easier to follow than long sentences. Write as concisely as you can, without losing essential detail. Avoid tautology such as 'In my opinion I think that', or padding such as 'It has frequently been thought that'.

That said, in law, scenarios and issues can be complex, and even if you write succinctly your interpretation and advice may be lengthy. Very long paragraphs can be off-putting and difficult to follow, so you should subdivide a long paragraph into several smaller paragraphs, and consider whether headings and subheadings would help the recipient to read your writing. For example, if you were writing about remedies in contract law, you might use paragraphs headed 'damages', 'rescission', and 'specific performance', rather than write about everything in one unwieldy paragraph. This would help the recipient both to identify the main remedies available and also to locate information easily about any one remedy in particular. With more lengthy pieces of writing, where you need to cross-refer to different paragraphs within the body of that work, consider numbering the paragraphs, so you can refer to 'paragraph 4' rather than, for example, 'the paragraph about damages'.

11.3.5 **Clarity**

You must write clearly and in the way that best promotes the recipient's understanding. Write in a way which shows you live in the modern world. Some students affect an archaic writing style, reminiscent of a Dickensian court room. Words and phrases such as 'henceforth' and 'it is hereby submitted' pepper their work. There is no real advantage to be gained by trying to make writing look or sound 'legal', and it can inhibit clarity of expression.

Choose language carefully. Generations of law students have used ambiguous language in essays to get round difficult issues they do not fully understand. Equally, passive language (see 11.3.3) can cause unintentional ambiguity. Ambiguous language is, by definition, unclear and you will not prosper if a tutor considers that you might not understand a particular concept. The modern case of *Levicom* v *Linklaters* (see the 'Further reading' section at the end of this chapter) shows the potential effect of ambiguity in legal practice. In this case, the court held that two letters of advice sent by lawyers to their client (about the client's likelihood of success in litigation proceedings) were negligent, not because of the views the lawyers held, but because the lawyers did not set out their views sufficiently clearly. Therefore, make sure not only that you understand the point you are making, but also that you state your point clearly and unambiguously so that anyone else reading it will also understand it.

11.3.6 **Tone**

We noted above that trying to sound 'legal' can inhibit clarity. Tone is another factor which affects the quality of legal writing and communication. While legal essays should not adopt the formal tone of an advocate addressing a Supreme Court judge, equally they should not be informal and 'chatty'. You should avoid the use of abbreviations such as 'shouldn't', 'won't', and 'haven't'. This will be good practice for writing professionally when you would also use the full words for expressions such as these, even if using email. The use of text messaging has also introduced new problems with abbreviation. To state the obvious, using text-speak such as '2' rather than 'to' or 'B' instead of 'be' is wholly inappropriate. It is, however, creeping into student emails, essays, and assessments—and even some professional communications—on an increasingly frequent basis.

11.4 Professional writing

The expectation that graduates should have good writing skills is directly related to the commercial requirements of professions and businesses. They operate in an increasingly competitive market and need to be effective and efficient in carrying out their operations. A major element of this is communication: both internally within the organisation, and externally with clients and customers. The latter will make a judgment about an organisation based on the quality of its professional communications. These communications need to be clear, concise, precise, in plain English and, above all, directed to the particular requirements of the recipient.

This section on writing and drafting examines these skills in the context, principally, of legal practice. However, written skills are transferable, that is, once developed, they can be applied in a different context. Therefore, the majority of information and suggested approaches provided below are equally applicable to any graduate career, whether in professional or public services, finance, manufacturing, or any other industry. You can also apply many of them when dealing with questions on your law programme that require you to advise. In all cases, the requirement for quality of communication does not vary. Whatever your career path, you can distinguish yourself through your written skills.

11.4.1 Why lawyers advise in writing

Lawyers need to commit their advice to writing for several reasons:

- lawyers advise on relatively complex issues, so recording advice in writing can help a client to understand that advice by:
  - setting out clearly what a lawyer has said;
  - providing a record which recipients can read in their own time and at their own pace;
- the recipient can show the written advice to others;
- written advice creates a permanent record for both the lawyer and the recipient in the event of a query, misunderstanding, or complaint.

11.4.2 Formats for professional writing

Lawyers, like other professionals, use a variety of formats to communicate their advice in writing. They include:

- a letter;
- an email;
- an internal memorandum;
- an attendance note;
- a research report.

Which format is chosen will depend on a number of factors, including whether it is an internal or external communication, who the recipient is, the subject matter in question, and the formality of relationship between the writer and recipient. The overriding factor is the requirement of the recipient: therefore, in the same way that the content must be relevant to the recipient, the format must be appropriate both for the content and the recipient. At 11.7 there are templates for some examples of the types of legal writing that you can start to practise as a student. These templates will help you with the structure, give you guidance as to the content and purpose of each format, and suggest how you can tailor them for different recipients.

While these templates demonstrate writing skills in the context of legal advice, very few of their aspects are limited to law in their application. Familiarising yourself with these templates will help you to develop good writing skills which are of general application wherever your career may lead. Set out below are some of the specific considerations which apply when advising in writing.

11.4.3 **Quality of advice**

That written advice to clients and colleagues should be of requisite quality should go without saying. Writing is not a skill ancillary to a lawyer's work: it *is* their work. The quality of that work is both intrinsic and based on the perception of the recipient. At 11.4.4 and 11.4.5 we look at two of the major factors which can affect that perception. First, however, we consider the intrinsic quality of advice. Quite simply, it has to be right.

The first step is to ensure full understanding of: the facts; the client's objectives; the relevant law; and how it applies to the client's situation. Only then can proper advice be formulated. This appears obvious but it is worth considering the importance of ensuring this quality of advice. If lawyers do not understand the law, they will be unable to make it clear to clients. If clients do not find the advice clear, they will, at best, be unhappy with the professional service being provided, and may not engage that lawyer again. As Chapter 16 explains, many lawyers rely on repeat business from clients, so failure to impress with quality work could lead to losing a client to a competitor. At worst, the lawyer's advice could be incorrect and, being written, it is in the form of permanent record which could be used in court in the event of a negligence claim.

11.4.4 **Tone**

One of the most common criticisms of the writing of trainees is that they struggle to adopt the correct tone. The aim should be to employ a tone which is both personal and professional, but neither over-familiar nor too terse.

Tone should be relatively measured in order to convey professionalism. For example, many junior lawyers find it difficult to know how they should express emotion in their professional writing. Everyone is different, and some people express their feelings more than others, however you need to avoid sounding 'over the top'. For example, if writing to a recently bereaved person, it is of course appropriate to express condolences, but 'You really must be absolutely devastated and I just cannot find words to express my absolute sympathy for your dreadful loss' might come across as a little disingenuous if there is no personal link to either the client or the deceased. Similarly, there should be no scope for exclamation marks in written advice to clients, no matter how alarming their predicament may be.

Once an ongoing professional relationship has been formed with clients, then it is easier to use a specific tone appropriate for them. Until that point, the best advice is to use a measured, professional tone, which still conveys approachability.

11.4.5 Jargon or 'legalese'

It may be appropriate to use legal terms without explanation when writing to another lawyer or a professional with some knowledge of the law in a particular field.

> **Example 9**
>
> A practising business lawyer will often be instructed by a company secretary. A company secretary is often a lawyer or, if not, will be familiar with areas of company law. This is an example when it may be appropriate to use jargon when writing to a client.

However, in writing to someone other than a lawyer, advice should be in language understandable to the recipient. Care should be taken not to take this too far, which can result in an impression of being patronising.

If jargon must be referred to, for example because the recipient will need to be familiar with it when reading some documents, or appearing in court, then it should be deciphered. Overall, consideration should be given to just how much legal detail it is essential to provide. While it is important for the *lawyer* to understand the legal background behind advice, the recipient *client* may not need or want to know the specific detail or even the name of the law that supports it.

While undoubtedly lawyers used to enjoy showing how clever they were by peppering their sentences with Latin and using as many words as possible that a non-lawyer would find difficult to understand, there has been a significant move away from this practice relatively recently. Increased competition within the profession has seen law firms market themselves on putting the client first. Clearly practices such as this did not put the client first in any way.

Similarly, a client is unlikely to be impressed by the use of needless legalese, such as 'vendor' or 'offeror' when 'seller' would convey the meaning perfectly well. Most respected senior lawyers now view the hallmark of the best lawyers as being not only able to understand legal complexities, but having the additional skill, which not all lawyers have, to break down those complexities and explain them in a way which a non-lawyer can understand.

The point is not that a client would be tempted to start looking for a new lawyer simply because his lawyer used the word vendor. However, if that client happens to come across one of these better lawyers who can and does use the same language that the client does, do not underestimate how impressed that client will be.

11.5 Drafting

11.5.1 Why lawyers draft

There is considerable overlap between writing and drafting. Drafting involves writing, but while the examples of writing above are communications of information, the term drafting tends to be used specifically to describe the task of creating a document. This could be anything from form-filling, to drafting company meeting documentation, to creating a written contract setting out legally binding rights and obligations. These documents can be a single page through to several hundreds of pages long, and range from the very simple to the very complex.

Lawyers frequently need to draft documents in order to give legal effect to their clients' instructions, and these documents must comply with all legal and procedural requirements. For example, you cannot circumvent the law on murder simply by drafting a document whereby a client agrees in writing that someone can kill her (as the ongoing public debate surrounding euthanasia has highlighted). So, as with legal writing, drafting must be underpinned by a sound knowledge and understanding of the relevant law and procedure. However, again as with legal writing, to draft within the law in a way which effectively and unambiguously carries out a client's instructions, calls for a skills requirement in addition to knowledge of the law.

11.5.2 Characteristics of good and bad drafting

The characteristics of good writing set out at 11.3 apply equally here. There are some additional considerations particular to drafting, and these are examined below.

Using and adapting a precedent

Law firms tend to maintain precedent banks of documents for their lawyers to use as a basis for their drafting. These precedents are drafted in general terms and must be adapted to suit the situation of individual clients. For example, a simple precedent licence may be adapted to suit any type of licensing, perhaps with some guidance notes about legal issues to be borne in mind depending on the situation (e.g. if the sale of alcohol is involved). Where a firm does not have its own precedents it may subscribe to other resources such as the online resources provided by Practical Law Company or the *Encyclopaedia of Forms and Precedents*. Details of both resources are set out in the 'Further reading' section at the end of this chapter.

Lawyers may also refer to a different type of 'precedent', namely the use of a document prepared by the firm previously that recorded a similar situation to that which a client needs. For example, a document drafted to grant a licence for the hire of a hall for a private event may then be amended by another lawyer to grant a licence to hold a festival in a field.

Precedents have significant advantages in that they promote efficiency (and so can help to keep costs down and allow firms to charge competitively) and they allow know-how to be passed on within a firm. However, they can have disadvantages too. First, the law is constantly changing, and so it can be a full-time job to make sure the firm's precedents are kept up to date. Indeed it is common for larger firms to employ **professional support lawyers** to do this job. If precedents are not kept up to date then they need to be treated with caution. The second disadvantage is that precedents can encourage and perpetuate poor drafting. Using a precedent which has been used before and appears to have worked can inhibit a lawyer from changing anything in it, even if it is not drafted as clearly as it might otherwise have been. Both of these disadvantages can be overcome if precedents are used responsibly. However, caution must be exercised in changing wording, as in some cases words have been specifically chosen for maximum benefit under the law: if the wrong deletion is made, the intended effect of the agreement may be reduced or even negated. A good precedent bank will contain explanatory notes to deal with issues like this.

Structuring a contract

Lawyers draft contracts for all sorts of different reasons. However, most contracts follow a similar structure. The contract template at 11.7.4 sets out the common structure and parts found in most contracts.

Consistency

It is common for many items to be repeated frequently within the body of any contract. It is important that any reference to the same item is consistent throughout the contract to avoid any ambiguity as to the intent of the parties. The use of definitions (seen in the contract template at 11.7.4) is a common means of ensuring consistency. The proofreading example at 11.5.3 sets out common inconsistencies that can appear in a contract in error.

Cross-referencing

Within contracts, clauses will often refer to other clauses for interpretation or meaning. Cross-referencing by clause number is a standard approach to ensure that the correct clause is referred to. This too must be consistent and, given that many contracts go through a number of drafts with many amendments to both the substance and number of clauses, it is good practice, on a final proofread (see 11.5.3), to check that each cross-reference refers to the correct clause.

Clarity

As a contract sets out legal rights and obligations, clarity is particularly important. In fact, there is a specific rule of law about contract interpretation, known as the **contra proferentum rule**, which reinforces this.

 Essential explanation

The *contra proferentum* rule

This rule provides that anything which is unclear or ambiguous will be construed against the party who included it in the contract.

Contracts commonly impose deadlines or timing provisions, and it is common to see examples of poor drafting in this regard.

11.5.3 **Checking work: proofreading**

A final stage in drafting, which is equally applicable to all pieces of legal writing (whether as part of your education or in your career), is to ensure, before it is sent, that the work looks exactly as intended. This checking requires the skill of proofreading.

Whatever your skills as a writer, you must take time to ensure no errors have crept into written work during the document production process. Many pieces of writing fall at this hurdle,

Example 10

Consider the following clause:

1. The Buyer must pay a deposit to the Seller of £1000 within 7 days.

The clause is unclear as to when the 7 days start to run. If this clause was in a contract signed on 1 September, could the deposit be paid on 8 September? The wording could be improved as follows:

1. The Buyer must pay a deposit to the Seller of £1000 within 7 days beginning with the date of this agreement.

Another example is:

1. The Buyer must pay a deposit to the Seller of £1000 before 22 December.

This can be improved as follows:

1. The Buyer must pay a deposit to the Seller of £1000 on or before [5pm on] 21 December.

as the practical processes of dictation (see 11.6) and word-processing afford ample opportunity for unexpected errors to be incorporated. These are often referred to 'typos' (short for **typographical errors**), which conveniently sounds if as the error is with the word-processing system rather than the person with responsibility for checking the document.

Generally, proofreading benefits from time and attention, which can be difficult when working under pressure. However, it also benefits significantly from practice. If time allows, putting work to one side for a while before proofreading it can be helpful.

 Practice tip

Proofreading changes made to larger documents is a common task for trainees in legal practice. One technique is that one trainee reads from the hand-amended 'marked up' document, and another checks that everything has been incorporated properly into the newly typed draft. Some firms draw up a 'checking rota' to make sure the burden is spread among all trainees regardless of which seat they are in.

Exercise 1 helps to illustrate some common proofreading errors. How did you do? Set out below are the errors, together with some practical steps to improve your proofreading skills.

Spelling

If you dictate a draft, or mark it up for amendment illegibly, this may result in spelling errors. Alternatively you may also be checking the work of another fee-earner who is not as good at spelling as you.

As described in this chapter, the on-screen spell-check facility can help here, but it will not identify some errors. For example, in clause 1.5, 'licence' (the noun) was spelled as 'license' (the verb) in error. The spell-check facility would not identify this as a spelling error.

Punctuation

As with spelling, punctuation errors may find their way into a draft. For example, clause 1.3 ends with a full stop rather than a semi-colon; clause 1.7 with a semi-colon rather than a full stop, and clause 2(iii) is missing a full stop.

Exercise 1

Test your existing proofreading skills by marking, in pencil, any errors on this draft section from a document granting a licence to store wine in part of a warehouse.

1. DEFINITIONS

In this Licence:

1.3 the 'Warehouse' means the building at Unit 4 Pickstock Industrial Estate, Pickstock, Yorkshire PK6 9NW edged green on the plan annexed to this licence.

1.4 "the Plan" means the plan attached to this agreement;

1.5 the 'Licence Period' means the period from and including the date of this license until and including the date on which the Hirer's rights under Clause 1 are terminated in accordance with Clause 4;

1.6 the "License Fee" means £800 including VAT; and

1.7 'the Storage Area' means the the area shown edged red on the Plan;

2. THE LICENCE

The Licensor gives the Hirer the exclusive right for the Licence Period to use:

2 (a)   the Storage Area (or such other area as the Owner may allocate by written notice to the Hirer;

2 (b)   the designated parking space for parking one car or van; and

2 (iii)   The entrance hall and corridors edged blue on the Plan for access to and from the storage area

Layout

Layout should be consistent. Here a double space was used in error between clause 1.6 and 1.7, and clause 2 is aligned differently to clause 1.

Numbering

It is common for word-processing software to lead to errors in numbering and cross-referencing. Here the numbering began with 1.3, and 2(c) had become 2(iii) in error. There also appears to be a cross-referencing error in clause 1.5; the cross-reference to the clause giving rights to the Hirer should be to clause 2, not clause 1.

Defined terms

Defined terms present several opportunities for error. First, if a term is defined, the defined term should be used throughout. Here clause 1.3 refers to the 'plan annexed to this licence' rather than the defined term 'Plan'. Second, ensure consistency. Here some definitions use single inverted commas, some use double; some include 'the' within the definition, some do not. Third, consider whether there is a need to define a term. There is no need to define a term which is used only once, but any term used several times should be defined. This document refers to 'Licence', 'licence', and 'agreement' when it should use one, clearly defined, term.

The 'find' function in word-processing software can help here. Use it to find each defined term throughout the document, and check the defined term is used consistently and looks the same throughout. There is no 'correct' format for a defined term; look to the firm's house style for guidance as to whether to use single or double inverted commas and whether to include 'the' within the definition.

General typographical errors

In this draft, clause 1.7 repeated 'the' in error, clause 2(a) did not close brackets, and clause 2(iii) begins with a capital letter.

11.6 Dictation

You are most likely aware that many lawyers and other professionals use dictation to record written communications and, in some cases, elements of drafting. Many find this a more efficient process, particularly if they cannot type at an appropriate speed. Dictation is the process of speaking into a dictaphone voice recorder or computer (if the latter has voice recognition word-processing software) what you want to write. A secretary, or a piece of software if you used a computer, will then transcribe your dictation for you to review. This process can be awkward when you start. Unless you use voice recognition software during your studies, your first attempt is likely to be in a law firm or other employment, either during work experience or at the start of your career. You may be sharing an office, or in an open-plan environment, so your performance will be relatively public. At first it can be very hard to think as you speak, structure your work properly, and also give appropriate instructions to the transcriber. With dictation, you must speak everything that you wish to find on the page, so you need to dictate punctuation, paragraphs, heading, fonts, capitals, spelling and so on. A kind secretary may plug the punctuation gaps for you, but it is something of a rite of passage to be presented with your first effort at dictation consisting of one long, useless, unpunctuated paragraph. If this happens to you, do not worry. You are not the first person this has happened to, and you will not be the last.

When you first begin to learn dictation, you may struggle to see how it could ever be a more efficient process than simply typing your own work. However, you should persevere, because although it may initially seem completely alien and inefficient, with practice it will suddenly click and, in retrospect, you will wonder why you found it so difficult in the first place.

Example 11

This is what you would have to dictate for the first few lines of the document used in the proofreading exercise at 11.5.3:

(Bold heading)(figure) one (then, all capitals) definitions (new line, capital I) in this (capital L) licence (colon, new line, figure) one point one the (open inverted commas, capital W) warehouse (close inverted commas) means the building at (capital U) unit (figure) 4 (capital P) pickstock (capital I) industrial (capital E) estate (comma) ... and so on through to ... (full stop).

11.7 Writing and drafting templates

11.7.1 Letter template

This should be in longform, e.g. 28 April 2013.

If you are not sure how familiar to be, err on the side of caution and choose Mr/Mrs/Miss. If you are writing in someone else's name, check the file to see how that person has addressed the recipient in previous correspondence.

If you do not know the recipient's marital status and she is female, this presents a difficulty. Although many do not like 'Ms', it has become widely used and is probably the best of a poor selection of options.

The most modern way is not to follow this with a comma. However, if you choose to use a comma here, you should be consistent and use a comma after 'Yours sincerely' (or faithfully) too.

Make sure the heading is not visible through any envelope window. If the matter is very sensitive, use a non-sensitive heading or dispense with a heading altogether. This is not a good way for a husband to discover his wife is divorcing him. Nor will a recent widow appreciate the heading 'Death of your husband'.

Firm's headed notepaper
Name of firm
Address

Recipient
Name
Address

Ref: 1234/5678
Date

Dear Recipient

Heading

The letter should begin with an opening sentence, explaining what it is about. You may need to remind the client why you are writing, for example if you are advising this client on several other matters. Consider the needs of the recipient you are writing to when deciding whether to include jargon, technical detail and citations, and the tone you wish to take.

Make your letter as clear and as easy to follow as possible. Layout and structure will help with this. Short sentences are easier to follow and also easier to write. Consider using paragraphs of an appropriate length, subheadings, and bullet points. Bullet points will be introduced with a colon:

- as a general rule
- consider whether they will help the recipient
- to understand what you are saying
- and decide whether you will
- Begin each bullet with upper or lower case
- and end each bullet point with or without a full stop.

Some lawyers do not like to see bullet points in a letter. You will get to know the preferences of the person you are working for, but bullets points can add clarity when used appropriately. Do not just use them in order to write in shorthand, however.

1. Consistency
   If you do use headings or numbering, check they too are consistent.

2. Orphan headings

The heading above would be an example of a 'hanging' or 'orphan' heading, if it had been left at the bottom of the page with its related paragraph beginning over the page. You should move any such headings so that they are on the same page as the paragraph to which they relate.

(continued . . .)

Firms have their own 'house style' which will be reflected in all of their precedent documents to provide a uniform brand. This means that fonts, colours, style, and layout will have been chosen for you.

If your firm does not have house style, or if you are writing before you join your firm, use a professional looking combination. Arial or Verdana size 10 are good modern choices and are used by larger commercial firms. Times New Roman size 12 is more traditional.

This is the client's file and matter reference. In practice, each client will be given a reference number (e.g. 1234), and each matter will be given a separate reference number (e.g. 5678). It is helpful to include these references here (e.g. 1234/5678) so it is clear where to file the letter and to ensure that any time spent on this letter, e.g. proofreading it, can be recorded to the correct file.

The text in this letter has been justified, which means that the text spreads uniformly from left to right. This looks modern, gives clean lines, and complements the use of modern fonts such as Arial. You can justify text quickly by highlighting it, then pressing the justify button. You can highlight all the text in a letter at the same time by pressing 'control' (or 'command') and 'a' together.

This paragraph has not been justified. It is aligned to the left, so you can see the difference. It is written in Times New Roman font. It looks a little outdated, however it is still used in house style by some, often smaller, firms.

You may wish to indent text. If so, always use the tab key, and never the spacebar.

If you are asking a client to consider several options, it is helpful to list them at the end of the letter so that the client can identify them and refer to them easily. Similarly, if you need the client to send you anything then you should list it clearly at the end of the letter. This is an example of using a good structure and clear language to make your own life easier. The clearer your instructions as to what you need the client to do, the more likely the client is to follow those instructions.

Your letter should end with an appropriate closing paragraph. Leave the recipient with a good impression.

Kind regards.
Yours sincerely/ faithfully

Name of lawyer or firm
Status

Side annotations (left column):

This is a professional way to close a letter, but it acknowledges your familiarity with the recipient. Note the lower case 'r' in re-gards. Some lawyers prefer not to use the word 'kind', and simply to write 'Re-gards'. Whichever you choose, with formal letters it is recom-mended that you follow it with a formal closing too (as here) as this looks professional and sufficiently formal if the letter ever needs to be produced in court proceedings.

If you have addressed the letter to the recipi-ent by name, you should use 'sincerely', and note that it takes a lower case 's'. If you have not used a name, but have written a 'Dear Sir' or 'Madam' letter, you must use 'faithfully' with a lower case 'f'.
   The most modern way to do this is not to follow with a comma. However if you choose to use a comma here, you should be consistent and use a comma after 'Dear X' too.

Side annotations (right column):

Some letters will be signed on behalf of the firm, and it is the firm's name which should appear here. In this case, you should write the letter using 'we' not 'I' throughout.
   Other letters you will sign personally, and it will be your own name that features here. In this case, you should write the letter using 'I' throughout.

If you are signing your own name, check house style. Some firms include your status (e.g. 'Trainee Solicitor)', others do not.

 Practice tip

In practice, a senior lawyer may delegate the writing of a letter to a more junior lawyer (see 12.3). She will then read, check, and make any amendments to the letter before she signs it. In other words, you **ghost write** the first draft of the letter to be sent by someone else.

This is a specific skill in itself. It involves you having to write in the style, manner, and tone of someone else. For example, if you would usually address the client as Miss Shephard, but the partner in whose name the letter will be sent out is on first name terms with the recipient, then you should write, for example, 'Dear Catherine' as the salutation in the letter rather than 'Dear Miss Shephard'. You should not leave any clues for the recipient that the person who read, checked, then signed the letter did not actually write it.

Your aim is to write the letter so well that the senior lawyer will be able to sign and send it without having to amend it substantially first.

11.7.2 Email template

Check very carefully that you are sending your message to the correct person(s), and not to anyone else. Check whether you wish to 'reply to all' or 'reply to sender'. Examples of errors include sending risqué jokes to the entire firm, disclosing negotiation tactics to the other side in error, and making disparaging remarks about someone who is copied in to a mail.

If the message is of a sensitive nature (e.g. about how to dismiss employees) always check that the recipient is happy to receive the message by email. Some people share their general email access with other members of their team or with their secretary, and have a separate address for confidential emails.

The comments on the letter template apply equally here.

Note this is the only example of written communication which does not refer to the client file and matter number.

From:
To:
CC:
BC:
Date:
Subject:

Dear Recipient

The guidance set out in the letter template applies equally here. You should write your email in the same professional manner as you would write a letter. Email emerged as an informal communication method but informality is no advantage should your document be scrutinised in court. You should use tone, rather than shorthand, to convey your sentiments.

Email can encourage lawyers not to pay as much attention to their writing as they would if they were writing a letter, and it is very easy to send a message without checking it first. Prepare the body of your email in a word-processing package, print, and check it. You can then cut and paste the text into your email.

If your email is quite long, consider whether it would be better to write a letter and attach it to an email instead. Bear in mind that if the recipient is reading the email from a smartphone, opening an attachment can sometimes present problems. You can enquire about this when you ask clients how they would prefer to receive letters.

Kind regards.
Yours sincerely

Name of Lawyer
Firm
Firm's address
Telephone number
Website

Use this with caution. Do you really need to blind copy the message to anyone? Consider what the recipient would think about this. If you really need someone else to see the message without the original recipient knowing, it may be best to forward that person the sent mail, with an appropriate covering message instead.

Bear in mind confidentiality here. The subject heading will be visible on screen whenever the recipients open their inbox, so err on the side of caution.

This information is usually contained in an autosignature, in house style if available, which you can prepare and arrange to be added to an email automatically when you send it. It may also include logos and references to Twitter and Facebook pages, but beware attaching anything that will annoy the recipient in terms of the amount of hard drive space it takes up.

11.7.3 Research report template

This template is set out at 8.4.2, and that chapter gives further guidance on legal research.

11.7.4 **Contract template**

You should define terms which you intend to use frequently in the contract. Then make sure you refer consistently to these terms in the body of the contract. Definitions should be in alphabetical order.

It does not matter whether 'the' is inside or outside the quotation marks, or whether the quotation marks are single or double, but you must be consistent.

This is an example of an active sentence. It makes clear who is granting the rights in a way that a passive sentence such as 'X is granted the following rights' would not.

Ensure numbering is consistent and squential.

AGREEMENT

Dated: [ ]
Parties: (1)
(2)

THIS AGREEMENT is made the day of BETWEEN

(1) [Name] of [Address] (the '[defined term]'); and
(2) [Name] of [Address] (the '[defined term]').

IT IS AGREED as follows:

1. DEFINITIONS

In this agreement:
1.1 the ' ' means [ ];
1.2 the ' ' means [ ]; and
1.3 the ' ' means [ ].

2. OPERATIVE PROVISIONS

This is where the clauses granting rights and imposing obligations will feature. You will structure the document so perhaps one clause grants rights, the next imposes obligations, the next deals with any payments, and so on.

3. GRANTING OF RIGHTS

The [ ] gives the [ ] the following rights subject to the provisions of this agreement:
3.1 to do X;
3.2 to do Y; and
3.3 to do Z.

4. OBLIGATIONS

[ ] must do A on or before [ ].

5. PAYMENT

[ ] must pay to [ ]:
5.1 a deposit of £[ ] on or before [ ] pm on [ ]; and
5.2 a further sum of £[ ] on or before [ ] pm on [ ].

6. OTHER CLAUSES TO REFLECT THE CLIENT'S SPECIFIC INSTRUCTIONS

You must make sure that your drafting carries out all of the client's instructions.

7. RESTRICTIONS

[ ] must not:
7.1 do A;
7.2 do B; or
7.3 do C.

(continued . . .)

Ensure cross-references are accurate.

8. BOILERPLATE CLAUSES

At the end of every agreement, whatever the context, you will find similar clauses referred to as boilerplate clauses. They include the following clauses.

9. LIABILITY AND INDEMNITY

[   ] must indemnify [   ] against [   ].

10. TERMINATION

The rights granted in clause 2 will end:

10.1 immediately on [   ]; or

10.2 on not less than [   ] month's notice expiring at any time given by either party to the other.

11. ASSIGNMENT

The benefit of this agreement [is] [is not] assignable.

12. NOTICES

All notices given by either party under any provision of this agreement must be:

12.1 in writing; and

12.2 addressed to [ ] at [ ] and served:

    12.2.1 by hand; or

    12.2.2 sent by registered post; or

    12.2.3 sent by recorded delivery; or

    12.2.4 sent by fax, provided that a confirmatory copy is delivered by hand or sent by registered post or recorded delivery on the same day.

SIGNED by [   ])
in the presence of)

SIGNED by [   ])
in the presence of)

You must choose the correct signing (or **attestation**) clause. Some documents need to be signed as a deed, others do not. Obtaining a witness is always helpful in any event, for evidentiary purposes. You should ensure that the signing clause is suitable for the person signing. If it is a company, consider how it will be signing—by company seal, or one or more of its officers?

Be clear by using 'or' or 'and' whether provisions are in the alternative.

Summary

- Legal writing is a fundamental skill developed during legal studies.

- Graduates are expected to display good levels of written communication skills.

- Through legal writing, you should be able to demonstrate understanding of the law and specific legal intellectual skills: both these factors can be determined from the title of a particular assignment.

- When writing a legal essay, follow the 5 'Ps': Purpose; Plan and Prepare; Perform; and Polish.

- Apply critical thinking: analyse arguments, evidence, and opinions before providing your own reasoned conclusion.

- Writing and drafting skills are a core part of the work of lawyers and other professionals.

- The level of writing skill displayed by a lawyer in communicating with clarity to a client will affect the latter's perception of the quality of advice given.

- In both legal studies and subsequent employment, considered and careful review of written work before submission or sending is vital.

What the professionals say

You soon realise that everything you write is either on the clock, against the clock, or both. That pressure, combined with the need to ensure everything you write is effective in the eyes of others and can withstand being crawled over with a fine tooth comb if it is ever scrutinised in court, soon instils a respect for Legal Writing skills that you didn't expect you would ever have.

Stedman Harmon, 2012–13 Trainee, DLA Piper

 ## Thought-provoking questions

1. Do you think it is fair for clients to expect a lawyer's written work to be entirely free from any proofreading errors? What are the arguments for and against? Which are you most persuaded by?

2. Think about your own writing. What are your strengths and weaknesses? What can you start doing now to address your weaknesses in good time before you start to apply for, or begin, your training contract?

3. When reading a newspaper, try to read one article critically for proofreading errors. Did you find any? If so, what steps would you take to prevent such errors in your own writing?

 ## Further reading

Judy Parkinson, *i before e (except after c)* (London: Michael O'Mara Books Ltd, 2007)
—this text contains plenty of useful memory tools for remembering grammatical rules.

Lynne Truss, *Eats, Shoots and Leaves: The Zero Tolerance Approach to Punctuation* (London: Profile Books Ltd, 2003)
—this entertaining book is a useful resource for sharpening up your punctuation skills.

BBC adult literacy website: http://www.bbc.co.uk/skillswise/english
—this site contains a great set of one minute videos to help you brush up on your grammar and writing skills.

Levicom v Linklaters [2009] EWHC 812 (Comm)
—a useful case for showing the potential effect of ambiguity in legal practice.

Practical Law Company: http://uk.practicallaw.com/; *Encyclopaedia of Forms and Precedents*, published by LexisNexisUK: http://www.lexisnexis.co.uk/our-solutions/legal/
—both of these online resources are sources of precedents, as used by firms. N.B. These sites are subscription access but you can read about their services.

 For the authors' reflections on the thought-provoking questions, additional self-test questions, podcasts offering a variety of perspectives on legal systems and skills, and a library of links to useful websites, visit the free Online Resource Centre *at* **http://www.oxfordtextbooks.co.uk/orc/slorach/.**

Part III

Professional Development and Commercial Awareness

It is a reality of life that all students need to consider employability and professional development at an early stage in their studies, and law students are no exception. This section is designed to assist students in developing a better understanding of the requirements of employers, and to provide guidance on how best to demonstrate knowledge, skills, and commercial awareness.

An employability skills chapter introduces law students to the skills and competencies which all employers, but particularly those in the legal services sector, value. It recognises that law students will meet practising lawyers during the course of their studies, while applying for work in the legal sector and otherwise. It not only provides students with guidance on how to develop their professional awareness, but also shows them how to demonstrate this awareness to potential employers.

Supported by a number of business case studies, sample interview questions, and activities, students are then challenged to reflect on and actively improve their own commercial awareness. They are encouraged to engage with the wider business environment in which the law operates, and are then introduced to law firms and the individuals and businesses that have recourse to the law.

12 Employability

 Learning objectives

After studying this chapter you should be able to:

- Appreciate the skills law firms are looking for in prospective trainees.
- Begin to develop these skills yourself.
- Understand how to show prospective employers that you have these skills.
- Understand the skills involved in working effectively with others.
- Prepare effectively for an assessment day at a law firm.

Introduction

Chapters 7 to 11 consider the essential legal skills which all lawyers need, whether they are in practice or not. This chapter focuses on the additional skills you will require if you intend to embark on a career in the practice of law particularly, although it is important to recognise that law graduates are found in a variety of sectors other than law (including accountancy, banking, finance, the civil service, the police, government, the armed forces, management, journalism, and academia) and rest assured these skills are eminently transferable and will be useful wherever your career takes you.

In today's competitive marketplace, employability skills are key. Law students tend to prioritise the acquisition of legal knowledge over the acquisition of legal skills, but this is not a good idea. This is because employability skills play a pivotal role in distinguishing a good lawyer from an average one, from both an employer's and a client's perspective.

The term 'solicitor' is an umbrella term to describe professionals who practise all areas of that broad and diverse subject known as law. You cannot possibly arrive at a law firm on day one of your training contract armed with a comprehensive knowledge of the specific area of law you intend to practise. Law firms understand this and will help you to supplement your existing legal knowledge as they train you on the job for practice in a particular legal sector. Clients, rightly or wrongly, will assume you have that legal knowledge. But although there is a limit on how much you will impress your employer or the client with your legal knowledge on day one of your training contract, it is possible to impress on day one with polished employability skills. By learning these skills early, you can stand out from your peers when you enter the world of professional practice. It is quite a transition between being a student and being a professional. This chapter will help to ease that transition for you when it comes, by showing what you can be doing now to prepare for professional life.

The term 'employability skills' includes all those skills which make you a covetable employee. Of course, it includes technical competence in law, which in turn requires the skills covered in this book, namely being able to read and understand the law, undertake legal research, solve legal problems, draft competently, and communicate effectively, both orally and in writing. However, effective lawyers deploy a host of other skills which we will consider in this chapter.

12.1 Personal characteristics

Effective lawyers share similar characteristics. They have a positive attitude to their work, approach work in a business-like manner, act with professionalism, and reflect on their work to develop their practice. These characteristics come more naturally to some rather than others, however the good news is that they can be learned and improved with practice, like any other skill. As a first step it is important simply to appreciate that they are vital components of a good lawyer. Eventually, most lawyers find they can demonstrate the following qualities when things are going well. However, law is a rewarding but demanding profession. It involves working under pressure, often during long and sometimes unsociable office hours. A really good lawyer will be able to show the same qualities when things are not going as well.

Law firms will be looking for evidence of these characteristics when they consider your application form and during the interview process. Let's explore further what they are and how you can show that you have them when you apply for a job. Work experience is excellent in terms of really bringing these points home. Spending time in any professional environment is a great idea at this stage, and will demonstrate clearly the points set out below.

12.1.1 Attitude

It is important to demonstrate that you have a positive attitude to your work. One of the most important things to show is enthusiasm, even (particularly) when you are given something to do which is relatively mundane. Taking responsibility for your own work, being proactive in identifying other work that might be required and being willing to do that work and showing commitment to your work are also examples of taking a professional approach to your work. The key point to bear in mind is that you must show that you are someone with whom other people would want to work. Lawyers work closely together and the hours can be quite intense. Being flexible, approachable, and having a sense of humour even when things are going wrong will count significantly in your favour. Do not underestimate how the personality of work colleagues can significantly affect life in the office. If you come across as someone who would enhance the experience rather than detract from it, you will make yourself a covetable employee. You can get into good habits now, by recognising when you are tired, stressed, or just cannot be bothered, and making a particular effort to try your best at these times. Try out different coping mechanisms to get you through these difficult periods, and find what works for you. Something as simple as going for a walk, listening to music, or taking a break and having a cup of tea can make a difference. Talk to others. Too many students isolate themselves when they feel overwhelmed, but if you talk to others you will tend to find (and it can be comforting to know) that everyone has concerns; some are just better at dealing with them than others. You can learn from your fellow students; consider who has an attitude you admire and would like to emulate, and talk to them about their coping strategies. Ask your tutors if they have any advice regarding any issues you are facing; they are likely to have advised many students with similar problems. You will continue to experience these feelings in professional life; there are just never enough hours in the day, so start now to discover what will help you through.

12.1.2 **Approach**

You must approach your work in a businesslike manner. Examples of behaviour which evidence this are being organised, demonstrating a high capacity for work, being resilient under pressure, self-aware, diligent, and paying attention to detail. In other words, you need to show that you are 'a safe pair of hands'. Of course, what you are doing right now, being a law student, lends itself to evidencing that you have these skills, but the fact is that some students are much more adept than others at organising their work. This is something you can improve immediately to make sure you are one of the good ones. Time management is crucial. You must be able to multi-task and achieve a balance between your work and social life, and this is no less true once you are a professional. It is not sustainable in the long run simply to work all the time at the expense of a social life. You can help yourself by being familiar with your timetable; importing it into your smartphone is best, so you always have it with you, but if this is not possible at least stick a copy on the fridge. Maintain a 'to-do' list; again you can do this on a smartphone so it is always with you. Set alerts to make sure you do not forget key events or deadlines. Ask your tutor how many hours a week the course demands of you, and timetable that into your diary, factoring in non-timetabled activities such as preparation, consolidation and revision, so you can then clearly ring-fence some leisure time. Start your work early, so you have time to look over it with a fresh perspective before the deadline. Know what you have to do, where you have to be, and when.

12.1.3 **Professionalism and ethics**

There is an understanding that professionals behave in a certain way. This behaviour includes being polite, approachable, reliable, honest, dependable, punctual, and dressing and behaving in an office-appropriate manner.

If anyone helps you, it sounds obvious but say thank you. This is equally the case if the help is by email. It is increasingly common for students and trainees simply not to reply to tutors and lawyers who respond to their queries by email. A quick email in reply just to say thank you will never be a waste of anyone's time.

Reliability, honesty, and dependability are particularly important qualities for a profession like law where professional ethics are held in high regard. Clients may need to disclose quite sensitive information to you so they must be able to trust you. Indeed the Solicitors Regulation Authority (see further 6.3), which regulates the profession, may not admit you as a solicitor at all if you have in your record certain matters which suggest that you are dishonest. Further information on this is set out in their Suitability Test which they publish on their website (details of which are set out in the 'Further reading' section below). It is important to realise that anything you do now which suggests dishonesty could impact quite seriously on your ability to join this profession, where honesty is valued above all else. So, for example, if you are found guilty of plagiarism, or are caught on a train without a valid ticket, this may have more serious consequences for you than for, say, your housemate studying the history of art (provided he is not planning to go on to convert to law by studying the Graduate Diploma in Law).

As Chapter 15 explains, a solicitor charges on a time basis (see 15.1.6). A client will not tolerate a solicitor taking longer than necessary over work, or keeping the client waiting unnecessarily. If you are a student who tends to be late to lectures on a regular basis then take heed and adopt good habits sooner rather than later.

In terms of dress, it can be difficult to pre-empt what is office-appropriate if you have not been inside a law firm before. Bear in mind that generally law firms are relatively conservative places. You have a working lifetime to express yourself through your clothes once you are more familiar with the firm and its culture. Initially however, as a rule of thumb it is a good idea to err on the side of formality if you are at all unsure. It is better to be too formal at first, and become less so, than to be too casual and have to smarten up. The look you are aiming for is that of a polished professional. The following guidelines may help:

- sober black, grey, or navy blue suits will never be out of place;
- for men, shirts should be light-coloured and long-sleeved, preferably without a pocket;
- women have more latitude in terms of colour, but should avoid anything too revealing;
- shoes should be polished;
- men should be cleanly shaved;
- hair should be clean and tidy;
- avoid anything 'novelty', including ties, socks, cufflinks, and jewellery;
- it is a good idea to wear your suit in the house for a practice run first, to identify any scope for a wardrobe malfunction.

Bear in mind that you will meet professionals during the course of your studies. They will visit your university and you will meet them at law fairs, while doing pro bono work and on vacation schemes. You should think carefully about how you can demonstrate that even at this stage you have the attributes of a professional. Like it or not, you will make an impression when you meet these people, and you need to give some thought as to what impression you want to make, then dress and act accordingly. Think carefully before making any permanent alterations to your appearance, such as having a visible tattoo or stretching the holes of your pierced ears. Something that you will feel comfortable sporting in the student union may make you feel very uncomfortable when you speak to lawyers at a law fair or enter a law firm for a vacation placement. Nor should you worry about your friends' reactions, for example, if you choose to wear smart clothing to a law fair. Have the confidence to be guided by your own instinct.

That said, law firms are not looking for clones and you should not be afraid to let your personality come through in your dress, provided you still fall within the description of a polished professional.

12.1.4 **Development**

Law firms are constantly looking for ways to improve, so that they can beat the competition. As an employee, the firm will expect you to operate a **reflective practice**, which means that you should reflect on your work at regular intervals and learn from your experiences, good and bad, to inform your practice going forward. This involves taking responsibility for your own learning and development, reflecting on your performance and learning from mistakes, seeking and accepting feedback and advice, and being willing and able to learn new skills.

Generally a supervising solicitor will be understanding if you make a mistake once, however she will be considerably less understanding if you make the same mistake again. The skill is to learn from your mistakes. This is one reason why it is important to secure a training contract where you will be given lots of practical experience. The sooner you are free to make mistakes, the sooner you will learn from them, and you will be a more impressive lawyer at an early stage in your legal career.

Reflective practice is something you can start to develop now, as a student. Analysing our own mistakes is never a comfortable exercise, but it pays dividends. When asked for their views, it is common to hear students say they would like more feedback on their

Example 1

The following example might help you to understand why law firms value the characteristics discussed above, but it is equally relevant to any other work experience you might undertake, such as working at a magazine publishing house (although the copying may be of slightly more glamorous documents).

Imagine you are a solicitor. It is 6pm. You are going to be working late and you have cancelled your plans for the evening. You ask your trainee, James, if he can copy the 150-page document which you will need to append to the document you will be drafting later in the evening. James' body language suggests he is not overly impressed with your request. He replies, 'OK, although I warn you I am not very on the ball when working late.' You leave your office for a while and return to find a pile of papers on your desk, and that James has left for the evening. The papers appear to be the photocopied document.

At 11.30pm, after several hours of drafting, you finish your document. However, when you try to append the copy document to your draft, you find that pages 148–50 are not in the pile of papers on your desk. You look for the original document, but it is not with the papers on your desk. You find it on James' desk, next to a half finished cup of coffee. Unfortunately pages 148–50 are also missing from the original document. You go to the photocopier and find that the lights on the copier are flashing to indicate a paper jam. You open the photocopier and fish out the original pages 148–50. You reset the copier. The copier is out of paper. You refill the copier. Finally you are able to add the photocopies of pages 148–50 to the appendix, email it to its destination, and go home at midnight.

As the solicitor in this scenario, what is your opinion of James? Consider again the personal characteristics which law firms value. Has James demonstrated any of them? Which ones has he definitely not shown? Analyse specifically what you would have liked him to have done differently. Now read the following:

Imagine you are a solicitor. It is 6pm. You are going to be working late and you have cancelled your plans for the evening. You ask your trainee, John, if he can copy the 150 page document which you will need to append to your document when you have finished drafting it. John looks up from his work, smiles and replies, 'Yes, of course'. You leave your office for a while and return to find two piles of papers on your desk, one with a label 'copy' and one with a label 'original'. John returns to your office with two cups of coffee, one of which is for you. He explains that he has counted the pages and two pages appear to be missing, so he is going to find them. Ten minutes later John returns with the two missing pages and puts them into the appropriate piles in the right place, explaining with a smile that he had just won a battle with the photocopier. He asks if you need anything else. You say no, thank him and say he should go home as there will be a few late nights ahead this week.

If both John and James were looking for a job in your department, it is likely that you would recommend John over James. John has made your life easier than James did. It is interesting to note what John did to earn your support. He was pleasant, smiled, did not complain, made you a coffee, checked the copying, and extracted two documents from the photocopier. None of these things in isolation is particularly burdensome. However it is these little things which can make a big difference to someone who asks for your help. Note that you did not have to do any of John's work. In contrast, it would probably have been more efficient for you to have done the copying yourself rather than give it to James. James runs the risk that you will not trust him again, and as a result he will not gather the same level of experience during this seat that John will.

work. However it can be that students who receive a poor mark find this so disappointing that they are tempted to file the work away without paying attention to the feedback provided. No matter how painful it may be, you must try to read feedback objectively, and discuss anything that you do not understand with your tutor. If you change your perception and view this as a positive process, by which you can move forward, it can help. It can also be useful to keep a reflective log, which might be referred to in practice as a personal development plan. The simpler you make this the more likely you are to use it, so if could just be a notes page on your smartphone which highlights areas of concern, and the steps you are taking to address them, which you can reflect on and update regularly to chart your progress.

12.2 Team-working

In the past, the image of a lawyer was perhaps of a professional sitting alone in an ivory tower, bestowing knowledge of the law onto grateful clients. Those days are gone. To be a good lawyer, or indeed any other professional, in the modern world you need to have good people skills and be able to work well with others. This includes working with those with whom you do not have a natural affinity. This is especially pertinent for a trainee lawyer, who will work in at least four different departments of a firm during their two-year training contract.

 Practice tip

Trainees sit with different departments during their training contract of two years. The time spent with one department is referred to as a 'seat', and when a trainee moves to a different department, this is called a 'seat move'. The majority of firms offer trainees four seats each lasting six months, but some firms offer more seats over the two-year period. Arranging seat moves can be a stressful time, as several trainees may indicate an interest in the same seat, and not all will obtain their first choice. It is important to give your best performance in all seats, even if you are not seeking to qualify into that department. Do not forget that the partner in your current department may well be acquainted with the partner in the department you want to go to next, and a positive or negative referral from one partner to another, however informal, may be pivotal in deciding whether you secure your first choice of seat move or not.

Most candidates who apply for any kind of employment refer in their curriculum vitae to good team-working skills. It is useful to give some thought as to what this actually entails.

12.2.1 What is team-working and why is it important?

You should be able to identify some examples where you have worked as part of a team. Playing team sports, being a member of a committee, or working as part of any other team, be it during work experience in a law firm or waiting tables, will all help you to give context to help you demonstrate that you are a good team player. If you have not done so already, start to examine your curriculum vitae for any gaps you need to fill in terms of team-working, and undertake activities now to plug those gaps. For example, you may need to take part in some extra-curricular activities such as joining a sports team or society (law-related, such as mooting, or otherwise). However, you may also be able to use examples you had not thought of to date as 'team work' such as working in groups during your face-to-face teaching, or setting up your own study group and establishing ground rules to help it work effectively.

A common question asked of prospective trainees at the interviewing stage is what exactly team-working involves. Some of the vital skills are highlighted below, in the order 'abcdef' to help you to commit them to memory.

- **A**cknowledging the contributions of others in the team.
- **B**uilding good working relationships.
- **C**ontributing to the team.
- Being able to **D**elegate, and be delegated to, **E**ffectively.
- Knowing how to **F**unction well as a team, including in team meetings.

We will explore these skills further in this chapter, and you can reflect on which component skills you may already have, and which you may be able to develop.

12.2.2 **Roles within a team**

It is worth spending some time reflecting on the role you like to take in a team, whatever team that may be. Most people have a preferred role that they find themselves adopting over again. Consider the scenarios in which you have worked as part of a team to date. Are you a dominant member of the team, or do you prefer to work away from the spotlight? Do you help the team to stay focused and on task, or are you a constant source of diverse creative ideas? Do you like to consider the detail, or do you prefer to think strategically but leave the finer detail to others?

There are several assessment tools available to determine how you can work to your full potential in a team, including *Belbin Team Roles*, which analyses the team role which would suit you best, and the *Myers-Briggs Type Indicator*, which analyses your personality type. It is common for employers, including law firms, to use these assessment tools as part of staff team-building days, to analyse how they might deploy their employees' skills to maximum advantage. Both the assessment tools referred to above require a fee to be paid, however they also have some useful free information available on their websites and the addresses are set out in the 'Further reading' section at the end of this chapter.

Whatever your preferred role, an employer will expect you to be aware of the strengths and weaknesses of that role. For example, if you are a dominant team member, you will have no problem in demonstrating that you contribute fully to the team, but are you aware that you may inhibit a valuable but quieter member of the team from contributing to the discussion? If you can both (i) identify the potential disadvantages of your personality type and also (ii) devise steps to address them, you are demonstrating high-level team-working skills. Professional employers will also be looking for employees with leadership potential. Regardless of the role you tend to adopt within a team, it is possible to show that working in any role within a team has allowed you to develop your own leadership skills. Team-working provides opportunities to reflect on your own strengths and weak-nesses, and those of others, and to devise strategies and develop communication skills which allow team members to participate in the team inclusively and in a way which plays to their strengths. It affords opportunities for you to practise how to identify a goal and work towards that goal effectively, and how to learn from the successes and mistakes you or others may make. If you can show that you have recognised these opportunities and learned from them, you will be able to demonstrate leadership potential, as they are all essential characteristics of a good leader.

12.2.3 Who might be in your team?

It is worth considering what teams you consider yourself to be working in at the moment. The number may surprise you. Team-working is an important skill for a lawyer because at any one time you might be working in several different teams. Let us consider the exam-ple of a trainee working in the commercial and corporate department of a law firm. What teams might she be working in? This is precisely the sort of question you may be asked at an interview. Simultaneously the trainee might be working in all of the following teams:

- **Team 1: trainee team.** The trainee may be one of an intake of several trainees. The trainees will support one another as peers and may work together in the same department or across other departments.

- **Team 2: department team.** The trainee is spending a finite period of time in the commercial/corporate department. During this time she must work effectively with the other trainees, fee-earners, partners, and secretaries in that department.

- **Team 3: transaction team.** The entire commercial/corporate department will not be advising on the same transaction (or 'deal'). Instead, a transaction team will be selected from the department to work on one particular transaction. Depending on the size of the transaction, this team will comprise one or more partners, fee-earners, and trainees.

- **Team 4: client team.** The transaction team may be advising a client which is a company. There will be a team of individuals at the company who are involved in putting the deal together, such as the company secretary (often a lawyer), the directors (who manage the company), and possibly a team of senior managers who are not directors. The trainee must be able to work with these people as part of a team.

- **Team 5: advisory team.** Typically the client will need other advice, in addition to legal advice, in order to complete the transaction. For example, the client's advisory team might consist of accountants, bankers, stockbrokers, and public relations professionals.

It is important to realise that you will not always have a natural affinity with those in your team. Nevertheless you will be expected to work seamlessly with these people as well as those towards whom you would more naturally gravitate. Law tutors may help you to develop these skills by encouraging you to sit with people other than your friends during workshops and seminars, and perhaps to adopt a role that would not be your first preference. This can help you to develop your team-working skills and will also help to prevent you always adopting the same role within a team (which you were encouraged to identify above). As part of the self-reflection process, and to work on the problem-solving skills referred to in Chapter 9, it is good to consider any problems you have or might experience while working as a team, and how you tried or might try to solve these problems. For example, you may come across someone who does not contribute to your group work. This may be for a number of reasons: perhaps he has not prepared, is shy, is reluctant to interrupt a more dominant group member, lacks confidence, does not understand the work, is tired, genuinely has a more pressing problem distracting him, and so on. How might you encourage this person to contribute? Should you? Does the reason that he is not contributing make a difference? How would you find out the reason? Should you? Get into the habit of learning from your experiences, and do not be afraid to admit that you handled a situation in a way you would not repeat. This is all part of your learning as a student, as much as reading *Donoghue* v *Stevenson*.

12.2.4 **Negotiating decisions as a team**

If there is no consensus in a team, how does it decide how to proceed? In a law firm, which has a hierarchical structure, it is often left to the most senior person to decide. This is not without merit, as she is often the most experienced team member. However, consider a partner who makes the decision that each of her junior lawyers should record one more hour of chargeable time each day. Clearly this is an example where she will need her team to buy in to the idea, or she could be left with no team to record any hours at all. Generally, teams functioning at a high level structure the decision-making process effectively and inclusively. With the arrival of alternative business structures (see Chapters 6 and 15), law firms are increasingly aware that they have to think like businesses, and they are looking to recruit people who might be able to bring business acumen into the firm. If team-working is an area which interests you, this is an area that lends itself to analysis outside the law firm bubble, and the following general team issues are worth considering. Negotiation itself is also a key skill for lawyers. You might like to try out some of the theory right now, as a student, in the teams you are currently in.

Aims and objectives

A team will have been brought together for a particular purpose, and it is worth making sure that all members of the team are aware of this purpose and the time period over which it must be achieved. Any plans for the team should be clear and divided into short-, medium-, and long-term plans.

Strategy

A well-managed organisation will have formulated and often publicly stated a clear strategy to achieve its aims and objectives. For example, a law firm may want to be known for the quality of its advice above all else, or it may wish to be defined as a cost-effective option. Decision-making within teams in the organisation must be consistent with the stated objectives and strategy.

Know-how

It is important to determine whether anyone in the team has any knowledge which would make them the best person to take a leading role in a particular decision. For example, if a team in a law firm is tasked with arranging a client marketing event, and you have a contact at a venue you think would be ideal, you should speak up. If your university law society is asked to start tweeting on a regular basis to raise its profile, and you have a particular interest in and experience of this, then again you should identify yourself as a team member with useful knowledge. Know-how does not always rest with the most senior member of the team.

Resolving disagreements

It is unlikely that all members of a team will agree with each other all of the time. The easiest way to move forward is to go with the majority. This is not always the best way, however, because it may be that there is a better way forward which could be identified by further debate. It can also encourage a competitive atmosphere within the team which can distort and obstruct the decision-making process. If the team can reach a position which every team member can live with and support, even if that decision does not reflect exactly the decision they would have made, this puts the team in a strong position. Each team member will have bought into the decision and will be able to engage with the process of taking it forward, as a team. You can see that, as referred to above, to reach this point a team needs a combination of individuals with different strengths to adopt different roles, for example someone to bring out the quieter members, someone with good powers of persuasion, a peace maker, and so on. Body language is also important in ensuring the team is functioning inclusively in negotiating a way forward.

12.3 Delegation

For a team to work most effectively, each member of the team should be working to their highest level. This involves the team members working together in a structured way, sharing

Example 2

In Shephard & Son, a partner charges £360 per hour, an associate £150 per hour, and a trainee £50 per hour. A client, Emma, has asked the planning team whether she can cut down a tree in her garden. The team needs to research the issue then provide some advice to Emma in writing.

The partner could do this. It would take her 15 minutes to research the law, and 10 minutes to draft the letter. The cost to the client would be £150 (£360/60×25).

Alternatively, the partner could delegate some of the task to the trainee. Let's assume that it would take the trainee 30 minutes to research the law and 30 minutes to draft the letter. The partner could then check and amend the work in 10 minutes. The cost to the client would be £110 (£50+(£360/60×10)).

Effective delegation has allowed the firm to charge competitively for the work for Emma, has freed the partner's time to work on a more complex problem for another client, and has given the trainee valuable experience.

the workload efficiently between them according to their training and experience. This is not restricted to law firms; consider, for example, why you have blood taken by a nurse but your appendix removed by a surgeon. It is particularly important however that lawyers work at an appropriate level, because clients pay each lawyer a different rate calculated specifically by reference to experience (see 15.1.6). If a senior lawyer with a high charge-out rate is doing basic legal work, there is a danger that the charge would be so expensive that the client would not pay it. Rather than 'write off' this time, which would adversely affect the firm's profits, it is better for more senior members of the team to delegate less complex tasks to the more junior members.

It can be very frustrating for both the person delegating and the recipient of the delegated task if this delegation is not done effectively. Unfortunately, poor delegation is very common. The following are common signs of poor delegation:

- Leaving a task until it is urgent before delegating it.
- Not giving enough thought about who to delegate to.
- Failing to give clear instructions as to what needs to be done.
- Not agreeing a deadline.
- Not being available to answer essential questions.
- Not passing on new information.
- Giving no feedback, or negative feedback with no scope to allow for learning from mistakes.

Why is poor delegation common? There are several contributing factors and understanding them can help you to be better both at delegating and being delegated to. Looking from the delegator's perspective, he may simply be too busy to have given enough thought to how to delegate effectively. Sometimes a delegator may feel too inhibited to delegate properly. He may be embarrassed at having to ask for help or worried about burdening other people. In some cases, there may be something on the file which the delegator would prefer others not to see, such as a complaint or a long delay on his part. From the delegatee's perspective, she may be inhibited and respond negatively to the delegator due to the fact she is already overloaded, or because of previous negative experiences of delegation, or simply because the work is not at the right level for her to take on.

Good delegation can avoid these problems, but it requires planning and forethought. The flowchart at Figure 12.1 will help you, as a guide to what to do if you are in the role of delegator, and to help you ask for appropriate guidance if you are a delegatee. As a student you may consider that you are more likely to be the delegatee, and this is true in terms of the role you will have while on work experience, or a law firm vacation scheme. However, if you think carefully you will probably be able to identify some times where you have taken, or should have taken, the role of delegator. For example, if your tutor gives you a group assignment to complete, how have you decided who is doing what and when? If you have held a charity cake sale, who has decided who will bake, who might sell some raffle tickets and who might be in charge of the money? On what basis were these decisions made? Whether you knew it or not, someone was delegating, and if you are going to be a good delegator it helps to realise this.

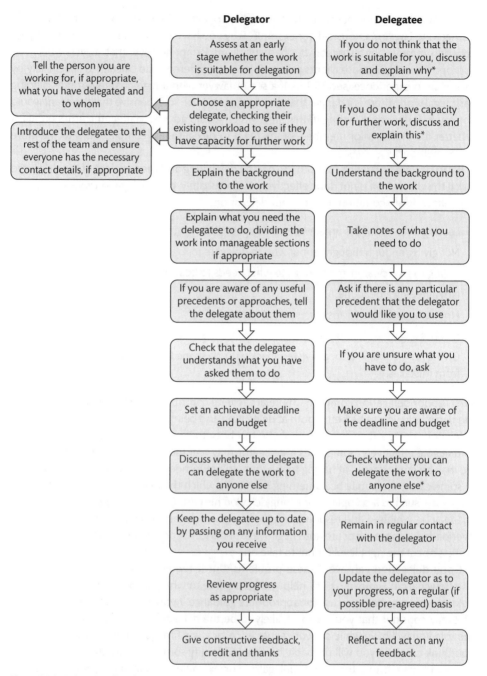

Figure 12.1 Delegation flowchart

* Take a cautious approach here. As a lawyer, you must be willing to take on challenging work in order to develop, and you must be willing to work hard. However, part of being a professional is also being able to manage your workload effectively, and knowing when to ask for help. If, for example, a supervisor mistakes you for someone else who is more senior, it would be appropriate to discuss that you are, say, a trainee. If you have been told by one supervisor that you should not take on any further work until you have completed a task for him, then again you would need to discuss this with the delegator. As ever, your tone and body language will be important here to make sure you do not come across as defensive, or simply saying 'no'.

12.4 Meetings

While initially you may have limited opportunities to change how meetings are run, it is nevertheless worth spending some time considering how meetings could be run most effectively, simply because meetings constitute such a considerable part of a lawyer's day. Lawyers will have external meetings (with clients, see 10.6) and internal meetings (with their colleagues).

12.4.1 Internal meetings

It will be probably be a while before you attend a meeting at a law firm or other professional office (although you may do so while undertaking pro bono work or on a vacation scheme or other work experience). However, as mentioned at 12.2.4 in the context of team-working, the arrival of alternative business structures (see Chapters 6 and 15) means that law firms are increasingly looking to recruit people who can bring business acumen into the office. If you are interested in this area, it is worthwhile considering how meetings can be run effectively while maximising profit.

While most businesses accept that external meetings should be run as efficiently as possible, typically internal meetings can be a significant source of frustration. It is a common complaint that businesses do not prioritise internal meetings, and law firms are no exception. While in theory they may appreciate that internal meetings should be on an equal footing with external meetings, it is not uncommon to witness lawyers who turn up late, allow themselves to be distracted and interrupted by their smartphones throughout the meeting, then leave early. Meetings can stray far away from the business they were called to discuss, or they may be called out of habit even though there is nothing to discuss. Internal meetings may fall into a regular pattern where each person repeats the same frustrating behaviour, be it one dominating voice, or someone complaining about the same old issue over and over again without suggesting any workable solution.

These issues may be familiar to you from meetings you have attended to date. However, when you factor in the cost of internal meetings in a law firm (by multiplying the time taken by their hourly salary, or indeed their hourly charge-out rate), it becomes clear that they are so expensive that solicitors particularly can ill afford to run them as they do.

Strategies to avoid some of these problems (and this could be the kind of question you might be asked in a law firm interview) include circulating an agenda in advance, establishing a practice of starting the meetings on time, nominating someone to chair the meeting to keep it focused and running to time, and restricting any record of the meeting to identifying the action required rather than recording exactly what everyone said. More creative ideas include conducting meetings with everyone standing up (to prevent meetings from running on too long) and imposing a time limit on contributions. These ideas obviously need to be implemented by someone with the power to force change; however as a student and a junior lawyer you can start as you mean to go on, develop your skills, and make a very good impression by thinking about how to make any meetings under your control (such as those of any club or society, or to organise the cake sale) run as efficiently as possible.

12.5 Client care

All businesses need to care for their customers, but some do this better than others. It is much more efficient to keep an existing, good client content than to lose that client and have to find another, but this is not always put into practice. For example, you might have experienced the frustration, as an existing customer of a bank or mobile phone company, of discovering that new customers are being offered better rates.

Without clients, businesses are nothing, and in an increasingly competitive marketplace all businesses, including law firms, need to keep their clients happy. When asked, law firms would say that they expect their employees to provide a good level of customer care, but anecdotally it would seem that many are yet to incorporate customer care into their training and development programmes. In the absence of any formal customer care training, the best guide is to consider the service you provide from a customer's perspective. This is good practice whatever the nature of the business. There are things you can be doing now to increase your understanding of customer care. If you have any experience of working in a service industry, such as in a shop, bar, or pro bono clinic, you will have a better understanding of what you can do to improve the customer's experience. Reflecting on this will help you to develop this skill now, and you will be able to showcase it on your curriculum vitae.

12.5.1 Common complaints (and how to avoid them)

Some of the most common complaints made by law firm clients are set out below, together with guidance to help you avoid being the lawyer they complain about. Again, this is exactly the sort of question that might arise in a law firm interview, but be aware that these complaints are not confined to law firms. Be alert to items in the news about customer care, and consider how they might transfer into areas relevant to your career.

Fees

Not surprisingly, bills can be a source of frustration for a client. A frequent complaint is that they are too high, but other complaints include that the bill arrived unexpectedly, contained obvious errors on its face, appeared to refer to work which was unnecessary or on which too much time had been spent, or included charges for disbursements (see definition) that seem very high or were unexpected.

 Essential explanation

A **disbursement** is a payment that the law firm has made on behalf of the client for goods or services. Examples include photocopying charges and fees paid to the Land Registry for land searches. They can amount to a significant proportion of a client's bill.

A good lawyer can help to avoid this by managing a client's expectations well. The bill should not come as a surprise to the client, nor should there be any surprises in the bill itself.

Jargon

Lawyers can become so used to using jargon or 'legalese' between themselves that they forget that a client will not understand what they are saying. Chapters 10 and 11 explain that all communication between lawyer and client should be clear and as succinct as possible. Clients will become frustrated if they cannot understand the advice they are paying for. A good lawyer can understand difficult legal concepts, but it takes a very good lawyer to be able to communicate those concepts clearly in a way that a non-lawyer can understand.

Listening

Everyone likes to be listened to and clients are no exception to this. Lawyers, like many other professionals, can be poor listeners, with a tendency to interrupt clients or make assumptions about what they think. As Chapter 10 sets out, this can have a catastrophic effect on the appropriateness of the work which a lawyer produces, but it can also leave the client feeling neglected and not valued. Asking lots of open questions, and listening to the answers without interruption, can help a client feel satisfied with your work. Chapter 10 explores this further.

Manner

It does not matter how technically brilliant you are if you have no interpersonal skills when it comes to delivering your advice. You need to develop a good 'bedside manner' with clients that is neither too patronising nor too abrupt. This will not be the same for each client. Once you know your clients and the work you will be doing for them, you can and should tailor your manner to suit. For example, advising a recently bereaved person may require a different manner to advising a company director on a multi-million pound deal. However, even this will depend on the individual concerned.

Keeping the client updated

Clients should not have to call you to find out what is happening with their matter. It is much better if you are proactive, and take the initiative to contact them, even just to convey a brief message that nothing has happened. It is particularly important to contact clients if they have tried to contact you. Failing to return a call is a common complaint. You may be able to think of an example from your own experience, such as trying to speak to your bank manager about a loan, and reflect on how it made you feel when your call was left unanswered. Admittedly as a lawyer it can be a difficult step to call a client to deliver an unpalatable message, such as your work is going to be late, or you have made a mistake in some way. However, experience dictates that clients will always appreciate an early and honest call rather than the alternative which is for them to wait, eventually call you and finally, when pressed, for you to confess to the delay or the error. Lawyers who covet the role of trusted adviser must develop good habits in keeping clients informed of everything they need to know, good and bad.

Poor-quality work

Chapter 11 explained that clients will judge you on the standard of your writing and drafting (often more so than the quality of your legal advice, which they will presume is accurate in the absence of any obvious error). Clients will complain about work which is clearly deficient in terms of spelling, grammar, and punctuation. Some errors which are undetectable using spell-check can actually cause offence. Consider the impact of 'Dear Gut' instead of 'Dear

Gus', or 'See you shorty' rather than 'See you shortly'. Common complaints surround poor use of punctuation (particularly the apostrophe) and sentence structure (particularly long letters with no paragraphs). While lawyers can argue that the work was actually of satisfactory quality given the circumstances in which it was done, for instance if they had to dictate a letter very quickly over the telephone, or draft a clause in the middle of the night, you can see that from the client's perspective these errors can be perceived as reflecting a generally substandard service.

Lack of continuity

Law firms are busy places and lawyers will be working for several clients at the same time. Client matters can also take a long time to resolve and even lawyers need holidays. It is a business reality therefore that from time to time you will have to pass work for one client to one of your colleagues. Most clients will understand this if the process is managed properly. However all too often, due to time pressure, the client is the last to know that someone else has taken over the work on his file, or will discover that the new lawyer may not have been brought fully up to date as to the progress on the file. Again, you might be able to reflect on your own experience; anyone who has had the experience of trying to contact a business only to find themselves passed from one person to another, having to explain the same issue to several different people, will appreciate how annoying this can be. Factor in that as a client of a law firm you are often paying by the minute for these repeated explanations and you will appreciate why this is a common client complaint. A few simple conversations, with the client and the lawyer you are handing over to, can remove these aggravating factors.

12.5.2 **Managing clients**

The key to good client relationships is to manage the client's expectations. For example, if a client is calling several times a day to check your progress, you clearly need to explain to her that you will provide a regular update and this will be a more cost-effective way for her to monitor your progress. Similarly, a client who expects you to be available to her or deliver work at unsociable hours needs to understand that this may be either unnecessary or may warrant a higher fee. The best time to discuss and establish all of this is at the outset, before the client instructs you.

12.5.3 **SRA Code of Conduct 2011**

You have read at 12.1.3 that lawyers must be aware of ethics (see also 6.3.4). The Solicitors Regulation Authority, which regulates the profession, has a Code of Conduct which solicitors must follow. Chapter 1 of the Code sets out obligations regarding client care. The Code reinforces the conclusions drawn above by placing an obligation on solicitors to provide clients with sufficient information about the services they require, how those services will be delivered, and how much they will cost. It also details how solicitors should make clients aware of their complaints procedure.

As referred to above, the Solicitors Regulation Authority also has requirements about how you must maintain confidentiality when dealing with clients. Students learn about this Code during their vocational stage of training, but useful information can be found on the Solicitors

Regulation Authority website, details of which are set out in the 'Further reading' section at the end of this chapter.

12.5.4 **Feedback**

It is good practice to seek feedback from any customer when you complete work for them. You may already have provided feedback to your university, for example on your course materials or the teaching you have received. This is so that the university can listen to your opinion, address any issues you raise, and ensure it continues to do everything that receives positive feedback. Thinking carefully about how you provide such feedback will develop your employability skills. For example, it is likely that you have been able to provide feedback anonymously to date, which has benefits in terms of freeing you to give your honest opinion, but has the drawback of allowing you to say things that you would not say to someone's face. When you enter the professional world your feedback will be attributable, so it is worth developing now the skill of providing feedback in a way that is constructive and which you would feel comfortable delivering face to face. As a professional, you will not just receive feedback but you will also have to give feedback to your colleagues and delegates, for example. Some businesses, including law firms, have formal procedures in place for this. Everyone likes to be asked their opinion, and indeed if business clients request feedback in their own business they may think it strange if you do not ask their opinion of your work at the end of the process.

12.6 **Networking**

Networking is a key skill for professionals, and although lawyers may have been relatively slow to embrace the need for this skill, it is now accepted that networking is part of a lawyer's job. Networking involves building new business relationships in order to generate business opportunities. Some people are very comfortable approaching and speaking to new people, and actively enjoy it, and to those people this skill will come more naturally. However for many lawyers, junior and senior, it is one that can take them outside their comfort zone. As ever, the keys to mastering this skill are preparation and practice.

There are networking opportunities everywhere and accomplished networkers will not only be able to identify these opportunities, but also work them to their advantage. As a student, you may encounter face-to-face networking opportunities through work experience, pro bono work, sitting in on court hearings, attending talks and law fairs, and also simply by socialising with your peers, who one day may be prospective and sought-after clients or employers. Social media such as Twitter and Facebook and the practice of blogging have also opened up networking opportunities online.

When you meet potential clients or employers, as the case may be, you want them to remember your name. If you have been given a name badge, wear it. It will be most prominent if you wear it on the side of your body you shake hands with. If you do not have a name badge, you need to develop another strategy to make sure the people you wish to secure as business contacts remember your name. If you have a business card, you can give them your card. Ask if they have a card, as not only do you want them to remember your name, you also need to remember theirs. If you are attending an event, it is helpful if you can see the attendee list in advance. Some event organisers are very good in this regard, and will send the attendee list, either directly to you or to the person in your organisation who has arranged your attendance. It is worth asking if one is available in advance. If it is not, there is often a sign-in sheet at the door of the event, and a quick glance can reveal whether there is anyone attending who you already know or who you would specifically like to make a business contact.

Then you need to start speaking to people. This is sometimes referred to as 'working the room'. It can be difficult to approach people, but remember that they too will be open to networking opportunities and are likely to welcome you. Use your communication skills, including good eye contact and body language, to signal to someone that you would like to join them.

Once you have the attention of the person you would like to meet, you need to be able to engage them. You can prepare in advance what you might be able to say if the conversation does not flow naturally from the outset. Remember that the other person is not privy to your preparation, so do not decide to talk about something so esoteric that, while impressive, will not allow the other person to participate in the conversation. The morning's headlines, or even something as simple as the good old weather, will be enough for most people to start the flow of conversation.

Another skill you will need is to be able to exit from a conversation. A good networker will seek to circulate as much as possible. Do not be inhibited about doing this (indeed the person you are speaking to will also want time to speak to others), but obviously there is a technique to exiting in a polite fashion. Classic techniques include excusing yourself to go to the toilet. Clearly however you cannot use this too many times. Going to get a glass of water or sandwich can also help you to exit in a polite fashion.

If you have been attending a talk, do not underestimate the value of staying behind to thank the speaker. Most attendees file out immediately, yet the five minutes after the talk can be an excellent opportunity for networking. Speakers will feel at ease, and will be happy to hear some feedback and answer questions which show that you have listened to and enjoyed what they had to say.

Remember to follow up the contacts you have made. Sending a short follow-up email, or, if appropriate, a short telephone call to say how you enjoyed meeting them, is a good idea. Social media, for instance the LinkedIn platform, can also be helpful to secure an ongoing contact, and this is explored further below. Use your instinct and skills to determine what it is appropriate to say in this follow-up communication. Depending on the individual concerned, and how your conversation went, sometimes it is not appropriate to do anything other than say thank you, while at other times a suggestion that you meet for coffee, or an expression of interest, such as in work experience or mentoring opportunities, can be appropriate and pay dividends.

Even reading this paragraph may have made your toes curl. To the uninitiated, networking can sound embarrassingly like you are trying to secure a date. In practice, take comfort from the fact that you will not be the only one in the room to be networking. It is now generally accepted that everyone in the room will be, or should be. Also appreciate the fact that most people will also feel a little out of their comfort zone. The more polished your networking skills, the more people will want to talk to you because, conversely, *you* will help to put *them* at ease.

Be aware that networking does not necessarily have immediate rewards. Do not feel frustrated if you attend an event and leave empty-handed, or people do not respond to your email. Networking will deliver benefits in the long term. It may only be after meeting someone for the fourth time, for example, that you feel comfortable in inviting that person to connect with you on LinkedIn, or to suggest you meet for a coffee. The only thing you can say with certainty is that if you do not attend events at all, you will definitely not extend your network.

You can practise your networking skills now. No matter how early a stage you are at in your career, you will already have a network you can access. Although they are likely to have no influence on getting you a training contract or other career just yet, your fellow students are excellent contacts as in the future they will go on to become lawyers and other professionals. The person you are sitting next to now might be the CEO of a company a law firm would love to bring in as a client in 15 years' time. Following the guidance in this book you can extend your current network to include alumni of your university and other legal professionals.

12.6.1 **Law fairs**

Law fairs offer a valuable opportunity to meet many firms under one roof. Many students choose to attend them, but often find themselves wandering rather aimlessly up and down many aisles of stands, perhaps managing to gather a few branded freebies on the way. Few students exploit their full potential.

At a law fair you will be able to speak to employees of many firms. Typically firms send a mixture of recruitment personnel, trainees, and other fee-earners. This is a huge expense for a firm, not least because the trainees and fee-earners are not fee-earning while they are at the fair. So think for a moment about why they bother to attend. They are hoping to attract good-quality candidates for training contracts. From this perspective, then, law fairs have the potential to be mini interviews where the firms have done all the work and come to meet you in one place. Put this way, it should be clear that no student considering a legal career should pass up the opportunity to attend a fair.

As many firms recruit years in advance, you should attend law fairs even in your first year of study. Although firms pay considerable sums to consultants to draft a set of values and to create a website which they feel reflects them uniquely, it is a common student observation that 'they all say the same thing'. The fairs offer a forum to meet and talk informally to firms and to get a real feel for their true culture and values.

The firms will be interested in meeting you. They will also expect you to be interested in meeting them. You need to prepare to make sure you leave the firm with a good impression of you and what you have to offer.

Preparation

The organisers of a law fair will circulate a list of attendees and a floor plan in advance of the fair. You need to study this to plan who to target, as the fairs are often so large you are unlikely to stumble across the firms you are looking for by accident. For example, if you are interested in working in a mid-sized regional firm which has a strong intellectual property presence, you need to work through the list in conjunction with a legal directory such as *Chambers and Partners* or the *Legal 500* and access to the firms' websites, and highlight those firms you would like to visit. Alternatively, if you have not yet narrowed your preference to that degree, you may like to make a varied selection of firms, from boutique practices to the largest Magic Circle firms, to start this process. Wherever you are in recognising where you want to practise, your aim should be to be able to produce a shortlist based on your experiences at the fair.

Presentation

Having drawn the conclusion that the fair offers an opportunity not unlike a mini interview, it follows that you should present yourself well. You will be making an impression on the law firms that you meet, and you should dress to convey the impression you would like to make. There is guidance at 12.1.3 about how to dress for an interview. You may feel more comfortable dressing in something a little more relaxed than a suit, however the guidance about general presentation in terms of your hair, shoes, and so on is just as applicable for law fairs.

Execution

Once you are at the fair, with a plan of action, you can expect to feel a little nervous. Take courage though, that the firms will appreciate that you might find the prospect of speaking to them quite daunting. If you can appear polite, well informed, and work on developing a veneer of confidence, this is all you need. The firms will want to speak to you, but this is easier for them if they have some information about you. Introducing yourself by name, shaking hands and telling them what you are studying, where, and what you are enjoying will help to start a conversation and strike up a rapport.

You should not ask questions you should already know the answer to. These include anything you could reasonably be expected to find on the firm's website. If you have prepared in advance you should already know the basics. This is not to say asking questions is wrong, far from it, but you should prepare questions which help to give you the edge in any subsequent application to the firm. For example, do not ask where the firm is based, or whether it has a property department (both of which you should have researched already), but, for example, you might ask whether the firm is planning to expand, geographically or strategically. Subtly show the firm that you have done your homework about them. Tell the firm what you are enjoying, and sound enthusiastic. Ask what you can be doing to impress in this area, give examples of what you are already doing, and what in the area has taken your interest.

After the fair, use the experience to prepare a shortlist of firms which you liked, and make a note of anything you learned which could help your application to that firm. A well-placed tweet can be helpful in putting a marker in the sand that you spoke to the firm, but be selective as the firms will be able to see who else you are tweeting.

12.6.2 **Mentors**

Having a mentor is a long-established and valued process by which you are guided by someone who has reached the place you are aiming for. The process has benefits for both the mentor and the mentee, and you will find that practising lawyers are often keen to take on the role of mentor. There are various ways of finding a mentor, and most universities have formal schemes which you can join. This is another valuable way to gain an insight into the profession, and learn valuable wider lessons about being a professional. Increasingly universities are harnessing their alumni network to help with mentoring current students, so this is a route you may be able to explore. Social networking may also lend itself to a more informal version of mentoring, as discussed above. Finally, do not forget the value in mentoring, and being mentored by, your fellow students. You will all have different skills and experiences to share and learn from, and appreciating at this early stage that you have something worthwhile to share will help you to reflect and identify your own individual strengths that you can showcase at interview.

12.6.3 **Work experience**

Employers will expect to see that you have sought and found work experience. Work experience will help you to develop your employability skills as well as give you an opportunity to impress those you are working with and learn what goes on in a law firm or in chambers. Mini-pupillages, vacation schemes, law tasters, opportunities to work as a paralegal, and other informal work experience are therefore things you need to seek out actively, and the sooner you do this, the better.

12.6.4 **Pro bono**

Pro bono means 'for the public good' and pro bono initiatives provide a superb opportunity to provide advice to real clients while helping members of society to access legal advice which they could not otherwise afford. There are numerous initiatives, covering the full spectrum of legal work. Universities often run law clinics in partnership with practice or charities, and there are also other external pro bono schemes, such as the Innocence Network UK. LawWorks is the Solicitors' Pro Bono Group. Together with the Bar Pro Bono Unit and the CILEx Pro Bono Trust, it forms part of the National Pro Bono Centre in Chancery Lane. Further information on pro bono is available online, for example on the website of ProBonoUK and on the Law Careers website. Further details are provided in the 'Further reading' section at the end of this chapter.

12.7 **Marketing**

Most businesses realise that they have to market the goods they are selling or the services they are providing, but some businesses will be more naturally adept at marketing than others. Lawyers do not tend to be natural salespeople. However, the market is now so competitive that everyone in the firm is expected actively to market their firm and bring in new business. In order to do this effectively, you need to understand the message that the firm wishes you to deliver. Most firms now have their aims, objectives, and/or strategy set out clearly on their website. When you join a firm, further information is likely to feature on the firm's intranet site. The earlier you are familiar with these selling messages, the better you will be at marketing. Of course the best form of marketing that you can deliver as a lawyer is to provide exceptional client service.

12.8 Information technology

There is no escape, you are likely to need sound IT skills wherever you work in today's world. From multinationals to local services such as your local car wash or gardener, businesses are using IT to increase their public profile and develop client relationships. The good news is that this is an area where youth is most definitely on your side. You are likely to have grown up around so much IT that your skills are well honed. Conversely, some of the partners in a law firm would not have had a single computer in their classroom during school and may have started out as a lawyer before mobile phones and the internet were in common use. You are therefore in a good position to dazzle them with your skills in this regard.

The firms will train you on their individual IT systems, which will include some or all of online time recording, dictation and precedent and information sharing systems. However the better you are with word-processing, spreadsheets, email, and typing, the more polished you will look and the more efficient you will be on arrival. Take advantage of the expertise you can tap into at university. Attend any courses you can which will polish your IT skills for the professional world.

12.9 Social media

Law firms are as alert to new business development opportunities as the next business and increasingly they are turning to social media platforms such as Twitter and Facebook to extend their reach. These platforms can also be useful networking opportunities for you as an individual. However, you must use them with care.

12.9.1 A word of caution

Remember that these are very public platforms, and you should not post anything on them which you would not be happy to say or show to a partner's face. Some professionals operate different Twitter accounts, one personal, and one professional. However, given the nature of the legal profession and the general availability of Twitter posts to the public at large, junior lawyers would be best advised to play safe and avoid using Twitter in a personal capacity. It is not uncommon for employers to check a prospective employee's Twitter feed. Clearly it is possible to use your feed to impress a potential employer if it evidences an interest in law or in other ways supports any claims you have made on your application form. However, your holiday snaps, or tweets about your latest big night out, might be best reserved for a more private forum. Facebook can be more private than Twitter, but you must take care to set your privacy preferences correctly, and choose your friends wisely. Again, given the potential for error it is advisable that you post only information that you would be happy for your employer to read.

12.9.2 Twitter

Twitter can be an effective networking tool if used correctly. By following firms and individuals in whom you have a professional interest, you can extend your professional network and access a wealth of relevant information, including employment opportunities. Tweeting itself improves your ability to summarise and distil information as you must restrict yourself to the limit of 140 characters. You can also increase your commercial awareness simply by following the right people then reading your timeline. Professionals, including employers and academics, tweet on a range of issues that can help you develop the skills in this book (see e.g. @missshephard which tweets about business law in practice, legal skills, commercial awareness, employability, law firms, and students). By re-tweeting or 'favouriting' tweets you can bring yourself to the attention of those you are following. However, if you are to do this you need to make a sustained effort. Several firms currently have a Twitter identity which is not managed on a regular basis, and this is revealed when they are copied into tweets which remain unanswered or are not commented on. If you no longer intend to maintain your account regularly, it is best to shut it down, otherwise you may well become known, but for the wrong reasons.

12.9.3 **Blogging**

A blog, or web log, is an online diary. There is extensive guidance available on the internet as to how you can create your own free blog. Maintaining a regular blog on a subject you are interested in, legal or otherwise, can help you to practise and improve your written communication skills and raise your profile among your professional network. You can use Twitter and Facebook to link to and promote your blog. Reading other people's legal blogs can also help to increase your own commercial awareness. Again, if you do decide to maintain a blog, take care to ensure the content is suitable for reading by a prospective employer.

12.9.4 **LinkedIn**

LinkedIn provides a professional social media platform on which you can showcase your curriculum vitae and capture your professional contacts, and it has been embraced by the legal sector. The process of putting together a profile will help you to focus your mind on your curriculum vitae, and the earlier you begin to think about your curriculum vitae the better it will be by the time you come to apply for a training contract. You will be able to link in to your peers immediately, and having your profile ready means that you are in a better position to capture any contacts you make while networking. The way the site works is that a standard message is sent to the contacts of your choosing, asking if they would like to connect with you. It is possible to personalise this standard message and this can be a good idea with contacts you are hoping to impress. As the site makes clear, however, you should only ask to connect to people you know well. As a rule of thumb, if the recipient will not be able to place you when your connect request arrives, you should probably not be sending them a contact request.

12.10 **The application process**

One of the reasons it is important to understand employability skills at an early stage in your studies is so that you will come across well when applying for a training contract or indeed any other graduate job.

Your careers adviser should have a wealth of information to help guide you through the law firm application process. You should consult a careers adviser, wherever you are studying, as soon as possible after you start your studies. Take as full advantage of the careers resources as you can. Find out any arrangements in place to contact alumni. Create a curriculum vitae the minute you start university and ask your careers adviser and personal tutor for help in identifying gaps and issues that you can work on while you are at university. Some tips about the application form and interview process are outlined below, to highlight how you can demonstrate your skills in the application process.

Further information is set out about presentations (12.10.4), group work (12.10.5), and socialising (12.10.6), which you may encounter on an assessment day or during any vacation schemes or work experience. It can be startlingly clear to an interviewer which candidates have not studied skills in a practical context, and which have. However, having read and engaged with the skills chapters in this book, you will be in a good position to show off your legal skills wherever you are currently in your legal career.

12.10.1 Timing your application for a training contract and vacation placement

The Law Careers website referred to in the 'Further reading' section of this chapter sets out firm specific application windows in relation to training contracts and work placements. The following will give you a sense of the general timescales of which you should be aware.

Larger law firms

The large law firms recruit two years in advance, so if you wish to apply to work for one of these firms you could be applying for interview in your *first year* of a two-year law degree or in your *second year* of a three-year law degree (hence the need to develop your employability skills now). If you manage to secure a training contract this way this would mean you could then complete your Diploma in Legal Practice immediately after your law degree and progress straight into your training contract.

Applications for both training contracts and vacations schemes tend to open in the autumn term, generally from October to December. Many vacation scheme applications close at the end of January, but some remain open as late as April. Training contract applications tend to close at the end of July. As the vast majority of these firms recruit from their vacation schemes, you should apply for both a vacation scheme and a training contract at the firm. Historically law firms did not take applications from first year students (on a three year degree) for vacation schemes, however this appears to be changing and more firms are introducing what they refer to as 'law tasters' for first year students.

You should look out for announcements that firms are recruiting to meet increased demand, as very occasionally the larger firms will realise they have under-recruited, perhaps as the market expands. Again, your careers adviser, Twitter, and your network of contacts will help in this regard.

Smaller law firms

Smaller firms recruit later, however the earlier you start to hone your employability skills, the better you will come across in any interview further down the line. These firms may recruit 12 to

18 months in advance, and may recruit trainees from their pool of paralegals. You should seek to obtain some work experience with these firms from your second year onwards, and if this goes well you may be able to secure part-time employment with these firms while you study. Generally these firms are more open to speculative applications.

12.10.2 **Application form**

The application form is likely to be the first impression you make on a law firm, so you need to make it stand out for the right reasons. Usually you will need to show that you have:

- a good academic record;
- good knowledge of the firm and the legal world (ideally referencing some work experience);
- the skills referred to in this book.

Many firms ask for forms to be typed and submitted electronically. Type in a word processing package first and apply a spelling and grammar check before you then cut and paste into the form. Despite the open acknowledgement that the application process for professional employment is highly competitive, it is all too common to find spelling and grammatical errors in submitted application forms. Firms receive huge amounts of forms and need to apply a filter system to identify which ones to reject. Those containing such errors typically will be rejected without further reading. You must not give the firms any easy excuse to reject your form. For firms which still require hand-written forms, it is obviously important that the form is legible and neatly presented. Follow any specific instructions, such as to write in capital letters using black ink. Failure to do so will help the employer narrow down the forms it needs to continue to read.

When composing the content of the form, of course you must highlight your strengths, but be aware that law firms remain relatively conservative places and so too many superlatives ('I am excellent at', 'I excel at') might dilute the overall effect. Analyse what you write from an objective perspective. If you are describing your academic results as excellent, consider whether they really are. Just because you describe results as excellent does not render them so. Be honest; identify what you think are your strong points and make sure your form highlights these strengths. Research the firm's stated objectives or strategy and make clear how your strengths will help the firm achieve its goals. Once you have identified your real strengths, do not be afraid to bring them to the interviewer's attention; it is not 'brash' or 'bragging', and you can be sure that the candidates before and after you will be drawing attention to what they do well.

It can come as a surprise to those new to the applications process that you also need to scrutinise your weaknesses. Is there anything in your record that stands out as being below your usual standard? If so, then you have two choices. You can either remain silent about it pending confirmation of an interview, or you can address the issue in the form. Whichever route you choose, be ready for an interviewer to ask you about your weaknesses. This is not necessarily a negative. Candidates who can show how they have learned from previous mistakes can make a very good impression. Those who refuse to acknowledge their mistakes will not come across well.

Don't be descriptive in your application. For example, if you worked in a bar in Corfu, say what you learned from it and how that will help the law firm's business needs, for example in terms of customer service, communication, language skills, punctuality, and complaints handling.

Analyse your form for any perceived inconsistencies, which you may need to explain either on the form itself or later if you are called for interview. For example, if you are applying to a corporate law firm, but your work experience to date has been with a high-street criminal practice, or you have chosen to study personal injury law, be prepared for an interviewer to question you about this. Again, it is not necessarily a negative, but being ill-prepared for what an interviewer considers an obvious question that your form raises will be deemed a negative.

12.10.3 **Interviews**

If you are called for interview you should feel a sense of achievement. You now have the opportunity to impress face to face. Naturally your communication skills (see Chapter 10) will be key in achieving this. First impressions count, so make sure you offer a firm handshake, look the part, pay attention to your body language and vocabulary, and are polite from the moment you arrive on the premises.

You are likely to feel nervous, but nevertheless you must be able to present with a veneer of confidence, both verbally and non-verbally. Try not to let nerves prevent your personality coming across. It is very easy for personable, enthusiastic individuals to turn unwittingly into overly intense, grim-faced interviewees. Remember that you want to convince the interviewer that she would like to work with you. Try to relax, smile, and make plenty of eye contact from the outset. You need to let your personality shine through the polished version of you that you are presenting to the interviewer. Never try to be someone you are not. It will be obvious to an interviewer and the chances are that the person you actually are is just as, or in fact more, appealing. Remember that you have been selected for interview on the basis of your application form, and this details all that *you* have achieved to date.

There are some techniques you can use to address the issue of nerves before an interview. Make sure that you arrive in good time. Aim to arrive at least an hour in advance, leaving plenty of time to allow for a late train or getting lost. When you arrive at the firm itself, you will be making an impression from the moment you open the door, so before you do that you may like to factor in some time to have a coffee nearby, where you can read through any notes, go through what you plan to say in your head, and check that you look presentable. If you can do all this 'off-site', the more professional and confident you will look when you arrive at the firm's offices.

Some students suffer more from anxiety than others. A certain level of anxiety can be helpful, as it can enhance your performance. However, if you know that anxiety is a particular problem for you, and can cause you to feel overwhelmed, you need to take steps to address this as it will inhibit your performance at interview. There are things that you can do to help. Regular exercise, relaxation, and talking to friends can all reduce stress levels which can lead to panic attacks, so try not to change your routine or isolate yourself in the run up to an interview, or spend too much time worrying about it. When you are at the interview, if you feel overcome, buy yourself some time by asking to be excused to go to the bathroom, practise good breathing techniques, and take a small bottle of water with you to sip as this can have a calming effect. Further guidance on how to control anxiety is set out in the 'Further reading' section at the end of this chapter.

During the interview process employers will be looking for good communication skills and in particular whether you can answer questions clearly, react appropriately, retain your composure, and listen to what others have to say. Your answers need to be fluent, comprehensive, and promote all those skills and experiences which, having read this book, you know that the employer is looking for. A good interviewer will help you to showcase your talents. However some interviewers do little in terms of guiding you through the process and simply ask open questions which leave it up to you to choose what to tell them. You need to be familiar with what you have written on your application form and show the interviewer that you (i) understand which skills they want you to have, and why, (ii) actually have those skills, and (iii) indeed can point to examples on your application form which prove this.

Do not be afraid of taking a moment to consider your answer before you speak. What can seem like a deafening silence to you is likely to sound simply like a natural pause from an interviewer's perspective. Remember that employers want employees to think carefully before they speak. Some employers will test whether you can do this specifically by asking you a question that you could not possibly have pre-prepared, for example 'what would you do with the Millennium Dome'? In fact, the actual answer to a question like this is unlikely to be of great import to the interviewer. Instead they will be looking to see how well you deal with the unexpected. If you did not pause for thought before such a question, your answer is unlikely to be good. You may start to stumble as you realise you need some thinking time, or in the heat of the moment you may simply say you do not know. This is not going to come across well. Instead, a candidate who responds by acknowledging that is an interesting question and requests a moment to think before answering is likely to come across well, even if ultimately his answer is not that feasible, such as 'I would turn it upside down and use it as a fairground ride'. You will not, of course be asked this example now as it was a topical question around the year 2000, but you can see how keeping up to date by reading a quality newspaper regularly, certainly in the month or so prior to interview, could give you an advantage in answering this type of question. Another example might be 'What should be done with the Olympic Stadium?', and there have been several press articles about whether the pitch is suitable for football club use, for example.

Conversely, make sure that your answers to any obvious questions, such as 'why law (or other profession)?', 'why this firm?', 'what is your main strength/ weakness?' or any question relating to the information on your application form, reveal that you have prepared well for the interview. Generally, you need to be prepared to talk about yourself, your interests, your strengths and weaknesses, challenges you have faced and how you tackled them, your team-working and leadership skills, what you are proud of, and precisely why the firm should choose you over another candidate.

You may also be asked questions about commercial awareness. Chapters 13 to 16 contain case studies and sample interview questions to get you thinking about how you might tackle these.

For all these questions the STAR technique can help you to structure your answer well:

- **S**ituation—give context.
- **T**ask—describe the challenge, why you were facing it, and the expectations of that challenge.
- **A**ction—describe what you did and how you did it.
- **R**esults—explain what they were and how you quantified them (e.g. did you obtain some recognition, make any savings?).

Being an impressive interviewee is a skill in itself, and as with all skills it improves with practice. Seek and take any opportunity to participate in a practice interview, and if possible record and review the practice interview yourself. Finally, remember that if you operate a reflective practice, then even if you do not succeed at interview, the process itself will have been a valuable one in terms of improving your interviewing skills for the next time. Remember you only need to succeed in one application to get into the profession, so stay positive.

12.10.4 Presentations

Chapter 10 considered the skill of presenting, and it is not unusual for an employer to test this skill by asking you to give a presentation as part of the assessment process (including on a vacation or other work experience scheme). This could be sprung on you when you arrive, or you may have been asked to prepare it in advance. The firm may set the title for you, or you might be able to select a topic of your own. Your audience may include other candidates, solicitors, partners, and/or members of the recruitment team.

   You will usually be given a target time frame for delivery of the presentation. Practise your presentation to make sure it will not go on too long, and have extra items you can bring in, or items you can cut out, to give you some flexibility to hit the target timescale. Often you will be given the option of preparing visual aids. When preparing these, bear in mind how long the presentation is and keep them to a minimum; a slide show may help to put you in your comfort zone but it rarely makes for a good presentation. The best presenters do not use cards, but if you really cannot do without a prompt, restrict yourself to bullet points on cards and never read out a pre-prepared presentation.

   When structuring you presentation make sure that it has a clear beginning, where you signpost the audience as to what is to come, a middle, and a definite end which draws every-thing together. In delivering your presentation, make sure you use the communication skills outlined in Chapter 10, and engage the audience by using effective body language (posture, eye contact, no distracting habits), looking professional (no leaning on the table or rushing around the room), projecting your voice (ask the audience if they can hear you), and trying to relax and smile. If you do not seem to be enjoying your presentation, the audience will really struggle to do so. Humour can be effective, but avoid being flippant and bear in mind you are unlikely to have had time to get to know your audience well. Remember to keep it simple. If you try to include too much detail you are likely to overrun. Include the essential informa-tion, and present it succinctly and clearly. Remember to try to relax, be yourself, and smile.

12.10.5 Group work

Assessment days can also include group exercises where the firm will test your team-working skills and how you work with others. You should bear in mind everything you have learned from Section 12.2 and seek to demonstrate you have these skills. Often the firm will have tasked particular employees to watch specific people. So the observer sitting at the back of the room might nevertheless be watching your every move. They will be looking to see what role you play in the group. You absolutely must make a contribution. However you must not be seen to dominate the discussion at the expense of the quieter members of the group. Showing that you have noticed someone who has not had the chance to contribute, and giv-ing her the chance to speak (without putting her on the spot) will work in your favour. If you always take the easy role, such as writing up others' ideas without contributing any of your own, the observers will notice. They will also be looking to see how you handle any disagreements between the group members, and whether you have any powers of persuasion.

12.10.6 Socialising

Often lunch or drinks are factored into an assessment day (or vacation scheme) to allow you to meet the people who work there. Do not make the mistake of letting your hair down too much at these events. While they have more of a sociable element than the rest of the day, there is no doubt that you are still being assessed. Enjoy these occasions, certainly, as they represent another opportunity to show how well you fit with the firm, its employees, and culture. However the clever applicant will use them as an opportunity to find out more information about the firm and its people, particularly information which can be used later in the assessment day. A simple mention in passing of the name of a person who is interviewing you later can often turn up a few useful facts (e.g. 'she is *the name* in corporate at the moment', 'I hope you're a United fan', 'that's him over there', 'he's a man of few words'). Often those attending the lunch or drinks will be asked if anyone particularly stood out, so use your networking skills to your advantage (see Section 12.6) and circulate, wearing your name badge, making a good impression, to give you the edge over other good candidates who have not yet honed that particular skill.

You can practise this skill now by attending more formal events at university. You will find that drinks receptions after talks are good places to try out these skills.

 Summary

- Technical ability is important for a lawyer, but the modern lawyer needs other skills, which are relevant to all businesses.
- Business skills such as client care, networking, marketing, and using IT and social media effectively are very important.
- Employers are not looking for clones. You need to show how your specific combination of skills will help the business to achieve its goals.
- A good team comprises individuals with complementary skills who work together effectively to achieve a common goal.
- Employability skills improve with practice and preparation.

Thought-provoking questions

1. What kind of personal characteristics would you like your colleagues to have? Consider ranking these attributes in order of importance, starting with those which you consider essential. Do you think you have these characteristics yourself? If so, are you able to show others that you have them?

2. What role do you tend to take when working in a group? Is this the role you like to take? What other role do you think you might flourish in?

3. If today you unexpectedly happened to meet a lawyer who works for a law firm you want to apply to, what would you say to him?

4. Think of a famous brand. How do you know about it? What did the company do to market its brand so well? What can a junior lawyer do to promote the firm's brand?

What the professionals say

What tips would I give a law student about employability? When it comes down to it, you can have the best legal knowledge in the world, but if you can't get on with people, they aren't going to trust you or engage with you. My mum advised me 'Do right by people and they do right by you' and it was sound advice for practice. Start the process now of learning 'people skills'. I'm passionate about pro bono work. If you have that on your cv, you have evidence that you got up and did something for someone else; that you've engaged at a human level. Pro bono also helps you to develop working relationships now at a level you are unlikely to be able to replicate until quite far progressed though your legal career.

Barry Matthews, Director of Legal Affairs at ITV plc

What did I learn from my work experience at ITV? I now understand the context in which law operates. As students we learn the law, but when I experienced law in practice I understood how it affected the client. The lawyers were in meetings sat next to and working together with people from all areas of the business, contributing to business ideas and saying things like, 'If you want to do that (commercially), then you have to do this (legally)'. I also learned that the skills I have acquired as a law student and in life are transferable into the workplace; it is not all about bestowing knowledge. For example I was acutely aware that I needed to be organised in everything I did, and I was reading and analysing documentation, such as file notes of meetings, and summarising information into timelines. I also undertook some legal research and drafted some terms and conditions. As a result I can now complete application forms with a better understanding of what employers expect from me as a lawyer. Rather than say, 'I am very interested in business law', I have clear examples to draw on to underpin what I am saying, for example 'I know that in team meetings that I would be expected to come up with creative solutions which not only work from a legal perspective but which also move the business towards its strategic goal and that aspect interests me because ...'. When I consider the application forms I completed before my work experience I can really see the difference work experience has made. It has really switched me on to an area of law I might otherwise have dismissed and made me enthusiastic and more informed about what lies ahead.

Serra Pheby, 2011 GDL student, The College of Law Manchester.

What advice would I give to mature students? It is easy to convince yourself that age and maturity may be viewed negatively by law firms. From my experience, nothing could be further from the truth. Your life experiences are attributes which will positively differentiate you from many of your legal contemporaries. Many of the skills which you have acquired to date will be transferable to your studies and later on in to practice.

In my first degree (pharmacy), which I studied straight after leaving school, I used to sit silently at the back of the lecture theatre, too unsure of myself to engage with the lecturers. By the time I came to study law several years later, I was determined to maximise the opportunity to learn. I was confident enough to ask questions and interacted with the tutors without fear of embarrassment. As a result, I really engaged with the subject and this undoubtedly came across during my training contract interviews.

During those interviews, I demonstrated to my potential employers how my experience as a pharmacist would benefit their business as a law firm. I already knew how to communicate effectively and behave professionally; I had acquired customer care skills; and I had background knowledge about the pharmacy sector which would benefit the firm's business. The bottom line is that many employers look for positive attributes in candidates which will differentiate them from all the other applicants clutching a 2:1. Work history, maturity and life experience are all positive differentiators for the mature student. Be prepared to use them confidently to your advantage.

To students who are not mature students, my advice would be to get stuck in to your studies and try not to worry too much about what others think. And invite the mature students to the odd party or two.

Richard Hough, Pharmacist and Associate Solicitor at Brabners Chaffe Street LLP

I attended a careers day at the university at the beginning of term. Some of the advice from the firms was a reality check, but the best thing I did was speak to the firms after they had finished their talks. I asked one of the firms if they might be interested in giving me some work experience, and they said they didn't really do this, but one of the lawyers gave me their card. I met the same person again at a pro bono fair a month later and following that I sent her a follow up email and she asked when I might be available. Around the same time I attended a law fair and talked to another representative of the same firm. She was really helpful and gave me some advice as to how to respond. I called the firm after the law fair, was given a telephone interview and I am now starting work experience with them in a month's time.

I have learnt that it is important to be proactive. My advice is to be prepared for rejection; do not let this dishearten you. Also ensure you start today what others will do tomorrow, and attend the careers days, pro bono events, law fairs, talks and other events that your university offers and publicises.

Mohammad Usman Choudhry, 2012 student, Postgraduate Diploma in Law, Manchester Metropolitan University

 ## Further reading

Solicitors Regulation Authority website: http://www.sra.org.uk
—this sets out information relevant to the profession including the Suitability Test for prospective solicitors (see 12.1.3), and the Code of Conduct (see 12.5.3).

Belbin website: http://www.belbin.co.uk; Myers & Briggs Foundation website: http://www.myersbriggs.org
—these both contain assessment tools to determine how you can work to your full potential in a team (see 12.2.2).

Bruce W. Tuckman, 'Developmental Sequence in Small Groups' (1965) 63 *Psychological Bulletin* **384 (also available from http://dennislearningcenter.osu.edu under 'Research')**
—this article provides further reading on team-working, and details a group development model by Bruce Tuckman which is commonly referred to in business.

Institute of Paralegals website: http://www.theiop.org
—if you are considering becoming a paralegal this website is a useful source of information.

LawWorks website: http://www.lawworks.org.uk; Innocence Network UK website: http://www.innocencenetwork.org.uk; ProBonoUK website: http://www.probonouk.net; National Pro Bono Centre website: http://www.nationalprobonocentre.org.uk
—these four websites all contain information about pro bono initiatives (see 12.6.4).

Law Careers website: https://www.lawcareers.net
—a resource for future lawyers, which works with the Law Society. Among other things it publishes information on pro bono (see 12.6.4), and on application deadlines (see 12.10.1).

Mind website: http://www.mind.org.uk/help/diagnoses_and_conditions/anxiety
—an online booklet on the causes of anxiety, its effects, and how to manage it.

 For the authors' reflections on the thought-provoking questions, additional self-test questions, podcasts offering a variety of perspectives on legal systems and skills, and a library of links to useful websites, visit the free Online Resource Centre *at* **http://www.oxfordtextbooks.co.uk/orc/slorach/.**

13

Businesses and the business environment

 Learning objectives

After studying this chapter you should be able to:

- Appreciate the importance of commercial awareness.
- Explain the main types of legal business structure, their organisation, and management.
- Explain different markets, sectors, and industries in which businesses operate, and the role of consumers within these markets.
- Understand a simple supply chain.
- Recognise the impact of competition within different markets.

Introduction

So far in this book, you have looked at what the law is, the legal systems that govern it, where to find it, and the legal skills that you need to use once you have found it. You have also thought about employability skills: the personal and professional skills that you need to get your training contract, and to succeed once you get into practice. It should be clear to you now that if you think that your career will *just* be about giving legal advice, then that career will be short lived. Lawyers, like everyone else involved in business of any sort, need to show commercial awareness. We explore what commercial awareness is and why you need it. We then look at law firms and their clients and the relevance of these issues for lawyers, but, in fact, commercial awareness is something that all students need, whether they they hope to be involved with the law, or any other profession or industry.

Chapters 14 and 15 introduce you to the fundamentals of commercial awareness. We look at business structures and organisation, basic economics, financial markets and banks, accounts, and insolvency. You may be wondering why any of these are relevant. At the beginning of your career, you cannot be expected to have the same commercial understanding as a partner who has been practising for 20 years. However, commercial awareness is an essential aspect of your professional development, and it is never too soon to start developing this knowledge. Commercial awareness is crucially important when completing your application forms and at interview. Law firms, and indeed all employers, expect you to be able to demonstrate a wide range of skills and competencies. An ability to learn is crucial, and you need to show that you have this ability, both before you get into practice and once you are in practice.

13.1 **What is commercial awareness?**

The problem with commercial awareness is that there is no neat definition. The term means different things to different people. If you think for a minute about what it means to you, you may come up with something along the lines of 'Commercial awareness is understanding how businesses work.' That is fine as far as it goes, but for lawyers, it means a bit more than this. Lawyers will have clients which are businesses, companies, partnerships, or sole traders; however, they will also have clients who are individuals and who come to them for advice on matters unrelated to business, for example buying a house or getting a divorce. Businesses are run by individuals, the directors of the company, or the partners in a firm. Businesses also have employees, customers, or clients. These are the people with whom lawyers will deal on a day-to-day basis.

You will be faced with typical concerns of those clients, both individuals and businesses: personal, financial, and legal. Understanding those concerns is the first step towards commercial awareness. Then there is one more step. Whether the clients are businesses or individuals, they will be affected by the same external factors. All matters will be affected by what is going on in the world: in other words, by the wider context within which the client operates, whether it be economic, political, social, or financial. So commercial awareness is about understanding businesses and the business and wider environment, which this chapter aims to help you to do, but is also about all of these other factors: your clients' personal concerns, the financial implications, and the wider environment in which they are operating.

You have seen in Chapter 9 that problem solving requires a lawyer to work through several stages before advising the client. The first thing that you will do is establish the facts (why they have come to you?) and then establish the main issues and the client's concerns (what are the client's objectives?). Usually, the client will tell you what she thinks are the relevant facts, what her concerns are, and what she is hoping to achieve. (These are her expectations.) The problem is that this will never be quite the whole story.

Once a client has outlined the matter about which she is consulting a lawyer, and explained her objectives, the next considerations will generally be financial: how much will the matter cost, what will be the financial consequences, and how can the client raise the finance needed to proceed. Once you start to dig a bit deeper, you will find out there are other relevant facts or concerns that the client has not told you about, which may change her objectives. Clients have 'latent' (or hidden) concerns and objectives, often based on facts that they have not even thought about. If you are commercially aware, you should be able to spot them.

The flowchart in Figure 13.1 shows the underlying considerations which lawyers should take into account when advising a client, and how they fit into the problem solving model that you were introduced to in Chapter 9.

Consider this straightforward example (Example 1).

Example 1

You are instructed by a client who tells you that he manages a shop in your local high street. A customer owes £2,500 for goods purchased on credit. The client wants to sue the customer for the amount owed.

The objective appears straightforward. He wants to you to issue proceedings to reclaim the £2,500. You advise the client accordingly.

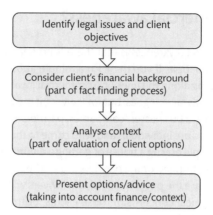

Figure 13.1 Commercial awareness steps

However, if you dig a bit deeper, you can see that this is not necessarily the advice which you should have given.

Example 1 (continued)

You are instructed by a client who tells you that he manages a shop in your local high street. **The shop is part of a national chain of retailers, making annual sales of over £1 million a year. An important corporate customer** owes £2,500. **The customer places regular orders, and there have never been any problems over payment before**. The client wants to sue the customer for the amount owed.

The objective is the same, but is that actually what is best for the company? Factors you should advise on include:

1. The amount owed is comparatively small—the company is a national chain. Does it really need to sue?

2. Litigation will be expensive—if the costs are going to amount to, say £1,500, is it going to be worth it?

3. You are told that the customer places regular orders—is it worth ruining this relationship for £2,500, especially if this is an oversight or a temporary blip?

4. In future, the client should conduct regular credit checks on customers.

None of this is legal advice (although point 2 is based on knowledge of a legal process). It is based on understanding the client's financial position, the environment in which he is operating, common sense, and experience. All of this is commercial awareness.

13.1.1 **Case studies**

These two case studies will help you to understand the importance of commercial awareness. The first is a question which students were asked to consider when applying for a holiday placement at a commercial firm: they were asked to summarise the impact of the BP oil spill in 2010 and to analyse the issues arising as a result. The second is a typical question which could have come up in any interview, legal or non-legal, corporate or non-corporate: what do you think should happen to the Olympic stadium? Once we have analysed these two questions, you will see why Chapters 14 and 15 are so important.

Case study 1

On 22 April 2010, one of BP's deep-water oil rigs in the Gulf of Mexico, the Deepwater Horizon, sank after an explosion. Eleven people died in the blast. The pipe which connected the wellhead to the rig became disconnected and began leaking oil, and the wellhead itself was leaking. Several attempts to reattach the pipe and stop the leak failed and 60,000 barrels of oil per day were leaking into the ocean. It was the US's largest ever oil spill, threatening wildlife along the coast, and bringing the fishing and tourist industries to a halt. President Obama suspended deep-water drilling in the Gulf of Mexico for six months. BP has incurred clean-up and other costs amounting to nearly $40 billion and suffered immense reputational damage as a result.[1]

What issues arise here?

This was an environmental and ecological disaster on an unprecedented scale. For BP, the legal issues resulted in huge pay-outs: 11 people died; BP has incurred the largest ever criminal fine in US history ($4.5 billion, or £2 billion);[2] it has settled compensation claims from fishermen and others whose livelihoods have been threatened; and been responsible for the clean-up costs. A quick internet search reveals that as of June 2012 BP had paid out a total of $8.8 billion (£5.6 billion) to individual, business, and government claims.[3] However, the effects are much more wide-reaching than the environmental and legal consequences.

First, BP is one of the world's largest multi-national public companies, with revenues of $375,517 million in 2011.[4] It is the third-largest company operating in the energy sector (after Royal Dutch Shell and Exxon Mobil[5]). Before you even start analysing the problem, consider whether you know the answer to the following questions:

1. What is a public company?
2. What is a multi-national company?
3. What do we mean by the energy sector?

BP's board of management was criticised for its management of the situation, especially in the US. BP's CEO, Tony Hayward, took part in a yacht race off the Isle of Wight while the oil washed up on the US coast,[6] and declared at the height of the crisis that he wanted 'his life back'. Shortly afterwards, he resigned.[7] Do you know:

1. What is the role of the board of directors of a public company?
2. What is a CEO?

---

[1] 'BP's PR campaign fails to clean up reputation after oil spill', *The Guardian*, 14 April 2011.
[2] 'BP gets record US criminal fine over Deepwater disaster', *BBC News*, 15 November 2012, http://www.bbc.co.uk/news/business-20336898.
[3] Jaimie Grierson, 'BP still paying for Gulf of Mexico oil spill', *The Independent*, 31 July 2012.
[4] http://www.bp.com.
[5] 'Global 500, 2012 annual ranking of world's largest corporations', *CNN Money*, http://www.money.cnn.com.
[6] 'BP chief Tony Hayward criticised for yacht trip', *BBC News*, 20 June 2010, http://www.bbc.co.uk/news/10359528.
[7] 'BP's Tony Hayward resigns after being "demonised and vilified" in the US', *The Telegraph*, 27 July 2010.

BP's share price fell sharply in June 2010, which means that the value of the company plunged. To meet its losses, BP is selling assets worth $38 billion (£24.4 billion) by 2013.[8] At one point *The Guardian* estimated that £45 billion (36%) had been wiped off the value of the company[9] and there were rumours that BP could face insolvency. This raises further questions:

1. What do you know about shares?
2. Do you know why share prices affect the value of a company?
3. What are assets?
4. Would you know where to look for a valuation of a company?
5. What is insolvency?

BP is one of the UK's largest companies, so inevitably millions are invested in its shares by UK shareholders. The fall in BP shares led a drop in the FTSE 100 leading shares.[10] As well as individual investors, institutional investors such as pension funds and unit trusts have significant holdings in BP. As well as the fall in the value of the shares, the company suspended dividend payments to investors. Can you answer the following questions:

1. What is the stock market?
2. What is the FTSE 100?
3. What are pension funds and unit trusts?
4. Why are share prices important economically?
5. What is a dividend?

The disaster significantly reduced oil production, especially in the US. This led to supply shortages of the world's most valuable commodity, oil. The result was a rise in oil prices, as the US was forced to source oil on the world commodities markets to meet demand. Oil is a fundamental raw material. It is not just the fact that petrol is more expensive at the pumps, but oil in one form or another is used throughout the supply chain, increasing manufacturing and food costs. In the UK, the knock-on effect was a rise in inflation threatening the fragile economic recovery. Further questions are:

1. What is a commodity?
2. What are commodity markets?
3. What sort of resource are raw materials?
4. What is the supply chain?
5. Why are supply and demand so important?
6. What is inflation?
7. Why does rising inflation have an effect on the economy?

---

[8] Jaimie Grierson, 'BP still paying for Gulf of Mexico oil spill', *The Independent*, 31 July 2012.

[9] Graeme Wearden, 'BP oil spill: shares fall further', *The Guardian*, 2 June 2010.

[10] Terry McAlister, 'BP facing multimillion-dollar legal claim from British pension fund', *The Observer*, 30 May 2010.

How did you do? It does not matter if the answer is 'Not very well.' The point here is that one question, which appears on the face of it to be about legal issues, gives rise to a large number of underlying issues covering economics, financial markets, business structures and organisation, accounts, and insolvency, and raises the sort of questions which you may meet in interviews. It does not matter how well you analyse the legal issues; if you do not know some of the basics of the topics that we are going to cover, you will not stand out. Incidentally, the firm that set this question was an LLP (see 15.2.4). If you got an interview with this firm, what would you find out first? At the end of the chapter, there is a question which you can answer on this.

If you are not considering corporate practice, you may be thinking that none of this has any relevance to you. This is not the case. You can easily give yourself away at interviews, by something as simple as calling a partnership a company, or not knowing why a company is a public or private company.

Throughout these chapters, we are going to look at some typical interview questions, which we will refer to as 'Sample interview questions', so that you can see how you might be expected to apply your commercial knowledge, in both corporate and non-corporate contexts. As a general rule, legal interview questions divide into categories: personal questions, legal questions, questions about the legal profession, questions about the firm, and current affairs questions of the type: 'Give your opinion on ...'. Case study 2 is an example of the latter. Case study 2 is the Olympic stadium example that was also mentioned in Chapter 10. Students were asked: 'What do you think should happen to the Olympic stadium now that the Games are over?' This is the sort of question you could be asked at any interview.

Case study 2

The Olympic stadium was built with public money at an estimated cost of £423 million. It had a capacity of 80,000 people for the Olympics, but was built in such a way that this can be reduced to 25,000. With the Olympics over, what do you think should be done with it? What are the issues here?

You have probably given no more than a passing thought to the Olympic stadium since the Games were over, and may have no opinion at all about what should be done with it. However, you need to provide an answer that shows that you are commercially aware.

If you can, you could start by showing you know what is going on, and putting the future of the stadium in context. You may know that the Olympic Park is going to be developed to provide housing in Stratford: over 6,000 new homes (a third will be affordable housing), with schools, nurseries, and playgrounds eventually will be built. If you do, it shows that you follow the news and are aware of topical issues. The need for housing, and especially affordable housing, is a topical social issue. In November 2012, the *Daily Telegraph* reported that 1,500 square miles of open countryside would have to be built on to solve a 'massive housing shortfall'.[11] You will consider some social issues when you look at life events in

[11] Christopher Hope, 'Government minister warns: "We must develop a third more land" to meet housing demand', *The Telegraph*, 27 November 2012.

Chapter 16, for example the problem for young couples buying their first house. Shortage of housing has fuelled property prices and rents have gone up, particularly in London. This is also an economic issue: prices are dependent on supply and demand, which we will consider in Chapter 14.

The stadium will need to fit in with this development. The Mayor of London has said that it will remain in public ownership, and bids for the lease have been received from four football clubs and from Formula One racing. You can give your opinion on the suitability of these bids. Will the athletics track be preserved? (Yes, according to the Mayor of London.) The future of British sport and especially school sport has been highly topical recently. (Incidentally, do you know who the current Mayor of London is?)

You could look at the transition from public to private ownership of the site. Responsibility for the development lies with the London Legacy Development Corporation (LLDC), which describes itself as 'a public sector, not for profit organisation' (a quango), set up after the Olympics by the Mayor of London.[12] There are a number of private and public companies involved in the development of the site. This will be a valuable boost for the construction industry. Can you talk with confidence about the public sector, not for profit organisations, or the difference between public and private companies?

Where will the money come from? The LLDC is looking for private as well as public finance, and has asked for pension fund investment amongst other sources. What do you know about investment and pension funds?

You could talk about what has happened to the Athens and Beijing stadiums after the 2004 and 2008 Olympics. These turned out to be white elephants. The Athens stadium, which was occasionally used for concerts, has fallen into disrepair, partly as a result of the euro and Greek government debt crisis. This gives you an opportunity to show that you can put seemingly unrelated issues into the wider economic context.

Chapters 14 to 16 are intended to provide the answers to some of these questions. You may not need the information all at once, but at some point either during your studies, when you go through the application process, or when you start a job, you will. As your career develops, you will need to adapt your knowledge for different clients, different firms, and as the world changes. The topics covered in this chapter are a starting point. If you look at some of the 'Thought-provoking questions' at the end of these chapters, they will give you an opportunity to practise this sort of analysis once you have read these chapters.

13.1.2 **Why you need it**

Building up commercial awareness cannot begin too early. It is relevant from the beginning of a degree course and into practice.

Studying

Having a level of commercial awareness can help to contribute to an understanding of various areas of black letter (academic) law.

---

[12] http://www.londonlegacy.co.uk.

Example 2

Take contract law: it is sometimes said that 'Contract follows the money'. If you look at some contract cases, you can see that an understanding of the economic context at the time throws light on these. In the 18th century, Britain's wealth was based on its maritime trade: many 18th-century cases involve ships. Until the 20th century, a person's main asset was often his horse: there are a huge number of cases involving horses. In the 19th century, the advent of the railway transformed Britain—leading to a number of railway cases. In the 20th century, technology has transformed the economy: suddenly, computers became the subject of some very important cases.

Employability

As you have seen in Chapter 12, from the moment you start applying for a training contract, employers will want to know that you are tuned into the wider world, that you have the ability to meet your clients' expectations and add value to your legal advice. They will expect you to know the law, but you have to show that 'edge' which sets you apart from other applicants. Chapter 12 explained the process, but we are going to consider this from a commercial perspective.

1. The first hurdle is the application form. Application forms will contain questions that are designed to test your commercial knowledge. You have already looked at the 2010 BP oil spill example as a good illustration of the sort of commercial understanding which will help to make your application stand out.

2. Once you get to an interview or assessment day, the questions will take this a little further. The Olympic stadium question is an example of how to use a seemingly non-commercial question to demonstrate some commercial knowledge.

3. Finally, you will be expected to have an insight into the firm itself, its structure, its position within the market, and who its clients are, and their position within the market in which they operate, so you will need to do some detailed research before you go. We will look at the sort of information you are looking for in Chapters 15 and 16.

Example 3

You have an interview with a commercial firm. You have researched the firm and its clients and know it acts for a number of manufacturers whose main export markets are in Europe. You are asked to comment on the impact of the euro zone crisis. Let's assume you have some idea about the economic causes and the consequences. However, you will impress your interviewers more if you relate these to the firm's clients, commenting on the disadvantages of a strong pound for exporters. You could ask whether the clients are considering or in a position to expand into new markets, such as the growing markets of Brazil, Russia, India, and China (the **BRIC** economies) especially now that the euro is in trouble.

Practice

Once you get into practice, you will see that law firms are businesses (see Chapter 15). A lawyer has to understand how businesses work. The partners of the firm will expect it, so that the lawyer can contribute to the success of the firm, and the clients will expect it, so that the lawyer can contribute to their business and financial success. We all know that the world of work is an increasingly competitive environment. Working as a lawyer is no exception. You need to stand out from the crowd by showing skills over and above your legal knowledge. One of the ways that you can do this is by demonstrating commercial awareness.

13.1.3 How to get it?

So how do you develop (and show that you are developing) commercial awareness? Much of this has been covered in Chapter 6, but we are now going to put a commercial slant on this.

Skills

Commercial awareness is often about people, your clients, and managing their expectations. The legal skills that you will be covering on your journey to becoming a lawyer, such as interviewing and problem-solving, are designed to help you to learn to do that and to improve your communication skills, both oral and written. This will all help you develop successful professional relationships as well as improving your ability to give effective advice.

Research

It is not just legal research which is going to further your career. You need to know about economic, social and political, and technological, as well as legal issues. You should:

- Read the quality daily newspapers—*The Times*, *The Guardian*, the *Daily Telegraph*, and *The Independent*—particularly the financial pages.

- Watch the television news. Listen to news items on the radio. As understanding develops, it is important to look at more advanced subject matter by reading *The Financial Times* and *The Economist*, and watching and listening to programmes which analyse economics and finance, like *Newsnight* or the *Today* programme.

- Be aware of what is going on in the legal press. *Legal Business*, *The Lawyer*, and (for students and trainees) *Lawyer2B* magazines are excellent sources of legal news, and help you to understand law firms as businesses, and the context within which they are operating. Although these should be used with caution, websites such as RollonFriday (RoF)[13] and Legal Cheek[14] provide legal 'gossip' and comment on law firms (including the salaries they pay) and the legal profession. They can be a useful source of information and give a further perspective on topical issues. RoF has a jobs database and provides other recruitment assistance.

Work experience

However much anyone reads, there is no real substitute for working in a commercial environment. Vacation placements in law firms or pro bono work with organisations such

---

[13] http://www.rollonfriday.co.uk.   [14] http://www.legalcheek.com.

as the Citizens Advice Bureau show commitment to the legal profession, and will inevitably help to develop commercial awareness. However, it is not just legal jobs which help to improve commercial know-how. Working for any business gives an insight into how businesses work, how they deal with money, and gives experience of working as part of a team as well as client/customer relationships. If you think about it, a job in a local supermarket teaches all these things in the same way as a job in a city bank. Law firms recognise such skills as transferable, that is provided you are able to demonstrate that you have acquired these skills, and how, they are less concerned about the context in which they have been acquired.

Networking

You have seen in Chapter 12 that networking is a crucial skill. Students should always use any contacts which they may have, particularly parents, friends' parents, and their friends. Most of them will have worked in some sort of commercial environment for years. Students can pick their brains to find out what the trends are within their businesses, what factors are influencing their business decisions, their customer/client experiences, and what contributes to success or failure.

Opportunities

Colleges or universities will usually arrange seminars and talks on subjects that are relevant to commercial awareness. There will be clubs and societies which help to develop this. Students should always make the most of these opportunities. It can all go into a CV.

13.2 Types of business structure

We will now follow through the BP example at 13.1.1 and start by giving you some of the information you need to demonstrate that you understand the business environment, and how businesses operate. Our starting point is business structures. There are five main types of legal business structures, which are illustrated in Figure 13.2:

1. Sole traders.
2. Partnerships.
3. Limited liability partnerships.
4. Private companies.
5. Public companies.

In every high street in every town in the country, there is a huge variety of different types of business of various sizes, operating in several sectors: retail, professional services, banking, and hospitality—cafes, restaurants, and bars. We will now use the high street as a model for considering the advantages and disadvantages of these different business structures.

It is crucial to understand that not all businesses are companies. The term business covers a wide range of business structures, each of which has its own legal status, which affects its conduct and performance. We will start by looking at some general principles.

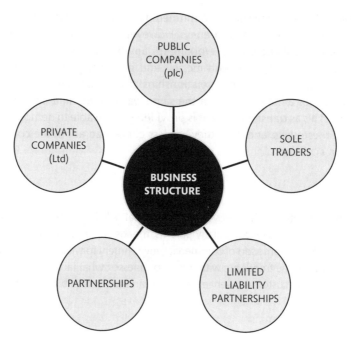

Figure 13.2 Types of business structure

 Essential explanation

Businesses can be either **incorporated** or **unincorporated**

1. An incorporated business must undergo a formal registration process before it is set up and before it can 'legally' exist. The most common examples are private limited companies, public companies, and limited liability partnerships.

2. An unincorporated business is not required to follow any formal process in order to be set up. All the owners need to do is open the doors and start trading. Unincorporated businesses include sole traders and partnerships.

13.2.1 **Legal personality**

 Essential explanation

Legal personality consists of a 'bundle' of legal rights and duties imposed by the law which govern every aspect of the lives of individuals or incorporated businesses. These rights and duties dictate their legal status.

Whether a business has its own legal personality depends on whether it is incorporated or unincorporated.

1. Unincorporated businesses have no legal status of their own. If the business fails, it is not just the business assets, such as the premises, stock, and shop fittings, but the owner's

personal possessions, such as her house, car, and savings which may be taken and sold to pay outstanding debts. If she cannot pay, she may be made bankrupt. This is known as **unlimited liability**. In addition, partners have 'joint and several' liability. Effectively, the actions of one partner can mean that the others could lose their house, car, or other assets, and in a worst-case scenario be made bankrupt. There is an old adage that you should 'choose your [business] partner more carefully than your spouse'.

2. Incorporated businesses do have their own legal personality, which gives them an independent legal existence, entirely separate from their owners. If the business fails, the owners lose the money which they have invested in the company, but no more. They cannot lose their personal assets in the same way that sole traders or partners may. This is known as **limited liability**.

In a famous case,[15] Lord Denning compared a company with a human body. Like a person, he described a company as having a brain and a nerve centre—the board of directors—which controls the entire body. The employees are their hands, and they carry out the instructions of the 'brain'.

13.2.2 Sole traders

The smallest, and most common, type of business entity is the sole trader. As the name suggests, this type of business is owned by just one person. Sole traders are the largest group of businesses in the UK. The Department of Business, Innovation and Skills (BIS) estimates that there were approximately 3.0 million sole traders operating throughout the UK at the start of 2012; 2.7 million of which had no employees.[16]

A sole trader may have a few employees but, according to the BIS statistics, over 75% have no employees at all (these are called **class zero businesses**). Most sole traders operate in the service sector: plumbers, builders, small retailers, and professionals. For example, on a typical high street, it is likely that the gift shop, butcher, and perhaps the accountant are run by sole traders. Table 13.1 shows the advantages and disadvantages for sole traders.

Table 13.1 Advantages and disadvantages for sole traders

Advantages	Disadvantages
Set up: A sole trader can set up with minimum administrative steps (the only thing that he will need to do is to inform the tax authorities (HMCR) for tax purposes).	**Start up costs:** The owner will be solely responsible for the start up costs.
Regulation: Sole traders are free to run the business as they wish. Day-to-day record keeping is unregulated and comparatively simple.	**Debts:** The owner is personally liable for all the debts of the business.
This is a good way to test the market for the new business.	**Expansion:** The owner must find the funds to expand the business himself.
	Management: The owner is responsible for all management decisions, and will have little support.

---

[15] *HL Bolton Engineering Co. Ltd* v *TJ Graham & Sons Ltd* [1957] 1 QB 159.
[16] BIS, *Business Population Estimates for the UK and Regions 2012* (17 October 2012).

13.2.3 **Partnerships**

For a partnership to exist, two or more people must own the business. For example, a boutique on the high street which is run by two friends will automatically be a partnership (unless they have set up a company). Partnerships are found in the same sectors as sole traders. They are particularly common in the professions. As well as the boutique, firms of solicitors, estate agents, or accountants could be partnerships, and it is equally possible that a gift shop or a butchers shop could be. The BIS figures show that there are nearly 450,000 partnerships in the UK. Over 60% consist of the partners only with no employees. Some of the City law firms on the other hand have over 100 partners and over 1,000 employees. Compare the advantages and disadvantages of sole traders with those of partnerships, as shown in Table 13.2.

13.2.4 **Companies**

Again, there is a wide range of company types, both in size and in the services they provide. There are about 2.7 million companies registered in the UK, with an estimated annual turnover of £2.9 trillion. Of these, 8,378 are public companies.[17] We have already looked at BP, Royal Dutch Shell, and Exxon Mobil as an examples of large multi-national companies. Most companies, however, are much smaller, employing fewer than four people. 41% of all limited companies have no employees, and are managed and run by a sole director. Now compare sole traders and partnerships with the advantages and disadvantages of setting up a company (Table 13.3).

Table 13.2 Advantages and disadvantages of partnerships

Advantages	Disadvantages
Set up: Partnerships can be set up with minimum formalities and administrative steps (apart from advising HMRC for tax purposes). A partnership agreement is advisable, but not required.	**Profits:** All profits belong to the partners, and are shared between them.
Regulation: Partners are free to run the business as they wish. Day-to-day record keeping is unregulated and comparatively simple.	**Debts**: The partners will be personally liable for all the debts of the business.
Management: Partners share management decisions, and each partner can specialise in, and concentrate on a particular area of the business, although with too many partners, decision making can be cumbersome.	**Joint and several liability:** If one partner cannot pay his share of the debts, the other partner or partners can be personally liable for that partner's share (as well as their own) from their own personal assets.
Start up costs: The partners will share the start up costs.	**Borrowing:** The partners must personally service all loans.
Expansion: With more owners, more finance can be raised so expansion is easier. If more money is needed, more partners can be brought in.	**Uncertainty:** If no partnership agreement has been entered into, this can lead to uncertainty.

[17] Companies House, *Register of Business Statistics*, http://www.companieshouse.gov.uk/about/businessRegisterStat.shtml.

Table 13.3 Advantages and disadvantages of setting up a company

Advantages	Disadvantages
Debts: Owners have limited liability so are not personally liable for the debts of the company.	**Setting up:** Companies must register with Registrar of Companies and obtain a certificate of incorporation.
Start up costs: Finance will be raised by issuing shares or borrowing.	**Profits:** Profits are shared between the shareholders.
Management: Board of directors responsible for day-to-day management	**Management:** Directors have extra legal duties and may be liable if these are breached.
Expansion: Further finance raised by issuing more shares or borrowing, which will be more readily accessible.	**Regulation:** There are ongoing regulatory requirements which must be complied with, e.g. companies have to file their annual accounts at Companies House, so financial information is made public.
Loans: Shareholders are not personally liable for servicing loans.	

13.2.5 Limited liability partnerships

A limited liability partnership (LLP) is basically a hybrid between a partnership and a limited company. Like a company, it must be incorporated, and as a result, it has its own legal personality separate from its owners. The owners are not personally liable for its debts, but it is run like a partnership. As with a partnership, there must be two or more people. There are approximately 45,000 LLPs in the UK. Many larger LLPs are professional firms (e.g. solicitors or accountants). Two of the largest LLPs are Clifford Chance LLP and Linklaters LLP, the City law firms. It is possible that your nearest high-street solicitors are an LLP.

13.2.6 Private and public companies

 Essential explanation

A **public** company can offer its shares to the public. 'Public' does not mean that it is a nationalised company owned by the government; these companies are known as **publically owned** companies. Examples of the latter include Royal Bank of Scotland and Northern Rock which the government rescued in 2008/9 to prevent their collapse. Conversely, **private** simply means that the company is not public and so it cannot make a public offer of its shares, which must be sold privately.

Private limited companies (ltd)

Most companies in the UK are private limited companies, many being small family concerns, such as hardware stores and hotels.

It is possible for a private company to be owned by a single shareholder and managed by a single director, usually the same person. Equally they can be large national companies. Richard Branson's Virgin Group Ltd is a private company. You can easily spot whether a company is a private company by looking at the name: a private company will have the abbreviation 'Ltd' for 'limited' after its name.

Public limited companies (plc)

A company has to comply with various statutory requirements to qualify as a public company. The most important is that it must have a specific amount of share capital, currently £50,000 or more. Again you can tell whether a company is a public company by looking at the name. You will see the abbreviation 'plc', for example, Marks & Spencer plc or Next plc.

A public company may be quoted, or listed, on a **stock exchange** in the UK. Private companies cannot be. There is no obligation on a public company to join a stock market. A company does not start out as a listed company. Companies tend to start small, expand, and once they reach a certain size, reputation, or level of growth, then they apply. To join the Main Market, a company must successfully complete a time-consuming and complicated procedure, known as a '**flotation**' or '**IPO**' (Initial Public Offering), but the rewards can be huge. (We will look at how the stock market works in Chapter 14). See Example 4.

Example 4

A recent high-profile example is the Facebook flotation on the New York NASDAQ exchange. Shares in the company were offered to the public at $38 each, and this meant that the company was valued at $104.2 billion. Caught in the hype of the largest IPO in history, investors flocked to buy. Mark Zuckerberg and the co-founders of Facebook become billionaires overnight. Within three days, the value of the shares had fallen by 15% and shareholders are suing Zuckerberg, Facebook, and the bankers involved in the IPO.[18]

13.2.7 Who owns a company?

When a company is set up, the owners buy shares in the company, and become, not surprisingly, the **shareholders** or '**members**' of the company. When someone buys shares, there are two results:

1. She owns a fraction of the assets of the company as each share represents a share of the ownership of the company. Shares also represent a fractional entitlement to the capital value of the company. The more shares owned, the greater the entitlement of that shareholder if, for example, the company was to be sold and its assets distributed to its shareholders.

2. She is entitled to receive a share of the profits. The amount of profit which she will receive depends, again, on how many shares she owns. The payment of profit which each shareholder receives is called a **dividend**.

Note that shareholders are not necessarily **directors**. There is no obligation on a shareholder to be a director. There is a distinct division between the roles and responsibilities of the two groups, which we will look at in 13.3.1, when we consider how companies are managed.

---

[18] 'Facebook founder Mark Zuckerberg sued by shareholders over IPO', *Daily Telegraph*, 23 May 2012.

13.2.8 **Other classifications**

Multi-national companies

A multi-national company is a company which trades worldwide and is quoted on more than one stock exchange. CocaCola and McDonald's are probably two of the best-known examples. On the high street, Barclays is a multi-national with operations in 50 countries, 140,000 employees, and it is listed on the London and New York stock exchanges. Starbucks has 18,887 stores in 55 countries, but does not meet the true definition of a multi-national as it only listed on one stock exchange in New York, the NASDAQ.

Micro, small, and medium sized enterprises

At the other end of the scale are **micro enterprises** and **small and medium sized enterprises** (**SMEs**). BIS defines these as businesses which have between 0 and 249 employees. 99.9% of all businesses are within the definition, and they account for 48.8% of all private sector turnover.[19] They include sole traders, partnerships, and companies. Historically, they have been responsible for stimulating the economy and driving competition. One of the side-effects of the credit crunch has been that many such businesses have been unable to get loans and investment to grow effectively, and thus have not been able to fulfil this function fully.

Groups of companies

Increasingly, companies are formed into groups. There is a **parent** (or **holding**) company and **subsidiary** companies, which together form one single economic entity. The subsidiaries are controlled by the parent. The parent company has a majority shareholding (51% or more) in the subsidiary and a right to appoint its directors. Figure 13.3 shows a typical group relationship.

Examples on the high street include Burton (a subsidiary), which is part of Sir Philip Green's Arcadia Group (parent company), which also includes Top Shop and Miss Selfridge (subsidiaries). Costa Coffee is a subsidiary of the Whitbread hotel and restaurant group (parent). Pizza Express (subsidiary) is part of the Gondola Group (parent). In other words, many successful, better-known companies are part of a larger group.

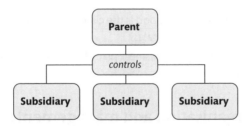

Figure 13.3 A group of companies

---

[19] BIS, *Business Population Estimates for the UK and Regions 2012* (17 October 2012).

Franchises

A franchise is where a business (the '**franchisor**') allows third parties ('**franchisees**') to use its name, concept, business format, and experience in return for payment. In particular, the franchisee can use the franchisor's intellectual property rights. Unlike a corporate group, where the parent controls the subsidiary, the franchisor does not own the franchisee, but has a contractual agreement which obliges the latter to operate in a particular way.

Franchising is becoming increasingly popular, and you will find franchises in various sectors. Well-known examples include McDonald's, KFC, and the Body Shop. If you go to McDonald's in any city in any part of the world, the restaurant set up is the same, the food is the same, the price is the same, and everything is sold under the McDonald's brand.

A franchise offers a franchisee a relatively cheap and comparatively risk-free way of opening a business, without starting from scratch. The franchisee is able to use a business concept which has been proved to work and an established brand. For the franchisor, franchising can also be a way of expanding into new or unfamiliar markets. For example, Next plc has 50 franchises throughout Europe, Asia, and the Middle East.

13.2.9 **Which is best?**

The role of the solicitor will be to advise a client who is setting up in business on the advantages and disadvantages of each type of business structure, but it will be up to the client to decide which is best for him, bearing in mind the advantages and disadvantages of each.

Commercial awareness, as we have seen, is not all about law and facts. Before a client makes a decision, it is important that he considers all the practical consequences of starting up a business. Examples of further factors which he should think about are:

1. **The economic climate**. Is this the best time to start up a business? What will be the effect of the continuing euro zone crisis?
2. **Personal factors.** Setting up a business is stressful and uncertain, not just for the client but for his family. Is he (and are they) ready for this?
3. **Change of lifestyle**. It takes commitment and motivation to get a business up and running. Is he ready to work long hours and weekends?
4. **The financial implications**. How will he manage financially before the business starts to earn money?
5. **The need for a new skill set**. How good is the client at financial planning, managing employees, logistics, marketing, and sales?
6. **Business plan**. Has the client got a business plan? Has he got the support of his bank/ small business adviser?

13.3 **Business organisation and management**

Your client may be a business but a business is run and managed by people—they may be very high-powered business executives, like Richard Branson of Virgin, or they may have limited business experience, like a plumber running a small business in a local town.

It is often said that vets have highly stressful jobs because not only do they need to be able to treat the animals effectively, but they also need to deal with the concerns of their owners. As a lawyer, acting for a business is similar. Lawyers need to know the law and advise on what is best for the business. However, lawyers are dealing not with the business itself (which, after all, is inanimate), but with a variety of individuals involved in business, such as the directors or managers of a company, or the partners of a firm. These are the people you will be dealing with on a day-to-day basis, and being a successful lawyer involves building good relationships with them. One of the things you need to know is what the people you are dealing with do within their organisation. They will not be impressed if you do not. Again, as we have seen from Case study 1, this background will help you at interviews and assessment days.

In this section, we will look at the management structure of businesses, and how they organise and plan their operations, concentrating particularly on larger public companies. Although management techniques and concepts are outside the scope of this chapter, we will cover some of the more important, so that you have an idea of the underlying rationale of company organisation, and understand some of the (sometimes seemingly incomprehensible) jargon used by those involved in management of companies.

13.3.1 Companies

We have already seen that there is a distinct division between the role of directors and the role of the shareholders. Shareholders do not need to be directors of the company and directors do not necessarily have to be shareholders, although often they will be required to do so by the company's constitution.

Directors

The directors take the day-to-day decisions on the running of the company at **board meetings**.

Directors have certain legal duties which ensure that they act in the best interests of the company and the shareholders, and do not take advantage of their position for their own benefit. In addition, there are certain things that they cannot do without the consent of a majority of the shareholders, for example, they cannot take a loan from the company. If directors or officers of the company are found to be in breach of their duties, they can be held liable.

Shareholders

The shareholders, although they are the owners of the company, do not take part in the day-to-day running of the company. In theory at least, they take the more important decisions affecting the company, because they are entitled to attend and vote at **general meetings**. In fact a majority of shareholders, particularly shareholders of public companies, never attend such meetings and take no part in the running of the company.

Public companies, but not private companies, have to hold an **annual general meeting** to allow the shareholders to elect new directors and question the directors on the annual report. The annual report is a report to the shareholders on how the company has performed during the year, and their plans for the following year. Again, most shareholders do not attend or vote. However, some do.

Example 5

The spring of 2012 saw several shareholder rebellions (collectively dubbed the 'Shareholder Spring' after the Arab Spring uprisings of 2011) against excessive executive pay rises at some top companies. At Barclays, where 27% of shareholders voted against CEO Bob Diamond's £17 million pay package, this was not a high enough percentage to succeed. However, at the AGM of the insurance company, Aviva, over 50% of shareholders blocked a pay rise for its CEO, who subsequently resigned, and shareholders at AstraZeneca, the pharmaceutical company, forced their CEO to resign after the company published poor financial results. In the long term, however, this has had a limited impact.[20]

13.3.2 Differences between private and public companies

Public companies by their very nature have far more complex management structures than private companies.

Private companies

Private companies have a board of directors which carries out the day-to-day management of the company. A private company may have just one director (a public company must have at least two). The shareholders of a private company are more likely to be the directors, but this will not necessarily be the case. For example, when a client sets up a company, he may issue shares to both himself and his wife. He will act as a director, but she may play no role in the running of the company.

Public companies

Figure 13.4 shows the hierarchy of the management structure for a plc. Like a private company, there will be a board of directors who will be responsible for decisions affecting the day-to-day running of the company. The board is also described as the **executive**, as it 'executes' decisions on behalf of the company.

Head of the board is the Chief Executive Officer (CEO). (CEO is a US term which is gaining popularity in the UK; you may also see the CEO referred to as the Managing Director (MD)). There may also be a Chairman above the CEO. The Chairman is often a figure-head, and acts in a **non-executive** or advisory capacity.

The board is responsible for strategic planning which sets the goals and objectives of the organisation. Below the board will be the managers of the company who are responsible for carrying out the board's decisions, and ensuring that the goals and objectives are achieved, through organisation and planning. In other words, they manage and organise the next level, the workforce. This gives a **cascade** effect. Decisions start at the top and cascade down towards those whose role it is to implement them. This is illustrated in Figure 13.4.

[20] Ruth Sullivan, '"Shareholder spring" muted', *FT.com*, 26 August 2012, http://www.ft.com.

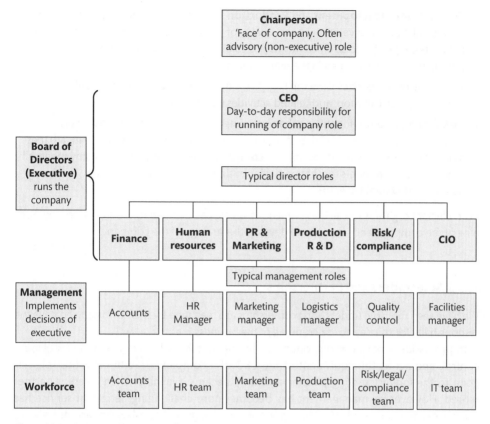

Figure 13.4 Management structure of a public company

Typical roles which directors may have include:

- **Finance** Director, who is responsible for all the financial decisions for the company. This is the most important role after the CEO. The **finance** or **accounts** department which she oversees is responsible for everything to do with money, for example the funding of the business, investment, paying suppliers, and ensuring that customers pay.

- Director of **Human Resources** or **People**, who takes decisions in relation to staffing, employment issues, and all other decisions affecting the workforce. His department's responsibilities include payroll, holidays and sick leave, performance, and disciplinary procedures. He will draft and implement company policies.

- **PR** or **Marketing** Director, who is responsible for promoting the company, dealing with customers, promotions, branding, and public relations. The PR department is responsible for dealing with the press and building the company's public profile.

- The **Sales** Director is responsible for actual sales to customers and account management.

- **Chief Information Officer (CIO)**, who is responsible for all the information technology. The ICT department deals with communication issues and the functioning of computers, networks, and telephones.

- **Research and Development** and **Production** Director, as the name suggests, will be responsible for the development and quality of products quality. He has to ensure that products are produced as efficiently as possible and have a technological advantage, putting the company ahead in the market place

- There may be a **Logistics** Director. Logistics is the modern term for procurement (purchasing), distribution, and related activities (see 13.4.4).

- **Risk management** is identifying the sorts of risks (or things that can go wrong) in a particular business, and ensuring that systems are put in place to avoid or mitigate these as far as possible. Those responsible for **compliance** ensure that the company meets all regulatory requirements for that particular business. They are often lawyers. There may be a separate **Legal Director**.

In an efficient organisation all these functions will be coordinated to ensure the smooth running of the company and, crucially, to develop the strategy of the company.

13.3.3 Sole traders and partnerships

We have seen that sole traders and partnerships are managed by their owners, who have the responsibility for the day-to-day running of the business.

In professional partnerships, often the senior partner will have overall management control, and act as the equivalent of the CEO of a company. Traditionally, this role has gone to the longest serving partner, and only became available when a senior partner retired. However, as management has become more challenging, length of service has not necessarily provided the necessary skills for the job. Good lawyers are not always good managers.

In law firms, larger partnerships and LLPs will often have a **managing partner**, who will have overall responsibility for the management of the partnership. The managing partner will oversee all the management roles mentioned above in relation to companies, personnel, finance, marketing, and so forth. A recent article in the journal *Legal Business* reported that this is not always an easy task. Lawyers tend not to be easily managed, and are often resistant to change. 'Lawyers are worst because they think they know best.'[21] Large city firms such as Linklaters, Lovells, and DLA Piper have tried to resolve this by sending their managing partners to Harvard Business School,[22] but clearly this is not going to be an option for all firms.

13.3.4 Strategies and objectives

Once you know how a business works, and who has responsibility for its management, it is important to know what it is hoping to achieve.

---

[21] Dominique Graham, 'It's a tough job...5 reasons not to be a managing partner', *Legal Business*, July/ August 2005, http://www.grahamgill.com/pdf/GG-A_tough_job.pdf.

[22] Ravinder Casley Gera, 'Business Schools for Lawyers', *The Chambers Magazine*, Issue 25, 2008, http:// www.chambersmagazine.co.uk/Article/Business-Schools-for-Lawyers.

Strategies

Business organisations, both large and small, should have a strategy.

 Essential explanation

A **strategy** sets out a long-term plan of what the business wants to achieve (its **vision**) and how it proposes to achieve it (its **mission).** You will sometimes see strategies referred to as the 'roadmap' for the business or its 'game plan'.

An organisation's vision and mission statements are usually published on its website, for example Microsoft, whose mission is to be 'the world's no 1 provider of innovative technical solutions' [23] and Coca Cola, whose mission is to 'refresh the world …'.[24]

These statements are closely allied to the organisation's **values and ethics**. When explaining its strategy, the organisation may state its values and/or culture, emphasising what makes a company unique within a particular market, or what binds it together. Taken together, the statement of values and the vision and mission statement set out **why** the company is in business.

Millions of pounds are spent by businesses developing strategies in order to improve their competitiveness within the market in which they are operating. However, there is no point in having a strategy if you cannot get your workforce to buy into it, or effectively communicate this to potential customers. The idea of a strategy is to motivate the workforce, which in turn will bring in customers and investment. In other words, the strategy needs to be effectively communicated and implemented. It is more likely to work in a business where everyone knows **what** they are required to do to achieve the strategy, **how** they are supposed to do it, and **who** is going to ensure that it is done.

If you go back to Figure 13.4 showing the management hierarchy, you can see how this can be achieved by a company.

- **Why**, the vision, mission, and values, is decided by the directors.
- **What**, the objectives, or targets of the business, again will be set by the directors.
- **How**, the tactical decisions how this is to be achieved are made by the management.
- **Who** is the workforce, which implement the tactics.

The relationship between each of the various levels should be clear so everyone knows who is responsible for, and to, whom. A business may have an **organogram**, which is a diagram showing the structure of the organisation and the interrelationship between directors, management, and the workforce. Figure 13.4 is a simplified organogram. If you are acting for any organisation, you will often find it useful to see its organogram, as it will clarify the role of the people you will be dealing with.

[23] http://www.microsoft.com/about/diversity/en/us/vision.aspx.
[24] http://www.coca-colacompany.com/our-company/mission-vision-values.

Objectives

 Essential explanation

An **objective** is a target. It is different from a strategy in that it is more concrete and immediate.

The target of many businesses is to make or increase a profit, for example increase profit by 10% per year for the next five years, or to achieve 50% return business. In order to ensure that targets are met they have to be achievable. Managers often use the SMART model in relation to objectives. You have already considered this in the context of a presentation, but the model has a range of applications, and is frequently used by business organisations. Objectives are SMART if they are:

- **S**–specific (clear and unambiguous)
- **M**–measurable (capable of being measured against objective criteria)
- **A**–achievable (can be accomplished by the workforce)
- **R**–relevant (suitable for and of appeal to the workforce)
- **T**–time-appropriate (achievable within an agreed time frame)

13.3.5 **Analysis**

A further role of management is analysis of its position within the market place. A variety of management tools are used, which you may also find useful in other situations. For example, if you are preparing for a negotiation, you can use a SWOT analysis to organise the information which you have, or you can use it when you research an organisation when you are looking for a job.

SWOT

 Essential explanation

SWOT is a management tool used to examine the strengths (S) and weaknesses (W), opportunities (O) available, and threats (T) confronting the business. **Strengths and weaknesses** are factors which are **internal** to the firm or business, whereas **opportunities and threats** relate to **external** factors. The results are usually shown in a grid form (see Figure 13.5).

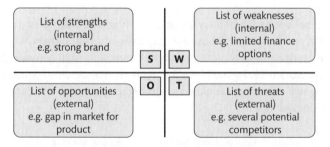

Figure 13.5 SWOT analysis grid

Using SWOT provides useful information for managers on the current position of the business and allows them to determine what their future priorities will be. It can be used on the business, its customers, or competitors. It is usually done when some change in business operations is likely, such as bidding for new customers, or expanding into new markets.

PESTLE

Just like the professionals who advise them, the owners and managers of companies need to think about the context in which they are operating.

 Essential explanation

PESTLE: political (**P**), economic (**E**), social (**S**), technological (**T**), legal (**L**), and environmental (**E**) changes that affect commercial activity.

All businesses are affected by changes brought about by these factors. They must take advantage of the opportunities offered and respond to the challenges and restrictions which they may impose. For example, political factors include the stability of the government, and its tax policy etc. Similarly, economic factors to be considered would include interest rates, the level of inflation, unemployment, projected economic growth or decline. Social factors include population growth rate and demographics, for instance the ageing population, social mobility, and public opinion. Technological issues include new ways of working and communication. Legal issues include trends in regulation and deregulation or employment legislation. Environmental issues are factors such as weather and climate change.

In Chapter 16, we look at a business case where a client is thinking of setting up an off-licence. There are concerns about binge drinking amongst young people and the increase in alcohol consumption amongst middle-aged professionals and the ensuing health problems. There is increasing debate about whether or not the government should intervene and legislate to restrict, for example, the opening hours of pubs, clubs, and off-licences in town centres. So a social concern will lead to political intervention and consequent legal constraints. The easiest way to control alcohol consumption is to increase the cost of alcohol by increasing taxes on all types of alcoholic drinks, making this an economic issue as well. All of this is bound to have an effect on the client's business. He will also need to think about the impact of technology.

Technology and social networking

We have seen that advances in technology have posed a significant threat particularly for smaller law firms. One of the challenges for any business is to harness and drive technology for its own ends. Whereas in the past, businesses had to go out and find customers, now the internet provides a forum for customers to find them. The development of cloud computing and the growth of social network sites like Facebook, Twitter, and LinkedIn have opened up important opportunities for businesses. The importance of social networking cannot be underestimated, perhaps illustrated by the fact that lawyers are beginning to consider what you should do with your 'digital assets', including your passwords, when you die.[25] The next opportunity could be a 'mouse-click' away. The marketing potential is immense. Facebook has 750 million users, 50% of whom log in every day. A survey has shown that 48% of small businesses are using social network sites to expand and grow:[26] 26% of those use Facebook, 25% use LinkedIn, and 21% use Twitter to promote their businesses.[27] Social networks provide infinite marketing opportunities. US corporations are increasingly setting up social media 'hubs' so that they can manage and respond to social media. A further benefit is that rather than the traditional recruitment process, social networks provide links to potential employees.

The accessibility of social networking sites works both ways. US employers are reported to be routinely asking interviewees for their Facebook logins so that they can check their profiles before making job offers.[28] Example 6 can be a warning to you of the power of social networks.

Example 6

After leaving University, Charlotte started looking for jobs as a PA. She had two successful interviews with a leading London property firm. The second interview went well and she was expecting to be called for a third interview. She heard nothing, and contacted her recruitment agent for feedback. She was told that she had interviewed well, but it was very unfortunate about the Facebook photograph. One of her friends had sent her a photograph of a lap dancer, to whom Charlotte bore an uncanny resemblance. Charlotte had posted this on Facebook, and jokingly changed her profile from unemployed to 'lap dancer'. The 'joke' had cost her the job.

13.4 The business environment

We now look at another important economic concept: markets and sectors. When we looked at the BP case study (see Case study 1), we saw that BP operated within the 'energy sector'. When we look at law firms, we will talk about the 'legal market'. The very act of selling goods or services creates a market. Businesses sell those goods and services to make money, and to make money they need to get as many buyers, or consumers, of the product as possible. The result is that within any market or sector businesses compete between themselves to be the biggest or the best, so markets and sectors are important because they generate competition. Healthy competition is good for businesses, as it drives growth, and it is good for the consumers of their goods or service, as it means that there will be more goods and services available, and prices will be lower. This section will consider what we mean by sectors and markets, the role of consumers, how products reach those consumers (the supply chain), and the influence of competition in providing goods and services for consumers. All of these issues will help make sense of why the BP oil spill was such a disaster.

---

[25] Oliver Embley, 'What happens to our online assets on death', *The Times*, 6 November 2012.

[26] Regus, 'SMEs lead way in social networking for business' (27 June 2011).

[27] YouGov survey, October 2011.

[28] 'Facebook passwords "fair game in job interviews"', *Daily Telegraph*, 23 March 2012.

13.4.1 Sectors and markets

The problem here is to define what exactly we mean by these terms, because you will see them used in all sorts of senses.

Economic sectors

 Essential explanation

An **economic sector** is a part or subdivision of the economy. It describes one of the areas into which the economic activity of a country is divided, and the proportion of the population engaged in particular activities.

There are four economic sectors:

1. **Primary:** extraction of raw material, such as mining, farming, or fishing. This is the oldest sector, as people have been engaged in farming since pre-historic times. Developed economies such as the UK or US will now have comparatively few workers involved in the primary sector.

2. **Secondary**: production, such as manufacture, construction, refining. There is a logical progression from extraction of raw materials to producing a finished product, like cars, houses, or textiles. The number of workers involved in manufacturing and related industries has declined in the UK in recent years, as more workers have moved into service industries. The decline of manufacturing industry is known as **deindustrialisation**.

3. **Tertiary**: provision of services, such as law, medicine, retail, entertainment, or tourism. This is the most important sector of the UK and other developed economies. As an economy develops, demand for services increases. The majority of workers in the UK are involved in the service sector, which accounts for about 75% of the UK economy.

4. **Quarternary**: research, design, and development, such as pharmaceuticals or computer programs. This is a comparatively new sector, but of increasing importance.

There is also a suggestion that there may be a fifth **quinary** sector, which includes workers who are involved in the highest decision-making processes, for instance top executives in media, culture, education, etc.

These are the main economic categories, but you will see further subdivisions. For example, energy, retail, industrial, hospitality, media, healthcare, financial, and so forth.

Public, private, and voluntary sectors

Public sector organisations, as we have seen, are those which are owned, financed, and controlled by the government. They provide services to the public, often free. Obvious examples are the National Health Service, or the BBC. The public sector is far wider than this and includes all central government departments, the central bank, local authorities, quangos, and government executive agencies. The London Legacy Development Corporation which is responsible for the development of the Olympic Park is a quango.

 Essential explanation

A **quango** is a 'quasi-autonomous non-governmental organisation'. It is funded by the tax payer, but it is not controlled by central government. Quangos are topical as the government promised in 2010 to get rid of nearly 200 as part of its austerity initiative.[29]

By contrast, the **private sector** is made up of all businesses which are run by individuals and companies for profit, whether they be sole traders, partnerships, or companies.

Voluntary sector organisations are charities and other organisations, such as clubs, which are not run for profit.

13.4.2 **Industries**

You will also see reference to **industries** and **industrial sectors**.

 Essential explanation

An **industry** is a group of businesses that produce the same goods, for example the electrical industry, the retail industry, or the pharmaceutical industry. These are then grouped into wider **industrial sectors**, for example the manufacturing sector, construction sector, or transport sector.

13.4.3 **Markets**

 Essential explanation

A **market** is any place where the sellers of particular goods or services can meet with the buyers who want to buy those goods or services. They can be actual physical markets or they can be 'virtual' markets.

Ever since people started trading, markets have existed. The very width of the definition shows there are going to be lots of different types of markets. If you watch *The Apprentice*, you will see that Lord Sugar tests his candidates by introducing them to a variety of 'market' experiences, and seeing how they cope in each one.

- Actual physical **retail markets** can be any type of market from the local market held each week in any typical market town to large scale markets which cater mainly for business customers.

- **Geographic markets** range from global markets (where trade takes place with every country in the world) to regional (e.g. the European Union) or local markets (a

---

[29] '"Bonfire of the quangos" revealed', *Channel 4 News*, 14 October 2012, http://www.channel4.com/news/bonfire-of-the-quangos-promised.

small defined area within one country). They are hugely important in assessing the competitiveness of a business.

- **Emerging markets** are markets which are experiencing rapid economic, social, and business growth. The main ones are Brazil, Russia, India, and China, the BRIC economies.
- **Product markets** are determined by the exclusivity of a product or whether, if this product is not available, consumers will buy another product instead. This is called **substitutionality**.
- **Labour markets** are markets where employers can find workers or workers can find jobs.
- **Financial markets**, including stock markets, currency, and commodity markets, are considered in Chapter 14.
- **'Virtual' markets** exist only online.
- **Consumer markets** are where businesses sell goods or services to consumers. These sales are referred to as **B2C** (business to consumer). In the legal profession, a typical example is the provision of domestic conveyancing services for individual clients.
- **Industrial markets** are where businesses sell to other businesses, selling the sort of goods or services that consumers would not normally buy, such as raw materials or industrial components. These sales are referred to as **B2B** (business to business). Again, within the legal sector, a typical example is the advice provided by the corporate departments of large City firms, for example in relation to equity or debt finance, which are considered in Chapter 14.

We are now going to concentrate on the last two categories, consumer and industrial markets, and think about how the goods you buy end up in the shops.

13.4.4 The supply chain

If markets are about buying and selling, it goes without saying that there have to be goods and services to buy and sell. Someone has to manufacture goods from raw materials, put them on the market, and make sure they reach the people who want to buy them.

 Essential explanation

The **supply chain** describes the steps it takes to get goods and services from a supplier to an end user, and includes every company that comes into contact with those goods in the process. Any break in the supply chain will cause shortages, and has the potential to increase prices.

One possibility is for a manufacturer to sell its goods direct to retailers, or wholesalers, who will sell on to other retailers or direct to the end user. This is, however, not the most usual arrangement, and often a 'middle man' in the form of either a distributor or an agent will be involved. Figure 13.6 shows a simple supply chain.

By looking at the diagram, you can see why the BP oil spill and the consequent shortage of oil (at the top of the supply chain) was such a disaster.

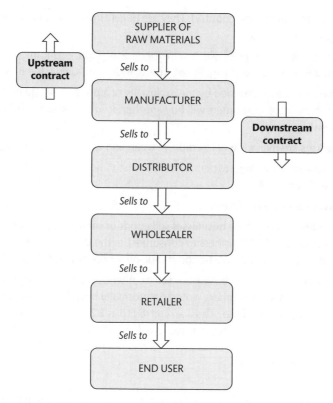

Figure 13.6 A simple supply chain

At the top end of the chain, the manufacturer will have two concerns:

1. First it has to produce the goods or services, its products, as efficiently and cheaply as possible. One aspect of the manufacturing process is the sourcing of the raw materials, services, and utilities necessary to produce the goods and enable the business to function effectively. Where necessary, materials have to be transported and stored. (This process is referred to as **supply chain procurement** or **logistics**.) As a result, the manufacturer enters into a series of contracts to enable it to produce the goods. These are known as **upstream contracts** (the manufacturer's money is flowing up the supply chain).

2. Next, it has to get the product to the ultimate consumer as cheaply and efficiently as possible. This process is known as **supply chain management**. Here the manufacturer organises a series of contracts to enable it to sell the goods. These are known as **downstream contracts** (the manufacturer passes the products down the supply chain, thus generating income for the business).

We have used a relatively simple supply chain example, where raw materials are being manufactured into a single product, but the logistics can be much more complicated, such as car manufacture. Cars are manufactured from a variety of component parts, such as doors, mirrors, windscreens, engine parts, electrics, nuts, bolts, and so forth. Possibly over 70% of the components will be manufactured by someone else and bought in, often from different countries. A supply chain of this sort can be immensely complex, a 'logistical nightmare' in the true sense.

13.4.5 **Consumers**

At the other end of the supply chain are the consumers.

 Essential explanation

Consumers are the end users of goods or services. They buy products for their own use, and not to use them in manufacture or to sell them on to other buyers.

They too want to buy the goods as cheaply as possible. Understanding the consumer market is vital for any business wishing to exploit its products successfully.

We live in a consumer society where the economy is highly dependent on consumer spending, and consumers are encouraged to buy material goods. The 1980s saw the rise of consumerism and a change in the way that people shopped. Rather than just buying necessities, people wanted luxury goods, for example designer clothes, mobile phones, computers, electrical goods, or luxury cars. The Office for National Statistics' report on household spending in 2012 shows that the percentage that consumers spend on **consumer durables** continues to rise despite the recession.[30]

 Essential explanation

Consumer durables are cars or vans, central heating, washing machines, tumble dryers, dishwashers, microwaves, telephones, mobile phones, satellite receivers, CD and DVD players, home computers and internet connection, etc.

There has been a consequential rise in the amount of money that people spend, partly as a result of the increasing availability of credit during the 1990s and the first decade of the 21st century. Spending on these items has been encouraged by advertising (and again, consequentially, increased the importance of mass and social media). There is much more emphasis on 'quick fix shopping' and shopping as a leisure activity. This, in turn, has led to a change in the types of shops people use, away from small retailers to supermarkets and national chains located in large shopping malls. For example, part of the Olympic Park development is the Westfield Shopping Centre in Stratford. It is the largest urban shopping centre in Europe, and cost £1.45 billion to build.[31] Increasingly, during the last decade, consumers are shopping online. For example, leading up to Christmas 2011, internet sales increased by 25% on 2009, totalling £6.8 billion.[32]

---

[30] ONS, *Family Spending 2012 Edition Release*, http://www.ons.gov.uk/.
[31] Rebecca Smithers, 'Inside Westfield Stratford City', *The Guardian*, 21 May 2011.
[32] Graeme Wearden, 'Online shopping hit an all time record in December', *The Guardian*, 21 January 2011.

13.4.6 **Consumer protection**

Despite their immense power as a group, individual consumers can be vulnerable, particularly at the hands of large producers. The rise of the consumer market has been accompanied by increasing regulation to protect consumers from unscrupulous suppliers. Consumer protection is a vast and specialist area of law, and it is very difficult to summarise. A good starting point is the website of the Office of Fair Trading, which tells you the bare minimum that a consumer who buys goods or services can expect.[33]

Chapter 7 looks at the Sale of Goods Act 1979 and the Unfair Contract Terms Act 1977, two of the main consumer protection measures. At the very least, goods must be of **satisfactory quality** (not faulty), be **fit for purpose** (do what the buyer expects them to do), and **match any description** that has been given (e.g. by a retailer, on the packet, in a brochure, or on a website).[34] If not, consumers can return the goods, claim a refund, or ask for a repair. Consumers who buy a service, like gym membership or hairdressing, can expect that the service will be carried out with **reasonable care and skill** (properly) within a **reasonable time** and at a **reasonable price**.[35] If not, consumers can get their money back. These are all statutory protections over and above any guarantee that a supplier or retailer provides to the customer.

In the early days, as more regulation was introduced, producers and retailers began to include clauses in contracts to protect themselves against liability (known as **exclusion clauses**) stating, for example, that faulty goods could not be returned and no refunds would be given. That was soon stopped, and there is extensive legislation preventing the exclusion of consumer rights in relation to goods and services.[36]

Regulation is all very well if consumers know about it, but to be effective consumers must be aware of their rights. Here are some examples of little known, but extremely useful, consumer protection measures:

- **Online sales**: If they buy goods online or over the phone, consumers have a right to change their minds (this is called a '**cooling off period**') and can send the goods back, usually within seven days. There does not have to be a reason. This applies even if the consumer has used the goods during the cooling off period and goods are no longer in perfect condition.[37]

- **Credit card sales**: Where a consumer has bought goods or services costing between £100 and £3,000 using a credit or debit card, the card company or bank is responsible if anything goes wrong.[38] The idea is that consumers should never be left in the position where they have to pay a debt for something that never arrives or cannot be used. This is a particularly useful provision if the company which has provided goods or services goes bust. Generally, where possible if you are buying anything that costs more than £100 it is much better to use your credit card, as you get double protection. This is illustrated by Example 7.

---

[33] http://www.oft.gov.uk/.   [34] E.g. Sale of Goods Act 1979.

[35] E.g. Supply of Goods and Services Act 1983.

[36] E.g. Unfair Contracts Terms Act 1977 and Unfair Terms in Consumer Contract Regulations 1999 (SI 1999/2083).

[37] Consumer Protection (Distance Selling) Regulations 2000 (SI 2000/2334).

[38] Consumer Credit Act 1977.

Example 7

You buy two pairs of shoes costing £150 each online using a credit card. You wear the first pair for one day at work, but they are uncomfortable. You wear the second pair for a week and the heel falls off. What are your legal options?

- **Pair 1**: Provided that you send the shoes back within the seven-day cooling off period, you can get your money back. It does not matter that you have worn them. In legal terms, all you need to do is to take 'reasonable' care of them during that time.

- **Pair 2:** Clearly these shoes are defective. In legal terms they are neither of satisfactory quality nor fit for their purpose. You have a statutory right to a replacement, repair, or refund. If you decide that you want your money back, because you paid with a credit card, you can choose whether to claim your money back from the seller or the credit card company.

13.4.7 Competition

Where two or more businesses operate within a particular market or sector providing the same goods or services, they will be competitors. If we return to the example of the typical high street in 13.2, there are several obvious competitors and some non-competitors within that geographical market.

For example, high-street competitors might include the following examples:

- Costa and Starbucks both sell coffee;
- Waitrose and M&S Simply Food are upmarket supermarkets selling food;
- Next, New Look, and the boutique sell ladies' clothes;
- Lloyds TSB and Santander provide banking and financial services.

These are competitors because they are operating in the same sector selling similar products. Non-competitors on the high street might include:

- the gift shop, phone store, and hardware store—if there are no others in the high street, they have no competition;
- solicitors, accountants, and estate agents are all operating within the service sector, but the services which they provide are complementary rather than competitive (if someone wants to buy a house, the estate agent may recommend the solicitors to do the property work and the solicitors may recommend the accountants to give any financial advice which their clients may need).

The high street illustrates how competition works, but it is only a very small local market. If we expand the geographical area, the amount of competitors will increase. For example, many towns have out-of-town shopping centres, where you will find large supermarkets, such as Tesco or Asda, which would clearly provide further competition for the food stores in the high street. There are likely to be other mobile phone providers. Large supermarkets will sell gifts, so the gift shop will face competition here. There may be a McDonald's or KFC which will increase the choice for fast food. At the other extreme, the two banks operate within a global market, competing for customers throughout the world.

The level of competition is determined by the number and size of the businesses operating in a particular market.

 Essential explanation

A **monopoly** is where one business dominates the market, such as Microsoft within the global market for computer operating systems.

An **oligopoly** is where a few businesses dominate the market, for example Tesco, Sainsburys, Asda, and Morrisons together have a 75.4% share of the UK grocery market.

A **competitive market** exists where there are hundreds or thousands of producers, none of which are particularly large or dominant. If you look, for example, in the Yellow Pages for any local area, you will see that there are hundreds of small businesses, such as hairdressers, pubs, or plumbing services, all competing within the same market.

A **cartel** is where two or more businesses join forces to dominate a particular market. An international example is OPEC (Organisation of Petroleum Exporting Countries) which dominates the world oil market.

The structure of the market and the market conditions will affect prices. If a business has a monopoly, or is operating as part of a cartel, it will be able to charge more than a business which is operating in a competitive market. This is clearly not a good thing for consumers.

In the same way that regulation exists to protect consumers from unscrupulous suppliers, there is considerable regulation to protect against anti-competitive practices. Competition law (which you may see referred to as **anti-trust** internationally) is designed to promote healthy competition. Understanding this area of law is vital for any business as breaking the law can have very serious financial consequences. Since 1990, Microsoft has been fined €1.64 billion for anti-competitive behaviour.[39] In 2009, Intel was fined $1.45 billion (£948 million) for trying to bully and bribe its customers into only buying its chips to keep its nearest competitor out of the market. It was said to have 'resorted to old-fashioned threats, intimidation and kneecapping' as well as paying ('bribing') manufacturers to use their chips rather than any others.[40]

13.4.8 **Environment**

The environment in which a business operates, its markets, its customers, and the competition it faces will influence all of the decisions which the managers of the business make. These factors are also important considerations for lawyers when advising any business. The emphasis throughout this chapter has been on the economic and financial environments, so those are what we will explore in Chapter 14.

 Summary

- Firms expect their lawyers to be commercially aware. In practice, commercial awareness is about understanding personal, financial, and business concerns of clients and the environment in which those clients operate. For students, developing understanding of these issues will help with your studies and employability skills.

---

[39] Charles Arthur et al., 'Microsoft loses EU antitrust fine appeal', *The Guardian*, 27 June 2012.
[40] Rupert Neate, 'Intel faces biggest ever EU competition fine', *Daily Telegraph*, 30 May 2009.

- In order to give effective advice to business clients you need an understanding of the main business structures—sole traders, partnerships, the different types of company—and the advantages and disadvantages of each. This involves understanding how those businesses are run and managed, and by whom and investigating a business's strategy and objectives.

- Finally, it is crucial to understand the environment within which a client is operating and take into account the factors that contribute to that environment: political, economic, social, technical, and legal. Businesses operate within a variety of sectors and markets; you need to be able to understand the market in which that client operates, how the client operates within the market, and the competition within that market.

 ## Thought-provoking questions

1. What are the main reasons why someone would choose to set up in business as a sole trader rather than a limited company?

2. What is an LLP? What are the advantages and disadvantages of these?

3. Research a company of your choice online. What are its vision, mission, and values?

4. What do you think are the main advantages of social media sites for businesses?

5. Research a law firm of your choice online. Use the SWOT analysis to identify one strength, weakness, opportunity, and threat for that firm's business.

 ## Further reading

Lucy Jones, *Introduction to Business Law* (Oxford: OUP, 2011)
—contains an accessible introduction to the structure and management of businesses.

Christopher Stokes, *All You Need to Know about Commercial Awareness* (London: Longtail Publishing Ltd)
—essential reading for information on how companies are run and managed. Aimed more at business people than lawyers, it still provides a unique insight into the subject. A revised version is published each year.

For the authors' reflections on the thought-provoking questions, additional self-test questions, podcasts offering a variety of perspectives on legal systems and skills, and a library of links to useful websites, visit the free Online Resource Centre at **http://www.oxfordtextbooks.co.uk/orc/slorach/**.

14 Essential economics and finance

Learning objectives

After studying this chapter you should be able to:

- Appreciate the importance of micro and macroeconomics in a business environment.
- Explain the role of banks and other financial institutions in the money markets.
- Recognise how the principles of business accounts affect businesses.
- Realise how personal and corporate insolvency may arise and their effects.

Introduction

In Chapter 13, you were introduced to different types of legal business structures and saw how businesses operate and are managed. We have stressed the importance of the environment in which individuals and businesses conduct their affairs. You have seen how the economy shapes the environment in which businesses operate and influences the everyday decisions of individuals. Whether or not you decide to pursue a career in the law, you will find that you need, at the very least, a basic understanding of how the economy operates. Now we consider that economic and financial environment, looking at the basics of economics, financial markets, and the major players within those markets. We look at the very fundamentals of money and finance: what money is, how to organise and account for it, and what happens when things go wrong.

14.1 Case studies: economics for employability

If we go back to our case studies, Chapter 13 should have filled any gaps which you may have had in your knowledge of business structures, organisation, and the business environment. However, the scenarios also raised economic and financial issues which you need to understand. To help you develop this understanding, we concentrate first on the most important economic concepts.

First, let's look again at the BP scenario.

> ## Case study 1
>
> On 22 April 2010, one of BP's deep-water oil rigs in the Gulf of Mexico, the Deepwater Horizon, sank after an explosion. Eleven people died in the blast. The pipe which connected the wellhead to the rig became disconnected and began leaking oil, and the wellhead itself was leaking. Several attempts to reattach the pipe and stop the leak failed and 60,000 barrels of oil per day were leaking into the ocean. It was the US's largest ever oil spill, threatening wild life along the coast, and bringing the fishing and tourist industries to a halt. President Obama suspended deep-water drilling in the Gulf of Mexico for six months. BP has incurred clean-up and other costs amounting to nearly $40 billion and suffered immense reputational damage as a result.[1]
> What are the economic and financial issues which arise here?

You saw that the disaster significantly reduced oil production, especially in the US. This led to supply shortages of the world's most valuable commodity, oil. The result was a rise in oil prices, as the US was forced to source oil on the world commodities markets to meet demand. Oil is a fundamental raw material. It is not just the fact that petrol is more expensive at the pumps, but oil in one form or another is used throughout the supply chain, increasing manufacturing and food costs. In the UK, the knock-on effect was a rise in inflation threatening the fragile economic recovery. The economic questions we thought about were:

1. What is a commodity?
2. What are commodity markets?
3. What sort of resource are raw materials?
4. What is the supply chain?
5. Why are supply and demand so important?
6. What is inflation?
7. Why does rising inflation have an effect on the economy?

You have looked at the supply chain, but the remaining questions will be covered in Sections 14.2 and 14.3.

BP's share price fell sharply in June 2010, which means that the value of the company plunged. To meet its losses, BP is selling assets worth $38 billion (£24.4 billion) by 2013.[2] At one point *The Guardian* estimated that £45 billion (36%) had been wiped off the value of the company[3] and there were rumours that BP could face insolvency. This raises further financial questions:

1. What do you know about shares?
2. Do you know why share prices affect the value of a company?
3. What are assets?

[1] 'BP's PR Campaign fails to clean up reputation after oil spill', *The Guardian*, 14 April 2011.
[2] Jaimie Grierson, 'BP still paying for Gulf of Mexico oil spill', *The Independent*, 31 July 2012.
[3] Graeme Wearden, 'BP oil spill: shares fall further', *The Guardian*, 2 June 2010.

4. Would you know where to look for a valuation of a company?

5. What is insolvency?

If you want to find out about company finances, you need to understand the basics of company accounts. Section 14.4 will cover these questions.

BP is one of the largest UK companies and millions are invested in its shares by UK shareholders, which includes individuals as well as institutional investors such as pension funds and unit trusts who have significant holdings. The fall in BP shares led a drop in the FTSE 100 index of leading shares.[4] As well as the fall in the value of the shares, the company suspended dividend payments to investors. There are further financial questions:

1. What is the stock market?

2. What is the FTSE 100?

3. What are pension funds and unit trusts?

4. Why are share prices important economically?

5. What is a dividend?

To answer these questions, you need to know what is happening in the City, which will be covered at 14.3.4.

> ### Case study 2
>
> The Olympic stadium was built with public money at an estimated cost of £423 million. It had a capacity of 80,000 people for the Olympics, but was built in such a way that this can be reduced to 25,000. With the Olympics over, what do you think should be done with it?
>
> What are the issues here?

This scenario also raised economic issues. We thought about the current housing shortage and house prices, which are dependent on supply and demand. This is one of the most fundamental economic concepts. We touched on the euro zone debt crisis.

14.2 Basic economics

What is economics? Economics is about wants and resources: the goods and services that individuals, businesses, and governments want, the resources that they have available to buy them, and the choices that are made when buying them. A central tenet is scarcity. No individual, business, or government can buy everything they want: neither goods and services nor resources are unlimited. In principle, and in economic terms, you have **infinite wants**, but you have limited resources with which to satisfy them—in economic terms, you have **finite resources**. The same is true for businesses, and for governments. Economics looks at how individuals, businesses, and governments manage this problem.

---

[4] Terry McAlister, 'BP facing multimillion-dollar legal claim from British pension fund', *The Observer*, 30 May 2010.

14.2.1 **Macroeconomics and microeconomics**

Faced with scarcity, everyone from the individual to the government is forced to make choices. The government may have to decide whether to spend more money on the NHS or on funding higher education, whilst a student might consider whether to spend money on a pair of jeans or a night out. Economists study how these choices are made. To do so, they divide economics into macroeconomics and microeconomics. 'Macro' means big, 'micro' means 'small'.

 Essential explanation

Macroeconomics is the study of how the entire economy works. It looks at the overall picture. Most television programmes and reports about the economy generally concentrate on macroeconomic concerns, such as unemployment, inflation, tax, or economic growth.

　Microeconomics is the study of individual businesses and consumers within the economy, and how they make choices about what to produce or how to spend money.

Clearly, there is an overlap between the two. Macroeconomic factors, such as tax and interest rates, affect individuals and businesses, and microeconomic activity is the basis for macroeconomic decisions, taken by the government and central banks. However, economists find it easier to keep the two separate. We will start with some microeconomics and then move on to macroeconomics, but first we need to consider some economic models and concepts.

14.2.2 **Economic models**

The detail of economics is highly complex. We are, after all, looking at the behaviour of governments, businesses, and individuals. Economists attempt to simplify things by making certain assumptions about how people and businesses behave, to produce economic models and theories which concentrate on the central issues. These are based on analysis of data and statistics. We shall therefore concentrate on basic economic concepts, and some of the accompanying jargon. Often, surprising as it seems, the use of jargon can simplify hugely complex concepts, which are summarised and conveyed by the use of one word or phrase.

Example 1

Economists look at things 'on the margin', for example 'marginal cost', 'marginal benefit', or 'marginal utility'. In economics **'marginal'** means **'one more'**. When you come across the word 'marginal' in any context, you know that it relates to, such as the benefit of producing or consuming one more unit of something. This does not have to be explained every time.

Models are based on theory, and are subject to criticism. They come in and out of fashion. For example, from about 1935 until the early 1970s, the government adopted a macroeconomic model for economic growth based on the theories of John Maynard Keynes (see also 6.4.3). These fell out of favour following the recession of 1972. Economic policy, particularly during the 1980s, was based on the theories of Milton Friedman, known as 'monetarism'. Since then the government has used a combination of the two.

 Essential explanation

Keynsian economics advocates active government intervention as a way of achieving economic growth and stability. Intervention takes the form of tax cuts and government spending to stimulate growth in times of recession, and tax increases and government cut backs to control inflation when the economy is healthy.

Monetarism is based on the idea that the quantity of money (the money supply) in the economy is what determines economic growth and inflation. Intervention by the government will eventually lead to higher prices (inflation). The role of the government is to control the money supply by controlling the amount of money within the economy, for example by increasing interest rates.

You may wonder why you need to know about economic theories. Interview questions could touch on the government's economic policy.

 Sample interview question

What do you think about the latest budget?

We will look at this in Chapter 16. For now, just bear in mind that to answer this effectively, not only would you need to know what the government's current economic policy is based on, but also what the alternatives could be.

14.2.3 Utility and opportunity cost

The concept of scarcity is fundamental to economics: given we cannot have everything we want, everyone has to make choices.

Economists start with the assumption that those choices are made to maximise human happiness. Happiness is not something you would automatically associate with economics, and it is, in fact, referred to as '**utility**'. Decisions are made by comparing the potential utility that each decision will bring and then choosing the one that will bring maximum utility, namely the one that has the highest utility and dismissing those that have a low or negative utility.

This all seems somewhat selfish, but economists also assume that one person's pursuit of happiness has the knock-on effect of increasing other people's happiness as well. For example, when you decide to buy a pair of shoes, you have decided that having a pair of shoes will bring you the greatest utility (given all the other options you have for spending your money). The shoe shop, however, is clearly not in business just to make its customers happy. It is in business to maximise profit, and so by buying a pair of shoes, you have contributed to the shoe shop's utility, whilst increasing your own.

There are, of course, consequences. Each decision has what is called an '**opportunity cost**', or the benefit that you have lost. Apart from no longer having the money spent on shoes, you have, for example, given up the opportunity to buy a handbag or jeans. So there is a choice to be made, but economists assume that consumers make it rationally.

You may be wondering what all this has to do with law. To give just one example, freedom of contract is partly based on the idea that parties to a contract choose to enter into 'deals' that are mutually beneficial.

14.2.4 **Basic microeconomics**

Microeconomics studies how businesses, workers, and consumers behave within markets, and the influence they have on prices, costs, and profits. We have already looked at several microeconomic issues, such as when we looked at pricing and sectors and markets at 13.4. At first glance, these may seem to be issues that are only relevant for businesses. However, they are the issues that underlie the decisions of the owners and managers of businesses, the people who will be your clients. Commercial awareness, as you saw in Chapter 13, is understanding these underlying issues and the 'latent' concerns of your clients. As a lawyer you need to be aware of them.

Resources and production

The starting point when looking at microeconomic issues is to think about what businesses do. Businesses take resources (referred to as **inputs** or **factors of production**) and convert them into a product (**outputs**). These outputs are not necessarily manufactured goods; they may be services. Outputs are dependent on resources. In economic terms, the resources which businesses have at their disposal are divided into four categories:

1. **Land**: includes raw materials, such as oil, gas, minerals, and agricultural produce, and also the weather, geothermal energy, and the electromagnetic spectrum.
2. **Labour**: the ability of individuals to work and thus contribute to production.
3. **Capital**: the physical 'things' which businesses use to produce other products, such as offices, machinery and plant, computers. It includes all sorts of other things like roads, sewers, electrical grids, and the internet.
4. **Enterprise**, or **human capital**: the human factor that transforms and drives the production process. Entrepreneurs are the people who have ideas, take risks, and invest in business. You tend to think about business people such as Richard Branson or Alan Sugar, but in fact, every shareholder who takes the risk of investing in a company is an entrepreneur.

All businesses, whatever their type, convert these resources into products, either goods or services. Law firms are no exception. They are converting the expertise of their solicitors into the legal service which they are providing to their clients, and as a result, law firms make a substantial contribution to the economy: £23.1 billion in 2009[5] (see Chapter 15).

Clearly there is a limited pool of resources. Unlimited production of any product is never going to be possible, and so the production of one product will always be at the expense of another. In economic terms, there is a **production possibility frontier** beyond which production is impossible. This is true for both businesses and economies in general.

---

[5] Ministry of Justice, *Plan for Growth: Promoting the UK's Legal Services* (2011).

Example 2

The easiest illustration of this is to imagine an economy which only produces two products, for example shoes and handbags. If all available resources were fully utilised and used to make shoes, there would be no handbags, but you would have the maximum number of shoes which could be produced, given the resources that are available. The result is that you have to reduce the number of shoes produced in order to produce handbags. In an ideal economy, a point would be reached where resources were fully utilised to produce an equal number of handbags and shoes.

However, businesses are not going to produce goods or services simply because they have the resources to do so. They are not going to produce anything unless they can make a profit from doing so. In other words, they have to be sure of two things:

1. The return is greater than the cost of production. This return will usually, but not always, be measured in monetary terms.

2. There is a market for the produce, in other words that they can sell it.

Economists calculate returns on production and analyse how consumers behave within the market. Both of these factors will affect the price of the goods or services.

Maximising profits

Economists assume that the main objective of any business is to maximise profits. In very simple terms, they do this by ensuring that revenue exceeds costs.

Economists take a different view of profits to that taken by accountants. Accountants simply look at the amount by which revenue exceeds costs. For example, if a car dealer buys a car for £2,000 (the cost) and sells it for £2,500 (the revenue), he will have made a profit of £500. Economists, however, give different meanings to profit, revenue, and costs. Economic profit, for example, takes into account opportunity costs. So in this example, if the dealer could have put the £2,000 in the bank instead of buying the car, and earned interest of £200, then the true cost is £2,200, reducing profit to £300.

Analysis of costs in relation to revenue enables businesses to set prices and work out how, what, and how much to sell to make a profit. In fact, price and output depend on a variety of other factors, such as the way that the business is run, the information which the business has, and the strategy which the managers of the business have decided to adopt. For example, managers may decide that their priority is to maximise the exposure of their brand, as this will give them a competitive edge in the long run. They may therefore, incur high marketing costs in the short term. (Marketing costs are known as **sunk** costs—costs which have been incurred and which cannot be recovered.)

Equally important are the characteristics of the market in which each business operates. We have already considered the effect of competition in Chapter 13. Clearly, the more competitive the market, the less opportunity there is to raise prices.

Supply and demand

The behaviour of the consumers who buy or use their products is also crucial to determining price and profit for businesses. This brings us on to one of the most fundamental economic concepts, supply and demand. Thomas Carlyle, a 19th-century economist, famously stated 'Teach a parrot supply and demand and you've got an economist', reflecting the fact that these are two of the most basic terms in economics.

 Essential explanation

Demand is how much of a product people want, that is we look at demand from the perspective of a consumer. The law of demand states that as demand for a product increases, prices will increase. If the price increases, demand will decrease. This is shown on a demand curve (Figure 14.1). Note that the demand curve slopes downwards.

   Supply is how much of a product is available, that is we look at supply from the point of view of the supplier. The law of supply states that as the demand increases, and prices go up, supply will increase to meet the rising demand. If prices decrease, businesses will produce less, because they will make a lower profit. This is shown on a supply curve (Figure 14.2), which by contrast slopes up.

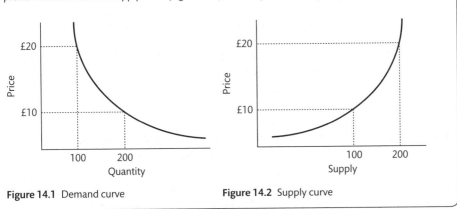

Figure 14.1 Demand curve   **Figure 14.2** Supply curve

The essential thing to understand here is the relationship between price, supply, and demand. Normally, in a free economy, markets regulate themselves.

- When demand goes up, prices rise until they 'peak'. People decide that they are paying too much for a particular product and either start to buy something else instead, **substitutes**, or stop buying that product at all.
- On the supply side, businesses will have seen that prices for a particular product are increasing, and high prices encourage production (so supply increases). Once the price 'peaks' there is no further incentive to produce more.

Example 3

Imagine that there is huge demand for lager, leading to shortages. Prices go up to £7 a pint, way beyond the price of other beers, which still cost £3 a pint. Manufacturers notice this and start producing more lager. At the same time, demand for lager will begin to fall because other beers now seem comparatively cheap. Unless lager is the only product people want to buy, they will start to buy other beers. The result is that the price will start to fall to a level where people are prepared to start buying it again. Supply will have gone up so there is now enough to go round. This will keep the price of lager stable at, say £3.50 a pint.

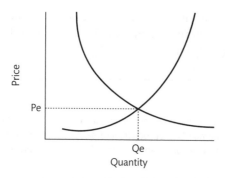

Figure 14.3 Equilibrium price

- Eventually, the price will fall to an equilibrium price where consumers are getting exactly the quantity they want at a price which they want to pay, and suppliers are selling exactly the quantity they want to sell at a price which ensures that they make a profit, that is to say everyone is happy. Supply equals demand. This is shown by Figure 14.3.

There are of course variables which may prevent this, such as consumer taste, the number and price of substitute goods, the market, and again the amount of competition are all significant.

Price elasticity

A further factor which businesses need to consider is price elasticity. Elasticity depends on the availability of substitute goods. The more substitutes there are for a product, the more elastic the demand will be, in other words, demand is highly responsive to price changes. Even a small change in price can lead to a large change in demand. Lager is a good example. There are hundreds of different brands of lager but other beers can be substituted, depending on taste. So if one manufacturer puts up prices, consumers will start buying another, or a different type of beer. The fewer the substitutes, the more inelastic the demand will be. Petrol is an example. The demand is likely to be inelastic as there is no real substitute. Although raising prices may mean that a few customers are lost, the price change is unlikely to deter a large number of customers.

Historically, it was always thought that professional services, like law and accountancy, were inelastic. Legal services are a necessity at certain times in an individual's life, but the supply of lawyers has been restricted by the need to pass exams and complete a lengthy training. However, this could all change with greater competition and deregulation, as discussed in Chapter 15. It is something to bear in mind when considering the threats and challenges to the legal profession.

An understanding of supply and demand is fundamental to your understanding of economics. Wherever you look, you can see that it has practical application. If we go back to Case study 1, the reason for the increase in oil prices following the BP oil spill was shortage of supply without a corresponding decrease in demand. Case study 2, looking at the analysis of the Olympic Park development, illustrated on the effect of supply and demand on house prices, more information on which can be found in David Smith's book *Free Lunch*.[6]

[6] David Smith, *Free Lunch* (London: Profile Books, 2008).

14.2.5 **Basic macroeconomics**

Macroeconomics is the study of how the entire economy works. The main macroeconomic issues are GDP (gross domestic product), inflation, unemployment, and what is called the current account, which is the difference between exports and imports. All of these are controlled to a certain extent by government policy. They are also the factors which businesses and those who manage them will need to consider before making any decisions. For lawyers, an understanding of these issues is vital when advising clients; for students, these are the issues which make the news and which you need to understand when you are applying for jobs, so we are going look at macroeconomics in more detail.

One of the problems about macroeconomic issues for students is that they are so central to our everyday lives that you will find that everyone—your tutors, employers and, when you get into practice, clients—tends to assume that you know what they are, and why they are important. If you have studied economics, you may do. If not, you need somewhere to find the information. This section is designed to give you some background, and help you with the sort of terminology and jargon which you will hear on the news, and which may come up at interviews. Refer to it when you need it.

Types of economy

We started looking at microeconomics by thinking about the problem of scarcity and resources. It is not possible to produce infinite quantities of any type of product, given limited resources. Resources need to be allocated to production. How they are allocated depends on the type of economy, of which there are three main types:

1. A **free market economy** is one where consumers and businesses decide what they want to buy and produce. Decisions about production will be determined by supply and demand, and the government plays a very limited role. This is also known as a 'laissez-faire' economy (which means in French 'leave to do [its own thing]'). Resources and the means of production are owned by individuals and businesses.

2. A **command** or **planned economy** is one where the government plans what will be produced, by whom, and how. Examples are the former Soviet Union and China under Chairman Mao. Resources and the means of production are owned by the people (in the form of the state). There are a few remaining planned economies (e.g. North Korea or Cuba).

3. In reality, most economies are **mixed economies**, where both market forces and government policy determine what goods and services are produced. In general, market forces will be the most important factor determining this, but the government does have a considerable influence through legislation, government spending, and welfare. Thus most resources and means of production are owned by individuals and businesses, but the government is responsible for the provision of some goods or, more likely, services, like education, health, and defence.

Figure 14.4 shows that in reality there is an overlap. There is no such thing as a completely free economy and most planned economies, such as the People's Republic of China, have started to introduce elements of a free economy, like competition.

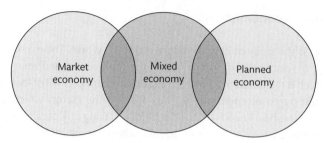

Figure 14.4 Economic systems

Supply and demand

Supply and demand are still important issues, but macroeconomics looks at **aggregate** supply and demand, namely the supply and demand in the whole economy.

 Essential explanation

Aggregate demand is the total of all consumption, investment, government spending, and net exports in the economy.

  Aggregate supply measures the volume of goods which can be produced in the entire economy at a given price level, namely the productive capacity available in the economy to *produce* goods and services, taking into account the available resources.

Again, there is a relationship between prices and aggregate supply and demand. If demand rises, prices will rise and, to achieve price equilibrium, supply will also have to increase. Equilibrium occurs when supply equals demand. This time, however, we are not looking at the price of individual items supplied by one business, we are looking at price levels across the whole economy.

  When times are good, government, business, and consumer spending and investment (i.e. demand) will be high, which will have the effect of driving up prices. This will not be a problem if supply can increase in tandem. However, aggregate supply depends on available resources, such as the supply of labour or land. In good times, there is likely to be full employment and land will be expensive, so finding a new factory or office, and staffing it, may be difficult and expensive. It will be difficult for businesses to produce any more. Prices therefore continue to rise, resulting in inflation. The economy 'overheats', which is often the first sign that the economy is going into recession. We will consider the causes of recession below.

Government intervention

In all types of economy, the government will intervene to a greater or lesser extent. Even in a free market economy, there may be reasons why a government might have to intervene. To take an extreme example, if there was no government intervention in the economy, it would be perfectly legitimate to sell Class A drugs (there would be a legitimate supply and legitimate demand), however harmful these may be. So the government needs to legislate on this for the greater good of society. The extent of government intervention in an economy can be measured by looking at the percentage of government spending and investment in relation to GDP, which we will consider below.

In the UK, as with all mixed economies, government intervention aims to achieve four main objectives:

- economic growth;
- stable prices/low inflation;
- low unemployment;
- favourable balance of payments.

Whatever else you need to know about the economy, you need to know about these. They are in the news all the time.

These objectives can be achieved by the use of fiscal and monetary policies. Policies which seek to control demand are known as **demand side policies** and, not surprisingly, those that seek to control supply are known as **supply side policies**.

Essential explanation

Fiscal policy involves the use of government spending, taxation, and borrowing to control **demand** and therefore economic activity. A 'tight' fiscal policy is where governments limit public spending. The current government's 'austerity programme' is a version of this. This is highly topical.

Monetary policy involves the use of interest rates to control the rate of aggregate demand, the **money supply**, and inflation. This is the responsibility of the central bank. The Bank of England is the UK's central bank. We will look at this at 14.3.1.

Gross domestic product or GDP

Essential explanation

GDP is the equivalent of **aggregate demand**. It is the sum of everything produced in the economy (inputs) less the amount it costs to produce (outputs). It is the sum total of everything that the government and millions of businesses and individuals are contributing, spending, and earning. It is measured quarterly (i.e. every three months) based on a huge survey of figures compiled by the Office for National Statistics (ONS). Figure 14.5 shows what contributes to GDP.

GDP is important because it is the chief measure of economic growth (i.e. the increase in economic output). It shows how well (or badly) the economy is doing. Ideally, the economy will grow at a consistent rate. In the UK there is no set target for economic growth, but on average the economy has grown at a rate of between 2% and 3%. At 2.5%, aggregate demand will grow at an equivalent rate to aggregate supply, so there will be low inflation and low unemployment. Slow or negative growth impacts on all sectors of the economy.

The business cycle

Growth does not remain constant. There are periods of boom, recession, slump, and recovery. These phases are known as the business, or economic, cycle.

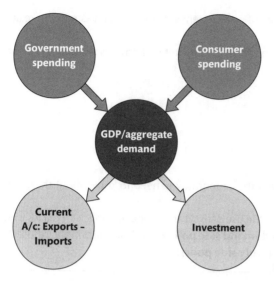

Figure 14.5 GDP or aggregate demand

 Essential explanation

A **boom** is when the economy grows.

A **recession** is when the economy shrinks for two or more quarters.

A **slump** is where a recession is severe and prolonged.

Recovery occurs when the economy begins to grow after a recession.

A **double-dip recession** is when the economy starts to recover, but then falls back into recession.

(See Example 4.)

Causes of recession

There are various causes of recession, but the most usual are inflation and 'economic shock'.

1. **Inflation**. As inflation increases, demand falls, and people start to save rather than spend. Businesses produce less, and generally start to lay off workers in order to cut costs

2. **Economic shock**. An 'economic shock' is a sudden and unexpected external factor which pushes the economy into recession. An example would be a sudden rise in oil prices. This is one of the reasons why the BP oil spill had such an impact.

Example 4

From 2008, the global financial crisis resulted in one of the deepest and most prolonged recessions on record. The economy began to grow in 2009, but since then recovery has been slow and there were periods during 2010–11 when either the economy showed no growth or shrank. The UK economy officially went back into recession when the GDP shrank by -0.3% in the final quarter of 2011 and -0.2% in the first quarter of 2012 (i.e. two quarters of negative growth). Since then it has improved, and in the third quarter of 2012 had grown by 1%.[7]

[7] http://www.ons.gov.uk.

Inflation

 Essential explanation

Inflation is the rate of change of prices for goods and services. There are a number of different measures of inflation, but the ones that you are most likely to see are:

- the Consumer Price Index (CPI); and
- the Retail Price Index (RPI).

To arrive at a figure, the government tracks the price of a hypothetical basket of over 650 goods each month. The 'basket' includes all the things which we use all the time, including food, drink, fuel, and entertainment. The RPI includes mortgage payments and council tax and is said to be more reflective of real prices than the CPI, which does not include these items. The quicker prices go up, the higher the rate of inflation.

The amount that the basket goes up is calculated as a percentage. If the cost of the basket goes up by 5% over a 12-month period, then the rate of inflation for that 12-month period is 5%. The same goods and services cost 5% more than they did 12 months ago. People will be worth 5% less in real terms, unless their incomes also rise by 5%. High rates of inflation therefore reduce living standards as individuals have less money to spend.

The current target rate of inflation is 2.0%.[8] The Bank of England has the responsibility of ensuring that inflation remains within that target. When inflation misses that target by more than 1%, the Chairman of the Bank of England is required to write an open letter to the Chancellor to explain why this has happened.

There are two main causes of inflation.

1. Demand grows faster than supply. This is known as **demand-pull inflation**. China is currently experiencing this type of inflation, as the wealth of its population increases and demand for consumer goods rises.

2. Production costs rise, for example the cost of raw materials and labour. Businesses pass these increased costs on to consumers. This is known as **cost-pull inflation**. An example is the cost of food. In November 2012 the *Daily Telegraph* reported that poor harvests leading to a sharp rise in the price of grain had put up food prices, consequently fuelling inflation.[9]

Inflation has a number of consequences for both businesses and individuals. As prices rise, resources become more expensive and profits for businesses fall. Wages fall in real terms. Labour becomes more expensive as workers seek wage rises. Forecasting profits and prices becomes more difficult, and businesses cut back, leading to higher unemployment. The knock-on effect will be that the economy contracts.

[8] http://www.bankofengland.co.uk, 19 February 2013.
[9] Rosie Murray-West, 'Food prices are rising and it's going to get worse', *The Telegraph*, 3 November 2012.

Unemployment

 Essential explanation

Unemployment measures all those who are willing and able to work, but who cannot find a job. The official level does not include those who are either unable or unwilling to work (e.g. because of disability). The government measures unemployment monthly. In October 2012, the number of people unemployed was 2.53 million in the UK (7.9% of the total workforce).[10] These workers are entitled to claim jobseekers allowance.

There are various causes of unemployment.

1. **Cyclical** unemployment is the most important at the moment. This occurs as a result of a downturn in the economic cycle. As we have seen, if demand within the economy decreases then businesses will lay off workers. Accordingly, it is also referred to **demand-deficient** unemployment.

2. **Structural** unemployment is the result of a particular industry going into decline. Workers who lose their jobs as a result do not have the skills to get jobs in other industries or sectors.

Labour is one of the main economic resources, so unemployment represents the waste of a resource. For the government, fewer people working means less income from tax and the need to pay out larger sums in benefits.

Balance of payments and the current account

As well as the situation within the UK, international trade also has to be taken into account when measuring the health of the economy. Businesses export their goods and services to countries outside the UK and businesses and individuals import resources, such as raw materials and products or services, like cars and electrical goods, from outside the UK.

 Essential explanation

The **balance of payments** measures the difference between the country's exports and imports, including all financial exports and imports. It measures all money flowing in and out of the country. The **current account** is the difference between exports and imports of goods and services (as opposed to sales and purchases of land or shares and bonds).

Ideally exports should exceed imports. This is a **trade surplus**. In this case, income from abroad is **injected** into the economy. However, in the UK the reverse is the case; we import more than we export, so the UK has what is known as a **trade deficit**. In September 2012 this stood at £10.1 billion.[11] The UK does have a strong record for the export of services, especially financial services, which is why the City of London is one of the major financial centres in the

[10] ONS, *Labour Market Statistics, October 2012.*
[11] ONS, *Balance of Payments Q2 2012,*

world, but as manufacturing has declined in the UK, we have imported more goods than we have exported.

The balance of payments is one of the measures of a country's financial health. It is an indicator of a country's ability to pay its way in the world. A trade deficit will mean that the government has to borrow more. It may also have an effect on the value of the currency.

The nature and extent of government intervention to control these factors will depend to a large extent on the political leaning of the government in power at the time. The current coalition government policy is one of austerity, cutting back government spending and borrowing, and increasing taxes (i.e. fiscal policy). At the same time, the central bank has made periodic injections of money into the economy, to increase the money supply (i.e. monetary policy), and stimulate demand. This is known as **quantitative easing**.

 Essential explanation

Quantitative easing is where the central bank buys financial assets from banks and private sector businesses with new, electronically created money. The purpose of injecting money into the economy is to stimulate activity and growth within the economy. It has been used because conventional monetary policy, namely lowering interest rates, is not possible as they are already at an all time low (0.5%).

The problem for the government is that it is rarely possible to solve all economic problems at one time. Improvements in one area come at the expense of others. For example, since March 2009, the Bank of England has kept interest rates at a record low of 0.5% in order to stimulate growth and help reduce unemployment levels, and the government has pursued a policy of austerity. Inflation has been above the target rate for over two years.

 Sample interview question

Do you think that austerity is working? (This is a variation on 'What do you think about the latest budget?') This is not an opportunity to give a forthright explanation of your own political views. Analyse the alternatives to show a balanced approach (see 14.2.2).

14.3 Banks, money, and the financial markets

Chapter 13 shows us that the financial markets are just another type of market or sector of the economy. In the UK, the City of London is the financial district of London. Although it is only approximately one square mile in the centre of London (and thus sometimes referred to as the 'Square Mile'), it is one of the world's leading financial centres, with financial institutions from all over the world based there. It is impossible to underestimate the influence of the financial markets and the City on the economy, and consequently the decisions taken by individuals and businesses. Today it is probably fair to say that everyone's lives have been touched by the banking crisis and the subsequent shortage of credit. In Chapter 16 we look at how individuals and business raise finance, and some of the difficulties they face as the result of the credit crunch. As a lawyer, whether you are acting for a young couple buying their first home, or for a corporate client involved in a large-scale corporate acquisition, you need to be aware of what is going on in the City, as it affects their ability to raise finance.

14.3.1 **Banks**

One of the most topical issues today is the influence of the banks within the financial markets and the economy. If you are going to understand the financial news today, you need to understand about banks and the banking system.

The central bank

The Bank of England is the central bank in the UK. It is not a bank in the usual sense as you cannot go and open an account there. Rather, it has overall responsibility for the rate of inflation, and is responsible for the implementation of monetary policy. It sets interest rates and issues bank notes. It issues money into the economy through the banking system and acts as a banker for the government and other banks. Unlike ordinary banks, the central bank does not lend money directly to either the banks or the government. It does so through the use of **financial instruments** such as stocks, bonds, and gilts (see 14.3.4).

Commercial and investment banks

Other than the central bank, banks are categorised into **commercial** (retail and wholesale banks) and **investment** banks.

1. **Commercial banks** take deposits from and lend to customers. They borrow money from other banks and the money market. They make their money by borrowing at one rate of interest and lending at a higher rate. There are two types of commercial bank:

   - **Retail banks** who lend to consumer customers and small businesses. They also offer financial services both to individuals, such as investment advice or providing foreign currency for holiday makers, and to small businesses, for example a start-up business can get advice from a small business manager who will help it through the basics of setting up and running the business.

   - **Wholesale banks** operate in the business-to-business market. They take very large deposits and arrange very large loans, both for other banks and for large corporate and commercial institutions.

2. **Building societies** perform the same role as retail banks, but they specialise in lending for the purpose of buying property. However, many have been taken over by banks, for example the Abbey National Building Society is now part of Santander.

3. **Investment banks** are not involved in the lending and borrowing process like commercial banks. Their customers are governments and large corporations. They deal with bond issues for the government and large companies and also organise takeover bids, flotation of companies, and issues of shares by companies.

Figure 14.6 shows the interrelationship between the banks.

Although some of the larger banks, like Barclays, Lloyds, or HSBC, do have an investment section, individuals and small businesses are unlikely to have dealings with this part of the

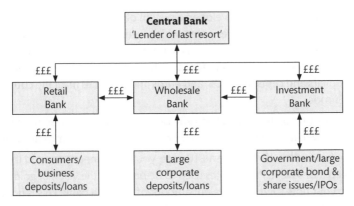

Figure 14.6 The banking system

bank or other investment banks, which are mainly located in major financial centres, like the City of London or New York. The retail sections of the banks, and the building societies, are based on most high streets.

The deposits which customers make enable banks to lend to other customers. When the economy is working well, the savings that one person makes are injected back into the economy in the form of loans. When it is not, there is the potential for huge problems because of the way in which banks borrow and lend.

Banks are said to **borrow short** and **lend long**.

- **Borrowing short**. When customers open either a current or ordinary deposit account at a bank, they are lending money to the bank. Although the deposit is a loan, customers with these types of account can withdraw their money at any time.

- **Lending long**. Banks lend money to customers, and charge interest for doing so. Loans are often long term, for example mortgages are generally for a term of 25 years, and unless the customer defaults on her interest payments, the bank cannot call them in.

This is not, as a rule, a problem. Most people trust their banks and are happy to leave their savings in the bank. However, if confidence in the bank falls for one reason or another, customers withdraw their money. A panic will lead to a 'run on the bank'. Loans cannot be called in to raise the cash needed to pay all the customers who are demanding their money, and the bank will technically become insolvent. This is what happened with Northern Rock in 2007. It was subsequently rescued by the government, and has now been bought by Richard Branson's Virgin Group.

14.3.2 **Money and the money supply**

What is money?

It is often said that 'money makes the world go round'. Money is central to the economy: the government, the banking system, individuals, and businesses alike. You probably think you know what money is, but in reality it has a variety of functions.

1. Money is a **medium of exchange**. It enables you to buy things. If there was no money, we would have to barter (i.e. swap goods or services for other goods or services, say two pairs of shoes for a handbag). Even early societies found this did not work well.

As early as 700 BC, the Chinese developed a system of money, based on metal coins, and about 118 BC introduced paper notes, which were easier to carry around. Gradually, all countries developed their own systems of notes and coins, which have been refined over the years. These are the **currencies** of each country, such as pounds and pence in the UK, dollars and cents in the US, and euros and centimes in all the countries of mainland Europe.

2. As money is the unit of exchange which we use to buy things, it is also used to set prices. All goods are given a monetary value, so money is said to be a **unit of account**.

3. Money also has a value. If you have a £10 note, you do not need to spend it immediately. You can keep it or save it. Paper notes used to be based on the value of gold, so you could swap your note for the equivalent amount of gold at a bank. This is no longer the case, but notes are now backed by the central bank, which guarantees payment. Money is also therefore a **unit of worth**.

The money supply

 Essential explanation

The money supply is based on statistics compiled by the Bank of England. It is the total amount of money in the economy at a given time. It consists of notes, coins, money held in bank and building society accounts, and M4 lending (i.e. loans from banks and building societies).

So money is not just cash in hand. Individuals and businesses also deposit money in banks and building society accounts. Those banks and building societies then lend money to other individuals and businesses. The money supply is made up of all these.

The money multiplier

Because the money supply takes into account loans, in reality not all money actually exists. Banks are continually 'creating' money by lending out the funds which customers have deposited with them. When a customer deposits money with a bank, the bank is required to keep a 'reserve' (i.e. a percentage of that deposit), but it can lend out the rest. The result of this lending is to expand the money supply. Below is a very simple example (Example 5).

Example 5

Bagit Ltd, a designer handbag company, sells ten handbags for £1,000 cash. It deposits this money with its bank. The bank keeps a reserve of, say, 10%, just in case Bagit does want to withdraw some money, and lends out the rest (i.e. the bank keeps £100 and lends out £900 to nine customers). Each customer borrows £100 and decides to buy a handbag from Bagit. So £900 of Bagit's money flows back into the economy. Bagit deposits this £900 in the bank, and the process starts all over again. The bank lends out £810 and so on. Bagit thinks it has £1,900 in the bank, but in reality most of that money is working outside the bank to increase the amount of cash in circulation.

Clearly, the higher the reserve requirement, the less money there is in circulation (i.e. the money supply is 'tight'). In the example above, if the reserve was 25%, the bank could only lend out £750 from a deposit of £1,000.

Understanding the money multiplier makes it easier to see how interest rates can control the money supply. When interest is high, people tend to save rather than borrow, so consequently there is less money flowing back into the economy. A tight money supply reduces demand, and economic growth.

A further problem arises where banks are unwilling to lend, which has been the case since 2008. Again, this reduces the amount of money in circulation.

14.3.3 Interest rates

We have looked at interest rates in the context of individual and business borrowing and credit, but now we are going to consider how these rates are arrived at. Again, interest rates are a highly topical issue, and something that could easily be the subject of interview questions. (See the sample interview question below.)

 Essential explanation

Interest is the cost of borrowing. There are various rates of interest, the **official bank rate** on which **market rates** are based, and **LIBOR**.

---

1. The Bank of England's Monetary Policy Committee (MPC) meets once a month to set the **official bank rate**. This is the rate which it charges to lend to other banks. We have seen that the Bank of England uses the official rate to regulate growth and control inflation. Currently interest rates are set at an all time low of 0.5%. The banks then set their base rate, which will generally follow the official bank rate.

2. **Market rates**. However, the official rate is not the rate at which banks lend to or borrow from their customers. When you look at the financial pages, you can see that there is a very wide variation in the interest rates offered to customers. Banks borrow at a rate which will attract customers and lend at a premium which will ensure that they make a profit. This premium is based on a number of factors, the most important of which are:

    –   Risk. With any loan, there is always a risk of default. The greater the likelihood that a customer will default, the higher the interest rate it will have to pay.

    –   The rate at which the banks can borrow from each other.

3. **LIBOR** stands for London Interbank Offered Rate. This is the rate at which banks will lend to each other. Unlike the official interest rate, it changes daily and is based on supply and demand. The rate is published by the British Banking Association (BBA) every day at 11 am, and has a very important effect on interest rates overall. When it goes up, banks find it more expensive to borrow, and this cost will be passed on to the consumer. Many financial institutions, such as mortgage lenders and credit card companies, base their rates on LIBOR, typically setting their rates at a percentage, say 2%, above LIBOR. The importance of LIBOR was illustrated by the scandal in 2012 when it emerged that the

investment branch of Barclays Bank had been fixing the rate.[12] This is a good example of how the actions of an investment bank can have an impact on the everyday lives of individuals. The fixing of the rate increased the price of borrowing for the ordinary consumer, and has had significant repercussions.

 Sample interview question

Why is the LIBOR rate so important?

14.3.4 **Financial markets**

 Essential explanation

A **financial market** is a market where traders come together to trade financial instruments, such as shares, bonds, or currencies.

There are various types of financial market, so now we will consider some of these and the main investors in these markets. The starting point is the **capital** markets, made up of the stock and bond markets.

Stock markets

When we looked at the BP scenario in Case study 1, we saw how the disaster had a devastating effect on the company's share price. This in turn had a knock-on effect on the stock market as a whole. This section is intended to give you the background you need to understand how this happened, and its importance.

Shares in public companies, and other stocks and securities, are normally bought and sold on a **stock market**, or **stock exchange**. The London Stock Exchange is an example.

The London Stock Exchange is effectively like a supermarket, where everyone who wants trade in shares can go to buy and sell. With advances in technology, there are now few actual physical market places. Trading is conducted through dedicated computer network systems, such as the National Association of Securities Dealers Automated Quotation (NASDAQ) system in the US.

There are two main markets in the UK: the London Stock Exchange Main Market and the Alternative Investment Market (AIM). This means that the London Stock Exchange has a 'two tier' system.

1. Larger companies join or are **listed** or **quoted** on the London Stock Exchange Main Market. About 1,400 companies from 60 countries are listed on the Main Market. In 2011, the combined assets of these companies amounted to £3.7 trillion: £20.8 billion of this had been raised on the Stock Exchange, £17.9 billion of that on the Main Market.[13]

---

[12] See e.g. 'Timeline: Libor fixing scandal', *BBC News*, 6 February 2013, http://www.bbc.co.uk/news/business-18671255.

[13] London Stock Exchange, *A Guide to Listing on the London Stock Exchange*, http://londonstockexchange.com/home/guide-to-listing.pdf.

2. AIM is a sub-market of the stock exchange. It was set up in 1995 so that investors could trade in shares which are not suitable for the Main Market. It is targeted at smaller companies which are hoping to grow in size, and is also popular with international companies. There are about 1,200 companies listed on AIM, including some football clubs, such as Watford or Tottenham Hotspur.

Share prices

Share prices are not fixed. Once a company has joined a stock market, its share price will be determined by the market (i.e. by supply and demand from investors). For each listed company, there is a fixed number of shares in circulation. Prices will rise when large numbers of people want to buy shares in that company and fall when they want to sell.

The fickle nature of market forces makes share prices volatile, and very difficult to predict. Any number of forces—social, political, economic, technological, or sometimes apparently inexplicable trends—can push share prices up and down. BP is a good example of a combination of political, economic, social, and ecological factors acting in tandem. Sometimes the fluctuations are based on rumour and sometimes on fact. You may have seen the terms 'bull market' and 'bear market'. These relate to the performance of the markets.

 Essential explanation

A **bull market** occurs when prices rise, confidence is high, and investors anticipate that prices will continue to rise for a consistent period.

A **bear market** occurs when prices are falling, investors are pessimistic and anticipate that prices will continue to fall for a consistent period.

 Sample interview question

Explain in layman's terms the difference between a bull and a bear market.

Indexes

To find out what a share is worth, and evaluate its performance, you consult an **index**. An index tracks a 'basket' of shares over a period of time (a bit like the RPI tracks the price of a typical basket of goods). In the UK, there are several indexes, the best known of which are those produced by the *Financial Times*, for example the FTSE 100 ('Footsie') which tracks the performance of the largest UK companies. If the share price of one large FTSE 100 company, like BP, falls sharply, this will bring down the FTSE, as we are looking at average prices.

Traditionally, the London Stock Exchange has been one of the leading stock markets in the world, although not necessarily the biggest. This has given the City of London a leading role in the international financial markets. There are other important markets such as the New York, Hong Kong, and Japanese stock markets. Each has its own index, such as the US Dow Jones Industrial Average (referred to as the Dow Jones, or simply the Dow) or the Hong Kong Hang Seng Index.

Bonds and the bond markets

The government and companies issue bonds and other debt instruments in order to borrow money (see 'Corporate finance' at 16.5.2). Government bonds are known as gilt-edged securities, or simply gilts. Public, but not private, companies can issue bonds as well as shares, and bonds are an important source of finance for public companies. Bonds can be bought or sold by investors. They are traded on the bond market.

When investors buy government bonds, they are lending money to the government and when they buy corporate bonds, they are lending money to a company. Bonds are generally considered to be the safest type of investment. Investors get a fixed rate of interest, and at the end of a specified period, they get their money back. As bonds are a relatively risk-free investment, the rate of return is relatively low.

Other financial markets

Investors do not just invest in shares and bonds. There are numerous other investment opportunities, which tend to be higher risk, but which also offer higher returns if investors get it right. There are markets for each of these types of investment.

1. **Currency markets** are global markets for foreign exchange (**Forex**), such as dollars, euros, yen, sterling, etc. Businesses need foreign currencies to trade abroad. Governments buy and sell currencies. Currencies can also be held as an investment. The price depends on supply and demand. Each day the financial news will report whether the pound has gone up or down in relation to other currencies, for example as against the dollar or the euro.

2. **Commodity markets** are markets where raw materials such as gold, oil, wheat, coffee, or cotton are traded. Commodity prices can be very volatile, namely going up or down very quickly depending again on supply and demand. The escalation in the price of oil is a current example. This ties into the BP analysis in Case study 1.

 Essential explanation

Currencies and commodities can either be traded on a **spot market**, where traders buy for immediate physical delivery, or they can buy **forward** for physical delivery at a specified date in the future.

---

3. **Futures markets**. Contracts to purchase currencies or commodities at a future date are sold on the futures market. Here there is no physical delivery of the commodity. The speculator simply buys the paper (futures) contract and takes on the risk of price fluctuations. If the price goes up before delivery he has made money; if it goes down, he has lost it. This type of investment is highly speculative.

4. **Derivatives markets**. Derivatives are investments the value of which is based on the performance of an underlying investment. When an investor buys a derivative, he is betting on the value of another investment. A futures contract, for example, is a derivative, as its value is based on the price of the underlying commodity. There are even 'weather derivatives' (which is effectively betting on weather conditions).

Who invests in the markets?

The individual (or retail) investor is a rarity. Not all investors are confident about investing in the markets. It is, after all, risky. Investors may be lucky, but generally they need a certain amount of knowledge and expertise. In addition, there are trading costs on deals, which can be very high. Usually, investors rely on professional advice. The result is that the main investors are institutions, which manage over 80% of the overall value of UK company shares. As they are the main players in the financial markets, we are now going to look at some of these.

1. **Investment funds**. An alternative to DIY for individual investors is to use the services of an investment, or managed, fund. Investors pay a management fee, but gain the benefit of a professionally managed fund and access to a far greater range of investments, and reduce the costs of investment.

2. **Hedge funds**. These have had a bad name recently, as there have been several high-profile frauds involving hedge funds reported in the media, and this is a topical issue. A hedge fund is simply another type of managed fund, but they are mainly used by wealthy individuals or institutional investors, rather than small investors.

 Essential explanation

Hedging is off-setting investments, so that for every high-risk investment (with the potential for making high profits, or return), the investor holds a low-risk investment (which will yield a far lower return). The gamble is that the high-risk investments will more than compensate for the low yields on the 'safe' investment.

Investors pay a management fee, but the managers also take a percentage of the profit, which can be very high. Hedge funds invest in everything from shares, futures, currencies, bonds, commodities, and property down to 'weather derivatives'.

3. **Pension funds and insurance companies**. Paying into a pension is the main way that people save for retirement. The money which investors have paid into pension schemes is managed by the pension funds. They are the biggest institutional investors, way ahead of the investment and hedge funds, insurance companies, and private equity.

You should now have a clearer idea about who is doing what in the City, which will help you to understand how the finances of both individuals and businesses work.

14.4 Business accounts

The key to understanding business finance is an understanding of the accounts of a business. We saw with BP that to understand some of the reports about the overall value of the company, you would need to look at its accounts. However, entering the world of accounting can seem like entering a parallel universe with mysterious rules and incomprehensible jargon, and students tend to assume that accounts involve complicated maths. Nothing could be further from the truth. Accounts do not involve complicated maths, simply some basic arithmetic. Accounts are logical. They follow the same structure, whether they are the accounts of a small business or a multi-national plc. Once you understand the basics, you are in a position to understand and interpret even the most complicated set of accounts.

14.4.1 **What are accounts?**

 Essential explanation

Accounts are summaries of financial information. They serve two purposes:

1. They are a record of the day-to-day financial transactions involved in the running of a business.

2. They are summaries of the financial performance of the business over a given period.

Not every set of accounts is exactly the same. There is some degree of both national and international regulation of accounts. This means that the information presented in any set of accounts will be consistent, but businesses and companies present their accounts using different conventions, layout, and terminology. However, the structure will always be the same. If you know the basic rules, you should always be able to extract the information you need.

14.4.2 **Accounts and lawyers**

Law students often query why they need to study accounts. Accounts provide essential information about both individual and business clients, and about the firm in which a lawyer is working.

Individual clients

Individuals need to know what their financial situation is in order to decide how to proceed with a variety of matters.

1. **Property**. Where clients are buying a house, their financial situation and creditworthiness will affect their mortgage application.

2. **Matrimonial**. In a family law context, where there is an acrimonious divorce, you may have to advise a client whether one of the parties is trying to hide their true wealth.

3. **Probate**. Where a client has died, and you are dealing with his estate, you will need details of his finances to advise how much the family will inherit.

4. **Tax**. You may need to give a client tax advice.

5. **Insolvency**. A client in financial difficulties may need advice on possible bankruptcy.

6. **Litigation**. The client's financial position is often crucial in deciding if, or when, to proceed with an action.

In all of these examples, you would get the information you need from their accounts. Even if they do not keep formal accounts, most people use basic accounting principles without realising it, by adding up income and deducting their expenses, and using these figures to prepare a budget. These everyday financial records kept by individuals are crucial to all areas of practice.

Business clients

Business clients need to know how the business is performing, and whether it is well managed.

1. **Owners, executives, and managers**. Everyone involved in the running of any business from the chief executive officer (CEO) of a multi-national corporation down to a small service business will use the accounts to make informed decisions about that business, either long-term business decisions, for example whether to expand the business, or everyday management decisions in relation to pricing, staffing, finance, and so on.

2. **Investors and lenders**. No one is going to invest in or lend to a business unless they know it is profitable and solvent. Investors will want to know that they will receive a return on their investment, and lenders that the loan will be repaid.

3. **Employees**. A business's employees will want to know that their jobs are secure and whether or not they have any prospects for a pay rise.

4. **Her Majesty's Revenue and Customs (HMRC)**. The tax authorities will look at accounts to ensure that the correct amount of tax is paid.

5. **Economists and analysts**. As we have seen, economists look at accounts of businesses in various sectors to forecast trends and growth and to analyse what is happening in the economy.

Law firms

1. **Solicitors' accounts**. Lawyers are required to deal properly with client's funds, and comply with the Solicitors' Accounts Rules. Solicitors' accounts are simply a slightly more specialised and regulated form of accounts.

2. **Performance**. Law firms, as we will see, are primarily businesses, so if you become a partner in a firm, you will need to understand your firm's business accounts so you know whether the firm is making a profit (and how much your partnership share is likely to be), and whether it is maintaining liquidity and solvency.

Students

Again, this is not an area that you can ignore until you get into practice. If you attend an assessment day with a potential employer, it is possible that you may be asked to do a numeracy test. This may be a straightforward test to see whether you have basic numeracy skills, but it may be based on a set of sales figures and you might be asked to calculate profits. This section will help you to know how to do that.

14.4.3 **Accounting definitions**

Figure 14.7 shows the main accounting definitions which are the basis of business accounts. These are all terms which you have met before. In Chapter 16 you will look at how income, expenses, assets, and liabilities contribute to the creation of individual wealth, and seen how businesses raise capital. Accountants define these terms more precisely.

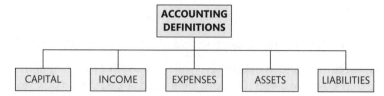

Figure 14.7 Basics of accounts

In Chapter 16, we introduce a case study involving a client, Tom Stevens, who is setting up in business as a wine merchant. We will consider the finance the business needs and how it gets it. We can use this as an example to look the activities of a business and consider what happens in accounting terms. Its entire financial life will be recorded, and form the basis of its accounts. Here is a summary of some of the transactions into which the business enters.

Example 6

1 September	Tom transfers £50,000 of his own money to the business bank account.
2 September	He negotiates a loan with the bank for £20,000, repayable in five years.
3 September	He rents premises in the High Street and pays the first instalment of rent (£3,000).
4 September	He buys shop fittings and fixtures, and a van.
5 September	He buys wine to stock the shop for £20,000 cash.
9 September	He buys £10,000 worth of champagne from a supplier on credit.
10 September	He opens the shop.
	He sells £5,000 worth of wine to customers for cash.
	He sells £6,000 worth of wine and champagne to a wine bar on credit.
11 September	He pays an electricity bill by cheque.
12 September	He negotiates an overdraft facility with the bank and draws down £5,000.

The first thing to bear in mind when looking at accounts is that all transactions will be considered from the point of view of what is happening to the *business* (not Tom). We will look at the entries in the order that they appear in the example.

Capital

 Essential explanation

Capital is the amounts owed to the owner(s) of the business.

The money which Tom has provided for the business is the capital of the business. It is money owed by the business to the owner. If Tom suddenly decided not to go ahead, or sold the business at a later date, the business would pay the capital back to him. This is a narrower definition than that used by businesses to describe their working capital (see 16.5).

Income

> **Essential explanation**
>
> **Income** comes from receipts of a recurrent nature.

When Tom sells the wine, he is earning income for the business. Income is what the business earns, either as a result of the labour of its owner and/or employees or as a result of investment of its capital, interest from bank accounts, or rental from property.

- Where you have a trading business, like Tom's, income will come from sales.
- Where you have a service business, like a firm of solicitors, income will come from professional charges.

You may also see these referred to as **turnover**, **revenue**, or **gross revenue**.

Expenses

> **Essential explanation**
>
> **Expenses** are outgoings of a recurrent nature, the benefit of which is used in the short term.

Expenses are the outgoings of a business, the benefit of which is used in the short term, and so will recur at regular intervals. Examples are rent, wages, electricity and other utilities, stationery, business rates (local taxes payable to the local authority), or bank interest. Expenses are necessary to maintain the earning capacity of the business. Tom's expenses were the rent, the electricity, and the purchase of his stock.

Assets

> **Essential explanation**
>
> **Assets** are resources owned by the business and used for its future benefit.

The cash that Tom has put into the business is an asset of the business. From our example, you will see that it has been used to buy other assets, such as the van and the fixtures and fittings, and it will be also be used to buy stock and pay the expenses of the business. In other words, that cash is working for the business.

When Tom sold the wine and champagne to the wine bar on credit, the business incurred another asset, a debt. The wine bar (the **debtor**) owes him money. Debtors *owe* money *to* the business. The debt is an asset because the wine bar will have to pay Tom at an agreed time in the future. In accounting terms, debtors are also referred to as **receivables**.

Assets are the product of expenditure by the business, either by spending cash or incurring a liability. They are an asset, as they are acquired for the long term (or future) benefit of the business. Assets are divided into categories:

- **Fixed assets**, such as premises, fixtures and fittings, vehicles, computers, furniture, and the like.
- **Current assets** are assets which are circulating in the business, such as cash and debtors.

The purchase of assets (which produces a long term result) is not the same as the payment of expenses (which produces a short term result).

There are three particular types of asset which need further explanation.

Intangible assets

A business will often be sold for a great deal more than the total value of its physical assets. This is because a purchaser is paying for the goodwill of the business and its intellectual property rights.

 Essential explanation

Goodwill is the value of a business over and above its (physical or tangible) asset value. It reflects the value of intangible assets such as a strong brand name, good customer relations, good employee relations, and any patents or other intellectual property rights.

Intellectual property rights (IPRs) are intangible property rights. They are often the most valuable asset of the business. The main ones are:

- **patents**, which protect inventions, either products or processes;
- **trade marks**, which protect names, brands, or logos;
- **copyright**, which protects creativity, for example literary, artistic, and dramatic works, and forms of media, like films and computer programs;
- **design rights**, which protect artistic, industrial, and product designs, both two dimensional (e.g. wallpaper designs) and three dimensional (e.g. furniture).

All these have a value to the business, and they can be bought and sold. They are therefore assets, and appear in the accounts of a business as intangible assets.

Cash and cash flow

Do not make the mistake of thinking that cash is income. Cash is an asset. Remember from Example 6 that some of the sales (the income) were cash sales, but others were on credit—no cash was received at that stage, but the business has still earned income by making the credit sales. So income can be represented by cash, but the cash itself is a current or **liquid** asset. As we have seen, it works for the benefit of the business. It is the most liquid (i.e. easily realisable) of a business's assets. The other current assets are **debtors** and **stock**.

The essence of a successful business is having enough cash. It is perfectly possible to have a business which is profitable, and owns lots of assets, but which does not have any cash.

Obviously, with no cash, a business is going to have problems paying its immediate expenses—in other words it has cash flow problems.

Essential explanation

Cash flow is the amount of money going through the business.

Cash flow problems are the commonest cause of business insolvency, particularly for start-up businesses. If a business cannot pay its debts as they fall due, it is insolvent and it may only be a matter of time before one of its creditors takes action and pushes it into either liquidation or administration.

We will now consider how this could happen. With Tom's business, you have seen that he has raised cash and has started buying and selling stock. Although some of his customers will pay cash, some, particularly business customers, will want a **credit period**, say 30 or 60 days to pay. Until they pay, they are debtors of the business. Figure 14.8 shows the relationship between the cash, debtors, and stock, and the problems which may arise.

If Tom has immediate liabilities (lots of bills to pay) and not much cash, he will have to try and come up with some solutions. He could run some promotions, or offer discounts on the stock to try to sell it more quickly. He could offer the debtors incentives to pay quickly. He could try to sell his debts. This is called **factoring**, and there are companies which specialise in the purchase of debts. Tom would not get the full amount of the debt, but it would raise some cash. In the short term, he could use his overdraft facility, but in the long term, that would increase his liabilities.

To raise cash, the first thing Tom could do is to sell the stock.

Problems with stock:
• How saleable is it?

Alternatively, he could try to get the debtors to pay up.

Problems with debtors:
• Can they pay?
• Has he given them long credit periods?

He may not be able to turn either into cash immediately.

Figure 14.8 Cash flow

Stock

Stock is a particular type of **expense**. The purchase of stock is one of the expenses which a business has to incur on a recurrent basis in order to make the sale—in simple terms, if a business does not have any stock, it has not got anything to sell and it will not earn any income. For Tom's business the wine is the stock. However, we have also referred to stock as an asset, so you may wonder what is going on. The answer is that not all stock will be sold in one accounting period. If, at the end of an accounting period, stock is left over, it becomes an **asset** of the business, referred to as **closing stock**, which will be sold in the next accounting period.

You may also see stock referred to as **inventory** or **inventories**.

Liabilities

 Essential explanation

Liabilities are amounts owed by the business to either the owner or outside creditors.

The bank loan has also injected cash (more assets) into the business, but this will have to be paid back in the future: in this case, in five years' time. Tom's business has incurred a liability as it owes money to the bank (its **creditor**). Creditors *owe* money *to* the business. They are also referred to as **payables**.

Tom has also bought the champagne on credit. Again, the business will have to pay for this in the future. His supplier is a **trade creditor**, and Tom will have been given a **credit period**, say 30 days. Liabilities are, therefore, sums owed by the business, and incurred for the long-term benefit of the business. They are also divided into categories:

- **Current liabilities** are liabilities which must be paid within 12 months, such as trade creditors or overdrafts.
- **Long-term liabilities** are those which are due after 12 months, such as the bank loan.

Note: **capital** is also a liability, as it is owed to the owner of the business.

14.4.4 **The accounting process**

Producing a set of accounts is essentially a three-stage process, with a beginning, middle, and end. Figure 14.9 shows the process.

Figure 14.9 The accounting process

Double entry book-keeping

All businesses keep records of their day-to-day financial transactions involved in the running of the business. These will be recorded using the **double entry book-keeping system**. These accounts are often referred to as 'the books' as historically these transactions used to be recorded in books containing ledgers—the employees responsible for keeping these records are, not surprisingly, known as 'book-keepers'. Nowadays, of course, this process will be computerised, using accounting software, for example SAGE.

Trial balance

At the end of each accounting period this information is collated into a **trial balance**, which categorises all the entries into income, expenses, assets, and liabilities.

Final accounts

The figures from the trial balance are then transferred to the **final accounts**. These are the summaries which a business provides at the end of an accounting year to give information about its financial performance, its assets, and its liabilities. The final accounts consist of two parts:

1. a **profit and loss account** (sometimes called an **income statement**) which lists all the income, deducts all the expenses, and shows how **profitable** the business is; and

2. a **balance sheet** which lists all the assets, deducts liabilities, and shows if the business is **solvent**, both in the short term (**liquidity**) and in the long term (**solvency**).

Figure 14.10 shows the basic format of a set of final accounts. The accounts are often accompanied by a **cash flow statement**, which shows how much cash is available within the business. This is not part of the accounts, but gives a clearer view of the cash position.

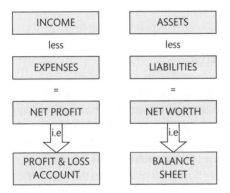

Figure 14.10 Simplified format of a set of accounts

14.4.5 **Interpreting accounts**

A set of accounts on its own is not very useful unless you know what to look for. Anyone looking at accounts will be asking the three same questions:

1. Is the business making a profit (**profitability**)? You look at the profit and loss account to see whether the business has made a profit.

2. Can the business pay its bills as they fall due (**liquidity**)? You look at the balance sheet to see what the total of the business's current assets are and whether they exceed its current liabilities. This will reflect the cash flow position.

3. What is the business worth (**solvency**)? You look at the balance sheet to see whether the business's total assets exceed its total liabilities. If liabilities are greater the business is insolvent in the long term.

Accountants make comparisons with the performance of the business over previous years and with other businesses. This puts the accounts in context, and provides realistic assessment of the health of the business. They analyse the information which they have by calculating percentages and ratios to work out trends and patterns, from which they can see how efficiently the business is operating.

14.4.6 **Audits**

Companies face greater regulation of their accounts than sole traders and partnerships. One of the more important company law requirements is that medium and large sized companies must have their accounts audited.

An audit is an independent report to a company's members as to whether the company has prepared its accounts and other financial statements in accordance with company law and the accounting standards, and that the accounts provide a 'fair and true view' of the company's finances. That means that the audited accounts are materially accurate and can be used to make informed decisions. If the auditors are unable to confirm this, the company's accounts should be treated with extreme caution.

Understanding accounts will help you understand our next topic: insolvency. Just like individuals, business that do not manage their income, expenses, assets, and liabilities will soon find themselves in difficulty. The ultimate outcome, sometimes of bad luck, but more often of bad management, is insolvency.

14.5 **Introduction to insolvency**

Borrowing money and using credit is a widespread and necessary part of modern, and particularly business, life. Debt, if sensibly managed, is not a problem. However, for a variety of reasons, individuals and businesses may find themselves in financial trouble. Insolvency is therefore an important part of the work of all solicitors. However, do you know the difference between bankruptcy and insolvency? People tend to use the terms interchangeably but this is not correct. We now consider why individuals and businesses become insolvent and the effect. The insolvency rules for companies and individuals are different, so we look at each separately.

 Essential explanation

Companies or individuals who are unable to pay their debts are **insolvent**.
  Bankruptcy is a process. It is one way that an **individual** deals with debts that she cannot pay. It does not apply to companies in the UK.

14.5.1 **Corporate insolvency**

There are two legal reasons for a company being insolvent.

1. The company is unable to pay its debts as they fall due (often referred to as the '**cash flow test**'). This is the most common cause of insolvency for any business. The business is simply unable to raise the cash to pay its bills.

2. Its assets are less than its liabilities (often referred to as the '**balance sheet test**'). This will be obvious from the accounts of the business.

Insolvency procedures

Insolvency means that the company is not viable in its current form and something needs to be done. It does not automatically mean that the company has to be wound up. This may be necessary, but it may also be possible to rescue the company. There are various options open to the company or its creditors, some of which may lead to it being wound up and some of which are designed to rescue the company.

1. **Liquidation**. The most extreme action which can be taken is to liquidate, or wind up, the company. A liquidator is appointed to bring the company's existence to an end by distributing its assets amongst its creditors and, if there is anything left, to its shareholders. This is unlikely if the company is insolvent.

2. **Receivership**. Receivers are usually appointed by banks when a company defaults on a secured loan. The security will usually be the company's premises. The receiver will repossess the asset and sell it on behalf of the bank, which gets back the amount of the loan. This usually results in the winding up of the company as, without its premises, it is unable to trade.

3. **Administration**. The purpose of administration is to rescue a company. An administrator, who will be an experienced insolvency practitioner, is appointed to run the company. Once this happens, the company cannot be put into liquidation for 12 months. This gives the company an opportunity to trade out of trouble. If this is not possible, the administrator will wind up the company. In 2012 there were several high-profile examples of companies which went into administration, including La Senza and Peacocks. Both have been sold and have continued to trade, although there has been considerable restructuring of both companies by their new owners.

4. **Company voluntary arrangement**. This is an arrangement with the company's creditors, who effectively agree to give the company a breathing space before they take action to claim the amount owed to them. They agree a plan for the repayment of all or some of the debts, and a supervisor is appointed to oversee the agreement. This again gives time for the company to trade its way out of trouble. An example is the gym chain, Fitness First, which reached an agreement with its creditors in January 2012 to avoid going into administration.

It is usually the company's largest creditors which will instigate action against an insolvent company. These are often the bank or HMRC, if it is owed unpaid tax. Essentially it is they that take the decision, based on what procedure is best for them. It could be that the creditors are in fact quite anxious for the company to survive and prosper. If it is unlikely that a creditor will get all its money back if the company is put into liquidation, it may decide administration is a better option in order to give the company a breathing space to get back on its feet.

14.5.2 **Insolvency of partnerships and sole traders**

If a partnership is unable to pay its debts, all the partners become personally liable for those debts, and may have to pay the partnership debts from their own personal assets. Partners are jointly and severally liable for the debts of the partnership, which means if one partner is unable to pay, then the creditors can recover the debt from any of the other partners, either jointly or individually. If a sole trader's business becomes insolvent, then he is personally liable. Insolvency of the business which is run as either a partnership or sole trader is likely to lead to personal insolvency of the owners.

Partnerships can offer their creditors a **partnership voluntary arrangement**, which is the equivalent of a company voluntary arrangement to give them time to settle their debts.

14.5.3 **Clawback**

When a business is in financial difficulty, and insolvency is inevitable, it is tempting to try either to hide company assets or put them out of reach of any liquidator, administrator, or trustee in bankruptcy (e.g. a sole trader might decide to 'give' the business premises to his wife). This will not work. Insolvency practitioners have wide power to investigate what has gone on in the period leading up to the insolvency and get the money back. This process is referred to as 'clawback' as the insolvency practitioner is clawing the money back for the benefit of the creditors.

14.5.4 **Directors**

Very often the reason for a company getting into difficulties is mismanagement by its directors. Liquidators can also investigate their behaviour in the period leading up to the insolvency. They may be required to make a personal contribution to the creditors if they are found to have behaved irresponsibly or fraudulently. In addition, directors may be disqualified for periods of up to 15 years.

14.5.5 **Knock-on effects of insolvency**

The collapse of any business is likely to have a knock-on effect for its suppliers, employees, landlord (if it is renting property), and others, who may find themselves in financial difficulties as a result. The insolvency of a large company can have a considerable impact up and down the supply chain. It is likely that a solicitor may be asked to advise clients who have been affected by the insolvency of a business, and who want to know how much they may be able to claim. Clearly the answer depends on how much is raised from the disposal of the assets of the business, the number of claims that are made, and what type of creditor the client is. Most creditors will not get back all of their money.

Trade creditors

Trade creditors are suppliers or customers to whom the business owes money. They are likely to be unsecured creditors (i.e. those who have not secured their loan by taking a charge over the company assets). When a company is wound up, or a sole trader or partners of a firm are made bankrupt, their creditors are paid in a particular order. Unsecured creditors will be paid after the secured creditors and after the liquidator, administrator, or trustee in bankruptcy have taken their money. Employees are also paid before the unsecured creditors. The unsecured creditors share what is left on an equal basis. The result will be that each creditor gets a (generally very small) percentage of what is left over. This is called a **dividend**. Example 7 shows how a dividend is calculated.

Example 7

Bagit Ltd, our handbag company, goes into liquidation owing £30,000 to its unsecured creditors. It owes £10,000 to its leather suppliers (LS Ltd) and £100 to Caroline who ordered a handbag which was not delivered before the company was wound up. After paying the secured creditors, his own fees and employees, the liquidator has £6,000 left. The liquidator divides the amount left (£6,000) by the amount owed (£30,000). Each unsecured creditor will get a dividend of 20 pence in the pound. LS Ltd will receive £2,000. Caroline will get £20.

Employees

1. **Wages**. If a business goes into liquidation, its employees may be owed some or all of their wages. Employees are preferred creditors. That means they can claim for unpaid wages up to a maximum of eight weeks' pay, with a limit of £450 per week; six weeks' holiday pay; and any unpaid pension contributions.[14] They will be paid before the unsecured creditors are paid, but after the secured creditors and the fees of the liquidator, administrator, or trustee in bankruptcy. To prevent immediate hardship, if there is not enough money for employees to be paid, they are entitled to be paid what they are owed by the Redundancy Payments Service (RPS), which makes immediate payments to employees up to set limits. The RPS is entitled to claim this money back from the liquidator when the assets of the company have been realised.

2. **Job losses**. If a business is wound up, all its employees will be made redundant. If a buyer can be found for the business, some employees may be kept on, and will be entitled to keep the same employment contracts. However, it is likely that many will still be made redundant in order to restructure the business as a viable concern. This is what happened with Peacocks and La Senza. A buyer was found for some parts of the businesses, but many of their shops were closed and the staff made redundant. Example 8 is a cautionary tale on the problems which this can cause.

Example 8

Six months after Peacocks went into administration, an ex-employee who had been responsible for booking travel and hotels for colleagues was sent a bill for £56,000 by American Express. Her name was on the credit card she used on behalf of the company. The administrators of Peacocks, KPMG, estimated that their unsecured creditors will get 1p in the pound, so Amex would only get £560.[15] They therefore tried to recover the money from the employee personally. They have now withdrawn the claim.

---

[14] https://www.gov.uk/your-rights-if-your-employer-is-insolvent.
[15] James McCarthy, 'Peacocks worker's shock over credit card bill for £56,000', *Wales Online*, 23 June 2012, http://www.walesonline.co.uk.

14.5.6 **Individual insolvency**

There were 28,723 individual insolvencies in England and Wales in the first quarter of 2012. This was down by nearly 5% from the same period in 2011.[16] Insolvencies 'peaked' in 2010. Interestingly, the Insolvency Service reported that in 2011 the number of women being declared bankrupt had reached 35,000 (58% of whom were aged between 25 and 44). Women have incurred excessive credit card debt, partly as a result of trying emulate celebrities, and partly because of the 'must have' culture during the decade leading up to the credit crunch. A good example of how easily this can happen was given by the journalist, Emma Messenger, writing in the *Evening Standard*. She described how she incurred nearly £20,000 of debt on a series of credit cards, to finance her shopping, holidays, nights out, and other luxuries which she could not afford to pay for from her salary. When she finally realised that she could not pay off the debt and confessed to her parents: 'They were horrified that someone supposedly so intelligent had got themself into such a mess.'[17]

An individual is insolvent if he is unable to pay a debt of over £750, or he has no reasonable prospect of being able to pay such a debt in the future. It is an increasing problem for individuals as well as sole traders and partners whose business has failed.

Personal insolvency procedures

The main formal options which are open to individuals are bankruptcy and individual voluntary arrangements.

1. **Bankruptcy** is effectively a formal declaration that an individual, sole trader, or partner is unable to pay her debts. Either a creditor or the individual herself can petition the court for a bankruptcy order, and a trustee in bankruptcy is appointed. The trustee controls her assets, which are used to pay her outstanding debts. Bankruptcy lasts for a year, after which the bankrupt is discharged.

   Examples of well-known bankrupts in the last few years include footballers Lee Hendrie of Aston Villa (unpaid tax) and John Barnes of Liverpool (unpaid tax, although the order was later rescinded on condition that he paid the tax), Westlife's Shane Filan (£18 million of debt following the collapse of his Irish property empire), four members of the reggae band UB40 (£750,000 of debt when their record company failed), and the TV presenter, Miquita Oliver (unpaid tax).

   The result of a bankruptcy order is that the bankrupt is discharged from her debts. Often, after months of considerable financial stress, it comes as a great relief that someone is managing her affairs on her behalf and dealing with her creditors. However it can have serious consequences. The individual can lose her home. Certain jobs are prohibited until the individual is discharged. An undischarged bankrupt cannot, for example, practice as a solicitor, as she will not be entitled to a practising certificate. If she does continue working, any income which she earns may be used to pay off her debts.

---

[16] Insolvency Service, *Insolvency Statistics*, http://www.bis.gov.uk/insolvency.

[17] Emma Messenger, 'Why I'm stuck in a never ending cycle of credit card debt', *London Evening Standard*, 10 October 2011.

Whilst she is bankrupt she cannot apply for credit of over £500. Banks may freeze her bank accounts, and might also refuse to open a new one in the future. After discharge, her credit rating will be very badly affected. She will have trouble getting credit and may have to pay higher interest rates when borrowing. Credit reference agencies keep details of bankruptcy orders for six years.

2. **Individual voluntary arrangements** are the individual equivalent of company voluntary arrangements. They have the advantage that very often, unlike in the bankruptcy process, the individual is able to negotiate to keep his home whilst being given the opportunity to pay off his debts. There are downsides. The debts are rescheduled, not discharged, and the individual must keep to the arrangement. If not, he may still be made bankrupt. The individual's credit rating may still be affected, although the consequences are not as severe as for bankruptcy.

3. **Debt relief orders (DROs)** are orders which provide debt relief for individuals with assets of less than £15,000, where the costs of the bankruptcy process would outweigh any amount likely to be recovered. They prevent action being taken against a debtor for 12 months, after which the debt is discharged.

4. **Debt management plans (DMPs)** help individuals to manage their debts, when they are unable to maintain their contractual payments to their creditors due to financial difficulties.

14.5.7 Non-legal help and advice

There are a number of organisations where individuals and (to a much lesser extent) businesses can go to get help and advice with debt problems. Such organisations offer help with, for example, negotiations with creditors or debt counselling. This sort of advice may be more suitable when financial difficulties begin to arise, and can prevent insolvency by helping individuals or small businesses to manage their debt. Examples for individuals include the Citizens Advice Bureau (CAB), the Consumer Credit Counselling Service, and charities such as the Debt Advice Foundation. Businesses can consult the Business Debtline. Law centres also provide advice for those who qualify for legal aid.

Debt management has become big business, especially during the current economic crisis. Debt management companies charge a fee for help with debt problems. They have the advantage that they will deal with creditors direct, and can often negotiate a better deal more quickly on repayments than debtors would be able to achieve for themselves. However, the fee is usually about 15% of the repayments, adding considerably to their cost. Many of these companies advertise extensively on daytime television (e.g. the Debt Advisory Line). Clients should be advised to choose a company with care. They are regulated and have to be licensed under consumer credit regulation. Some provide an excellent service, but the Office of Fair Trading (OFT) took action against 35 companies in 2011 for misleading the public and non-compliance with OFT guidelines.

14.5.8 Law firms

Insolvency will not just be relevant for your clients. Law firms have suffered in the recession with less work coming in (lower income) and rising costs (higher expenses) resulting in lower profits, and lower partnership shares. Like any other business, law firms can fail and the recession has seen some high-profile casualties.

The collapse of the US firm Dewey & Leboeuf, which filed for bankruptcy in the US in May 2012, is the biggest law firm failure ever. It employed 1,300 lawyers, and had offices in 15 countries throughout the world including London and Paris. In 2009, trainees in London were paid £40,000 in their first year and pay went up to £75,000 on qualification, together with performance-related bonuses.[18] It collapsed with debts of $300 million. The US part of the operation filed for bankruptcy and the London office, which is a separate legal entity, was placed in administration, and is likely to close with the loss of 200 jobs. The former partners have been asked to pay between $25,000 (£16,000) and $3 million (£1.94 million) each as part of a settlement which will release them from future liability.

In the UK, the northern firm Halliwells went into administration in 2010, owing over £190 million. Given the size of the debt, administration was never going to be a realistic option and the firm was put into liquidation. The liquidators have sued 32 former partners for £21 million as part of a clawback action.[19] The matter is still in dispute.

Like all businesses, law firms are faced with unprecedented economic difficulties, and, as you have seen in Chapter 6, a changing market for legal services, so they cannot assume that they are safe. Competition is on the increase, whilst public perception of the profession is poor. In July 2012, the *Law Society Gazette* reported the findings of the Legal Services Consumer Panel into legal services. Far from the reforms brought about by the Legal Services Act in 2007 fulfilling their purpose of increasing public confidence in the profession, only 43% of those surveyed were found to trust the legal profession.[20] A *Law Society Gazette* blog claims that insolvency practitioners who specialise in legal insolvency have seen an increase in the number of firms using their services during 2012.[21] To survive, law firms must now find ways to ensure that they run their practices as successful businesses. This is what we will look at in Chapter 15.

➕ Summary

- An understanding of some basic economic concepts is essential to understand the economic environment in which businesses and individuals operate. Lawyers need to appreciate the distinction between macroeconomics—the study of how the entire economy works—and microeconomics—the study of business activity within the economy—and the most important economic principles in relation to each.

- The City of London is an international financial centre. The role of the central bank and commercial and retail banks is central to the money supply and the domestic economy. It is important that lawyers should know how the financial markets work and the role of other key financial institutions in the City of London in order to understand the issues faced by business clients and individual investors.

[18] 'Dewey & LeBoeuf', *Legal Week*, 14 December 2009.

[19] Katy Dowell, 'Halliwells: Picking at the carcass', *The Lawyer*, 23 January 2012.

[20] John Hyde, 'Panel identifies consumer trust shortfall', *Law Society Gazette*, 25 January 2012.

[21] '2012—the year of insolvency?', *Law Society Gazette*, 2 March 2012, http://www.lawgazette.co.uk/blogs/blogs/in-business-blog/2012-year-insolvency.

● The accounts of a business record its day to day financial transactions, and provide a picture of its financial health. An understanding of the basics of business accounts is also essential to analysing and assessing a business's financial circumstances, strengths, and weaknesses.

● In a difficult economic climate, insolvency is on the increase, for both individuals and businesses. Clients in financial difficulties may need legal advice on their options, requiring an understanding of the main insolvency procedures and their consequences for both companies and individuals.

 ## Thought-provoking questions

1. Can you now answer all the questions raised by the BP case analysis?

2. Do you think a knowledge of economics is important for lawyers? Be prepared to justify your answer.

3. Why do you think share prices are so important for the economy?

4. Using the financial pages in a quality newspaper, track the FTSE 100 for a few weeks to see whether it goes up or down.

5. Why do you think cash flow is so important for businesses?

6. Do you think it is justified that bankrupts should be discharged after one year?

 ## Further reading

Andrew Gillespie, *Business Economics* (Oxford: OUP, 2nd edn, 2013)
—a comprehensive guide to economics in a business context, explaining why economics are so important for business clients, with insights from business practitioners.

David Smith, *Free Lunch* (London: Profile Books, 2008)
—one of the most readable (and entertaining) summaries of economic issues. It has a useful glossary of economic terminology. Bear in mind that this was written before the full effects of the credit crunch had been felt.

Romesh Vaitilingam, *Using the Financial Pages* (Harlow: Pearson Education Ltd, 6th edn, 2011)
—a comprehensive guide to the City that gives a clear insight into who does what, and contains useful chapter summaries.

**The Bank of England, 'Your Money: What the Bank Does', http://www.bankofengland.co.uk/
about/Documents/pdfs/whatthebankdoes1.pdf**
—a useful pamphlet published by the Bank of England on its role which is worth looking at to get a further insight into the role of the Bank in the economy. The website also has an 'Education' section, where you can find further information about the bank and the economy.

**The London Stock Exchange, 'A Guide to Listing on the London Stock Exchange', http://www.
londonstockexchange.com/home/guide-to-listing.pdf**
—a useful starting point to learn about the stock market.

 For the authors' reflections on the thought-provoking questions, additional self-test questions, podcasts offering a variety of perspectives on legal systems and skills, and a library of links to useful websites, visit the free Online Resource Centre *at* **http://www.oxfordtextbooks.co.uk/orc/slorach/.**

15 Law firms as businesses

 Learning objectives

After studying this chapter you should be able to:

- Recognise that, as well as providing legal services, law firms are businesses.
- Explain the different types of law firm and their clients.
- Understand the competition and challenges which law firms face.

Introduction

Chapters 13 and 14 have introduced you to commercial awareness and its importance. You have seen that commercial awareness is an addition to all the other employability skills that you need to find a job. Now we are going to look at the next stage: once you have found that job. When you finish your studies, if you decide to move into practice, the first thing you need to understand is that the organisation you are working for is, first and foremost, a business. The Ministry of Justice's Action Plan, published in May 2011, reported that the legal services sector generated £23.1 billion (or 1.8% of the UK's gross domestic product) in 2009 and constituted £3.2 billion in exports—nearly three times more than a decade earlier.[1] So law firms are part of the modern economy in the same way that every other business is.

A recent television documentary, *The Briefs*,[2] followed lawyers from the successful criminal legal aid practice, Tuckers, in Manchester,[3] as they defended criminal clients. You might imagine that such lawyers would see their role primarily as helping vulnerable clients. However, its senior partner, Franklin Sinclair, ended the programme by stating:

> firstly let me point out that we are a business, and if we don't make any profit, we won't survive, and there won't be any criminal law firms defending anybody. And as a senior judge recently said, nobody else protects the vulnerable as well as criminal lawyers do.

Like any other business, law firms 'sell' a product—legal services—and the object of doing this is to make money. Being a successful lawyer is, therefore, not just about knowing the law and advising clients; it is also about understanding what makes a law firm a profitable business.

What does this mean for students? One of the associate directors of Hogan Lovells, the large Anglo-American City firm, was quoted in the *Daily Telegraph* as saying that when they are recruiting they are looking for candidates who 'demonstrate a keen understanding of what a legal career involves and [are] ambitious, with a flair for identifying business opportunities'.[4] In other words, you will need to be both a lawyer and businessperson.

---

[1] Ministry of Justice, *Plan for Growth: Promoting the UK's Legal Services* (2011).
[2] Franklin Sinclair, *The Briefs*, ITV, 2 August 2012. [3] http://www.tuckerssolicitors.com.
[4] *Daily Telegraph*, 11 February 2012.

Lawyers, as we shall see, have to make money for their firms and manage the expectations of their clients, whoever they may be. Now we take that a little further and consider the business environment in which you will be working. We look at law firms, their clients, and the business skills that will be required of students once they are in practice. Many of these skills are not unique to lawyers. They will be relevant for all students, whether you hope to be involved with the law, or any other profession or industry. From the beginning of your studies, you should take every opportunity to enhance your business skills. Never forget that when you go for an interview, it is a two-way process. You want to find out what the business can offer you if you decide to take the job. However, you will not be offered the job unless you can show that you can make a valuable contribution to that business.

15.1 Law firms in a business context

Law firms within the commercial sector differ vastly, as we shall see in Section 15.2. At one end of the spectrum are the massive City firms with hundreds of partners, dealing with multinational corporate clients, and at the other end are high-street firms with perhaps one or two partners, who deal mainly with individual clients or small local businesses. However, large or small, law firms have the same financial motivations and pressures as any other business.

- They need money (**investment**) to set up, and then to survive and grow.
- They must earn money (**income**) from their clients and convert this into **profit**.
- They need to attract customers (**clients**).
- They need to stay ahead of other law firms (**compete**) in an increasingly difficult market.
- They need to consider the impact of the **environment** in which they are operating.

You will need to understand where this investment comes from, and how law firms make a profit, how law firms attract and retain their clients, and the nature of the competition which law firms face in doing so. All businesses operate within an economic, political, social, legal, and technological environment which will influence their commercial performance and decisions. Law firms are no different, so you will be thinking about the effect of all of these factors on your firm.

15.1.1 **Investment**

Most law firms are partnerships, although there are over 3,500 sole practitioners practising in the UK. The owners, the sole practitioner or the partners, will provide the funding when the firm is set up by investing a lump sum and sometimes assets, such as premises.

Once a firm is set up, it may need more money to expand and grow. If the firm is facing financial difficulties, more money may be needed to tide it over. A sole practitioner will have to provide the finance herself. Where there is a partnership, the partners can each put in an additional lump sum. The problem here is that the partners may not be able to predict when such additional finance is needed, and they may not have the money readily available. To avoid having to find substantial amounts of money at unknown intervals, partners may agree that they will pay a certain amount into the firm each year. Often this contribution will be taken out of their earnings. This means that once they have been practising for a period of time, they will have a considerable amount of money invested in the partnership. Usually, where a firm is taking on additional partners, these partners will also be required to put a lump sum into the partnership or to contribute annually. This will also add to the amount of funding.

The partners' overall investment is known as the **equity** in the firm and the partners who have contributed the investment are known as **equity** partners.

15.1.2 **Borrowing**

Not all funding will come from the owners of the business. Realistically, they cannot be expected to put their hands in their pockets for every eventuality. Some of the funding for the firm may come from borrowing, either by getting a long-term loan, such as from a bank, or borrowing in the short term, such as by way of **overdraft**. Borrowing is a necessity for most businesses. Borrowing as a source of finance will be dealt with in detail in Chapter 16.

15.1.3 **Profit**

When you looked at business accounts in Chapter 14, you saw that businesses make a profit if their income exceeds their expenses. Like any other business, a law firm makes its profit by earning as much income as possible and managing its expenses as efficiently as possible.

Law firms earn income by charging their clients fees for providing a service. The most successful and well known are those that earn the most money (their income or revenue). Their main expenses will be the wages of their staff. Like any business, the more efficient the firm, the better they manage their expenses, and the higher their profit margin, so there will be more profit to share between the partners. Partners are not paid wages, like employees, but take a share of the profits each year. They can agree amongst themselves the amount of profit which they take out of the business. The amounts which each partner takes out are known as drawings.

Law firms have league tables, just like schools and universities. Some of these tables are based on how much income they earn each year, while others are based on the size of the firm (i.e. the number of partners and lawyers), profit per partner, or the number and size of deals. Each year, in September, the details of the revenue of the top 200 UK firms are published in the legal press, for example *The Lawyer* or *Legal Business*, together with details of how much profit each of the equity partners is getting.

 Essential explanation

The amount of profit which each equity partner in a law firm receives annually is known as **profit per equity partner** or **PEP**. It is one, but by no means the only, measure of the financial performance of law firms.

Table 15.1 contains some extracts based on *Legal Business's* figures in September 2012. You will see that at the top, DLA Piper's revenues for that year were well over £1 billion. Average PEP depends on a number of factors, not least the number of partners, and profit margins. The firms with the highest revenue are not necessarily the most profitable. The top PEP in 2012 was earned by the ten partners of Parabis Law. Placed at 100 is Wedlake Bell, where the figures are more modest.

Table 15.1 Top 100 law firms 2012

Firm	No of equity partners	Revenue (ranking)	Profit margin (ranking)	PEP (ranking)
DLA Piper	459	£1,440,000,000 (2)	25.1% (45)	£766,000 (14)
Slaughter & May	120	£448,800,000 (11)	49% (1)	£1,833,000 (2)
Parabis Law	10	£108,000,000 (33)	17% (81)	£1,840,000 (1)
Wedlake Bell	24	£24,000,000 (97)	13.8% (92)	£138,000 (100)

Source: Legal Business, September 2012.

Clearly, no firm will be a successful business if it cannot attract and retain clients, so the next consideration is how law firms can do this.

15.1.4 **Marketing**

A business trying to compete in the modern market will not be able to get clients without an effective marketing strategy. Marketing is based on an understanding of client relationships. For solicitors, it is about finding ways to provide services that your clients want, promoting these services so that your clients and prospective clients know that you can meet their expectations, and ensuring that the firm meets those needs profitably. To achieve this, businesses need to understand the 'marketing mix' or 4 Ps.

 Essential explanation

The '**marketing mix**' or the 4 Ps:

1. **Product** (producing a product which people want).
2. **Placing** (ensuring that product is available for the people that want it).
3. **Promotion** (making those people want to buy it).
4. **Price** (striking a balance between incentive and profit).

Marketing is a little different for law firms than some other businesses. Most marketing is aimed at promoting a product, but when a client comes to a solicitor he has generally decided what product it is that he wants. For example, someone buying a house knows that he wants a property lawyer to do his conveyancing. There is no need to 'sell' him the product. What solicitors must do is show why clients should come to that firm, and not the firm down the road, so the firm needs to stand out.

Marketing must be tailored to the appropriate audience. There is no point in a small firm trying to attract large corporate clients. In any event, smaller firms are unlikely to have large marketing budgets. Large firms on the other hand have dedicated marketing departments. The purpose of their marketing activities, however, is the same for all firms: to develop a reputation or **brand** within your own market.

Advertising

Solicitors were not allowed to advertise until 1986, and even since then the content of legal advertising has been strictly regulated, first by the Law Society and now by the Solicitors Regulation

Authority. The result has been that solicitors have tended to use advertising with caution, and rely on their reputations. This means that most solicitors have minimal 'brand recognition', although there are some exceptions (e.g. Linklaters). In a recent article, *The Lawyer* reported that when Sir Nigel Knowles, the CEO and managing partner of DLA Piper, appeared on BBC Radio 5's *Wake Up To Money* show, he was asked why the host had never heard of DLA Piper, one of the largest law firms in the world. He had to agree that law firms need to do more raise their profiles.

On the other hand, unrestrained advertising can never be a good thing. A recent article in *The Guardian*[5] gives an example of a television advertisement for a Florida firm of divorce lawyers, DivorceEZ. (The name could give you a clue of what is to come.)

> If you and your spouse hate each other like poison and want to get out of the hellhole you call a marriage, you've come to the right place ... You're on your way to getting rid of that vermin you call a spouse.

Clearly, such an advertisement would not be compatible with the UK ethos of conciliation and mediation, but, done appropriately, it is important that lawyers should promote their services and brand.

Brands

 Essential explanation

A **brand** represents a business's image. Its purpose is to create an association in the minds of customers and potential customers which persuades them to 'buy in' to a product or idea. It may be a word, a sentence, or a logo. The best-known (and most valuable) brand in the world is 'Coca Cola', worth $71,861,000,000.[6]

Each law firm needs to develop a brand that will represent the firm's identity and values. It does not need to spend a fortune on developing a sophisticated brand. A simple sentence or 'tagline' could produce this result. For example, a sole practitioner who feels that the unique feature of his firm is the personal service which it provides uses the tagline: 'Working with you. Working for you'.[7] Larger firms will have developed sophisticated brands, based on established reputations. In the Superbrand ratings of the top 500 UK brands, Linklaters comes in at number 175 after British Gas.[8]

Marketing activities

Once a firm has attracted clients, it cannot then relax and think that these clients will always come back to the firm. Marketing is an ongoing process which should encourage client loyalty. When you start in practice you will find that one of the roles of any solicitor, from a trainee to the partners, is to help with marketing, either directly or indirectly. This is something that you should be aware of when you go for an interview, and any sales or marketing experience which you may have had will be an invaluable addition to your CV. Example 1 shows the sort of marketing a firm might expect a newly qualified solicitor to undertake.

[5] Neil Rose, 'UK Lawyers start to take advertising seriously', *The Guardian*, 23 November 2010.
[6] Interbrand, *Best Global Brands 2012*, http://www.interbrand.com.
[7] Warren Boyes & Archer, http://warrensboyesandarcherlaw.co.uk/.
[8] Superbrands, *Business Superbrands 2013*, http://www.superbrands.uk.com/.

Example 1

Naila qualified as a solicitor in 2009. At the time, her firm, a mid-sized London firm, was unable to offer her a job as a newly qualified solicitor, but was confident that it would have a position for her in its employment department in six months. As a result, Naila was offered a six-month contract in the firm's marketing department. The firm considered this to be in both their interests. The experience would improve her ability to handle client relationships, and the firm would benefit from her direct marketing expertise. Her duties included:

- working on the firm's brand;
- updating the firm's website;
- maintaining databases with lists of key clients;
- using this information for cross-referrals (**cross-selling**) within the firm;
- use of social media, such as Twitter and LinkedIn, to raise the firm's online presence and thus the profile of the firm;
- firm advertising and sponsorship;
- liaising with public relations (PR) agencies to publicise high profile cases and ensure that the firm's experts have articles published in both the legal and national press (e.g. if a national newspaper runs an article on tax planning, one of the firm's solicitors contributes the legal background);
- organising in-house seminars on updates to the law for key clients and other lawyers and professionals;
- producing newsletters for clients with legal updates;
- organising networking events, for example entertaining clients at external hospitality events such as sporting events, or in-house social events such wine-tasting or quiz evenings.

15.1.5 Pricing

Pricing is an integral part of marketing and it is important to get it right. There is no point in a firm providing a spectacular level of service to a client, if this cannot be done at a profit. Law firms earn income by charging their clients in the form of fees. The amount of those fees is crucial. Charge too much and clients will go elsewhere; charge too little and the firm will sacrifice its profits. It may seem that clients and businesses are looking at prices from opposite ends of the spectrum. In fact when you look at what professional businesses consider when setting a price, and what clients think about when deciding whether or not to accept, often you will see that they are not that far apart.

- Clients want value for money. This does not necessarily mean getting the cheapest price. Clients will look, for example, at the level of service provided, the experience of the person providing the service, the choice of providers at that level with that experience, and the importance of the matter. The more important the matter, the more a client will be prepared to pay. Experienced business clients understand that an excellent service commands high prices, and a compromise on price could mean a compromise on service. In other words, they know that they 'get what they pay for'. Hence the City firms can command very large fees.
- For the business, making a profit does not necessarily mean charging the highest price. Factors to consider include the importance of the client, the potential for future work with that client, and the complexity of the matter. Sometimes it is better to forego some profit to ensure that the client comes to the firm, and stays.

Both sides have to accept that all matters carry a degree of risk, that is they have the potential to go wrong. The matter may take longer than anticipated or the outcome may not be exactly as planned. Acting for a client is no different from any other business deal: the firm must allocate this risk between the parties. To an extent this is done using different fee structures.

15.1.6 How law firms charge

Lawyers use a variety of pricing structures. The main ones are:

- hourly rates;
- fixed fees;
- contingency and conditional fees ('no win, no fee' arrangements).

Hourly rates

As the name suggests, solicitors are charged out at a rate per hour, depending on their seniority. These rates vary considerably, depending on the type of firm. Table 15.2 shows some typical rates for partners and newly qualified (NQ) solicitors in 2011.

Where the firm charges an hourly rate, the risk is on the client. If the matter takes longer than expected, clearly the client will end up paying more.

Fixed fees

A price is fixed at the outset of the matter. Here the risk is on the firm. There is no margin for error: if the matter overruns, the firm will not be able to charge more.

Contingency and conditional fees

The client does not have to pay unless there is a successful outcome for the case. They are mainly used in litigation matters, for instance personal injury or employment claims. There is a difference between the two:

- **Contingency fees**: if the client wins, he pays the solicitor a percentage of the damages which have been awarded.
- **Conditional fees**: even if the client wins, he does not have to pay his solicitor anything. (This is usually because the solicitor will be able to recover the fees from the losing side.)

Table 15.2 Hourly rates

	Magic Circle	City firm	National/regional	High street
Partner (per hour)	£600–700	£425–600	£325–450	£200–250
NQ (per hour)	£300	£215–300	£175–240	Variable

Source: Jim Diamond's Hourly Rate Survey 2011, http://www.jimdiamond.com.

Clients have access to legal advice and representation with minimum risk, and without having to pay out large sums of money whilst the matter is unresolved. If things go wrong, they do not have to pay anything at all. The risk is on the solicitor.

Scale of fees

There is a very wide difference between fees charged by the leading City firms and those charged by a high-street firm. This is because there is a variety of ways in which a firm can maximise its fee income.

 Essential explanation

Professional work types fall into three categories, known as the **three Es**:

1. **Expert work** (high cost/high fees).
2. **Experience work** (mid-cost/competitive fees).
3. **Efficiency work** (low cost/often fixed fee).

At one end of the scale, the City firms offer a high level of expertise to a relatively small number of corporate clients. The work is highly specialised and will be carried out by partners or highly skilled lawyers. The result is that these firms can charge high fees, and the clients expect to pay this as they know that they are getting value for money. This type of work is known as **expert** work. Example 2, taken from the Am Law, a US legal publication, illustrates this point.[9]

Example 2

In September 2008 the investment bank Lehman Brothers collapsed, leading to the global banking crisis. In March 2012, Am Law reported that the total costs paid to lawyers, accountants, and other professionals as a result of its insolvency amounted to $1.6 billion. Lehman's insolvency was described by a US bankruptcy judge as 'the biggest, the most incredibly complex, the most impossibly challenging international bankruptcy that ever was'. The Anglo-American firm Weil Gotshal & Manges, which had acted for Lehman since it filed for bankruptcy, has earned $383 million (£243 million) in fees and expenses. It seems a huge amount of money, but there are few firms which would have the expertise to undertake this type of challenge.

At the other end of the scale, smaller firms carry out a high volume of work for a large number of clients, but they charge much less than the City firms. The idea is to attract enough low-value work to bring in a high level of profit. The work is far less specialist and requires less expertise, and so will be carried out by lower paid, often unqualified staff, such as paralegals. This type of work is known as **efficiency** work. An example is the sort of property work carried out by licensed conveyancers which is described at 15.1.8.

---

[9] 'As Lehman Exits Bankruptcy, Weil's Tab Stands at nearly $383 Million', *The AmLaw Daily*, 6 March 2012, http://www.americanlawyer.com/amlaw_daily.jsp.

In between is what is known as **experience** work. This sort of work is not highly challenging and does not require a high level of expertise. Once a lawyer has carried out one or two transactions, she learns what she needs to do, where to find suitable precedents, and to appreciate the various pitfalls. Most lawyers can do this type of work with practice. Drafting commercial contracts or leases would come into this category.

15.1.7 **Targets**

To maximise the income coming into the firm, law firms need to ensure that their fee earners are working at full capacity, in other words, they are fully **utilised**. One way of doing this is to set targets.

Chargeable hours

All fee earners will be given a number of target hours per day which they must charge to a client. It is important to realise that during a working day, a fee earner cannot spend the whole day on chargeable matters. He will need to take rest breaks or make a cup of coffee; some time will be spent working on non-chargeable matters such as marketing, management, training etc. Most solicitors will probably be able to record one chargeable hour for every two that they spend in the office. Each chargeable hour will be recorded on a time sheet, which will be used for the purposes of working out the client's bill. It is therefore absolutely essential that fee earners complete their time sheets accurately.

Billing

The firm must also ensure that it gets paid as quickly as possible. The problem for professional firms is that clients do not generally pay up front; they pay when they are sent a bill. Work which the fee earner has done for a client, but has not yet billed, is called **work in progress** or **WIP**. To maximise profits, firms need to ensure that clients are billed promptly, and they are not left with large amounts of unbilled (and therefore unproductive) WIP.

> **Essential explanation**
>
> The length of time it takes a firm to produce a bill from when the work has been done until being paid by the client is known as **lock up**, as the firm will not make any profit until payment is received. Reducing lock up thus increases the profitability of the firm.

Fee earners will also have a billing target. They have to put in bills totalling a certain amount every month or three months. The amount will depend on the firm.

Targets are sometimes tied into bonuses. To offer further incentives, fee earners who exceed their targets may receive a bonus based on a percentage of the amount of the bills that they have delivered in a specified period.

Targets are based on how much each fee earner costs the firm. As we have seen, income has to be turned into profit. All the expenses of the firm have to be paid for out of fee income, so if expenses are very high, profits will be reduced. The main expense for a law firm is its staff, and the more qualified and experienced they are, the more expensive they will be. For each fee earner, there is the expense of support staff, for example secretarial, accounts, and IT. A further expense is the cost of the premises.

- In a small law firm, a fee earner needs to earn income of three and a half times her salary to cover the expense of employing her. (It is said that one-third covers the cost of employing her, one-third covers the overheads, and the rest is profit for the firm.)
- In a larger firm it will be six times her salary to meet the higher costs of, for example, larger premises, higher marketing costs, and more support staff.

15.1.8 Competition

To survive as a successful business, law firms must stay ahead of the competition, and they are operating in an increasingly competitive environment. They have always faced competition from other firms operating in the same areas and providing the same expertise, but nowadays other law firms are just the tip of the competition iceberg.

The first challenge came in the late 1980s when, for the first time, licensed conveyancers were allowed to set up independent practices, breaking the legal profession's monopoly over conveyancing (see 6.4.5.2). At the time, this was predicted to be a nail in the coffin of small high-street practices. In the event, this development coincided with a downturn in the property market, and licensed conveyancers have never really proved a material threat to solicitors' practices.

The next development came when will writers were allowed to prepare wills for customers independently of the legal profession. Clearly this does provide competition, and has often led to problems for consumers, and the Law Society is now looking for greater regulation. The President of the Law Society, Lucy Scott-Moncrieff, has stated: 'Without regulation, there is not enough protection for consumers from poor-quality advice, or in the worst cases unscrupulous advisors—with a real risk of painful and expensive consequences.'[10]

 Essential explanation

Licensed conveyancers specialise in property law. They are not qualified solicitors. They are regulated by the Council for Licensed Conveyancers (CLC) and have to pass exams set by the CLC.

Will writers, who again are generally not qualified solicitors, have a self regulatory professional body, the Institute of Professional Will Writers. Membership requires an entrance examination, but it is still possible to set up as a will writer without becoming a member.

15.1.9 Changes in the provision of legal services

As you have seen in Chapter 6, there are fundamental changes taking place in the way that legal services are provided. These changes reflect the demand from consumers and businesses for more accessible legal advice. It is estimated that there is an untapped market for 'instant' legal advice worth between £15 and £24 billion.

---

[10] Catherine Baksi, 'Will writing should be reserved, super regulator recommends', *Law Society Gazette*, 27 September 2012.

Technology

One challenge faced by law firms today is new technology. This gives consumers instant access to solicitors without the need for face-to-face meetings. There are a growing number of online providers of legal services, such as Keystone Law and DAS. Although it was originally thought that these providers would principally threaten the consumer market, it is clear that online providers are also aiming at cornering the business market. Keystone advertises online services in the commercial field using a 'sophisticated IT platform'.[11] DAS provides online legal documents, forms, and templates for both individuals and businesses. For solicitors providing face-to-face services, this is undoubtedly something that they need to address.

However, not everyone wants to conduct their legal business online. Technology can be used in other ways and law firms should harness the opportunities available. For example, a blog on the *Law Society Gazette* online states that 1.8 million searches are made each month for the term 'solicitor'. Firms should not underestimate the importance of an effective and accessible website, and the opportunities for digital marketing.[12]

Deregulation

The second development is the deregulation of the legal profession following reforms introduced by the Legal Services Act 2007. You have looked at the development of multi-disciplinary practices and alternative business structures at 6.4.5.

To give you an idea of how new entrants to the market intend to attract potential legal consumers, we can look at Lawyers2You and Quality Solicitors as examples (see Example 3).

Example 3

In 2011, the Midlands firm, Blakemores, set up its franchise (see 13.2.8). Lawyers2You. It was one of the first firms to register as an ABS. Operating from what are called 'heavy footfall' locations, such as train stations and shopping centres, it set up stands manned by paralegals. Potential clients were referred to a franchise firm in their area who provided fixed fee legal services, thus threatening serious competition to smaller high-street practices. However, in March 2013 (see NLJ, 14 March 2013), it was announced that the SRA had intervened to close Blakemores as a result of severe financial difficulties, raising doubts about the viability of this business model.

However, Quality Solicitors is operating a similar model successfully from 500 branches of WH Smith around the country, having been one of the first law firms to secure private equity backing.

In November 2012, there were 36 firms which had successfully registered as alternative business structures. Until recently, it was thought that the main threat from these new providers was to small high-street firms, as their target market is the consumer or individual market. However, DLA Piper has acquired an interest in another alternative business structure, LawVest, which in 2013 launched Riverview Law, a firm that, for an annual fee, provides unlimited access to legal advice for businesses with over 1,000 employees.[13] Other organisations

[11] http://www.keystonelaw.co.uk.

[12] Stephen Moore, 'Competing with new entrants', *Law Society Gazette*, 1 November 2012.

[13] http://www.lawvest.co.uk/riverview-law.html.

may join, and some private equity firms are showing considerable interest. Parabis Law, which operates as a limited company, was the first firm backed by private equity to gain registration as an alternative business structure. You will see from Table 15.1 that it has shot up to the top of the PEP rankings, after entering the rankings only in 2010.[14]

These new entrants to the legal scene are using television and other media advertising in a way that traditional law firms tend not to. This will undoubtedly give them a competitive advantage.

Referral fees

Another shark in the legal monopoly waters is the growth of so-called 'factory law' (see 6.4.5.2). If you watch daytime television, you will probably have seen advertisements for personal injury solicitors, claiming to be able to assist you in claiming substantial amounts if you have had an accident or been injured at work. Colloquially, these firms are sometimes referred to as 'ambulance chasers'. Advertising is one way that these firms get work, and you can easily find any number of these firms online.

Another way is through referral fees. Insurance companies sell personal injury details to law firms, who then contact the client and offer to act for them in pursuing their claim. The same sort of thing happens with property work. Estate agents offer to pass clients on to firms in return for a fixed fee, say £120 per transaction. Both practices have been severely criticised, as inevitably the result is an increase in costs for the client. However, supporters of referral fees argue that this is simply an alternative to marketing. Smaller firms do not have the time or expertise to market their services, and this is a workable alternative.

The government intends to ban referral fees, in an attempt to curb what has been described as the 'compensation culture',[15] but so far they have only concentrated on personal injury claims, and nothing has been mentioned about estate agents' referral fees. These prejudice small firms which are not prepared to pay and find that, as a result, the agents have discouraged potential clients from using them, referring them instead to firms that are prepared to pay the fee.

Legal aid

A further recent threat to small firms has been government cutbacks in legal aid as a result of the Legal Aid, Sentencing and Punishment of Offenders Act 2012. The legislation is predicted to cut £350 million from the £2.2 billion legal aid budget, mostly in the fields of social welfare, immigration, clinical negligence, and private family law. Family litigation has always been one of the mainstays of smaller firms, and this poses significant challenges in an already tough environment.

There is no doubt that there is a multi-million pound untapped consumer market out there, and law firms, especially smaller firms, may have to rethink their tactics to gain a share of it. The plus side is that by the time a first-year law student starts applying for jobs, the new entrants to the legal market may be providing significant employment opportunities, although their critics argue that by 'swamping' the market, they may keep salaries down. At the moment, these issues are highly topical. Students could well be asked to give their opinion

[14] 'UK200 2011', *The Lawyer*, 12 October 2011.
[15] Legal Aid, Sentencing and Punishment of Offenders Act 2012, ss. 56–60.

on these developments at an interview. The sample interview questions require you to show an understanding of the topics. Research in these areas is crucial before any interview.

 Sample interview questions

1. What do you think are the main challenges/opportunities facing the legal profession?

2. What do you know about alternative business structures?

3. Do you think that the franchising of law firms helps to provide better services for clients?

4. Should all referral fees be banned by the government?

5. What do you think about the recent reforms of legal aid?

6. What do you think about the effects of the Legal Aid, Sentencing and Punishment of Offenders Act 2012?

15.1.10 Environment

Like all other businesses, law firms need to consider the environment in which they are operating, in particular the political, economic, social, technological, and legal context (**PESTLE**).

 Essential explanation

PESTLE: political (**P**), economic (**E**), social (**S**), technological (**T**), legal (**L**), and environmental (**E**) changes that affect commercial activity. (See also 13.3.5.)

At 13.3.5, you saw that all businesses are affected by changes brought about by these factors. They must take advantage of the opportunities offered and respond to the challenges and restrictions which they may impose. Law firms are no exception. They are subject to all these factors themselves, but they also need to be aware of the impact of these factors on their clients, both individual and commercial.

A clear example is the economic climate. The credit crunch has had a devastating effect on businesses, both large and small. Smaller firms have been hit by the slowdown in the property market, which has affected both individuals and commercial clients. In an increasingly nervous market, the cost of professional indemnity insurance (see 15.2.3) has risen sharply over the last few years. Banks and mortgage companies which used to instruct small firms to act in conveyancing transactions have withdrawn their instructions and moved the work to larger firms. All of these factors have a cumulative effect. It is not just the small firms that have been hit. Some of the large corporate firms found that lucrative work declined, such as when the merger and acquisitions market dried up in 2009, although it is now showing signs of improvement.

Never think that a knowledge of what is going on in the economy is irrelevant for you. Here is another question that students have been asked at an interview with a law firm, although it is the sort of question that you could be asked when applying for a job with any profession or business.

 Sample interview question

How do we recession-proof our industry?

15.2 Consumers of legal services

As we have seen in Chapter 13, all businesses operate within a 'market'. Within each market there are sellers (producers) and buyers (consumers). We tend to think of buyers and sellers in terms of the sale and purchase of goods, but businesses produce all sorts of products. Some produce goods, others provide services.

 Essential explanation

Goods are 'things', namely physical items which you can look at, touch, and inspect before you buy, like your mobile phone, your clothes, or food. **Services** are not tangible. For instance if you employ a plumber to mend a dripping tap, or have your hair done at the hairdresser, that is a service. You cannot inspect the service or see what you will be getting before you buy. Both goods and services are '**products**'.

Law firms operate within the legal market, producing a product, legal services. The 'consumers' of that product are the clients.

We will now consider who those clients are, and why they chose a particular firm. Clients vary from individuals to multi-national corporations, so it is impossible to generalise. Successful firms have built up a reputation which attracts high-profile, big-spending corporate clients. Smaller firms are looking to attract more local clients and will be concentrating on the consumer market. The lawyers acting for these different clients will have different skill sets to manage the expectations of their respective clients. Lawyers acting for multi-national companies need to understand completely different markets, strategies, investments, and contexts from the lawyer acting for a local plumber.

The fact that clients cannot inspect what they are getting means that they will rely partly on the reputation of the firm which they chose, and we have seen the importance for a law firm of developing a strong brand (see 15.1.4). However, this will not be the only factor in influencing their decision. Law firms must also anticipate and manage the expectations of their clients. The best lawyers provide the sort of service which is tailored to the needs of their clients, so that clients come to the firm and keep coming back (client retention).

Awareness of the different types of law firm and different types of client is essential for students from an early stage. When you are applying for training contracts, you need to show that you know the type of work that a lawyer in that firm will be undertaking, and the type of work the clients bring in, and thus understand the commercial issues at stake. Assessment days and interviews will be based on exercises designed to show that you have done your research and can demonstrate your understanding of the expectations of these types of client.

15.2.1 Types of law firms and their clients

Our starting point is to think about the different types of firm, and the types of clients which they attract. In November 2011, there were 159,524 solicitors practising in the UK and, although the numbers increased in 2011, they fell back in 2012.[16] Solicitors' practices

---

[16] John Hyde, 'Crisis, what crisis? Number of solicitors soars to all time high', *Law Society Gazette*, 14 December 2011; compare Law Society Gazette blog, 17 April 2013.

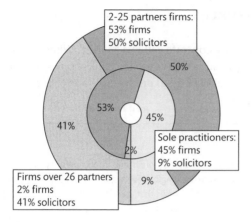

2-25 partners firms:
53% firms
50% solicitors

50%

53%

45%

41%

2%

Sole practitioners:
45% firms
9% solicitors

Firms over 26 partners
2% firms
41% solicitors

9%

Figure 15.1 Make-up of law firms

are organised in various ways. The Law Society's statistics show that just over 45% practise as sole practitioners and 53% are in partnerships, including limited liability partnerships, of various sizes. There are a small number of firms that are incorporated as companies. Figure 15.1 shows the breakdown between sole practitioner and partnership practices, based on the Law Society's figures.[17] Note how the largest firms (about 2%) employ over 40% of all practising solicitors.

If you do decide to go into the law and start to look for training contracts, you will need to consider carefully what type of firm you want to work for. To be successful, you should do extensive research into the firms to which you are applying. A useful starting point is *Chambers Student Guide*.[18] The Guide classifies law firms into categories, so we will use their classification to help you understand the main types of law firms. Then we will look at the websites of some typical firms in each category, which gives you a good indication of what sort of clients they act for. This will also be useful knowledge for interviews. Any firm that you apply to will expect you to have a detailed knowledge of the firm, its structure, its clients, and its competitors. Here are some possible interview questions.

 Sample interview questions

Why do you want to work for this firm? How is this firm different from its competitors? These are variations on the question: What do you know about this firm?

Magic Circle

This is the name given to the top five 'elite' City firms: Allen & Overy, Clifford Chance, Freshfields Bruckhaus Deringer, Linklaters, and Slaughter & May. These are the firms that earn the most money with massive global revenues. Many of these firms earn more from their legal businesses outside the UK than their UK operations. They act for high-profile corporate and financial clients, and deal with a significant number of international clients. Most have

---

[17] Law Society, *Annual Statistical Report 2011* (2012).   [18] http://www.chambersstudent.co.uk.

offices worldwide. Linklaters, for example, have 27 offices in 19 countries and employ 2,200 lawyers and 4,800 staff overall. Their turnover (revenue) in 2011–12 was over £1.2 billion. They advise 25 of the UK's 100 largest (FTSE 100) companies, including British American Tobacco plc, Lloyds Banking Group plc, and Vodafone Group plc. Their website states that they are 'Everywhere our clients need us to be' and that they advise on 'multi-jurisdictional projects and transactions across the world'.[19]

Silver Circle

The next five commercial City firms, Ashurst, CMS Cameron McKenna, Herbert Smith Free-hills, Hogan Lovells, Simmons & Simmons, and SJ Berwin are sometimes described as 'Silver Circle' firms. There is not really a great deal of difference between them and the 'Magic Circle' firms in terms of the type of work, but their incomes are slightly lower. For example, Herbert Smith's turnover was £480 million in 2011–12. Now merged with Freehills, it has over 2,800 lawyers, with offices worldwide. It also advises 25 of the FTSE 100 companies, including British Sky Broadcasting Group plc, the Daily Mail Group and Trust plc, and Moneysupermarket.com Group plc. Its website claims that: 'As one of the world's leading law firms, we advise many of the biggest and most ambitious organisations across all major regions of the globe.'[20]

US London firms

There are a significant number of US firms based in London, for example Weil Gotshal & Manges and Mayer Brown. Again, they deal mainly with international corporate clients. Weil Gotshal & Manges employs 1,200 lawyers in 12 countries. Its turnover was $1.229 billion in 2011. Weil's website states that: 'Faced with high-stakes legal challenges, the world's most sophisticated clients count on Weil to listen hard, understand their business, and deliver un-equivocally sound judgment.'[21]

Recently, some of these firms have merged with top London commercial firms. For exam-ple, Lovells merged with Washington-based Hogan & Hartson in May 2011 to create one of the world's ten largest legal practices, with 2,500 lawyers, and Denton Wilde Sapte merged with Chicago-based Sonnenschein Nath & Rosenthal, resulting in combined law firm with offices in 33 countries.

Other London commercial firms

These fall into two categories:

1. **Mid-sized commercial**: examples are Macfarlanes or Trowers and Hamlins. Again, these firms deal mainly with commercial/corporate clients. However, both have, in addition, long-established private client or 'private wealth' departments. Macfarlanes are best known for their corporate work. They have a turnover of over £90 million. They have one office in London and employ over 150 solicitors and 71 partners. According to

---

[19] http://www.linklaters.com. [20] http://www.herbertsmithfreehills.com.
[21] http://www.weil.com.

their website, they are 'advisers to many of the world's leading businesses and business leaders' offering 'discerning clients an alternative to the world's legal giants'.[22]

2. **Smaller commercial**: examples are Wedlake Bell or Collyer Bristow. Both these firms are traditional, long-established law firms, based in Bedford Row, London. Both deal with a mix of commercial/corporate clients, media and intellectual property, private client, and property work. Wedlake Bell has a turnover of £18.6 million. They state on their website that they 'provide a full service to corporate and private clients ... and offer a personal service with a high level of partner accessibility'.[23]

National and 'multi-site' firms

Chambers uses this classification to cover firms which have offices throughout the UK and are expanding rapidly into the international market. The examples given include Eversheds and DLA Piper, both of which have offices throughout the UK and overseas. They have a large number of offices in the UK so that they can serve local businesses, and so are not limited to the City, but the term 'national' disguises the fact that they are also very much international in outlook. The number of offices internationally means that these types of firm are among the largest in the world. Eversheds, for example, has 24 offices and 4,000 staff worldwide, and a turnover of £366 million. Eversheds brands itself as an 'International Innovative Law Firm' and DLA Piper as a 'Global Law Firm'. DLA's global revenue was over £1.4 billion in 2012. The focus for these firms is still commercial/corporate, but from DLA Piper's website you can see that the emphasis is very slightly different: 'Unlike many law firms, we ... provide clients with a range of essential business advice, not just on large scale mergers and acquisitions and banking deals but also on people and employment, commercial dealings, litigation, insurance, real estate, IT, intellectual property and plans for restructuring.'[24]

Regional firms

Regional commercial firms are based outside London and, although some have offices outside their home cities, they do not have a strong national presence. Examples are the Newcastle-based firm Dickinson Dees or the Leeds firm, Walker Morris. The larger regional firms still act for large corporate clients, and have the advantage of charging less than the London or national commercial firms. Walker Morris's website states that they 'are proud to be a major employer in Yorkshire and have developed a centre of excellence which engenders the nurturing of close, long-term relationships with our clients of which 71% are based outside Yorkshire. We have developed the firm to have the capacity to support our clients' national legal requirements throughout the UK.'[25]

Increasingly, however, regional firms are opening offices in London, a recent example being Wilsons, the Salisbury-based private client firm. Smaller regional firms tend to concentrate on more local clients, such as (the wonderfully named) Wright Hassall who are based in Leamington Spa and who 'are large enough to provide an all-round skill set whilst local enough to give personal attention'.[26]

[22] http://www.macfarlanes.com.   [23] http://www.wedlakebell.com.
[24] http://www.dlapiper.com.   [25] http://www.walkermorris.co.uk.
[26] http://www.wrighthassall.co.uk.

Niche or boutique firms

Niche or boutique firms specialise in particular areas of law such as employment, family, media, aviation, shipping, intellectual property, etc. Examples are Actons in Nottingham who specialise in horses (equine law), or larger firms such as Thomas Cooper Partners, who specialise in maritime, trade, and finance law. Clearly, such firms will have a select clientele.

General practice/high-street firms

There are hundreds of small high-street firms of varying sizes throughout the country. They will have broad-based practices, and act for local businesses and individual clients. These are the firms that carry out the majority of legal aid work. They are unlikely to have dedicated commercial or corporate departments, but so-called CoCo departments (combined commercial/corporate) will deal with matters such as setting up private companies or partnerships, and dealing with consumer issues. The emphasis, however, will be on property, litigation, family law, wills, and probate work.

Figure 15.2 summarises the different categories of law firm and the types of client who instruct them.

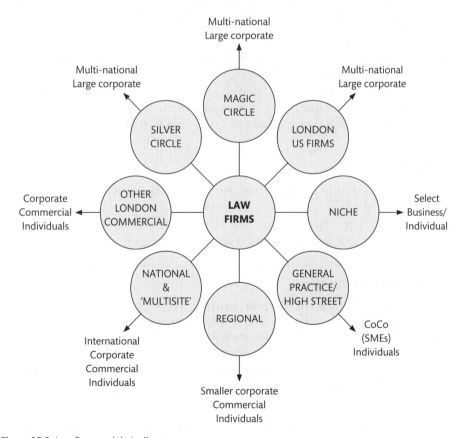

Figure 15.2 Law firms and their clients

Figure 15.3 Client retention: categories of client

15.2.2 **Client retention**

The vast majority of clients choose a firm based on recommendation, and individuals often return to the same firm throughout their lives. However, bear in mind that not all clients stay with the same firm forever. As their needs change, they may change firms, and 'up-grade'. For example, when a client sets up his first business, he will probably use a local firm which he knows about, for example the same firm that he may have used for his conveyancing. However, as the business expands, he may decide that they no longer have the expertise to cope with increasingly complex business decisions, and he will be able to pay more for legal services.

The converse is true for law firms. As they grow and expand, they will be able to increase their prices, and inevitably, their client base will change. Some existing clients may no longer be able to afford this increase, and the firm will gradually shed less profitable clients, whilst gaining new and more profitable ones.

However, most law firms work hard to retain their clients. There is a tendency to think that a firm constantly needs to get in new clients in to survive. In fact, research shows that it is between 5 and 12 times more expensive to get a new client than it is to exploit the full potential of your current or past clients. In marketing terms, clients fall into four categories, depending on their value to the firm. Figure 15.3 shows the different categories of clients.

'Hot' clients

Once a firm is established, its most valuable clients are its existing, 'hot', clients. Each firm will have 'core' clients, the important clients who contribute substantially to their income. They are the ones that keep coming back. There is an interesting theory, the Pareto Principle, which helps to explain why your core clients are so important.

 Essential explanation

The Pareto Principle (or 80-20 Rule/Law of the Vital Few): *In any set of circumstances, 20% of causes (inputs) are responsible for 80% of the results (outputs).* 80% of profits of a business come from 20% of (core) customers (and, incidentally, 80% of work in a business is done by 20% of the workforce).[27]

Managing customer relationships is essential to ensure that once one matter is concluded, these core clients will use the firm again. If we look at the next two categories, we will see that

---

[27] This is named after the Italian economist Vilfredo Pareto (1858–1923), who put forward the principle in *Manual of political economy* (1906).

existing clients are invaluable, not just for the matter in hand, but for the potential which they have to bring in new business. It is thus crucially important to stay in touch with your clients, and nurture the relationship. Little things will ensure that they stay 'on side': whilst the matter is ongoing you should keep them informed about the progress of a matter—you may know what is going on, but clients will not unless you tell them, so you should ring them before they have to ring you. Be approachable—clients need to be able to talk to you—and avoid bamboozling them with legal jargon. Exceptional client care is central to getting repeat business.

'Warm' clients

Existing clients should not 'escape the net' once one matter is concluded. Once a matter is finished, they should not be ignored, and firms need to work hard so that they return. In addition, firms may be 'under-exploiting' the potential of their existing clients. A firm should ensure that a key client who, for example, consults their corporate team, is aware of the service that can be provided by, for example, the private client department so she continues to use the firm for her tax planning, or the property department if she buys a property. You have already seen the importance of 'cross-selling' at 10.6.11. It is vital to exploit this potential. Marketing departments have software to help their firms to do this.

'Lukewarm' clients

A great deal of work for lawyers comes as a result of a recommendation and referrals, which is why your existing clients are so valuable. They are, in effect, the best advertisement for a firm. If existing or past clients are happy with the service, they will recommend the firm to others, and they have the potential to bring in different sorts of work. For example, if a client changes job, he may recommend the firm to his new company, bringing in valuable corporate work. It is therefore important to keep in touch with past clients once a matter is concluded. Again, you have already looked at networking at 12.6. It is a crucial marketing activity for lawyers.

'Cold' clients

Firms would quickly stagnate without new clients. However, far harder work, and thus more expense, is required to get in clients who have no connection with the firm at all. Here it is all about marketing, which we considered at 15.1.4. Once a new client comes to the firm, it is essential that the potential value to the firm of that client is carefully assessed. Taking on a new client often involves a significant time investment, in acquiring knowledge of that client's business, business processes, and the sector in which it is operating. Firms have to assess whether the effort will be worth it.

15.2.3 **What happens when things go wrong?**

When consumers buy faulty goods, they can take them back and get a refund. When customers receive a poor level of service, the position is not quite so straightforward. They cannot give a service back. The provision of legal services always carries an element of risk and has the potential to go wrong: for instance, a lawyer may miss a time limit, or fail to include an important provision in a contract. Sometimes the client may simply feel that the solicitor has provided a poor service.

If things go badly wrong, the right to redress lies first with the common law and the tort of negligence. If a poor level of service is provided, the Solicitors Regulation Authority (SRA) provides a complaints procedure to which all solicitors must adhere.

Professional negligence claims

 Essential explanation

Solicitors owe a **duty of care** to their clients. This means that they must not place their clients in a position where they suffer unnecessary harm or loss. If they do, then they will be negligent. Where a solicitor has not met the duty of care, the client may be able to sue for **professional negligence** (sometimes referred to as **pro neg**) and obtain compensation.

Actions for professional negligence are becoming increasingly common, and a quick search on the internet will bring up hundreds of firms who will advise on this. This is an unfortunate downside of the 'compensation culture'.

The result is that all solicitors are required to take out **professional indemnity (PI) insurance** to meet the cost of such claims. (In the US, this type of insurance is referred to as 'errors and omissions' (E&O) insurance, which makes its purpose very clear.) In the UK, the SRA regulates indemnity insurance, and solicitors are not allowed to practise without it. This has advantages and disadvantages: it means that solicitors are able to meet the cost of claims, but the premiums are expensive and a significant cost for law firms, especially smaller firms, which have seen their premiums rise by thousands of pounds over recent years, due to an increasing number of claims.

Complaints against solicitors

A client cannot bring a professional negligence claim simply on the grounds of poor service, but all firms are required by the SRA to have a complaints procedure, which they must bring to the attention of their clients, and as a last resort clients can complain to the Legal Ombudsman.[28]

Clearly no firm wants a series of complaints about its service. However, a complaint can be used to improve services and does not have to have a continuing negative impact. If acted on swiftly and responsively, it can be an opportunity to demonstrate to a disgruntled client the firm's commitment to client care and retention.

Complaints about costs

Solicitors must set out how much the costs of a matter will be at the outset. Where it is not possible to give an exact quotation, a firm should give a 'best estimate'. Complaints about costs are the most frequent client complaints. In a recent interview conducted on behalf of the College of Law Future Lawyers' Network with Adam Sampson, the Legal Ombudsman, he said that he

---

[28] http://www.legalombudsman.org.uk.

receives about 80,000 to 90,000 complaints a year about solicitors, the majority to do with costs.[29] Complaints are likely to arise where the client feels that she has received poor service, or simply has not received value for money. Generally, this can be resolved by negotiation, but as a last resort a client can apply to the court to examine the bill and, if appropriate, reduce it.

15.2.4 Added value

Most importantly, to retain clients, lawyers need to add value. We keep coming back to this point, so why is this so important? The answer is that it is a bit like buying a mobile phone. If you look at this practically, all you need is a device from which you can make phone calls, and you could buy the cheapest phone on the market, but in reality, that is not what you want to buy. Given completely free choice you may well choose to buy an iPhone 5. Why? To many loyal fans of Apple, it has that 'extra something'—its design, its image, its versatility—that creates a 'must buy' urge. Law firms also need to provide that 'extra something'.

If you wish to become successful in securing employment in the legal services industry, you will surely need in-depth knowledge of the law, but given the stiff competition for training contracts and many graduate jobs, how can you differentiate yourself, both at application stage and on an ongoing basis throughout your career? The 'extra something' you can develop is an in-depth understanding of your clients and an ability to manage their expectations. This knowledge and skill would indeed give you equal benefit in many non-legal graduate careers. When you interview an individual client for the first time, you need to find out as much as you can about their background, particularly their financial background. It does not matter that some of this may have nothing to do with the matter in hand, it will help you understand those expectations.

You should always find out what the client does, how and why he does it, and understand the context within which the client operates. When you advise a business client, certainly for the first time, you should do in-depth research into the business so that you find out the answers to those same questions. As we have seen, it is important to think beyond the basic facts and identify your clients' 'latent' concerns. This is the commercial awareness part of the 'added value' element. It helps you to anticipate whether a particular outcome is impossible, impractical, or commercially inadvisable, and advise accordingly. This is also an approach which will give you an edge with potential employers.

 Sample interview question

How do you think you could make a client confident that you are commercially aware of their business and their needs?

The starting point for providing your clients with this 'added value' element is to understand why they are seeking legal advice in the first place, what are the underlying considerations, and what are the implications—personal, legal, and financial—using the structure which we looked at in Figure 13.1. To enable you to do this effectively, Chapter 16 will look at typical concerns of both individual and business clients.

[29] College of Law, Future Lawyers Network, http://www.college-of-law.co.uk/futurelawyers.

Summary

- Firms expect their lawyers to be commercially aware. An important part of this commercial awareness is understanding that a law firm is a business, with all the challenges and opportunities faced by every other business. You need to understand how a firm makes its profit, how it attracts its clients, the competition which it faces, and the environment in which it operates.

- Like every business, law firms provide a product—legal services—for their customers—clients—and must tailor their services to their customer base. Commercial awareness involves understanding those clients, why they instruct a particular firm, and their expectations from that firm.

Thought-provoking questions

1. In order to improve their profits law firms must increase their income and reduce their expenses. Can you think of ways that might help to achieve these aims?

2. Watch the Quality Solicitors' advertisement 'For Whatever Life Brings'. http://www.youtube.com/user/QualitySolicitors. Do you think that this sort of advertising poses a threat to traditional high street solicitors?

3. Find some recent examples of institutions which have successfully registered as alternative business structures.

4. Choose a law firm and research its website. Explain what sort of clients that firm is trying to attract, identify some of its clients and some high profile cases in which it has been involved.

Further reading

Whether you are preparing for an interview or creating your own professional development plan, you may find it useful to access some of the websites referred to in this chapter.

Law Society website: http://www.lawsociety.org.uk
—contains comprehensive information on the legal profession, including invaluable information for students, for example on training contracts and 'Top tips for applications'.

Chambers Student Guide: **http://www.chambersstudent.co.uk**
—an excellent starting point for finding out about law firms, their practice areas, and clients. It contains essential information for students when researching and applying to law firms. The 'True Picture' feature gives insight into the life of a trainee at 120 firms.

However much anyone may tell you about an individual firm, it is always best to find out for yourself. Make sure that you look at (at least one) website for each of the categories of firm mentioned.

 For the authors' reflections on the thought-provoking questions, additional self-test questions, podcasts offering a variety of perspectives on legal systems and skills, and a library of links to useful websites, visit the free Online Resource Centre *at* **http://www.oxfordtextbooks.co.uk/orc/slorach/.**

16 Understanding clients: individuals and businesses

 Learning objectives

After studying this chapter you should be able to:

- Identify life events that will require individuals and businesses to have recourse to the law.
- Describe how individual wealth is created.
- Explain how businesses finance their operations.

Introduction

Whatever sort of business you go into when you finish your studies, at the heart of that business is its customers or clients. In Chapter 15, we saw the importance of 'adding value' to the advice you give to your clients. We looked at an interview question which asked you whether you could demonstrate to clients that you can anticipate their needs. This applies whether they are individual or business clients. Anticipation is key to commercial awareness. If you can anticipate clients' needs, you can manage their expectations. You will find that this is not rocket science. Most clients' legal needs are based on ordinary life events, and understanding those life events—the personal, social, financial, or business concerns which arise and their legal impact—will add a further dimension to your commercial awareness. In this chapter we consider this in a legal context, but much of the information will be relevant to many other professions or occupations. We look at some more interview questions, and some topical issues which will be useful whether or not you are looking for a career in the law.

At some point in their lives, most people will need some sort of legal advice, usually as a result of some life event, or change in their circumstances, such as buying a house, marriage, death, divorce, employment problems, or a criminal prosecution. Different life events give rise to different legal rights and duties, on which law firms can give advice. Businesses, like individuals, have a life cycle. They grow and develop, and experience changes in circumstance, for instance buying premises, taking on employees, changing the status of a business from a sole trader to a partnership or company, all of which give rise to equivalent legal rights and duties. Businesses often need the same sort of advice as individuals, it is just that the emphasis is a little different.

In this chapter we are going to use a client case study to explore typical life events in more detail. We take finance a little further and look at how both individuals and businesses raise money. This raises different issues from those which we have looked at before. We have thought about economics and finance, and money generally, but we have not yet thought about social and personal issues. We have seen that commercial awareness is about people, your clients, so you need to understand these issues as well. An example is the Olympic stadium scenario, which raised a variety of social issues.

This chapter gives you some more sample interview questions. Bear in mind that not all these questions will be asked. Different questions are relevant for different types of firm, and different types of client base. Interviewers tend to tailor their questions to your CV, so if you have expressed an interest in private client work, you might be asked questions on what you know about the tax implications in the latest budget, or if you want to practise welfare and immigration law, you might expect questions on welfare reform.

16.1 Why individuals and businesses have recourse to the law

16.1.1 Individuals

In 1967, Thomas Holmes and Richard Rahe, two psychiatrists, conducted a survey to see how stress contributed to illness. They listed typical life events (which they called Life Event Units or LFUs) and gave them a stress score. (The conclusion, although not really relevant for our purposes, was that the higher the score, the more likely the subject was to become ill.) Table 16.1 shows an extract of the top 6 LFUs, (and the lowest scoring one, so that you can make a comparison).

These are all events about which individuals are likely to consult a solicitor. (Number 42, incidentally, is Christmas, which carries 12 stress points. Clearly this is not an event which will send someone rushing to see their solicitor, but, interestingly, more couples consult a solicitor about matrimonial difficulties in the period immediately following Christmas than at any other time of the year.) From the table, you can see that the most stressful life events all involve a change in circumstances for the worse, and it is undoubtedly true that a lawyer will often be advising clients when they are most vulnerable.

However, the life of a solicitor is not all doom and gloom. Often clients' circumstances change for the better, for example they get married, have children, or buy their first home.

Table 16.1 Extracts from the Holmes and Rahe Stress Scale

	Event	Stress score
1	Death of spouse	100
2	Divorce	73
3	Marital separation	65
4	Jail term	63
5	Death of close family member	63
6	Personal injury or illness	53
...	....	...
43	Minor violations of law	11

Source: Thomas H. Holmes and Richard H. Rahe, 'The Social Readjustment Rating Scale' (1967) 11 *Journal of Psychosomatic Research* 213.

Client case study

Let's look at some clients and think about the sort of legal advice a law firm might provide (see Case study 1).

Case study 1

Tom Stevens is 29. He works as a procurement (purchasing) manager for a national chain of wholesale wine retailers. He earns £30,000 a year. Tom's fiancée, Anna Evans, is 28. She teaches English and Drama at a local Community Academy near Cambridge. She earns just over £27,000 a year.

Anna and Tom are planning to marry in July next year. They are both agreed that they would like to have two children. Anna hopes to carry on working once she has had the children. Both Tom and Anna's parents are willing to help with childcare, and there is a good local nursery near where they are looking for a house.

At the moment, Tom and Anna rent an unfurnished flat, but they are hoping to buy a house to move into once they are married, and have saved enough money.

Tom has recently paid off his student loan, and has started saving for the house. Tom's grandmother died a year ago, and left him £10,000 which he will use as part of the deposit. Anna has not yet paid off all her loan, so she will not be able to contribute as much to the house as Tom. They both have credit cards. Tom pays his off every month. Anna tries to do this, but occasionally has a balance outstanding on hers.

Tom and Anna operate their finances separately. They have separate bank accounts and they each pay their share of the rent and split bills equally. Once they are married, they intend to pool their finances and open a joint account, from which they will pay the mortgage and the bills.

Tom has a car as part of his job. Anna drives a ten year old car, which she has had since she was a student, but it is unreliable. She realises that she will need to buy a new one before too long, and it would be sensible to get one which is suitable for children.

Tom is passionately interested in wine, which he regards as his hobby as well as his job. He is hoping to start up his own business as a wine merchant in a year or two's time. He plays golf and football for his local team. He is a bit of a gadget man: he has an iPhone 5 and the latest iPad. Anna loves the theatre and clothes, and reads a lot. She plays tennis and goes to a local gym to keep fit. They like eating out when they can afford it. The both enjoy travelling, and have been on several holidays together, both long-haul and in Europe. They hope to continue taking annual foreign holidays, and family holidays once they have children.

Tom and Anna do not lead particularly exceptional lives. Tom is in management, and Anna is one of the 6.037 million people employed in the public sector. They have the same sort of hopes and aspirations as many young couples—a family, a house, two cars, annual holidays. They are fairly 'typical' clients who experience 'life events'—events which change their lives to a greater or lesser extent. There will be legal consequences when each one of these events occurs.

Legal personality

Each phase of life or 'life event' will bring with it corresponding rights and duties imposed by the law. In legal terms, all human beings are born with a 'bundle' of legal rights and duties imposed by the law which govern every aspect of their lives. For example, at the moment, Tom and Anna are renting a flat. The law gives them a right to live in the property without disturbance, but imposes an obligation on them to abide by the terms of the lease. When they buy their own house, these rights and duties change. They no longer have a landlord to whom they must pay rent, but property ownership brings other obligations, for example if they have borrowed money to buy the property, they will have to pay this back. This 'bundle' of rights and duties makes up what is described as an individual's **legal personality**. The exact extent is determined by each person's status: married or single, employer or employee, house owner or tenant, and so on. Just like human personalities, legal personalities develop as individuals mature.

16.1.2 **The role of a lawyer**

On the basis of what we know about Tom and Anna so far, let's look at the sort of work a law firm is likely to be able to do for them.

1. **Property work**. When Tom and Anna buy their house they will want legal advice on the property transfer and how to finance their purchase. They may need advice on ending the tenancy on their current flat, for example if they have a problem getting the deposit back.

2. **Finances**. They may need some advice on the implications of pooling their finances, especially as Anna is going to contribute less to the house than Tom. At this stage in their lives, they probably do not even want to consider this, but what will happen if they do not live happily ever after, and the marriage ends in divorce?

3. **Wills**. It is always advisable to make a will on marriage or when you cohabit with someone, so that you can be sure that your partner will inherit your property on your death.

4. **Probate**. When Tom's grandmother died, the people who were responsible for administering her estate (her executors) may have come to the firm for advice about the administration of the estate (the probate).

5. **Contract law**. Individuals make contracts every day of their lives. When Anna buys her new car, she will enter into a sale of goods contract with the seller.

6. **Company/commercial**. When Tom sets up his new business he will want advice on this. We will be looking at this at 16.1.3.

7. **Employment**. Hopefully, Tom and Anna's jobs are reasonably secure, and there will be no problems here. (Employees who lose their jobs often consult solicitors if they think that they have been dismissed unfairly, or the correct procedure has not been followed.) However, when Tom sets up his own business, a lawyer may need to look at his contract with his current employers to see whether it contains any restrictions preventing him from working in the same area or approaching the company's clients. These are **restraint of trade** clauses, and protect employers against competition from employees once they have left the business.

8. **Welfare and benefits**. If at any time in the future either Tom or Anna is out of work, they may need advice on the benefits to which they may be entitled.

9. **Tax**. At the moment, Tom and Anna's tax affairs are straightforward. Their employers will deduct tax (PAYE) and national insurance (NI) from their salaries and send the correct amount to Her Majesty's Revenue and Customs (HMRC). However, once Tom sets up his own business, he will need more detailed tax advice.

10. **Retirement and pension provision**. Once they have funded the purchase of their home, and paid off their student loans, Tom and Anna will need to think about starting to save for their retirement. This may seem a long way away, but it is still an important consideration.

Most people will not go to a solicitor until they buy their first home. When they do approach a solicitor, the solicitor will advise them about their legal position on their house purchase but, as we can see, if Tom and Anna remain clients of the firm, over the years the solicitor will give advice on a variety of legal rights and duties.

16.1.3 **Business clients**

We are now going to fast-forward a few years and think about Tom's business as an example. You will remember that Tom wanted to start up business as a specialist wine merchant. Businesses, like individuals, have a life cycle from start-up (birth) through expansion (growing to maturity) to when they cease to trade (death). They employ people, and must look after them (a bit like having children). Businesses merge or acquire other businesses (marriage). In the same way that individuals need somewhere to live, businesses need premises to trade from, which they will either rent or buy. They need money to set up, buy assets, survive, and expand. Like individuals, businesses have certain legal rights and legal duties, which govern their day to day lives. The life of the business is ongoing, and the advice which they need will also be ongoing. Let's look at the sort of legal advice that Tom's business may need:

1. **Company/commercial**. Tom will need advice on the type of business structure which is most suitable for his business, and the legal issues which affect each type. Once it is up and running, although the lawyer will be dealing with Tom, the business will be the client. Businesses do not stay the same for ever: Tom will want the business to grow and develop. At each stage of its development, he will need advice.

2. **Property**. Tom will have to decide whether to rent or buy his business premises. In either event, he will need legal advice on the lease or property transfer. If the business expands, it may need to move into larger premises.

3. **Financial**. Tom will have to raise money to start trading, and will need advice on the implications of either putting his own money into the business, or borrowing the money he needs. Again, as the business expands, it may need to raise more finance. Tom may need advice on the options available and on banking law.

4. **Employment**. Tom may be taking on employees, such as sales staff, so he will need advice on his obligations as an employer, the rights of his employees, and the employment legislation which protects them. He will need to think about their contracts, working conditions, and health and safety, for example.

5. **Tax**. Once Tom starts up his own business, he will be responsible for his own tax and the tax affairs of his business.

6. **Licensing and other regulatory matters**. As Tom is setting up a wine business, there are certain licensing requirements with which he must comply.

7. **Consumer issues**. Apart from basic contract law which affects everyday sales, there is a great deal of complex legislation which protects consumers in relation to the provision of goods,

services, and credit, particularly where a business is selling online. In particular, there are **data protection** issues to consider in relation to collating and holding customers' personal details.

8. **Insolvency**. It is a sad fact that many start up businesses fail. If this is the case, the lawyer may need to advise Tom on the implications of the business becoming insolvent, and, in a worst-case scenario, how this can have a knock-on effect and result in his own **personal bankruptcy**.

As well as economic and political context, there are other factors which influence an individual's choices. Life does not stay the same forever. As their life circumstances change, so will their legal needs, and we have seen that Anna and Tom are making plans for their long-term future together. So next we need to look into the future and consider some of these life events, both for Tom and Anna as individuals and for Tom's business.

16.2 Typical life events: individuals and the law

If Tom and Anna's plans work out, their legal personalities will undergo a series of changes. We now look at some of these developments. We explore the concerns and expectations of the clients at each stage of their lives, the environment in which they are taking place, the financial implications, and then think about the underlying legal issues. You can see how an individual's legal personality develops and the impact of seemingly every day events. One point that should become clear is that clients are not always primarily concerned with legal issues. Their life plans and often their finances are more likely to be at the forefront of their minds. To go back to the sample interview question at 15.2.4, an understanding of those underlying concerns will help you anticipate your clients' needs.

16.2.1 **The wedding**

Client concerns

Tom and Anna's main concern when planning their wedding will be that everything is perfect on their 'big day'. They will be arranging all the details of the event: the ceremony, the venue for the reception, the food and drink, the photographer, the flowers, Anna's dress, the bridesmaid's dresses, and so on. This is where their attention will be focused.

Financial considerations

According to *Wedding Magazine*, in 2013 the average cost of a wedding is likely to be £16,164.[1] Clearly an important consideration is how to finance this. Traditionally, the bride's parents usually foot the bill for their daughter's wedding, and we will assume that they will do so in this case. Anna's father (who is 62) has said that he will draw down part of his pension fund. This means that he will take a lump sum, say £20,000, out of his pension fund, as a way of releasing some of his savings. This is one way that older people can benefit from a lifetime of saving, but obviously the fund will be worth £20,000 less, and provide proportionately less income when he retires. We will consider pensions in more detail at 16.4.5.

---

[1] 'Budgeting: Average wedding costs 2013', *Wedding Magazine*, http://www.ukweddingbelles.com.

Legal considerations

Whilst planning the wedding, Tom and Anna are very unlikely even to think about legal issues. However, underlying all their plans there will be legal implications.

First, and most obviously, the marriage must be valid. It has to be conducted according to the requirements of the Marriage Acts; couples cannot just go and say their vows to each other on top of a mountain and be married. The marriage has to be in a recognised format, in a licensed venue, and properly witnessed. It has to be consummated. So if Tom and Anna have a massive row at the wedding reception and never speak to each other again, the marriage will be void.

Getting married changes a person's legal status, giving different rights and obligations from those of single people or cohabitees who are not married. There are rights in relation to a spouse's (husband's or wife's) property if they die. If a couple want to end a marriage, they cannot just walk away and be free to marry again. They must either obtain a divorce or show that there is a valid reason for annulment of the marriage. Both of these are court-based procedures, requiring legal advice. The couple's finances are crucial to any settlement that they may reach on divorce or separation.

The moment that a couple get married, any will which either of them may have made previously is automatically 'revoked' (i.e. it becomes invalid). A common mistake that many couples make is thinking that they will automatically inherit each other's property should one of them die. This is not the case. In the absence of a will, there are legal rules which determine who gets what.

As we have seen, the couple must consider their finances carefully, for example if they decide to have a joint bank account. There are tax reliefs which apply on gifts of property between married couples and on death, so a lawyer can advise on the implications of pooling their finances and tax planning.

Then there are the legal implications from the organisation of the wedding itself. Tom and Anna are entering into a series of contracts for the supply of goods and services. If something goes wrong, they have the benefit of consumer protection legislation, which governs the sale and supply of both goods and services.[2]

16.2.2 The house

Client concerns

Tom and Anna also want to buy a house. Their main concern will be to find a house which they like, with the right accommodation, in the right area. As they are planning a family, they will probably want to find a suitable family home at a price that they can afford. They will need to make sure that once they have found the right house, there is nothing structurally wrong with it. Once they have bought it, they will need to fit it out and furnish it.

Financial considerations

In December 2012, the average house price was £162, 080.[3] As we have seen, Tom has £10,000 and some savings, but that is not going to cover the cost of a house. The couple will have to borrow some money, that is to say approach a bank or building society for a mortgage.

[2] E.g. Sale of Goods Act 1979, Supply of Goods and Services Act 1982, Consumer Protection Act 1987.
[3] Land Registry, *House Price Index*, http://www.landreg.gov.uk.

Essential explanation

A **mortgage** is another word for a property loan. It is a loan which allows you to borrow a large amount of money in order to buy a property. The loan is **secured** against the value of the property, and you pay it back, with interest, over an agreed period of time. The term 'secured' means that if you **default**, in other words fail to make the payments as agreed, the lender has the right to **repossess** your property, in other words to sell it to recover the money which it has lent.

(The word mortgage actually means the security provided for the loan but the term is now used to cover the whole transaction, i.e. the loan and the giving of security.)

Economic factors may also play a role in their decision, for example they may be concerned about the impact of the recession on house prices. In 1995, the average UK house price was just over £62,000. Between 1995 and 2012, house prices have increased by 257.5%. In times of recession, however, house prices tend to stagnate or fall, though historically, once a recession ends, house prices have recovered and outstripped inflation. There have been 'peaks and troughs' but the overall trend is upward. Overall, there is a shortage of housing (particularly affordable housing), which has the effect of pushing up house prices and increasing rents for those who cannot afford to buy.

The shortage of housing in the UK is fast becoming one of the most important social issues of the decade, and the government has intervened to try to stimulate house building by, for example, reforming planning laws.[4] To go back to the Olympic stadium question (see Case study 2 at 14.1), you could use this information to demonstrate awareness of social and political issues. There are economic implications too. This is a simple example of how supply and demand works in a seemingly everyday context (see 14.2.4).

One problem for Tom and Anna is that no bank or building society is going to lend them the whole amount they need for their house purchase, so they will have to put up a proportion of the purchase price as a deposit. The average deposit for first time buyers has risen from £6,793 in 1990 to £27,500 in 2012.[5] As a result, the average age for someone to enter the housing market has risen from 26 to 35. In addition, following the credit crunch, it has been difficult for first-time buyers to borrow money.

 Sample interview questions

1. What do you think the impact of the rise in house prices/shortage of first time buyers would be on this firm?

2. Do you think that the government's initiatives to stimulate house building will have an effect on the property market?

It is important that the couple should be encouraged to seek independent financial advice as to the timing of the purchase, the security of the investment, and how to raise the money they need.

---

[4] Rachel Lee, 'Planning reform: can we get Britain building again?', *The Guardian*, 1 November 2012.
[5] James Hall, 'Average first time buyer is now 35, research finds', *The Telegraph*, 11 September 2012.

Legal considerations

Starting with their legal personalities, home ownership confers a variety of rights and obligations, which, as we have seen, are different from those which affect someone who is renting
a property.

The first thing that they may need advice on is how they want to own the house.
Even if Tom is putting more money in than Anna, they could choose either to own the
house in equal shares, or, alternatively, in proportion to the amount of money that they
have put in: for instance if Tom puts in two-thirds of the money, he will own two-thirds
of the property and Anna will own one-third. This makes it easier if they should ever
divorce. Their solicitor will need to talk this through with them so that they can decide
which is best for them.

When Tom and Anna agree to buy the house, they are entering into a contract.
Contracts for the sale and purchase of property are a particular type of contract. Clients
will need advice on the terms of the contract and must be made aware that once they
have signed the contract, they are committed to the purchase and will be liable if they do
not go through with it. They must ensure that they have all their finances in place before
they sign.

Primarily, their solicitor will deal with the transfer of the ownership, or **title** to the property
from the people who are selling to Tom and Anna. However, this raises all sorts of legal issues.
The title to the property may be freehold or leasehold. If the property is leasehold, the solicitor will need to check the terms and conditions of the lease.

A solicitor starts by doing searches to ensure that the property does not have any fundamental problems, for example they do not want to find that there is planning permission
for 1,000 houses to be built on adjoining land, or that the road that runs past their house is
subject to a road improvement scheme which will turn it into a motorway, or that it has been
built on contaminated land. The solicitor will make enquiries to see what exactly is being sold,
for example, does the sale include the fixtures, such as lights, and fittings, such as carpets and
curtains or any items of furniture.

Once the purchase has been completed, Tom and Anna will be able to move into their
property. However, the solicitor has to be sure that all the formalities have been completed.
He must register their purchase at the land registry. Stamp duty, which is a form of property
tax, has to be paid.

Tom and Anna also need to consider what will happen to the house if one of them dies. If
this has not been provided for, they should update their wills.

Furnishing and fitting out the house will involve more contracts for the sale of goods
and services.

16.2.3 **The children**

Client concerns

Tom and Anna want to have children. Again, they will probably not be thinking about the
legal implications of this decision. They will consider how many children they want, and
when they want to start a family. Their main concern will be that the children are healthy and
have a happy family upbringing.

Financial considerations

A recent article in *The Guardian*, based on figures from the insurer LV=, estimated that the average cost of raising a child from birth to 21 was £218,000. The main cost is child care and education.[6] Clearly, although a huge amount of money overall, the cost is at least spread over 21 years, and most will be met out of income, but there may be times when Tom and Anna will need to borrow money, either by way of short-term loan or overdraft, or by using their credit cards for exceptional expenses. For example, the average cost of Christmas presents for children is £112 per child. Using credit cards is fine if they are able to pay off the credit card each month, but failure to pay off credit card debt is one of the most common causes of individuals finding themselves in financial difficulties.

Legal considerations

When Anna becomes pregnant, she will have certain rights in relation to her employment. She will be entitled to maternity leave of up to a year, and maternity pay during her leave. Tom will also be entitled to paternity leave of up to two weeks. Anna has the right to return to her existing job at the end of her maternity leave.

Once a child is born, like all individuals, it has its own legal personality. A new-born child has few rights and duties, but as the child grows up and assumes more responsibilities, these increase. The rights of children are mainly governed by the Children Act 1989, which governs parental responsibility and obligations, as well as providing for situations where parents are unable to look after their children or where children are suffering from abuse.

As a married couple, Tom and Anna will share responsibility for their children and will be responsible for their basic needs. The welfare of children is of paramount importance legally. It is assumed that all children, for example, have the right to health care and education, and the right not to be abused. Most parents take this for granted and provide the best of care for their children. However, where there is evidence that a child is not being properly looked after or is out of control, the child may be taken into local authority care. Family lawyers deal with this sort of work.

Parents do not generally seek legal advice in relation to children unless they separate or divorce. The parents then have to decide who the child should live with, and how to arrange contact between the child and the absent parent. If the parents cannot decide, these matters may need to be settled by court order. Absent parents are responsible for the child's maintenance, and financial orders may be made if the parents are unable to agree the amount.

These are all worst-case scenarios. However, all families may face certain legal problems, e.g. if they are unable to get a child into the school of their choice, they may need legal advice on the appeals procedure to try and sort this out.

Parents are entitled to certain benefits. Most mothers are entitled to child benefit for each child until it reaches 16, subject to income constraints. Single parents can claim various additional benefits. Welfare and benefits are a highly specialised and topical area of law.

---

[6] Rebecca Smithers, 'Cost of raising a child rises to £218,000', *The Guardian*, 26 January 2012; LV=, *Cost of raising a Child: From cradle to college, 2012 report*, http://www.lv.com/upload/lv-rebrand-2009/pdfs/other/11665_LV_COAC.PDF.

Although this is not something that will affect Tom and Anna, a topical interview question which involves children is given below.

 Sample interview question

Do you think the constitution should be changed so that a first-born girl can succeed to the throne?

16.2.4 **The car**

Client concerns

Anna needs a new car. Again, it is not something about which she will consult a solicitor. Her concerns will be what make and model to buy, its performance, safety features, economy, colour, and so forth. She will have to think carefully about the finance.

Financial considerations

The average cost of a new car in February 2013 was £28,940[7] (admittedly, that takes into account every type of car from a Lamborghini down to a Smart car, and Anna probably will not be spending that much), but even if she buys a second-hand car, the average cost of a family-size used car was £8,540.[8]

Whichever option Anna chooses, she will not be able to pay for this out of income, so she will have to borrow the money, either by getting a short-term loan from the bank or perhaps from a finance company. Most car dealers have arrangements with finance companies to enable buyers to finance the cost of a new car.

Legal considerations

If Anna buys a new car from a dealer, she will again be entering into a sale of goods contract, which will protect her as a consumer in the event that the car turns out to be defective. There is, however, less protection if she buys a defective second-hand car privately. In either event, she may find herself involved in litigation and will need legal advice. Her finances will be important in deciding whether or not to sue or whether it is better to settle the dispute.

If she borrows the money or enters into a finance deal, again as a consumer, she will be protected by consumer credit legislation, which is designed to protect individual borrowers from being taken advantage of by loan sharks and other unscrupulous lenders when borrowing money or entering into contracts for credit. We look at this legislation in more detail at 13.4.6.

As a motorist, Anna has certain obligations to other motorists, such as to obey speed limits and drive with 'due care and attention'. Failure to do so may lead to criminal prosecution under the Road Traffic Act 1988. Over 1 million traffic offences are dealt with by the magistrates' courts each year, including drink driving, careless driving, and use of mobile phones. In 2011,

---

[7] *New Car Price Index—February 2013*, http://drivendata.inluk.com.
[8] 'Used car prices fall to their lowest level for more than a year—but some regions miss out on the best deals', http://www.thisismoney.co.uk, 14 January 2013.

there were 955,459 incidents of speeding in Britain, punishment for which includes fines and penalty points on driving licences.[9] Serious offences, such as causing death by dangerous driving, can lead to imprisonment. Road traffic offences are a common cause of individuals consulting their solicitors and there are specialist firms of solicitors for this type of work.

All motorists must take out insurance to cover any damage or injuries to third parties in the event of an accident. Driving without insurance is also a criminal offence. An insurance contract is a specialised form of contract.

16.2.5 Holidays and hobbies

Client concerns

Tom and Anna hope to take annual holidays, and they both have hobbies and interests which they pursue. This seems innocuous enough, but in reality this will involve more expense and there are still legal implications.

Financial considerations

According to *Travel Weekly*, the average cost of a holiday per person in 2010 was £701.43,[10] and the cost is going up, partly as a result of increased fuel costs and tax for airlines. *Which?* reports that the average cost of gym membership is £442 a year.[11] The average joining fee for a golf club is £738.[12] Hobbies can generally be paid for out of income, but holidays are the sort of expense that many people put on their credit cards or pay for with an overdraft or loan.

Legal considerations

Again, contract law is central to holiday bookings and membership of clubs. The main purpose of these types of contract is pleasure and enjoyment, so if something goes wrong, there are additional remedies to compensate for disappointment. There has been an important test case brought by the Office of Fair Trading involving unfair terms in gym contracts.[13]

16.2.6 Old age and death

Client concerns

By now, you will be able to see that with every life event come financial and legal implications. This is true from birth to death. Tom and Anna will probably give little consideration to these 'events' (old age and death) at this stage in their lives. They may have started thinking about

---

[9] 'Figures reveal rise in speeding drivers', *The Telegraph*, 29 March 2012: estimates from LV= car insurance, quoted in the article, suggest 1.5 million drivers faced 2.2 million penalty points and £41 million in fines in 2011.

[10] 'Price "still dominant factor" in Brits holiday choices', *TravelWeekly*, 25 August 2010, http://m. travelweekly.co.uk.

[11] 'Brits waste 37 million on unused gym memberships', *Which?*, 19 January 2011.

[12] British Golf Industry Association, http://www.bgia.org.uk.

[13] *Office of Fair Trading v Ashbourne Management Services Ltd and others* [2011] EWHC 1237 (Ch).

saving for their old age, but that will probably be about as far as they have got. Early planning is crucially important. A further consideration is their parents, or other older relatives, who may need care in their old age.

Financial considerations

With an increasingly ageing population, individuals who retire in their mid-sixties will have to provide a pension fund to live off for 20 to 30 years or more. Anna, as a teacher, will get a teacher's pension, paid by the government. Currently, a teacher who retires on a salary of £37,800 will get a pension of £25,200 a year. Tom will have to save for his pension himself. To get the same as Anna, he would need a pension fund of £700,000. If he saves £50 a month in a pension fund, he would only have a fund of about £190,000 on retirement.

An article in *The Guardian* reported that the average cost of dying, including the cost of the funeral, probate fees, and a headstone, is £7,248.[14] People do plan ahead for this, and you will see advertisements for funeral plans, which are savings schemes to finance your funeral (another form of contract), but Tom and Anna will hope to have a few years to think about this.

Legal considerations

Pension law is becoming an increasingly important area of law as individuals become more concerned about saving for their old age.

As people get older, they may become ill or infirm and not be able to manage their affairs. We have seen how important it is to make a will at various stages of life. Once individuals lose their 'capacity' to do so, for example as a result of dementia, it is too late. It is also important to make arrangements for someone to manage their affairs if they become unable to do so for themselves. Individuals should take advice on these things both for themselves and for elderly relatives.

During their lives, as we shall see, Tom and Anna will substantially increase their wealth. When they die, this will be taken into account in calculating how much their estates are worth. There are legal formalities which have to be completed before the money in the estate can be released to whoever is entitled to the money. Tax may be payable on the estate. Often, though not always, solicitors will be involved and complete the legal processes on behalf of the relatives. The larger the estate, the more likely it is that a solicitor will be instructed to administer it.

16.2.7 **The context**

So far, we have thought about the client's concerns, and financial considerations and the type of legal advice that might be given. A lawyer should also think about the economic environment and its effect on the client. Over a lifetime, the economic climate will change dramatically. There will be times of economic prosperity and phases of economic downturn, as now. You looked at the **business cycle** at 14.2.5.

The current recession has had a profound effect on most individuals' finances and standard of living. In an article in 2010, the Labour leader, Ed Miliband, referred to people living on

---

[14] Rebecca Smithers, 'Cost of dying rises above £7,000', *The Guardian*, 14 September 2011.

average incomes as 'the squeezed middle', that is to say individuals who are seeing their standard of living fall as a result of rising prices, rising taxes and pay cuts.[15] Tom and Anna could be seen as falling into this category.

This has had a knock-on effect on the legal profession, and the sort of advice which clients seek. Consider Example 1, which sets out the experiences of a private client lawyer in the recession.

Example 1

You have seen how many life events make it essential for a client to make a will. Jane is a private client lawyer who has worked for a successful high-street practice for ten years. The firm has a policy of cross-referring their property clients to Jane, so when clients buy a property, they are encouraged to make or update their wills. Until 2008, clients were keen to take advantage of this complete package. During the recession, she has found that they are reluctant to spend more money once their purchase is completed. If they do, they want competitive rates or fixed fees regardless of what is involved, sometimes making this unprofitable.

16.3 Typical life events: businesses and the law

Like individuals, each phase of a business's lifecycle will involve its owners thinking about the context in which the business is operating, its long term plans, and finance. The main considerations are commercial, but there are underlying legal issues and practical concerns on which business clients will need advice. Often these will be the same as for an individual. Again, you should anticipate the client's business needs, by having an in-depth understanding of the business and the concerns of the owner(s). To do this, we are going to fast-forward a few years and look at Tom's business as an example (see Case study 2).

Case study 2

You will remember that Tom wanted to start his own wine business. He has found an empty shop for his business in the high street of a picturesque local market town. He is confident that this is a good location. It is an affluent small town in the commuter belt.

He has conducted some market research and feels that there is a gap in the market for a specialist wine merchant which can offer its customers a wide range of wines, from affordable to top end prices, with specialist advice. He realises that he will not be able to undercut the supermarkets and larger wine retailers, but he has come up with a marketing concept to attract customers. He has a name for his business, The Wine Seller, which he hopes to use to develop its brand.

The business will offer wine tasting 'experiences', accessible advice and education, with regular talks from wine journalists and experts in the wine trade. Customers will have access to an online wine magazine, *Seller's Sips*, with recommendations, and he hopes to develop an app for customers' phones. Using the latest technology, he is hoping to expand to offer a similar online service, which he hopes to run on the lines of LoveFilm.com. Customers will pay a subscription for regular tasting samples, email recommendations, reminders, and the online magazine.

---

[15] 'Ed Miliband: my vision to rebuild trust', *The Telegraph*, 25 September 2010.

16.3.1 **Start up**

Client concerns

When he starts up the business, Tom's main concern will be whether this a viable business, and whether he will be able to make a profit.

Financial considerations

Before the business even opens its doors, Tom will need to spend money to get the business going. He needs suitable premises to operate from, stock to sell, and customers to sell to. There will be expenses like legal fees, marketing materials, doing up the shop, or buying in the wine to sell. He will have to buy assets for the business, such as shop fittings, computers, telephones, cash registers, or wine storage units. He may need to pay rent in advance to his landlord, and put up a deposit (as you have to do when you rent a flat). There are various things that Tom will need to organise, and therefore pay for, before he starts to trade. These are illustrated by Case study 3.

Case study 3

Tom is hoping to open his business on 7 September. He gives up his job at the beginning of August and starts to prepare for the opening of the business. The following transactions take place:

1 August	Tom transfers £50,000 of his own money to the business bank account.
2 August	He negotiates a loan with the bank for £20,000, repayable in five years.
3 August	He rents premises in the High Street. He pays a deposit of £4,500 and the first instalment of rent (£3,000). He pays for insurance on the property (£230).
10 August	He buys shop fittings and fixtures, and computers.
12 August	He orders marketing materials, stationery, and business cards.
15 August	He buys wine for £20,000 cash to stock the shop.
16 August	He pays a web designer for designing and setting up the business website.
5 September	He obtains and pays for his licence to sell alcohol (£985).
6 September	He pays the shop fitters who have installed the fixtures and fittings. He pays his solicitor (£1,000 plus VAT) for general advice on business set up, licensing, and checking the lease on the property.

Often, clients setting up new businesses tend to underestimate start up costs, and forget that it will take time to get the business going before it starts to generate income. In our example, all of the money that Tom has paid out between 1 August and 7 September are his start up costs. This is just a simple example. In reality, the process may take much longer, and involve more money (e.g. to obtain a licence to sell alcohol, the shop owner must attend a training course and sit an exam).

On a personal level, he will need to consider how he is going to pay his everyday living expenses whilst he is setting up the business.

It is essential that anyone starting up a business has a realistic business plan.

Essential explanation

A **business plan** is a written document that describes a business, its objectives (what it hopes to achieve), its strategies (how it hopes achieve them), its products, the market it is operating in, the potential for growth within that market, and its financial forecasts. A business should have a plan at every stage of its development, not just when starting up.

The best option for Tom is to get independent financial advice. He will need a good accountant and a sympathetic business relationship manager at his bank.

Legal considerations

Ownership of a business will change Tom's individual legal personality. The rights and responsibilities which he had as an employee will be replaced by a new set of rights and obligations as a business owner/employer. As a result, Tom may need advice on a range of legal issues.

To begin with, Tom will need advice on the legal structure of the business. From the facts that we have, it looks as though he will be running the business by himself as a sole trader. Tom has full responsibility for the business both financially and legally. There are other types of business structure, such as partnerships or limited liability companies. His solicitor will need to advise him on the implications of running the business as a sole trader and the advantages and disadvantages of other types of business structure so that he can decide whether this is really the best option (see 13.2).

Tom is going to borrow money from the bank to fund the business. He may need help with the terms of the loan. The bank may require some form of security to ensure that if the business runs into difficulties, it will get its money back, for instance it may ask Tom for a further mortgage on his house. There are other options for raising finance. Again, Tom may need advice on the advantages and disadvantages of each of these (see 16.5).

Tom is renting the business premises under the terms of a lease. He will need advice on these, especially to ensure that there are no restrictions preventing him from selling alcohol.

 Essential explanation

A **lease** of premises is a contractual arrangement which grants the right to occupy the premises for a fixed period, subject to the terms and conditions set out in the lease (e.g. payment of the rent). The lease of business premises may contain restrictions as to the type of business activity which can be carried out on the premises.

Tom is entering into a series of contracts for goods and services with various suppliers, and for the installation of the fixtures and fittings. Like an individual, he has certain rights if any goods or services turn out to be defective. However, as a business customer, he does not have the benefit of consumer protection legislation. He may need advice on the terms of his supply contracts to ensure that he is not agreeing to terms which will be prejudicial to the business.

To promote his business, Tom has ordered some marketing materials. He needs to be aware of what he can and cannot say in advertisements and promotional material.

He has arranged insurance. This involves a further type of contract. Running a business exposes the owner(s) to various risks, for example liability should either customers or employees

injure themselves on the premises, or if the business sells defective products. Risk management is crucial for every business, so Tom may need advice on the risks which are likely to
arise, and the type of insurance cover the business needs.

Before he starts up, Tom should get advice on the tax implications of setting up the business
and how to minimise his tax. There will be further tax implications once the business is up and
running. He should be made aware of these before he starts the business, and advised to get
an accountant to oversee the business finances.

Tom is selling alcohol and will therefore require a licence. He will need advice on the statutory requirements in relation to the sale of alcohol and how to obtain a licence.

Tom has a name for the business, 'The Wine Seller'. Before he starts to use the name, he will
need to check whether any other business is trading under this name, or he may be infringing that other business's intellectual property rights (e.g. its trade mark). The name will be his
brand. He will need advice on how to protect his brand and other intellectual property rights.

16.3.2 **Running the business**

Client concerns

Once Tom opens the doors of his business, his aim will be to make a profit. He will be concerned with all the day-to-day running of the business.

Financial considerations

To make money, businesses have to spend money. Case study 4 gives some simple examples,
showing the constant expenditure involved in running a business.

Case study 4

On 7 September, Tom opens the shop.

7 September	He sells £5,000 of wine to customers who pay cash.
	He sells £6,000 of wine and champagne to a wine bar on a 30-day credit period (i.e. the customer does not need to pay his bill for 30 days).
	He buys champagne for £10,000 from his supplier on a 14-day credit period (i.e. he has to pay his bill within 14 days).
	He pays the next instalment of rent and insurance (£3,230).
8 September	He pays an electricity bill of by cheque.
	He buys a van for £15,000, and employs a delivery driver.
9 September	He negotiates an overdraft facility with the bank and draws down £5,000 to buy more stock. (He pays the bank an arrangement fee for setting up the overdraft.)
10 September	He pays his phone and internet bill (£850).
	He makes further cash sales of £3,000.

Assume further sales and purchases during the rest of the month

30 September	He pays the van driver's wages (£1,090).
	He pays Mastercard and Visa for use of credit facilities.
	He pays bank charges and interest of £550.
	He employs a cleaner for five hours a week at £10 an hour.

Tom will have to ensure that he maintains his stock of wine. The wine will not sell itself, and he may need to employ sales staff in his shop. At the moment, he is just employing a driver and a cleaner, and selling the wine himself.

Throughout the year, he will be paying rent, rates, utility bills, and other outgoings. All this is fine, provided that he continues to sell the wine. There will be some days when he sells a fair amount, and he should use this to build up a reserve. In our example, on 7 September, Tom has sold £11,000 of the £20,000 worth of wine which he bought to stock up the shop, although he is not paid for all of this immediately. On the same day, however, he has bought £10,000 worth of champagne, but it is possible that none of his customers will want champagne until Christmas. All businesses need to keep a reserve for periods when trade is slow. (A rough guide for a business with start up costs of £50,000–£70,000 is a reserve of £20,000–£30,000.)

Legal considerations

The day-to-day transactions—the sale of the wine—will be governed by contract law. Where Tom is selling to consumers, he will have to bear in mind consumer protection legislation.

Where he is offering credit to consumers, consumer credit legislation offers them further protection. He may also need advice if his customers fail to pay, for example on debt collection.

Once the business is making a profit, there are tax implications. Tom, as a sole trader, will be liable for tax on those profits. In addition, once the total sales (turnover) of the business reach £77,000, he must register for VAT.[16]

 Essential explanation

VAT is an indirect tax on consumers charged on most goods and services sold by VAT registered businesses. It is not paid by the business itself. It is paid by the customers and the business collects it and passes it on to HMRC.

This means that Tom must charge VAT at 20% on everything which he sells, although he will be able to reclaim any VAT which he has paid on his own purchases. He will have to complete VAT returns for HMRC every three months.

Tom has employed a driver, and it is likely that as the business grows he will take on sales staff. All employees are protected by employment legislation. Employees have rights in relation to their contracts, pay, working hours and conditions, holidays, pensions, and also the right not to be dismissed wrongly or unfairly. They have the right not to be discriminated against on the grounds of race, sex, disability, religion, age, and so forth. Employment law is a highly complex area, and Tom will need advice when he takes on employees, particularly in relation to their employment contracts. Employment protection is not all one-way traffic. The converse is true; the employees should look carefully at their contracts, and understand that they have certain obligations towards their employer, for example to work their contracted hours and not 'moonlight' (i.e. work for someone else at the same time).

Employers are responsible for paying their employees' tax (called PAYE), which they take directly out of their wages and pass on to HMRC (see 'Tax' at 16.4.3).

---

[16] Rates for the tax year 2012/13.

The cleaner is more likely to be self-employed than an employee. If this is the case, the cleaner will not have the employment rights which the other employees enjoy, but it is important that Tom establishes the status of all of those working for him before he takes them on.

16.3.3 Expansion

Client concerns

Let's assume that Tom's business has been running successfully for five years, and he is considering whether or not to open a second shop. He has the option to buy another wine merchant's business in a neighbouring town.

He is also considering combining his shops (known as the '**bricks and mortar**' part of his business) with expansion of the online (**e-commerce**) part of the business. If he expands, he is thinking about incorporating his business, to raise funds and to give himself the protection of limited liability.

Financial considerations

If Tom expands his business, he will have all the same expenses, but on a larger scale. For example, he will have additional premises, and so he will have to pay more rent and his utility bills will go up. He may incur additional marketing costs to promote the business in its new venue or format. There will be legal and other professional fees (e.g. accountancy fees). More storage space will be needed to store more stock, so Tom may have to rent a warehouse, and pay for rent and utility bills for that as well. He may take on more sales staff, and administrative support will be needed. He may need a fleet of vans and so have to employ more drivers.

For the e-commerce venture, he will need to invest in the relevant technology, and the staff to operate this, in particular IT support. Often the result of incurring additional expenses is that profits decrease, especially initially, before the benefit of the expansion takes effect. Once the profits do increase, a further consideration is that there will be extra tax (e.g. VAT).

If all goes well, however, expansion should mean that Tom can achieve '**economies of scale**'. This effectively means that as his business expands, costs per unit sold will decrease, allowing him to make a higher profit, and reduce prices. Instead of buying for one shop, he will now be buying for two and will be supplying his online customers. If he buys more, he may be able to get lower prices. Some of the costs will be spread across all parts of the business, such as advertising, professional, or administration costs. An example of how this works is the big supermarkets. They are able to cut prices as the sheer size of their operations enables them to get lower prices from their suppliers. However, economies of scale tend to work less well for smaller than for larger businesses.

Legal considerations

There are various ways that a business can expand, and so Tom may need advice as to the best way of doing it. He can expand by just buying the shop in the neighbouring town (i.e. acquiring a new asset). This means that he will develop his existing business from two outlets. Alternatively, he can buy the business itself as a going concern, with all its assets, thus combining the two businesses. Finally, he could go into business with the owner of the other wine merchant and merge the two businesses.

Essential explanation

An **acquisition** is the purchase of one business by another. This will not result in a new business being formed.

A **merger** is where two businesses merge or combine their existing operations to form a new business.

Certainly, if you are interested in corporate practice, you should know the difference. Again, it is the sort of question you might be asked at an interview.

 Sample interview question

What is the difference between a merger and an acquisition?

If Tom decides to buy the business as a going concern, his solicitor will carry out a 'health' check on the business by examining all the documentation, financial records, and other material facts relating to the business to ensure that the business is sound and there are no problems that have not been revealed during the purchase negotiations. This process is known as **due diligence**. If he decides only to buy the shop, the solicitor will need to investigate the title to the premises and ensure that ownership is transferred to Tom.

As the business grows, Tom will need ongoing advice on many of the issues that we have already considered, such as contractual and employment issues, tax, and debt collection.

16.3.4 **Insolvency**

The BIS Insolvency statistics show that nearly 17,000 companies went into liquidation in 2011, an increase of 5.1% on 2010.[17] Insolvency practitioners warn that worse is to come. Several very well-known companies and organisations either ceased trading or were taken over as a result of insolvency in 2012 alone, for example Comet, La Senza, Peacocks, and Rangers Football Club to name but a few.

16.3.5 **The context**

Again the final stage is to analyse the commercial factors and the economic environment in which the business is operating. If Tom decides to start his business now, he will be setting up during the most prolonged recessions since the 1930s. The Chancellor's autumn budget statement in 2012 made it clear that the economy is growing more slowly than predicted and it is expected to take until 2015 to reach growth of 3%.[18] It is crucial that Tom is aware of the possible consequences.

For example, at each stage of the life of a business, there is always the spectre of insolvency hanging over it, and this is an increasingly real prospect in times of recession. The knock-on effect is very often the bankruptcy of the proprietor of the business. Insolvency is covered at 14.5.

---

[17] Insolvency Service, *Insolvency Statistics*, http://www.bis.gov.uk/insolvency.

[18] 'Autumn Statement 2012: At a glance summary of key points', *BBC News*, 5 December 2012, http://www.bbc.co.uk/news/uk-politics-20606382.

Start up companies are particularly vulnerable in the current economic climate. We have seen that Tom will have significant start up costs before he begins to make any money. Even once he is up and running, many small businesses have struggled to survive the recession, as often they find it difficult to borrow money, and owners may have to use their own money to keep afloat.[19] Over-expansion is a further common cause of insolvency.

The type of business and the market in which it operates is important to its success. Although statistics show that alcohol sales have fallen slightly during the recession, Tom is aiming primarily at an affluent market, where consumption has increased. The latest Office of National Statistics survey shows that 54% of adults drink alcohol at least once a week and many adults aged over 45 drink every day.[20] Another important fact that Tom should bear in mind is that this is a seasonal market, with sales increasing, for example during the period leading up to Christmas and the New Year, and then falling off. This may cause him cash flow problems, so he should run a tight credit policy following up bills and ensuring that they are paid, and it is important to keep reserves for these periods.

On the plus side, some of his wine stocks will be sourced from major wine producers abroad, particularly in France. Tom's business will benefit from the strength of the pound (sterling) against the euro, as a result of the recent euro zone crisis. Export clients and those buying from abroad are very much at the mercy of developments in the currency markets. Understanding currency fluctuations and the advantages and disadvantages of a strong or weak pound is a crucial part of commercial awareness, and something that you can demonstrate at interviews.

We have now seen why individuals and businesses have recourse to the law, and the legal and financial impact of everyday events. We are next going to think further about the financial concerns of both individuals and businesses, and how clients of both types raise finance.

16.4 Forms of individual finance

You have seen that as individuals and businesses progress through their lives, their financial concerns are paramount. In short, everyone needs money. Now we are going to consider how individuals get money and what they do with it. We will look at individual wealth, in its broadest sense, thinking about what individuals are worth in terms of their total assets and the effect that this may have on their financial decisions.

16.4.1 Background

To fully understand their clients, lawyers need to be aware of their financial background. There are four main aspects to consider, which taken together represent an individual's wealth:

- how much money your clients earn (**income**);
- how they spend it (**expenses**);
- what property and savings they have (**assets**); and
- how much money they have borrowed (**liabilities**).

---

[19] 'Small firms "surviving" recession', *BBC News*, 9 November 2009, http://news.bbc.co.uk/1/hi/business/8349308.stm.

[20] ONS, *General Lifestyle Survey 2010* (March 2012), http://www.ons.gov.uk.

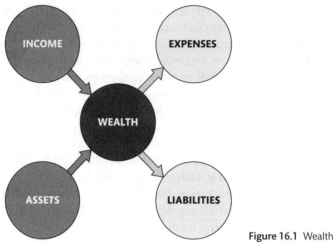

Figure 16.1 Wealth

Figure 16.1 shows how all of these factors contribute to an individual's wealth.

'Wealth' is a bit of a buzz word at the moment. The annual *Sunday Times* 'Rich List'[21] and the attention which it attracts shows how fascinated people are by the concept of wealth. It shows that if you add up the wealth of the 1,000 richest people in the UK, it comes to over £414 billion.[22] Top of the list is the steel tycoon, Lakshmi Mittal, whose wealth totals £12.7 billion. Many law firms no longer have 'private client' departments, they have 'private wealth' departments, which advise clients on financial planning, tax issues, inheritance, wills, and probate. However, this gives a totally false impression of what wealth is. Having wealth does not necessarily mean that you are rich. It is simply a measure of what you own.

 Essential explanation

An individual's **wealth** is what she is worth, taking into account income, expenses, assets, and borrowings. Clearly, the more you own, the richer you are. In practice, you will be looking at the impact of a client's 'wealth', whether you are working in a large commercial firm or a small high-street firm.

Most people try to budget carefully. They work out how much income is coming in each month, and what their main expenses are. If anything is left over, they can use the money to reduce their liabilities, buy extra assets, or put the excess into savings, all of which will increase their wealth. At 14.4 you saw that this is basic accounting. However, there are variables, which will affect their budgets. As well as inflation, we have already seen that typical life events cost money, and sometimes they cost a large amount of money. Not all of an individual's expenses can be met out of income, and generally people will not want to sell assets. One way of raising finance is to borrow money, creating liabilities.

---

[21] *Sunday Times Rich List 2012*, 29 April 2012, http://www.thesundaytimes.co.uk/sto/public/richlist.
[22] Patrick Sawyer, 'Wealth of richest grows to record levels', *The Telegraph*, 28 April 2012.

16.4.2 **Code of Conduct**

It is crucial at this stage to realise that, as a lawyer, you will not be giving detailed financial advice to your clients. Most of this information will be background only to your advice to your clients. This is because there are very strict conduct rules which govern what sort of financial advice a solicitor can give. The fundamental principle of the Solicitors Regulation Authority's Code of Conduct[23] is that solicitors can only advise if they have the necessary skill and expertise to do so. If not, they will not be acting in their client's best interests. Most solicitors will not have financial expertise, but even if they do, they (and all professionals who offer financial advice) are regulated by the Financial Services and Markets Act 2000, which prevents professionals giving specialist financial advice of any sort unless they are authorised to do so. Most solicitors are not authorised, and so would commit a criminal offence were they to do so. This is punishable by a two-year prison sentence and/or a fine.

You can give general advice, for example explain the nature of shares or bonds, and that shares are a riskier investment than bonds. However, you cannot go on to give more specific advice, such as you think that shares in BP are not the best investment to make at the moment, because of the fall-out from the Gulf of Mexico oil spill. You may be right, but you need to refer your client to an independent financial adviser, like a stockbroker.

16.4.3 **Income**

1. **Income**. Income is what you earn. Most individuals' income comes from their salaries as employees. The average salary in 2011 was £26,200 a year (gross) for full-time employees in the UK.[24]

2. **Benefits**. For those who are unemployed, benefits are the main source of income. A recent survey of households by the insurance company, Aviva, showed that 21% of households rely on benefits.[25] There are a variety of different benefits which people who are unemployed may claim. The main ones are jobseekers' allowance and employment support (which used to be called incapacity benefit). Lone parents, carers, and the disabled are also able to claim. The welfare system again is highly topical, because of the welfare cuts which are part of the government's austerity programme.

 Sample interview question

Do you think the welfare system needs to be reformed?

---

3. **Savings**. Individuals may also have savings and investments which earn income, e.g.:

  - interest from savings accounts, or bonds;
  - dividends from investments in shares;

---

[23] SRA Handbook, Code of Conduct 2011 and Accounts Rules 2011, http://www.sra.org.uk.

[24] Matthew Sparkes and Sebastian Payne, 'Average salary falls 3pc in face of high inflation', The Telegraph, 23 November 2011.

[25] Aviva, Family Finances Report, January 2013, http://www.aviva.com/data/report-library/Family_Finances_Report_Jan_2013.pdf.

• rent from property. Individuals may invest in residential or other investment properties which they let out for profit. It is estimated that there are over 4.8 million buy-to-let properties in the UK.

Tax

As Benjamin Franklin famously remarked, 'in this world nothing can be said to be certain, except death and taxes'. Most income is subject to tax. An employee is paid a net salary, that is after deduction of tax. Tax on employment income is known as Pay As You Earn (PAYE). The employer calculates the tax due each month and takes it out of the employee's salary before payment. Employees also pay National Insurance (NI) contributions to the government. This is deducted at the same time. NI helps to fund the welfare state, and in particular affects the final amount of an individual's pension.

 Essential explanation

Gross income is income before tax has been deducted.
　Net income is the amount received after the deduction of tax.

The rate of tax depends on the amount which the employee earns. A taxpayer can earn up to £8,015 without paying any tax. Once someone's income goes above this figure, they start to pay tax. The rates of tax are set each year in March by the Chancellor of the Exchequer in the budget statement, which is the yearly update on the state of the economy. The budget is of vital importance for individuals and businesses alike. It is one of the political events of each year which you should always know about. Apart from anything else, it could well be the subject of an interview question.

 Sample interview question

What are your views on the latest budget?

Inflation

You have considered inflation and its impact on the economy at 14.2.5. It is a vital factor when advising clients. In September 2011 inflation went up to 5.2%. At that time, private sector pay rises were 2.6%, just over half the rate of inflation, which would have meant that workers were considerably worse off in real terms. If pay deals fail to match inflation, there is a gap between actual wages and real wages. In November 2011 *The Telegraph* reported that workers had seen a 3% fall in wages in real terms since 2010.[26] This is illustrated by Example 2.

---

[26] Matthew Sparkes and Sebastian Payne, 'Average salary falls 3pc in face of high inflation', *The Telegraph*, 23 November 2011.

Essential explanation

Actual wages are wages before taking into account inflation.
   Real wages take into account inflation.

Example 2

If an employee's actual wage is £1,000 a month (net), and inflation for that month is 3%, his real net wage is £970.

16.4.4 Expenses

Recent ONS statistics show that households spend an average of £474 a week.[27] Most people's expenses are housing (rent or mortgage payments), utilities (gas, electricity, and water), running the car, and food. They will have to pay council tax (tax paid to the local authority) on the property. They probably have other expenses as well, such as their mobile phones. Hobbies cost money. They may be paying interest to the bank on any overdrafts which they have, or on any unpaid balance on their credit cards.

Some expenses have increased beyond the rate of inflation. The cost of commodities has risen significantly over the last couple of years. Transport is a significant expense because of high fuel prices. Food is expensive, and the average household gas and electricity bill went up by £224 during 2011. Example 3 shows that many people are struggling as their expenses increase.

Example 3

A survey of professional households in 2009, conducted by the insurance company Hiscox, suggested that even on an income of £93,000 a year, most of those surveyed still found it hard to manage, and 'felt broke'. They said they would need to earn over £150,000 before they felt 'wealthy'.[28] No doubt they would feel that they need considerably more today.

16.4.5 Assets

An individual's assets are the various items of property which he owns. An asset has a value. It can be sold and converted into cash. Examples include land and buildings, bank accounts, investments, cars, furniture, and electronic equipment. The sum total of an individual's assets is sometimes referred to as his **capital**. Some assets are more easily converted into cash (i.e. are more 'liquid' than others). Cash is the most liquid of assets. You can go to your bank and get all your cash out of your account, but it may take some time, for example, to sell your car.

[27] ONS, *Family Saving, 2011 Edition Release*, http://www.ons.gov.uk.
[28] Hiscox, *Wealth Review 2009*, http://www.hiscox.co.uk/shared-documents/Hiscox-wealth-review-2009.pdf.

House ownership

In England, 14.5 million people (or 66% of households)[29] own their own home, which will be by far their most valuable asset. Other important assets are savings and investments.

Savings

Savings provide individuals with a fund for the future, and in the meantime produce an income. There are various ways that individuals can save.

1. **Savings accounts with banks and building societies**. These are the most common way of saving, as they carry little risk, but the problem for savers is that interest rates are low at the moment so the return on these savings is minimal.
2. **Individual Savings Accounts (ISAs)**. These are tax-free savings schemes. In simple terms, they are ordinary bank savings accounts or portfolios of stocks and shares but which are subject to tax exemptions.

Pensions

One of the main ways that many people save is by paying into a pension. A pension is an investment policy which provides income when you retire. Everyone is entitled to a state pension, paid by the government, funded from NI contributions paid during an individual's working life. The basic pension for an individual is £107.45 a week,[30] which only gives limited support. It is advisable to supplement the state pension by paying into a private scheme and build up a fund which will provide income for your old age. Pension provision is a complicated area and there are various types of private pension schemes.

Public sector workers, such as doctors, the police, teachers and civil servants, get a pension funded by the state, and based on their final salary. Outside the public sector, however, government research shows that millions of people are not saving anything at all into private pensions. This has led to large-scale reform of pension law, and by 2016 all employers will be obliged to enrol all their workers automatically into an employer funded pension scheme.[31]

Saving for a pension has other advantages apart from providing for retirement. You get tax relief on pension contributions. Most pension schemes allow policy holders to withdraw a lump sum from the pension 'pot' which they have saved once they reach 55, which can be a useful way for older people to raise money.

Investments

Investments are a form of saving, in that they provide a fund for the future and an income (e.g. investors receive dividends on shares), but they also have the potential to increase in value. Paying into a pension fund can be regarded as an investment, in that a pension fund should

---

[29] Department for Communities and Local Government, *English Housing Survey. Headline Report 2010-11* (February 2012),

[30] https://www.gov.uk/state-pension.   [31] Pensions Act 2008, in force from October 2012.

increase in value over the years, whereas cash in the bank or building society is not. In real terms, cash will decrease in value, because of inflation. Savings can take various forms:

1. Bonds, shares, and unit trusts, all of which will produce an income (see 14.3.4).

2. The purchase of a house is also an investment but, unlike other investments, houses do not provide an income (unless bought to let). However, since the 1980s, house prices have gone up dramatically, and more quickly than inflation, and thus provide **capital growth**.

Tax

Some assets are subject to **capital gains tax (CGT)**. This means that if an asset is sold or given away, a proportion of any increase in value is subject to tax. In addition, on death, all an individual's assets are added together to form her 'estate'. If the total value exceeds a certain limit, or threshold known as the nil rate band (currently £325,000),[32] then **inheritance tax** has to be paid.

Sample interview question

Do you think it is fair that the inheritance tax threshold should stay the same?

16.4.6 Liabilities

An individual's liabilities are the amounts which he owes (his debts) to his creditors.

Essential explanation

A **debtor** is someone who borrows, or **owes**, money.
A **creditor** is someone who lends, or is **owed**, money.

Borrowing and credit

Since the 1980s, with the rise of consumerism, borrowing and credit have been an important part of the everyday lives of individuals in the UK. As a result, in October 2011, *The Telegraph* reported that households in the UK owed £1.5 trillion. The average adult owes £29,500.[33]

Essential explanation

An individual's **credit** is the amount of money which is available for him to borrow. It is called credit because it is based on the trust that the amount will be repaid in the future. Loans, mortgages, overdrafts, and credit cards are all forms of credit.

---

[32] As at February 2013.
[33] Jeff Randall, 'The debt trap time bomb', *The Telegraph*, 31 October 2011.

The provision of credit is very highly regulated in order to protect consumers. Banks and other financial institutions which provide credit to consumers must be licensed, and follow prescribed guidelines in relation to the information which they give when a credit contract is formed, and procedures to follow during the term of the agreement and when the agreement comes to an end.[34]

Credit rating

Knowing about credit ratings is one of the most important bits of financial knowledge that you can have, both for your clients and in relation to your own affairs. The amount of credit available to any individual depends on her credit rating. This is an assessment of her credit-worthiness based on her assets and liabilities, past borrowing, and repayment history.

Credit reference agencies collect financial information on individuals, looking at all aspects of their financial lives, such as how many credit cards and mobile phone contracts they have, and whether they have missed payments on those. They then draw up credit reports which they sell to banks and other institutions. When you apply for a loan or a credit card, the bank or card provider will 'score' you, based on how well, (or badly) you have managed your finances in the past. It also looks at non-financial information such as court orders against you, and whether you are on the Electoral Roll.

A poor credit score makes it difficult to get credit. However, anyone can improve their credit rating, by taking a few simple steps that make it look as if they are managing their finances responsibly, such as always paying bills on time, not exceeding overdraft limits, reducing debts, and, perhaps surprisingly, getting a credit card (but you must repay it on time every month).

The cost of borrowing

Banks and other commercial lenders make a profit by charging interest on borrowing. Interest rates vary, depending on the type of loan and the risk involved. Lenders may also charge fees when the loan is taken out, and this will put up the cost of the loan. It is sometimes far from clear how much interest is actually payable. Lenders are required by consumer credit legislation to state how much it will cost per year to take out a loan. It is vital to understand this calculation.

 Essential explanation

The **Annual Percentage Rate (APR)** is the annual cost of a loan. It includes the interest on the loan and any associated fees that are automatically included for that type of loan. It is possible that the interest rate is 10%, but the APR is, say, 12% because the costs of the loan put up the APR.

Borrowers should always check the APR before taking out any form of loan, so as to make a comparison between various loans, and see what is being charged for. Many borrowers are unaware of the significance of APR. Emma Messenger writing in the *Evening Standard* reported that 50% of people do not bother to check what the interest rate is before applying for credit.[35]

---

[34] Consumer Credit Act 1974, as amended.

[35] Emma Messenger, 'Why I'm stuck in a never-ending cycle of credit card debt', *London Evening Standard*, 10 October 2011.

Secured loans

> **Essential explanation**
>
> A **secured loan** requires the borrower to put up an asset, or **collateral**, to back the loan. The term secured means that if the borrower **defaults** (i.e. fails to make the payments as agreed), the lender has the right to **repossess** the asset (i.e. to sell it to recover the money which it has lent).
>
> An **unsecured** or **personal loan** does not require the borrower to put up any collateral. The lender relies on the borrower's promise to repay the loan.

Mortgages

The most common type of secured, long term loan is a mortgage, where the loan is secured against the value of the property. Banks and building societies offer mortgages and there are also specialist mortgage lenders. The lender is the **mortgagee** and the borrower is the **mortgagor**. The loan is repaid in one of two ways:

- **Repayment** mortgages: the mortgagor makes monthly payments for an agreed period, or **term**. These payments cover the interest and an amount to repay the capital of the loan itself. The usual mortgage term is 25 years.
- **Interest only** mortgages: the monthly payments cover the interest only on the loan. At the end of the term, the mortgagee has to find the money to pay off the capital.

There are a wide variety of mortgage types, and a range of interest rates to choose from. It is essential to advise clients that they should seek specialist mortgage advice to decide which type of mortgage is most suitable for them, how much they can afford each month, and how much they will be able to borrow.

They also need to be aware that because the loan is secured against their house, they could lose the house. The mortgage agreement will give the bank or building society the right to **foreclose** if the mortgagor does not keep up with the payments. The bank will take possession of the house, and sell it to pay off their loan.

This does not necessarily mean that the clients will lose all the money which they have invested in the house. The mortgagee is only entitled to the amount of the loan. If the house is worth more than the loan, then the client keeps the balance. That balance is the **equity** in the house. Consider Example 4.

Example 4

If someone buys a house for £250,000 and borrows £150,000 from the bank, secured by a mortgage, the **equity** in the house is £100,000. If the borrower defaults on the loan, the bank can repossess and sell the house. Assuming that the house is sold for £250,000, the bank will get £150,000 and the borrower (the mortgagor) will get £100,000 (equity) from the sale. If the value of the house has fallen and it is worth less than £150,000, this is described as **'negative equity'** and the bank will not recoup its loan.

Unsecured loans

Unsecured borrowing takes a variety of forms. Individuals enter into unsecured loans every day. When you borrow £10 from your friend for a night out, that is a simple form of unsecured loan. The Aviva household survey shows unsecured borrowing is on the increase, with a typical UK family owing £11,101 in unsecured borrowing.[36]

Without security, unsecured loans are riskier for the lender, and interest rates tend to be higher than for secured loans. The main types are:

1. **Credit and store cards**. The most usual form of unsecured credit is purchases made on a credit or store card. The average family owes £6,055 on their credit cards.[37] Credit cards are a convenient way of financing purchases, and offer the cardholder a short period of interest free credit, provided that the amount is paid off at the end of each month.

   Problems arise if a cardholder is unable to pay off the balance each month. Interest rates are high, depending on the credit rating of the cardholder. For example, *Which?* reports that the average APR on store cards is 25.2% (60% higher than the Bank of England base rate of 0.5%).[38] The highest rates are just under 31%. Some providers also charge late payment and other fees. Interest is added to the balance, and then next month interest is charged on that total. Month by month the balance adds up and can lead to serious debt problems.

2. **Personal loans**. These are a cheaper way of funding smaller purchases than using credit cards. They are generally used to finance the purchases of items between £500 and £25,000, such as home improvements, car purchases, furniture, or domestic appliances. The repayment period is usually set at anything between one and ten years, with the borrower paying an agreed monthly sum to clear the loan. A typical family has £8,591 of personal loans.[39]

3. **Hire purchase and conditional sale agreements**. Often stores or dealers offer to arrange finance for their customers to purchase items such as domestic and electrical appliances or cars. The stores or dealers are not providing the finance themselves. They enter into an agreement with a credit provider who buys the goods from them, and then hires the goods to the customer in return for monthly payments over an agreed term, so the customer does not own the goods until she has finished paying for them. If the customer defaults on any of the payments, the credit provider still owns the goods and can take them back.

4. **Overdrafts**. As almost every student will be aware, you go into overdraft when you spend more from your bank account than you have in it. Many people will arrange an authorised overdraft facility with their bank. This enables them to overdraw their account up to a

---

[36] Aviva, *Family Finances Report January 2013*, http://www.aviva.com/data/report-library/Family_Finances_Report_Jan_2013.pdf.

[37] Aviva, *Family Finances Report January 2013*, http://www.aviva.com/data/report-library/Family_Finances_Report_Jan_2013.pdf.

[38] 'What are store cards?', *Which?*, http://www.which.co.uk/money/credit-cards-and-loans/guides/store-cards/what-are-store-cards.

[39] Aviva, *Family Finances Report January 2013*, http://www.aviva.com/data/report-library/Family_Finances_Report_Jan_2013.pdf.

certain limit, in return for an agreed rate of interest or fee, although some authorised overdrafts are interest free. The average family has an overdraft of £3,955.[40]

 Essential explanation

An **overdraft facility** is an agreement with the bank which allows a customer to overdraw his account up to an agreed maximum limit (say £1,000). The customer only borrows (or 'draws down') the money when he needs it. Interest is only paid on the amount actually borrowed, not the full amount of the facility.

Unauthorised overdrafts incur higher penalties and are expensive. The characteristic of an overdraft is that the bank can 'call in', or require the loan to be paid, at any time.

5. **Pay day loans**. For individuals with poor credit ratings it can be extremely difficult either to arrange an overdraft or get credit card or loans from a bank. This can cause problems for people who run out of money for one reason or another in the middle of the month before they are paid. Pay day loan businesses lend money to 'bridge the gap'. They charge large fees for the loan and very high interest rates, often at a time when poorer people are at their most vulnerable (e.g. 14% of single parents resort to pay day loans).[41] One company which advertises online offers an APR of 3,214.07%.[42] As a result of borrowing a comparatively small sum, the borrower may end up owing very considerable amounts of money, with no prospect of repaying.

16.5 Forms of business finance

Just as individuals need money to finance their ever changing lifestyles, businesses need to finance their development. Without the requisite funding, a business will fail and have to be wound up. Now we are going to consider how businesses raise money at each stage of development.

There are two main sources of business finance: equity finance and debt finance.

 Essential explanation

Equity finance is raised from individuals or businesses putting money into a business in return for a share in the business and a share of the profits.

    Debt finance is money which is lent to the business. Lenders are not entitled to a share in the business or profits, but will be paid interest on the loan. The loan will usually be secured to guarantee repayment. The money which is put into the business is its **capital**.

You may think that debt and equity finance is about large corporate deals, involving millions of pounds, so this is something you only need to know about if you are going into corporate practice. This is not the case. All businesses raise finance: if you decide to start up a business

---

[40] Aviva, *Family Finances Report January 2013*, http://www.aviva.com/data/report-library/Family_Finances_Report_Jan_2013.pdf.

[41] Aviva, *Family Finances Report January 2013*, http://www.aviva.com/data/report-library/Family_Finances_Report_Jan_2013.pdf.

[42] https://www.poundaccess.co.uk.

and your parents help you by investing £5,000 in the business, that is equity finance; if your parents lend you £5,000 for your business, that is debt finance. If a multi-national corporation raises £50 million from its shareholders, that is equity finance; if it borrows £50 million from its bank, that is debt finance. Whether large or small amounts are involved, the terminology is the same.

 Sample interview question

What is the difference between debt and equity finance?

16.5.1 Sources of equity finance

Owner funding

Initially, most businesses will be funded by their owners, either using their savings or through borrowing. If you go back to Case study 3, this is how Tom financed his business. This initial funding will be the original capital of the business.

Anyone who provides equity finance for a business (i.e. invests in the business) will want some stake or share (equity) in the business, which ensures a return on their investment. The larger the investment, the bigger the share that they will want. The type of stake will depend on the type of business.

1. **Sole traders**. A sole trader will provide all the capital (equity) for the business himself, and so, as the sole investor, will own the business and be entitled to the entire profit of the business.

2. **Partnerships**. If the business is to be run as a partnership, there will be two or more investors, who will each be given a partnership share. This will entitle them to receive a share of the profits. The share in the business and entitlement to the profit should be agreed between the partners and set out clearly in a partnership agreement. The agreement may also entitle investors to interest on their investment. If investors do not want to take part in the management of the business, they may be **sleeping partners**. They would still have a share in the business and be entitled to a share of the profits and interest if agreed, but would not need to participate in the everyday running of the business.

3. **Companies**. If the business is to be run as a company, the original investors will be given shares in the company. There are various types of shares which a company can issue to its investors, in return for voting rights and, generally, dividends, which represent a share of the profit. The most common type of shares in small limited companies are ordinary shares, which do not necessarily guarantee a dividend but do give the holder voting rights. However, if a company fails to pay dividends it is unlikely to attract further investment, and existing investors may pull out.

The original owners of the business may be able to provide enough finance when a small business starts up, but if the business has an ambitious plan or as the business grows, it will need larger sums of money. It will need to look to outside sources. There are a variety of options.

Share issues

When a company starts up, shares are issued to the original investors, who are usually the promoters of the company. As the company grows, and seeks to expand, they may wish to raise finance through further share issues. Public companies can issue shares to the public. Private companies can also issue shares, but these can only be offered privately. The disadvantage is that once a company issues more shares to outside investors, more people have a stake in the company and are entitled to dividends, and the company's original shareholders will take correspondingly less and have less control of the company.

As you saw at 14.3.4, where a company is seeking to expand and raise capital for growth, joining a stock market or the Alternative Investment Market (AIM) is another way to raise finance. A stock market listing is not suitable for small or start up companies, but for larger businesses seeking to expand, it is not only a useful way of raising capital but can raise the public profile of the business and attract investment.

Business angels

Business angels are wealthy individuals who invest in high-growth businesses in return for a share in the ownership of those businesses (equity in the business). Examples are the 'Dragons' in the television programme *Dragons' Den*. Not only do they provide funding for the business, but as they are successful entrepreneurs themselves, they have the business experience, management skills, and contacts to help businesses either to start up or expand. The 'Dragons' work with the owners of the business.

Private equity

Private equity firms manage private pools of funds for investors. They raise funds from private sources, usually pension funds and wealthy individuals, as well as borrowing. They buy controlling interests in undervalued or underperforming companies which they have identified as having the potential to improve. They then use their controlling interest to turn the company around and sell it on at a profit at a future date, usually within five to ten years. Well-known examples of private equity-backed firms are Ben Sherman, KwikFit, and New Look. Although private equity is more suitable for larger companies which are seeking to grow than for start ups or small businesses, this is again not entirely a corporate issue. Private equity firms are becoming increasingly interested in law firms (e.g. James Caan's private equity company, Hamilton Bradshaw).[43] Again this is a topical issue, and could well come up at interviews.

 Sample interview questions

1. Do you think that private equity investment is suitable for law firms?
2. Do you think that the involvement of private equity in law firms will improve their business performance?

---

[43] http://www.hamiltonbradshaw.com.

Venture capital funds

Venture capitalist firms again provide investment in return for equity in the business. They manage funds on behalf of individual investors who want to invest in businesses with high growth potential. They sit somewhere between business angels and private equity firms. Whereas private equity firms invest in larger businesses, venture capitalists provide funds for start ups and smaller private businesses. They invest larger sums of money than business angels and are often prepared to take on higher risk ventures than either private equity firms or business angels.

Crowdfunding

You may not have heard of crowdfunding, as it is a relatively new form of investment. Crowdfunding sites, such as Kickstarter in the US or Crowdcube in the UK, invite investment from the public over the internet. Individuals invest small amounts of money—usually between £100 and £10,000—into a business. The individual investments are then pooled together to help a business reach its funding target. This is a suitable investment option for small, often high-risk innovative businesses, which may have difficulty raising finance from more conventional sources. For example, Kickstarter raised over $3.3 million (£2 million) from 87,142 backers in just over eight hours for a San Francisco company, Double Fine Productions, to develop the computer game 'Double Fine Adventure'. Investors do not necessarily get a share in the business. They provide funds solely to enable the business to start up or finance a particular project. The return for a small investment in Double Fine was a copy of the finished version of the computer game.

Other forms of investment

Although these are the main options for equity finance, there are other possibilities, for example family and friends may be prepared to invest in the business, and initially are an important source of finance for small businesses. Government-backed schemes such as the enterprise investment scheme (EIS) offer tax advantages to small limited companies.

16.5.2 Sources of debt finance

Bank finance

Businesses can borrow money in the short term (i.e. it has to be paid back within one year) or long term (an agreed term of over a year). Most loans will come from a bank.

1. **Long-term loans**. Banks or other lenders will usually require some form of security for the loan in the form of a charge over assets of the business. The type of charge will depend on whether the business is a sole trader, partnership, or company. If the business owns its premises, it will be easier to get a loan as this is the best form of security for a lender, which will take a mortgage over the premises. Companies give different types of charge, known as fixed and floating charges, but the effect is the same. If the company does not keep up its payments, the lender can recover the amount owed from the sale of the charged asset.Limited liability means that shareholders of a company are not personally liable for the debts of the company (see 13.2.1). Unlimited liability means that

if the company defaults, the bank will require the directors themselves to repay the loan from their personal assets. The bank may also require personal guarantees from the directors. If a sole trader or partnership does not own its own premises, the bank may require the owners to grant a charge over their own properties.

2. **Overdrafts**. These are the most common form of short-term loan for a business. Businesses will arrange an overdraft facility and borrow money when they need it. Overdrafts are particularly useful when a business is up and running to prevent short-term cash flow problems. Overdrafts can, however, be expensive, as interest is charged on a daily basis.

Corporate finance

Public companies can issue bonds and other debt instruments in order to raise capital. Whereas the value of shares is based on the **equity** value of a company, bonds are based on **debt**. These are effectively loans which are not backed by any form of security. The company issuing the bond agrees to repay the amount of the bond at an agreed date (on 'maturity') and to pay interest to the holder of the bond until maturity. For the investors, bonds have the advantage that, like any other investment, they can be sold and the investor gets her money back. The interest will be paid to the current holder of the bond, who will claim the capital sum on maturity (see 14.3.4).

Other sources of debt finance

Although most debt finance comes from banks, there are other options available, especially if the business has a poor credit rating or has existing high levels of borrowing which make it difficult to raise money. The most obvious example of non-bank finance is borrowing from family or friends, who may charge a lower interest rate or be able to make loans over a longer period than a bank. Other sources are commercial loan providers, which provide financial services like loans and credit facilities, though they cannot take deposits like banks. In addition, the government offers a variety of grants and loan schemes for small businesses, for example Small Business Administration Loans.

16.5.3 **Credit rating for businesses**

Businesses have credit ratings in the same way as individuals do (see 16.4.6). Large corporations (and even countries) are credit rated so that investors can decide whether or not to invest in their shares or bonds. Businesses will run credit checks on business customers before offering credit, if they are uncertain whether they are creditworthy.

Business lenders rely on a similar credit scoring system to decide on the risk of lending to a particular business. There are credit reference agencies which report to banks and other lenders on businesses. The main one is Dun & Bradstreet, which issues a **Paydex** score. Unlike individual credit scores, Paydex only takes into account whether a business makes payments on time and meets creditors' payment terms. Businesses are scored from 0–100. If a business scores 80 or above, it means it pays on time. The later the business pays its bills, the lower the score.[44]

[44] http://www.dnb.com/company/our-data/rating-paydex-and-score-tables.html.

Government and corporate credit ratings

When buying government bonds, or bonds and shares in public companies, investors will want to know that the investment is safe. The three main credit reference agencies for investment purposes are Moody's, Standard and Poors (S&P), and Fitch IBCA. Their ratings help investors determine the risk associated with investing in a specific company, or indeed, country. Triple A (AAA) is the highest credit rating, and C or D (depending on the agency issuing the rating) is the lowest, which is sometimes referred to as **junk quality**. For example, in March 2012, at the height of the euro zone crisis, Moody's rating for Greece was Ca, which is the lowest rating it can give before a country or company defaults on its loans. This is why Greece could not borrow money on the markets and has had to be bailed out by the euro zone countries. Germany has a AAA rating, but Moody's downgraded the UK from AAA to AA1 in February 2013.

16.5.4 **Equity finance vs debt finance**

Whether debt or equity finance is better depends on the situation of the business. Factors to think about include:

- the type of business;
- the amount of financial capital the owner of the business has to invest;
- whether there are other potential investors, and the amount of capital which they have available to invest;
- tax considerations;
- the relative costs of borrowing or raising equity finance.

16.6 **Conclusion**

We started Part 3 by looking at a couple of topical scenarios as examples of commercial knowledge that you may need. Throughout these chapters, you have seen that commercial awareness is closely tied to employability. It is an important skill. In the same way that you will need to demonstrate, for example, communication or research skills both to find a job and once you are in practice, you will also be tested on commercial awareness. We now conclude by looking at one final scenario.

You will have researched the firm and its clients, and are prepared for questions about these, as well as personal and legal questions. If, however, you were asked about the budget statement or related issues, would you now be prepared for that? Let's just run a quick checklist to see which of these issues we have covered (see Table 16.2).

You can conclude that the last four chapters have given you the commercial background you need. Over the next few years of your studies you can build on this knowledge, gradually adding to the checklist. When you come to start looking for jobs, you can attend any interview knowing that you can answer questions designed to test your commercial awareness with confidence.

Case study 5

Imagine that you have an interview for a training contract. It is two days after the Chancellor's autumn budget statement in December 2012. Some of the key points reported in the press were:

- the Chancellor has had to downgrade predictions for economic growth;
- the government has failed to meet its targets for reducing debt as a percentage of GDP;
- austerity will continue until 2018;
- despite increases in income, inheritance, and capital gains tax thresholds, tax increases of £7 billion are predicted for 2015;[45]
- there are to be deep cuts in welfare payments, tax allowances for pensions; and maternity pay;
- interest paid on government bonds decreased;
- unemployment is expected to peak at 8.3%, although it should then fall;
- help is to be provided for small and medium size enterprises (SMEs);
- ISA limits will go up;
- funding is to be provided for 120,000 new homes.[46]

(Inflation targets are not included in the autumn statement. These are set in the main budget statement in March.)

There was some speculation that the UK could lose its AAA credit rating as a result of not meeting its deficit targets. Surprisingly, however, over the next two days, on the stock market, the FTSE went up and the pound held its value on the currency markets.[47] However the UK's AAA rating was later downgraded to AA1 in February 2013.[48]

Table 16.2 Essential commercial awareness checklist

Budget statement	✓
Economic growth/GDP	✓
Income, inheritance, and capital gains tax	✓
Welfare cuts and reform	✓
Pensions	✓
Maternity pay	✓
Housing	✓
SMEs	✓
ISAs	✓
Unemployment	✓
Bonds	✓
Credit ratings	✓
Stock market and FTSE	✓
Currency markets	✓

[45] James Kirkup and Rowena Mason, 'Autumn Budget: family bombshell over new black hole', *The Telegraph*, 6 December 2012.

[46] Paul Owen, 'Autumn statement 2012: key points', *The Guardian*, 5 December 2012.

[47] Alice Ross, 'Pound steady after Autumn Statement', *Financial Times*, 5 December 2012.

[48] 'Britain's loses AAA credit rating', *Daily Telegraph*, 23 February 2013.

Summary

- There are a variety of reasons why individuals and businesses will have recourse to the law. Often the need for legal services is triggered by some form of important life event, such as moving house, divorce, or setting up a business.

- All life events, some seemingly mundane, will have a legal and financial impact on individuals and businesses. Lawyers need to be anticipate their clients' needs in the light of this.

- 'Wealth' is the term used to describe what an individual owns, taking into account all his financial circumstances, including income, expenses, assets, and liabilities. Lawyers acting for individual clients must be aware of their financial background in order to advise their clients effectively.

- Adequate funding is crucial for businesses not only when they start out, but also for the everyday running of the business and as they expand and grow. Businesses raise funds in a variety of ways. Lawyers acting for businesses should understand the difference between equity and debt finance and the advantages and disadvantages of each.

 ## Thought-provoking questions

1. Think of a life event that has affected you. How did it impact on your finances? What were the legal implications?

2. Calculate your wealth. What could you do now to increase it?

3. Find out how to check your credit rating. What do you think you could do to improve it?

4. What are the main advantages and disadvantages of debt and equity finance?

5. Go through Chapters 13 to 16 and expand the Essential Commercial Awareness Checklist to cover areas that you consider could form the basis of interview questions. Check your understanding of all these.

 ## Further reading

Follow up some of the websites referred to in this chapter. They will give a useful insight into some of the issues discussed. Much of the information in this chapter is background knowledge that you can acquire by reading quality newspapers on a daily basis. Make sure that you do so.

Office of National Statistics (ONS): http://www.ons.gov.uk
—the national statistical institute of the UK. It collects, compiles, and analyses statistics on all aspects of social, economic, and demographic issues. It provides invaluable information on a variety of topics and is often a useful starting point for research into social and economic factors.

Aviva Family Finances Report: http://www.aviva.com/research-and-discussion/report-library/
—if you are interested in socio-economic factors, thisprovides useful further information.

**Department of Business, Innovation and Skills: https://www.gov.uk/government/organisations/
department-for-business-innovation-skills**
—information on funding for businesses, including a straightforward guide, *Business Finance Explained*, at https://www.gov.uk/business-finance-explained.

 For the authors' reflections on the thought-provoking questions, additional self-test questions, podcasts offering a variety of perspectives on legal systems and skills, and a library of links to useful websites, visit the free Online Resource Centre *at* **http://www.oxfordtextbooks.co.uk/orc/slorach/.**

Court facts

Statistics taken from *Judicial and Court Statistics 2011* (Ministry of Justice, 2012).

1. Magistrates' courts

Number of courts	245
Magistrates	Three sit on the bench. Not normally legally qualified, assisted by a clerk on legal matters.
Number of magistrates	24,200 (with a small number of district judges and deputy district judges).
Criminal jurisdiction	<ul><li>Issue of summonses and warrants for search or arrest.</li><li>Hearing bail applications.</li><li>Trial of summary offences.</li><li>Mode of trial procedure to decide whether a case should be tried summarily in magistrates' court or on indictment in Crown Court.</li><li>Committal proceedings whereby certain cases are formally sent up to Crown Court for trial sentence.</li><li>Youth Courts.</li></ul>
Civil jurisdiction	Magistrates also have limited civil jurisdiction, e.g. licensing and certain types of family proceedings.
Defendants proceeded against	1,620,000
Number of trials	166,808
Average period from offence to completion	120 days

2. County courts

Location	165 county courts across the country.
Judges	<ul><li>Circuit judges.</li><li>District judges (a junior appointment; must be legally qualified for seven years).</li></ul>
Civil jurisdiction	General types of work:<ul><li>contract or tort actions;</li><li>equity jurisdiction, e.g. mortgages;</li><li>disputes over wills;</li><li>recovery of land;</li><li>some family proceedings, etc.; and</li><li>disputes under the Consumer Credit Act 1974.</li></ul>County courts do not have any criminal jurisdiction.
Cases (non-family)	1,553,983
Trials and small claims hearings	15,941 trials; 36,719 small claims hearings.
Time taken from issue of claim to decision	56 weeks (trials); 30 weeks (small claims hearings).

3. The Crown Court

Number of centres	76 (across six circuits).
Judges	Depends on the gravity and/or nature of work:

- High Court judge (mainly QBD) or circuit judge or recorder (part-time appointment, e.g. solicitor or barrister).
- Magistrates may sit with judges on appeals.
- Jury for trial.

Criminal jurisdiction	

- Trials on indictment (with jury).
- Committals for sentence from magistrates' courts where the magistrates' sentencing powers are inadequate. (Maximum of six months' imprisonment and/or £5,000 fine.)
- Appeals by defendants convicted summarily in magistrates' courts.

Civil jurisdiction	Very limited.
Defendants proceeded against	91,910 for trial; 42,981 for sentencing only.
Guilty pleas	70%
Average waiting time	140 days.

4. The High Court

Location	The court sits at the Royal Courts of Justice, Strand, London ('The Law Courts'); The Rolls Building, Fetter Lane, London; and also at provincial centres (e.g. Manchester). There are 137 district registries.
Judges	Usually one High Court judge will sit alone. If necessary, a circuit judge, senior QC, Lord Justice, or a retired judge, may sit instead, e.g. on appeals from magistrates' courts.
Divisions	The High Court is one court, but it is divided into three divisions.
Queen's Bench Division	Jurisdiction:

- contract and tort actions;
- criminal appeals; and
- contempt of court.

It also incorporates various specialised courts, e.g. the Commercial Court and the Technology and Construction Court.

The QBD also has some appellate jurisdiction, the Divisional Court where two or more judges sit. Of particular interest is the hearing of appeals by way of case stated from magistrates' courts.

The Administrative Court falls within the QBD, and deals with cases of judicial review.

2011 proceedings commenced: 13,928.

Chancery Division	Jurisdiction: ● wills and probate; ● trusts; ● land and mortgage actions; ● company law; ● intellectual property; and ● bankruptcy. There are specialised courts within the Chancery Division, including the Patents Court and the Companies Court. 2011 proceedings commenced: 35,238.
Family Division	Jurisdiction: 'Family' matters, including: ● wardship and adoption; and ● divorce.

5. The Court of Appeal

Location	Royal Courts of Justice, Strand, London
Judges	Usually three, but sometimes five or seven Lords Justices of Appeal. Amongst those entitled to sit are: ● Supreme Court Justices; ● the Lord Chief Justice; ● the Master of the Rolls; and ● High Court judges as requested. The majority decision prevails (so an odd number of judges will normally sit).
Jurisdiction	Entirely appellate
Criminal Division	Appeals: ● Crown Court by the defendant; ● Attorney-General's reference procedure, on a point of law or against an unduly lenient sentence; and ● referrals by the Criminal Cases Review Commission. 7,475 appeals considered in 2011.
Civil Division	Appeals from: ● High Court; ● county court; and ● certain tribunals, e.g. Employment Appeal Tribunal. 1,269 appeals considered in 2011.
Procedure	As an appellate court, the Court of Appeal does not receive evidence from witnesses, but reads documents and hears argument.

6. The UK Supreme Court

In 2009, under the Constitutional Reform Act 2005,[1] the Supreme Court took over the functions of the Appellate Committee of the House of Lords.

Location	Parliament Square, Westminster.
Judges	Between three and nine (but usually five) Supreme Court Justices. (Formerly known as the 'Law Lords', Lords Justices of Appeal in the Ordinary.)
Jurisdiction	Almost entirely appellate. It is the final court of appeal not only for England & Wales but also for Scotland (in civil cases) and Northern Ireland.
Criminal jurisdiction	Appeals in criminal cases from: ● Court of Appeal (Criminal Division); ● QBD (Divisional Court); and ● Northern Ireland (not Scotland).
Civil jurisdiction	Appeals in civil cases from: ● Court of Appeal (Civil Division); ● High Court ('leapfrog' procedure); and ● Scotland and Northern Ireland.
Appeals disposed of	81 in 2011.
Procedure	Like the Court of Appeal it does not receive evidence from witnesses but reads documents.

7. The Judicial Committee of the Privy Council

Location	Parliament Square, Westminster.
Judges	At least three and (usually five) of: ● Supreme Court Justices; ● Lord President of the Council; ● members of the Privy Council who have held high judicial office; and ● Commonwealth judges who are members of the Privy Council.
Jurisdiction	● Appeals from some Commonwealth countries. ● Questions relating to the competences and functions of the devolved authorities in Scotland, Wales, and Northern Ireland.
Procedure	No 'judgment' is delivered; the judges give 'advice' to the Queen. There is one 'opinion' though dissenting opinions are allowed.
Appeals disposed of	45 in 2011.

---

[1] Constitutional Reform Act 2005, s. 23.

8. The Court of Justice of the European Union

Location	Luxembourg
Constituent courts	The CJEU comprises three courts: ● The Court of Justice (ECJ), the EU's highest court. ● The General Court, formerly the Court of First Instance, There is a right of appeal on matters of law to the ECJ. ● The Civil Service Tribunal.
Judges	Judges are appointed by agreement among the governments of the Member States (at least one judge from each). The judges are assisted by Advocates General.
Jurisdiction	● Ensuring European law is applied uniformly in all member states. ● Actions against member states to determine whether they have failed to fulfil their obligations under the Treaties. These may be brought either by the Commission or by one member state against another for failure to fulfil its Treaty obligations. ● Limited power to deal with actions brought by individuals.
Procedure	In keeping with its 'civil law' traditions, one judgment is delivered. The Advocate General assigned to the case assists the court by presenting an opinion (analysis) and recommendations to the court.
Length of proceedings	A House of Lords report in 2011 stated that competition cases took an average of 2¾ years to reach a conclusion.
Completed cases	574 in 2010 for the ECJ and 2,463 for the General Court; both have many more pending.[2]

9. The European Court of Human Rights

Location	Strasbourg
Judges	Judges are appointed from each state which is a party to the European Convention on Human Rights of 1950 (ECHR).
Jurisdiction	● Individuals can complain of breaches of the ECHR. ● N.B. Convention rights are directly enforceable in UK domestic courts under the Human Rights Act 1998.
Length of proceedings	The Court states that it 'endeavours to deal with cases within three years after they are brought'.[3]
Workload	In 2010, 61,300 applications were made, and the backlog was 119,300.[4] In 2010 there were 1,499 judgments. Since 1959, state violations have been found in 83% of cases.

[2] http://www.civitas.org.uk.   [3] European Court of Human Rights, *The ECHR in 50 Questions* (July 2012).
[4] Council of Europe report (February 2012).

Index

Introductory Note

References such as '178-9' indicate (not necessarily continuous) discussion of a topic across a range of pages. Wherever possible in the case of topics with many references, these have either been divided into sub-topics or only the most significant discussions of the topic are listed. Because the entire work is about 'legal systems' and 'skills', the use of these terms (and certain others which occur constantly throughout the book) as an entry point has been restricted. Information will be found under the corresponding detailed topics.